T0213386

Lecture Notes in Computer Science 10027

Commenced Publication in 1973
Founding and Former Series Editors:
Gerhard Goos, Juris Hartmanis, and Jan van Leeuwen

More information about this series at http://www.springer.com/series/7408

Pekka Abrahamsson · Andreas Jedlitschka
Anh Nguyen Duc · Michael Felderer
Sousuke Amasaki · Tommi Mikkonen (Eds.)

Product-Focused Software Process Improvement

17th International Conference, PROFES 2016
Trondheim, Norway, November 22–24, 2016
Proceedings

 Springer

Editors
Pekka Abrahamsson
Norwegian University of Science
  and Technology
Trondheim
Norway

Andreas Jedlitschka
Fraunhofer Institute for Experimental
  Software Engineering
Kaiserslautern
Germany

Anh Nguyen Duc
Norwegian University of Science
  and Technology
Trondheim
Norway

Michael Felderer
University of Innsbruck
Innsbruck
Austria

Sousuke Amasaki
Okayama Prefectural University
Soja
Japan

Tommi Mikkonen
Tampere University of Technology
Tampere
Finland

ISSN 0302-9743   ISSN 1611-3349   (electronic)
Lecture Notes in Computer Science
ISBN 978-3-319-49093-9   ISBN 978-3-319-49094-6   (eBook)
DOI 10.1007/978-3-319-49094-6

Library of Congress Control Number: 2016955998

LNCS Sublibrary: SL2 – Programming and Software Engineering

Printed on acid-free paper

This Springer imprint is published by Springer Nature
The registered company is Springer International Publishing AG
The registered company address is: Gewerbestrasse 11, 6330 Cham, Switzerland

Preface

The 17th International Conference on Product-Focused Software Process Improvement (PROFES 2016) brought together software researchers and industrial practitioners to Trondheim in Norway, during November 22–24, 2016. The hosting organization was the Department of Computer and Information Science (IDI) from the Norwegian University of Science and Technology. It is notable that this was the first time the PROFES conference was held in Norway, which is a country known for its advanced IT services and infrastructure. Norway is quickly becoming the hotspot of ICT development and innovations in Scandinavia. In the spirit of the PROFES conference series, PROFES 2016 focused on how the challenges of improving software development within the different practice areas such as requirements, design, construction, testing, maintenance, process, methods, management, etc. The conference has always encouraged submissions of research papers based on empirical evidence ranging from controlled experiments to case studies and from quantitative to qualitative studies.

This year we received 82 submissions of which 24 were selected as full papers and 21 as short papers. The scientific works were strictly scrutinized by international Program Committee members. Scientific papers in the PROFES conference received three or four reviews each.

As a novelty for 2016, we introduced a new track for the conference called "Radical Challenge Track." The intent was to draw ideas from the scientific and professional software communities who are searching ways to build the next paradigm for software development. The contributions in such a track are less scientific in their nature but are argued in a compelling way. We wanted to provide an opportunity for the community to present ideas that generate discussion and have the capacity to push the field forward in an unexpected way. The submissions were still to be peer-reviewed to ensure the quality and they were to be included in the technical conference proceedings. Both full papers and short papers on radical challenges were welcomed. However, it appears that the community is not ready for such track because we did not receive any submissions under the heading of radical challenges. We were able to attract a few papers dealing with the future of computing and were thus able to conclude the conference with these presentations and a panel dealing with issues of tomorrow. We will continue to motivate the community and especially the more senior scientists to begin undertaking ambitious endeavors dealing with tomorrow's challenges. We are well aware of the fact the digitalization process, Internet of Things, and big data require a lot of software to run them effectively and such issues should be raised under discussion sooner rather than later.

Another topic in the academic circles in the past years, which also includes the PROFES community, is the participation of the industrial community in the discussions, presentations, and experience sharing. Since 10–15 years ago, the development has actually been heading in the opposite direction. Industrial practitioners appear to organize themselves organically among certain topics quite effectively and are less keen in participating in classic scientific conferences. PROFES 2016 recognized this and organized tutorials on topics and themes of industrial interest. There were nine tutorials held on topics such as regulated software development, DevOps, lean start-ups, innovation, and software security. Scientific software engineering research needs industrial attention to survive and prosper.

The keynote speakers this year were of high quality. Mikko Terho is the CTO for Mobile Software and the site manager of Huawei's R&D center in Finland. As one of the founding board members of Symbian, at the time the leading open mobile operating system, Mikko Terho has had a significant influence on, and made a substantial contribution to, the development of the mobile industry as a whole. He was one of the few persons who were appointed as Nokia Fellow. Dag Sjøberg is Professor in Software Engineering and works at the Department of Informatics in University of Oslo in Norway. He is one the brightest software researchers around and has had a significant impact in the field. Dag Sjøberg sees that software systems form the foundation of the economic, political, social, cultural, and scientific spheres of modern information society. Such systems are, for example, crucial to solving global humanitarian and environmental problems.

We are thankful for having had the opportunity to organize PROFES 2016 in Trondheim. The Program Committee members and reviewers provided excellent support in reviewing the papers. We are also grateful to the authors, presenters, and session chairs for their time and effort that made PROFES 2016 a success. We are especially thankful to Prof. Letizia Jaccheri, the head of the Department of Computer and Information Science at NTNU, for providing the conference with the financial backing and helping in the organization. We would like to thank the PROFES steering group members and organizations (University of Oulu, VTT Technical Research Centre of Finland and Fraunhofer IESE) for the guidance and support in the organization process. Finally, we would like to thank the NTNU IDI's student and staff volunteers for making PROFES 2016 an experience that will live in the memory of the participants for years to come.

September 2016

Pekka Abrahamsson
Andreas Jedlitschka
Anh Nguyen Duc
Michael Felderer
Sousuke Amasaki
Tommi Mikkonen

Organization

 **NTNU**
Norwegian University of
Science and Technology

PROFES 2016 was hosted by the Norwegian University of Science and Technology, Department of Computer and Information Science.

General Chair

Tommi Mikkonen   Tampere University of Technology, Finland

Program Co-chairs

Pekka Abrahamsson   Norwegian University of Science and Technology, Norway
Andreas Jedlitschka   Fraunhofer IESE, Germany

Organization Chair

Jingyue Li   Norwegian University of Science and Technology, Norway

Proceedings Chair

Anh Nguyen Duc   Norwegian University of Science and Technology, Norway

Short Paper Co-chairs

Michael Felderer   Innsbruck University, Austria
Sousuke Amasaki   Okayama University, Japan

Publicity and Social Media Co-chairs

Daniel Méndez   Technische Universität München, Germany
Daniel Graziotin   University of Stuttgart, Germany

Poster Co-chairs

Tanja Suomalainen   VTT Technical Research Center of Finland
Masud Fazal-Baqaie   S&N CQM, Germany

Design Chair

Juhani Risku   Norwegian University of Science and Technology, Norway

PhD Symposium Co-chairs

Xiaofeng Wang   University of Bolzano, Italy
John Noll   The Irish Software Research Center, Ireland

Workshop and Tutorial Co-chairs

Daniela S. Cruzes   SINTEF, Norway
Sabrina Marczak   PUCRS, Porto Alegre, Brazil

Program Committee

Andreas Birk   SWPM, Germany
Anh Nguyen Duc   Norwegian University of Science and Technology, Norway
Andreas Jedlitschka   Fraunhofer Institute for Experimental Software Engineering,
                                      Germany
Barbara Russo   Free University of Bolzano/Bozen, Italy
Bruno Rossi   Masaryk University, Czech Republic
Daniel Rodriguez   The University of Alcalá, Spain
Daniel Méndez   Technische Universität München, Germany
    Fernández
Daniel Graziotin   University of Stuttgart, Germany
Davide Falessi   Cal Poly, USA
Dietmar Pfahl   University of Tartu, Estonia
Dietmar Winkler   Vienna University of Technology, Austria
Frank Houdek   Ulm University, Germany
Hironori Washizaki   Waseda University, Japan
Jens Heidrich   Fraunhofer Institute for Experimental Software Engineering,
                                      Germany
Jingyue Li   Norwegian University of Science and Technology (NTNU),
                                      Norway
Jonas Eckhardt   Technische Universität München, Germany
Jürgen Münch   University of Helsinki, Finland
Klaus Schmid   University of Hildesheim, Germany
Kurt Schneider   Leibniz Universität Hannover, Germany
Lech Madeyski   Wroclaw University of Technology, Poland
Luigi Buglione   Engineering.IT/ETS, Canada
Marco Kuhrmann   University of Southern Denmark, Denmark
Marco Torchiano   Politecnico di Torino, Italy
Marcus Ciolkowski   QAware GmbH, Germany
Maria Teresa   Università degli Studi di Bari A. Moro, Italy
    Baldassarre

Maurizio Morisio	Politecnico di Torino, Italy
Masud Fazal-Baqaie	S&N CQM, Germany
Maya Daneva	University of Twente, The Netherlands
Michael Felderer	University of Innsbruck, Austria
Noriko Hanakawa	Hannan University, Japan
Oscar Dieste	Universidad Politécnica de Madrid, Spain
Paolo Panaroni	INTECS, Rome, Italy
Reinhold Plösch	Johannes Kepler Universität Linz, Austria
Rini van Solingen	Delft University of Technology, The Netherlands
Risto Nevalainen	FiSMA Association, Finland
Silvia Abrahão	
Sousuke Amasaki	Okayama Prefectural University, Japan
Tomi Mannisto	University of Helsinki, Finland
Yoshiki Higo	Osaka University, Japan

Main Sponsors

 **NTNU**
Norwegian University of
Science and Technology

Department of Computer and Information Science, Norwegian University of Science and Technology

 The Research Council of Norway

Norwegian Research Council

City of Trondheim

Contents

Methods and Tools

Verification and Validation

Process Improvement

Speed and Agility in System Engineering

Requirements and Quality

Process and Repository Mining

Business Value and Benefits

Emerging Research Topics

Future of Computing

Invited Papers

2nd International Workshop on Human Factors in Software Development Processes

Keynotes

The Relationship Between Software Process, Context and Outcome

Dag I.K. Sjøberg[1,2(✉)]

[1] Department of Informatics, University of Oslo, Oslo, Norway
dagsj@ifi.uio.no
[2] SINTEF ICT, Trondheim, Norway

Abstract. Most practitioners and researchers agree that when developing software, process affects product, and the usefulness of a process depends on the context. However, which processes are most useful for a specific company or project is generally unknown. When studying the relation between context, process and product, one challenge is that experiments often lack realism, which makes the transfer of results to industry difficult. In contrast, most of the important factors vary beyond the researcher's control in case studies, which makes it difficult to identify cause and effect relationships. This paper reports a study where realism was combined with control over certain context and process factors. Four companies developed the same system, and the price varied by a factor of six. Certain patterns of relationships were expected (expensive company, low cost, schedule overrun); others were unexpected (cheap company, maintainable system because of small code). The community needs to identify the most important relationships among process, context and outcome.

Keywords: Software process improvement · Controlled multiple-case study · Software industry · Theory · Software engineering folklore · Measurement

1 Introduction

I am regularly contacted by various organizations for help regarding their software processes. They range from small, private companies to large, public sector agencies, some of whose projects failed to the order of hundreds of millions of euros. These organizations are not interested in general, overall principles regarding process; they are interested in what would work for them. They expect us, as researchers in the field, to know "what works for whom, where, when, and why" [1].

In a few cases, I have immediate suggestions for improvement, such as introducing automated testing if the number of defects is out of control. But in most cases, I cannot propose anything without working with the organization for some length of time. Identifying and measuring the factors that should be taken into account when proposing process changes are far from trivial; the software engineering literature does not give much help in concrete settings. The current body of knowledge is mostly too general or too specific; see Fig. 1.

© Springer International Publishing AG 2016
P. Abrahamsson et al. (Eds.): PROFES 2016, LNCS 10027, pp. 3–11, 2016.
DOI: 10.1007/978-3-319-49094-6_1

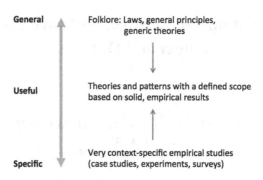

Fig. 1. Useful theories and patterns

Software engineering folklore guides processes to some extent. For example, a collection of "laws" and principles that have emerged over the years can be found in [2–4]. One of the laws stated by Endres and Rombach [4], attributed to the work by Boehm [5], is: "Errors are most frequent during the requirements and design activities and are more expensive the later they are removed." This "law" encourages processes that emphasize the analysis and design phases. However, what does this mean in practice? Should one spend, say, 10 to 30 percent of the total effort of a development project in these phases? Because of varying contexts, software engineering folklore is often contradictory. For example, much effort has been devoted to developing process models that include a large number of activities, practices and roles together with formal, detailed project documents. In contrast to such heavy processes are the light processes recommended in agile development.

Few empirical studies in software engineering discuss the contexts to which the results may be generalizable. Experiments in software engineering generally have few subjects and almost all of them use convenience sampling [6]. Most case studies are of single cases, and few attempt to generalize the results through theories with a well-defined scope of validity [7]. Surveys collect people's subjective opinions, which are based on knowledge and experience gained in specific contexts. The results of surveys also need to be related to theories to become generally useful.

Nevertheless, a premise in software engineering is that there is a relationship between software processes and success of a project or task. The success is typically described in terms of the quality of the delivered software, how long it takes to develop it and how much it costs. It is also commonly agreed that this relationship is moderated by the context of the processes, as illustrated in Fig. 2. It is reasonable to assume that an optimal process varies with context; for example, a small team may not benefit from activities designed to help large teams.

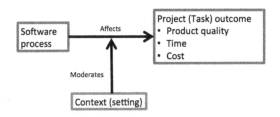

Fig. 2. Relationship between process, context and outcome

The ideal model would be a deterministic one, in which a set of given context and outcome parameters would determine the optimal process, and a given process and context would determine the outcome. However, it is unlikely that we will manage to develop such models given that software development is a mostly human activity and we are unable to describe human behaviour deterministically in general, even though certain theories describe human behaviour in specific situations, for example, the prospect theory [8].

Although we are far from a scenario where we can fully determine which process gives which result in a specific context, our community can improve in identifying patterns and proposing theories for the relationships among process, context and outcome. This paper reports on a study that is an ongoing attempt in that direction.

2   Design of Study

The empirical software engineering community conducts both controlled experiments, which focus on cause and effect, and case studies, which focus on realism. How to identify cause–effect relationships in realistic settings is a challenge. What if we hire several companies to develop the same system and see what happens? Some years ago, our research group had such an opportunity. We needed a web application to store information about all the empirical studies of the group. We developed a requirement specification and sent a call for tender to 81 consultancy companies and received bids from 35 of them. A study of this bidding process was reported in [9].

The striking difference in the bids, given that we provided a well-defined 11-page requirement specification, led us to use price as the selection criteria. We wanted to study the effect of price on process and outcome. Thus, in four price segments, we selected the company that appeared most likely to develop a good system based on the quality of the bid documents. The companies are named *A* to *D* in this paper, in the order of bid price; see Fig. 3.

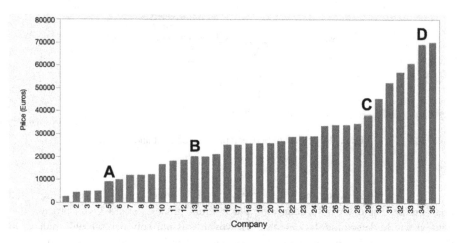

Fig. 3. Four out of 35 companies selected for development

The data sources in this study are comprehensive. They include daily time sheets on tasks and subtasks of each developer, weekly snapshots of all documents including source code produced during the projects, full history provided by the configuration management and issue tracker tools and other information collected from defect logs, e-mail communication and team interviews.

From this study, we published an investigation on reproducibility and variability in software engineering [10] and a study of effort estimation based on use case points [11]. The code developed by the four companies has also been used in follow-up studies on maintenance metrics [12] and effects of code smells [13]. (In this paper, the companies are named according to bid price, while in the papers already published, the order was alphabetic. Company C is now Company A, Company A is now Company B, and Company B is now Company C. Company D remains Company D.)

A detailed investigation of the effect of process and context has not yet been published. Initial results are reported here.

3   Context

We controlled parts of the context to make them the same for all the companies; other context factors were specific to each company. The controlled ones included:

- Requirement specification
- Application domain (web document management)
- Functional size of the system (57 unadjusted use case points [11])
- Low complexity of system
- Customer (our research department)
- Programming language (Java, Javascript and SQL)

- Tools (IDE: Netbeans or Eclipse, Build & Deploy: Ant, Configuration management: CVS; note that these tools were selected by the companies themselves but they happened to be the same by accident)
- Team composition (1 project manager and 2 developers, except in Company B, which had 1 developer and 1 interaction designer)
- Uniform interaction between development team and customer (e.g., use of same issue tracker, acceptance tests by the same customer team)
- Intermediate skill level of the developers

Regarding skill level, we selected the developers on the basis of their CVs. All of them had at least three years of formal education in programming and three years of industrial experience with the technology to be used. Ideally, we should have tested the developers using a validated skill evaluation instrument [14], but in the absence of such an instrument at that time, the developers were tested for their Java skills by taking part in a one-day exercise in which they performed the same Java programming tasks used in a former experiment [15]. Their performance was thus compared with that of 77 other Java programmers. Similarly, the developers were tested for their design skills by taking part in a half-day UML exercise where they performed the same tasks used by 28 persons in a former experiment on use cases and class diagrams [16]. We did not observe any clear relationship between the skills of the team and project outcome.

Table 1 shows context factors that varied among the companies. Some factors were specific to the development organization; others were specific to this development project. Note that the bid by Company D, of 69,000 euros, shown in Fig. 3, was negotiated down to the 56,000 euros, shown in Table 1.

Table 1. Varying context

Aspect	Variable	Company A	Company B	Company C	Company D
Development organization	Size (# employees)	Appr. 8	Appr. 100	Appr. 25	Appr. 13,000 worldwide
	Nationality	Domestic	Domestic	Domestic	International
	Ownership	By employees	Private	By employees	Listed exchanges
	Location	Bergen	Oslo	Oslo	Oslo, 20 countries
	Process models	Light	Intermediate	Intermediate	Heavy
Project	Firm price	€8,750	€20,000	€45,380	€56,000
	Agreed time schedule	41 days	55 days	73 days	62 days
	Estimated effort	100 hours	220 hours	341 hours	650 hours
	Allocation	Part-time	Part-time	Part-time	Full-time
	Co-location	No	No	No	Yes

The table shows several internal relationships among the factors. Company A is small and can therefore only run fairly small projects with small teams. Their organization-level process models are therefore light. The low price offered to build the system is followed by an expectation of a short lead time, a low number of effort hours, and the need for the developers to work on several projects in parallel. At the other end, Company D is large and has a heavy organization-level process model. The high bid allows higher estimated effort and allows developers to work full time on this project.

4 Processes

As an example of process data, Fig. 4 shows the number of hours the companies spent on various development activities. Note the one-to-one correspondence between the effort spent on the activities "Implementation" and "Analysis and Design". There is no indication here that much effort spent on analysis and design reduces the effort needed on implementation, or vice versa. Remember that the amount of functionality is fixed. Figure 5 shows the hours spent on the activities as the projects were running.

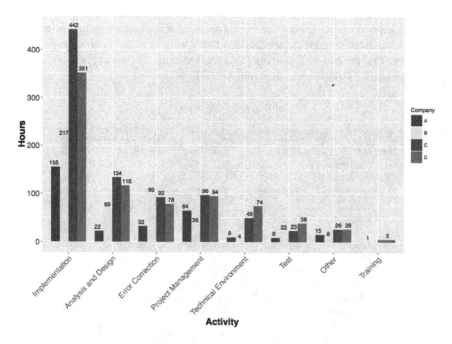

Fig. 4. Effort spent on various activities

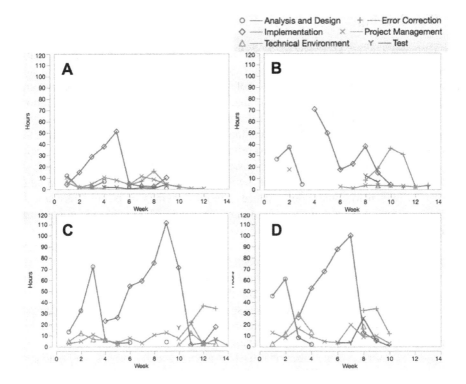

Fig. 5. Effort on activities along the way

5　Outcome

The outcome of a process or project may be measured along many dimensions. For the four systems, we assessed reliability, usability and maintainability. Reliability was measured by investigating the defects found over a period of two years when the systems were operational [10]. The usability was measured through a dedicated experiment [17] and maintainability in a follow-up experiment [13]. Table 2 shows the results and also includes measurements of effort and lead time.

Table 2. Outcome variables

Aspect	Variable	Company A	Company B	Company C	Company D
System	Reliability	Poor	Good	Good	Fair
	Usability	Fair	Good	Fair	Good
	Maintainability	Good	Fair	Poor	Fair
Effort	Actual effort	315 hours	562 hours	894 hours	796 hours
	Overrun effort	215 %	155 %	74 %	22 %
Lead time	Actual lead time	79 days	87 days	90 days	65 days
	Overrun lead time	93 %	58 %	23 %	5 %

6 Relationships

Did the rather extreme price differences, of a factor from 1 to 6, lead to corresponding differences in outcome? Generally not. Company A had given the lowest bid and accordingly spent the least effort on the whole development, particularly on analysis and design and on testing. In a sense, this company developed a "quick and dirty" solution, but the small size of their Java code led to the most maintainable system. The low number of lines of Java code trumped other maintainability metrics [12]. On the other hand, the low focus on testing resulted in the least reliable system and required us as a customer to spend much more effort on testing than we did for the other companies. In total, we spent almost twice the number of effort hours on Company A as we did on the other companies, which to some extent reduces the cost savings of hiring Company A. Furthermore, we were a competent customer; an incompetent customer might have resulted in a failed project.

Company B scored best on the system quality dimensions on average. Given the next lowest price, one may consider their project as the best value for money.

Company C over-designed their system, which resulted in excess code size, which in turn resulted in poor maintainability. But they scored top on reliability.

Company D had relatively heavy processes and a highly competent project manager. The developers worked full-time and were co-located. Their project seemed to have full control all the way and resulted in the lowest lead time and very little overrun.

We have observed many other relationships among context, process and outcome, but much analysis remains. We hope to reveal interesting patterns that may shed new light on existing theories or be the basis for new theories.

References

1. Dybå, T., Sjøberg, D.I.K., Cruzes, D.S.: What works for whom, where, when, and why? On the role of context in empirical software engineering. In: ACM-IEEE International Symposium on Empirical Software Engineering and Measurement. ACM (2012)
2. Brooks Jr., F.P.: The Mythical Man-Month: Essays on Software Engineering. Addison-Wesley Publishing Company, Reading (1975)
3. Glass, R.L.: Facts and Fallacies of Software Engineering. Addison-Wesley Professional, Reading (2002)
4. Endres, A., Dieter Rombach, H.: A Handbook of Software and Systems Engineering: Empirical Observations, Laws, and Theories. Pearson Education, New York (2003)
5. Boehm, B.W., McClean, R.K., Urfrig, D.E.: Some experience with automated aids to the design of large-scale reliable software. IEEE Trans. Softw. Eng. 1, 125–133 (1975)
6. Sjøberg, D.I.K., Hannay, J.E., Hansen, O., Kampenes, V.B., Karahasanovic, A., Liborg, N.K., Rekdal, A.C.: A survey of controlled experiments in software engineering. IEEE Trans. Softw. Eng. 31(9), 733–753 (2005)
7. Sjøberg, D.I.K., Dybå, T., Anda, B.C., Hannay, J.E.: Building theories in software engineering. In: Shull, F., et al. (eds.) Guide to Advanced Empirical Software Engineering, pp. 312–336. Springer, London (2008)
8. Kahneman, D., Tversky, A.: Prospect theory: an analysis of decision under risk. Econometrica 47(2), 263–291 (1979)

9. Jørgensen, M., Carelius, G.J.: An empirical study of software project bidding. IEEE Trans. Softw. Eng. **30**(12), 953–969 (2004)
10. Anda, B.C.D., Sjøberg, D.I.K., Mockus, A.: Variability and reproducibility in software engineering: A study of four companies that developed the same system. IEEE Trans. Softw. Eng. **35**(3), 407–429 (2009)
11. Anda, B., Benestad, H.C., Hove, S.E.: A multiple-case study of software effort estimation based on use case points. In: International Symposium on Empirical Software Engineering, pp. 407–416 (2005)
12. Sjøberg, D.I.K., Anda, B.C., Mockus, A.: Questioning software maintenance metrics: a comparative case study. In: ACM-IEEE International Symposium on Empirical Software Engineering and Measurement (2012)
13. Sjøberg, D.I.K., Yamashita, A., Anda, B.C., Mockus, A., Dybå, T.: Quantifying the effect of code smells on maintenance effort. IEEE Trans. Softw. Eng. **39**(8), 1144–1156 (2013)
14. Bergersen, G.R., Sjøberg, D.I.K., Dybå, T.: Construction and validation of an instrument for measuring programming skill. IEEE Trans. Softw. Eng. **40**(12), 1163–1184 (2014)
15. Arisholm, E., Sjøberg, D.I.K.: Evaluating the effect of a delegated versus centralized control style on the maintainability of object-oriented software. IEEE Trans. Softw. Eng. **30**(8), 521–534 (2004)
16. Anda, B., Sjøberg, D.I.K.: Investigating the role of use cases in the construction of class diagrams. Empirical Softw. Eng. **10**(3), 285–309 (2005)
17. Følstad, A., Anda, B.C.D., Sjøberg, D.I.K.: The usability inspection performance of work-domain experts: An empirical study. Interact. Comput. **22**(2), 75–87 (2010)

Early Phases in Software Engineering

Eight Paths of Innovations in a Lean Startup Manner: A Case Study

Mikko Raatikainen[1](✉), Marko Komssi[2], Harri Kiljander[2], Laura Hokkanen[3], Jukka Märijärvi[4], and Omar Mohout[5]

[1] Aalto University, Espoo, Finland
mikko.raatikainen@aalto.fi
[2] F-Secure Inc., Helsinki, Finland
{marko.komssi,harri.kiljander}@f-secure.com
[3] Tampere University of Technology, Tampere, Finland
laura.hokkanen@tut.fi
[4] Landon Ltd., Helsinki, Finland
jukka.marijarvi@landon.fi
[5] Sirris, Heverlee, Belgium
omar.mohout@sirris.be

Abstract. Software companies face high pressure to develop innovative products and services at increasing speed. However, a traditional new product development (NPD) process is not always a sufficient means for doing this. We report experiences from an explorative multiple case study covering eight cases from four companies of different sizes and business characteristics. Each case aimed to streamline the development of a product or service innovation in a Lean startup manner as an alternative to the traditional NPD. We present eight life-cycle paths that together exemplify the use of the five organizational alternatives, such as internal startup and company subsidiary. Driving force to choose the organizational alternative is novel business endeavor rather than being depended on the company. Using even multiple organizational alternatives is possible during the innovation life-cycle as long as the speed and independence for the innovation is achieved.

Keywords: Internal startup · Lean startup · Subsidiary · Institutional entrepreneurship · Intrapreneurship · Case study · Industrial experience

1 Introduction

Software companies face high pressure to develop innovative products and services at increasing speed. The traditional *new product development (NPD)* process, such as presented by Cooper [1], seeks to enable the creation of new innovative products. However, the NPD process is fuzzy and difficult from the beginning [2]. In particular, NPD is a complex higher-order capability that involves multiple organizational functions, capabilities, and competencies [3]. However, forming a traditional NPD program may not be always a sufficient

© Springer International Publishing AG 2016
P. Abrahamsson et al. (Eds.): PROFES 2016, LNCS 10027, pp. 15–30, 2016.
DOI: 10.1007/978-3-319-49094-6_2

to take care of the full life-cycle of developing and commercializing a new software product — creating new innovations may require more flexibility in terms of experimentation and learning from failure than is characteristic of the traditional NPD process [4]. For example, fast-paced, revolutionary, or disruptive innovations could be done differently, as exemplified by startups.

Recently, new means have emerged to reshape the work done in the traditional NPD programs. For example, *Customer development* [5] and *Lean startup* [4] are methods that try to streamline the innovation development process. However, in order to be able to gain the benefits of such methods, software companies need to establish ways in which to carry out the Lean startup process. Different types of company ventures — seeking to efficiently capture and monetize new innovations outside established business lines — can be used for this purpose [6]: For instance, the software company can incubate the idea in a separate strategic unit and, later, form an internal startup or even a separate subsidiary to effectively search for new business [7].

However, the experiences on different types of company ventures are still scarce. The research problem addressed in this paper is the structures and life-cycles of means of going beyond the traditional NPD. To shed light on the topic from the industrial perspective, we carried out an explorative case study about NPD programs that decided adopt also the other than traditional NPD structures over their life-cycles. Based on the eight cases, we describe and synthesize (1) the structures that were established, (2) the points in the life-cycles when decisions were made about the structures, and (3) the justifications for the structures.

The paper is organized as follows. Section 2 describes the life-cycle of an innovation program as background. Section 3 outlines the research method. Section 4 provides the case accounts. Section 5 analyses the findings. Section 6 provides discussion in the light of related work. Section 7 concludes.

2   Background: The Life-Cycle of an Innovation

For the scope of an innovation project, the four stages can be mapped and summarized as follows (Fig. 1):

Idea stage: The innovation program should focus on gaining a detailed understanding of the problem or need that it wants to tackle. At the end of this stage, the startup should have a holistic understanding of the problem domain, and a minimal viable product (MVP) or concept to initiate concept validation with real customers and users. Ideas are handled as hypotheses that need to be validated using the MVP to collect customer feedback. The primary goal is learning.

Problem/solution fit: In this stage, the innovation program should focus on further developing the concept as an optimal solution for the first lead users and customers. The MVP offers a path of very rapid iteration of customer requirements followed by testing and validation. This stage is called 'going from 0 to 1' by Peter Thiel [9]. Experimenting with (innovative ways of) customer acquisition is the second key activity of this stage.

Idea Stage	**Problem/Solution Fit**	**Product/Market Fit**	**Scaling**
It all starts with an idea. At this stage, all that matters is to understand in detail the problem or need that you want to tackle.	Once the opportunity is framed, it's time to create the optimal solution and to get the first users or customers on board.	This is the magical point proving that you found a sticky market for your product or service. You will also test your business model and pricing strategy.	Congratulations, you have found a market and a business model. Now it's time to move from being a startup to a scale-up. You need resources for that: money and people.
The main activity is gaining market insights through customer discovery.	The main activity is solution validation through customer acquisition.	The main activity is market validation through retention.	The main activity is scaling by accelerating growth while increasing the organizational maturity.

Fig. 1. Four stages of the startup life-cycle [8].

Product/market fit: Once the optimal solution for the lead users is ready and the innovation program has been able to acquire new customers and users, its focus should move to customer retention and further generation of the business model. In this stage, the innovation program should particularly focus on retention, the business model, and a pricing strategy.

Scaling: When the innovation program has found a scalable business model, the focus should shift to actual scaling. In this stage, the innovation program should focus on accelerating the business. The acceleration typically requires large investments in marketing and business development. This stage is called 'going from 1 to n' by Thiel [9].

The four stages form a value chain: No idea creates value until you embody it in a product or service; no product or service captures value until you embody it in a business model and pricing strategy; and no business model becomes sustainable until you figure out distribution.

The lengths of these phases vary largely, and the stages can partially overlap and are not clear-cut. It is also not possible to set a deadline for product/market fit. By moving from one stage to another, the risks are reduced because assumptions are validated. This is of paramount importance, because markets are simply unpredictable for innovative products and services. According to our experience from the field, the main focus of each innovation program typically follows these stages over the startup life-cycle. Furthermore, they are similar to other life-cycle models presented in [4, 10, 11]. If the project does not succeed, it will face its end and discontinue: That can take place during any of these phases.

3 Research Method

The research follows the explorative case study methodology, meaning a study about a contemporary phenomena in industry [12]. As the research topic is emergent, the selection of cases was done opportunistically and purposefully on the basis of innovation programs that the authors were familiar with in order to explore different kinds of cases. The main criterion for selecting the cases was that they did not follow a traditional NPD program but started to apply some other kind of organizational alternative during the life-cycle. However, the idea stage started within an existing company rather than as an independent start-up in each case. The study was carried out to investigate the following cases: F-Secure's F-SOS, DF-Data, Freedome, Key, Lokki and Sense; Qentinel's Quality Intelligence (QI); Aptual's Johku; and OP Financial Group's Pivo. These are all Finnish companies developing software-intensive solutions.

The collected data was qualitative and relied mostly on interviews. The Johku and QI cases were each based on a one-hour interview with the CEO of the company. During the interview, the interviewee was asked to describe the life-cycle of the case. Additional clarification questions were asked during the interviews. Two researchers conducted the interviews and took notes. Sense, Freedome, KEY and Lokki are based on the interview with the responsible vice president at F-Secure as well as interviews with two representatives from each of these cases. Pivo is based on an interview with the head of New Business Development who has been responsible for Pivo from the start. All these interviews were carried out by researchers who did not work in the case company. F-SOS is based on a previous case study by one of the authors [13,14] complemented with re-analysis and an additional informal interview with a key person in F-SOS. Moreover, two of the authors have been a part of or had a supporting role in the five cases (Lokki, Key, Freedome, Sense, and DF-Data). These authors' participatory role in these programs were used to enrich the data. Furthermore, the authors have gained additional informal knowledge about the cases through personal collaboration.

Based on the acquired data, case accounts to summarize each case were constructed. The accounts were read for corrections by at least one representative of each case: Typically, the interviewee or alternatively someone equally familiar with the case read the account.

We analyzed each of the cases along the life-cycle as introduced in the previous section as follows. For each case, we identified the organizational alternatives that the case applied. Furthermore, we analyzed the decisions and justifications to understand the rationale for each decision. The analysis was carried out in a bottom-up manner, so that different organizational alternatives emerged and were formulated as we analyzed the cases. As different organizational alternatives emerged over the life-cycle, we were able to illustrate and synthesize the paths that the cases had taken in a two-dimensional space. Finally, we cross-analyzed and synthesized the rationales, decision points along the paths and benefits over different cases.

4   Case Descriptions

F-Secure F-SOS. F-Secure Corporation is an Internet and cyber security company. F-Secure founded a company subsidiary called F-SOS to establish a new business concept and model. F-SOS used F-Secure's existing technology without developing the core technology further and even without direct access to the technology. Rather, the key idea was to build new service-oriented business and service concept based on the existing technology. The first release was not especially successful, but a year later the second solution's release showed major success. After being in operation for one year, the F-SOS service and solution were merged back into the F-Secure mother company and the solution became strategically important, and eventually the most important of F-Secure's business areas for several years. The key idea of the solution was to build a Software as a Service (SaaS) business model around F-Secure's existing technology. Around the same time, F-Secure reshaped its business by discontinuing other product offerings. Later, F-SOS operated inside F-Secure as its own unit and the cross-functional F-SOS team tried to establish other similar SaaS-type solutions that turned out to be moderate successes, at best.

F-Secure DF-Data. F-Secure has a subsidiary called DF-Data for testing and validating any new kinds of product or business concepts. Although products and services are developed and marketed under this incubating subsidiary's brand, these products are using the subsidiary as a test bed without generating any revenue. Overall, DF-Data operates as an incubator, for example to explore and test social media marketing practices; to test beta products; and to test concept products and technologies. All this is accomplished without the risk of sacrificing the mother companys brand name. The company has been used as the publisher of beta versions for several products, such as FS Cloud and FS Protection. Product concepts include Secure Selfie Camera, Funny Hat Stickers, and Snapwallet: Photo Safe, that are available as apps for Android smartphones.

F-Secure Lokki. Lokki was the first internal startup that F-Secure established within the business organization. The company strategy renewal in 2012 identified Family Protection to be a prospective new security product and business area. A new family location-sharing service concept was developed by a small concept design team. The company leadership team decided to productize the concept and bring it to the market with a rapid schedule, and the guidance from the company CEO to the concept creation team leader was to "work like a startup!". The Lokki service reached some tens of thousands of users through moderate marketing efforts but it was eventually ramped down as it did not fit well enough within the company's strategy framework. The learnings of the internal startup way of working, together with some of the software features are being deployed and further developed as part of current F-Secure consumer security and privacy products and services. The Lokki service itself was open sourced and Lokki is currently managed by University of Helsinki.

F-Secure Freedome. The second F-Secure internal startup, called Freedome, was founded within the company strategy unit. The startup's product leveraged some existing technologies, while some parts were developed from scratch. After the commercial launch of the MVP, the internal startup was seen as a great success in terms of the defined objectives such as the number of downloads and new users, as well as positive reviews. The internal startup was later integrated into the F-Secure consumer business organization. More recently, the product has been adapted for business customers and has been subject to other kinds of market and channel extensions, e.g. from B2C to B2B. However, the scaling of the business from consumers to B2B customers has not been completely straightforward due to different customer needs and expectations.

F-Secure KEY. The idea of the third internal startup, KEY, was incubated as a technology proof-of-concept within the company strategy unit. After a strategic decision, the internal startup was transfered to the consumer security business organization. The initial hypothesis for the product was to compete in the direct consumer business (B2C), but after this was found to be an uphill battle against the dominant incumbent players, the more lucrative B2B2C channel was chosen as the primary business opportunity. At the moment, various business models are being experimented with, ranging from a standalone product to using the product as a tactical add-on in a larger security service bundle.

F-Secure SENSE. By the strategic decision of the company management, the fourth internal startup, called Sense, was founded at F-Secure. A significant investment is being made to develop a security software and hardware solution to protect new kinds of IoT (*Internet of Things*) devices in smart homes. The hardware product developed in-house is the first of its kind for F-Secure. However, an essential element of the total product has been developed using existing F-Secure software security technology. The product is currently available for pre-ordering and the internal startup team is currently finalising the MVP to start commercial deliveries.

Qentinel Quality Intelligence (QI). Qentinel is a quality assurance company and most of its services are based on knowledge-intensive consulting. Around 10 years ago, Qentinel started to plan to shift its business toward a more sophisticated understanding of quality through the concept of value, resulting in a traditional NPD program (2007–2008) that eventually became known as QI. QI was a drastic change for Qentinel because the objective was to develop the company's own products and services with protected IPR that was different from Qentinel's existing consultancy-based business model. However, the project was not a business success at first, and the existing business of Qentinel continued to be successful, which hindered the concept development of the new business. In 2008 the strategy work of Qentinel resulted in establishing runtime quality monitoring in information systems as a new area as one of its three strategic areas. A company specialized in the technical monitoring of IT services was acquired in 2011. This technology-based service became a key part of the QI offering, and at the same time was expected to finance the development of the other parts of QI. However, the QI project was still relatively time-consuming and used resources from the other profitable consultancy-based business with constant cash flow. The organizational culture hindered rather than boosted the development of QI. To clarify the role of QI, Qentinel ended up turning QI into an internal startup staffed with dedicated people. This somewhat clarified QI's identity. Less than a year later, Qentinel decided to restructure its organization. As part of this, the QI internal startup was moved to a separate corporate subsidiary. Although the move caused some uncertainties at first, things started to go better. QI obtained independence without the burden of the old organization and the QI employees realized that they had the sole responsibility for acquiring new prospects and customers. At the moment, QI is growing but its business is not yet making profit because of the heavy development investments.

Aptual Johku. Aptual is a small company that focuses on creating better marketing communications and exploring new frontiers for its customers. The company has historically carried out customer-specific projects that it has further developed and commercialized. This has resulted in a set of small solutions that have each had a good problem/solution fit for a single customer. However, a poor product/market fit has required a significant amount of customer-specific work with the next customers for scaling. Therefore, Aptual decided to narrow down its number of solutions to three. One of these three was Johku, which is today a software-based solution for travel service providers, such as cottage renters. The intial version of Johku was developed as a typical Aptual NPD project. However, Aptual carried out different kinds of analysis about the market, resulting in a decision that the value proposition of Johku needed reshaping and sharpening as a part of a significant development project. As a result, Aptual decided to establish an internal startup for Johku that was financed by the two other revenue-generating solutions. The essence of the internal startup was to make an explicit internal investment and clarify the role of Johku as an upfront investment in development rather than trying to productize existing projects. The internal startup developed an MVP and started to search for product/market fit. A startup that takes care of Johku was spun off very recently. While the startup considers the existing MVP to be ready for scaling, validation from larger markets is lacking.

OP Pivo. The OP Financial Group is the largest of the major players that dominate the Finnish banking market. Three to four years ago, the company recognized the importance of mobile payments but the topic did not find a clear owner in the organization. A team familiar with mobile payments was established and they started working on the problem. A new research and development unit was set up in the city of Oulu, far from the headquarters, because there was a lot of experience available due to the citys past life as one of Nokia's major sites in Finland. Most people were new hires, but the owner of the problem was an OP Financial Group veteran, bringing in a wealth of banking experience.

The team started using the Lean startup paradigm relatively strictly, and was a an internal startup inside the OP Financial Group. The Lean startup methodology was found to be successful, but it also became clear that if one follows the model strictly, it is a very disciplined model and one needs to be prepared for it. Initially the team created a set of assumptions, which looking back were all wrong, and they were changed later in the project. However, fast learning is key in the setup – being initially wrong does not matter as the Lean startup methodology tests the assumptions early and then brings in end-user feedback to re-direct the project. Currently, Pivo is its own company with its own management, being separated from the OP Financial Group so that the app can be used by customers from any banks.

5   Analysis

Decisions need to be taken at the company level regarding the types of innovation programs to be used. In particular, the decision-makers need to understand that a traditional NPD program is only one option, while other alternatives exist. In this section, we analyze the organizational alternatives to the traditional NPD program that were identified from the cases. As another orthogonal concern, we use the life-cycle phases of an innovation program from the stage of idea incubation to that of business scaling, and map the path through the phases and structures of the cases. The key decisions and rationales are also analyzed along these paths. Finally, we highlight the key benefits of applying other structures than the traditional NPD program that have emerged from the cases.

5.1   Organizational Alternatives

The following structures were observed in the cases. The difference between the alternatives is that the relative independence from the parent company increases as we progress through the list. The cases that apply each structure is summarized in Table 1.

- **NPD (new product development) project.** This is broadly any kind of traditional innovation or development project or programs for products or services within a company relying on established structures. It typically includes

Table 1. The structures and supporting cases.

Structure	Case
NPD	*(All)*
Internal startup	Freedome, Key, Lokki, Sense, Johku, Pivo
Company subsidiary	QI, F-SOS, Johku, Pivo
Company startup	Johku
Incubating subsidiary	DF-Data

the company's strategic work and follows the company's established practices and structures. We differentiate an NPD because all cases were selected so that the start was in an NPD.

- **Internal startup.** Internal startups take place within a company but work much more independently than an NPD, even entirely independently. As a results, internal startups have different levels of freedom from the companys standard policies.
- **Company subsidiary.** A company can found a child company to take care of an innovation program. A subsidiary is fully owned by the originating company. Such a subsidiary has more freedom, responsibilities and financial incentives than an internal startup.
- **Company startup.** Innovation programs can also take place in more independent startups of which the originating company has no full control. However, often the originating company or its owners have influence over or ownership of the company startup, and a company startup still has ties to the originating company: For example, employees can have working contracts in both companies or work through subcontracting arrangements.
- **Incubating subsidiary.** A variant of the company subsidiary is an incubatory subsidiary. The subsidiary is not founded for one particular innovation program, but the same subsidiary exists continuously and a series of innovation projects are carried out within it.

5.2   Rationales and Success Factors

There were varying rationales for establishing an alternative structure to the NPD program, but one common characteristic was that something novel or a significant change to the existing business was being planned. F-SOS developed a new SaaS-based business model. Sense had some new features such as including hardware and targeting new kinds of devices, although its main functionality was basically the same as other security products. DF-Data focused on different kinds of new concepts. Sense, Freedome, Key and Lokki each targeted new markets, although they were strategically in the same security business area. In general, these three products were considered internally as completely new offerings rather than features of existing products, even though some existing technology was utilized. The Aptual's internal startup Johku was a means to make an investment decision and to give Johku the independence, freedom and resources to develop the new solution as well as a change in business model. Similarly, gradually moving QI through the phases of traditional NPD program, internal startup, and subsidiary seems to have been a successful business model transformation and service development path. Nevertheless, founding a subsidiary does not necessarily explain the recent success of QI fully. During the transformation, the QI offering has also matured, the market seems to be more ready, and the technologies used within the major digitalization trend have shaped the business environment.

When establishing any of the alternatives to a traditional NPD program, a certain level of independence was looked for, and the independence seems to have been a prerequisite and a success factor in all cases. The structural alternatives are not better or worse per se, but rather a means to an end. Independence needs to be realized by a clear mandate to be able to work toward the objectives. Independence also minimizes the disturbances of the existing organizational culture, resulting in less unnecessary interaction.

One means of establishing an organizational structure as well as a factor positively affecting success seems to be the use of external people such as new recruits in these organizational alternatives. The external people are not tied to the old organizational culture and business models. For example, F-SOS had many new recruits in the team and likewise Pivo recruited most of the team from outside of OP group.

There is a risk, especially in establishing an internal startup, that it may remain too close to the existing business areas whereas a corporate subsidiary, being relatively more independent, can be a means for assuring independence. Business lines do not seem to natively support novel or disruptive ideas that can even be destructive to their current business or ideas beyond their current goals. This is exemplified by the QI case, where the organization did not initially realize the value of QI. Established business organizations also tend to be primarily focused on the short term or quarterly business priorities, not allowing a new business or product entry to be developed and iterated sufficiently, and a revenue stream may be expected too soon, when the new product is still going through the Problem/Solution Fit phase, as with Lokki. Business lines seem to focus on evolutionary ideas and concepts rather than revolutionary ones. As the CEO of Qentinel stated, "The more successful your business is, the more likely your transformation is to fail". If the business is successful, there is less pressure to change or invent something new, and the organization may not necessarily want a change. However, there is then a risk that a competitor can establish a new business and take over the market. Thus, it seems that a strategic or research unit is a good choice for internal startups when business lines are inhibiting rather than catalyzing structures. The more radical or disruptive the innovation is, the better a corporate subsidiary or other means of being made independent can be, as indicated by F-SOS and QI. Even in more general terms, independence seems to be a good indication for good operations or freedom from existing hindering or controlling practices.

5.3   The Different Paths

Combining the organizational alternatives described above and the life-cycle phases results in a two-dimensional space through which each innovation program takes its path. This space and the paths of each program within the space are illustrated in Fig. 2. The horizontal axis shows the different phases as well as the progress but does not indicate the absolute length of the phases, e.g. in terms of months, but is roughly propositional in relation to the phase length, such as whether transformation was carried out at the beginning or end of the phase. For example, the life-cycle of Lokki and QI are presented in this same figure but the life-cycles were roughly one and eight years, respectively. The vertical axis lists the different organizational alternatives as described above. The vertical position of different paths within each box has no meaning. Due to the case

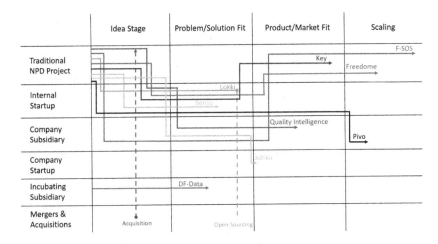

Fig. 2. The paths that different cases have taken through organizational alternatives over the life-cycle of the cases.

selection, all paths start as a traditional NPD program. Some of the cases apply several structures. Direct vertical lines over structures is used for illustrative purposes for changes while horizontal lines indicate that a structure is applied; for example, F-SOS that became a subsidiary from NPD without being internal startup in between. The end of a line as an arrow indicates that particular cases are still in progress, while Lokki has been discontinued at F-Secure and the code has been open sourced.

In the following, we elaborate key points of the phases and decision points along the paths.

Origins of the idea. As all cases represent an alternative means for structuring an NPD, the ideation phase was typically carried out as part of the strategic work within the company in the form of an NPD program or a pre-phase for such a program. After the idea had reached a certain degree of maturity, an alternative structure to the NPD program was established. An incubating subsidiary was also used in DF-data, but even then, the ideas followed the company's strategic initiatives due to its close links to the main company. QI relied partially on M&A for part of the technology, but even then the strategic work was the basis for the idea that the M&A decision supported.

When to make the change. It is feasible to even incubate the idea for a long time as a traditional NPD program but the idea phase seems to be a good point at which to make a change. That is, all of the cases resulted in an organizational alternative other than a traditional NPD program during the idea phase through the establishment of an internal startup or a subsidiary. However, the length of ideation and the maturity of the idea differed largely. For example, especially QI but also Freedome and Key were ideated and were a part of strategic process for a long time as a traditional NPD program. On the one hand, the QI case indicates that delaying the decision does hinder the progress. On the other hand, it is unclear whether too immature a concept can survive on its own too early. In contrast, Lokki was established as an internal startup relatively quickly as the result of a strategic initiative.

Multiple changes. Although making several changes is not necessarily the optimal strategy, multiple changes can be a less risky method and suitable for certain situations. QI started as an NPD followed by an internal startup and finally ending up becoming a subsidiary; and Johku started similarly as an NPD followed by an internal startup but was finally spun off to an independent startup. The development of QI might have been slowed down as an NPD and internal startup, but the slow progress allowed the idea to mature and was not in the end that delaying to the progress. For Johku, the multiple changes were justified by investment decisions and the changes do not seem to have had too much of an effect. Moreover, unlike in the other cases, the leaders of QI and Johku were also the CEOs of their parent companies, and therefore, had more power to make decisions and changes.

The end of the life-cycle. The structural alternatives can be temporary. An internal startup in particular typically has a limited lifetime. At the end of the life-cycle, the developed innovation can be brought back into the main company or a spinoff company can be established, for example. However, only some of the studied cases are at the end of their life-cycle: F-SOS was turned into a scalable business within the existing business line, but F-SOS has later been able to repeat the success only moderately; Lokki was discontinued in F-Secure during the internal startup stage on the basis of a strategic decision and open sourced; DF-Data products have not been discontinued but not all of them are being developed actively and some are being used for other purposes such as testing and learning new marketing strategies; and Key and Freedome have been brought back to the business lines and are searching for a scalable business model within them.

It seems that after the end of the life-cycle of the alternative structures, being too closely related to business lines can be problematic, especially for novel innovations. A reason for this could be that, especially if the resulting innovation is not mature enough, it does not fit into the daily routines and objectives of the business line. In fact, one important consideration during the end of the life-cycle is whether the appropriate home for the developed concepts lies in the existing business lines, or is it worth establishing a new business line for the new innovation or a subsidiary to take care of the business, as is the case with QI and Johku.

The length of the life-cycle. The length of the life-cycle and phases can vary largely. Too fast progress in terms of finding solutions before fully understanding the problem or aiming at scaling before appropriate market fit that is, rushing to the next life-cycle phase too early seems in general to not be recommended, as for any innovation program. For example, a too early search for a scalable model and merging into a business line might have taken place in Freedome before a proper market fit was found, whereas the long idea stage of QI matured and helped to clarify its value proposition. In particular, at the end of the life-cycle of an organizational alternative such as an internal startup, it seems that the solution should have completed the objectives of the phases properly in addition to finding a relevant home.

In general, it seems that internal startups should continue until at least the product/market fit stage has been reached properly, while corporate subsidiaries and other more independent entities should continue at least until the scaling stage.

5.4 Benefits

Effects to the innovation program. The experience from the cases show that, one the one hand, the alternatives to NPD, such as internal startups and subsidiaries, can be more undisciplined as well as radical and quicker to test something new. The independence of an innovation program means minimizing the disturbances from, e.g., other employees, management, and even customers. The existence of fewer such interfaces mean faster speed that then enables fast changes and faster learning. On the other hand, compared to startups that do not have any back-up from the originating company, they can be financially in a better position to not rush, for example starting scaling too early, which adds interfaces and naturally slows the team down.

Effects to the existing business. A successful innovation can even be a boost to the existing business. In the case of QI, the main business ended up with a new business area to complement their current business. F-SOS drastically changed the business models of F-Secure toward the SaaS model, even in other business lines. Although not everything results in flourishing new business, the cases show several other benefits and usages. Lokki continues its life as open source. Funny Hat Stickers from DF-Data was first developed as a funny add-on to cloud services, but once the F-Secure cloud services had been discontinued, there was no strategic use for Funny Hats. However, the Funny Hat Stickers app had users and worked on its own. Thus, Funny Hat Stickers was changed to be a testbed for trying new things such as learning and testing the usage of social media channels for various purposes.

6   Discussion

In recent years, new methods and models have been introduced to tackle the challenge of bringing new products to market in a timely manner. While digital products can be distributed globally by even the smallest startups, competition to find scalable business models fast enough is getting tighter. Customer development [5] and lean startup [4] seek to answer to this need where methods like the NPD stage gate model [1] or the new concept model for Fuzzy Front End (FFE) [15] fall short. Emphasizing interaction and testing hypotheses with real customers to gain validation before investing heavily in development, Lean startup takes advantage of global digital markets as a test bench for new product innovations. However, these experimental methods also need specific attention to avoid biases that result in false validation [16]. Moreover, utilizing such methods in established companies often requires more freedom for the executing team in order for them to be able to react quickly to the insights gained. Company ventures can enable the development of new business with more freedom while fostering entrepreneurial culture [17] and also enable the recruitment of talent to complement the current skillset inside the company [6].

This paper introduced four alternative organizational structures for traditional NPD: Internal startup, company subsidiary, company startup, and incubating subsidiary. While none of the study's alternatives are novel, the findings from the selection and usage of each alternative offer practical insights from the Finnish companies. In fact, one of the alternatives, internal startup, was used in six out of eight of the study's cases during the life-cycle of new business endeavors. Indeed, there is a growing interest in initiating internal startups, or at least adopting the principles of the Lean startup method in software companies. To our knowledge, however, internal startups have not been widely studied (with that term) in the software business research field. On the other hand, the term and idea of the intrapreneur have been used in large software companies for over thirty years [18]. Edison et al. [19] have recently studied internal startups in one of the companies that is also part of our study. Their study focused on the characteristics and implementations of internal startups, whereas our findings emphasize that the internal startup seems to be a suitable but only a temporary organizational structure in the early and middle phases of NPD.

Previous work exists on the factors that determine whether new business opportunities are exploited by starting a new venture for an employer (i.e., nascent intrapreneurship) or independently (i.e., nascent entrepreneurship) [20]. In our study, the former refers to internal startups and the latter to company spinoffs, such as subsidiaries and startups. Individual, organizational, and product characteristics all affect the decision to exploit an opportunity via intrapreneurship or entrepreneurship [20]. Our findings highlight that the decision does not have to be one or the other. A software company can also begin a business endeavor with intrapreneurship and move to entrepreneurship later. Actually, one of the cases shows that the order can also be the other way around. This implies that decision-makers need to continuously evaluate, not just at the beginning, the alternatives for organizational structures over the life-cycle of NPD.

In the four cases of our study, spinoffs (either company subsidiaries or startups) were created. Interestingly, all of them have been successful business-wise so far. Based on our findings, however, we cannot draw the conclusion that company subsidiaries or startups are always a better choice business-wise than, for instance, internal startups. However, Rice et al. [6] and Mazur [21] conclude that depending on business goals and available funding, spinning out can bring advantages in terms of more flexible funding possibilities as well as increased motivation through increased freedom, responsibility, and personal risk. In addition, it can be beneficial to recruit experienced venture capitalists and other experts to advise the new spinoff [6]. Chammanur and Yan also claim that spinoffs are associated with an increase in long-term operating performance [22]. According to them, however, an incumbent management team is required to give up control to a rival management team in the case of a spinoff, which may motivate the incumbent management team to work harder to avoid loss of control. Interestingly, however, companies are announcing increasing numbers of new but smaller and smaller spinoffs [23]. Indeed, a small spinoff will not take a lot of power from the incumbent management team. Our study's findings also showed that the parent company's CEO can become the leader of the new spinoff.

Our findings are exploratory and preliminary representing cases only in one country. Further studies on the same topic in different countries are recommended. Our findings also raise further research topics. First, what are the business performance differences between internal startups and company spinoffs over the NPD life-cycle? Secondly, if internal startups (or Lean startups inside corporations) are becoming increasingly popular, how can we better integrate the strengths of spinoffs, such as financial freedom and incentive mechanisms, into those internal startups?

7   Conclusions

We presented an explorative case study of innovation programs applying different organizational alternatives than traditional new product development (NPD). We outlined the life-cycle of such innovation programs along their path through the life-cycles of ideation, problem-solution, product/market fit and scaling the business. Along this path, we showed how an innovation program approach can apply different structures: internal startup, component subsidiary, company startup, or incubating subsidiary. Finally, we elaborated on the nature of different decision points, changes, and prevailing mechanisms.

Acknowledgments. The authors would like to extend their gratitude to the participants of the study. They also acknowledge the financial support of TEKES as part of the Accelerate program and Need for Speed (N4S) program of Dimecc.

References

1. Cooper, R.G.: The new product process: a decision guide for management. J. Mark. Manag. **3**(3), 238–255 (1988)
2. Wowak, K.D., Craighead, C.W., Ketchen, D.J., Hult, G.T.M.: Toward a "theoretical toolbox" for the supplier-enabled fuzzy front end of the new product development process. J. Supply Chain Manag. **52**, 66–81 (2015)

3. Bendoly, E., Bharadwaj, A., Bharadwaj, S.: Complementary drivers of new product development performance: cross-functional coordination, information system capability, and intelligence quality. Prod. Oper. Manag. **21**(4), 653–667 (2012)
4. Ries, E.: The Lean Startup. Crown Business, New York (2011)
5. Blank, S.: The Four Steps to the Epiphany. K&S Ranch, Pescadero (2013)
6. Rice, M.P., OConnor, G.C., Leifer, R., McDermott, C.M., Standish-Kuon, T.: Corporate venture capital models for promoting radical innovation. J. Mark. Theor. Pract. **8**(3), 1–10 (2000)
7. Fosfuri, A., Rønde, T.: Leveraging resistance to change and the skunk works model of innovation. J. Econ. Behav. Organ. **72**(1), 274–289 (2009)
8. Mohout, O.: Startup master class ii: Exodus – problem-solution fit (2015). http://www.slideshare.net/omohout/exodus-problem-solution
9. Thiel, P., Masters, B.: Zero to One: Notes on Startups, or How to Build the Future. Crown Business, New York (2014)
10. Cooper, R.G.: What's next?: after stage-gate. Res. Technol. Manag. **57**(1), 20–31 (2014)
11. Overall, J., Wise, S.: An s-curve model of the start-up life cycle through the lens of customer development. J. Private Equity **18**(2), 23–34 (2015)
12. Yin, R.K.: Case Study Research, 2nd edn. Sage, Thousand Oaks (1994)
13. Komssi, M., Kauppinen, M., Heiskari, J., Ropponen, M.: Transforming a software product company into a service business: case study at F-Secure. In: IEEE International Computer Software and Applications Conference, pp. 61–66 (2009)
14. Komssi, M., Kauppinen, M., Ropponen, M., Palomäki, P.: Transformations of a solution strategy: a case study. In: Regnell, B., Weerd, I., Troyer, O. (eds.) ICSOB 2011. LNBIP, vol. 80, pp. 140–153. Springer, Heidelberg (2011). doi:10.1007/978-3-642-21544-5_12
15. Koen, P.A.: The fuzzy front end for incremental, platform and breakthrough products and services. In: PDMA Handbook, pp. 81–91 (2004)
16. York, J.L., Danes, J.E.: Customer development, innovation, and decision-making biases in the lean startup. J. Small Bus. Strategy **24**(2), 21 (2014)
17. Hass, B.H.: Intrapreneurship and corporate venturing in the media business: a theoretical framework and examples from the german publishing industry. J. Media Bus. Stud. **8**(1), 47–68 (2011)
18. Pinchot, G.: Introducing the 'intrapreneur': successful innovators in large companies sometimes function as in-house entrepreneurs, running projects as independent innovators would. IEEE Spectr. **22**(4), 74–79 (1985)
19. Edison, H., Wang, X., Abrahamsson, P.: Lean startup: why large software companies should care. In: Scientific Workshop Proceedings of the XP2015 (2015)
20. Parker, S.C.: Intrapreneurship or entrepreneurship? J. Bus. Ventur. **26**(1), 19–34 (2011)
21. Mazur, M.: Creating m&a opportunities through corporate spin-offs. J. Appl. Corp. Finan. **27**(3), 137–143 (2015)
22. Chemmanur, T.J., Yan, A.: A theory of corporate spin-offs. J. Finan. Econ. **72**(2), 259–290 (2004)
23. Zenner, M., Junek, E., Chivukula, R.: Shrinking to grow: evolving trends in corporate spin-offs. J. Appl. Corp. Finan. **27**(3), 131–136 (2015)

On the Distinction of Functional and Quality Requirements in Practice

Jonas Eckhardt[1(✉)], Andreas Vogelsang[2], and Daniel Méndez Fernández[1]

[1] Technical University of Munich, Munich, Germany
{eckharjo,mendezfe}@in.tum.de
[2] Technische Universität Berlin, Berlin, Germany
andreas.vogelsang@tu-berlin.de

Abstract. Requirements are often divided into functional requirements (FRs) and quality requirements (QRs). However, we still have little knowledge about to which extent this distinction makes sense from a practical perspective. In this paper, we report on a survey we conducted with 103 practitioners to explore whether and, if so, why they handle requirements labeled as FRs differently from those labeled as QRs. We additionally asked for consequences of this distinction w.r.t. the development process. Our results indicate that the development process for requirements of the two classes strongly differs (e.g., in testing). We identified a number of reasons why practitioners do (or do not) distinguish between QRs and FRs in their documentation and we analyzed both problems and benefits that arise from that. We found, for instance, that many reasons are based on expectations rather than on evidence. Those expectations are, in fact, not reflected in specific negative or positive consequences per se. It therefore seems more important that the decision whether to make an explicit distinction or not should be made consciously such that people are also aware of the risks that this distinction bears so that they may take appropriate countermeasures.

Keywords: Quality requirements · Functional requirements · Survey

1 Introduction

In literature (e.g., [9,13–15,18]), requirements are often categorized in *functional requirements (FRs)*, *quality requirements (QRs)*, and *constraints*. FRs are characterized as "things the product must do" contrasting QRs as "qualities the product must have" and constraints as "organizational or technological requirement". Although this categorization is common sense to some degree, there are still debates about the precision of the categories (e.g., [7]). There are other academic groups that suggest to rather distinguish between *behavior* (e.g., response times) and *representation* (e.g., programming languages) [3].

In a previously conducted study [6], we analyzed 11 requirements specifications from industrial environments with a particular focus on requirements labeled as "quality". We found out that (i) there is a distinction between QRs

© Springer International Publishing AG 2016
P. Abrahamsson et al. (Eds.): PROFES 2016, LNCS 10027, pp. 31–47, 2016.
DOI: 10.1007/978-3-319-49094-6_3

and FRs in the documentations, and that (ii) many requirements labeled as QR actually describe system behavior and, thus, could also be labeled as FR. However, our previous investigation focused on analyzing artifacts after the fact and we still have little knowledge about what difference it makes in a development process if a requirement is labeled as FR or as QR and what the resulting consequences are. In response to this question, we conducted a survey with 103 practitioners which we report in this paper.

In particular, we contribute: (i) a quantification of company practices regarding the style of documenting functional and quality requirements, (ii) a list of reasons why practitioner do or do not document FRs and QRs separately, (iii) a list of consequences for the two styles of documentation that helps engineers to make conscious decisions.

2   Research Objective

The goal of this study is to understand whether practitioners consider product-related requirements labeled as FR differently from those labeled as QR. We are further interested in the reasons for this distinction and the resulting consequences for the development process. We derive the following research questions:

RQ1: Do practitioners handle FRs and QRs differently? In this RQ, we want to analyze whether QRs are documented in practice, whether there is a distinction in the documentation, and whether this distinction makes a difference in the development process. To this end, we formulate the following sub-RQs:

   RQ1.1 Do practitioners differentiate between QRs and FRs in the documentation? We want to know whether the accepted categorization of product-related requirements as FRs or QRs is reflected in the style of documentation as used in practice.

   RQ1.2 To what extent do development activities for QRs differ from activities for FRs? A possible consequence of a requirement categorization is that different categories of requirements are handle differently in the development process. We want to investigate whether this is the case in practice and how this is influenced by the style of documentation.

RQ2: What are reasons for distinguishing or not distinguishing between QRs and FRs in the documentation? While categorizations only provide definitions, we are interested in the underlying reasons that lead practitioners to distinguish or not distinguish between QRs and FRs in the documentation.

RQ3: What are positive and negative consequences of distinguishing or not distinguishing QRs and FRs in the documentation? A decision for or against a separate documentation may have positive or negative consequences that practitioners should be aware of.

3   Research Methodology

Our goal was to reach out to a broad spectrum of practitioners and capture their perceptions of their own project environments. To this end, we used (online) survey research as our main vehicle. We intentionally designed the survey such that respondents required as little effort as possible to complete it; we kept the number of questions at a minimum, the instrument was self-contained and it included all relevant information. We further limited the response types to numerical, Likert-scale, and short free form answers as suggested by Kitchenham and Pfleeger [10]. As a validation of our instrument and its alignment with the audience, we piloted the survey with three practitioners, who completed the survey and afterwards participated in an interview, where questions and answers where checked for misunderstandings.

3.1   Subject Selection

We deliberately targeted practitioners who work with requirements. This includes practitioners who write requirements (e.g., *requirements engineers*) but also practitioners whose work is based on requirements (e.g., *developers* or *testers*), and also practitioners who manage projects or requirements. Our survey was further conducted anonymously. Since we were not able to exactly control who is answering the survey, it was especially important to follow Kitchenham and Pfleeger's [10] advice on the need to understand whether the respondents had enough knowledge to answer the questions in an appropriate manner. For this, we excluded data from respondents who answered that they do not use requirements specifications at all, or respondents who stated that they did not know how requirements are handled in their company. We finally offered respondents the chance to leave an email address if they were interested in the results of the survey.

3.2   Data Collection and Instrument

We started our data collection on February 4th, 2016 and closed the survey on February 22nd, 2016. For inviting practitioners to participate, we did not select a specific closed group of practitioners but, instead, contacted as many practitioners as possible via the authors' personal contacts from previous collaborations, via public mailing lists such as *RE-online*, and via social networks. In the following, we introduce the main elements of our instrument used. The full instrument can be taken from our online material[1].

Demographics: We collected a set of demographic data from the respondents to interpret and triangulate the data with respect to different contexts of the respondents. The demographic data included the role of the participant, the experience, the company's size, the typical project size, the geographical distribution of project members, the paradigm of their applied development process

---

[1] http://www4.in.tum.de/~eckharjo/SurveyResults.zip.

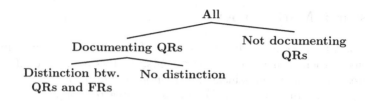

Fig. 1. Categorization of respondents by their style of documenting QRs.

(on a scale from agile to plan-driven), the industrial sector, the type of developed systems, and the role of the requirements specification within the company. To better understand the participant's focus and project context, we additionally asked respondents for the importance of different types of QRs in their projects. The respondents were asked to assess the importance of quality factors[2] taken from ISO/IEC 25010 [8] for their typical projects on a 5-point Likert scale.

Practices of Handling QRs: As a first step towards comparing different practices for handling QRs, we asked the respondents how strongly development activities differ between QRs and FRs in the phases *requirements engineering, architecture/design, implementation,* and *testing.* As a follow up, we provided a free form text field and asked the respondents to explain the differences in detail.

We were especially interested in the question whether it makes a difference for the development process if project participants distinguish between QRs and FRs and how this distinction is documented. Therefore, we asked the respondents two conditional questions. First, we asked whether QRs are explicitly documented in their projects. If this was the case, we asked whether the respondents explicitly distinguish between QRs and FRs in the documentation, i.e. whether they are labeled differently (e.g., some requirements are labeled as *performance* or *maintainability*) or documented in different sections (e.g., special sections for *performance* or *maintainability*). The answers to these questions categorize the responses into three groups (see also Fig. 1).

Problems/Benefits of Current Practices: Given the categorization into the three groups, we asked our respondents for specific reasons why they do or do not distinguish between QRs and FRs. Additionally, we asked for benefits and problems that arise from the way they consider QRs (i.e., not documenting QRs, mixing QRs and FRs in the documentation, or distinguishing between QRs and FRs in the documentation). For these questions, we provided free form text fields to be filled out by the respondents.

3.3 Data Analysis

Our data analysis constitutes a mix of descriptive statistics and qualitative text analysis. To answer RQ1, we analyzed in particular the answers that the respon-

---

[2] These were functional suitability, performance/efficiency, compatibility, usability, reliability, security, maintainability, and portability.

dents provided for the following survey questions: (i) *Are QRs documented in your typical projects*, (ii) *In the documentation (e.g., in a requirements specification), do you distinguish between QRs and FRs*, (iii) *Considering the following phases, how much do the activities for handling QRs differ from those for FRs*, and (iv) *Considering your work, for what activities does it make a difference if you consider an QRs vs. an FR.* For RQ1.1 and RQ1.2 we analyzed the results of the first, second, and third question, respectively. As the answers for the fourth question are open, we analyzed the answers in detail to provide more insights in the activities and the differences.

To answer RQ2 and RQ3, we analyzed the data our respondents provided for the following survey questions: (i) *Are there specific reasons why you do (or do not) distinguish between QRs and FRs in the documentation*, (ii) *Do you experience negative consequences in your current work that result from distinguishing (not distinguishing) between QRs and FRs in the documentation*, and (iii) *Do you experience positive consequences in your current work that result from distinguishing (not distinguishing) between QRs and FRs in the documentation*. The answers to the questions are free text answers. To analyze the results, we coded the provided answers in pairs of researchers to assemble a conceptual model of reasons and consequences for distinguishing between QRs and FRs in practice. The qualitative coding technique was chosen as recommended by (Straussian) Grounded Theory [16], but differs in that the central categories were previously defined following our research questions. To visualize our results from the text analysis, we used cause-effect diagrams (also known as Ishikawa diagrams).

4 Study Results

4.1 Sample Characterization

In total, 283 people clicked on the link to our survey, 172 started the survey (61 %), and 109 completed it (39 %). From these 109 respondents, we excluded 6 as they matched our exclusion criteria. The respondents seem quite experienced as 93 % stated that they have more than 3 years of experience with requirements, 5 % one to three years, and only 2 % with less than a year. Furthermore, a majority of the respondents work in large companies: 57 % work in companies with more than 2000 employees, 25 % in companies with 250–2000 employees, and 17 % in companies with less than 250 employees. However, typical projects of the respondents showed a variety of small to large projects: 24 % stated that in a usual project in their company up to 10 people are involved, 46 % that 11–50 people are involved, 24 % that more than 50 people are involved, and 6 % did not know. Most of the respondents (59 %) answered that their team is distributed over multiple locations in more than one country, 23 % that the team is distributed over multiple locations but in one country, and 17 % that all team members are in one location. The employed process paradigm is balanced between agile and plan-driven: 41 % of the respondents answered that their development process is rather agile, 21 % that it is rather plan-driven, 37 % that it is mixed, and 1 % did not know. The type of systems the respondents develop is quite balanced (except for consumer software): 24 % develop embedded systems, 37 % business information systems, 5 % consumer software, and 34 % hybrid systems. Most of the respondents use requirements specifications for in-house development (57 %), 23 % create them and an external company is responsible for the development, and 19 % are subcontractors using requirements specifications (e.g., as basis for development or testing).

4.2   RQ1: Handling of QRs in Practice

RQ1.1: Do practitioners differentiate between QRs and FRs in the documentation? 88 % of the respondents answered that they document QRs in their projects, while 12 % answered that they do not document QRs at all. We contextualized this distribution w.r.t. the process paradigm the respondents use in their projects. Figure 2a shows that all respondents with a plan-driven process document QRs, while in agile processes only 77 % document QRs.

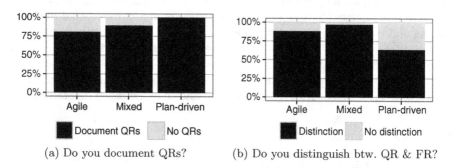

(a) Do you document QRs?   (b) Do you distinguish btw. QR & FR?

Fig. 2. Relation between process paradigm and the style of documenting QRs.

From the respondents who document QRs (91 in total), 85 % answered that they distinguish between QRs and FRs in the documentation and 15 % answered that they do not. We also contextualized this distribution w.r.t. the process paradigm. Figure 2b shows that a higher percentage of the respondents in agile processes distinguish between QRs and FRs compared with respondents in plan-driven processes. As a second contextualization, we analyzed the importance of quality factors w.r.t. the style of documentation. Figure 3 shows how the respondents ranked the importance of different quality factors for their daily work on a five point Likert scale. *Reliability* and *Performance/Efficiency*, for example, stand out as they are considered more important by participants who do not distinguish between QRs and FRs.

RQ1.2: To what extent do development activities for QRs differ from activities for FRs? Figure 4 shows how the respondents ranked the difference in the phases requirements engineering, architecture/design, implementation, and testing on a three point Likert scale. As a contextualization, we analyzed whether

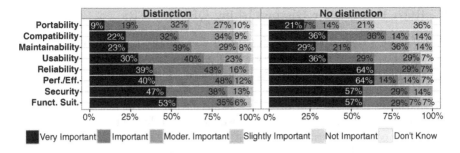

Fig. 3. Relation btw. importance of quality attributes and style of documentation.

there is a difference in how respondents rank the difference in the development phases w.r.t. whether they do or do not distinguish between QRs and FRs. The figure shows that the phase architecture/design was reported to differ stronger by respondents who distinguish between QRs and FRs.

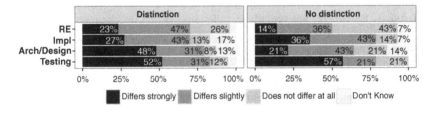

Fig. 4. Relation between process differences and style of documentation.

To further detail this response, Table 1 shows exemplary statements that respondents gave explaining the differences in the development activities. According to the answers, there is a different maturity of the processes for treating FRs vs. QRs (see Statement A). Furthermore, when it comes to project planning, FRs are planned in detail but QRs are considered in an unplanned way and only documented on a high-level (see Statement B). In testing, there are approaches for deriving test cases from FRs but none for deriving them from QRs (see Statement C). Moreover, different stakeholders are involved in testing QRs vs. FRs (see Statement D). In architecture and design, QRs need to be considered early in the project as they have a high impact on the architecture. In contrast to this, it is sufficient to consider FRs at an abstract level in early stages (see Statement E). In the implementation, QRs need to be monitored continuously, whereas FRs can be implemented successively (see Statement F). In requirements engineering, FRs are more fixed than QRs as QRs can be negotiated with the customer while FRs usually cannot (see Statement G).

4.3   RQ2: Reasons for Distinguishing QRs and FRs

Figures 5 and 6 show the cause-effect diagrams for the reasons for and consequences of (not) distinguishing between QRs and FRs in practice. On the left-
hand side of the diagrams, the mentioned reasons for distinguishing (Fig. 5) or
not distinguishing (Fig. 6) between QRs and FRs are indicated. On the right-
hand side of the diagrams, the mentioned consequences of the decision are shown.
The upper part contains the positive consequences while the lower part contains
the negative consequences. The different entries of the diagrams (e.g., *QRs have
different nature* in Fig. 5) correspond to codes that we identified in the data and
their number of occurrences. Furthermore, we structured the codes in categories
that are represented by the arcs in the diagram.

Reasons for Distinguishing QRs and FRs: The left-hand side of Fig. 5
shows the resulting reasons for distinguishing between QRs and FRs. In total,
49 out of the 77 respondents (64 %) that distinguish between QRs and FRs provided an answer to this open question. We identified 24 codes in the answers
for this question. For clarity, we only show codes that occurred at least twice in

Table 1. Exemplary answers about differences in the development process.

#	Phase	Answer
A.	General	*"[QRs] are usually treated less transparent: not clearly documented, not explicitly tested, but somehow considered in RE, design and coding as common sense background, e.g., in terms of [QRs] considering IT security, performance or reliability."*
B.	General	*"FRs are documented and planned in high detail [...] Working on [QRs] are often unplanned activities and only high level documented."*
C.	Test	*"Test cases for FR[s] can quite easily [be] derived from functional models or textual requirements [... but there is no] method for deriving test cases from [QRs]."*
D.	Test	*"Test planning, preparation and execution for [QRs] are handled by different stakeholders ([QRs] are [...] strongly architecture related) and personnel (performance and load tests are performed by specialists usually not part of the project team)."*
E.	Arch.	*"[QRs] are often architectural drivers and therefore have to be evaluated and considered very early in the project when defining the architecture. Whereas in an early stage of the project a more abstract view on the functional requirements is sufficient."*
F.	Impl.	*"[QRs] require continuous monitoring, as achievements (e.g., performance) may degrade during implementation."*
G.	RE	*"[In contrast to FRs,] [QRs] can be negotiated, if they are technically not reachable."*

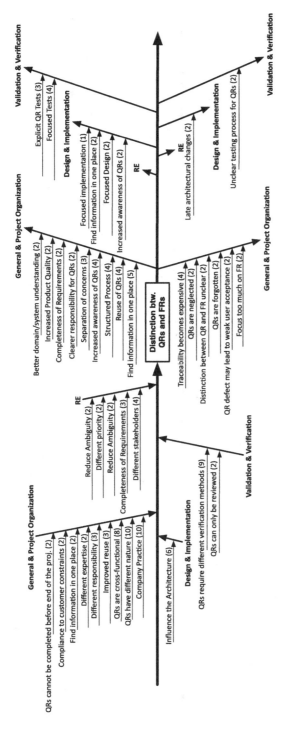

Fig. 5. Reasons for and consequences of distinguishing between QRs and FRs (Condensed version containing codes that occurred at least twice. The comprehensive diagram containing all codes is available at http://www4.in.tum.de/~eckharjo/DistinctionFishbone.pdf). The left-hand side shows the mentioned reasons and the right-hand side the mentioned consequences. The upper part of the right-hand side contains the positive consequences while the lower part contains the negative consequences.

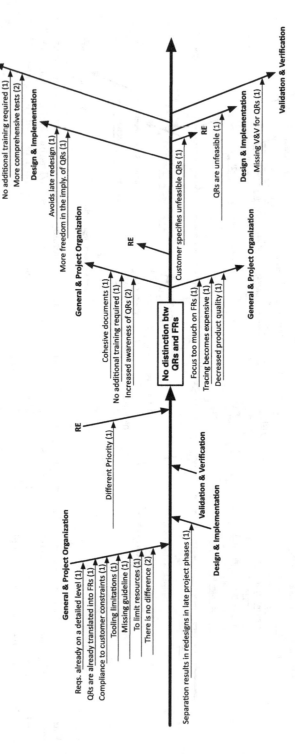

Fig. 6. Reasons for and consequences of not distinguishing between QRs and FRs. The left-hand side shows the mentioned reasons and the right-hand side the mentioned consequences. The upper part of the right-hand side contains the positive consequences while the lower part contains the negative consequences.

Fig. 5.[3] Reasons that we coded as *QRs have different nature*, *Company Practice*, and *QRs are cross-functional* occur frequently in the category *General & Project Organization*. Furthermore, in the category *Design & Implementation* the reason *Influence the architecture* and in the category *Validation & Verification* the reason *QRs require different verification methods* also occur often.

Reasons for Not Distinguishing QRs and FRs: The left-hand side of Fig. 6 shows the mentioned reasons for not distinguishing between QRs and FRs. In total, 7 out of the 14 respondents (50%) who do not distinguish between QRs and FRs provided an answer to this open question. We identified 8 codes in the answers for this question. Figure 5 shows all identified codes, which all occurred only once in the data (except for *There is no difference*).

4.4   RQ3: Benefits and Problems

Benefits and Problems of Distinguishing QRs and FRs: The right-hand side of Fig. 5 shows the consequences of distinguishing between QRs and FRs. The upper part shows the positive consequences while the lower part shows negative consequences. In total, 45 out of the 77 respondents (58%) that distinguish between QRs and FRs provided answers to the open question about positive consequences. Regarding negative consequences, 16 out of the 77 respondents (21%) provided answers. We identified 35 codes in the answers for positive consequences and 13 in the answers for negative consequences. As shown in the diagram, the code that we identified most in the mentioned benefits is *Find information in one place* in the category *General & Project Organization*. In this category, there are also other benefits that occurred frequently (e.g., structuredness of the process, completeness of the requirements, separation of concerns, and increasing the awareness of QRs). We coded the benefit *Increased awareness of QRs* also three times in the category implementation. For validation and verification, the most frequent benefits are *Focused Tests* and *Explicit QRs Tests*. The code that we identified most in the mentioned problems is *Traceability becomes expensive*. Further problems that were mentioned are that QRs are neglected or forgotten, that the distinction between QRs and FRs is unclear and that the distinction results in a weak user acceptance. Moreover, in the category *Validation & Verification*, the problem *Missing testability* was mentioned.

Benefits and Problems of Not Distinguishing QRs and FRs: The right-hand side of Fig. 6 shows the consequences of not distinguishing between QRs and FRs. The upper part shows the positive consequences while the lower part shows negative consequences. In total, 9 out of the 14 respondents (64%) that distinguish between QRs and FRs provided answers to the open question about positive consequences. Regarding negative consequences, 5 out of the 14 respondents (36%) provided answers. We identified 7 codes in the answers for positive consequences and 6 in the answers for negative consequences.

---

[3] The complete diagram including all codes is available at http://www4.in.tum.de/
~eckharjo/DistinctionFishbone.pdf.

5   Discussion

From the results presented in the previous section, we conclude that practitioners are split into two groups; one advocating a distinction between QRs and FRs and one advising against it. Interestingly, the respondents stated contrary reasons as arguments for or against a distinction (e.g., *"Both are requirements"* vs. *"We distinguish them because they are different"*). Similarly, we found the same benefits stated by respondents of both parties: *"If you distinguish, then QRs are considered better"* vs. *"As soon as QRs are treated equally to FRs it is a clear win-win situation such that QRs get the same attention."* Additionally, our results indicate that it is not clear to practitioners what the difference between both classes of requirements actually is, even though they stated reasons, benefits, and problems of a distinction: *"Most people have problems to distinguish between them, so they mix"* or *"[Not distinguishing] avoids unnecessary confusion at the requirements authors' side. Adding the distinction QR/FR would require additional training, QS, etc. without adding value to the projects"*. Some respondents see this as a reasons why they do not distinguish between them: *"[. . .]There is just no real guideline how to do it"*.

The most prevalent reasons for distinguishing between QRs and FRs are in line with those that are often found in literature (e.g., QRs have a different nature and are cross-functional, influence on architecture, require different verification methods). However, we cannot underpin any of those reasons with negative consequences in the cases where QRs and FRs were not distinguished. Therefore, we conclude that there seems to be confusion about this topic in practice and handling QRs seems to be driven by expectations rather than by evidence.

In the following, we will detail and discuss some conflicting or even contradictory statements. We believe that these are topics that need to be investigated further in the future, or, in case of a clear scientific position about a topic, we need to invest more into the dissemination of the results into practice.

QR Testing – A Double-edged Sword: One of the top reasons mentioned for distinguishing QRs and FRs was the need for different verification methods (especially w.r.t. testing). Figure 4 also shows that testing is the activity that differs most for QRs and FRs. When considering consequences of distinguishing between QRs and FRs in testing, we found both positive and negative. While some respondents said that a distinction leads to more focused and specialized tests for specific QRs, some also stated that a distinction leads to the fact that some QRs are not tested at all. For example, *"Performance tests are recognized as [a] key success factor by project managers"* vs. *"Main issue is how to handle the [QR] tests before product release"*. On the other hand, respondents who do not distinguish between QRs and FRs also reported positive and negative consequences regarding testing: *"[. . .]the mapping [of FRs to QRs] should ensure that this testing also covers [QRs]"* vs. *"[When not distinguishing,] corresponding V&V suffers"*. We conclude from this that distinguishing QRs and FRs supports the awareness for specialized tests of important QRs but, simultaneously, bears the risk of neglecting tests for less important QRs.

Company Practice – Never Change a Running Game: Another commonly stated reason for distinguishing between QRs and FRs is that this is common practice in the company or that this is required by customers. However, these reasons were almost never questioned or justified. For example, *"[. . .]Our specification template prescribes a structuring w.r.t. [QRs] and FRs"* or *"[we distinguish] as requested by the customer"*. Additionally, the respondents did not mention any positive or negative consequences that result from complying with customer constraints. We consider this as a sign of inadvertent handling of this topic. It would be interesting to ask customers to explicitly state reasons why they request a distinction of QRs and FRs.

QRs – Drivers for the Architecture: Several respondents stated that the architecture of a system is specifically influenced by QRs. For example, *"[QRs] are often architectural drivers and therefore have to be evaluated and considered very early in the project when defining the architecture"*. This was often used as an argument to distinguish between QRs and FRs: *"The separation allows architects to get a quick (and in-depth) understanding of the QRs without needing to know all the functional requirements"*. FRs, on the contrary, were considered to be more local and do not need to be fixed at the beginning of the project: *"[It is] easier to find[. . .]special FRs for developing a single use case"* or *"[. . .]in an early stage of the project a more abstract view on the functional requirements is sufficient"*. Surprisingly, some respondents stated that it has a positive impact for the implementation when QRs and FRs are not strictly distinguished: *"[QRs] and FRs are handled as features. They are not separated, which avoids the redesigns e.g., due to performance problems"* and *"[When not distinguishing,] we have much more freedom during the implementation iterations[. . .]to find solutions that fit the customers' expectations and the possibilities that come with the architecture and technology we use"*.

Awareness Matters: It seems that an increased awareness for QRs was considered as one of the most prominent benefits. Both parties claimed this as a benefit of distinguishing respectively not distinguishing between QRs and FRs: *"[Distinction] ensures that [QRs] are also in the focus"* vs. *"[Not distinguishing] helps keeping the team aware that the device does not only need to have certain features, but that these features also need to work e.g., at a high temperature"*. It seems that awareness can be increased with both strategies. The crucial point seems to be that there is a clear and explicit relation between FRs and QRs, which leads to the following observation.

Tracing – The Good, the Bad, and the Ugly: One trade-off that we found in the data is an inherent challenge that does not seem to be resolved in practice. Some respondents stated that a distinction between QRs and FRs is beneficial because it keeps associated information in one place and, thus, supports different viewpoints on the requirements: *"People who are particularly concerned with QRs, such as architects and performance testers, find relevant information in one place"* and *"As most [QRs] apply across components, they are more easily retrieved in a separate specification"*. However, this benefit also comes with clear disadvantages considering tracing and the risk of forgetting requirements: *"Consistent documentation of relationships between FRs and [QRs] is difficult"* and *"The development team needs to be fully aware about all sources for requirements. Ostrich strategy causes a high yield of trouble"*. Respondents who do not distinguish reported on benefits regarding the cohesiveness of their specifications: *"Some documents benefit from this, as they turn more cohesive"* or *"[...]the feature is really ready if installed and not only 80 %"*.

6   Limitations and Threats to Validity

We now discuss the threats to validity and mitigation measures we applied.

Participant Selection: One limitation in the study is the missing lack of control over the respondents given that we distributed the survey invitation over various networks. Apart from an unknown response rate, this means that we cannot control how representative the responses are. We removed those respondents from the population that stated that they do not deal with requirements. Also, although the introductory texts explicitly stated that the survey is aimed at addressing practitioners perspective, we cannot guarantee that all the views taken really result from practitioners.

Survey Research: Further threats to the validity result from the nature of survey research. We cannot control on which basis the respondents provide their answers, the respondents might be biased, and there exists the possibility that they have misinterpreted some of the questions or even the concept of QR/NFR. We reduced the first threat by asking questions to characterize the context of the respondents. We cannot mitigate the second threat, but reduced it by conducting the survey anonymously. We minimized the third threat by conducting a pilot phase in which we tested the instrument used and the data analysis techniques applied.

Subjectivity of Coding: A further major threat to validity, however, arises from the data analysis, i.e., the coding process, because coding is a creative task. Subjective views of the coders, such as experiences and expectations, might have influenced the way we coded the free text statements. A threat arises from the fact that we cannot validate our results with the respondents given the anonymous nature of our survey. We minimized this threat by coding in pairs (researcher triangulation).

Representativeness of the Codes: Finally, one limitation stems from the result set itself and its expressiveness. Our focus was to collect and code practitioners experiences on how they consider QRs. We quantified the results to get an overview of whether certain codes dominate others. However, a potentially high frequency of codes does still not allow for conclusions on the criticality of those codes. In particular, the fact that we got more answers about reason for and consequences of a distinction between QRs and FR than for no distinction might have distorted our interpretation of the results.

7   Related Work

The literature on categorizations of requirements is very extensive. Major contributions address categorizing non-functional requirements (e.g., [5,7,13]), of which most rely on quality (definition) models (a detailed discussion can be found in [6]). Pohl [13], for instance, discusses the misleading use of the term "non-functional" and argues to use "quality requirements" for product-related NFRs that are not constraints. Glinz [7] performs a comprehensive review on the existing definitions of NFRs, analyzes problems with these definitions, and proposes a definition on his own. Mairiza et al. [11] perform a literature review on QRs, investigating the notion of QRs in the software engineering literature to increase the understanding of this complex and multifaceted phenomenon. They found 114 different QR classes. Contributions such as those have fostered valuable discussions on the fuzzy terminology used and the concepts applied, but they did not focus on the implications of these categorizations on development processes in practice.

Chung and Nixon [4] investigate how practitioners handle QRs. They argue that QRs are often retrofitted in the development process or pursued in parallel with, but separately from, functional design and that an ad hoc development process often makes it hard to detect defects early. They perform three experimental studies on how well a given framework [12] can be used to systematically deal with QRs. Svensson et al. [17] perform an interview study on how QRs are used in practice. Based on their interviews, they found that there is no QR-specific elicitation, documentation, and analysis, that QRs are often not quantified and, thus, difficult to test, and that there is only an implicit management of QRs with little or no consequence analysis. Furthermore, they found that at the project level, QRs are not taken into consideration during product planning (and are thereby not included as hard requirements in the projects) and they conclude that the realization of QRs is a reactive rather than proactive effort.

Borg et al. [2] analyze via interviews how QRs are handled in two Swedish software development organizations. They found that QRs are difficult to elicit because of a focus on FRs, they are often described vaguely, are often not sufficiently considered and prioritized, and they are sometimes even ignored. Furthermore, they state that most types of QRs are difficult to test properly due to their nature, and when expressed in non-measurable terms, testing is time-consuming or even impossible. Ameller et al. [1] perform an empirical study based on interviews around the question *How do software architects deal with QRs in practice?* They found that QRs were often not documented, and even when documented, the documentation was not always precise and usually became desynchronized.

In all of the investigations, FRs and QRs are treated separately, and the investigations take an observational perspective on how practitioners deal with QRs in that context. The goal of our study is to analyze whether practitioners handle FRs and QRs differently, which reasons motivate the way they consider QRs, and what consequences this has on the development process.

8   Conclusions

In this paper, we reported on a survey conducted with 103 practitioners to explore whether and, if so, why they handle requirements labeled as "functional" differently from those labeled as "quality" as well as to disclose resulting consequences for the development process. Our results indicate that practitioners document QRs and most of them do make an explicit distinction between QRs and FRs in the documentation. Furthermore, our data suggests that the development process strongly differs depending on a distinction between QRs and FRs, especially in interconnected activities such as testing. The rationale of practitioners is that QRs are different to FRs, i.e. they are of different nature, are cross-functional, strongly influence the architecture, and require different verification methods. In our previous study [6], we found, however, that many requirements labeled as "quality" might as well be categorized as "functional" and prior to the study presented here, we had the simple speculation that if a blurry distinction determines how the following development activities are performed, we should find problems that arise because the activities do not really fit the corresponding requirements. Still, our results indicate that the question whether to make a distinction or not is without a direct linkage to negative or positive consequences per se. Therefore, we argue that the decision whether to make an explicit distinction should be made consciously such that people are aware of the risks that this distinction bears so that they may take countermeasures.

Acknowledgements. We would like to thank M. Broy, K. Beckers, J. Mund, S. Smith-Eckhardt, and M. Glinz for their helpful comments and suggestions.

References

1. Ameller, D., Ayala, C., Cabot, J., Franch, X.: How do software architects consider non-functional requirements: an exploratory study. In: 20th IEEE International Requirements Engineering Conference (RE) (2012)
2. Borg, A., Yong, A., Carlshamre, P., Sandahl, K.: The bad conscience of requirements engineering: an investigation in real-world treatment of non-functional requirements. In: 3rd Conference on Software Engineering Research and Practice in Sweden (SERPS) (2003)
3. Broy, M.: Rethinking nonfunctional software requirements: a novel approach categorizing system and software requirements. In: Software Technology: 10 Years of Innovation in IEEE Computer. John Wiley & Sons (2016)
4. Chung, L., Nixon, B.A.: Dealing with non-functional requirements: three experimental studies of a process-oriented approach. In: 17th International Conference on Software Engineering (ICSE) (1995)
5. Chung, L., do Prado Leite, J.C.S.: On non-functional requirements in software engineering. In: Borgida, A.T., Chaudhri, V.K., Giorgini, P., Yu, E.S. (eds.) Conceptual Modeling: Foundations and Applications. LNCS, vol. 5600, pp. 363–379. Springer, Heidelberg (2009). doi:10.1007/978-3-642-02463-4_19

6. Eckhardt, J., Vogelsang, A., Méndez Fernández, D.: Are non-functional requirements really non-functional? An investigation of non-functional requirements in
   practice. In: 38th International Conference on Software Engineering (ICSE) (2016)
7. Glinz, M.: On non-functional requirements. In: 15th IEEE International Requirements Engineering Conference (RE) (2007)
8. ISO/IEC: Systems and software quality requirements and evaluation (SQuaRE).
   ISO/IEC 25010, Geneva, Switzerland (2011)
9. ISO/IEC/IEEE: Systems and software engineering – Life cycle processes – Requirements engineering. ISO/IEC/IEEE 29148:2011(E), Geneva, Switzerland (2011)
10. Kitchenham, B.A., Pfleeger, S.L.: Personal opinion surveys. In: Guide to Advanced
   Empirical Software Engineering. Springer, London (2008)
11. Mairiza, D., Zowghi, D., Nurmuliani, N.: An investigation into the notion of non-
   functional requirements. In: 25th ACM Symposium on Applied Computing (2010)
12. Mylopoulos, J., Chung, L., Nixon, B.: Representing and using nonfunctional
   requirements: a process-oriented approach. Trans. Softw. Eng. **18**, 483–497 (1992)
13. Pohl, K.: Requirements Engineering: Fundamentals, Principles, and Techniques.
   Springer, Heidelberg (2010)
14. Robertson, S., Robertson, J.: Mastering the Requirements Process: Getting
   Requirements Right. Addison-Wesley (2012)
15. Sommerville, I., Kotonya, G.: Requirements Engineering: Processes and Techniques. John Wiley & Sons Inc., Hoboken (1998)
16. Stol, K., Raph, P., Fitzgerald, B.: Grounded theory in software engineering
   research: a critical review and guidelines. In: 38th International Conference on
   Software Engineering (ICSE) (2016)
17. Berntsson Svensson, R., Gorschek, T., Regnell, B.: Quality requirements in practice: an interview study in requirements engineering for embedded systems. In:
   Glinz, M., Heymans, P. (eds.) REFSQ 2009. LNCS, vol. 5512, pp. 218–232.
   Springer, Heidelberg (2009). doi:10.1007/978-3-642-02050-6_19
18. Van Lamsweerde, A.: Goal-oriented requirements engineering: a guided tour. In:
   5th IEEE International Symposium on Requirements Engineering (2001)

A Survey on Software Release Planning Models

David Ameller, Carles Farré$^{(\boxtimes)}$, Xavier Franch, and Guillem Rufian

Universitat Politècnica de Catalunya, Barcelona, Spain
{dameller,farre,franch}@essi.upc.edu,
guillemonl3@gmail.com

Abstract. Software release planning (SRP) is the problem of selecting which features or requirements will be included in the next release or releases. It is a crucial step in software development, which happens to be extremely complex given the need to reconcile multiple decision making criteria, (e.g., business value, effort and cost), while considering several constraints (e.g., feature precedencies, resource availability). For this reason, several SRP models have been proposed in the literature. The objective of this paper is to provide an updated review of SRP approaches reported in the literature.

Keywords: Software release planning · Next release problem · Resource optimization · Software evolution · Literature survey · State of the art

1 Introduction

According to Lehman's First Law of software evolution [6], software must be continually adapted or it becomes progressively less satisfactory to be used in its environment. Software changes are usually not implemented all together but incrementally [5]. Major enhancements are planned and incorporated, together with other minor changes, in each new release or upgrade. According to Sommerville [12], the main activities in an evolution loop are feedback, impact analysis, release planning, system implementation, and system release.

Software Release Planning (SRP) is the problem of finding the best combination of features to implement in a sequence of releases. SRP seeks to maximize business value and stakeholder satisfaction without neglecting the constraints imposed by the availability of adequate resources and the existence of dependencies between features, among other constraints [11]. There are several factors that make SRP a computationally complex problem: the number of features and their interdependencies; the number of stakeholders involved, their different levels of priority, and their conflicting interests; the variety of variables to be considered (e.g., business value, effort, cost); and the uncertainty and incompleteness of the available information [10].

Given its importance, many approaches to SRP have been proposed. Svahnberg et al. [14] presented a comprehensive survey of SRP models formulated until 2008. These models were analysed under different perspectives (inputs considered, industrial application, etc.). Since then, other proposals have been formulated.

The goal of this paper is to update the results of the survey [14] by considering these recent approaches to SRP. For attaining this goal, we have searched, analysed and

© Springer International Publishing AG 2016
P. Abrahamsson et al. (Eds.): PROFES 2016, LNCS 10027, pp. 48–65, 2016.
DOI: 10.1007/978-3-319-49094-6_4

discussed the different SRP models that have been proposed in the scientific literature related to this question by performing a snowballing-based literature review.

Following the four perspectives for describing a goal in the Goal-Question-Metric (GQM) approach [2], the goal of our study is defined as follows:

- Purpose: find and characterize
- Issue: the proposed models in the academic literature since 2009
- Object: for software release planning
- Viewpoint: from the viewpoint of project managers and software developers.

The rest of the paper is organized as follows. In Sect. 2, we introduce the research method followed in the paper, with special attention to the snowballing procedure and the research questions. In Sect. 3, we extract the results of the surveyed papers in relation to the research questions. In Sect. 4, we analyse the results and provide the most relevant observations from it. Finally, in Sect. 5 we present the conclusions and future work.

2   Research Method

As stated above, we built on top of the knowledge gained in the Systematic Literature Review (SLR) conducted by Svahnberg et al. [14] that surveyed the SRP approaches proposed until 2008. We proceeded according to the following steps:

- Our research questions were based on those in [14].
- Given its high citation count and prominent venue of publication, we assumed that any sound primary study on SRP models published in the period 2011–2015 has cited [14]. Therefore, we based our search of primary studies on forward snowballing from this paper.
- For the period 2009–2010, we checked the references appearing in the papers found in the forward snowballing. In addition, this reference analysis (backward snowballing) was used also to check any further relevant work in the period 2011–2015.
- Finally, we conducted an expert consultation step and added a few extra references that were considered relevant.

The rest of the section presents in detail the research method applied under these general guidelines.

2.1   Research Questions

In this study, we kept two of the research questions (RQs) from the SLR presented in [14] while discarding the other two that were more specific and related to specific interests of the authors. We also decided to decompose the two remaining RQs into sub-RQs to structure the data collection and analysis.

The most fundamental RQ of our study is: *What SRP models have been presented since 2009? (RQ1)*. We decompose it into four sub-questions:

- *RQ1.1. What are the main motivations for the models?*
- *RQ1.2. What are the inputs processed by the models?*
- *RQ1.3. What are the outputs generated by the models?*
- *RQ1.4. What are the algorithms or techniques applied by the models?*

We also want to know *to what extent have the SRP models surveyed in RQ1 been validated? (RQ2).* We have decomposed this RQ into:

- *RQ2.1. Are the models supported by tools?*
- *RQ2.2. How has been industry involved in the models?*
- *RQ2.3. What are the major threats identified on the models?*

2.2 Selection of Studies

As mentioned above, we combined forward and backward snowballing using [14] as starting point plus an additional final check with experts. Snowballing refers to using the reference list of a given paper (backward snowballing) or the citations to the paper (forward snowballing) to identify additional literature [16].

We defined the following inclusion criteria to select the relevant studies:

1. The paper is a full research paper published in any of: JCR-indexed journal belonging to Q1–Q3 quartiles; proceedings of one of the following main software engineering or software evolution conferences: ICSE, ESEC/FSE, ESEM, HICSS, ICSM, ICSME, CSMR; or any JCR-indexed journal, CORE A or B conference/ workshop proceedings if at least one of the authors has an industry affiliation. In addition, we included PROFES because it is the most recurrent venue in the papers found by [14], together with IEEE Software.
2. The paper describes an SRP model.

The rationale about the restricted selection of venues in the first criterion is that the most relevant studies should be found published in the most renowned journals and conferences. The reason for which the selection of these venues is relaxed for studies with authors having industrial affiliation is that we want to find as many as possible proposals where a full-scale industrial validation of the proposed SRP model is conducted. We think that, in line with the conclusions and recommendations given in [14], industrial validation is a key issue when assessing an SRP model.

The process was implemented in three different iterations as depicted in Fig. 1. For the *first iteration*, we used both Scopus and Google Scholar to find the references that cite directly [14]. This search was performed on 2 October 2015 and we retrieved 56 references from Scopus, while Google Scholar provided us 101. All the references returned by Scopus, except two, were also in the set provided by Google Scholar. Most of the 47 Google Scholar references not included in Scopus were excluded later on (see application of inclusion criteria below), but a few of them were considered. These ones were references to papers published in major journals as "online first", without being assigned yet to a concrete journal issue.

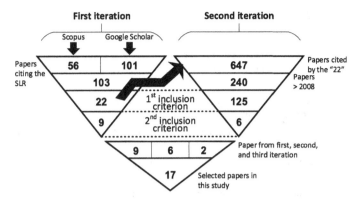

Fig. 1. Papers selected in each iteration.

From the grand total of 103 studies, 81 studies were excluded by the first inclusion criterion. The titles and abstracts of the remaining 22 studies were read to apply the second inclusion criterion. In the cases where that information was not sufficient to make a decision, the full text was also considered [16]. This resulted in the selection of 9 relevant papers listed in Table 1 (see the References section for full details).

Table 1. Papers selected from the forward snowballing iteration.

Ref.	Year	Paper title
M1	2012	A hybrid release planning method and its empirical justification
M2	2011	Quantitative release planning in extreme programming
M3	2013	Multi-sprint planning and smooth replanning: An optimization model
M4	2012	Solving the large scale next release problem with a backbone-based multilevel algorithm
M5	2013	Analyzing an industrial strategic release planning process - a case study at Roche diagnostics
M6	2013	Continuous release planning in a large-scale scrum development organization at Ericsson
M7	2015	Software requirements prioritization and selection using linguistic tools and constraint solvers — a controlled experiment
M8	2014	Industrial evaluation of the impact of quality-driven release planning
M9	2014	Theme-based product release planning: an analytical approach

For the *second iteration*, we used the 22 papers from the first iteration (i.e., the selected papers before applying the second inclusion criterion) and retrieved all their references. We retrieved 647 references overall, without taking into account any inclusion criteria. These references included papers, books, manifestos and programs. For the second iteration we used the same inclusion criteria, with the exception that from the 647 references we only considered those that were published after 2008. Then for the remaining 240 papers we applied the first inclusion criterion. Finally, the titles and abstracts of the 125 remaining papers were read to apply the second inclusion

Table 2. Papers selected from the backward snowballing iteration.

Ref.	Year	Paper title
M10	2009	Software project planning for robustness and completion time in the presence of uncertainty using multi-objective search based software engineering
M11	2010	Rigorous support for flexible planning of product release - a stakeholder centric approach and its initial evaluation
M12	2011	Conceptual scheduling model and optimized release scheduling for agile environments
M13	2015	Differential evolution with Pareto tournament for the multi-objective next release problem
M14	2010	An integrated approach for requirement selection and scheduling in software release planning
M15	2014	Bi-objective genetic search for release planning in support of themes

criterion. This resulted in the selection of 6 relevant papers listed in Table 2 (see the Reference section for full details).

For the *third iteration*, we asked for additional references to experts participating in the SUPERSEDE H2020 European project (www.supersede.eu). We received 5 proposals of papers which were considered relevant in the context of this project. From these 5 references, we discarded 3 of them: Ruhe's book because it was not providing new models but a compilation of knowledge [10], a paper by Durillo et al. [4] (see justification below) and a tool demo report since it was only 4 LNCS pages long [1]. The two remaining papers are listed in Table 3.

As a result, we selected 17 papers from this period starting in 2009 until date. This number is quite aligned with the total number of papers surveyed in [14], a total of 28 papers found in the period 1997–2008.

Table 3. Papers selected after recommendation in the SUPERSEDE project.

Ref.	Year	Paper title
M16	2016	Risk-aware multi-stakeholder next release planning using multi-objective optimization
M17	2010	Analytical product release planning

It is worth to mention that the second inclusion criterion left out some papers that are relevant to the SRP field but are not directly related to the goals of this research. We highlight four categories of papers that have not been included:

- Papers that present some experimentation (through benchmarks) on advanced algorithms that are applied to SRP (e.g., Durillo et al. [4] performing a sensitivity analysis of three genetic algorithms or Luna et al. [9] which surveys different metaheuristics for solving a multi-objective based formulation of the problem).

- Papers that assess the quality of SRP techniques or practices (e.g. Lindgren et al. [8] proposing a capability maturity model for release planning or Didar-al-Alam et al. [3] identifying release readiness improvement factors).
- Papers that focus on activities that may or must take place during SRP but do not focus on this particular context (e.g., Lehtola et al. [7] analysing requirements prioritization).
- Papers that add a small delta to previous publications (e.g., Szőke [15] adding assignment of features to distributed teams which does not change significantly the model proposed by the same author in another journal paper selected in our study).

2.3 Data Extraction and Analysis

For the data extraction we used a set of variables associated to each research question and the metadata used for the selection criteria (see Table 4). For the analysis we extracted data and categories as a basis for our results, and we revised the relevant papers for each particular topic to provide valuable information.

Table 4. Data extraction criteria

Metadata		Article title
		Authors' name
		Journal/conference
		Retrieval search query
		Date of publication
RQ1	Context	What is the main motivation for the model
	Models	What are the inputs that the model processes
		What are the algorithms/techniques used for computation
		What are the outputs that the model produces
RQ2	Tool	Tool availability
	Study	Study from academia or industry
		Description of threats to validity
	Adoption	Model proposed in literature or in industry
		Model validated in academy or in industry
		Model adopted in academy or in industry

2.4 Threats to Validity

Construct Validity. The selection of primary studies followed a strict protocol; however, the use of snowballing has some inherent, well-known limitations. The most important threat is that snowballing narrows the search scope to the referenced papers, therefore some papers may be left out. We consider that this threat was mitigated by the fact that we used an SLR published in a main software engineering journal as departing paper because such SLRs are normally cited by many researchers. A second mitigation action was to include a third iteration based on experts' opinion.

Internal Validity. Each paper was analysed in depth by one researcher of this study; however, it is known that it is easy to have different views or interpretations on the same paper depending, e.g., on the research background or past experiences in similar studies. Therefore, papers were checked by a second researcher when doubts arose.

External Validity. As in most literature reviews, this study does not aim to generalize results because there is no statistical basis to claim that the selected papers are a representative sample of the population (i.e., all the papers ever published about SRP). Therefore, any claim made in this study is limited to the set of studied papers. Moreover, the study only covers the works published in the literature, any model made available by other means (e.g., commercial tools) has not been considered.

Conclusion Validity. We defined a precise protocol of the steps to be followed, however as in any other literature review, we relied on the result of search engines which may offer different results in the future. Therefore, a replication of this study could lead to different selection of primary studies, and thus to different results.

3   Results

This section summarizes the results of the analysis of the 17 selected SRP references in relation to the RQs formulated in Sect. 2.2.

3.1   RQ1. *What SRP Models Have Been Presented Since 2009?*

Eleven [M2–M4, M6, M7, M10, M12–M16] out of the 17 papers that we have examined propose new models. The 6 remaining models [M1, M5, M8, M9, M11, M17] are extensions of the EVOLVE II model (being itself an extension of EVOLVE) and its implementation as a commercial tool, ReleasePlanner. Given this fact, we analyse separately the two families in the RQ. They are summarized in Tables 5 and 6 whose contents will be detailed in the rest of this subsection. Table 6 focuses on the customization that the different approaches propose on EVOLVE II.

Table 5. Summary of responses to RQ1: new SRP models

Ref	Motivation	Input factors	Output	Technique
M2	Planning in agile	RD • EC • SiF • VF	Next release • User stories • 3 priority levels	Nested knapsack problem, solved with branch and bound
M3	Planning in agile	RD • EC • VF • RF	Multi-release • User stories	Generalized knapsack problem, solved with branch and cut

(continued)

Table 5. (*continued*)

Ref	Motivation	Input factors	Output	Technique
M4	Scalability	RD • B&CC • SiF	Next release • Requirements	Backbone-based multilevel algorithms
M6	Scalability	B&CC • VF • RF	Next release • Features	Human assessment
M7	Scalability	SiF	Next release • Requirements • Prioritized list	Satisfiability modulo theory supported by NLP and AHP
M10	Robustness and completion time	RD • RC	Tasks assigned to developers	Genetic algorithm
M12	Planning in agile	RD • RC • EC • TiC • SiF	Multi-release • Features	0-1 multiple knapsack problem, solved with branch and bound
M13	Development cost and customer satisfaction	B&CC • SiF	Next release • Requirements	Evolutionary algorithm
M14	Time schedule +diversity of precedences	RD • RC • TiC	Next release • Requirements • Time schedule	Knapsack problem +resource-constrained scheduling problem, solved with branch and bound
M15	Grouping features by themes	RD • RC • EC • SiF • VF	Next release • Features	Evolutionary algorithm
M16	Risk assessment and stakeholder prioritization	B&CC • SiF	Next release • Requirements	Satisfiability modulo theory

Table 6. Summary of responses to RQ1: EVOLVE II-based models

Ref	Motivation	Input factors	Output	Technique
M1	Dealing with complex constraints	RD • TeC • RC • SiF	Multi-release • Features	ReleasePlanner+Constraint Programming Solver
M5	Scalability	RD • RC • SiF	Multi-release • Features	ReleasePlanner

(*continued*)

Table 6. (*continued*)

Ref	Motivation	Input factors	Output	Technique
M8	Quality aspects	RD • QC • RC • SiF	Multi-release • Features	ReleasePlanner
M9	Grouping features by themes	RD • RC • SiF	Multi-release • Features	Graph clustering +ReleasePlanner
M11	Active stakeholder involvement	RC • SiF	Multi-release • Features	ReleasePlanner +Weighting-Based techniques
M17	Introducing data analysis	RD • B&CC • SiF	Multi-release • Features	Crowdsourcing+Data Analysis+ReleasePlanner

RQ1.1. *What are the main motivations for the models?*

Among the 11 new models, we have identified a first group [M2, M3, M12] whose main concern is to address SRP in agile contexts, characterized by the uncertainty related to working with estimations (e.g., project velocity) and the flexibility required by agile projects (e.g., continuously changing customer needs, especially when the model is intended to plan more than one iteration as [M3, M12] do). Other approaches do also propose a solution in an agile context (e.g. [M14]) but the problems they face are not inherent to this paradigm (e.g., different type of requirement precedencies).

A second group of new models seems more concerned in proposing solutions that scale up in the presence of large sets of requirements ([M4, M6, M7]).

Another group [M10, M13] emphasise the contradictory nature of some SRP objectives: robustness (defined as a solution that satisfies expectations of project manager) vs. completion time [M10] and development cost vs. customer satisfaction [M13].

For the remaining new models, the motivations differ: grouping related features into themes to be scheduled preferable together [M15], considering different sorts of dependencies between requirements [M14], taking into account the requirements inherent risks [M16] or tightly integrating time [M14] into the solution.

For the 6 models that extend EVOLVE II/ReleasePlanner, the motivations are also different in each case. The resulting extensions, thus, are orthogonal and complementary with respect to the others. In [M1], for example, there is the need of dealing with requirements selection constraints that are more complex and richer than the ones that ReleasePlanner accepted as input. In [M5], the original motivation is to apply ReleasePlanner in an industrial case study and, as a result, a new extension is proposed to address the problem of feature generation. In [M8, M9] the proposed extension of EVOLVE II is driven by the need of dealing with quality aspects and features grouped into themes, respectively. In [M11] the main aim is to promote and support the active participation of the stakeholders in the planning process. Finally, in [M17] the motivation is to define a generic framework to solve different sorts of release planning problems by applying analytical methods on a diversity of data available from internal and external sources of information.

RQ1.2. *What are the inputs processed by the models?*

Here we replicate the analysis of input factors done in [14] by applying the same taxonomy of requirements selection factors. The taxonomy is as follows:

- Hard Constraints: include those factors that may restrict the order and time when certain features or requirements can be implemented. They are classified as:

  - Technical Constraints: Requirements Dependencies (RD), Quality Constraints (QC), and Other Technical Constraints (TeC).
  - Other hard constraints: Budget & Cost Constraints (BCC), Resource Constraints (RC), Effort Constraints (EC), Time Constraints (TiC).
- Soft Factors: include those factors that are more difficult to estimate and provide exact numbers on. They are classified as: Stakeholders' Influence Factors (SiF), Value Factors (VF), Risk Factors (RF), and Resource Consumption Factors (RCF).

In Table 7 the factors appear in their original formulation and, between parenthesis, their mapping to the taxonomy of requirements selection factors.

Table 7. Requirements selection factors per SRP model

Ref	Factors in model
New models	
M2	Technical precedencies (RD) • Story sizes+Velocity estimate (EC) • Preference (customers wish) precedencies (SiF) • Story & theme values (VF)
M3	Correlation & Precedence among stories (RD) • Story efforts (EC) • Story values (VF) • Story risks (RF)
M4	Requirements dependencies (RD) • Requirement costs (B&CC) • Customer satisfactions (SiF)
M6	Feasibilities (B&CC) • Profitabilities (VF) • Risks (RF)
M7	Keyword prioritization by user (SiF) • Pairwise comparisons between requirements by user (SiF)
M10	Task dependencies (RD) • Available resources/staff (RC) • Different skills (RC).
M12	Feature dependencies (RD) • Resource capacities (RC) • Business priorities and efforts (EC) • Iteration-delivery times (TiC) • Requirement priorities (SiF)
M13	Requirement costs (B&CC) • Client values (SiF) • Client weight factors (SiF)
M14	Task dependencies (RD) • Available employees (RC) • Employee salaries and dedications (RC) • Deadline of the project (TiC)
M15	Task dependencies (RD) • Available resources (RC) • Task efforts (EC) • Stakeholder values (SiF) • Theme & feature values (VF)
M16	Requirement costs (B&CC) • Stakeholder values (SiF)
EVOLVE-based models	
M1	Coupling and precedence dependencies (RD) • Constraints solvable by CP solvers (TeC) • Resource constraints (RC) • Stakeholder scores to features (SiF)

(continued)

Table 7. (*continued*)

EVOLVE-based models	
M5	Coupling and precedence dependencies (RD) • Resource constraints (RC) • Stakeholder scores to features (SiF)
M8	Coupling and precedence dependencies (RD) • Quality constraints (QC) • Resource constraints (RC) • Stakeholder scores to features (SiF)
M9	Coupling and precedence dependencies (RD) • Resource constraints (RC) • Stakeholder scores to features (SiF)
M11	Resource constraints (RC) • Stakeholder scores to features (SiF) • Stakeholder pre-selected features (SiF)
M17	Advanced feature dependencies (RD) • Budget capacities (B&CC) • Stakeholders' cost predictions (SiF) • Stakeholders' willingness to pay (SiF)

The input factors considered in EVOLVE II/ReleasePlanner are coupling and precedence constraints between features (RD), resource constraints (RC), as well as the stakeholder scores to features, given for a flexible number of criteria (SiF) [M1]. Some of the models that extend EVOLVE II/ReleasePlanner do not require extra input [M5, M9]. In addition, [M1] accepts as input any constraint that can be also expressed as an input of a Constraint Programming Solver (e.g., a constraint expressing mutual exclusion between features, or productivity investments). In the case of [M8], some quality aspects are added to the model. In [M11], the model adds a pre-selection of candidate features from stakeholders. Finally, [M17] presents a case study where the decision of what to release considers advanced feature dependencies, stakeholders' predictions on feature costs, budget capacities over different time periods, and the price that stakeholders would pay for each feature.

RQ1.3. *What are the outputs generated by the models?*

In the case of the new SRP models, we report three main categories of outputs. Eight approaches [M2, M4, M6, M7, M13–M16] produce as output the list of stories/requirements/features to be included in the next release. Moreover, in [M2] this list is divided into three groups with different priority: must-have, should-have and could-have stories. Going further, [M7] produces a list of prioritized requirements for the next release. In [M14] the output combines the list of next-released requirements with a schedule of the relative time at which these tasks should be performed by the development teams. Two approaches [M3, M12] produce a multi-release plan, more specifically an assignment of user stories or features to consecutive sprints. One approach [M10] does not produce release plans but an assignment of different tasks to different developers taking into account the specified constraints (i.e., the focus is only on the operation release planning).

The models that extend EVOLVE II/ReleasePlanner produce the same output than the original model/tool: an assignment of features to the releases in which they have to be implemented.

RQ1.4. *What are the algorithms or techniques applied by the models?*

In spite of their diversity, most of the approaches build on top of a very simple formulation of the SRP problem: calculate an assignment from a feature set $\{f(1), ..., f(N)\}$ to a release plan $x = (x(1), ..., x(N))$ such $x(j) = k$ means that $f(j)$ is offered at release k. The solution is required to maximize the value of some utility or objective function. Except for naïve assumptions, the problem becomes a multi-objective problem and the approaches differ mainly in the techniques proposed to solve this NP problem.

Some approaches [M2, M3, M12, M14] formulate the problem as an instance of the knapsack problem, using some kind of branch and bound algorithm to solve it. The number of releases to plan and the type of constraints managed configure the exact type of knapsack (nested, generalized, ...). [M14] combines this solution with additional techniques from resource-constrained project scheduling problem solving.

Other family of approaches use optimization-related techniques. Satisfiability modulo theory is among the preferred ones [M7, M16]. In addition, [M7] uses natural language processing (NLP) for extracting information from requirements, and the analytic hierarchy process (AHP) to fine-tune the prioritization of requirements. Evolutionary algorithms [M13, M15] and genetic algorithms [M10] are also used to implement the multi-objective problem. Finally, a backbone-based multilevel algorithm was tune to the SRP problem in [M4].

On a completely different setting, [M6], which is based on a large-scale industrial case at Ericsson for agile processes, presents a model which does not use any particular model. In fact, one of the motivations of the case study is to overcome the limitations posed by model-based approaches, especially in relation with the assumptions for their application. Therefore, all the release planning is integrated in the traditional agile lightweight agile process.

On the other hand, the EVOLVE-based models are implemented using the ReleasePlanner tool. From these approaches:

- [M5, M8] use the tool as it is.
- [M9, M11] complement the tool with some extra functionalities. For instance, [M11] includes a weighting-based technique to consider the influences that every stakeholder has in each iteration requirements.
- [M1, M9] integrate ReleasePlanner with some other software component. In [M1], ReleasePlanner is used to generate a first solution that feeds a constraint programming solver to find the best solution with an enlarged set of constraints. Conversely, [M9] uses the output of a graph clustering algorithm to feed ReleasePlanner.
- [M17] embeds ReleasePlanner into a more complex system which seeks maximizing a utility function.

3.2   RQ2. *To What Extent Have the SRP Models Surveyed in RQ1 Been Validated?*

To answer RQ2, following we summarize our findings for the three sub-RQs.

RQ2.1. *Are the models supported by tools?*

Nearly half of the works found in this state of the art mention some kind of tool, but is worth to differentiate those works that use a tool just to validate their approach (i.e. a prototype or just an ad-hoc solution specific for the paper) from those that are presenting a ready-to-use tool; in this second case, the most remarkable case is ReleasePlanner, mentioned in [M1, M5, M8, M9, M11, M17] (the models based on EVOLVE-II).

The papers that use a prototype or ad-hoc solution mention the following technologies: CP-Solver [M1], LP-Solve (an OSS linear programing tool) [M2], and CPLEX [M3]. In general, we can see that all the academic contributions use problem solvers to determine what features will be implemented in the next release.

The rest of papers ([M4, M6, M10, M12–M16]) did not report any kind of tool.

RQ2.2. *How has been industry involved in the models?*

All selected papers are academic works (i.e., all or most authors have an academic affiliation). In 4 cases [M5, M6, M8, M10] there was one author from the industry. It is worth noting that these works were the only ones that provide real case studies as part of their contribution. The rest of works were validated using experiments with the exception of [M9], which had a case study (using students).

All the proposed models except one were originated in academic research. The exception is an approach proposed by Ericsson [M6], which is also the only one that is being adopted by the industry (by the same company).

RQ2.3. *What are the major threats identified on the models?*

We found 5 papers [M5, M6, M7, M8, M10] with a wide analysis of the threats to validity (i.e., including internal, external, construct and conclusion validity threats). In 5 cases [M1, M4, M9, M11, M15] there were some threats explained but without any kind of structure and in 7 cases [M2, M3, M12–M14, M16, M17] there was no mention of threats to validity.

From those that mention the threats to validity, the most recurrent ones are: lack of testing in an industrial setting, the difficulty to generalize the results (e.g., due to the different skills of the testing participants, variability, and different domain applications), and that some formalizations do not contemplate all the possible dependencies.

4 Discussion

In this section discuss the most remarkable observations coming from the analysis of the results.

4.1 RQ1. *What SRP Models Have Been Presented Since 2009?*

One family of models prevails in the field, namely those coming from the EVOLVE-II/ReleasePlanner proposal. This fact is not surprising due to the high prevalence of the EVOLVE family in SRP before 2010 as reported in [14].

RQ1.1. *What are the main motivations for the models?*

Pursuing scale. In contrast with the results reported in [14], we have found more proposals aimed to scale in presence of large sets of requirements, which is a necessary step towards a full industry application. Unfortunately, the theoretical approaches have not been complemented with a proper validation in true industrial settings (see below).

RQ1.2. *What are the inputs processed by the models?*

Incomplete input factors. In a recent survey conducted through interviews with the three companies participating in the SUPERSEDE project [13], any SRP model should be able to deal with the following input factors in order to fit industry needs:

- For each requirement: the required effort to implement it (measured in person hours or similar), the developer skills required to implement it, its deadline (optional), its dependencies with respect to other requirements and its priority or its business value assessed by its stakeholders.
- For each release: its deadline and the list of available developers, for whom it is necessary to know:
  - his/her skills (to be matched with the ones required to implement requirements)
  - the amount of effort (measured in hours per week or similar) that s/he can invest in the release.

While requirements dependencies are taken into account by almost all the studies, other constraints like time (deadlines) are only addressed by two papers [M12, M14], and only one other paper [M10] take into account the different (developer) skills required and available to implement the requirements. On the contrary, soft factors like stakeholder consideration have been considered by a great share of approaches.

RQ1.3. *What are the outputs generated by the models?*

Simple outputs. Most of the SRP surveyed models produce a "binary" yes/no result that simply tells which requirements should be implemented for the next release (s). Only in the case of the models presented in [M10, M14], a richer type of results, in terms of requirement implementation scheduling and resource (developers) allocation, is provided. Clearly, this latter type of results is the one that matches better with the needs of software companies, in accordance with the input factors that they think that should be taken into account as reported above.

RQ1.4. *What are the algorithms or techniques applied by the models?*

SRP as a multi-objective problem. Most approaches recognize the existence of different and often conflicting objectives that need to be reconciled in the planning of releases. Solutions aim at reducing the inherent NP nature of the algorithms into linear-time implementations still able to find an optimal release plan. Experimentation is a key instrument for these works in order to demonstrate the accuracy and efficiency of the proposed technique.

4.2   RQ2. *To What Extent Have the SRP Models Surveyed in RQ1 Been Validated?*

RQ2.1. *Are the models supported by tools?*

Lack of ready-to-market tools. Only one tool (among the mentioned in the selected papers) can be considered a ready-to-market tool, namely ReleasePlanner. In fact, the product, while created in an academic context, is the core business of a spin-off company created around it. On the positive side, this commercial nature may be an indicator that there is a market share for this kind of tools. However, it is true that other tools are available in the market (e.g., Tempo Planner, a plug-in for JIRA) but none of them got their way into the selected papers. Another important observation is that 8 of the selected papers (out of 17) that did not mention any tool support; this circumstance makes very difficult to assess the suitability of these approaches.

RQ2.2. *How has been industry involved in the models?*

Scarce industrial contributions. Very few authors from the surveyed papers came from industry, in most cases as providers of a case study. Only in one single case the industrial authors were providing the SRP model. On the other hand, as commented before, there are other commercialized tools without representation in the academic literature. This situation may imply that the observations made in this paper are slightly deviated towards the academic perspective because there is a part of the big picture underrepresented in the academic literature.

RQ2.3. *What are the major threats identified on the models?*

Non-optimal consideration of threats to validity. For a literature survey focused on journals and main conferences, it is a bit surprising to find as much as 7 papers (from 17) with no mention at all at threats to validity. The absence of their analysis hampers the applicability of the presented models.

4.3   SRP Field Evolution

It is interesting to analyse the evolution of the SRP field by comparing the results from [14] and ours. As a first observation already stated in Sect. 4, the EVOLVE family of SRP models keeps its prevalence. In our literature review, we have found 6 papers out of 17 (35.3 %), less than the $16/28 = 57.1$ % found by [14] but still the biggest share by far. No other method has shown prevalence in the field since 2009. In particular, in the case of papers not belonging to the EVOLVE family, none of the authors of models reviewed by [14] appear in the new models that we have studied, except for the case of [M14]. This means that although these researchers have made interesting proposals from a research point of view, the transferability to industry is not reported.

Svahnberg et al. [14] found that most models focused on a limited set of input factors, mainly hard constraints. Only a 57.1 % of the reviewed models considered soft factors. In our study, 15 out of the 17 models (88.2 %) do include soft factors. Noteworthy, soft-constraints that implied some kind of stakeholder involvement (SiF constraints) are considered in 13 out of the 17 models (76.5 %) that we have found, whereas that in [14] only 7 out of 28 (25 %) took them into account. An interpretation to this observation is that the proposals until 2008 needed to focus on algorithms able to solve such hard constraints in a comprehensive and efficient manner, while newer proposals could build on top of these results and focus on the business-related issues pointed out by soft factors.

As for model validation, we have already stated in Sect. 4 that industry involvement in the validation of the SRP models has decreased in the proposals found by our study compared to those in [14]: while in [14] the amount of models validated in the industry was 56 %, in the last years the participation of the industry has decreased to 23.5 % (4/17). This can be somewhat compensated by the fact that we have found more models, in proportion, considering larger sets of requirements, which is a factor supporting transferability of the models to industry.

5   Conclusions

In this paper, we have presented the state of the art on SRP models in the period 2009-2016. We have investigated two research questions analysing the characteristics of these models and their validation state. We have used the results of a previous systematic literature review published in 2010 [14] as main reference to our research methodology. The main results (detailed in Sect. 4) show some progress with respect the previous proposals in the period 1997–2008 surveyed in [14], in particular:

- Special attention to the scalability of the models (cf. RQ1.1).
- Increasing emphasis on soft factors like consideration of stakeholders and business value (RQ1.4).

On the contrary, some other observations make evident that SRP scientific proposals have not yet reached the maturity required by industrial contexts:

- Incomplete input factors considered (RQ1.2) and simple output produced (RQ1.3).
- Proof-of-concept tool support, except for the case of the EVOLVE-ReleasePlanner family of proposals (RQ2.1).
- Poor validation due to scarce industry validation (RQ2.2) and non-optimal consideration of threats to validity (RQ2.3).

We may conclude that the current state of the art claims for an increasing effort in making SRP models closer to industry requirements like those surveyed in [13].

Acknowledgements. This work is a result of the SUPERSEDE project, funded by the EU's H2020 Programme under the agreement number 644018.

References

1. Aydemir, F.B., Mekuria, D.N., Giorgini, P., Mylopoulos, J.: Next Release Tool. ER 2015
2. Basili, V., Caldiera, G., Rombach, D.: Goal/question/metric paradigm. In: Encyclopedia of Software Engineering, vol. 1, Wiley, New York (1994)

3. Didar-Al-Alam, S,M., Shahnewaz, S,M., Pfahl, D., Ruhe, G.: Analysis and improvement of release readiness – a genetic optimization approach. In: Jedlitschka, A., Kuvaja, P., Kuhrmann, M., Männistö, T., Münch, J., Raatikainen, M. (eds.) PROFES 2014. LNCS, vol. 8892, pp. 164–177. Springer, Heidelberg (2014). doi:10.1007/978-3-319-13835-0_12

4. Durillo, J.J., Zhang, Y., Alba, E., Harman, M., Nebro, A.J.: A study of the bi-objective next release problem. Empir. Softw. Eng. **16**(1), 29–60 (2011)

5. Grubb P, Takang AA. *Software maintenance: concepts and practice*. World Scientific, 2003

6. Lehman, M.M.: On understanding laws, evolution, and conservation in the large-program life cycle. J. Syst. Softw. **1**, 213–221 (1979)

7. Lehtola, L., Kauppinen, M., Kujala, S.: Requirements prioritization challenges in practice. In: Bomarius, F., Iida, H. (eds.) PROFES 2004. LNCS, vol. 3009, pp. 497–508. Springer, Heidelberg (2004). doi:10.1007/978-3-540-24659-6_36

8. Lindgren, M., Land, R., Norström, C., Wall, A.: Towards a capability model for the software release planning process -- based on a multiple industrial case study. In: Jedlitschka, A., Salo, O. (eds.) PROFES 2008. LNCS, vol. 5089, pp. 117–132. Springer, Heidelberg (2008)

9. Luna, F., González-Álvarez, D.L., Chicano, F., Vega-Rodríguez, M.A.: The software project scheduling problem: a scalability analysis of multi-objective metaheuristics. Appl. Softw. Comput. **15**, 136–148 (2014)

10. Ruhe, G.: Product Release Planning: Methods, Tools and Applications. CRC Press, Boca Raton (2010)

11. Ruhe, G., Saliu, M.O.: The art and science of software release planning. IEEE Softw. **22**(6), 47–53 (2005)

12. Sommerville, I.: Software Engineering, 10th edn. Pearson (2015)

13. Stade, M., Seyff, N., Perini, A., Marco, J., Nadal, S., Franch, X.: D3.1: Requirements for Methods and Tools. SUPERSEDE EU project deliverables (2015)

14. Svahnberg, M., Gorschek, T., Feldt, R., Torkar, R., Saleem, S.B., Shafique, M.U.: A systematic review on strategic release planning models. Inf. Softw. Technol. **52**(3), 237–248 (2010)

15. Szőke, Á.: Optimized feature distribution in distributed agile environments. In: Ali Babar, M., Vierimaa, M., Oivo, M. (eds.) PROFES 2010. LNCS, vol. 6156, pp. 62–76. Springer, Heidelberg (2010). doi:10.1007/978-3-642-13792-1_7

16. Wohlin, C.: Guidelines for snowballing in systematic literature studies and a replication in software engineering. In: EASE 2014

Primary Studies Found in the Literature Survey

M1. Przepiora, M., Karimpour, R., Ruhe, G.: A hybrid release planning method and its empirical justification. In: ESEM 2012

M2. van Valkenhoef, G., Tervonen, T., de Brock, B., Postmus, D.: Quantitative release planning in extreme programming. Inf. Softw. Technol. **53**(11), 1227–1235 (2011)

M3. Golfarelli, M., Rizzi, S., Turricchia, E.: Multi-sprint planning and smooth replanning: an optimization model. J. Syst. Softw. **86**(9), 2357–2370 (2013)

M4. Xuan, J., Jiang, H., Ren, Z., Luo, Z.: Solving the large scale next release problem with a backbone-based multilevel algorithm. IEEE Trans. Softw. Eng. **38**(5), 1195–1212 (2012)

M5. Zorn-Pauli, G., Paech, B., Beck, T., Karey, H., Ruhe, G.: Analyzing an industrial strategic release planning process–a case study at Roche diagnostics. In: REFSQ 2013

M6. Heikkilä, V.T., Paasivaara, M., Lassenius, C., Engblom, C.: Continuous release planning in a large-scale scrum development organization at ericsson. In: Baumeister, H., Weber, B. (eds.) XP 2013. LNBIP, vol. 149, pp. 195–209. Springer, Heidelberg (2013). doi:10.1007/978-3-642-38314-4_14

M7. McZara, J., Sarkani, S., Holzer, T., Eveleigh, T.: Software requirements prioritization and selection using linguistic tools and constraint solvers—a controlled experiment. Empir. Softw. Eng. **20**(6), 1721–1761 (2015)

M8. Felderer, M., Beer, A., Ho, J., Ruhe, G.: Industrial evaluation of the impact of quality-driven release planning. In: ESEM 2014

M9. Agarwal, N., Karimpour, R., Ruhe, G.: Theme-based product release planning: an analytical approach. In: HICSS 2014

M10. Gueorguiev, S., Harman, M., Antoniol, G.: Software project planning for robustness and completion time in the presence of uncertainty using multi objective search based software engineering. In: GECCO 2009

M11. Heikkilä, V., Jadallah, A., Rautiainen, K., Ruhe, G.: Rigorous support for flexible planning of product releases - A stakeholder-centric approach and its initial evaluation. In: HICSS 2010

M12. Szőke, A.: Conceptual scheduling model and optimized release scheduling for agile environments. Inf. Softw. Technol. **53**(6), 574–591 (2011)

M13. Chaves-González, J.M., Pérez-Toledano, M.A.: Differential evolution with Pareto tournament for the multi-objective next release problem. Appl. Math. Comp. **252**, 1–13 (2015)

M14. Li, C., van den Akker, M., Brinkkemper, S., Diepen, G.: An integrated approach for requirement selection and scheduling in software release planning. Requir. Eng. **15**(4), 375–396 (2010)

M15. Karim, M.R., Ruhe, G.: Bi-objective genetic search for release planning in support of themes. In: Goues, C., Yoo, S. (eds.) SSBSE 2014. LNCS, vol. 8636, pp. 123–137. Springer, Heidelberg (2014). doi:10.1007/978-3-319-09940-8_9

M16. Pitangueira, A.M., Tonella, P., Susi, A., Maciel, R.S., Barros, M.: Risk-aware multi-stakeholder next release planning using multi-objective optimization. In: Daneva, M., Pastor, O. (eds.) REFSQ 2016. LNCS, vol. 9619, pp. 3–18. Springer, Heidelberg (2016). doi:10.1007/978-3-319-30282-9_1

M17. Nayebi, M., Ruhe, G.: Analytical product release planning. In: The Art and Science of Analyzing Software Data. Morgan Kaufmann (2015)

Organizational Models

A Power Perspective on Software Ecosystem Partnerships

George Valença[1(✉)], Carina Alves[1], and Slinger Jansen[2]

[1] Centro de Informática, Universidade Federal de Pernambuco, Recife, Brazil
{gavs,cfa}@cin.ufpe.br
[2] Department of Information and Computing Sciences,
Utrecht University, Utrecht, The Netherlands
fs.jansen@cs.uu.nl

Abstract. To address today's market demands for continuous enhancement of systems capabilities, software producing organisations have increasingly formed or joined software ecosystems. In these complex and networked settings, they define partnerships to complement each other's features, acquire new skills, divide R&D costs and share customers. Such business model entails mutual dependence on companies for survival and effectiveness. It creates a flow of influence among them and makes the ecosystem resemble power-law distributions. Drawing on established concepts from Social and Behavioural Sciences, we performed an exploratory case study of six software companies to investigate their power-dependence relationships in an ecosystem environment. A prime result of this research is showing that it is possible to understand how power and dependence influence the behaviour and coordination of partner firms within a software ecosystem.

Keywords: Software ecosystem · Open business model · Partnerships · Power · Dependence · Case study · Software product management

1 Introduction

Software companies have increasingly recognised that product and process innovation alone are no longer sufficient to successfully market their technology. To stay competitive in current fast-moving economy, they have adopted innovative business models by changing the dominant logic of doing business [26]. The emergence of cloud platforms, the explosion of data and the development of new avenues for information have led these firms to gradually build proprietary software ecosystems around their products. In parallel, free software is a promising platform for open-source software ecosystems, which are leveraged by active collaboration of community developers.

These ecosystems result from the strengthening of multiple, bi-lateral alliances among complementors. As competitors in the IT industry and collaborators in joint development initiatives, software firms have embraced coopetition, i.e. relationships between companies that cooperate in some activities while compete in others. They are constantly facing the interplay of power and dependence, which are driving forces of their partnerships. The power exerted by companies in business-to-business contexts

© Springer International Publishing AG 2016
P. Abrahamsson et al. (Eds.): PROFES 2016, LNCS 10027, pp. 69–85, 2016.
DOI: 10.1007/978-3-319-49094-6_5

influences business models for value co-creation as well as market dominance. Hence, power is a critical aspect of interfirm relationships in business networks [19].

This paper reports on an exploratory case study that analysed power-dependence relationships between partners in proprietary software ecosystems. We interpret this phenomenon in light of established work from Social and Behavioural Sciences theorists, using a conceptual framework of multiple facets of power. Furthermore, we discuss our findings from the perspective of ecosystem governance and health [1].

Our contribution is twofold. First, we describe different power types and a structured way of modelling power directions in a dyad. We then analyse the power flows in the partnerships and their outcomes in the ecosystems. Second, we offer empirically grounded knowledge and raise a theoretical discussion that is relevant for future research on software ecosystems [9], as a growing field in software engineering (SE).

The rest of the paper is structured as follows: in Sect. 2, we present the research fundamentals. In Sect. 3, we detail the research design. Section 4 describes the results, while Sect. 5 discusses these findings. Finally, in Sect. 6, we conclude the paper, with implications and future work of this research.

2   Background

2.1   Software Ecosystems

The notion of *software ecosystem* adopts concepts from business and biological ecosystems to analyse the dynamics of today's software industry [2]. For Jansen and colleagues [13], a software ecosystem consists in a set of businesses functioning as a unit and interacting with a shared market for software and services, together with relationships among them. It represents a disruptive open business model strategy that proposes novel ways for a central firm to collaborate with partners, and for them to create and capture value from the network [26].

According to Campbell and Ahmed [3], one can describe a software ecosystem from a business, architecture and social dimension. The *business dimension* comprises factors such as vision, innovation and strategic planning. It involves the definition of business strategies (e.g. profit and revenue models) and partnership model (e.g. membership models serving participants). The *architecture* or *technical dimension* focuses on technological aspects of the ecosystem. It is concerned with products from third parties, generally developed and integrated through a common platform. Finally, the *social dimension* consists in the relationships among software firms/developers in the associated social ecosystem. It includes the motivations to build alliances, rules for social interaction, and opportunities to show and enhance actor's capabilities [17].

There are two main types of software ecosystems: proprietary and open source [17]. In a *proprietary* ecosystem, the source code and other artefacts produced are protected and new players usually need to be certified to join the network. It is the case of iOS ecosystem, in which external developers guarantee a steady flow of apps for Apple's iPhone, or SAP ecosystem, in which a thriving community of resellers enables SAP to be Europe's largest software company. In its turn, an *open-source* ecosystem has a generally flexible certification criteria and actors who participate independently from receiving revenues from their activity. Android is an open source ecosystem, with participants that develop apps or plug-ins for the software platform.

Actors in software ecosystems play different roles, with specific duties. The *keystone* or *orchestrator* is a company, community or independent entity responsible for running a technological platform, creating and applying rules (e.g. quality standards), and managing the participation of actors. *Niche player* is a company, person or entity that complements the platform by developing specific features that customers require. *Value-added reseller* (VAR) is a company that makes profit from selling ecosystem products. Finally, *users* acquire and use an ecosystem solution or service to carry out their business or perform personal activities [9, 17].

The keystone is the main responsible to orchestrate ecosystem members and coordinate development efforts on top of the software platform. Moreover, this firm is responsible for *software ecosystem governance*, which involves the creation of procedures to control, maintain, or change the ecosystem [1]. It includes business and technical aspects such as management of the platform and interfaces, definition of a sustainable business model, and development of partners [25]. A successful governance strategy leads to a healthy software ecosystem. It brings a growing number of opportunities for participants and a great ability to innovate by transforming inputs into new products and services with lower costs [1, 10, 12].

2.2 Power and Dependence

According to Emerson [8], *power* is not a property of an actor or group. It derives from the existence of a relationship, which implies on specifying over what/whom power is exercised. The power of an actor A is thought to be the inverse of the dependence of an actor B, bringing the idea of a *power-dependence relationship*: the power of A over B is equal to, and based upon, the dependence of B upon A.

Lawler [16] considers power as a structurally based capability of an actor. Hence, an actor can rely on a *power capability* (PC) to exert influence over another party. This PC can be positioned according to French and Raven taxonomy [20], which is formed by five core *power types* or *bases*: coercive power, expert power, legitimate power, referent power and reward power. We depict these forms of power in Table 1.

Table 1. Main types of power [20].

Power type	Description
Coercive (CO)	It is based on B's perception that A has the ability to mediate punishments for him
Expert (EX)	It is based on B's perception that A has some special knowledge or expertise. Obs. *informational power* can be seen as a specific type of expert power that involves the control of relevant information
Legitimate (LE)	It is based on B's perception that A has the right to prescribe behaviour for him
Referent (RF)	It is based on the identification of B with A, i.e. feeling of oneness of B with A or desire for such identity. If A is an attractive group, B will desire to join in
Reward (RW)	It is the perception that A has ability to provide rewards and benefits for B

The total amount of power in a relationship is not fixed, but variable [16]. It means that power is a contingent and dynamic construct, which is constantly negotiated in the course of a relationship [15]. Hence, there may occur shifts of existing power, e.g. one party gains power while the other's power remains constant. Such dynamism results from changes in an actor's sources of power. They represent tangible or intangible resources or outcomes that he exploits to affect the behaviour of another actor [6]. Any change in the availability or demand for such power sources may affect power distribution in a dyad (i.e. interaction between a pair of firms).

The analysis of power is a means to explain behaviour and balance a dyad. When mutual dependence differs, there is a power advantage for one party, e.g. if A acts as less dependent and more powerful, B may comply with requests from A, since B is less able to resist. By tactically manipulating his PCs, an actor can obtain a power advantage and rebalance a relationship. Too imbalanced dyads may be dysfunctional, since a powerful actor may pursue short-term exclusive interests. This actor may also appropriate a larger portion of overall benefits accruing from the dyad [4]. In addition, certain forms of power may not sustain long-term development of the relationship, as there shall be undesirable exchange conditions and levels of uncertainty for one party.

Emerson's definition is a common operationalisation of power in studies on inter-organisational settings, with increased academic interest in recent years [18]. These studies primarily draw on the power base theory from French and Raven, which was originally presented in the book 'Studies in Social Power', in 1959, and is one of the most adopted conceptualisations of power [7]. These authors underpin the conceptual framework that we use in this paper to analyse power-dependence relationships between studied companies in a software ecosystem.

3   Research Method

This research analyses the interplay of power and dependence in software ecosystems. We translate this goal in the research question: *how power and dependence manifest in partnerships between companies participating in a software ecosystem?* To answer it, we performed an exploratory case study, which is appropriate when there is little evidence about a phenomenon and researchers seek new hypotheses [22]. The qualitative data collected enabled us to examine specific aspects of the phenomenon, such as situations when a firm gains power, and decisions that reduce the dependence of a partner. The study involved six companies that participate in a software ecosystem.

3.1   Data Collection

We collected empirical data through semi-structured interviews, which provided an in-depth understanding of the exercise of power and the consequent notion of dependence in an ecosystem. The interview protocol[1] covered partnership strategies, technical and social issues. We guaranteed that the same basic structure was followed in each

---

[1] The interview protocol is available via this link https://goo.gl/LbvSLL.

interview, although we asked new questions according to interviewees discourse. To map other partnerships and ecosystems, we used a snowball sampling and asked interviewees to recommend other firms and participants based on their expertise.

The case study started with the CRM Software Company, where we interviewed the CEO and a developer. This company is a Microsoft VAR and has partnerships with the software firms here named as Data Integration Company, E-mail Marketing System Company, Financials Software Company and Insurance Software Company. We also interviewed the CEOs of the Insurance Software Company and Financials Software Company to enrich partnerships information provided by the CRM Software Company. In addition to the interviews, we adopted the analysis method from Romano and colleagues [21] to examine web-based qualitative data. We retrieved data from the websites of these firms to analyse their product portfolio, partners, marketplace and news pages. We also searched IT news portals, since most of these firms have an international operation that makes them subject of evaluations from such websites.

3.2 Data Analysis

Initially, one researcher generated the interview transcripts and another researcher verified them to validate the text, clarify interviewees' expressions and discuss the findings. This procedure turned the findings more concrete by reducing misunderstandings. In addition to interviews data, we collected evidence from firms' portals and news websites. We adopted Thematic Analysis (TA), which is one of the most common methods for synthesising evidence in SE and particularly useful in case studies [5]. TA aims to identify, analyse and report patterns within data. This coding procedure generated themes and sub-themes related to the ecosystem scenario, such as 'technological platform' and 'software product management'. This structure helped us to organise the data set in rich detail, preparing it for a conceptual analysis.

In this subsequent step, we relied on our theoretical framework, without which TA would have limited interpretative strength. We used an abductive reasoning and adopted established theories from Social and Behavioural Sciences (c.f. Sect. 2) to describe our findings. We considered Emerson's statement that power resides in the other's dependency [8] to examine the power-dependence relationships, here represented by the partnerships. We identified the power capabilities (PC) [16] held by partners, which enabled us to denote situations of power exercise in the ecosystem. We just considered PCs identified by our data analysis, since we are not performing a general investigation of the companies in their segments. It means we only listed PCs supported by collected evidence. This decision increases the validity of our study, since we kept a clear chain of evidence while drawing our conclusions. We labelled each PC with the code *PowerType_CompanyCode_Number*, where *PowerType* means the form of power exercised by the firm (cf. Table 1), *CompanyCode* indicates the firm (CA - CRM Software Company, CB - Data Integration Company, CC - E-mail Marketing System Company, CD - Financials Software Company, CE - Insurance Software Company and CF - Microsoft) and *Number* is the number of the PC (01, 02, and so on). For instance, LE_CA_02 means the second power capability of legitimate power type exercised by the CRM Software Company over an ecosystem partner.

We created schemes to represent the use of power capabilities by companies in a software ecosystem. A directed arrow indicates an activity that expresses a form of power exercised by a firm in a given situation of the partnership. In addition, the schemes indicate the correspondent source(s) of power used by partner companies.

3.3 Case Companies

The *CRM Software Company (CA)* was founded in mid 90 s. It has 30 employees and serves about 400 customers from IT and financials markets in Benelux. The firm's business model completely depends on Microsoft: it is a VAR of Dynamics CRM. It adapts the product to different verticals by offering templates (functional modules), toolbox (solution to build such templates) and connectors (solution that enables data exchange between Dynamics CRM and other systems). It has focused on software integration via connectors to act as niche player in multiple software ecosystems.

The *Data Integration Company (CB)* was founded in 1995 and is a leading provider of CRM integration solutions worldwide. The company built an ecosystem around an integration platform, which has over 1.200 partners. Integration providers get access to 12.000 clients from diverse markets after joining the partner program as VARs or system integrators. They build their solutions on the platform or sell existing ones. Its Microsoft partner program provides standard connectors for Microsoft Dynamics.

The *E-mail Marketing System Company (CC)* is a 10-year-old company with 40 employees. The company provides solutions for the marketing domain and has over 2.700 customers. Based on its e-mail marketing system, it raised an ecosystem of over 130 partners. It particularly invests in integration partners, e.g. firms that develop connectors that allow clients to send newsletters from their ERPs or CRM systems.

The *Financials Software Company (CD)* has existed for more than 30 years. It is a market leader for cloud accounting in Benelux, with 500 employees and a portfolio of products for financial, accountancy and related domains. It has an expanding software ecosystem around its solutions, with more than 160.000 clients. A third party can join this network after becoming an app centre partner. Generally, partners build extensions in the form of connectors that the firm will later offer in its online marketplace.

The *Insurance Software Company (CE)* is a 30-year-old firm with 180 employees. It provides a cloud-based and modular SOA insurance system, with policy and claim handling modules, for Netherlands, UK, Belgium and South Africa markets. It has gradually created an ecosystem as a means to go forward in Netherlands competitive software industry. It focuses on its competencies and relies on small implementation partners who provide complementary features and consultants who sell its products.

Finally, *Microsoft (CF)* was founded in 1975 and it is the world's largest software vendor in terms of revenue. Its Microsoft Dynamics solution consists in a line of ERP and CRM applications. Dynamics CRM focuses on sales, marketing, and service sectors, relying on an ecosystem of 640.000 partners who use a .NET-based framework to build customisations. Microsoft certifies these firms as VARs and enables them to access cutting-edge technologies and potentially reach a base of 40.000 customers.

4   Results

This section answers the research question by describing how power and dependence manifest in partnerships within a software ecosystem setting. Our analysis takes the perspective of the CRM Software Company as VAR of Dynamics CRM ecosystem and niche player of other ecosystems, in which it provides connectors for Dynamics CRM. We adopt the three-dimensional view of software ecosystems from Campbell and Ahmed [3] to describe power distribution in the partnerships and introduce the power capabilities of the companies based on French and Raven power forms [20].

4.1   Business Dimension

The *business dimension* involves the creation of an ecosystem vision, which generally consists of disseminating product and platform goals to inspire participants to follow them. This dimension embraces the definition of an innovation strategy to support the continuous improvement of processes and products. It also includes the creation of a strategic plan to understand how, when and who will perform the goals [3, 23]. In particular, the keystone may open up governance policies and allow the community to influence them. In this case, this firm gives power to partners as they start to participate in ecosystem decision-making process [14].

The studied networks are in an expanding phase and their initial keystones (Data Integration Company, E-mail Marketing System Company, Financials Software Company, Insurance Software Company and Microsoft) are in charge of ecosystem governance. It differs from open ecosystems, where this duty is generally shared in a committee (e.g. product managers, partners and users). Keystones define how much power is left to members and how much they keep for themselves. Frequently, studied firms not just provide partners with a comprehensive view of the platform and product roadmaps, but also share decision rights. For instance, the Data Integration Company has a voting system for partners to make trade-off decisions that a product manager does. They register feature requests to improve integration tools and assess the value of other partners' ideas. The keystone then shows its dependence on partners to fulfil untapped needs and leverage ecosystem innovation, as perceived in the arguments of the Financials Software Company CEO: *"to what extent I want to be a certain product (or) leave it to others? I said (this) when he (marketing director) asked me how to build this ecosystem: 'create space; if (partners) don't have space, they gonna suffocate and there is no money for anybody; nobody is gonna work with (the ecosystem)"*.

Partners such as the CRM Software Company obtain the **legitimate power** to influence management plans of the ecosystem (LE_CA_01). By sharing this power with external actors, studied keystones allow partners to adjust ecosystem focus, e.g. technologies to develop, features to include in future release. Hence, keystones benefit from the convergence of development efforts in the network. Figure 1 shows this power.

Fig. 1. Legitimate power (LE) of the CRM Software Company over keystones

4.2 Social Dimension

The *social dimension* of an ecosystem involves the factors promotion, utilitarianism and knowledge sharing. Other aspects related to this perspective are recognition from peers, reputation, learning and sense of code ownership, for instance [2, 3]. The keystone must explore these factors and not simply open a platform to obtain extensions from third parties. The success of a software ecosystem depends on how adequately a firm engages with other peers and creates a collaborative and innovative environment.

By structuring a software ecosystem and positioning itself as a keystone, a firm reinforces its **expert power**, i.e. superior abilities or information. The recognition of such expertise by external actors may generate a feeling of membership and desire to join the network. The reliance of the CRM Software Company on the vast know-how and robust products of Microsoft (EX_CF_01) motivated the firm to define Dynamics CRM as a foundation for its solutions. It also trusts the platform and tools of the Data Integration Company (EX_CB_01) to develop connectors for SaaS, cloud or hybrid scenarios, as cited by the CRM Software Company CEO: *"They (Data Integration Company) are a market leader in connectors"*. Partners' knowledge is critical for the firm, which previously had to develop connectors from scratch, using web services.

Despite the expertise of the E-mail Marketing System Company, Financials Software Company and Insurance Software Company, respectively, in e-mail marketing (EX_CC_01), finances control (EX_CD_01) and policy/claim handling (EX_CE_01), they depend on the CRM Software Company to extend their product portfolio. The CEO of the Insurance Software Company CEO explained the importance of complementors to fuel the ecosystem with specific features: *"we have organisations such as CRM Software Company around us that provide additional functionality to our own (, which is) not that special need that we want to develop ourselves"*. The need for the expertise of partners was also mentioned by the Financials Software Company CEO: *"these are the areas that we don't cover with our own product – this is where we are going to find apps; you won't be able to do it without an emergent ecosystem"*.

The dependence of these companies gives power to the CRM Software Company. Hence, this firm expresses its expert power on CRM (EX_CA_01). It links Dynamics CRM with other solutions via connectors, resells this product and enables clients to optimise it with a toolbox and templates. *"For certain verticals you have to adapt it (Dynamics CRM); we got 4 templates (and) developed an editor where you can build templates; there is a need for CRM and they (partners) don't want to build it themselves;*

we build this connection; we got expertise in this product; it is integration; connector sales", detailed the CRM Software Company CEO.

This context describes the role of expert power in a partnership, which involves the knowledge a firm has in a given domain, product or technology, as shown in Fig. 2.

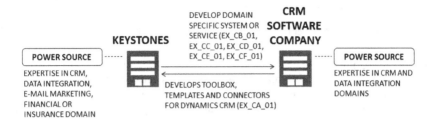

Fig. 2. Expert power (EX) of the CRM Software Company and keystones

Microsoft and other keystones may directly promote ecosystem participants via an associate model, which enables them to obtain and manage partners. In a proprietary ecosystem, a partnership model defines roles and duties that external actors may play in the network while they manipulate software artefacts and information [24]. This instrument specially states the benefits resulting from the adoption of the platform and presents strategies to generate value from the partnership. By creating incentives, the keystone highlights ecosystem utility and fosters partners' engagement. In their turn, partners enable the keystone to offer complements and access new technologies [23].

We perceived that all firms have the ability to generate advantages for a partner, which denotes their **reward power**. Microsoft benefits the CRM Software Company with Dynamics CRM VAR certification (RW_CF_01), which involves technical support in product deployment and maintenance, and commercial support via licensing, pre-sales and marketing actions. Moreover, it lists the solutions of the CRM Software Company at Microsoft Pinpoint, a wide marketplace for clients to search applications and services based on Microsoft technologies. *"This one (Dynamics CRM ecosystem) has 40.000 customers"*, explained the CEO of the CRM Software Company.

Microsoft ecosystem also offers a key asset to partners: Microsoft's strong image as one of the world's most valuable and successful firms. *"CRM is a bigger ecosystem; if they (partners) say 'this is CRM Software Company add-on', no one knows the firm; if they (clients) see Microsoft logo, they click and buy"*, argued the CEO of the CRM Software Company. This niche player recognises Microsoft's **referent power** (RF_CF_01), using such reputation to promote its sales (Fig. 3). This visibility is far more relevant than that of small-to-medium partners of the CRM Software Company such as the E-mail Marketing System Company or Insurance Software Company.

An indirect benefit from Microsoft VAR certification is enabling the CRM Software Company to reach other networks. The firm was certified as system integrator in the software ecosystem of the Data Integration Company, which has a Microsoft partner program (RW_CB_01). This keystone provides partners with an API and integration tools as well as developers to support connectors' construction. In addition, the Data Integration Company enables partners to access an online marketplace and promotes

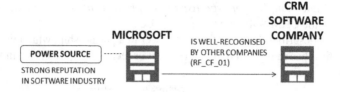

Fig. 3. Referent power (RF) of Microsoft over the CRM Software Company

their expertise by publishing customer stories involving the extensions. The CRM Software Company developer reinforced the success of this ecosystem: *"(It) is a new platform; there are lots of partners developing connectors for it"*.

The E-mail Marketing System Company grants an integration partner certification (RW_CC_01) to the CRM Software Company. It does campaigns about the CRM Software Company connector on its website, where customers can buy it and receive further assistance. Similarly, the Financials Software Company certifies the CRM Software Company as app centre partner (RW_CD_01). The benefits include free access to APIs, participation in workshops and developer resources. It also publishes partners extensions at an apps centre, enabling them obtain new customers: *"they have business apps from third parties and we are one of them; (its) online (platform) is an accountancy program (with) 160.000 customers"*, described the CRM Software Company CEO. In addition, the Financials Software Company organises business events to foster interaction among niche players.

In Fig. 4, we represent the dynamics of reward power in the relationship between keystones and the CRM Software Company in the software ecosystems.

Fig. 4. Reward power (RW) of keystones over the CRM Software Company

The Insurance Software Company presents partners' products to potential clients in pre-sales (RW_CE_01), as cited by its CEO: *"in our portfolio, these products are lined up just as our own products are; we sell (CRM Software Company) efficiency, compliance or commercial possibilities"*. The partner receives a purchase order, with an agreement per client, or it may be hired as contractor in joint sales. In this specific relationship, the CRM Software Company offers a kickback fee (RW_CA_01) once there are recommendations/potential sales generated by this partner. The CEO of the Insurance Software Company described this agreement: *"if a partner does something on his own, he provides a kickback and you get a small percentage of (the business deal)"*. Figure 5 shows reward power forces in the relationship between the Insurance Software Company and the CRM Software Company.

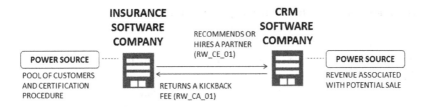

Fig. 5. Reward power (RW) of the CRM and Insurance Software Companies

The studied keystones obtain reward power by increasing the dependence of niche players on opportunities accruing from ecosystem customer base. The CRM Software Company CEO described this context: *"you are depending but on the other side you are using big marketing machine ecosystems of very big companies; (and) the marketing is done by those players; we are here on their website"*. In its turn, the CRM Software Company gains power once creating a dependence in the Insurance Software Company with respect to monetary payment for deals this partner promotes.

However, the Insurance Software Company has the right to cease all opportunities offered to a partner if his extensions do not satisfy acceptance criteria. Since these features may pose a risk to the image of the system and affect company's reputation, the partner can be removed from the ecosystem. The CEO of the Insurance Software Company draws an analogy to explain this practice: *"the quality of our partners is a risk to our brand; if you have a low battery quality, you have an issue (for the whole car); all cars (have) rubbish (and) there is only one part that has been replaced, which is rubbish; it has been a natural situation"*. Such careful quality control may involve the substitution of partners who offer low quality features. This penalty denotes the **coercive power** of the Insurance Software Company (CO_CE_01) (Fig. 6).

Fig. 6. Coercive power (CO) of Insurance Software Company over CRM Software Company

4.3 Technical Dimension

It is imperative that the keystone coordinates the contributions of multiple and varied actors from a technical perspective. Hence, the *technical dimension* embraces software platform management in terms of domain engineering, products' commonalities and variabilities, among other issues. Such open software enterprise model also requires changes in software product management processes [14], e.g. on a tactical-operational level, the keystone shall inform partners about policies related to quality requirements, certification and intellectual property (IP) of products in the ecosystem.

Such rules that guide the partnerships involve implicit and explicit rights of the companies, which configure their **legitimate power** in the ecosystem. The ownership of Dynamics CRM provides Microsoft with full control of changes over system functionality. Thereby, value-added resellers cannot change core features of Dynamics CRM (LE_CF_01). This means that the CRM Software Company can only develop extensions. Frequently, the company has to explain to clients that their customisation requests cannot be satisfied. *"We are only partners; we can't just change (Dynamics) CRM; (it) is a Microsoft product"*, argued the CEO of the CRM Software Company.

The expertise of the CRM Software Company in CRM domain enables it to determine how each connector will be built (LE_CA_02), as indicated by its CEO: *"the whole thing about connectors is defined by us"*. The firm is in charge of requirements and technologies specification, whereas partners generally have short influence on connectors' development due to their usual lack of knowledge in CRM. *"The [CRM Software Company] owner is very convincing saying 'we are the specialists, we will dictate what the requirements are'; Insurance Software Company isn't a CRM specialist"*, cited the developer of the CRM Software Company.

In particular, the E-mail Marketing System Company obtained the right to specify the scope of the connector since it paid the CRM Software Company to develop it (LE_CC_01). It demanded the CRM Software Company to follow a requirements document. *"They had a document (with) how the connector should work; it was mainly a connector that was placed (by us) into their requirements to get it working"*, described the CRM Software Company developer.

Although the CRM Software Company uses the platforms and app stores of partner ecosystems to build and offer the connectors, it owns the intellectual property of connectors. Thereby, it has the prerogative to control the evolution of connectors (LE_CA_03), as argued by the CEO: *"the plan is to phase it (E-Mail Marketing System Company connector) out, because we want to bring down our portfolio; we have a lot of little products and we want to focus on a couple of things"*.

While the CRM Software Company defines how connectors are built and maintained, the Data Integration Company demands that the final version of the connectors go through a certification procedure (LE_CB_01). This prerogative stems from the Data Integration Company ownership of the technology and marketplace used by the CRM Software Company. It also results from the fact that connectors will be available in other firms' sales channels, carrying the mark of the Data Integration Company.

Similarly, the Financials Software Company controls the submission of partners' extensions to the apps centre via a lengthy quality review (LE_CD_01). *"They (partners) submit the application referral, (which) is reviewed by market and tech departments; we request them to do a demo (to) see how it works (and) publish (in the) apps centre"*, detailed the Financials Software Company CEO.

The Insurance Software Company imposes a code restriction to partners. It has the right to define degrees of access to source code of its system (LE_CE_01). Hence, the CRM Software Company only deals with the system via interfaces: *"so far we have not let partners into our code base; they can adjust or add codes; change parameterisation; (but) not customise"*, cited the Insurance Software Company CEO. It denotes the legitimate power of the firm to manage system architecture in the ecosystem.

In Fig. 7, we represent the interplay of legitimate power forces among studied software companies. For instance, it shows that the CRM Software Company cannot apply its power to define connector requirements (LE_CA_02) over the E-mail Marketing System Company. This is a right of this partner due to his payment for the connector (LE_CC_01). Therefore, the E-mail Marketing System Company supersedes the right of the CRM Software Company to define development details.

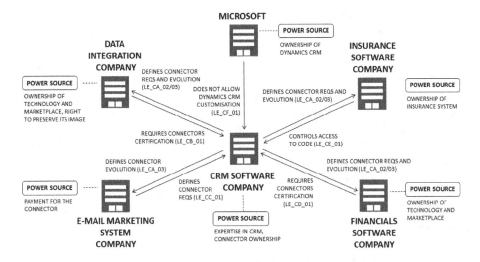

Fig. 7. Legitimate power (LE) of keystones and CRM Software Company

5 Discussion

The previous section described the forms of power and respective sources used by the companies in investigated partnerships. The representation of power enabled us to understand their relationships from multiple views, such as knowledge recognition and use (**expert power**), rights and roles definition (**legitimate power**), and benefits sharing (**reward power**). This analysis of what directs power configuration is a relevant input to propose effective business strategies and define suitable governance mechanisms in a software ecosystem environment. Our findings reveal that certain power capabilities allow partnerships to flourish. The keystones' strategy of sharing decisions provides niche players with the **legitimate power** to influence changes in product and platform plans [1]. In turn, this strategy fosters innovation in the ecosystem. The keystone firms could also nurture value creation by exercising a specific **reward power**: support partners with low implementation costs and even provide financial resources [25]. In addition, external players would have an important incentive to join and stay in the network. By adopting this strategy, keystones would reinforce their role and power position in the expanding software ecosystems.

The **legitimate power** of keystones and niche players to control the platform and complementary products reflect their rights, as rules that govern partnerships. For instance, keystones have the right to perform quality evaluations of extensions built by partners, who accept this rule due to their dependence on the ecosystem. However, keystones must ensure that these standards and certifications do not decrease the productivity of niche players. It is not the case of the Data Integration Company, whose legitimate power to review partners' connectors implies on a lengthy certification process. Similarly, the Insurance Software Company has the power to restrict the access to core code of the insurance system, which constraints the development of complements and may affect ecosystem productivity [12].

If certain exercises of legitimate power may cause conflicting relationships, the use of **coercive power** can compromise the success of the business model adopted in the ecosystem. The coercive behaviour of a keystone may promote the migration of a niche player to another network where he could obtain similar opportunities but with less intimidating rules. The survival rate of participants then decreases, affecting ecosystem robustness [10]. We observed that the Insurance Software Company simply substitutes a partner once the quality of his features may threaten the reputation of the firm and hamper the development of its referent power. Instead of exercising such negative form of power over partners, it should define mechanisms for them to properly develop complements (e.g. open platform, with published interfaces, or integration services) and guarantee their approval (e.g. quality requirements for a release).

Studied keystones also invest in the use of **reward power**. They provide a firm such as the CRM Software Company with a partner certification. This often involves the promotion of partner products in online sales channels or via recommendations to clients. Such capability provides partners with business prospects, increasing their market share. It reveals a governance mechanism to attract and retain firms in the network over time by offering benefits that are critical for small players. A specific reward power of the Financials Software Company is a key asset for a software ecosystem to thrive: it creates incentives for partners to close new deals via workshops and business events for ecosystem members. This keystone increases the connections among participants once it fosters networking. Thereby, it strengthens the structure of the network, which contributes to the robustness of the ecosystem [10].

By offering a technological platform, keystones enable third parties to fuel the ecosystem with additional functionality. Through this strategy, partners can show their **expert power** in the network. In particular, keystones such as the Data Integration Company and E-mail Marketing System Company reinforce the expertise of niche players by publishing successful cases about their complements. They promote the knowledge available in the ecosystem and diffuse innovation among members [10].

Big players such as Microsoft naturally hold **referent power**. The strong business reputation is a significant power capability for a keystone as it creates a feeling of respect and admiration for the firm. To develop their referent power, other keystones may highlight their growing position in the market as well as the attractiveness of their platforms and economics of their network [11]. Such promotion strategies rely on external actors recognising the status of both the firm and the ecosystem.

In Table 2, we provide an overview of our case study analysis. It presents the different types of power and their observed outcomes in a software ecosystem.

Table 2. Forms of power used by companies and outcomes on the software ecosystems.

Power type	Outcomes
Coercive	It fosters partners' migration to other ecosystems due to tensions entailed by negative attitudes of the keystone, which may also directly remove members from community
Expert	It raises the trust of partners and external actors on the expert company. It enables the firm to enter niche markets, build complements and create value for the ecosystem
Legitimate	It represents rules that guide partnerships, delineating firms' rights and roles. Once there is a keystone, this firm formally defines such rules, as governance mechanisms
Referent	It provides the company with strong respect and reputation, increasing its ability to attract external actors interested in gaining visibility and opportunities
Reward	It enables partners to fulfil each other's business and financial expectations. It helps value co-creation in the ecosystem

6   Conclusion and Future Work

The in-depth analysis of power-dependence dyads is a useful lens for researchers to explore ecosystem partnerships. From the view of practitioners, it is a valuable tool for firms to have insights on how to affect the resources flow, obtain a higher position in the ecosystem or manage the degree of dependence on competitors. By analysing power distribution, keystones can also define governance strategies that enable them to use existing power to effectively manage the ecosystem [11].

Studied keystones foster ecosystem success by leveraging complementors: they exalt partners' expert power and exercise reward power by raising business in the network. Besides, they often do not use the influence resulting from their status to apply coercive power. They also avoid using power to take actions solely in their favour and get a bigger slice of the pie, which could harm ecosystem performance.

The findings represent our interpretation of partners' reality. To support credibility, we used multiple sources of data and discussion of results among authors. Together with details about data collection and analysis, these strategies also ensured reliability.

In future studies, we plan to (i) increase the number of participants per company (e.g. obtain more input from technical staff about power in partnerships) and (ii) verify our findings in final interviews (respondent validation). Our broad goal is to develop a substantive theory to describe power exercise by software ecosystem partners.

Acknowledgement. We thank Yang Zherui Ryan for his constructive feedback on early versions of this paper.

References

1. Alves, C., Oliveira, J., Jansen, S.: Software ecosystem governance – a systematic literature review and research agenda. Inf. Softw. Technol. (In submission)
2. Barbosa, O., Pereira, R., Alves, C., Werner, C., Jansen, S.: A systematic mapping study on software ecosystems from a three-dimensional perspective. In: Jansen, S., Cusumano, M. A., Brinkkemper, S. (eds.) Software Ecosystems: Analyzing and Managing Business Networks in the Software Industry, pp. 59–81. Edward Elgar Publishing (2013)
3. Campbell, P.R.J., Ahmed, F.: A three-dimensional view of software ecosystems. In: Fourth European Conference on Software Architecture, pp. 81–84 (2010)
4. Casciaro, T., Piskorski, M.J.: Power imbalance, mutual dependence, and constraint absorption: a closer look at resource dependence theory. Adm. Sci. Q. **50**(2), 167–199 (2005)
5. Cruzes, D.S., Dybå, T.: Recommended steps for thematic synthesis in software engineering. In: International Symposium on Empirical Software Engineering and Measurement, pp. 275–284 (2011)
6. Dahl, R.A.: The concept of power. Behav. Sci. **2**(3), 201–215 (1957)
7. Elias, S.: Fifty years of influence in the workplace: the evolution of the French and Raven power taxonomy. J. Manage. Hist. **14**(3), 267–283 (2008)
8. Emerson, R.M.: Power-dependence relations. Am. Sociol. Rev. **27**(1), 31–41 (1962)
9. Hanssen, G., Dybå, T.: Theoretical foundations of software ecosystems. In: 4th International Workshop on Software Ecosystems, pp. 6–17 (2012)
10. Hartigh, E., Tol, M., Visscher, W.: The health measurement of a business ecosystem. In: Annual Meeting of European Chaos and Complexity in Org. Network, pp. 1–39 (2006)
11. Hurni, T., Huber, T.: The interplay of power and trust in platform ecosystems of the enterprise application software industry. In: European Conference on Information Systems (2014)
12. Iansiti, M., Levien, R.: Strategy as ecology. Harvard Bus. Rev. **82**(3), 68–81 (2004)
13. Jansen, S., Finkelstein, A., Brinkkemper, S.: A sense of community: a research agenda for software ecosystems. In: 31st International Conference on Software Engineering, pp. 187–190 (2009)
14. Jansen, S., Brinkkemper, S., Souer, J., Luinenburg, L.: Shades of gray: Opening up a software producing organization with the open software enterprise model. J. Syst. Softw. **85**(7), 1495–1510 (2012)
15. Lacoste, S., Johnsen, R.E.: Supplier-customer relationships: a case study of power dynamics. J. Purchasing Supply Manage. **21**(4), 229–240 (2015)
16. Lawler, E.: Power processes in bargaining. Sociol. Q. **33**(1), 17–34 (1992)
17. Manikas, K., Hansen, K.M.: Software ecosystems - A systematic literature review. J. Syst. Softw. **86**(5), 1294–1306 (2013)
18. Meehan, J., Wright, G.H.: The origins of power in buyer–seller relationships. Ind. Mark. Manage. **41**(4), 669–679 (2012)
19. Olsen, P.I., Prenkert, F., Hoholm, T., Harrison, D.: The dynamics of networked power in a concentrated business network. J. Bus. Res. **67**(12), 2579–2589 (2014)
20. Raven, B.H.: The bases of power: origins and recent developments. J. Soc. Issues **49**(4), 227–251 (1993)
21. Romano, N.C., Donovan, C., Chen, H., Nunamaker, J.F.: A methodology for analyzing web-based qualitative data. J. Manage. Inf. Syst. **19**(4), 213–246 (2003)
22. Runeson, P., Höst, M.: Guidelines for conducting and reporting case study research in software engineering. Empir. Softw. Eng. **14**(2), 131–164 (2009)

23. Santos, R.P., Werner, C.: Treating business dimension in software ecosystems. In: International Conference on Management of Emergent Digital EcoSystems, pp. 197–201 (2011)
24. Van Angeren, J., Kabbedijk, J., Jansen, S., Popp, K.M.: A survey of associate models used within large software ecosystems. In: 3rd International Workshop on Software Ecosystems, pp. 27–39 (2011)
25. Van Angeren, J., Alves, C., Jansen, S.: Can we ask you to collaborate? Analyzing app developer relationships in commercial platform ecosystems. J. Syst. Softw. **113**, 430–445 (2016)
26. Weiblen, T.: Opening up the business model: Business model innovation through collaboration. Ph.D. Thesis. University of St. Gallen, Bamberg (2015)

No More Bosses?

A Multi-case Study on the Emerging Use of Non-hierarchical Principles in Large-Scale Software Development

Helena Holmström Olsson[1(✉)] and Jan Bosch[2]

[1] Department of Computer Science, Malmö University, Nordenskiöldsgatan 1,
211 19 Malmö, Sweden
helena.holmstrom.olsson@mah.se
[2] Department of Computer Science and Engineering, Chalmers University
of Technology, Hörselgången 11, 412 96 Göteborg, Sweden
jan.bosch@chalmers.se

Abstract. Organizations are increasingly adopting alternative organizational models to circumvent the challenges of traditional hierarchies. In these alternative models, organizations have leaders instead of the traditional boss and teams operate using self-management and peer-to-peer advice processes. Although the adoption of these models have primarily been seen in smaller companies and startups, examples of long-established organizations that have adopted these models to restructure themselves and move away from their traditionally slow hierarchies are starting to appear. In this paper, we explore how seven large software-intensive companies in the embedded systems domain are adopting principles of non-hierarchical organizations in order to increase empowerment. Based on our empirical findings, we provide recommendations for how to manage this transformation and we develop a model that outlines the steps that companies typically take when transforming from hierarchical towards empowered organizations.

Keywords: Empowered organizations · Non-hierarchical principles · Self-management · Autonomy

1 Introduction

In most organizations, formal structures and hierarchical layers define tasks, roles and behaviors [1, 2]. In such organizations, job descriptions outline the responsibility and the authority that is associated with each person and each role and there is a clear separation between different teams, departments and divisions in the organization. Typically, hierarchical organizations have a top-down management structure and are characterized by centralized decision-making and strategy [2]. While hierarchical organizations benefit from advantages related to e.g. efficiency and control, they suffer from being slow and less responsive to rapidly changing market and customer needs. In addition, they are often found less motivating and engaging for employees, as they tend to restrict individual and team autonomy.

© Springer International Publishing AG 2016
P. Abrahamsson et al. (Eds.): PROFES 2016, LNCS 10027, pp. 86–101, 2016.
DOI: 10.1007/978-3-319-49094-6_6

Recently, a number of alternative organizational models have started to appear as a response to the many challenges identified with traditional hierarchies, and to better address the rapid changes in today's market environment. Also, and as a major characteristic, these models recognize the increasing need for organizations to attract, retain and advance top talent by supporting employees in adopting the critical new behaviors necessary to keep pace. Therefore, and instead of hierarchies and managers as central decision-makers, these models focus on self-management, autonomy and empowerment and rather than managers they advocate leaders with the role to support and guide the organization. Based on a number of recent examples [2–7], it is argued that companies adopting non-hierarchical principles to increase empowerment early will significantly improve their competitiveness.

However, although some examples exist, non-hierarchical principles and initiatives to increase empowerment have been challenging to adopt in larger companies due to existing structures and formal hierarchies. Typically, these organizations are large, globally distributed and producing systems of high complexity that need to satisfy strict certification and regulatory demands. As a result, the organizational structures tend to be highly hierarchical and centralized.

In this paper, we report on recent attempts to adopt non-hierarchical principles to increase empowerment also in large organizations. We explore how seven large software-intensive companies in the embedded systems domain are adopting principles of non-hierarchical organizations in order to increase empowerment. In our study, we provide qualitative empirical evidence on situations in which the organizations we studied were able to by-pass formal hierarchies by adopting alternative ways-of-working that allowed for outcomes that the traditional structures do not support.

The contribution of the paper is twofold. First, we present qualitative empirical evidence on how large software-intensive companies are adopting non-hierarchical principles. Based on our empirical findings, we present four areas in which the companies adopted alternative ways-of-working and how these allowed them to act more rapidly and with increased engagement and autonomy by teams. In addition, we provide a number of recommendations that help facilitate the adoption of non-hierarchical ways-of-working in large organizations. Second, we develop a model that identifies the steps that companies typically take when transforming from hierarchical towards empowered organizations.

The continuation of the paper is organized as follows. In the background section, we describe the characteristics, the strengths and the weaknesses of hierarchical organizations as outlined in literature. Also, we identify and describe a number of new organizational models that have recently emerged as a response to the weaknesses experienced in hierarchical organizations. In Sect. 3, we present the case companies involved in the study and we describe the research method that was chosen for the study. In Sect. 4, we present the findings from the empirical study and we outline four areas in which the case companies adopted alternative ways-of-working characterized y non-hierarchical principles. In Sect. 5, we discuss our findings and we develop a model that show the steps that companies typically take when moving towards empowered organizations. Finally, in Sect. 6, we conclude the paper.

2 Background

2.1 Hierarchical Organizations

Traditionally, and as can be seen in most larger companies including the ones we studied, organizational structures are formed around hierarchies [1, 2, 7–9]. In such hierarchies, people and roles are typically defined by job descriptions that outline the responsibility and the authority that is associated with each person and role. While the advantage of this is that each person in such an organization has a well-defined task and clear boundaries within which to operate, it comes with the drawback of having each person doing exactly what they are asked for instead of being encouraged to explore new interests and take on more challenging tasks. Also, job descriptions are often imprecise as they are rarely updated. Therefore, the risk is that they reflect an outdated and illusionary understanding of an organization rather than an accurate and valid one. Moreover, hierarchical organizations have strong top-down management with dele-gation of authority being rare. Managers limit delegation of decision-making and even when they do their decisions ultimately trump. As a result, the organizational structure is mandated from the top and rarely revisited as that could reveal re-organization opportunities that might threaten existing power structures. Finally, hierarchical organizations are often characterized by implicit rules and "shadow beliefs" that slow down change and favor people and assumptions that are well known and well estab-lished in the organization. In Table 1, we summarize the strengths and the weaknesses that are typically associated with hierarchical organizations, and as described in pre-vious literature [1, 2, 7–9].

Table 1. Strengths and weaknesses of hierarchical organizations.

Strengths:	Weaknesses:
• Effective for scaling	• Slow decision making processes
• Efficient for controlling many people from a central position	• Power driven by position rather than by capability
• Efficient for repeatable tasks and replicable processes	• Tendency to be internally focused
• Harmonization of processes	• Easily gravitates to politics
• Globalization	• Highly resistant to changes
• Handles low complexity situations well	• Challenged by high-complexity situations

As can be seen in the table, hierarchical organizations scale well, they are efficient for managing large groups of people and they support the execution of repeatable tasks in large organizations even if geographically distributed. Also, they are regarded superior for tasks and situations of low complexity as they advocate stability and rigor rather then flexibility and elasticity. However, and as mentioned already in beginning of this section, hierarchies suffer from a number of weaknesses that make them less suited for certain business environments. They are considered to slow down decision-making processes, as it is typically time consuming to coordinate within an hierarchy that involve a number of layers of people and roles. Also, they easily gravitate towards internal politics and they favor people and opinions that are already well established. Finally, and as the main drawback for organizations that operate in turbulent and fast changing business environments, they are less suited for highly complex situations where there are no predefined rules or known variables.

2.2   New Organizational Models

In response to the weaknesses that have been identified in relation to hierarchical organizations, a number of new organizational models have emerged. Instead of managers, top-down decision-making and formal reporting structures these models emphasize self-management, peer-to-peer advice processes and informal, temporary structures that support the task or situation at hand. Examples of such organizational models are e.g. agile development [3, 4, 10], holistic/authentic organizations [2], holocracy [5], and exponential organizations [7]. Although different in some aspects, they all emphasize principles of empowerment and self-management, wholeness and evolutionary purpose. This means that they advocate organizations with coordination mechanisms and natural leadership instead of managers with positional power, temporary hierarchies instead of formal ones and open and accepting cultures in which people act according to whom they are instead of what is expected in order to "to try to fit in". Also, all models emphasize the wisdom of the crowds instead of central decision-making. Opposite to hierarchical organizations, these models encourage people to shoulder one or more roles, independent on place in the organization, and they provide support for coordination of work between people. Throughout the organization, everyone has the authority and autonomy to make decisions that pertain to their role or roles. All relevant stakeholders need to be asked for advice before any decision is made, but this is not to be confused with consensus. Any individual can decide to disregard the advice given as long as all stakeholders that are affected by the decision have been asked for their input. In such organizations, roles, activities and agreements evolve constantly in mutual agreement and agreements are entered voluntarily.

In looking more closely at the concept of empowerment, empowered organizations are described as having fewer levels of rank and hierarchy, making them flat, lean and nimble [11]. Typically, decisions are made at every level within the organization instead of handed down from the top as orders to be followed, and all employees are encouraged to expand their expertise in various roles rather than climb a ladder of titles. Empowered organizations are driven by teamwork [3, 4, 12]. Employees proven to be capable are made responsible for making decisions that impact the company, and are held accountable for the results of their decisions. In larger empowered organizations, employees form teams to control various aspects of the organization. Employees may move around to different teams over time, which can increases their expertise in various roles and their value as employees overall. Instead of the traditional management role, empowered organizations have 'leaders' that guide the direction of the company by enabling employees to create, to take risks and to work interdependently, and as such uncover the direction for the company as an organization as part of its evolving purpose. Hence, a leader is less a person of authority and more a person of support.

It should be noted that organizational models that emphasize empowerment is not a new phenomenon. Already in the early 1980's, Henry Mintzberg presented five organizational types for designing effective organizations and shows how most organizations are typically hybrids of two or more of these types [8, 9]. In his research, Mintzberg focuses on collaboration mechanisms, power distribution and structural issues and identifies mutual adjustment as one of the coordination mechanisms that allow individuals to coordinate their own work. The adhocracy type is an example of an organizational moel focused on empowerment.

Table 2. Organizational models that emphasize empowerment, self-management and autonomy.

Organizational model:	Characteristics:
Agile development	• Empowered teams • Voluntary commitment • Coordination through communication (daily standup meetings) • Close and frequent customer collaboration (short development sprints) • Team mission is to do "right" by the customer
Holistic/authentic organizations	• Self-managed teams • Wholeness as in "be yourself at work" • Evolutionary purpose • Organizations as increasingly driven by autonomous teams • Peer-to-peer review and advice processes as the basis for decision-making
Holocracy	• Roles are defined around the work, not around people, and are updated regularly • People fill several roles and are associated with several tasks • Authority is distributed to teams and roles and decisions are made locally • The organizational structure is regularly updated via small and frequent iterations and every team is self-managed • Everyone is bound by the same rules – the CEO included. • These rules are transparent and known by everyone in the organization
Exponential organizations	• Strives for nimbleness by accessing, renting or sharing of people and assets rather than owning them ("staff on demand") • Engagement through digital reputation systems and incentive prizes • Organizational metrics are transparent and visible to everyone in the organization • Emphasizes risk-taking and failure to learn rapidly (lean startup) • Self-managed and multi-disciplinary teams and individuals that operate with decentralized authority

In Table 2, we provide an overview of some of the new organizational models that have recently gained increasing interest in management literature as well as among practitioners in the field [2–5, 7]. While we are aware that the models we outline are not the complete set, and that there exist variations of each of these, we believe that the ones we identify reflect the main characteristics and therefore, provide a solid background for understanding the fundamentals of the many new organizational models that are currently gaining momentum.

While the organizational models identified above are indeed gaining momentum, they have so far been challenging to apply in large and distributed organizations with multiple teams working on a broad product portfolio. Today, most successful examples originate in smaller companies or in startups where non-hierarchical principles and a culture of empowerment can be more easily implemented from the start, and where communication and coordination is by nature less complex. However, there are examples of long-established organizations that have restructured themselves with great success [2, 7, 11], and there are several aspects of these models that help larger organizations move away from their traditionally slow hierarchies towards more rapid and competitive ways-of-working. In what follows, we report on seven companies in the embedded systems domain that have managed to adopt principles of empowerment. As can be seen in our research, they did so in relation to certain tasks and they were able to accelerate performance by bypassing formal organizational structures. Below, we outline the case companies involved in our study and the research method that we choose.

3 Research Method

The research reported in this paper builds on on-going multi case study research [13, 14] in close collaboration with seven companies in the embedded systems domain. The project was initiated in July 2015 and is on-going. In the sections below, we provide a short description of each company and the roles that we met with so far, and we describe the research design that was chosen.

3.1 Case Companies

See Table 3.

Table 3. The seven case companies and the roles involved in the study.

Company A	A provider of communication systems and equipment for mobile and fixed network operators. For the purpose of this study, we met with five people with expertise in product and project management, change management, software development and methods and tools.
Company B	Offers network cameras and camera applications for professional IP video surveillance. For the purpose of this study, we met with four people with expertise in software architecture, product and project management and methods and tools.
Company C	A manufacturer and supplier of transport solutions for commercial use. For the purpose of this study, we met with two people with expertise in technical lead within software engineering and management.
Company D	An automotive telematics service provider providing manufacturers of cars and commercial vehicles with complete and customized telematics services to end-customers. For the purpose of this study, we met with two people with expertise in product and project management and technical management and connectivity.

(continued)

Table 3. (*continued*)

Company E	A software company specializing in navigational information, operations management and optimization solutions for airlines. For the purpose of this study, we met with three people with expertise in software architecture, software development and product and project management.
Company F	A manufacturer producing pumps for heating, air conditioning and for water supply. For the purpose of this study, we met with three people with expertise in product and project management, solutions and services development and emerging technologies and connectivity.
Company G	A company that serves the global market with products, services and solutions from military defense to civil security. For the purpose of this study, we met with two people with expertise in software development, architecture and product and project management.

3.2   Case Study Design

The findings reported in this paper are based on longitudinal multi case study research in seven software-intensive companies in the embedded systems domain. The research project was initiated in July 2015 and is on going. So far, we have conducted a number of workshops and focus groups in all companies. Also, we have developed and piloted an on-line survey to be used in our future research.

In total, we have met with sixteen people representing the seven companies and we have organized six cross-company workshops and two reporting workshops. At each workshop, the researchers introduced a selected topic by giving a short presentation. Examples of topics are emerging organizational models, empowerment and self-management, non-hierarchical principles in software development and non-hierarchical principles for business decisions. To prepare for each workshop, the company representatives got a few questions related to the selected topic, and after the introduction and presentation by the two researchers each company was asked to present and share a few examples/cases in relation to the questions. In this way, the workshops became a mix of research presentations, company presentations and group discussions focusing on the selected questions and topics. During the workshops, one of the researchers took notes to document the discussions and the answers to the pre-defined questions. Also, each company provided a presentation slide deck that they shared with the researchers and that summarized the examples/cases they presented. Finally, many illustrations were made on a white board during the discussions and all these were captured as input to the empirical data collection process.

During analysis, the workshop notes, the company presentations and the graphical illustrations were used as the basis for interpretation and coding of the data. The data was coded and analyzed following the conventional qualitative content analysis approach [14] where we derived the codes directly from the text data. As soon as any questions or potential misunderstandings occurred, we verified the information with the representatives from the companies.

To strengthen the construct validity of our study [15], we continuously validated our interpretations and findings with the company representatives. Also, we combined data from different sources and we were two researchers who independently could assess the data, as well as together discuss our interpretations. The results of the study cannot directly translate to other companies. However, and considering the external validity of our study, the case companies represent current state-of-practice of large-scale software development and therefore, we believe that the results we present are valid also for other large-scale software development companies.

4 Findings

In this section, we present our empirical findings. Our findings build on group discussions and company presentations from the cross-company workshops that we organized for the purpose of this research. First, we provide an overall description of the companies and the business domain in which they operate. This description serves as a basis for understanding their current ways-of-working and the type of products and systems they provide. Although the companies operate in different domains and therefore embrace different characteristics, they have a number of similarities in relation to the way they are organized, the organizational principles they apply and the restrictions and regulations they face.

Second, we present examples of situations in which the companies have moved away from their hierarchical and formal ways-of-working and where they have instead adopted non-hierarchical ways-of-working to achieve outcomes that were considered difficult to achieve within the traditional organizational structures. These examples reflect attempts to increase empowerment and to adopt principles that emphasize informal rather than formal structures and autonomous rather than hierarchical ways-of-working.

4.1 Case Company Contexts and Current Ways-of-Working

The seven companies involved in this study are all large companies within the embedded systems domain. This domain has gone through significant changes over the last decade. Whereas this domain was originally driven by mechanics and hardware, now software makes up the key differentiation in virtually any industry, ranging from telecommunications to automotive and from aeronautics to defense. For instance, some reports claim that modern high-end cars have up to 100 million lines of code [16]. In addition, embedded systems typically have significant security and safety requirements that limit the freedom that these companies have to adopt continuous deployment and other modern software development technologies. Finally, as embedded systems often are highly interconnected in order to deliver the desired product functionality, the complexity of the system is not only due to size but also due to the high connectivity between different parts of the system.

The characteristics of software-intensive embedded systems have significant implications on the organizational approaches that these companies typically employ. As these organizations are large, globally distributed and have to satisfy certification and regulatory demands, the organizational structure tends to be highly hierarchical and centralized. Over the last decades, this structure has evolved as the most effective to deliver large and complex systems while satisfying the requirements of all stakeholders. However, with the emergence of modern collaboration technologies, automated ways of ensuring regulatory and certification requirements as well as the increasing need for continuous deployment for differentiation purposes, also embedded systems companies are now experiencing the limits of hierarchical organizations and have started to experiment with principles reflecting self-management and empowerment.

4.2   Adoption of Non-hierarchical and Empowered Ways-of-Working

Below, we present examples that illustrate situations in which the companies moved away from their formal and typically hierarchical ways-of-working and where they instead adopted non-hierarchical ways-of-working reflecting empowerment. We present our findings by categorizing them into four areas within which all companies report on new ways-of-working. We summarize our findings in Table 4.

Table 4. Summary of the four areas in which the case companies adopted alternative ways-of-working.

Area:	Principles of empowerment:
New strategic focus	• Self-managed teams • Voluntarily engagement
areas/innovations	• Advice and peer-to-peer processes • Formal organization as a "guiding star"
Customer/research collaborations	• Purpose and vision-driven initiatives • Direct customer communication • Exploratory experimentation • Voluntarily engagement
Adoption of new development practices	• Autonomous teams that run in parallel with the formal organization • Rapid feedback cycles • Bottom-up adoption of new practices
Competence development in new core areas	• Cross-functional teams • Teams decide on methods and tools • Short iterations with a "build-test-refine" approach

Area 1: New Strategic Focus Areas/Innovations
In all case companies, strategic focus areas are typically put together and presented by top management. Often, they consist of a list of ideas that are identified as critical for the coming years. These ideas are then shared with the organization to be evaluated and "tested" on people in order to understand whether they are indeed the right things to focus on. Common examples of focus areas in the companies are continuous integration, continuous deployment and development and adoption of new technologies etc.

Typically, strategic focus areas involve technical development and new technology as well as adoption of new ways-of-working and process initiatives. As a common characteristic, they don't involve specific funding but rather they have synergies that integrate well with the existing formal organization. When it comes to involving in such an initiative the companies use a self-management approach in that they don't assign the traditional roles. Instead, role assignment is flexible and people choose in what initiative they want to involve. No specific requirements are defined for the involvement. Instead, people engage based on their own interest and in order to benefit from synergies in relation to their formally assigned tasks. When starting a strategic focus area or innovation initiative, the companies identify key people that can work as ambassadors and that can help drive the initiative in the different units. By having a good mapping and alignment between the formal organization and the new initiatives commitment from key people is ensured. Also, the mapping and alignment is critical for securing an impact on the organization as a whole. From a management perspective, only brief guidelines are provided in terms of 'how' to address and solve a specific challenge in order not to restrict creativity in the units.

During the initiative, those involved meet with, and report to, the formal organization on a regular basis. However, the formal reporting structure is only used as a "guiding star" that helps setting direction and steer the initiative towards a goal. It is not used for guiding ways-of-working or detailing what methods and processes to use. In all case companies, people report on a wide variety of methods and processes and the opportunity to more flexibly adapt to the task at hand. Throughout the initiative, an advice process is used to invite the larger organization to workshops and presentation sessions where they get the opportunity to provide feedback on the initiative and the focus and direction of the work. In this way, the team gets ideas and comments that can be used to structure the work and to understand the direction in which the larger organization is aiming in the coming years.

Area 2: Customer/Research Collaborations

A common area in which principles of non-hierarchical and autonomous ways-of-working are seen in all companies, are customer and research collaborations. The case companies report on examples where individual engineers shortcuts the formal hierarchies and instead initiates direct customer contact in order to accelerate and achieve a certain outcome. Typically, this happens when there is a purpose and vision-driven initiative rather than requirements-driven initiatives. The purpose and vision driven initiatives are more open in scope, they often involve stakeholders that the companies don't typically collaborate with and they require alternative ways-of-working to be successful. In such initiatives, the time people put in is "synergy funded" which means that they don't get time allocated. Instead, the problem they solve and the effort they put into this generate advantages and benefits in other tasks and in their formal assignments.

In some of the companies, these initiatives are used, as examples for customers in order to show them that the organization is capable of doing new things in new ways and things that might not be recognized in the formal organization and its processes. As such, innovative customer collaborations are used to show other customers that the organization manages to explore new opportunities by using alternative ways-of-working at the same time as it is able to fulfill the requirements in relation to the traditional tasks. Internally, the companies find the opportunity for people to work on things where there are no formal requirements and "no right way" very motivating. In similar, the companies use alternative ways-of-working in collaborations with different research teams. The companies in our study are all involved in several larger research collaborations in which different academic partners are involved. In such collaborations people involve when they find it interesting and if they find it beneficial to their work. In some cases, the companies agree more formally on time and resources, but often there is flexibility and people decide themselves. The goal is to create a situation where people can choose to be part of projects that they pick themselves and where they feel they get support by the larger organization without having to put the traditional structures and processes in place.

Area 3: Adoption of New Development Practices

All the case companies are large and successful software-intensive companies in the embedded systems domain. If not market leading, they have strong positions in their business ecosystems and they manage to stay competitive despite fierce business environments and disruptive technologies. One of the reasons for this is the ambition to accelerate the adoption of new development practices. All companies have continuous integration practices in place, and some of the companies are implementing continuous deployment. In order to drive the adoption of new development practices, several of the companies report on the potential to have specific and "non-traditional" initiatives as a means to accelerate the process. As an example, one of the companies started a project with the aim to re-architect the platform to reduce its complexity. But rather than viewing this as the only goal, the responsible team recognized the potential to also have this project help drive continuous deployment in the organization. What typically happens, and as experienced in several of the companies, is that an initiative that aims to improve product and process performance often benefit from alternative ways-of-working where the responsible team can operate outside, or in parallel, with the formal organizational structure to increase speed. In the case of the platform initiative mentioned above, it became a larger initiative that aligned well with the organizational goals and that added benefits to a number of roles and units, but that was run in parallel with the formal organization and outside the traditional unit boundaries. This allows for cross-functional and innovative ways-of-working where teams can operate more autonomously and where they can drive the process. As recognized in one of the companies, this reflects a bottom-up approach to process improvement and as a result the new practices are better manifested and aligned with the organization in which they are intended to be used.

Area 4: Competence Development in New Core Areas

The majority of the case companies use alternative ways-of-working when learning skills that are outside their core practices. For example, one of the companies in the automotive domain is experiencing a strong need to catch up when it comes to software development as they are traditionally a mechanic company. To do so, they apply more flexible ways-of-working that allow for cross-functional teams to work together and they let the teams decide what methods and what tools they want to use when practicing the new skills. Still, the teams interface with the formal organization by using standardized exchange formats, but these are meant to facilitate knowledge sharing and not to restrict team creativity. In this area, the other companies describe similar initiatives where they are able to have teams explore new ways-of-working while at the same time contribute to the larger goals and initiatives of the formal organization. Since the focus is on competence development for areas that are regarded important for future development, they are prioritized by the organization and the teams that choose to work on these enjoy the opportunity of being more flexible and explorative. In most cases, the teams work in a "build-measure-learn" fashion [17] instead of the traditional "specify-understand-agree-build-test" model, and some of the companies explore agile contracting as part of the initiatives.

5   Discussion

In this section, we discuss and summarize our findings and we present a number of recommendations that facilitate the adoption of empowerment in large organizations. In addition, we present a model in which we outline the transformation towards empowered organizations by identifying the different steps that companies typically take when moving from traditional towards more empowered ways-of-working.

5.1   Towards Empowerment in Large-Scale Software Development

Traditionally, and as recognized in previous research, hierarchical organizations have severe challenges meeting rapidly changing markets and customer needs [2, 5, 7]. Due to formal structures and communication and coordination overhead between the different organizational layers hierarchical organizations often struggle to innovate. As a result, these organizations run the risk of being disrupted by competitors that are able to act nimble and adopt more effective ways-of-working. This was recognized already in the beginning of the 1980's when a number of organizational structures were presented in order to increase the understanding for the many different ways in which organizations operate [1, 8, 9]. Also, the introduction of the agile development methods significantly increased the emphasis on flexibility and speed as organizational principles [10, 12]. More recently, and in response to the challenges that hierarchical organizations face, a number of alternative organizational models have started to emerge. Typically, these models originate from successful startups, from online companies or from smaller companies that have managed to grow based on highly engaged and skilled teams that operate independently and that spend little, if any, time navigating through administrative, managerial and political layers [11]. While traditional hierarchies support repetitive tasks, control of large groups of people and scaling of processes, these alternative models emphasize empowerment and self-management and they seek to facilitate autonomy to increase speed and responsiveness throughout the organization.

Although very attractive, the adoption of alternative organizational models in large-scale companies is challenging and so far examples of such adoption are few. However, and as reported in this paper, attempts to facilitate empowerment are emerging also in larger organizations and we are starting to discern situations in which also these companies move away from their traditionally slow hierarchies towards more empowered ways-of-working. In our study, we see how the companies have adopted principles that helped them increase flexibility and responsiveness, and that encouraged individuals and teams to take responsibility, to accelerate innovation and to improve creativity. Based on our empirical research and the lessons learnt in the case companies, we summarize our findings by presenting a number of recommendations. The recommendations reflect considerations that should be taken to facilitate the adoption of empowerment in large software-intensive organizations.

- **Recommendation 1:** Non-hierarchical ways-of-working and initiatives that challenge traditional organizational structures need to align well with the overall business goals in order to have an impact and to attract long-term commitment of key people in the organization.
- **Recommendation 2:** Non-hierarchical ways-of-working and initiatives that emphasize informal and emergent structures need to align with, contribute to and help accelerate already existing formal and approved structures.
- **Recommendation 3:** Non-hierarchical ways-of-working and initiatives that challenge the traditional organizational structures should aim at strengthening customer relationships and collaborations by shortening feedback loops and allowing rapid communication and coordination channels.
- **Recommendation 4:** In moving towards non-hierarchical and autonomous ways-of-working, large organizations need to balance bottom-up autonomy and non-hierarchical problem solving with top-down strategy and central decision-making.
- **Recommendation 5:** In moving towards non-hierarchical and autonomous ways-of-working, large organizations need to balance long-term and strategic decision-making made centrally within existing management, with short-term and tactic implementations made locally within self-organizing teams.

5.2   Transforming Towards Empowered Organizations

During our research, and supported by previous research, we see that companies evolve their software development practices over time [17]. Similarly, companies evolve their organizational practices and their ways-of-working. Typically, and in relation to the focus of this paper, there is a pattern that companies typically follow as they evolve and as they transform towards becoming empowered organizations. We illustrate this evolution in Fig. 1 by outlining the steps from traditional organizations characterized by formal hierarchies to empowered organizations characterized by decentralized decision-making and leaders instead of managers.

To further detail our model, and to recognize the different organizational levels at which principles of empowerment can be adopted, we outline each step in relation to four organizational functions that are found in most organizations (Table 5). We refer to these levels as 'local' as principles characterizing the culture between multiple R&D teams, 'inter-team' as in principles characterizing the culture between departments such as e.g. R&D and Product Mgmt. (PdM), 'General Mgmt.' as in principles characterizing the culture between high-level divisions and, finally, 'Culture' as in principles characterizing the culture in the entire company.

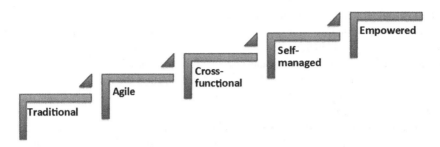

Fig. 1. From traditional towards empowered organizations.

Table 5. Summary of each step in the model (Traditional – Empowered), and how different organizational functions operate at each of these steps.

	Traditional	Agile	Cross-functional	Self-managed	Empowered
Culture	Hierarchical	Hierarchical	Hierarchical	Hierarchical	Empowered
General Mgmt.	Hierarchical	Hierarchical	Hierarchical	Empowered	Empowered
Inter-team (PdM/R&D)	Hierarchical	Hierarchical	Empowered	Empowered	Empowered
Local (R&D)	Hierarchical	Empowered	Empowered	Empowered	Empowered

Finally, it should be noted that although the principles of empowered organizations are both attractive and rewarding, the adoption of these depend on the type and mission of a company. In organizations that operate in domains that are characterized by highly standardized and repetitive ways of doing things, a hierarchical organizational model is typically the best form. In such organizations, the short-term can be to stay hierarchical while the long-term goal should probably be to automate manual practices rather than focusing on the transformation towards more empowered ways-of-working.

6   Conclusion

In this paper, we explore how seven large software-intensive companies in the embedded systems domain are adopting principles of non-hierarchical organizations in order to increase team autonomy. Typically, such principles are seen in smaller companies and in startups but so far they have been challenging to adopt in larger companies due to formal structures and existing hierarchies. However, and as reported in this paper, attempts to facilitate empowerment and self-management of teams are rapidly emerging also in larger organizations. In our study, we provide empirical evidence on situations in which the organizations we studied were able to accelerate innovation and by-pass formal hierarchies by adopting alternative ways-of-working that allow outcomes that the traditional structures do not support. Also, we show how non-hierarchical principles help large-scale software development companies to act more rapidly and with increased engagement and autonomy by teams. We provide recommendations for how to facilitate the adoption of non-hierarchical and autonomous ways-of-working and we develop a model that outlines the typical evolution path when transforming towards autonomous organizations.

While our research is limited to seven software-intensive companies in the embedded systems domain we have good reasons to believe that the challenges they face, and the opportunities they currently explore, are valid also for other similar companies. As any hierarchical organization has severe challenges in meeting rapidly changing markets and customer needs, and as alternative organizational models are appearing to address these challenges, we foresee a future in which companies that manage to adopt this paradigm shift early will significantly improve their competitiveness.

References

1. Malone, T.W.: Modeling coordination in organizations and markets. Manage. Sci. **33**(10), 1317–1332 (1987)
2. Laloux, F.: Reinventing organizations. Nelson Parker, Brussels (2014)
3. Larman, C., Vodde, B.: Practices for Scaling Lean & Agile Development: Large, Multisite, and Offshore Product Development with Large-Scale Scrum. Addison-Wesley, Upper Saddle River (2010)
4. Leffingwell, D.: Scaling Software Agility: Best Practices for Large Enterprises. Addison-Wesley, Upper Saddle River (2007)
5. Robertson, B.J.: Holacracy: The New Management System for a Rapidly Changing World. Henry Holt and Company, New York (2015)
6. Endenburg, G.: Sociocracy. The Organization of Decision-Making 'No Objection' as the Principle of Sociocracy. Eburon, Delft (1998)
7. Ismail, S., Malone, M.S., Van Guest, Y.: Exponential Organizations: Why New Organizations are Ten Times Better, Faster, and Cheaper than Yours (and What to Do About It). Diversion Books, New York (2014)
8. Mintzberg, H.: Structure in fives: a synthesis of the research on organisation design. Manage. Sci. **26**(3), 322–341 (1980)
9. Mintzberg, H.: Designing Effective Organizations. Prentice-Hall, New Jersey (1983)
10. Eckstein, J.: Agile Software Development in the Large: Diving into the Deep. Dorset House, New York (2004)
11. http://smallbusiness.chron.com/structure-empowered-organization-44194.html. Accessed 23 June 2016
12. Highsmith, J., Cockburn, A.: Agile software development: the business of innovation. In: Software Management, pp. 120–122 (2001)
13. Yin, R.K.: Case study research. Design and Methods, 3rd edn. Sage, London (2003)
14. Maxwell, J.A.: Qualitative Research Design: An Interactive Approach, 2nd edn. SAGE Publications, Thousands Oaks (2005)
15. Adler, P.A., Adler, P.: Observational Techniques. In: Denzin, N.K., Lincoln, Y. (eds.) Handbook of Qualitative Research, pp. 377–393. Sage, Thousand Oaks (1994)

16. Ebert, C., Jones, C.: Embedded software: facts, figures, and future. Computer **42**(4), 42–52 (2009)
17. Ries, E.: The Lean Startup: How Constant Innovation Creates Radically Successful Businesses. Penguin Group, London (2011)
18. Olsson, H.H., Alahyari, H., Bosch, J.: Climbing the "Stairway to Heaven": a multiple-case study exploring barriers in the transition from agile development towards continuous deployment of software. In: Proceedings of the 38th Euromicro Conference on Software Engineering and Advanced Applications, Cesme, Izmir, Turkey, 5–7 September 2012

Supporting Management of Hybrid OSS Communities - A Stakeholder Analysis Approach

Hanna Mäenpää[1]([✉]), Tero Kojo[2], Myriam Munezero[1], Fabian Fagerholm[1],
Terhi Kilamo[3], Mikko Nurminen[3], and Tomi Männistö[1]

[1] University of Helsinki, Helsinki, Finland
{hanna.maenpaa,myriam.munezero,fabian.fagerholm,
tomi.mannisto}@cs.helsinki.fi
[2] The Qt Company, Espoo, Finland
tero.kojo@qt.io
[3] Tampere Technical University, Tampere, Finland
{terhi.kilamo,mikko.nurminen}@tut.fi

Abstract. In Hybrid Open Source Software projects, independent and commercially oriented stakeholders collaborate using freely accessible tools and development processes. Here, contributors can enter and leave the community flexibly, which poses a challenge for community managers in ensuring the sustainability of the community. This short paper reports initial results from an industrial case study of the "Qt" Open Source Software project. We present a visual stakeholder analysis approach, building on data from the three systems that provide for the Qt project's complete software development workflow. This overview, augmented with information about the stakeholders' organizational affiliations, proved to help the project's community manager in finding potential for encouraging contributors and to identify issues that can potentially be detrimental for the community.

Keywords: Hybrid open source · Community management · Stakeholder identification

1 Introduction

Using Open Source Software (OSS) has proven effective for companies as it removes many barriers to code reuse and modification. By collaborating with OSS communities, companies can benefit from the knowledge and work of external developers and flexibly integrate their input to the company's internal development processes. OSS communities provide a low cost means for testing the quality of products which reduces the time to market and cost of software releases [5,12]. In hybrid OSS projects a mix of independent and commercially oriented

---

The original version of this chapter was revised: The chapter title has been corrected. An erratum to this chapter can be found at DOI: 10.1007/978-3-319-49094-6_66

© Springer International Publishing AG 2016
P. Abrahamsson et al. (Eds.): PROFES 2016, LNCS 10027, pp. 102–108, 2016.
DOI: 10.1007/978-3-319-49094-6_7

stakeholders build software collaboratively. While independent developers are inspired by intrinsic reasons such as improving their skills or supporting an ideology [6,11], companies focus on achieving business goals. In some hybrid communities (including our case community, Qt) a community manager works to ensure that the community is healthy and heading in a sustainable direction. As the scope of OSS projects is typically large, knowledge about stakeholders' needs has to be synthesized manually from various sources. This encumbers the work of the community manager significantly.

Previous attempts to identify stakeholders and their roles have focused on single data sources such as code repositories [7,10], bug databases [3] and mailing lists [2,8]. Fewer address the complete software development process from requirements engineering to delivery of the code. The contribution of this short paper is to report experiences of the latter strategy from the practical viewpoint of a community manager's work.

2   Case Qt

Qt is an open source software that is used to create platform-independent applications for Android, iOS and Windows operating system environments. Its users include independent application developers and companies from a wide variety of industries including electronics, automotives, defense and media. The Qt software's hybrid licensing model offers both an Open Source[1] and commercial options [4]. The chargeable licenses allow for making applications proprietary, to access new software components and to receive varying levels of support from hosting organization: The Qt Company. Development of the Qt software is driven by a versatile, open community for which the company provides software development tools. The company holds decision power for timing and packaging of releases and employs an internal software development unit to strengthen the community driven development process. To advance interoperability and dissemination of the software, the company hosts a partner consortium. The community manager describes dynamics of the ecosystem as:

"Adoption of the Qt software by developers leads to increased participation in community activities. This disseminates knowledge about the software, as information is shared among developers, leading to a stronger, healthier community. This translates into improvements in the product itself. From a commercial perspective, an active community presents more potential to existing stakeholders and builds attractiveness of the product and its surrounding business ecosystem."

He continues:

"A high-performing community member is very active on multiple platforms or extremely active on one of those. Some contributors shine out of the usage statistics of distinct tools but without looking at multiple platforms the best do not stand out."

---

[1] GPL, LGPL v2.1, LGPL v3.

The manager hopes to get a data-centric, visual overview of all the stake-holders who develop the software. With this, he hopes to streamline his work process and to identify individuals that are entering the community, have potential for increasing contributions and those that have previously been active, but are fading away.

3   Research Approach

This study highlights relevant issues for community management in its real context [9,13]. By using data from tools that provide for the project's complete development workflow, we hoped to reveal those stakeholders that are active in multiple roles. A random three-month period was chosen because it represents a typical release span of the software. A sample was extracted from the task management system Jira, code review tool Gerrit and source code repository Git in June 2015, focusing on the currently latest release of the software (version 5.5).

We yielded records of 248 unique work requests, 2194 code review actions and 3363 increments to the software code. As the data sources were separate, cross-sample matching was required to eliminate false identities that were due to variations in spellings and the several email addresses persons had used in registering to the systems. 284 unique stakeholders from 139 organizational affiliations were discovered and network visualizations with force-directed layout [1] were created in July 2015 using the Gephi tool. Three semi-structured interviews with the community manager followed within the timespan of 6 months to evaluate benefits and deficiencies of the approach.

4   Results

A developer could have: (A) created a work task, (B) being assigned to one, (C) performed a code review or (D) authored a code increment. 12 different combinations of these roles (referred to later as "activity groups") were found. Figure 1 overviews the 284 individuals who are represented as small nodes while the large central nodes (A,B,C,D) represent types of the activities they had performed. Table 1 displays sizes of the activity groups.

A total of 139 affiliations of developers were grouped into four groups: employees of the Qt Company[2], members of its partner consortium[3], employees of commercial companies[4] and independent individuals[5]. Shares of these affiliation types in each activity group are presented in Fig. 2, highlighting the host company's influence on different stages of the workflow.

---

[2] theqtcompany.com, digia.com, qt-project.org.
[3] kde.org, kdab.org, redhat.org.
[4] jolla.com, mrisoftware.com, basyscom.com.
[5] gmail.com, yeandex.ru, hotmail.com.

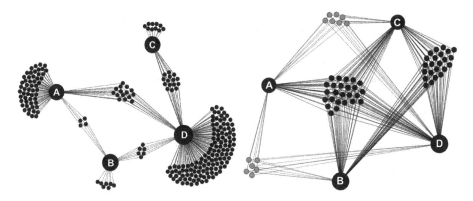

Fig. 1. Developers associated with 1–2 activities (left) and 3–4 activities (right). (A) Creating a work task (B) being assigned for work (C) performing a code review (D) authoring a code increment.

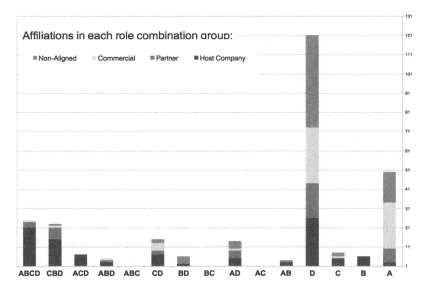

Fig. 2. Distribution of affiliations in each activity combination group. Column height is related to group size.

4.1   The Manager's Viewpoint

The community manager (Later, CM) was provided with interactive network visualizations where names of developers were distinguishable. At the same time Fig. 2 provided shares of different affiliations among each of the activity groups. The following subsections summarize the observations.

Company Involvement. One of the benefits of the OSS development approach is that by combining expertise and knowledge of versatile stakeholders, a

Table 1. Number of developers that have performed in an activity or a combination of activities. # = number of individuals.

	Description	#	%
Person that has performed one activity N = 185 (65 %)			
A	Created work task	50	18 %
B	Assigned for work	6	2 %
C	Performed a code review	8	3 %
D	Authored code increment	121	43 %
Two activities N = 39 (14 %)			
A,B	Created, Assigned	4	1 %
A,C	Created, Reviewed	0	0 %
A,D	Created, Authored	14	5 %
B,C	Assigned, Reviewed	0	0 %
B,D	Assigned, Authored	6	2 %
C,D	Reviewed, Authored	15	5 %
Three activities N = 35 (23 %)			
A,B,C	Created, Assigned, Reviewed	0	0 %
A,B,D	Created, Assigned, Authored	5	2 %
A,C,D	Created, Reviewed, Authored	7	2 %
C,B,D	Assigned, Reviewed, Authored	23	8 %
Four activities N = 25 (9 %)			
A,B,C,D	Created, Assigned, Reviewed, Authored	25	9 %
		Total of 284	100 %

better quality of software products can be expected. The CM was delighted to see that a mix of company external stakeholders dominated both reporting new work issues (A) and delivering source code increments (D). As groups (ABCD), (BCD,ABD,ACD) and (CD) consisted of the developers who actively run the project, the CM identified that having stakeholders from the partner organizations complemented the host company's dominance.

Potential for Growth. Acquiring new contributors and increasing the involvement of existing ones are essential for ensuring sustainability of OSS communities. The CM found value in seeing names of individuals in the visualization, as contacting people for rewarding or encouragement could then be a next step. He also saw the potential for identifying and following entry paths of new developers. As reporting defects (A) is often the first thing a person can do, combinations (AD) and (ABD) could reflect the increasing or decreasing of their involvement. As the combination groups were small compared to (A), a need for encouraging the current stakeholders was identified. This was also the case for (D) as delegating work for others while working on the source code (AD) would be desired.

Code reviewers (C) are the most fundamentally integrated to the community since this task requires deep expertise, which is gained through personal learning and peer-to-peer mentoring. 55 % of developers that performed code reviews with any other combination were employees of the host company. Increasing the share of active code reviewers from outside the host company was thus desired.

Alarm Signals. A healthy hybrid OSS community consists of both commercial and non-aligned stakeholders. If the overall number of independent developers in any activity group would suddenly drop, a conflict between community-driven and commercial motivations would be evident. Here, a rapid investigation into the reasons and planning an intervention would be required. Secondly, some activity groups reflect the way the software development process is organized and how it is performing. The lack of group (BD) was mentioned as indicative of the Gerrit tools fitness to support coordination of the code review process. Also, if the number of people performing only work coordination (AB) would grow, a management overhead would be evident.

5   Limitations

External validity of the empirical evaluation is compromised by the single-case study design and involvement of only one interviewee. However, as hybrid OSS projects typically form around business-driven, platform-like products, the ecosystem itself can be considered representative. The limited time span of the sampling does not allow continuous analysis, which is particularly interesting for understanding development of the community. However, we hope the results give a way for future research on community management in hybrid environments.

6   Conclusion

This single case study explored ways of supporting management of hybrid OSS communities. Based on an initial visualization approach, several indicators that contribute to the health of the community could be observed by overviewing stakeholders that actively participate in tasks related to work coordination, code review and code delivery of the project. Based on these, the community manager was able to pinpoint individuals whose contributions to the project could be encouraged and to contemplate how the effectiveness of these actions could be evaluated. Knowledge of stakeholders' affiliations helped in evaluating the influence of different organizations on the development process. The manager also reported increased awareness of phenomena that might be indicative of problems in the organization of the community-driven software development process.

As future work, we have identified several places of improvement. These include using a longer time span for sampling, which would reveal the the in-

and outflow of developers and help to identify those who are the most dedicated to the community. Highlighting the frequency of contribution would also add to the value of the visualization and to help identify high performers on single platforms. Finally, combining the approach with software process metrics, e.g. throughput of work requests can bring new, meaningful insight on the phenomena that prevail in hybrid OSS environments.

Acknowledgments. This research is funded by DIMECC's Need4Speed program (http://www.n4s.fi/) and the Finnish Funding Agency for Innovation Tekes (http://www.tekes.fi/en/tekes/).

References

1. Adamic, L.A., Baeza-Yates, R.A., Counts, S. (eds.): Proceedings of the Fifth International Conference on Weblogs and Social Media, Barcelona, Catalonia, Spain, July 17–21, 2011. The AAAI Press (2011)
2. Concas, G., Lisci, M., Pinna, S., Porruvecchio, G., Uras, S.: Analysing the social networks constituted by open source communities. In: International Electronic Conference on Computer Science, vol. 1060, pp. 147–150 (2008)
3. Crowston, K., Howison, J.: Hierarchy and centralization in free and open source software team communications. Knowl. Technol. Policy **18**(4), 65–85 (2006)
4. Digia annual report (2014). http://vuosikertomus2014.digia.com/filebank/132-Digia-Annual-Report-2014.pdf. Accessed 08 Sep 2015
5. Free software definition (2015). http://www.gnu.org/philosophy/free-sw.html. Accessed 18 Sep 2015
6. Lakhani, K., Wolf, R.G.: Why hackers do what they do: understanding motivation and effort in free/open source software projects. In: MIT Sloan Working Paper No. 4425-03 (2003)
7. Long, Y., Siau, K.: Social network structures in open source software development teams. J. Database Manage. **18**(2), 25–40 (2007)
8. Oezbek, C., Prechelt, L., Thiel, F.: The onion has cancer: some social network analysis visualizations of open source project communication. In: Proceedings of the 3rd International Workshop on Emerging Trends in Free/Libre/Open Source Software Research and Development (FLOSS 2010), pp. 5–10 (2010)
9. Runeson, P., Höst, M.: Guidelines for conducting and reporting case study research in software engineering. Empirical Softw. Eng. **14**(2), 131–164 (2009)
10. Shen, C., Monge, P.: Who connects with whom? A social network analysis of an online open source software community. First Monday **16**(6) (2011). http://firstmonday.org/ojs/index.php/fm/article/view/3551
11. Von Krogh, G., Haefliger, S., Spaeth, S., Wallin, M.W.: Carrots and rainbows: motivation and social practice in open source software development. MIS Q. **36**(2), 649–676 (2012)
12. Watson, R.T., Boudreau, M.-C., York, P.T., Greiner, M.E., Wynn Jr., D.: The business of open source. Commun. ACM **51**(4), 41–46 (2008)
13. Yin, R.K.: Case Study Research: Design and Methods. Sage publications, Thousand Oaks (2014)

Architecture

A Process Framework for Designing Software Reference Architectures for Providing Tools as a Service

Muhammad Aufeef Chauhan[1,3(✉)], Muhammad Ali Babar[1,2], and Christian W. Probst[3]

[1] CREST-Centre for Research on Engineering Software Technologies,
Software and Systems Section, IT University of Copenhagen, Copenhagen, Denmark
muac@itu.dk
[2] CREST-Centre for Research on Engineering Software Technologies,
The University of Adelaide, Adelaide, Australia
ali.babar@adelaide.edu.au
[3] Formal Methods Section, Department of Applied Mathematics and Computer Science,
Technical University of Denmark, Kongens Lyngby, Denmark
cwpr@dtu.dk

Abstract. Software Reference Architecture (SRA), which is a generic architecture solution for a specific type of software systems, provides foundation for the design of concrete architectures in terms of architecture design guidelines and architecture elements. The complexity and size of certain types of software systems need customized and systematic SRA design and evaluation methods. In this paper, we present a software Reference Architecture Design process Framework (RADeF) that can be used for analysis, design and evaluation of the SRA for provisioning of Tools as a Service as part of a cloud-enabled workSPACE (TSPACE). The framework is based on the state of the art results from literature and our experiences with designing software architectures for cloud-based systems. We have applied RADeF SRA design two types of TSPACE: software architecting TSPACE and software implementation TSPACE. The presented framework emphasizes on keeping the conceptual meta-model of the domain under investigation at the core of SRA design strategy and use it as a guiding tool for design, evaluation, implementation and evolution of the SRA. The framework also emphasizes to consider the nature of the tools to be provisioned and underlying cloud platforms to be used while designing SRA. The framework recommends adoption of the multi-faceted approach for evaluation of SRA and quantifiable measurement scheme to evaluate quality of the SRA. We foresee that RADeF can facilitate software architects and researchers during design, application and evaluation of a SRA and its instantiations into concrete software systems.

Keywords: Cloud Computing · Software Reference Architecture (SRA) · Tools as a Service (TaaS) · Architecture Design · Architecture evaluation

1 Introduction

A Software Reference Architecture (SRA) provides an abstraction for designing and reasoning about a concrete software architecture of a specific system domain [1, 2]. Whilst a concrete architecture is designed for a specific project according to well-defined

© Springer International Publishing AG 2016
P. Abrahamsson et al. (Eds.): PROFES 2016, LNCS 10027, pp. 111–126, 2016.
DOI: 10.1007/978-3-319-49094-6_8

business goals and requirements, a SRA usually aims to address generic business goals and domain requirements. A SRA consists of not only details on architecture components and its view, but also encompasses best practices for describing the architecture and the process guidelines for analysis, design and development of the architecture [3]. Though describing stakeholders concerns in terms of architecture view points and presenting the details of a SRA using multiple views [4] is important, it is equally important to describe the design-time and run-time quality characteristics of a SRA and the use of appropriate architecture styles and patterns [5]. A SRA is primarily designed for two main reasons: (i) to standardize existing available concrete architectures or (ii) to propose a preliminary SRA that can facilitate concrete architecture design for a specific domain. Whilst a SRA standardization effort focuses on extracting reusable architecture elements from a number of concrete architectures, a SRA preliminary proposition focuses on recommendations for SRA documentation, guidelines for SRA design and evaluation as well as SRA adoption and evolution.

In this paper, we present a software Reference Architecture Design process Framework (RADeF) for designing cloud-based systems in general and cloud-based Tools as a service workSPACE (TSPACE) in particular. RADeF reports a set of key specifications and SRA design guidelines. Whilst cloud-based systems provision on-demand computing as Infrastructure as a Service (IaaS), Platform as a Service (PaaS) and Software as a Service (SaaS) [6], a TSPACE is characterized by as an activity or a task specific selection and on-demand provisioning of Tools as a Service (TaaS) as part of an integrated cloud-enabled workspace [6]. We assert that designing and evaluating a TSPACE SRA is more challenging than SRAs of general cloud-based systems because of the involvement of diversified tools and tenants with varying functional requirements and quality concerns. For example, performance and scalability can be more important for tenants and users of software development and testing TSPACE, whereas integration can be more important for tenant and users of architecture analysis and design TSPACE. Furthermore, instantiation of a TSPACE SRA for different domains can require customization (e.g. addition of new components or only selecting a subset of a SRA), which requires a mechanism that can be used to analyze quality and completeness of the instantiated architectures. Although there have been attempts to provide a systematic approaches for reference architecture design, documentation and evaluation [2, 3, 7], to the best of our knowledge, there has been a little work done on providing a process framework for SRA design given the specific needs of SRA design and evaluation of the TSPACE. Our work reported in this paper aims to address the following research objectives:

- Provide a systematic approach that can lead to a SRA's design elements identification, requirements analysis and detailed design.
- Provide insight to the specific needs of TSPACE SRA evaluation and instantiation into concrete architectures.
- Demonstrate application of RADeF on SRAs of software architecture design and implementation TSPACEs.

The organization of the paper is as follows. Section 2 provides the details of RADeF. Section 3 describes the results of the case studies of applying RADeF for describing and

implementing TSPACE. Section 4 provides an overview of the related work and
Sect. 5 concludes the paper by sharing lessons learned and experiences.

2 Reference Architecture Design Process Framework (RADeF)

A SRA is expected to provide guidance for designing and evaluating a concrete architecture. A SRA description usually includes reusable solutions in terms of architectural
goals, architectural styles, design patterns, design principles and decision and guidelines
for initiating a SRA. That is why it is important that a SRA description includes as much
details as possible. It is also important to have a clearly described process that can be
used to design and evaluate a SRA [2]. In this section, we describe RADeF, the process
that can lead to TSPACE SRA development, evaluation and implementation. We also
discuss important factors that should be considered at each stage of TSPACE SRA
design. A pictorial representation of RADeF is presented in Fig. 1. RADeF is an iterative
process framework and information produced in preceding stages is used as input for
the proceeding stages of the process and as shown in Fig. 1.

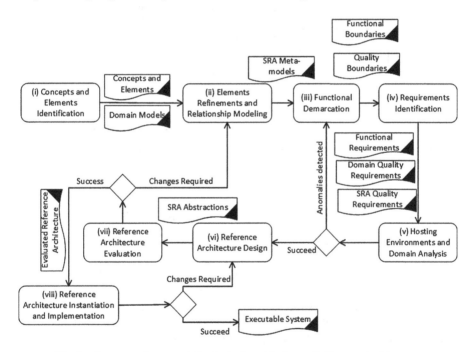

Fig. 1. A process framework for designing a Software Reference Architecture

2.1 Identification of a Reference Architecture's Concepts and Elements

First step in designing a SRA of a cloud-based TSPACE is to identify the concepts and
elements that constitute TSPACE. A SRA consists of not only SRA requirements and

SRA views, but it also provides guidelines for SRA evaluation. A generic view of the SRA elements is depicted in Fig. 2(a). The required concepts an elements are identified through a high-level analysis of a particular domain. TSPACE SRA elements can be classified into: Tenants, Tools, Provisioning Infrastructure, Artifacts, Context and Integration Methods. Each of the elements is tailored and extended with respect to the domain requirements for which the SRA is to be enacted.

Participants' Roles: End users, Requirements Analysts and Software Architects.
Artifact(s) Consumed: Business Requirements.
Artifact(s) Produced: High-level relationship models for TSPACE concepts and elements.

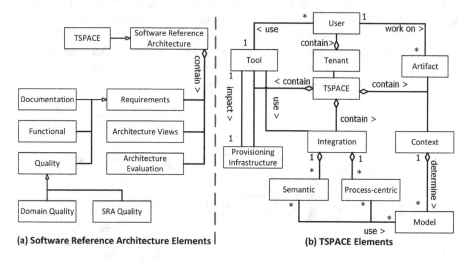

Fig. 2. Software Reference Architecture elements

2.2 Refinement of Domain Element and Relationships Modeling

The activities identified for this stage are aimed at refining the identified elements in previous stage, establishing the hierarchical structure of TSPACE elements and modeling relations among the elements. Domain models are considered the main sources of the information for this stage. The domain models can provide standardizations for elements, their hierarchical structures and the relationships among the elements. However the domain models need to be extended in order to cover all the dimensions of TSPACE including the tools, the development processes which govern the provisioning and usage of the tools, data integration and exchange formats among the tools, and any additional functional aspects that are required by TSPACE in a specific domain. Figure 2(b) shows TSPACE elements and relationships among the elements. The artifacts that are produced at this stage, serve as a foundation for the detailed requirements analysis and architecture design of the components that are responsible for tools bundling and integration in the TSPACE.

Participants' Roles: Business Analyst and Software Architect.
Artifact(s) Consumed: Documentation approaches, documentation templates and architecture design abstractions.
Artifact(s) Produced: TSPACE conceptual models that consists of concepts and elements that encompass TSPACE and relationship among the concepts and models.

2.3 Functional Demarcation Between the Reference Architecture Elements and the Tools to Be Provisioned

This stage of the activities deals with demarcation of functional requirements to be handled by a SRA and functional requirements for which TSPACE can rely on the tools (that can be provisioned by TSPACE). The artifacts that are produced at this stage provide a foundation for TSPACE functional requirements. The high-level architecture design with specific focus on the identification of components responsible for the TSPACE features.

Participants' Roles: Requirements Analyst, Business Analyst and Software Architect.
Artifact(s) Consumed: Domain models.
Artifact(s) Produced: Documents describing functional demarcation of TSPACE and encompassing tools.

2.4 Requirements Identification and Classification

The TSPACE SRA requirements can be classified into service model, integration and quality requirements as discussed below.

Service Model Requirements: This task aims at identifying the requirements for tools bundling, provisioning and enactment. For example, one of the primary objectives for providing a software architecting TSPACE is to provide the bundled suite of tools on demand as part of a TSPACE. It is critical to determine bundling and provisioning constraints and parameters. The tools bundling mechanism should be flexible enough to cater integration needs of different types of the tools to be used in a particular domain. In certain cases, there can also be some constraints with respect to the underlying virtualized infrastructure (e.g., IaaS cloud virtual machines) that can host the tools to enable their operations within acceptable runtime quality parameters (e.g., performance, scalability and reliability). The artifacts that are produced in this activity provide guidelines to identify integration needs of the tools in a TSPACE and guide the SRA analysis and design process.

Integration Requirements: Integration requirements focus on integration needs of the tools that can be provisioned in TSPACE. With reference to software architecting domain, the integration mechanism should be flexible enough to accommodate different proprietary and standardized formats as well as support integration among heterogeneous types of tools (e.g. desktop-based, web-based and cloud-based tools). The tools that are provisioned in a TSPACE instance can vary and the integration mechanism should be flexible enough to adapt to the tools' integration requirements of the provisioned tools. The integration mechanism should also support workspace require-ments, such as awareness of the operations that are performed on the artifacts as a result of the users' activities [8]. The artifacts that are produced at this stage guide the reference architecture design and analysis process of integration.

SRA Quality Requirements: The SPACE is aimed at providing a bundled suite of tools following a service model. As a result, the TSPACE SRA needs to incorporate archi-tecture quality requirements of cloud-enables services based system such as scalability [9], multi-tenancy [10] and dynamic provisioning [11]. The activities that are performed at this stage aim to identify important quality characteristics with reference to the domain in which the TSPACE is to be used. For the software architecting domain, scalability, multi-tenancy and dynamic provisioning are important. For another domain such as software testing, elasticity [12] and reliability [13] can be important. The artifacts that are produced as a result of this activity provide a foundation for runtime architecture quality requirements of TSPACE.

Participants' Roles: Business Analyst and Software Architect.
Artifact(s) Consumed: Design time constrains and tools bundling constraints, TSPACE functional boundaries, required activities and tasks, and tools enactment/provisioning parameters and constraints, Collaboration and integration models.
Artifact(s) Produced: Integration and collaboration models. Design time constrains, tools bundling constraints and tools' provisioning/enactment parameters. TSPACE runtime architecture quality requirements.

2.5   Impact of Potential Cloud Hosting Environments on the Domain

The suitability of the underlying IaaS or PaaS platform can impact the way a reference architecture is designed. E.g. PaaS environments can be a suitable choice for testing domains in which autonomous scalability of the resources is more important. Whilst IaaS environments can be suitable for hosting tools implemented using different tech-nologies as IaaS clouds provide customizable hosting environments.

Participants' Roles: Software Architect.
Artifact(s) Consumed: List of potential cloud hosting environments.
Artifact(s) Produced: Selected cloud hosting environments.

2.6   Reference Architecture Documentation, Analysis and Design

This stage of the activities focus on analyzing architecture documentation approaches and preliminary analysis of the maturity of the domain for which a SRA is designed. The analysis of the documentation approaches determines the most appropriate strat-egies for capturing the architecture of the domain for which TSPACE is designed. A comprehensive analysis of the SRA documentation approaches is reported in [2, 3]. Angelov et al. have recommended that a reference architecture documentation include information about the context, goals and design decisions. The context dimension covers the purpose, the organization(s) that is (are) developing a reference architecture and its maturity stage (e.g., preliminary or classic) [2]. The goal dimension encompasses business goals and quality attributes as well as the purpose of defining a reference architecture (e.g., to standardize concrete architecture or to facilitate design of concrete architecture). The design dimension elaborates whether a SRA is concrete or abstract and whether the SRA has been described using formal, semiformal or informal approaches. Avgeriou et al. [3] propose that a SRA description should have three main elements: (i) description of the approach used to document a SRA, (ii) guidelines on instantiation of a SRA and (iii) evaluation of a SRA corresponding to desired functional requirements and quality attributes. The outcome of this activity determines the approach used for describing a SRA, the level of abstractions to be covered in the SRA documentation, the objectives and the selection of the approaches for evaluation and instantiation of a SRA. Outcome of this activity has impact on all the proceeding stages of the reference architecture design process. A summary of a SRA design dimensions is shown in Fig. 2(a).

A SRA design should be based on reference models and architecture styles and patterns [14, 15]. If a TSPACE SRA is to be used for mission-critical and safety-critical tools, then it is also important to have metrics that can be used to measure runtime quality parameters of an architecture. An empirical investigation of the SRAs have revealed the absence of important views [4] in a SRA and the details of the supporting algorithms and formalization to achieve the required functionality of the reference architecture [4] impact a SRA's adoption and applicability. Hence, a SRA should encompass all the important views according to some well-known approaches such as 4 + 1 view model [4].

Participants' Roles: Software Architect.
Artifact(s) Consumed: Architecture documentation templates and models.
Artifact(s) Produced: SRA documentation approaches used, filled templates, details of the abstractions to be used, evaluation and initialization approaches and views.

2.7 Evaluating a Reference Architecture

Evaluation of a SRA is an important step for analyzing its feasibility and applicability. Different considerations for evaluating a reference architecture have been proposed [3, 7, 16]. Avgeriou et al. [3] have proposed to evaluate a SRA using scenarios and prototyping. Scenarios based approaches enable an implementation-independent evaluation. The evaluation scenarios need to be focused on important design time and runtime qualities of the architecture. The prototyping helps analyze the suitability of the implementation decisions such as platform choices and programming languages for the design decisions incorporated in a SRA. Angelov et al. [7, 16] have argued that straightforward adoption of architecture evaluation methods such as Architecture Tradeoff Analysis Methods (ATAM) [17] and Software Architecture Analysis Methods (SAAM) [18] is not feasible because: gathering all the stakeholders and generating scenarios for a SRA evaluation may not be possible, there can be a significantly large diversity of stakeholders and the levels of abstractions in the designed components can be quite high. Hence, it is important to identify the most relevant architecture requirements by involving domain experts or domain models and then preparing scenarios by involving a SRA's potential users [7, 16].

Other than the above-mentioned challenges, a TSPACE SRA evaluation activity has some additional complexities. For example, a TSPACE provision the tools for performing the different activities; hence there is a need for tools integration and workspace specific functions in a *aaS model. An evaluation activity focuses on the parts of a SRA that are embodied by TSPACE boundaries rather than by the tools to be provisioned. Some of the key quality characteristics are inherited from *aaS model for evaluating a TSPACE SRA's abilities of on-demand provisioning of tools in a particular domain, whose quality attributes should drive the evaluation activities. Hence, the evaluation activity should focus on identifying and analyzing the relevant quality attributes for the given domain. Moreover, as the SRA's elements (i.e. components or services) and design decisions collectively constitute to SRA quality, traditional architecture analysis and evaluation methods such as utility tree [17] from ATAM are not sufficient because these are unable to quantify architecture quality. We advocate for leveraging an new approach inspired from attack-defense trees [19] to enhance the utility tree for analysis of the completeness of a SRA. Figure 3(a) shows the structure of the enhances utility tree. Sub-nodes of the utility tree corresponding to each quality can be assigned with three types of operators: logical OR operator which identifies that opting any of the branch can achieve a quality attribute, logical AND operator that indicates that opting all of the branches will be essential to meet a quality criteria, and a Seq-AND (sequential AND) operator indicates that the design decisions corresponding to the branches need to be executed in a specific sequence in order to achieve the corresponding quality characteristic. In some cases, it might be required to analyze overall quality and completeness of the SRA. For this purpose, the probability values for the effectiveness of the design decisions can be assigned to each branch of the quality attribute nodes (such that maximum probability of all design decisions corresponding to each quality attribute do not exceed one). When probability values are used, OR operator takes minimum, AND takes sum and SeqAND takes sum of the probability values of all the branches of a quality attribute sub-tree. Finally, to evaluate the tools bundling and integration approaches, a prototype based evaluation is considered more effective. That means a TSPACE SRA prototype can play a critical role for the SRA evaluation and the tools that are selected for provisioning using the prototype can help to cover the most critical

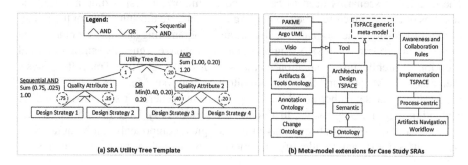

Fig. 3. SRA utility tree template and models

evaluation scenarios. The outcome of evaluation activity can trigger modification in the artifacts that were generated in previous stages as depicted in Fig. 1.

Participants' Roles: User, Requirement Analyst, Business Analyst and Software Architect
Artifact(s) Consumed: TSPACE Software Reference Architecture.
Artifact(s) Produced: Evaluation results.

2.8   Reference Architecture Instantiation and Implementation

As a SRA provides a generic architecture solution for a specific domain, its instantiations can require appropriate tailoring, sometimes significant. As a result, some of the components can be excluded from the instantiated architecture and some additional components can be incorporated. The enhanced utility tree (Fig. 3(a)) presented in Sect. 2.7 can facilitate the analysis and quantification of the concrete architecture.

Participants' Roles: Business Analyst, Software Architect and Developers.
Artifact(s) Consumed: Evaluated TSPACE Software Reference Architecture.
Artifact(s) Produced: Instantiated system.

3   Two Cases of Applying RADeF

We have followed RADeF to support the design of a SRA for two types of TSPACE: software architecting tools domain and software implementation tools domain. The two case studies of applying RADeF for analysis, design, evaluation and implementation of the TSPACE aimed at provisioning integrated suite of tools for the domains. The tools commonly used for software architecture design and software implementation were selected for the case studies and TSPACE was designed by following RADeF steps. In this section, we provide the insight gained from our experiences from applying RADeF.

First and second stage of RADeF is to *identify concepts and elements of a SRA* and *establish relationships between the elements*. The generic model presented in Fig. 2(b) provides a foundation for TSPACE elements identification and relationship modeling. Though the generic model needs to be extended to cater the needs of a specific type of tools and the operations that can be performed using the tools. Figure 3(b) shows the extensions to the generic model for software architecting and software implementation domain. The tools used for software architecting have different types of the artifacts, e.g., architecture knowledge artifacts, design decision artifacts and architecture design diagrams. Since software architecture artifacts can be at different levels of abstractions, and there is no need to exchange complete artifacts (although selected information exchange is required) among architecting tools, which can be integrated through semantic integration technologies. We have leveraged IEEE 1471-2000 [20] and ISO/IEC/IEEE 42010:2011 [21] to build the semantic integration model for SRA of the architecting tools. Figure 3(b) shows a high-level view of the elements of the semantic model (the details can be found in [22]). The software implementation need to exchange the artifacts for collaborative work. For example, in a scenario where a UML modeling tool is used to design class diagrams, the code skeleton generated using the UML modeling tool (forward engineering) has to be used as input by Integrated Development Environments (IDEs). For example, process-oriented tools bundling requires process-centric integration. At this stage the SRA integration models are produced that provide foundations for the detailed architecture design.

Functional demarcation between the requirements to be incorporated by a SRA and the requirements to be incorporated by the provisioned tools is an important step for the *requirements identification*. As in the case studies, our focus was on providing software architecting and development tools, the SRAs focused on tools provisioning, tools integration and awareness of the operations that are performed on the artifacts using the tools. Whereas, individual tools were responsible for providing support for specific activities such as architecture knowledge management, architecture design decision management, architecture design and software implementation. Table 1 shows details of the SRA and the tools'. requirements classification. The details of the requirements can be found in [22, 23]. Multi-tenancy and scalability are domain specific quality requirements to support a large number of tenants [24]. *Analysis and identification of cloud hosting environments* for software architecting and implementation domains requires using IaaS cloud because of heterogeneity of the tools. A combination of desktop and web-based tools are used for software architecting and implementation. The IaaS provides flexibility to host the existing tools by configuring the virtual machine templates.

Table 1. Functional demarcation and requirements

Functional Demarcation			
	Tools Requirements	Architecting	Knowledge management, design decision management, architecture modeling.
		Implementation	Software development, unit testing.
	SRA Requirements	Functional	Autonomous provisioning, semantic integration, process centric integration, awareness of the operations.
		Quality	Flexibility, interoperability, completeness and adaptability.
	Domain	Quality	Multi-tenancy, scalability

For the TSPACE *SRAs detailed design,* we have used a layered architecture [5] and a view-based approach [4] to represent different parts of the SRA. A layered architecture can facilitate easy modifiability of a TSPACE SRA, whose different dimensions can be represented using a view-based approach. The TSPACE meta-model (Fig. 2(b)) and the detailed models (Fig. 3(b)) produced in the second stage of RADeF are used as a foundation for the detailed design. Table 2 shows the key architecture design decisions for software architecting and software implementation of a TSPACE SRA design. We have reported the details on the architecture views and design decisions in [6, 23].

Table 2. Decisions for software architecting (Arc.) and implementation (Impl.) case studies

Architecture Design Decisions	Case Study	
	Arc.	Impl.
Service Oriented and REST Architecture	✓	✓
Centralized Repository to have common semantic integration models	✓	✗
Use of pipes and filter patterns to support multi-tenancy and easy scalability	✓	✓
Tenant specific integration, information discovery and awareness rules	✓	✓
Process-centric integration	✓	✓
IaaS cloud for hosting tools	✓	✓

As discussed earlier, the inclusion of heterogeneous tools producing and consuming artifacts at different levels of abstractions makes the evaluation of a TSPACE SRA a challenging activity. We have adopted multi-faceted approach to *evaluate the TSPACE SRAs* for the reported case studies. (i) We evaluated the TSPACE SRAs and their respective implementations for functional completeness corresponding to the functional and quality requirements. (ii) We implemented the prototype systems for TSPACE SRAs using Amazon IaaS cloud[1]. Interface modules of TSPACE have been implemented using Service Oriented Architecture (SOA) [25] and REST [26] architecture styles using JavaEE service technologies (JAX-RS[2], JAX-WS[3]) for enabling easy interoperability of different types of tools with the systems. The semantic integration has been implemented using Apache Jena Framework[4]. The process-centric integration has been implemented using jBPM[5] process workflow engine. (iii) We used quantitative architecture evaluation approach that is presented in Sect. 2.7, which is based upon utility tree of ATAM, but can quantifiably measures the TSPACE SRA's quality. The evaluation was carried out by six potential stakeholders, who had experiences (of architecting and implementation) of software development tools, process-based applications, cloud-based systems and collaborative software development systems.

A subset of the enhanced utility tree (described in Sect. 2.7) constructed in the evaluation session is presented in Fig. 4. The participants of the evaluation session were asked to assign each of the design decisions with values 0, 0.25, 0.50, 0.75 or 1.00. Then the average of the value score was taken for each of the design decisions to be assigned to a specific quality attribute on a utility tree branch. In case, if there were more than one design decisions corresponding to a specific quality attribute, an average was divided by the total number of design decisions to keep the maximum probability value under 1 corresponding to each of the quality attributes. If some of the design decisions are important than others, then weighted averages can be used. Whilst we considered all of

---

[1] http://aws.amazon.com/.

[2] http://jax-rs-spec.java.net/.

[3] https://jax-ws.java.net/.

[4] https://jena.apache.org/.

[5] http://www.jbpm.org/.

the design decisions of the equal importance, the enhanced utility tree branches corresponding to each of the quality attributes (and sub attributes) had either AND, OR and SeqAND operators (as discussed in Sect. 2.7). The evaluation participants found the proposed operators (that were assigned to the enhanced utility tree) helpful to quantify the architectural quality of the TSPACE SRA. Figure 4 shows the evaluation results corresponding to four key quality attributes of the TSPACE SRAs for software architecting and implementation TSPACE. An average of the quality score (average of the score given by the six evaluators) is shown in the figure corresponding to each of the design decisions of the quality attributes. Sum and Min functions (as described in Sect. 2.7) are used to calculate the aggregated quality score of the reference architectures.

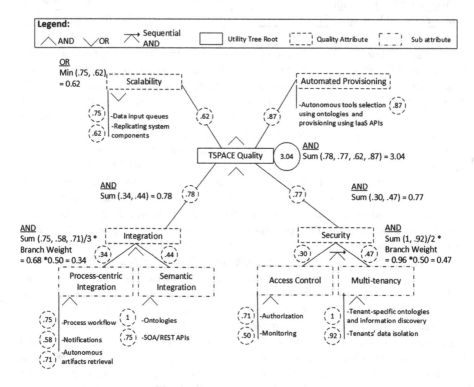

Fig. 4. SRA evaluation utility tree

4   Related Work

Given the increasing importance of SRAs for guiding the designing and evaluating of concrete architectures in different domains, several researchers have attempted to provide a set of standardized activities and frameworks for designing and documenting reference architectures. One of the most comprehensive and detailed guidelines have been reported by Angelov et al. [1, 2, 7, 16]. Their work provides a classification technique of the reference architectures based upon the domain-specific maturity and how the reference architectures are designed. For the mature domains, the aim of a reference architecture is to provide the standardization of the architectures, whereas, for the emerging domains, the purpose is to facilitate the design of concrete architectures in multiple organizations. Some of the problems associated with designing a reference architecture are missing design methods, challenges in defining non-functional requirements, problems with selecting appropriate views, lack of suitable architecture documentation methods and relatively little support for evaluating the reference architectures [1]. In our TSPACE SRA design process, we have explicitly catered all of the above-mentioned challenges to support the process of designing the reference architecture and have explicit stages for design and documentation methods, define non-functional requirements, select appropriate views and choose appropriate evaluation strategies.

Avgeriou [3] suggests representing a reference architecture using multiple viewpoints of Rational Unified Process (RUP) including logical viewpoint, deployment viewpoint, implementation viewpoint and data viewpoint. Avgeriou has emphasized that the reference architecture should be evaluated using both scenario-based and architecture prototype-based evaluation with respect to development-time and run-time qualities [3]. Nakagawa et al. [27] have proposed the use of ontologies to identify different components of the reference architecture. Fernandez et al. [28] have described the key documentation elements of a software reference architecture. The documentation elements include technical design, architecture knowledge and experiences and management documentation. For TSPACE SRA, we have described the details about the technical design and architecture knowledge. However, the management of the documentation (during applications of the software reference architecture in different setting) is out of the scope of this work.

5   Discussion and Conclusions

The cloud-enabled tools not only need to be compliant with specific quality requirements but also need to provide support for different activities, just like desktop-based tools. Whilst tools in every domain have their specific challenges, there are some generic characteristics that tools in every domain need to address. We share our experience from different activities of designing the TSPACE SRA.

Adoption of Appropriate Methodology to Formalize relations among TSPACE Elements: To establish relationship among the artifacts that are maintained by cloud-based tools with other tools is a critical characteristic and can play a significant role in cloud-based tools adoption. Hence, it is important to identify the integration needs for the tools to be provisioned from a cloud-enabled workspace. Our experience has shown that an ontology driven semantic model can provide support for tools selection, relating different artifacts with each other even though the artifacts are maintained by using different proprietary data structures, and awareness needs in a cloud based workspace. As different tools have different requirements for integration, there is a need to have appropriate semantic integration models corresponding to the artifacts' formats used by the tools.

Incorporating Workflows with Tools Provisioning: In some cases, the tools that are provisioned as part of a tools suite need to exchange information according to project specific development processes (e.g., to manage collaboration in distributed architecture evaluation processes [29]). In such cases, the integration support for the tools needs to be complemented by a workflow based process on the cloud so that artifacts among the tools can be exchanged according to the specific software development processes.

Quality of Individual Tools in TSPACE: In our proposed TSPACE SRAs, we have considered each of the provisioned tools as a black box and have not considered the management of quality characteristics of each individually provisioned tool during the lifecycle of a TSPACE instance. However, for certain tools that produce executable artifacts, e.g. model driven tools used to generate code, may require extra computing, memory or other resources during their life cycle depending on the tasks to be executed. In such cases, a TSPACE for the tools needs to incorporate the metrics and corresponding prediction models so that additional resource needs can be predicted and resources can be acquired according to the needs of a specific task.

Impact of software reference models: Availability of standardization models for respective domain impact the reference architecture design process. Whist designing TSPACE software reference architecture for software architecting domain, we have leveraged IEEE 1471-2000 [20] and ISO/IEC/IEEE 42010:2011 [21] architecture documentation models as a baseline for the identification of the TSPACE architecture elements and the TSPACE ontology meta-model design. The meta-model has been further enhanced by analyzing architecting TSPACE requirements. The incorporation of standardized domain model in the reference architecture design ensures the applicability of reference architecture for broader range of tools. Unavailability of the standardization models for the respective domain or not using them during the reference architecture design can negatively impact the applicability of a reference architecture.

Selection of Appropriate underlying IaaS Clouds and Cloud Deployment Models: As tools in a TSPACE SRA are considered as black box, the tenant specific constrains on artifacts' storage location are applied onto the tools that are provisioned on the location that is compliant with the constraints (in our prototype implementation, we have used Amazon EC2 location specific provisioning features). However, for more complex use cases, where location constraints on the artifacts can change during their lifecycle, Virtual Machines (VMs) hosting the tools might need to be migrated from one location to another. In such cases, the capability of underlying IaaS to support VMs migration would play a critical role. Hence, IaaS cloud selection and selection of cloud deployment model (e.g., public, private or hybrid) should be carefully made. A cloud environment that supports the desired features should be selected.

Multi-facet approach for TSPACE SRA Evaluation: Considering a generic nature of TSPACE SRA and a broad range of potential stakeholders, multiple architecture evaluation techniques need to be adopted for evaluating a reference architecture from different perspectives. We have evaluated the TSPACE software reference architecture using scenario-based evaluation approaches [18], architecture tradeoff analysis method

[17] and a prototype implementation of the reference architecture. Scenario-based evaluation approaches can help evaluate completeness of a SRA with respect to reference architecture objectives and requirements. Architecture tradeoff analysis method enables the identification of strong and week points of a SRA. A prototype is a viable way to demonstrate the feasibility of a SRA. The proposed TSPACE SRA evaluation methodology facilitates the quality score of not only the SRAs but also their concrete representations. For example, if a concrete implementation of the SRA corresponding to evaluation tree presented in Fig. 4 adopts different parts of the design decisions and corresponding components for different tenants, the quality of the instantiated architecture and corresponding system can be computed on the fly, especially for SaaS based systems.

In future, we intend to apply RADeF on software reference architecture design and analysis of other types of cloud-based systems. We also intend to carry out empirical evaluations on our proposed quantification mechanism for SRA evaluation utility tree to analyze its impact on long-term management of the software reference architectures.

References

1. Angelov, S., Trienekens, J., Kusters, R.: Software reference architectures - exploring their usage and design in practice. In: Drira, K. (ed.) ECSA 2013. LNCS, vol. 7957, pp. 17–24. Springer, Heidelberg (2013). doi:10.1007/978-3-642-39031-9_2
2. Angelov, S., Grefen, P., Greefhorst, D.: A framework for analysis and design of software reference architectures. Inf. Softw. Technol. **54**(4), 417–431 (2012)
3. Avgeriou, P.: Describing, instantiating and evaluating a reference architecture: a case study. Enterp. Archit. J., 24 (2003)
4. Kruchten, P.B.: The 4 + 1 view model of architecture. IEEE Softw. **12**(6), 42–50 (1995)
5. Buschmann, F., et al.: Pattern-Oriented Software Architecture: A System of Patterns, p. 457. John Wiley & Sons Inc., New York (1996)
6. Chauhan, M.A., Ali Babar, M., Sheng, Q.Z.: A reference architecture for a cloud-based tools as a service workspace, In: 2015 IEEE Conference on Service Computing (SCC). IEEE, New York (2015)
7. Angelov, S., Trienekens, J.J.M., Grefen, P.: Towards a method for the evaluation of reference architectures: experiences from a case. In: Morrison, R., Balasubramaniam, D., Falkner, K. (eds.) ECSA 2008. LNCS, vol. 5292, pp. 225–240. Springer, Heidelberg (2008). doi: 10.1007/978-3-540-88030-1_17
8. Dourish, P., Bellotti, V.: Awareness and coordination in shared workspaces. In: Proceedings of the 1992 ACM Conference on Computer-Supported Cooperative Work, pp. 107–114. ACM, Toronto (1992)
9. Sodhi, B., Prabhakar, T.V.: Application architecture considerations for cloud platforms. In: 2011 Third International Conference on Communication Systems and Networks (COMSNETS), p. 1–4. IEEE (2011)
10. Domingo, E.J., et al.: CLOUDIO: a cloud computing-oriented multi-tenant architecture for business information systems. In: 2010 IEEE 3rd International Conference on Cloud Computing (CLOUD), pp. 532–533. IEEE (2010)
11. Calheiros, R.N., et al.: The Aneka platform and QoS-driven resource provisioning for elastic applications on hybrid Clouds. Future Gener. Comput. Syst. **28**(6), 861–870 (2012)

12. Han, R., et al.: Enabling cost-aware and adaptive elasticity of multi-tier cloud applications. Future Gener. Comput. Syst. **32**, 82–98 (2014)
13. Brandic, I., Music, D., Dustdar, S.: Service mediation and negotiation bootstrapping as first achievements towards self-adaptable grid and cloud services. In: Proceedings of the 6th International Conference Industry Session on Grids Meets Autonomic Computing, pp. 1–8. ACM, Barcelona (2009)
14. Bass, L., Clements, P., Kazman, R,: Software Architecture in Practice, p. 640. Addison-Wesley Professional, Boston (2012)
15. Avgeriou, P., Zdun, U.: Architectural patterns revisited–a pattern (2005)
16. Angelov, S., Grefen, P.: An e-contracting reference architecture. J. Syst. Softw. **81**(11), 1816–1844 (2008)
17. Kazman, R., et al.: The architecture tradeoff analysis method. In: 1998 Proceedings of the Fourth IEEE International Conference on Engineering of Complex Computer Systems, ICECCS 1998 (1998)
18. Kazman, R., et al.: SAAM: a method for analyzing the properties of software architectures. In: 1994 Proceedings of the 16th International Conference on Software Engineering, ICSE-16 (1994)
19. Kordy, B., et al.: Attack–defense trees. J. Logic Comput., exs029 (2012)
20. IEEE Recommended Practice for Architectural Description of Software-Intensive Systems. IEEE Std 1471-2000, pp. i–23 (2000)
21. ISO/IEC/IEEE Systems and software engineering – Architecture description. ISO/IEC/IEEE 42010:2011(E) (Revision of ISO/IEC 42010:2007 and IEEE Std 1471-2000), pp. 1–46 (2011)
22. Chauhan, M.A.: Foundations for Tools as a Service Workspace: A Reference Architecture. Ph.D. Dissertation, IT University of Copenhagen, Denmark (ITU-DS; No. 118) (2016)
23. Chauhan, M.A., Babar, M.A.: PTaaS: Platform for Providing Software Developing Applications and Tools as a Service. Technical report TR-2014-176 (2014). https://pure.itu.dk/ws/files/74130379/TR_2014_176.pdf
24. Azeez, A., et al.: Multi-tenant SOA middleware for cloud computing. In: 2010 IEEE 3rd International Conference on Cloud Computing (CLOUD), pp. 458–465. IEEE (2010)
25. Huhns, M.N., Singh, M.P.: Service-oriented computing: key concepts and principles. IEEE Internet Comput. **9**(1), 75–81 (2005)
26. Fielding, R.T.: Architectural Styles and the Design of Network-Based Software Architectures, p. 162. University of California, Irvine (2000)
27. Nakagawa, E.Y., Barbosa, E.F., Maldonado, J.C.: Exploring ontologies to support the establishment of reference architectures: an example on software testing. In: Joint Working IEEE/IFIP Conference on Software Architecture, 2009 & European Conference on Software Architecture, WICSA/ECSA 2009. IEEE (2009)
28. Martínez-Fernández, S., et al.: Artifacts of software reference architectures: a case study. In: Proceedings of the 18th International Conference on Evaluation and Assessment in Software Engineering. ACM (2014)
29. Ali Babar, M.: A framework for groupware-supported software architecture evaluation process in global software development. J. Softw. Evol. Process **24**(2), 207–229 (2012)

Should We Adopt a New Version of a Standard? – A Method and Its Evaluation on AUTOSAR

Corrado Motta[1($\boxtimes$)], Darko Durisic[1($\boxtimes$)], and Miroslaw Staron[2]

[1] Volvo Car Group, Gothenburg, Sweden
{Corrado.Motta,Darko.Durisic}@volvocars.com
[2] Chalmers University of Gothenburg, Gothenburg, Sweden
Miroslaw.Staron@cse.gu.se

Abstract. The development of large software systems is usually based on a number of industrial standards that define a set of features and their requirements. In order to use new features specified in the standards, new releases of the standards need to be adopted together with their requirements. This requires a thorough impact analysis of the changes in the requirements that can be time-consuming considering their potentially high number. In order to facilitate the adoption of new releases of industrial standards in large software systems, we present a method based on both quantitative and qualitative analysis of requirements evolution. The method is evaluated in a case study of AUTOSAR - a standard used in the development of automotive software systems in cooperation with Volvo Car Group. The evaluation results show that the use of the proposed method can identify the most unstable AUTOSAR specifications and their requirements whose changes may have a significant impact on the automotive systems. This knowledge can increase the speed of adoption of new AUTOSAR releases by automotive vendors.

Keywords: Requirement evolution · Metrics · Industrial standards

1 Introduction

Analyzing the evolution of system requirements is an important and inevitable phase in the development of large software systems [8], especially for OEM (Original Equipment Manufacturers) that base their development on industrial standards. This is because features specified in the standards and their requirements are usually driven by a number of competitive companies. The process of updating one system with new standardized features brings a series of advantages, such as making use of a number of standardized requirements that are proved to be valid in practice and buying cheaper off-the-shelf software packages from software vendors. However, it also brings new challenges such as working with requirements not written by OEMs and dealing with their fast evolution.

For this reason, the process of analyzing the evolution of standardized requirements without a suitable methodology and tool support can be time-consuming

© Springer International Publishing AG 2016
P. Abrahamsson et al. (Eds.): PROFES 2016, LNCS 10027, pp. 127–143, 2016.
DOI: 10.1007/978-3-319-49094-6_9

and can require significant engineering effort. Furthermore, adopting new standardized features in the development projects without having a clear knowledge whether the standardized requirements related to them can be fulfilled in practice can lead to the introduction of new faults into the system. Therefore, dealing with the evolution of standardized requirements is one of the primary objectives of large companies in order to be able to update their systems faster and cheaper.

Although several solutions have been proposed mostly originating from the academia, the evolution of standardized requirements is still considered one of the most challenging practical problems in the development of large software systems [8]. The objective of this work is to define a suitable methodology for efficiently analyzing the evolution of standardized requirements as well as improving the process of updating large software system with new standardized features. We aim to provide an answer to the following research question: *How can we assure efficient adoption of new releases of standards in the development of large software systems by analyzing the evolution of standardized requirements?*

As outcome of our work, this paper presents a method, named SREA (Standardized Requirements Evolution Assessment), that consists of four steps that are based on both quantitative and qualitative analysis of requirements evolution. All steps of the method can and should be performed automatically with the help of a software tool in order to reduce the time of analysis. Despite the fact that we focus on the analysis of standardized requirements where the proposed method is particularly helpful as certain requirements changes are driven by other companies, the method can also be applied on the evolution of company internal requirements as part of the common requirements engineering process.

In order to evaluate the proposed method, we applied it in the automotive domain in a case study of AUTOSAR (Automotive Open System Architecture) standard [3], that specifies a reference architecture and methodology for the development of automotive software systems. In particular, AUTOSAR provides a set of standardized requirements for the design of the automotive architectures (i.e., language for the architectural models), that consists of a number of Electronic Control Units (ECUs) responsible for executing software functionalities, and requirements for the ECU middleware. The rest of the functional ECU requirements are left to be defined by each OEM. As AUTOSAR represents a big industrial standard that counts more than 150 partners and 21.000 requirements, we believe it qualifies as a valid case for evaluating the SREA method.

The study is conducted in collaboration with Volvo Car Group (VCG) whose engineers helped us to understand and prioritize AUTOSAR releases and their specifications for the evaluation of the proposed method. The results of our evaluation show the importance of performing automated analysis of requirements evolution. In particular, they show that the use of SREA method could help automotive engineers in analyzing the evolution of the AUTOSAR requirements faster by providing the engineers with information such as which specifications are unstable (e.g., their requirements change with every release), which requirements are changed and the actual content of the changed requirements.

Knowledge about the unstable specification can be useful for making strategic decisions about the set of standardized features that are mature enough to be implemented in the system. Knowledge about the changed requirements has a potential of saving lots of time spent on reading tents of AUTOSAR specification with thousands of requirements manually. For example, in all specification with design requirements between AUTOSAR releases *4.2.1* and *4.2.2*, we identified 1563 requirements and presented relevant changes (additions, removals and modifications) for only 172.

The rest of the paper is organized as follows: Sect. 2 presents the related work; Sect. 3 provides the background of AUTOSAR as our unit of analysis; Sect. 4 describes the research methodology we used during this project; Sect. 5 defines the proposed *SREA* method; Sect. 6 presents the results of evaluation of the *SREA* method on AUTOSAR; Sect. 7 discusses the validation of the proposed method and provides recommendations; finally, Sect. 8 concludes our work and describes our plans for future work.

2 Related Work

Several studies of requirements evolution are related to our study. In particular, Wang et al. [15] provide a general method for studying changes in the requirements in order to find relations between them and the number of software defects. The method relies on the quantitative analysis. Although their approach was considered as a starting point for our work, our focus was on the impact of requirements changes on the system under development.

Similar but more exhaustive studies were conducted in the avionics context by Anderson et al. [1,2] who show how to conduct an empirical analysis of requirements evolution starting from a general point and moving to a product-oriented one. They perform the following two steps: (i) collecting information from the avionics domain using the *Requirement Maturity Index* (*RMI*), *Historical Requirement Maturity Index* (*HRMI*), and *Requirement Stability Index* (*RSI*) metrics and (ii) refining the information gathered in the first step using the qualitative approach. We rely on a similar work-flow based on the RMI metric that shows the stability of requirements changes in relation to the past releases. We did not consider RSI and HRMI metrics since a great number of requirements changes can lead to a non-meaningful (e.g., negative) number.

For the quantitative analysis of requirements evolution, we considered the study of Shi et al. [13] that aims to identify requirements that are most likely to be changed in the future using a number of metrics, e.g., *Sequence*, *Frequency* and *Lifecycle*. However, these metrics cannot be used for identifying the requirement specifications that are mostly affected by changes, that is one of our major goals.

For efficiently studying the evolution of system requirements, Nurmuliani et al. [11] provided a taxonomy of changes for categorizing different types of requirements changes, reasons for their change and the origin of changes. This study inspired us to define a taxonomy of changes for the AUTOSAR requirements.

Additionally, Stark g. et al. [14] proposed a method for analyzing the evolution of requirements in two steps. We adopted the first step called *micro* analysis in order to get a preliminary view on the requirements architecture, structure of the requirements specifications and possible types of requirements changes.

Finally, in order to understand the development of automotive software systems based on AUTOSAR, several automotive papers were considered. Two studies of Durisic et al. [6,7] were useful for improving our general knowledge of AUTOSAR, its architecture, methodology and complexity. More generally, the paper from Broy et al. [4] was useful for identifying trends in the evolution of the automotive software, even though they do not explain how it can be measured.

Although there is a significant number of methods related to the analysis of requirement evolution, the majority of them are not applied in a real industrial context in which large software systems are developed. This paper aims to fill this gap by combining the existing studies with our considerations and metrics in order to develop an efficient method for analyzing the evolution of standardized requirements that can facilitate this activity in the real industrial contexts.

3   Case Study Evaluation Context

In the automotive domain, OEMs are usually responsible only for the design of automotive systems while the actual implementation of software and hardware components is done by a hierarchy of suppliers. In order to standardize the methodology of work in such a distributed environment and a reference architecture for the distributed realization of the automotive systems using a number of ECUs, AUTOSAR standard has been introduced. The proposed ECU architecture is based on the following common three-layer architecture:

1. Application software layer that consists of a number of software components responsible for certain vehicle functionalities.
2. ECU middleware layer (a.k.a. basic software - BSW) that consists of a number of BSW modules responsible for, e.g., signaling and diagnostic services.
3. ECU hardware layer responsible for executing the allocated software components and BSW modules.

Since ECU basic software does not contribute to the realization of high level car functionalities that could make a competitive advantage for one OEM (e.g., autonomous drive), it is completely standardized by AUTOSAR that provides a set of requirements specifications for each BSW module. On the other hand, the functionality of the application layer is generally not standardized, although there are some predefined software components. However, AUTOSAR provides a meta-model followed by a set of design requirements that define the language for the architectural models of the application layer in order to facilitate the exchange of models between OEMs and suppliers [6]. This meta-model and design requirements serve as basis for the development of AUTOSAR modeling tools.

Based on the described methodology, we can distinguish between the following three types of requirements in the AUTOSAR based development process:

1. *Functional requirements* for the application software specified by OEMs.
2. *Design requirements* for the system models standardized by AUTOSAR.
3. *BSW requirements* for each BSW modules standardized by AUTOSAR.

In this paper, we focus on the last two types that are standardized by AUTOSAR. Design requirements are described in the specifications called "templates" (*TPS*) and they can be either *specification items* or *constraints* (checked by modeling tools). BSW requirements are described in the software requirement specifications *SWS*. An example for each type is provided below:

- **Specification item example:** The 1:n multicast routing is supported with the definition of several *IPduMappings* classes.
- **Constraint example:** The value of *windowSize* shall be greater or equal 1.
- **BSW requirement example:** CAN module shall allow that Multiplexed Transmission functionality is configurable (ON — OFF) at pre-compile time.

Apart from these types of requirements, AUTOSAR builds a requirements traceability hierarchy starting from the explained requirements until the general AUTOSAR features and objectives. These requirements are, together with the OEM-specific functional requirements, not considered in our analysis as they do not produce a direct impact on the development of automotive systems.

All AUTOSAR requirements specifications including the meta-model are released simultaneously. There are three types of AUTOSAR releases:

1. *Major release:* first digit change, contains backwards incompatible features.
2. *Minor release:* second digit change, contains backwards compatible features.
3. *Revision:* third digit change, contains bugfixes only.

4 Research Methodology

In order to provide the answer to the research question addressed in this study that is presented in the introduction, we developed a method named *SREA* that aims to reduce the costs and time associated with the process of analyzing the evolution of standardized requirements and evaluated it in a case study [12] of the AUTOSAR requirements, in collaboration with VCG.

We defined the SREA method by relying both on the existing and novel approaches. First, we conducted a literature review on the existing approaches for monitoring the evolution of system requirements using the *snowball* method [16]. In order to identify the starting set of papers, we searched for papers mentioning *requirements evolution* and *requirements volatility* keywords in their title, abstract and keywords sections using *Google Scholar, IEEE Xplore* and *Scopus* databases. We selected papers [2,9,13] as the starting point and continued to look for references and citation in these papers. We performed three iterations in total and analyzed in details 23 out of 42 relevant papers. Second, we improved our understanding of the case study context in semi-structured interviews, workshops and meetings with AUTOSAR experts from VCG. These two steps served as input for defining the SREA method.

Finally, we evaluated the method using AUTOSAR requirements as a unit of analysis from the chosen set of AUTOSAR releases. We chose all AUTOSAR releases from the latest major release *4.0.1* until the latest revision *4.2.2*. We decided not to consider previous AUTOSAR releases as their specification are not structured in the same way which makes them hard to be analyzed automatically. Nevertheless, AUTOSAR has a lot of significant changes in the last major release. Finally for the detailed analysis of changes between two releases, we decided to focus on the changes between *4.0.3* and *4.2.2* releases.

In order to be able to cope with the size of AUTOSAR that counts more than 21.000 requirements in its latest release (*4.2.2*), we developed a configurable software tool for gathering data and calculating and presenting the results to the AUTOSAR engineers at VCG. The tool compares different versions of the AUTOSAR requirements specifications in PDF and creates a structured report. The report presents the following information for the analyzed specifications: types of requirement changes in all analyzed releases, change history of each requirement and the number of requirements, cumulative number of requirements, number of changes and cumulative number of changes for each AUTOSAR release.

Finally in order to validate the proposed *SREA* method, we distributed a survey with 10 questions to six AUTOSAR experts at VCG. The questions were based on both quantitative and qualitative results of the method applied on AUTOSAR requirements, e.q., which AUTOSAR specifications are mostly unstable, and they aimed to assess whether the results of the method are in line with the expectation of the experts who participated in the development of the AUTOSAR standard. The experts were not aware of the method results.

5   The *SREA* method

The *SREA* method we propose in this paper consists of the following steps:

1. Define taxonomy of requirement changes in order to design the right metrics for performing the quantitative analysis in the next step.
2. Perform quantitative analysis of evolution of the requirements specifications in order to be able to correctly prioritize them in the next step.
3. Prioritize individual requirements specifications in order to select groups of specifications for the qualitative analysis in the next step.
4. Perform qualitative analysis of changes in order to accurately assess their impact on the system under development.

Step 1: Define taxonomy of changes: The first step of the *SREA* method aims to define the taxonomy of changes by:

1. Defining which types of changes shall be considered, e.g., added requirements, in order to define the metric for each type.
2. Defining the metrics for different types of changes, e.g., *NoA* as the number of added requirements, in order to calculate the total number of changes.

3. Defining the total number of changes, i.e., *NoC*, as the (weighted) sum of results of the previous metrics, in order to perform quantitative analysis.
4. Defining the taxonomy of modifications (which modifications shall be considered), e.g., requirements title, in order to perform qualitative analysis.

First three points aim to define the types of changes that shall be considered in the requirements evolution analysis, as not all changes have impact on the system under development (e.g., split requirements with low probability of occurrence). We specified the following metrics for each type of identified change:

1. *NoA* for the number of added requirements.
2. *NoS* for the number of split requirements.
3. *NoU* for the number of merged requirements.
4. *NoD* for the number of deleted requirements.
5. *NoM* for the number of modified requirements.
6. *NoC* for the total number of changed requirements.

The *NoA*, *NoS*, *NoU*, *NoD* and *NoM* are simple metrics that are calculated by counting the number of occurrences of each type of change. The *NoC* metrics is calculated as the sum of the results of other metrics, as shown in Formula 1:

$$NoC = a * NoA + b * NoS + c * NoU + d * NoD + e * NoM \tag{1}$$

The coefficients a, b, c, d and e are there to indicate which simple metrics shall be considered in the *NoC* metric, i.e., value 0 means that this particular type shall not be considered whilst value 1 means that it shall be considered.

The last point aims to define the taxonomy of requirements modifications that shall be considered in the analysis. Requirements that are added, split, merged and deleted are usually easily detectable based on their unique IDs or names. However, requirements that are modified require checking whether their content was changed. In practice, not all modifications to the content of the requirements are relevant, e.g., fixing spelling mistakes does not require effort for fulfilling the analyzed requirements. There are no general rules for deciding which modification are not relevant, so they have to be defined. Table 1 shows the taxonomy of the general types of modification we encountered in our study.

Additionally, it is advisable to implement the taxonomy of modifications in the tool responsible for calculating the metrics in a configurable way so that the inclusion/exclusion of each type could be done automatically.

Based on the defined taxonomy of changes, we can exclude from both quantitative and qualitative analysis all types of changes in the requirements that do not affect their semantics. This in turn is very valuable for the engineers analyzing the evolution of requirements as they are presented with the precise measure of requirements change considering only those requirements that actually require certain effort to be fulfilled by the system under development.

In order to successfully perform points 1–4 from the first step for a specific industrial case, a preliminary analysis of the requirements behavior shall be conducted. We propose the *micro* analysis method [14] that enables a comparison

Table 1. Taxonomy of modifications

Types of modifications	Description
Grammar and spelling corrections	Grammar and spelling improved in a new release.
Encoding modification	The specifications can be encoded in different ways and the output could slightly change.
Format modification	The format can change, e.g., how requirements are structured in tables or text.
Change in the technical term name	Changes in the name of, e.g., an API or a class.
Title modification	The title of a requirement can change.
Content modification	Modification in the content of a requirement.
Reference modification	Change of requirement's traceability reference

of two different versions of one significant (in terms of number of requirements and their scope) requirement specification for each category of requirements, e.g., functional requirements, design requirements, etc. This comparison aims to identify both different types of changes and different types of modifications. The outcome of the *micro* analysis should be a table with one row for each requirement changed and one column for each type of change encountered in the analysis, i.e., deleted, split, modified, merged and added requirements. Depending on the results of the *micro* analysis, we could then decide not to consider certain types of changes if their occurrence is insignificant for the analysis.

Step 2: Perform quantitative analysis of requirements evolution: In this step we aim to quantitatively analyze the evolution of standardized requirements in order to identify specifications that are mostly affected by changes. Our qualitative analysis relies on the *NoC* (Number of Changes) metric that counts the number of added, deleted, split, merged and modified requirements according to the defined taxonomy of changes. We analyze the evolution of requirement specifications in two ways: (i) by calculating the *NoC* and (ii) by considering the percentage of changes, based on the *RMI* metric that is derived from *NoC*.

The first one gives an overview of the amount of changes and which specifications contain the biggest number of changed requirements. The other one does that same taking also the total number of requirements into account. For example, although a specification with one thousand changes has a significant *NoC*, it could be quite stable, i.e., with a low percentage, if it contains ten thousands requirements. For this reason, we aim to assess the stability of each requirement by measuring *RMI* in the way defined in Formula 2.

$$RMI = \frac{R_t - NoC}{R_t} \tag{2}$$

Rt represents the total number of requirements for a specific version while *NoC* represents the total number of changed requirements between this version and the previous one. Substructing the results of the *RMI* metric from *Rt* can be used for calculating the percentage of changed requirements. Note that the percentage could exceed 100 % in some cases because *RMI* considers all types of changes including merged and deleted requirements. For example, one specification could have 199 *NoD*, 20 *NoA*, and 47 *NoM*, hence 266 *NoC* from one version to another. However it could have just 200 requirements in the last version.

Step 3: Prioritize individual requirements specifications: The third step of the proposed method aims to collect a group of specifications based on the results of the previous step and the importance of each specification for the system under development. One specification is usually considered important if its requirements are needed for adopting a specific standardized feature in the system. The set of prioritized specifications are then grouped according to their semantics (e.g., relevant standardized features) in order to serve as input to the next step of the method. We do not specify the number of specifications that should be prioritized and grouped because it depends on the needs, e.g., adopting one small standardized feature can affect only a few requirements specifications while adopting an entire new release of a standard may affect many.

Step 4: Perform qualitative analysis of changes: The last step of the *SREA* method is focused on the qualitative analysis of changes in the prioritized group of requirement specifications. The analysis of the actual changes in the requirements is done by comparing their content (i.e., whether their textual representation is the same or not) between different releases of the standard. The outcome of this step is a report for each prioritized specification or for a group of specifications related to the analyzed feature. In order to increase its readability, we propose to structure the report in the following way:

1. *Table of Contents* contains a list of sections and subsections of the report.
2. *General Data* contains the results of the *NoC* metric, for each type of change, and *RMI* metrics, calculated again for the prioritized specifications.
3. *List of Changed Requirements* contains the list of all types of changes considered by specifying the ReqId, title and content of each requirement.
4. *Detail of Modified Requirements* contains the comparison between the content of all modified requirements emphasizing (e.g., bold or coloring) the modified text according to the taxonomy defined in step 1.

Since the main goal of *SREA* is to increase the speed of analysis of standardized requirements evolution, automated tool support for performing both quantitative and qualitative analysis described in the steps above is an important part of the method. This tool should also be able to generate the final report based on the configured taxonomy of changes, as already explained.

6   Evaluation of the *SREA* Method on AUTOSAR

In this section, we show partial results from the evaluation of the *SREA* method on the evolution of AUTOSAR requirements for a specific objective: to facilitate updates of the AUTOSAR modeling tools with new releases of AUTOSAR.

This implies focusing on the analysis of AUTOSAR specifications containing design requirements. We organize this section according to the steps of the method.

Step 1: Define taxonomy of changes: We initially performed *micro* analysis using two AUTOSAR specifications: *AUTOSAR_TPS_SystemTemplate*, containing design requirements, and *AUTOSAR_SWS_Com*, containing BSW requirements. Figure 1 shows an extract of the results for *SWS_COM*.

	Mod	Mer	Split	Del	Add
[SWS_Com_00675]	▓				
[SWS_Com_00863]					▓
[SWS_Com_00736]				▓	
[SWS_Com_00789]	▓				
[SWS_Com_00393]				▓	

Fig. 1. Short extract of the *micro* analysis

Based on the complete results of the *micro* analysis of the *SWS_COM* and *TPS_SystemTemplate* specifications, we concluded that the number of merged and split requirements is very low and therefore insignificant for our study. Therefore, we decided not to consider split and merged requirements because of their low probability of appearance and increased difficulty in detection. The decision not to consider these types of requirement changes resulted in the definition of the *NoC* metric we used for AUTOSAR evaluation presented in Formula 3.

$$NoC = 1 * NoA + 0 * NoS + 0 * NoU + 1 * NoD + 1 * NoM \qquad (3)$$

Based on the taxonomy of modifications, and in the discussion with the engineers from VCG, we decided to consider only the following types of modification for the quantitative analysis performed in step 2: *Change in the technical term name*, *Title modification* and *Content modification*.

Step 2: Perform quantitative analysis of requirements evolution: The results of the quantitative analysis of the AUTOSAR requirements evolution are presented in Fig. 2. We considered all minor releases and revisions of the AUTOSAR major release 4 (i.e., releases from *4.0.1* to *4.2.2*).

We can observe the evolution of the AUTOSAR standard in Fig. 2 from two different perspectives: (i) the *NoC* across consequently releases (left chart) and (ii) the total number of requirements (right chart). Based on these charts, we can see that AUTOSAR is continuously changing through its releases. Furthermore, we can also see that AUTOSAR is continuously *growing*: In *R401* AUTOSAR had 14.000 requirements whilst in the last version (*R422*) it counts more than 21.000 requirements. Finally, we can see that minor releases of AUTOSAR (*R411* and *R421*) bring more changes to the requirements than revisions.

In order to analyze the specifications that are mostly affected by the evolution of the AUTOSAR standard, we sorted them based on the results of the *NoC* and

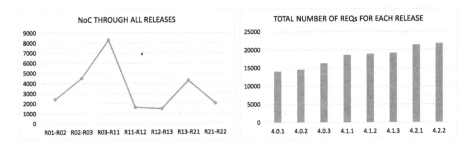

Fig. 2. Results of the quantitative analysis of the AUTOSAR requirements evolution

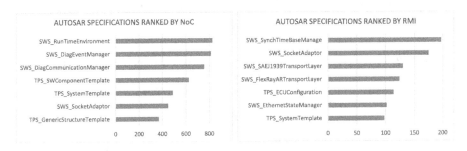

Fig. 3. AUTOSAR specifications ranked according to the *NoC* and *RMI*

RMI metrics calculated between the chosen AUTOSAR releases *4.0.3* and *4.2.2*. Figure 3 shows the first 7 (over 84) specifications.

The results of the *NoC* metric show that *SWS_RunTimeEnvironment* and *SWS_DiagEventManager* specifications are mostly affected by the changes (more than 800 changes). Although they have a significant *NoC*, we can not directly conclude that these specifications are also the most unstable ones. To assess this, we ranked them by the results of the *RMI* metric in order to investigate the relations between the two lists. We can see that *SWS_SynchTimeBaseManager* and *SWS_SocketAdaptor* specifications have the highest *RMI* value. By combining the two lists, we can also see that *SWS_SocketAdaptor* and *SWS_SystemTemplate* are the only two specifications that are considered highly affected by the evolution based on the results of both metrics. Generally, all the specification that have high values of *NoC* and *RMI* are good candidates to be analyzed first, depending on their importance for the actual system under development.

Step 3: Prioritize individual requirements specifications: In this step, we focused on the main objective of this analysis: facilitate the updates of the AUTOSAR modeling tools based on a new release of AUTOSAR. Therefore, we asked the AUTOSAR engineers from VCG which specifications are considered the most important for the analysis of impact on the AUTOSAR modeling tools. They agreed on the following three specifications: *TPS_SystemTemplate*, *TPS_SWComponentTemplate* and *TPS_ECUConfiguration*.

Based on this prioritization and the outcome of the previous step that identified specifications mostly affected by the changes, we decided to focus on the qualitative analysis of *TPS_SystemTemplate* and *TPS_SWCTemplate* in the first phase. The *TPS_SystemTemplate* specification contains general design requirements on how the system shall be designed, e.g., description of ECUs connected with electronic buses and transmission of signal on the electronic buses. The *TPS_SWComponentTemplate* specification contains general design requirements on how software components should be designed with their data interfaces.

Step 4: Perform qualitative analysis of changes: In the last step we performed qualitative analysis on the prioritized specifications by running the tool we implemented and by providing a detailed report. In this report, we first show the results of all proposed metrics, as presented in Table 2.

Table 2. Report - results of the metrics applied on the chosen specifications

Metric	TPS_SystemTemplate	TPS_SWCTemplate	Total
NoA	472	374	846
NoD	4	24	28
NoM	13	228	241
NoC	489	626	1115
RMI	0,01	0,41	0,28

The only significant difference in results between the two specifications is for the *NoM* metric. *TPS_SystemTemplate* counts only 13 modifications whilst *TPS_SWComponentTemplate* counts 228 modifications. Nevertheless, the *RMI* metric indicates higher stability of the *TPS_SWComponentTemplate* (0,41) in comparison to the *TPS_SystemTemplate* (0,01). This is because the number of requirements in the last version of the *TPS_SWComponentTemplate* is much higher than in the last version of the *TPS_SystemTemplate* (1069 compared to 494) with much smaller difference in the *NoC* value (626 compared to 489).

After showing the results of all metrics, we list in the report all added, removed and modified requirements emphasizing the textual modifications in the modified requirements in bold. The example of the presentation of one modified specification items in the report is shown in Fig. 4.

One interesting discovery that we came across by analyzing changes in the AUTOSAR requirements was the fact that change in the name of certain technical terms (e.g., API or meta-class names) can have a significant impact on the results of the metrics. For example, we located an unexpected increase in the results of the *NoM* metric between AUTOSAR releases *4.2.1* and *4.2.2*. After investigating the causes of this, we found that AUTOSAR renamed one requirement specification from *SWS_DevelopmentErrorTracer* to *SWS_DefaultErrorTracer*. As a consequence of this renaming, all requirements that contained the word *development* (in this context) have also been renamed to *default*.

5.54 [TPS_SWCT_01209]

————content————

previous version:
ClientServerAnnotation

the clientserverannotation can be used to provide more information with respect to the operation of the port.

current version
ClientServerAnnotation

the clientserverannotation can be used to provide more information with respect to the **clientserveroperation** of the **portprototype**.

———————————————

Fig. 4. Example of modification of a specification item

In order not to invalidate the results by this change that has no impact on the semantics of the analyzed requirements, we provided an option in our tool for the engineers to specify which changes in the names of the technical terms shall be ignored (e.g., every change of a single word from *development* to *default*). Using this option, engineers can add these types of modifications to the configuration file every time they encounter them and run the tool again. We discovered that ignoring these types of replacements can significantly decrease the total *NoM* and therefore the size of the report providing more accurate results to the users. For example, excluding the *development* to *default* replacement reduced the total *NoM* between the two analyzed releases by 27%.

7   Discussion

We validated the proposed *SREA* method by distributing a survey to the AUTOSAR experts at VCG in which we asked them a number of questions related to the evolution of the AUTOSAR requirements specifications, e.g., which specifications they think are mostly affected by the changes between two AUTOSAR releases. Our goal was to assess whether the results of our method meet their expectations. We concluded that the results of the *SREA* method fully met the answers from the VCG experts in 66% of questions and were significantly different in just 1%. In 17% of questions we did not get an answer from the experts and in 16% of questions the answer was slightly different than the one provided by our method, e.g., the experts indicated that the second most affected document according to our method was mostly affected by the changes. More details about the validation including survey questions and answer can be found in [10].

Based on the results of the validation, we concluded that the proposed method can indeed be used for analyzing the evolution of standardized requirements of AUTOSAR and identifying the requirements specifications, together with the actual requirements, that are mostly affected by the changes. However, additional validation of the true benefits of the proposed method and the tool in reducing the amount of time spent analyzing the evolution of standardized system requirements is yet to be performed, as we explained in the future work.

In order to assess different threats to validity for our study, we followed Cook and Campbell's list of threats [5], i.e., threats to internal, external, construct and conclusion validity. Due to space limitation, we describe in this paper the most important threats to internal validity, that concerns accuracy of our results, and external validity, that concerns generalization of our results.

The most important threat to the internal validity of our study is related to what is considered a requirement in the AUTOSAR specifications. According to AUTOSAR, not only specification items and constraints described in this paper can be considered as requirements, but also plain text written in the specifications as it is mandatory to be followed when developing AUTOSAR compliant systems. However, we realized during our micro analysis that most of the important statements are part of specification items (and constraints), whilst the remaining text usually represents examples, rationales, and figures. For this reason, we believe that the internal validity of our results is still high as we managed to analyze the most important content of the requirements.

The most important threat to the external validity of our study is related to the generalizability of our results to systems that are developed based on other industrial standards and their requirements. Although we cannot claim that the *SREA* method can provide equally good results in other domain without evaluating it in additional case studies, we believe that the this is likely due to the fact that we designed the steps of the method considering the existing literature and studies performed and validated in different domains (e.g., avionics).

Finally, we can recommend to other companies who would like to analyze the evolution of standardized system requirements to start by defining the taxonomy of possible requirements modifications and the types of changes according to their knowledge about the analyzed standard. We believe that the other steps of the method are applicable to other contexts/domains as well.

8   Conclusion

In this paper, we present and evaluate the method named *SREA* that can be used to facilitate the process of adopting new releases of industrial standards and their features. The method is based on the quantitative and qualitative analysis of evolution of the standardized system requirements and is able to:

- Identify, based on the *NoC* metric, requirements specifications that are mostly changed in the new release of a standard, indicating that they should be considered first in the analysis of impact of adopting the new release.

- Identify, based on the *RMI* metric, requirements specifications that are mostly unstable during the evolution of one standard, indicating that features described in these specifications may contain defects.
- Present the actual content of added/removed and modified requirements in the concrete specifications of one release of a standard to the engineers performing the analysis, thus significantly reducing the time of analysis.

We apply and validate the *SREA* method on the case of AUTOSAR standard by developing the software tool that implements the method. We used the proposed method and the tool to study and assess the impact of AUTOSAR requirements evolution on the automotive software systems based on AUTOSAR. Our results show that the requirements standardized by AUTOSAR and their evolution should be analyzed and measured in a structured and automated way, i.e., by following a clearly defined method supported by a software tool to automate the process of gathering results. This approach helped automotive engineers from Volvo Car Group to faster assess the impact of AUTOSAR design requirements changes, related to a set of new AUTOSAR features, on the AUTOSAR modeling tools used in the development process.

In particular, we show that by applying the *SREA* method to different versions of the AUTOSAR standard, it is possible to identify the most important requirements specifications to be analyzed in the first phase. As an example, we showed the analysis of the two specifications - *TPS_SystemTemplate* and *TPS_SWComponentTemplate* - shall be done first in order to assess the impact of switching from the AUTOSAR release *4.0.3* to release *4.2.2* on the used AUTOSAR modeling tools. We also show that the method is able to provide a report containing only relevant information on the added, removed and modified requirements to the automotive engineers in order to increase the speed of analysis. For example in case of the *TPS_SystemTemplate*, the report contained 269 pages of relevant information about the changes whilst the same specification provided by AUTOSAR have around 1500 pages. Without the proposed method, these pages would need to be compared manually between the analyzed releases.

The information provided by the *SREA* method can therefore help organizations responsible for managing large software systems in understanding which areas of the system will be mostly affected by the changes in the standardized requirements and therefore faster adopt new releases of the standard.

We identified several potential areas of interest for further work. Since requirements evolution is today considered to be a challenging task for both industry and academia, this study shall be considered as a first step in defining the methodology for performing this task. There are several interesting ways for improving and/or extending the method we propose, in particular:

1. Calculate the actual engineering effort that is saved by using the *SREA* method. This would increase the validity of the presented results.
2. Apply *SREA* to other industries that develop system based on standards. This would increase the generalizability of the presented results.

3. Extend the proposed method to provide effort estimates for adopting new standardized features in the development projects. This would additionally help companies in allocating resources for supporting specific features.
4. Extend the proposed method to include a model for estimating the number of changes to the requirements specifications that will occur in the future releases of the standard. This would help standardization organizations in allocating resources for working with the most critical specifications early.

The tool we used for the analysis of AUTOSAR requirements can be downloaded from here: https://www.chalmers.se/en/projects/Documents/SREA.zip

Acknowledgment. The authors would like to thank Swedish Governmental Agency for Innovation Systems (VINNOVA) for funding this research (grant no. 2013-02630) and the AUTOSAR team at Volvo Car Group for contributing to the work.

References

1. Anderson, S., Felici, M.: Controlling requirements evolution: an avionics case study. In: Koornneef, F., Meulen, M. (eds.) SAFECOMP 2000. LNCS, vol. 1943, pp. 361–370. Springer, Heidelberg (2000). doi:10.1007/3-540-40891-6_31
2. Anderson, S., Felici, M.: Requirements evolution from process to product oriented management. In: Bomarius, F., Komi-Sirviö, S. (eds.) PROFES 2001. LNCS, vol. 2188, pp. 27–41. Springer, Heidelberg (2001). doi:10.1007/3-540-44813-6_6
3. AUTOSAR, www.autosar.org: Automotive Open System Architecture (2003)
4. Broy, M., Kruger, I., Pretschner, A., Salzmann, C.: Engineering automotive software. Proc. IEEE **95**(2), 356 (2007)
5. Cook, T., Campbell, D.: Quasi-Experimentation: Design & Analysis Issues for Field Settings. Houghton Mifflin, Boston (1979)
6. Durisic, D., Staron, M., Tichy, M.: ARCA - Automated analysis of AUTOSAR meta-model changes. In: International Workshop on Modelling in Software Engineering (2015)
7. Durisic, D., Staron, M., Tichy, M., Hansson, J.: Evolution of long-term industrial meta-models - a case study of AUTOSAR. In: Euromicro Conference on Software Engineering and Advanced Applications, pp. 141–148 (2014)
8. Ernst, N., Borgida, A., Jureta, J., Mylopoulos, J.: An overview of requirements evolution. In: Mens, T., Serebrenik, A., Cleve, A. (eds.) Evolving Software Systems, pp. 3–32. Springer, Heidelberg (2014)
9. Li, J., Zhang, H., Zhu, L., Jeffery, R., Wang, Q., Li, M.: Preliminary results of a systematic review on requirements evolution. In: Proceedings of the IEEE Conference on Evaluation Assessment in Software Engineering, pp. 12–21 (2012)
10. Motta, C.: Analyzing the Evolution of System Requirements. Chalmers — University of Gothenburg (2016)
11. Nurmuliani, N., Zowghi, D., Fowell, S.: Analysis of requirements volatility during software development life cycle. In: Proceedings of the Australian Software Engineering Conference, pp. 28–37 (2004)
12. Runeson, P., Host, M.: Guidelines for conducting and reporting case study research in software engineering. In: Proceedings of the Conference on Empirical Software Engineering, pp. 131–164 (2009)

13. Shi, L., Wang, Q., Li, M.: Learning from evolution history to predict future requirement changes. In: Proceedings of the International Conference on Requirements Engineering, pp. 135–144 (2013)
14. Stark, G., Skillicorn, A., Smeele, R.: A micro and macro based examination of the effects of requirements changes on aerospace software maintenance. In: Proceedings of the IEEE Conference on Aerospace, pp. 165–172 (1998)
15. Wang, H., Li, J., Wang, Q., Wang, Y.: Quantitative analysis of requirements evolution across multiple versions of an industrial software product. In: Proceedings of the 17th Conference on Asia-Pacific Software Engineering, pp. 43–49 (2010)
16. Wohlin, C.: Guidelines for snowballing in systematic literature studies and a replication in software engineering. In: Proceedings of the 18th International Conference on Evaluation and Assessment in Software Engineering (2014)

Choreography Modelling Language for the Embedded Systems Domain
Empirical Evaluation and Lessons Learned

Nebojša Taušan[1(✉)], Jari Lehto[2], Jouni Markkula[1],
Pasi Kuvaja[1], and Markku Oivo[1]

[1] M3S Research Group, University of Oulu, Oulu, Finland
{nebojsa.tausan,jouni.markkula,pasi.kuvaja,markku.oivo}@oulu.fi
[2] Research and Development, Management and Automation,
NOKIA, Espoo, Finland
jari.lehto@nokia.com

Abstract. Choreography, as a service-oriented architecture-specific viewpoint, is increasingly present in the embedded systems domain. Existing languages for choreography modelling, however, are insufficiently expressive to capture the complexities that are typical in the embedded systems domain. To address this, a new language for choreography modelling was designed. This study presents an empirical evaluation of the language and findings based on the evaluation. The empirical evaluation was conducted with experts from four software companies and two university research groups. Data were collected using focus group method and analysed with template-based thematic analysis. The findings of the evaluation revealed (a) software testing and protocol development as areas in which the new language can be applied, (b) design requirements for the language improvement, and (c) practical challenges regarding the use of the language. For practitioners, the findings confirmed the applicability of choreography modelling in protocol development and that users' level of expertise has a significant influence on the introduction of the language into practice. For researchers, the findings revealed how choreography can by used beyond its original purpose in the testing phase and identified new aspects that can be considered during choreography modelling language design.

Keywords: Choreography · Focus group · Evaluation · Embedded systems

1 Introduction

Service-oriented architecture is increasingly used in embedded systems (ES) development as an approach to manage the growing complexity of ES [13,21]. Systems based on service-oriented architecture consist of distributed services as their main building blocks and rely on service interactions to realise system-level goals. There are two viewpoints on service interactions: choreography and

P. Abrahamsson et al. (Eds.): PROFES 2016, LNCS 10027, pp. 144–159, 2016.
DOI: 10.1007/978-3-319-49094-6_10

orchestration [18]. Choreography implies decentralised coordination and focuses on the flow of service interactions from a neutral point of view. Orchestration implies centralised coordination and focuses on the flow of tasks from the point of view of a single participant.

Although orchestration is more frequently studied, several studies indicate that there is increasing interest in choreography among practitioners and researchers of SOA-based ES. For example, Kaur et al. [8] suggest that choreography is a more suitable viewpoint for capturing the behaviour of large-scale control systems. Modelling and execution of service choreography were chosen over orchestration as an approach to broaden the industry manufacturing system with features of event-driven architecture in [24]. Following this approach, an execution of choreography with strong real-time requirements in the context of manufacturing was implemented in [11]. Specifying a choreography viewpoint in ES, however, is a challenging task for two reasons. First, general purpose modelling languages used to specify service interactions are not expressive enough to capture the complexities that are typical in the ES domain [1,7,14]. Second, custom-developed languages for choreography modelling in ES are tightly-coupled with the specific development area they aim to support [28]. Once used in the development process, which emphasises other development areas, these custom-developed languages become only partially applicable.

To address these problems, one of the goals of the AMALTHEA international research project [20], of which this research is part, was to design a choreography modelling language that is applicable in ES development. To design the language, the authors conducted several studies focusing on challenges in software architecture development [25], the influence of middleware features on choreography language [26] and the design requirements for choreography modelling in ES [28] within this project. Based on the findings from these studies the authors designed a new choreography modelling language (CML) that is sufficiently expressive for use in the ES domain.

This study builds on the previously mentioned studies. Its goal is to learn about the applicability of the designed CML in the ES domain using experts' evaluations. Based on this goal, the following research question was derived:

RQ: To what extent is the designed CML applicable in the ES domain from experts point of view?

This research question was answered using a focus group for expert evaluation. Findings based on the evaluation complete the study goal by revealing how experts see the applicability of the CML in the ES domain and by highlighting directions for further improvements.

The presentation of the CML[1] evaluation consists of the following sections. Section 2 presents previous evaluations of the choreography modelling languages. Section 3 presents the way in which focus group approach was adopted to evaluate the CML, while Sect. 4 presents the research findings. The lessons learned from these findings are presented in Sect. 5. Techniques for ensuring the trustworthiness of our findings are presented in Sect. 6. Section 7 concludes the study.

---

[1] The CML and its editor are publicly accessible and can be obtained from [3].

2   Background

Several studies have focused on evaluating choreography modelling languages. The support for basic and complex control structures offered by three existing languages for choreography modelling was evaluated in [2]. The study characterised the offered support for control structures, and indicated potential improvements for the languages. A sub-set of language constructs for choreography modelling from the Business Process Model and Notation (BPMN, bpmn.org) was evaluated using the extended semiotic quality framework in [4]. The study concluded that, despite several limitations, the BPMN is appropriate for capturing choreography. Future choreography modelling language evaluations can benefit from the quality model for choreography presented in [16]. This quality model focuses on external quality attributes such as the functionality, efficiency and security and represents a step toward a full quality model for choreography specifications.

The focus of the study presented in this article is the evaluation of the designed CML (See Footnote 1), which was intended to address the limited expressiveness and partial applicability of existing choreography modelling languages used in the ES domain. This evaluation differs from the previously mentioned evaluations since (a) it represents an empirical evaluation that is conducted with experts, and (b) it considers the needs of the ES domain. The CML that is evaluated is designed based on the knowledge from our analysis of the state of the art and practice. This knowledge is presented in [28] and includes a set of design requirements, language implementation technologies, and reasons for selecting BPMN as an existing choreography modelling language that is suitable for redesign according to the design requirements.

3   Research Design

The goal of this study is to evaluate the applicability of the CML that was designed for ES during the AMALTHEA research project, and for this purpose we chose the focus group (FG) method [15]. The main reason for choosing the FG method is that it is a well-accepted method to collect data in the software engineering field [12] and a suitable method to obtain initial evaluations about new artefact designs [10,29]. The FG method utilises FG inquiry sessions as the main method of data collection and allows various data analysis methods to be used to produce the findings. In this study, FG inquiry was supported by the affinity grouping technique [6], while the data analysis relied on thematic analysis with templates [9] and was supported by frequent collaboration with experts. A summary of these methods is presented below.

Focus group inquiry referes to a session in which a moderator asks a group of people about their opinions, attitudes and beliefs about the phenomenon under study [15]. During an inquiry, a moderator encourages participants to discuss and, if needed, align their opinions. This type of inquiry, therefore, produces qualitative data from both participants' answers and their discussions.

The affinity grouping technique is a brainstorming method suitable for generating ideas about a phenomenon under study. Once ideas are collected, participants can easily organise them into meaningful categories based on similarities between the ideas [6].

The thematic analysis with templates (TAT) method was used to analyse the experts' feedback [9]. TAT is a variant of thematic analysis method, which is a qualitative method used for identifying patterns, themes, and their interpretations within collected data [17]. What differentiates TAT from the conventional thematic analysis is the use of a template during analysis. The template represents an initial set of themes that will be studied in the collected data. This set of themes is developed based on researchers experience and exploration of the phenomenon under study. The set is a flexible structure that evolves as the analysis progresses. According to King [9], TAT is less time-consuming and more flexible than other variants of thematic analysis. In additon to these reasons, TAT was chosen for this study since it is a suitable technique for analysing FG data that is collected during the design of artefacts [29].

Collaboration with experts refers to meetings, workshops, demonstrations, and email conversations during which the experts and researchers participating in this study discussed various issues and aspects of the CML.

Figure 1 summarises the organisation of these methods in this study. The methods and findings are presented as rectangles grouped based on whether they are used for data collection, data analysis, or representation of the study findings. The dotted arrows indicate the relation between methods and between methods and findings, while solid arrows represent the order in which these methods were utilised.

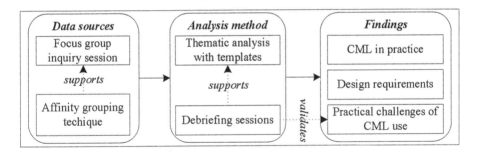

Fig. 1. Research design

Evaluation of the CML using the FG approach follows the steps proposed in [10]: (a) definition of the research problem, (b) planning the FG session, (c) selecting participants, (d) conducting the FG session, (e) analysing the data, and (f) reporting the results.

Definition of the research problem. The CML evaluated in this study is designed for ES development and, was based on experts' needs and existing knowledge found in the literature [27]. The research problem in this study addresses the lack of knowledge and understanding about how experts see the expressiveness of the CML and its applicability in ES development. By understanding experts' viewpoints on the use of CML for ES, additional refinements can be made and more focused evaluations in the field can be performed, thus leading to better acceptance of the CML by the ES development community.

Planning the FG session. Two FG sessions were planned. They consisted of three phases: opening, central discussion and the closing. The opening phase included an introduction to the general rules, study objectives and participants' backgrounds. In the central discussion and closing phases, experts' feedback was elicited. To elicit feedback, the moderator asked questions recommended in [10]. These questions, which were adopted for our study, are as follows: (1) Is the CML comprehensible? (2) How can it be deployed into a working context? (3) What are the potential problems in using or understanding the CML? The first two questions were asked during the central discussion phase while the third question during the closing phase. We planned to use the affinity grouping technique to support the closing phase. The planned duration of the FG sessions was ninety minutes.

Selecting participants. Experts who participated in the FG sessions were from two large software development industries (LI), two small and medium sized enterprises (SME) and two university research groups (EDU). Two LIs are global vendors with thousands of employees whose product portfolios include various hardware environments, many types of embedded and non-embedded software and, domain-specific languages (DSL) and tools. These LIs also participated in the AMALTHEA project. One SME focuses on the development of software tools and solutions for systems integration, which can be used for the development and integration of ES. The other SME focuses on modelling solutions based on open-source technology. The two research groups (EDU) closly cooperate with industries regarding modelling and methodological improvements. Table 1 summarises the companies at which the experts are employed.

Table 1. Companies and their characteristics

ID	Size	Country	Domain	Product
A	LI	Finland	Telecom	Hardware, ES and non-ES
B	SME	Finland	SW Products	System integration solutions
C	LI	France	Tools and DSLs	ES, tools, modelsand DSLs
D	SME	France	Tools and DSLs	Models, tools and methods for ES development
E	EDU	France	Modelling	
F	EDU	Belgium	Modelling	

Nine experts from the presented organisations participated in the FG sessions. All participants were software engineers with more than ten years of experience in software development. These participants were suitable for this inquiry due to their expertise in models, modelling languages and modelling technologies. Experts from companies that participated in the AMALTHEA research project were also involved in the development of the CML under evaluation. The experts' backgrounds are presented in Table 2.

Table 2. Focus group participants and their characteristics

Expert	Involvement in CML design	Role	Role description
1	1 year	Software architect	Design and management
2	3 years	Process improvement engineer	Product creation, improvement and renewal
3	1 year		
4	Minimal		
5	Minimal	Test architect	Testing improvement
6	Not involved	Software architect	Models, tools and method engineering
7	Not involved		
8	Not involved	Researcher and designer	Model design and innovation
9	Not involved		

Conducting the FG sessions. The FG sessions took place during the winter and spring of 2015. Prior to the sessions, all experts received materials describing the CML to study and participated in a workshop in which the developed CML was presented and discussed. For six FG participants, this workshop was their first exposure to the CML. As planned, the FG sessions consisted of opening, central discussion and closing phases.

In the first phase, the moderator introduced FG participants to the objective and general rules of the discussion and the experts presented their backgrounds. In the second part of the session, the moderator asked experts to discuss the comprehensibility of the CML and its deployment in their work contexts. During the last part of the session, experts discussed potential problems with using or understanding the CML. The affinity grouping technique was employed in this phase. In short, experts were asked to write down problems with the CML. Then, researchers formed categories based on the similarities between the listed problems and used these categories during the analysis. The first FG sessions lasted eighty minutes, and the second session lasted fifty minutes. The sessions were audio-recorded and transcribed.

Data analysis. We adopted TAT in this study and implemented it in three phases: (a) template development, (b) coding, and (c) interpretation. *Template development.* TAT starts with the development of a template that consists of the initial themes that are considered relevant to evaluation of the CML. These themes were created based on collaboration with industry partners on CML design, relevant literature, and questions asked during the FG sessions. The initial set of themes is presented in the first column of Table 3.

Table 3. Initial and final set of themes

Initial theme	Final set of themes	Final set of sub-themes (codes)
CML in practice	1. CML utilization	(a) software testing practice
		(b) protocol development
Drawbacks	2. Drawbacks	(a) communication layer
		(b) real-time execution
		(c) Data visualization
		(d) Interaction visualization
Challenges	3. Practical challenges of using the CML	(a) abstraction level
		(b) interactions
		(c) integration
		(d) task automation
Comprehension	4. Comprehension	No sub-themes
Benefits	Merged with 1.a and 1.b sub-codes	No sub-themes

Coding. After developing the template, researchers encoded the FG transcripts. During the encoding process, researchers assigned the codes to themes to further refine them. This process created hierarchical structures that formed the basis for the interpretation of the themes. Final set of themes and sub-themes is presented in the second column of Table 3.

Comparison of the initial and final template reveals the template evolution during the analysis process. The following changes occurred: (a) the text coded under the benefits theme was merged with the software testing and protocol development sub-codes since benefits are related to those development areas; (b) comprehensibility remained a top-level topic but did not receive further characterisation since all the experts agreed that the CML is comprehensible and did not discuss the topic in more detail; (c) a new theme, *practical challenges of using the CML*, was added; and (d) text under the challenges theme was rearranged under several sub-codes.

Interpretation. Researchers interpreted the derived themes, and experts verified these interpretations during workshops and meetings (collaboration). During both the interpretation and the coding processes, researchers used the NVivo [19] tool, which is a software package that automates a number of qualitative research-related tasks.

Reporting of the results. The themes in the final version of the template (presented in Table 3) represent a structured view of the experts' evaluations of how the designed CML helps solve the study problem. The first theme (ID 1) shows that the CML's expressiveness is sufficient for its application in the two identified areas of ES development. The second theme (ID 2) consists of identified drawbacks, correction of which can increase the expressiveness of the CML. The third theme (ID 3) reveals practical challenges to using the CML. Addressing these challenges can contribute to better acceptance of the CML by future users, thus contributing to its wider applicability. The fourth topic (ID 4) reveals that experts see the CML as comprehensible, which can also contribute to better acceptance by future users. Since the group did not discuss the CML's comprehensibility in more detail during the FG sessions, this theme was not interpreted further as part of the research findings.

4   Research Findings

The research findings consist of three parts. The first part reveals how the CML can be used as part of software testing and protocol development practices within one of the participating companies. The second part lists the design requirements considered important for choreography modelling in ES that the CML does not address. The third part describes and clarifies the challenges experts identified regarding CML use in practice.

4.1   CML in Practice

Software testing. Software testign practices rely on techniques such as unit testing, functional testing, regression testing, and debugging. The management of testing practices and techniques is organised with regard to the way in which user requirements are structured. Analysis of the relation between testing practices and the requirement structure revealed an area in which choreography modelling can contribute to more informative and understandable test specifications and to shortening of the testing time. This area is highlighted in Fig. 2 and explained further below.

The company uses 'request' to denote what customers wish to have in the product and 'requirements' to express how the request affects the product. Upon receiving a new customer request, requirement engineers generate a hierarchical structure consisting of requirements and sub-requirements. A top requirement is broken down to sub-requirements until clear acceptance criteria can be defined for those sub-requirements. Defined acceptance criteria are one of the main indicators of the completeness of a user request specification and are important in the testing phase.

In the testing phase, the derived (sub-) requirements and their corresponding acceptance criteria are used for verification of new or modified software functionalities based on those (sub-) requirements. The UML activity diagrams (http://uml.org/) present the steps for the verifying sub-requirement acceptance criteria. In practice, steps in one activity diagram often rely on the steps in other activity diagrams. This is especially the case when the verifying sub-requirements which are derived from a common requirement.

Figure 2 presents one such exemplary case in which one requirement, two sub-requirements and their acceptance criteria are derived from a customer request. In the testing phase, the software functionality created based on the customer request is verified against the acceptance criteria. Two activity diagrams (labelled A and B) represent this process. The verification processes, however, are not isolated from each other. This means that the verification steps, which

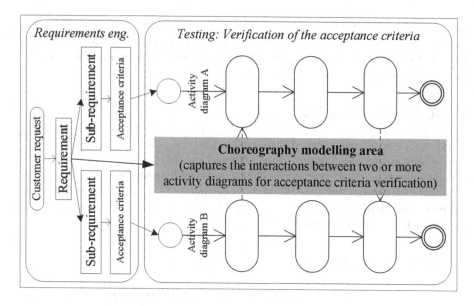

Fig. 2. Choreography modelling area in testing

are presented as ovals, need to interact with steps from other processes in order to advance the verification process.

Figure 2 presents the interaction between the verification steps with dashed arrows. These interactions represent the areas experts identified as suitable for choreography modelling and thus can be specified using the CML. Once specified, the choreography scenario supplements the appropriate testing specification by showing the verification of acceptance criteria from the higher level of abstraction. To represent this, Fig. 2 relates the choreography with the requirement from which the two sub-requirements are derived. Compared to verification of individual sub-requirements, verifying the software functionality against the requirements is expected to shorten the length of testing by reducing the number of test cases required to guarantee product quality.

Protocol development. Analysis of the FG discussion and characterisation of the ES product developed by one of the companies revealed that protocol development is an area that is suitable for CML use. The ES developed by the company can be characterised as a large-scale distributed system in which communication between distributed parts (e.g. components built by autonomous development teams or companies) occurs by passing messages. The companys current practice is that the rules that define the communication dialogs are hard-coded (or implicit) in software components. This way, upon receiving a message, each component has to analyse whether the message is correct and required by that particular component. Since the components participate in a large number of different dialogs, hard-coding the communication rules for each dialog makes the component prone to error, requiring demanding maintenance work, while the analysis of each received message leads to degradation of the components' performance.

To address this problem, the experts proposed making the dialog between communicating entities more explicit by developing a communication protocol. Communication protocol, according to [23], specifies the interactions between communicating entities by defining acceptable dialogs between them and, therefore, enabling independent implementation and maintenance of the system parts while retaining the correctness of their integration within the system. From the company's perspective, there are at least two expected benefits of protocol development. The first is the removal of hard-coded rules from the components' code and their allocation in the protocol. The second is the possibility to centrally manage and monitor protocol enactment during ES execution by implementing or using existing monitoring services. Experts expect that these benefits can reduce the amount of maintenance required and improve the performance of the components. Since the CMLs syntax natively supports the specification and timely ordering of interactions, experts saw choreography and the CML as suitable tools for specifying communication protocols.

4.2   Design Requirements for the CML

Analysis of the FG data showed that some of the experts needs are not supported with the CML. This study presents these needs using a structure similar that used in our previous study [28]. This structure consists of the context and problem description. The context describes the details related to experts' needs while the problem description identifies the implications of those needs for CML. The context and problem description result in the identification of design requirement (DR).

Differentiation of the communication layers. Context: Systems built by FG participants can be characterised as large, distributed, message-based systems. These systems consist of several autonomous parts, which are often distributed and communicate via message exchange. Communication or message exchange can occur on different communication layers depending on the purpose of the communication. Examples of different communication layers in the telecom domain include the exchange of messages for delivering user data delivery (data plane), for defining the routes for data delivery (control plane) and for configuring system (management plane). Problem: The choreography specified using the CML does not differentiate interactions in terms of communication layer. To address this, the following design requirement is derived: *DR1: The CML should differentiate the communication layer on top of which the interactions being modelled are occurring.*

Real-time execution. Context: Parts of the ES built in the experts' companies have various real-time (RT) requirements. Our previous study identified the need to capture RT information with the CML [28], but this analysis revealed that additional RT data need to be supported. For example, the experts highlighted that synchronisation problems between participants can occur in continuous and discrete time paradigms. Problem: RT information in the CML is too generic and insufficient for practical use in the ES development process. To overcome this, additional data that is specific to the application domain or industry branch under consideration must supplement the CML. Accordingly, the following requirement is derived: *DR2: The CML should capture real-time information that is specific to the application domain or industry branch under consideration.*

Visualisation of data. Context: The ES built in one of the companies supports multiple communication technologies. Each of these technologies defines their own message and data types, that are included in the message being exchanged in the choreography scenario. Problem: The CML includes data that are sufficient only for generic representation of the data that are included in the message. The CML does not support the data needed to differentiate message payloads. This need motivated the following design requirement: *DR3: The CML should include the information needed to visualise the data that is included in a message.*

Visualisation of interaction. Context: The number of interactions in ES tends to increase until visualising them in the choreography scenario becomes difficult or even impossible. In these cases, the added value of the choreography scenario becomes questionable because the sizes of these models increase (rather than decrease) developers' cognitive burden. Problem: The CML does not contain data to support the clustering or selective presentation of interactions on the diagrams. The following design requirement addresses this need: *DR4: The CML should support definition of criteria for clustering interactions.*

4.3   Practical Challenges of Using the CML

During the FG sessions, the experts strongly emphasised the changes in the development organisations that were caused by the introduction of the CML. According to their claims, successful integration of the CML into existing work practices is strongly related to users' understanding of the language and the value it brings to the company. To contribute to better understanding, experts identified and clarified practical challenges regarding CML use.

How to keep the scenario on the right abstraction level? This question summarises the experts' concerns about whether use of the CML brings value to the development process. Experts noted that, if it includes too many details, the model becomes a burden and decreases the value of the specification. CML model developers should be guided to retain the value of the specification at the optimal level of abstraction. Two criteria determine the level of detail in a specification. The first criterion is users' expertise. Users use specifications to implement ES and users with more expertise and knowledge about the ES under development may require fewer details compared to novice users, who usually require more details. Consequently, the level of detail in a specification should be aligned with the users' level of expertise. The Second criterion is customer demand. Customers can demand that the specification include various points of view at various levels of detail. These demands, for example, can be related to compliance wiht standards.

How to impose an exact CML semantic? The need to ensure an exact semantic in CML constructs was strongly emphasised by the experts for two reasons. First, an exact semantic helps users perform their work in a way that leaves less space for individual interpretations and the development of workarounds. Second, it allows the development of compilers and simulators that can automatically verify various properties of the specified models. One approach to imposing an exact semantic is to clearly define the construct based on the application context and consider end users terminology, metaphors and ways of working. Once defined, the semantic of the CML should be disseminated to end users through training, manuals and the tools built-in help system.

How to enable users to work only with meaningful interactions? During the FG sessions, experts pointed out the possibility of encountering a large number of interaction steps in a specification and proposed the need to develop a mechanism to enable them to work only with interactions that are meaningful from their perspective. One way to address this is to categorise interactions based on the needs of different stakeholders. The CML editor can later highlight the specification details that are relevant to the users roles and hide the details that are not.

How to ensure integration with other models? Experts raised concerns regarding the integration of the CML with changing technologies and the other models that are used in the development process. The CML is built on Eclipse technologies, which allow easy modification of both the CMLs meta-model and the visual representation of its language constructs in the CML editor [28]. To address this, individuals responsible for maintaining the CML should be familiar with the flexibility of these technologies and trained to make necessary modifications to the CML.

Which tasks are automated by the CML editor? During the FG sessions, the experts expressed concerns regarding the automation of tasks such as detection of faults, interaction clustering and predictive fault correction. The current CML editor does not support the automation of these tasks, but they will be supported in future versions of the editor. To aid acceptance of the CML in organisations, these features of the editor need to be clearly communicated to future users.

5   Lessons Learned

The goal of this study was to learn abuot the applicability of the CML in ES by analysing experts' opinions. The analysis indicated how the CML can be used in practice, additional design requirements and potential challenges during its use. Four lessons learned were derived based on these findings.

The first lesson is that choreography modelling can be used beyond its original purpose. The typical understanding of choreography is that it captures the interaction between participants services (which are autonomous units that offer distinct functionalities for its users) from a global or neutral point of view. This study revealed its potential to capture the interactions between verification steps in the ES testing phase. In the testing phase, instead of presenting the sequence of service interactions needed to fulfil system goals, choreography models are related with the verification of the requirements that are being tested. To the authors knowledge, this is the first study to present the use of choreography in this context.

The second lesson is that choreography can be used in protocol development. Choreography modelling was used to capture the communication protocols among devices for ocean observation, as in [5]. This study confirms that choreography modelling can be used for protocol development in large-scale distributed ES.

The third lesson is that four design requirements can be derived from the analysis of the experts opinions. These requirements complement the requirements that were identified in our previous study [28] and highlight the aspects of ES development that should be considered when designing a CML for ES. Consequently, these requirements were seen as additions to the knowledge base of modelling language design.

The fourth lesson is that alignment between developers level of expertise and the level of detail in a modelling language is important for the languages acceptance in practice. For the modelling language to be accepted and used by its potential users, company managers should consider the users level of expertise and balance the level of detail in the modelling language accordingly. A balanced level of detail in a modelling language prevents ambiguous interpretation of models without imposing an additional burden on model developers. In this way, the developed models convey the necessary information to its users, thus facilitating communication among them.

6   Trustworthiness of the Study

This study used TAT, a qualitative method for data analysis, and relied on the techniques for ensuring the trustworthiness of qualitative studies proposed by Shenton [22]. These techniques address the study's credibility, transferability, dependability and confirmability.

Credibility of the study was ensured by applying the following techniques. *Adaption of well-established research methods.* This study relied on FG and affinity grouping for data collection and on TAT for data analysis. These data collection methods are well known and accepted in the software engineering field, and the questions asked during the FG session are recommended for collecting experts' feedback on novel artefacts. The TAT was chosen due to its flexibility and suitability for analysis of FG data collected during the development of novel ICT concepts.

The development of early familiarity with the culture of participating organisations. The authors have much experience cooperating with the companies whose experts participated in the FG sessions. The AMALTHEA project is one of several research projects during which the authors and experts built mutual understanding and trust and learned about each others organisations.

Sampling. The FG participants were chosen for their experience in software engineering, modelling, modelling technologies and languages, and their familiarity with the work of AMALTHEA.

Frequent debriefing sessions. During the analysis of the collected data, the experts and researchers frequently collaborated to validate and clarify the concepts that were not discussed in depth during the FG sessions. Before taking their current form, the study findings underwent a process of refinement during which the researchers presented and discussed the findings with the experts.

Thorough description of the phenomenon under study. This study is part of a larger research project that aims to design a CML. Intermediary studies conducted as the CML design progressed describe various aspects of the CML design, which is the phenomenon considered by this study.

Transferability of the study was ensured by providing a description of the context in which the study was executed. These data include a number of companies and participants, participants' backgrounds and involvement with the CML, data collection and analysis methods, the sessions' length and the period of time over which the data was collected. Based on these data, readers can determine the extent to which these study findings are applicable in their contexts.

Dependability of the study was ensured by describing the way in which research methods were used for data collection and analysis. These descriptions, together with other published work on the CML design, are seen as sufficient for readers to develop an understanding of how the study was conducted.

Confirmability of the study was ensured using two techniques. The first technique is thorough methodological description, which, like previous criteria, allows the study findings to be scrutinised. The second technique is recognition of the shortcomings of the study. The main shortcoming is that the experts who were involved in the CML design could provide biased evaluations during the FG sessions. To a large extent, FG sessions with experts who were not involved in the CML design mitigated risks related to this shortcoming. Additionally, only a single expert who was involved in all of the CML development phases also evaluated the CML. Other experts in CML design were involved with limited tasks such as providing company-specific documentation and explaining their company's ES development process. Consequently, these experts were seen as suitable participants in FGs.

7 Conclusion

In this study, the CML developed for the ES domain was evaluated by collecting and analysing experts' opinions. The lessons learned from the evaluation are considered relevant for both practitioners and researchers. For practitioners involved in protocol development, the lessons learned confirm that choreography modelling is a useful technique and indicate that its use may reduce the maintenance burden and improve performance. For practitioners interested in introducing a modelling language in their practice, the lessons learned indicate that alignment between users expertise and the level of detail in language constructs is important for future users to accept the language.

The lessons learned are of interest to researchers due to this study's unique finding about the adoption of choreography modelling in ES testing and the design requirements it identified. The use of choreography to capture the sequence of interactions between the verification steps of ES testing shows that it can be used beyond its original purpose, and further research should investigate its use in this and other similar contexts. The identified design requirements complement the requirements that were identified in our previous study and represent the knowledge that is relevant for designing CMLs for the ES domain.

Acknowledgments. The authors are grateful to FG participants for their time and effort and to the AMALTHEA partners for their cooperation. This study was supported by ITEA2 and Tekes, the Finnish Funding Agency for Technology and Innovation.

References

1. Bond, G., Cheung, E., Fikouras, I., Levenshteyn, R.: Unified telecom and web services composition: problem definition and future directions. In: Proceedings of the 3rd International Conference on Principles, Systems and Applications of IP Telecommunications, p. 13. ACM (2009)
2. Cambronero, M.E., Díaz, G., Martínez, E., Valero, V.: A Comparative Study between WSCI, WS-CDL, and OWL-S. In: IEEE International Conference on e-Business Engineering, ICEBE 2009, pp. 377–382. IEEE (2009)
3. Choreography Modelling Language and Editor (publicly accessible version) (2015). http://www.oulu.fi/sites/default/files/content/cml.zip
4. Cortes-Cornax, M., Dupuy-Chessa, S., Rieu, D., Dumas, M.: Evaluating choreographies in BPMN 2.0 using an extended quality framework. In: Dijkman, R., Hofstetter, J., Koehler, J. (eds.) BPMN 2011. LNBIP, vol. 95, pp. 103–117. Springer, Heidelberg (2011). doi:10.1007/978-3-642-25160-3_8
5. Hu, R., Neykova, R., Yoshida, N., Demangeon, R., Honda, K.: Practical interruptible conversations. In: Legay, A., Bensalem, S. (eds.) RV 2013. LNCS, vol. 8174, pp. 130–148. Springer, Heidelberg (2013). doi:10.1007/978-3-642-40787-1_8
6. Hut, P.M.: Affinity Diagram - Kawakita Jiro or KJ Method (2015)
7. Iwai, A., Oohashi, N., Kelly, S.: Experiences with automotive service modeling. In: Proceedings of the 10th Workshop on Domain-Specific Modeling. ACM (2010)
8. Kaur, N., McLeod, C.S., Jain, A., Harrison, R., Ahmad, B., Colombo, A.W., Delsing, J.: Design and simulation of a SOA-based system of systems for automation in the residential sector. In: 2013 IEEE International Conference on Industrial Technology (ICIT), pp. 1976–1981. IEEE (2013)
9. King, N.: Using templates in the thematic analysis of texts. In: Cassell, C., Symon, G. (eds.) Essential Guide to Qualitative Methods in Organizational Research, pp. 256–270. Sage, London (2004)
10. Kontio, J., Lehtola, L., Bragge, J.: Using the focus group method in software engineering: obtaining practitioner and user experiences. In: Proceedings of the 2004 International Symposium on Empirical Software Engineering, ISESE 2004, pp. 271–280. IEEE (2004)

11. Kothmayr, T., Kemper, A., Scholz, A., Heuer, J.: Schedule-based service choreographies for real-time control loops. In: 20th Conference on Emerging Technologies & Factory Automation (ETFA), pp. 1–8. IEEE, Luxembourg (2015)
12. Lethbridge, T.C., Sim, S.E., Singer, J.: Studying software engineers: data collection techniques for software field studies. Empirical Softw. Eng. **10**(3), 311–341 (2005)
13. Lewis, G., Morris, E., Simanta, S., Smith, D.: Service orientation and systems of systems. IEEE Softw. **28**(1), 58–63 (2011)
14. Lin, L., Lin, P.: Orchestration in Web Services and real-time communications. IEEE Commun. Mag. **45**(7), 44–50 (2007)
15. Litosseliti, L.: Using focus groups in research. A&C Black (2003)
16. Mancioppi, M., Perepletchikov, M., Ryan, C., Heuvel, W.-J., Papazoglou, M.P.: Towards a quality model for choreography. In: Dan, A., Gittler, F., Toumani, F. (eds.) ICSOC/ServiceWave-2009. LNCS, vol. 6275, pp. 435–444. Springer, Heidelberg (2010). doi:10.1007/978-3-642-16132-2_41
17. Miles, M.B., Huberman, A.M.: Qualitative Data Analysis: An Expanded Sourcebook. Sage, Thousand Oaks (1994)
18. Peltz, C.: Web services orchestration and choreography. Computer **36**(10), 46–52 (2003)
19. QSR-International: NVivo 10 research software for analysis and insight (2014)
20. AMALTHEA. www.amalthea-project.org (2014). Accessed 25 May 2014
21. Scholz, A., Gaponova, I., Sommer, S., Kemper, A., Knoll, A., Buckl, C., Heuer, J., Schmitt, A.: SOA-service oriented architectures adapted for embedded networks. In: 7th IEEE International Conference on Industrial Informatics (INDIN 2009), pp. 599–605. IEEE, Cardiff (2009)
22. Shenton, A.K.: Strategies for ensuring trustworthiness in qualitative research projects. Educ. Inf. **22**(2), 63–75 (2004)
23. Sridhar, T.: Designing Embedded Communications Software. CRC Press (2003)
24. Starke, G., Kunkel, T., Hahn, D.: Flexible collaboration and control of heterogeneous mechatronic devices and systems by means of an event-driven, SOA-based automation concept. In: 2013 IEEE International Conference on Industrial Technology (ICIT), pp. 1982–1987. IEEE (2013)
25. Taušan, N., Aaramaa, S., Lehto, J., Kuvaja, P., Markkula, J., Oivo, M.: Customized choreography and requirement template models as a means for addressing software architects challenges. In: The Ninth International Conference on Software Engineering Advances, ICSEA 2014. IARIA XPS Press, Nice (2014)
26. Taušan, N., Lehto, J., Kuvaja, P., Markkula, J., Oivo, M.: Comparative influence evaluation of middleware features on choreography DSL. In: The Eighth International Conference on Software Engineering Advances, ICSEA 2013, pp. 184–193. IARIA XPS Press (2013)
27. Taušan, N., Markkula, J., Kuvaja, P., Oivo, M.: Choreography in Embedded Systems Domain: A Systematic Literature Review (submitted for publication, 2016)
28. Taušan, N., Markkula, J., Kuvaja, P., Oivo, M.: Choreography modelling in embedded systems domain -requirements and implementation technologies-. In: 4th International Conference on Model-Driven Engineering and Software Development, MODELSWARD 2016. Scitepress, Rome (2016)
29. Tremblay, M.C., Hevner, A.R., Berndt, D.J.: Focus groups for artifact refinement and evaluation in design research. Commun. Assoc. Inf. Syst. **26** (2010). Article 27

Methods and Tools

An ISO 26262 Compliant Design Flow and Tool for Automotive Multicore Systems

Maria Trei[1], Salome Maro[2]($^{\boxtimes}$), Jan-Philipp Steghöfer[2]($^{\boxtimes}$), and Thomas Peikenkamp[1]

[1] OFFIS e.V., Eschwerweg 2, 26121 Oldenburg, Germany
{maria.trei,peikenkamp}@offis.de
[2] Chalmers | University of Gothenburg, Gothenburg, Sweden
{salome.maro,jan-philipp.steghofer}@gu.se

Abstract. Model-based design processes in the automotive industry must support standards like ISO 26262. Especially for smaller suppliers developing software for OEMs, large-scale methodologies like AUTOSAR are impractical. Instead, smaller, focused processes that still allow ISO 26262 compliance are required. In addition, the steps in the process must be well-supported by the development tool-chain, in particular when developing complex multicore systems. In this paper, we show such a process based on existing design flows and the current state of an automotive modelling tool. We structure the design flow to ensure compliance with the ISO 26262, where necessary complementing it with required steps to ensure safety. Furthermore, supporting tools extending the modelling tool are discussed. As a result, the presented design flow covers all development phases.

1 Introduction

With the development of new functions that are needed for new car generations—in particular in the context of autonomous driving functions—a massive performance increase of electric and electronic (E/E) systems is needed. The needed performance boosts are demonstrated not only by new car generations, but also several research projects—backed up by key industrial partners—that investigate how to use current multicore technologies. Projects like AMALTHEA4public and ARAMIS address concrete challenges imposed by exploiting multicore technology in model-based design processes.

These processes are very much focused on providing functional aspects of multicore systems. However, the domains in which the final system is deployed and the complexity of multicore development make it necessary to put a particular focus on safety aspects [12]. We address this need by presenting a safety-oriented design workflow, where state-of-the-art modelling and analysis concepts

The work has been partially funded by the German Ministry for Education and Research (BMBF) under the funding ID 01IS14029H (AMALTHEA4public) and ID 01IS15031H (ASSUME) and Vinnova AMALTHEA4public.

P. Abrahamsson et al. (Eds.): PROFES 2016, LNCS 10027, pp. 163–180, 2016.
DOI: 10.1007/978-3-319-49094-6_11

for the development of multicore systems are structured to support the fulfilment of ISO 26262 requirements. The underlying work was carried out in two phases that are also reflected in the structure of this paper: First, an analysis was carried out, identifying *design steps* applied in current industrial automotive processes and the *design concepts* involved in these design steps. The second phase was an analysis of the ISO 26262, identifying requirements that affect the execution of these design steps, including the relevant information to be included in the previously identified design concepts.

This paper is structured as follows: Sect. 2 introduces ISO 26262, method engineering, and related work. In Sect. 3, we discuss the AMALTHEA platform and design flow which is extended with concepts from ISO 26262 in Sect. 4. We conclude the paper with a summary and an outlook on future work.

2   Background and Related Work

The international standard ISO 26262 ("Road vehicles – Functional safety") focuses on safety issues in the development of E/E systems of passenger cars with a maximum gross vehicle mass up to 3500 kg. It describes the safety lifecycle of automotive E/E systems, including management, development, production, operation, service and decommissioning. A central element is the hazard analysis and risk assessment in the beginning of the safety lifecycle, where *Automotive Safety Integrity Levels (ASILs)* are defined. Based on this classification, requirements for avoidance of residual risk are defined and validation methods are recommended or prescribed. The procedure of how to develop the *system under development (SUD)*

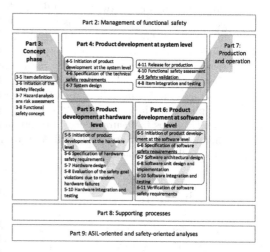

Fig. 1. V-Model of ISO 26262

is given by a V-model, that divides engineering processes into phases of system, hardware, and software development based on the safety concept as shown in Fig. 1. This paper addresses the phases shown in bold, where the clauses highlighted with black boxes are already partially supported by the design flow. The organisation of requirements and their correspondence to elements of the SUD is prescribed to allow validation of the design and verification against the safety concept.

Since ISO 26262 mostly focuses on safety aspects of the development, additional method content must be provided for the functional part. Such adaptation can be done in a systematic fashion using approaches such as *situational method*

engineering (SME) [9] or *process lines* [13]. The former approach uses standard-
ised fragments to compose a process based on an analysis of the needs of a
specific team and project. The latter extends SME by making the variability
of the fragments explicit and using variability modelling primitives provided by
process modelling tools. The need for tailoring ISO 26262 to a company's process
guidelines has been acknowledged [8].

The authors of [7] model ASPICE, IEC 61508, and ISO 26262 in a process
line with the aim to allow companies to derive processes conforming to one or
more of these safety standards. Functional aspects are not modelled explicitly.
Our work, in comparison, aims at combining a design flow for the functional
aspects of the system with one for the safety aspects. We envision its use in the
context of SME with specific adaptations for teams and projects.

The migration towards an ISO 26262 compliant process is the focus of [4].
Importantly, the authors identify the need to integrate the practices of the standard with the ones of existing processes at the companies. This is in line with
what we have done by studying the existing process and deriving the superset
of activities that are now combined with safety practices from ISO 26262.

3   The AMALTHEA Platform and Design Flow

AMALTHEA and AMALTHEA4public are ITEA funded projects running since
2011. They concentrate on software development for multi- and many core systems. One of their outcomes is the AMALTHEA platform [1,14] (APP4MC),
a tool solution to aid the design of many and multi-core systems. The design
flow has been developed in this context as the result of a survey of current
development activities in the projects.

3.1   AMALTHEA Platform

Overview. The AMALTHEA platform is an open source tool platform developed
mainly for engineering embedded systems in the automotive area. It supports
many design activities as well as complex partitioning and mapping for embedded systems. Further, the platform assists engineering processes with the ability
of handling product lines and executing simulation and validation tools. It is continuously extended to integrate more facets of system engineering processes such
as verification, safety, and formal validation of timing requirements. Conformity
to ISO 26262 is one topic to be addressed. A first step was the identification of
correlations and needs between both the standard and the meta-model of the
platform in form of a gap analysis [3]. The platform supports an iterative workflow to accommodate rapid prototyping and feedback from validation activities.
Engineers are supported by the AMALTHEA platform in many steps ranging
from component modelling to partitioning and mapping activities. The trace
model, e.g., a result of the simulation of the system, provides helpful information
about the execution times of specific system parts as a basis for the improvement
of the existing architecture.

Data Models. APP4MC uses a top-level *System Model* that is subdivided into more fine-grained sub-models. They allow modelling based on the platform to derive the description of hard- and software used in the overall system down to the lowest level of abstraction. We will give a brief overview of the most important features.

The SUD can be represented from the system, software and hardware point of view. The *hardware model* is composed of (hardware) systems, ECUs, microcontrollers and cores. Networks and memories can be defined. Similarly, software can be subdivided into processes, tasks, runnables, and Interrupt Service Routines (ISRs) using the *software model*. The technical architecture in terms of components and their interfaces is part of the *components model*. Requirements on the behaviour of the system can be described by the *constraints model*, which consists of constraints on timing, data age and runnable sequencing or grouping, aspects particularly important in multicore development. This also includes requirements of the dynamical architecture, whereas interactions of software and hardware are covered by the *property constraints model*. The *partitioning model* describes how the software is broken down into *runnables* which are in turn aggregated in tasks [10]. The final allocation of software to hardware is given by the *mapping model*. The system model is completed by a *stimuli model, common model, event model, configuration model* and the *OS model*. The *trace model* contains information about the simulation/execution of the software on the hardware.

3.2   AMALTHEA Design Flow

Methodology. The design steps are the result of an extensive data collection process in which the project partners in AMALTHEA4public provided detailed information about the concrete steps they follow when developing multicore embedded software, especially in the automotive domain. Data was collected from five industrial partners and five academic partners. While the academic partners provided information mostly from their experience with different industrial partners they cooperate with in research projects, the industrial partners contributed with their concrete practical experience. The overall design steps, along with a rationale and additional information are published in [2]. The design steps are mainly concerned with development of functionality. Interestingly, safety aspects were not mentioned by any of the partners during the data collection.

Design Steps. Table 1 gives an overview of the design steps that are the result of the analysis. Note that no order in which these steps are carried out is implied since defining a concrete development process with a concrete lifecycle is generally company specific. A wide variety of lifecycles can be applied, including the V-model that is implied by ISO 26262 and AUTOSAR. While some steps are carried out sequentially, others can be done in parallel. The dependencies between the design steps at times imply an iterative approach where they are repeated or at least revisited after other work has been performed. Such an approach is common in iterative-incremental lifecycles. The identified steps cover most aspects of a traditional software development effort, starting from contract negotiation and scope identification and ending at the delivery of the software (with the exception of software maintenance). Some steps and circumstances are specific in the context of the automotive domain, e.g., the differentiation of system and software. Another re-occurring theme is product line issues and variants, even though this theme will not be regarded in detail in the context of this paper.

Table 1. Overview of the identified Design Steps

DS 1: System Requirements Engineering	DS 7: Variant Configuration
DS 2: System Architecture Design	DS 8: Implementation
DS 3: Software Requirements Engineering	DS 9: Validation and Testing
DS 4: Derivation of Product Variants	DS 10: System Integration
DS 5: Definition of Software Architecture	DS 11: Handover
DS 6: Behaviour Modelling	

Some of the design steps we elicited, such as Requirement Engineering and Architecture Design, can be found in nearly all development processes in a similar form. However, there are specific steps steps that are only relevant in multicore development: *Partitioning, Task Creation and Target Mapping* are, e.g., part of **DS 10: System Integration**. We discuss these design steps in more detail in Sect. 4.3.

4   Analysis of Compliance Towards ISO 26262

Based on the phases and clauses of ISO 26262 as well as the identified design steps, we analyse the recommended design flow to satisfy compliance with the standard and which support APP4MC provides. Further, we will show necessary extensions and the steps to achieve them. This will be presented constructively so as to show how the elicited design flow can be extended and how the platform capabilities tie into the flow.

The resulting extended design flow as shown in Fig. 2 represents the functional design steps outside the "V" and is enriched by six design steps related to safety inside the "V". The top of the given V-model stands for the vehicle/system-part of the V-model of ISO 26262 while the bottom represents the software part. As our focus lies on the design process derived for software development, we will only briefly relate to hardware development in the following subsections. However, many design steps, e.g., partitioning or definition of property constraints, require the formulation of hardware assumptions that are needed during software development.

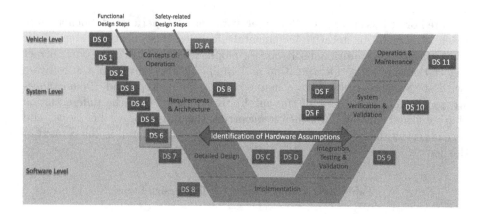

Fig. 2. Overview of the extended Design Steps

Briefly summarized, the new design flow lifts the development lifecycle up to the vehicle level, where in **DS 0** functional requirements are defined, which is important to initiate the *safety lifecycle* and therefore to support the concept phase (**DS A**) of ISO 26262. Safety requirements are introduced at system and software level (**DS B** and **DS C**). Integration and testing at software level for safety-related software elements is described by **DS D**, where the integration into the system and the item is given by **DS E**. **DS F** covers integration and validation activities at vehicle level. Since validation is against safety goals which are part of the concept phase at vehicle and item level, **DS F** can be seen as system and vehicle part. Before discussing our analysis of the different ISO 26262 phases, we first give an overview of common models that are used in all the development phases.

4.1   Generic Models Addressed in All Development Phases

ISO 26262 describes the development of an item based on the functional behaviour which is intended by each element of the item on the one hand, and the hazardous events concerning these elements which might lead to the violation of safety requirements on the other hand. As the different levels of abstraction during this development process lead to different features of safety requirements it is necessary to define the intended behaviour using concepts of certain levels of abstraction. Analogously, occurring errors of elements of the item have to be modelled at every level.

The overall functional system behaviour, as well as the specific aspects of the functional behaviour of the hardware and the software are captured in a *Behaviour Model*. The functional requirements on the vehicle level are broken down into respective parts for all levels and corresponding behaviour and thus defined on each level. Depending on the level, the specific models can take different forms such as algorithms, interaction protocols, state machines, etc. The model is captured in **DS 6: Behaviour Modelling** which is performed for each of the levels.

Further, it is necessary to introduce *modelling of errors* to analyse how faults of elements of the item affect their behaviour. On the modelling side, this requires a model that allows to perform safety activities related to the development of such a safety concept. To this end, we are using a generic error model that has been developed in the ITEA project SAFE [6] shown in Fig. 3.

Basically it captures failure behaviour, in particular how internal and external failures are propagated through the functions or components of the system. Once these propagations have been identified, *safety requirements* can then be derived and allocated to the architectural elements. Using this allocation scheme, the corresponding Automotive Safety Integrity Level (ASIL) can be derived for each of the allocated requirements. The ASIL describes the risk

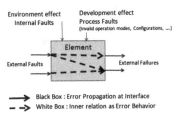

Fig. 3. Error model from SAFE project

associated with each requirement based on the severity of a hazard, the likelihood of its occurrence, and how well the hazard can be controlled. This error model will be used at vehicle level to support the definition of the functional safety concept (ISO 26262-3:2011, 8), and at system level for definition and allocation of technical safety requirements (ISO 26262-4:2011, 6–7). Refinement of technical safety requirements to software and hardware safety requirements entails to also introduce error models at software and hardware level. Error models on system, hardware and software level have to include faults related to multicore scheduling, which are much more complex than faults occurring in a singlecore system. This is due to the fact that the scheduling does not only rely on the basis of timing and priorities of tasks, but also on the commonly shared memory available, temperature behaviour of the system and, going into the structure of the hardware a little deeper, shared buses or power supply.

4.2   Concept Phase (ISO 26262 Part 3)

Processes provided by ISO 26262. The safety lifecycle given by the international standard ISO 26262 starts with the concept phase in ISO 26262-3:2011, which consists of the clauses given in the first column of Table 2.

Description of the SUD, called *item* in terms of ISO 26262, takes place at the vehicle level and includes dependencies on, and interaction with, other items and the environment of the item. Functional and non-functional requirements need to

Table 2. Concept phase

Clause	Supporting DS	Support by APP4MC
5: Item definition	**DS 0, DS A**, DS 6	(Property) Constraint Model, Component Model
6: Initiation of the safety lifecycle	**DS A**	ProR, Papyrus, Yakindu statecharts
7: Hazard analysis and risk assessment	**DS A**	Papyrus, Yakindu statecharts
8: Functional safety concept	**DS A**	ProR

be defined, as well as constraints given by the environment and other items. Note that at this point not only safety-related requirements are considered. Operating modes, interfaces and boundaries on them have to be specified to enable hazard analysis and risk assessment on the one hand and the development of the item with its intended behaviour on the other hand. Based on the item definition, the safety lifecycle is initiated in ISO 26262-3:2011, 6, which means that the development category of all parts of the item is analysed.

Processes during the hazard analysis and risk assessment of ISO 26262-3:2011, 7, systematically describe possible *hazardous events* and their consequences. They need to be classified using metrics for the *severity* of potential harm, the *probability* of exposure of operational situations, and the *controllability* of each hazardous event. As a result the *ASIL* can be calculated for each hazardous event. A *safety goal* is derived for each hazardous event, inheriting its ASIL. These safety goals serve as top-level safety requirements, from which further functional safety requirements will be derived, in particular those characterizing the *Functional safety concept*.

The definition of a functional safety concept requires to analyse how component faults can contribute to the identified risks. On the modelling side, this requires a model that allows to perform safety activities related to the development of such a safety concept (ISO 26262-3:2011, 8). To this end, we are using the generic error model introduced in the previous section and shown in Fig. 3. Basically it is able to capture failure behaviour, in particular how internal and external failures are propagated through the components of the system. Once these propagations have been identified, *functional safety requirements* can then be derived and allocated to the architecture according to ISO 26262-3:2011, 8.4.2 and 8.4.3. Using this allocation scheme, the corresponding ASIL can be derived for each of the allocated requirements.

Activities in the Design Flow. We extend the elicited design steps by introducing **DS 0: Functional Requirements Engineering**. In this step the functional requirements of the item at vehicle level will be collected. They provide a basis for the functional design of the system, software and hardware on the one hand and the initiation of the safety lifecycle on the other hand. As our design flow does not include the *development* of hardware, but has to represent all important information about the hardware available, if appropriate, it is recommended to define hardware properties already at this early stage of development. This can be, e.g., the intended number of available cores, the size of memory, and the interaction with other systems. The higher complexity of multicore systems compared to singlecore architectures may affect the exposure of certain hardware failures, which has to be considered both at system and at software level again. Further, the activities given by clauses 6–8 and discussed above need to be represented. For this, we introduce **DS A: Derivation of the Functional safety concept**, where the hazard analysis and the risk assessment take place to define the corresponding safety goals as top-level safety requirements.

Support by APP4MC. As shown in Table 2, APP4MC can only support the Item definition clause by allowing the definition of the system through the Component Model and constraints through the Property Constraint Model. Other open source eclipse-based requirements management tools such as ProR[1] can be used in the Item definition clause to describe the requirements of the item as text. Papyrus[2] and Yakindu statechart tools[3] can be used to describe the relationship between the item and the environment through component models. Description of the safety lifecycle, hazard analysis and risk assessment and functional safety concept can be done by text in ProR. However one needs to add safety related attributes such as *implementation categories, safety goals* and *hazardous events* to the requirements.

4.3   Product Development at the System Level (ISO 26262 Part 4)

Processes provided by ISO 26262. Development of the product on the system level defines how both hardware and software capabilities form the overall system. The division into seven clauses according to ISO 26262 is shown in Table 3. In clauses 5–7, requirements for the system to be developed as well as its overall structure are defined. Then, hardware and software development takes place (cf. Sects. 4.4 and 4.5), before clauses 8–11 manage the integration of hardware and software components into the overall system, further verification activities and, later on, the release for production.

Central work products of the former steps are the *Technical safety requirements specification* (ISO 26262-4:2011, 6.4) and the *Technical safety concept* (ISO 26262-4:2011, 7.4.) Both contain the set of safety-related requirements that are used to implement functional safety requirements. This hierarchical structure of requirements must be traceable back to the top-level safety goals and to the corresponding system elements. Basic information about the intended use of particular software and hardware resources shall be considered during these steps. Safety mechanisms qualified to prevent parts of the system from failing need to be described in terms of the underlying system architecture. Technical safety requirements inherit the ASIL of the corresponding functional safety requirements following the rules for ASIL decomposition given in ISO 26262-9:2011.

The *System design specification* and the *Hardware-software interface specification* (ISO 26262-4:2011, 7.4) consist of the overall system architecture and a first view on the separation into hardware and software. The system design shall be based on the functional concept, in particular not just the safety-related parts and the technical safety concept. If technical safety requirements are allocated to certain parts of the system design, their ASIL shall be attached to these parts respecting amongst others the criteria for coexistence given in ISO 26262-9:2011. Note that the hardware-software interface specification is going to be refined during hardware and software development.

---

[1] http://eclipse.org/rmf/pror/.

[2] https://eclipse.org/papyrus/.

[3] https://marketplace.eclipse.org/content/yakindu-statechart-tools.

Table 3. Phase 4: product development at the system level

Clause	Supporting DS	Supported by APP4MC
5: Initiation of product development at the system level	**DS B**	✗
6: Specification of the technical safety requirements	DS 1, **DS B**	(Property) Constraint Model, Component Model
7: System design	DS 2, DS 6	Component Model
8: Item integration and testing	DS 10	Mapping Model, (Property) Constraints Model, OS Model, Trace Model, Stimuli Model, Event Model, Configuration Model, Hardware Model
9: Safety validation	**DS E**	✗
10: Functional safety assessment	**DS F**	✗
11: Release for production	DS 11	✗

Other work products concerned with *planning* integration, verification and validation activities must also be considered. The relevance of verification even this early on during system development must be noted.

Execution of integration, verification and validation is part of ISO 26262-4:2011, 8–11. Integration takes place on different levels, where, roughly described, first hardware and software is integrated to systems, second systems are integrated to the item, and third the item is integrated to the vehicle. The compliance of the ASILs of different objects must be analysed, as well as the correctness of the functionality of the system design. Together, these steps form the work products *Integration testing specifications* and *Integration testing reports*. Clauses 9–10 describe in more detail which methods are recommended for certain verification and validation processes.

Activities in the Design Flow. The activities in the design flow on the system level are concerned with requirements engineering, overall system design, and system integration. We combine these aspects concerning the functional system with safety-specific aspects by introducing new, safety-focused activities.

DS 1: System Requirements Engineering is concerned with the elicitation and definition of system requirements as well as of platform and product requirements in case a product line approach is used. The system requirements can be captured in different ways and describe the system as a black-box, focusing mainly on what the system does (goals and scenarios), who the users are and what other systems will it interact with [5]. Model-based systems engineering methods provide a set of partial models to capture system requirements. Examples of the partial models are environment models which describe the SUD in its context, application scenarios which capture the different use cases of the SUD and requirements models which capture additional functional and non-functional requirements. The relevant artefacts created in this step are the *System Model (preliminary)* and the *System Requirements Specification Document*.

There is a strong correspondence between the described artefacts of the design flow and the *Technical Safety Requirements Specification* and the *Technical Safety Concept* of ISO 26262, even if safety is not yet regarded. System requirements with an impact on safety questions of the SUD should be treated separately from system requirements as system *safety* requirements with necessary attributes to correlate to technical safety requirements of ISO 26262. This includes amongst others the introduction of safety mechanisms and ASILs for these requirements. We therefore introduce **DS B: System Safety Requirements Engineering** which consists of at least the following sub-steps:

1. planning verification/validation activities at system level;
2. definition of system safety requirements based on results of **DS 1** and **DS A**, including safety-related assumptions caused by the multicore structure of the SUD.

DS 2: System Architecture Design addresses the design of the overall system architecture according to the elicited system requirements. This system architecture consists of several partial models that describe the system, sub-systems, their respective structure and behaviour, and the relations and interactions of the system with the environment. The relevant outcome of this step is the *System Architecture* that contains the architecture of the entire SUD. Along with the functional behaviour on the system level defined in **DS 6: Behaviour Modelling**, this complies in many points with the *system design specification* of ISO 26262. Accordingly, traceability of different system elements and underlying (safety) requirements should be enabled in this design step to ensure that safety-related sub-systems with their corresponding ASIL can be identified. Safety-related interference must be represented to allow validating if criteria for coexistence are met by objects defined during the system design. This includes, for instance, the problem of space and time partitioning, which describes the concurrency of resources and is therefore related to hardware and software development, but has to be regarded at system level. Therefore the behaviour modelling also relates to ISO 26262's *hardware/ software interface specification* as part of the system, software, and hardware design.

After the hardware and software development has been performed, the next relevant step is **DS 10: System Integration** in which executable tasks from the system are created, partitioned and mapped to the target hardware. This is where multicore development differs from singlecore development: multiple tasks can run at the same time and efficiency and consistency must be guaranteed. Therefore creation, partitioning and mapping of tasks as discussed below are essential activities.

Task Creation. In this step, tasks that contain a set of Runnables are created from the software model. Task creation also takes into account the constraint model in order to decide which Runnables can be grouped together. The results of this step are stored in an augmented *Software Model*. At this point, the rate at which the tasks are activated, e.g., periodic, single, or sporadic activation is determined and stored in a *Stimulation model*.

Partitioning. In this step, tasks are identified to derive possible partitions that can be executed in parallel. Partitioning includes possibilities to group Runnables by their activation reference and group independent sets of Runnables to come up with graph structures that have the most efficient potential when running tasks in parallel. This step leads to a *Partitioned Software Model* and a *Constraint Model*.

Target Mapping. The aim of this step is to find a valid and optimal distribution of software elements to hardware components. Data from *Software and Hardware Models*, as well as the tasks activation from the *Stimulation Model* are used to calculate such a distribution. Additionally, a *Property Constraints Model* may be included during the mapping process which is used to narrow down the solution space, e.g., some tasks may require the target platform to have a certain amount of memory. The results of this step are stored in a *Mapping Model*. Moreover, a preliminary *OS Model* is generated, which contains a scheduler for each of the cores of the hardware platform.

The artefacts of **DS 10** correspond to inputs of the *hardware-software interface specification* (HSI) of the ISO 26262 system level, which is already supported by **DS B**. But the elicited design steps do not contain explicit support for verification of safety system requirements after the integration. This will be corrected by introduction of **DS E: Safety Validation** and **DS F: Functional Safety Assessment**. **DS E** consists of testing activities to verify that the safety requirements are satisfied and **DS F** assesses the functional safety concept defined in **DS A** and its implementation.

Finally, **Design Step 11: Handover** handles acceptance testing, delivery of the product and sign-off. All acceptance tests must pass before the product can be delivered to the customer. Including safety-related tests, this corresponds in many points to the *Release for production* given by ISO 26262-4:2011, 11.

Support by APP4MC. APP4MC provides a *Hardware Model* which is dedicated model that supports the mapping process. The model allows for definition of the available hardware by specifying the number of cores, the speed, memory and other hardware related properties [11]. This model can then be used together with the software model and the constraint model to create an optimal distribution of the software to a specific hardware platform. The property constraints model also offers the possibility to define safety-related constraints, e.g., to separate safety-critical from non-safety-critical software running on different hardware components. This could be necessary in a development process to guarantee freedom of interference of certain artefacts. Another use case of separation related to safety is the principle of redundancy, which means that some safety-critical parts of a system are implemented twice to prevent the single-point-failure for a certain part.

4.4   Product Development at the Hardware Level (ISO 26262 Part 5)

Processes provided by ISO 26262. Due to space constraints, we restrict development activities on the hardware level to the derivation of hardware safety requirements (ISO 26262-5:2011, 6) as shown in Table 4 and do not dive into the hardware design or its evaluation (ISO 26262-5:2011, 7–9). We cannot drop this clause since hardware safety requirements have to be consistent with the technical safety concept and the system design specification (ISO 26262-5:2011, 6.1), imposing non-trivial relationships between the hardware and system level on one side, and between hardware and software level on the other side. The hardware elements relevant for the hardware-software interface have already been identified as shown in Sect. 4.3.

Activities in the Design Flow. Description of required hardware and its components can be captured in the *Variant Model* and the *Hardware Model* derived during **DS 4: Derivation of Product Variants** and refined in **DS 6: Behaviour Model**. An important aspects to be considered when designing a multicore systems is the distribution of safety-related software to certain hardware elements such as ECUs, cores, or memory. Depending on such a classification, hardware can then also be categorised as safety-related or not which affects to what extent testing activities are required. This again emphasizes why traceability of all kinds of information is very important in the development of safety-critical systems. The elicited design flow did not contain an explicit step for definition of hardware safety requirements. Therefore we suggest that this is addressed as early as in **DS B: System Safety Requirements Engineering**. When system safety requirements are defined, hardware safety requirements should be defined as well. These can later be refined when the actual design and development of the hardware takes place.

Support by APP4MC. Table 4 shows the tools available in APP4MC, that can be used to support clause (ISO 26262-5:2011, 6). All necessary elements for a description of the hardware-software interface are available in the Hardware model, including descriptions for *ECU*, *Microcontoller*, and *Core* and their associated memory access and communication characteristics. Since hardware safety requirements have to address the effectiveness of safety mechanisms (ISO 26262-5:2011, 6.4.2), an error model used to represent hardware failures is required for a precise description of these. Although it has the same role as the error model on concept level shown in Fig. 3, this model has to be rich enough to allow for the (later) evaluation, integration and testing activities (ISO 26262-5:2011, 7–10). Due to this detail in the hardware safety requirements it is possible to evaluate the impact of hardware failures on system level (ISO 26262-5:2011, 7.4.4) even before the hardware is available. The support by APP4MC for the definition of hardware safety requirements is given by the usage of ProR on the one hand and the Property Constraints Model on the other hand, where requirements and constraints on hardware can be defined.

4.5   Product Development at the Software Level (ISO 26262 Part 6)

Processes provided by ISO 26262. ISO 26262 provides the clauses shown in Table 5. *Software safety requirements* based on the technical safety concept specified at system level need to be defined. The HSI is updated to accord with these

Table 4. Product development at the hardware level

Clause	Supporting DS	Support by APP4MC
6: Specification of hardware safety requirements	**DS B**	Hardware Model, (Property) Constraint Model, ProR

requirements before regarding a first version of the overall software architecture in ISO 26262-6:2011, 7. The *Software architectural design specification* describes *software components* and their interactions, i.e., their hierarchical structure and interfaces, and properties that influence their implementation such as scheduling properties (ISO 26262-6:2011, 7.4). Based on this, the *Software unit design specification* is derived (ISO 26262-6:2011, 8.4). The next step is to generate source code, which is followed by verification and testing activities (ISO 26262-6:2011, 8–9). The goal of these activities is to ensure that the implementation satisfies requirements on the software units. These requirements are not limited to safety-related parts of the software, even if testing activities in ISO 26262 only focus on them. Integration of the software elements to the embedded software in ISO 26262-6:2011, 10, consists of regarding the implementation results with respect to the software architectural design specification, whereas satisfaction of software safety requirements is part of ISO 26262-6:2011, 11. Relations concerning the hardware-software interface must be considered.

Table 5. Phase 6: product development at the software level

Clause	Supporting DS	Supported by APP4MC
5: Initiation of product development at the software level	DS C	✗
6: Specification of software safety requirements	DS 3, DS 4, **DS C**	Software Model, (Property) Constraint Model
7: Software architectural design specification	DS 5, DS 6, DS 7	Software Model, Component Model
8: Software unit design and implementation	DS 8	Software Model
9: Software unit testing	DS 9	Trace Model
10: Software integration and testing	DS 9	✗
11: Verification of software safety requirements	**DS D**	✗

Activities in the Design Flow. The activities in the functional design flow cover all aspects of the software development lifecycle, starting from requirements, to analysis and design, to coding, and validation. **DS 3: Software Requirements Engineering** addresses the elicitation of requirements pertaining to the software part of the system. Sources for requirements are system requirements and customers or potential users of the software. Software units shall be described so that a partitioning can be executed to prepare the software for mapping to the hardware. For multicore development, it is very important to describe any kind of requirements on relations between software units, such as sequencing and dependent deadlines. This step is usually done in several iterations. The collected requirements are recorded in the *Software Requirements Specification Document*. *Acceptance Tests* are defined based on the requirements to validate that the agreed-upon system is being built.

As for the system level, requirements engineering at the software level needs to be extended with respect to safety to comply with ISO 26262. We introduce **DS C: Software Safety Requirements Engineering** which, similar to **DS B**, consists of

1. planning verification/ validation activities at software level,
2. the definition of software safety requirements based on **DS B** (and the system design), and the
3. validation of the software safety requirements against the software requirements (i.e., the part that is not safety-related).

Also, it must be ensured that the software safety requirements are correct, complete, and consistent with respect to the safety goals and the system design.

DS 5: Definition of Software Architecture can produce design artefacts such as component models which contain all the software components and their dependencies and interaction models to describe communication between these components. The architecture of a software can be described using more than one model in order to capture different perspectives of the software or to further refine it into a lower abstraction level. All models are captured in the *Software Architecture Document*. The development of software is further supported by **DS 6: Behaviour Modelling**, where the behaviour of software components can be specified, such as the communication between components. An iterative review process ensures consistency and completeness of the architecture.

In **Design Step 8: Implementation**, the required code is produced, tests are developed and executed, the software is integrated and the code is reviewed. The main resulting artefacts are *Source Code* and different sets of *Tests* (unit, component, integration) as well as the *Integrated Software and its Documentation*.

The final activity in this phase is **Design Step 9: Validation and Testing**. It involves testing of software components to validate if they are working as desired, i.e., according to the specified requirements. For software components that will interact with hardware components, simulations are run in order to fix as much defects as possible before the component can be tested on the actual hardware. *Deployable Control Software* is a packaged integrated software that is ready to be deployed on a specific hardware.

In parallel testing methods given by ISO 26262 should be introduced to support the verification of the embedded software against the software safety requirements. Depending on the ASIL of each safety goal, different technologies and testing environments are feasible, as e.g. fault injection tests or interface tests. We define **DS D: Verification of software safety requirements** to be the design step supporting these activities.

Support by APP4MC. The platform provides the Software Model that can be used to model the runnables, tasks and processes that make up the software. For software architecture specification, the Component Model can be used, as well as the Property Constraint Model to define software constraints. Additionally, the platform provides a Trace model to assist software testing. The trace model gives details on time consumed by tasks to allow refinement of the model to get the most efficient one.

4.6   Tool Support

As can be seen in the tables that show tool support for the design steps in APP4MC, mainly parts introduced by the clauses related to safety assessment and verification in ISO 26262:2011 are missing natively. Therefore, it is necessary to accompany APP4MC with one or more additional tools that can fill those gaps. Where open source eclipse tools are available(e.g., ProR and Papyrus), we have proposed their use in combination with APP4MC. However, not all phased can be supported by open source tools, for instance for functional safety activities a commercial tool like medini analyse[4] which supports Item Definition (ISO 26262-3:2011, 5; **DS 0, DS A, DS 6**), Initiation of the Safety Lifecycle (ISO 26262-3:2011, 6; **DS A**), Hazard Analysis and Risk Assessment (ISO 26262-3:2011, 7; **DS A**), and Functional Safety Concept (ISO 26262-3:2011, 8; **DS A**) may be used. This covers the entire concept phase. Validation and assessment capabilities, supporting Safety Validation (ISO 26262-4:2011, 9; **DS E**), Functional Safety Assessment (ISO 26262-4:2011, 10; **DS F**), and Verification of Software Safety Requirements (ISO 26262-6:2011, 11; **DS D**), can be provided by, e.g., BTC EmbeddedValidator[5].

In addition, APP4MC interfaces with a number of requirements management and modelling tools that are commonly used in the industry. Some like IBM Rational DOORS are integrated through the use of OSLC adapters or other means, while many such as the different modelling environments integrate

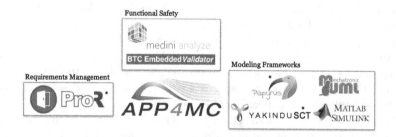

Fig. 4. Tools providing support for clauses not covered directly by APP4MC. The star indicates which tools are shipped with the distribution of the platform.

---

[4] http://www.kpit.com/engineering/products/medini-functional-safety-tool.
[5] www.btc-es.de/index.php?idcatside=40&lang=2.

seamlessly into the Eclipse environment provided by APP4MC. If a direct integration or the use of standards like OSLC is not feasible, the export and import capabilities of APP4MC and the tools must be used. This potentially introduces synchronisation issues, however. For design steps that are not repeated very often and occur towards the end of the development cycle—such as **DS D: Verification of software safety requirements**—this problem is negligible since exported artefacts do not need to be synchronised with the tools where they were originally created. An overview of the tools that are currently in use to support development with APP4MC is shown in Fig. 4.

5   Summary

An efficient way of working in an ISO 26262 compliant fashion with effective tool support is vital to maintain the relationship between OEMs and their suppliers. In this paper we have shown how a design flow elicited from actual development practices at such companies can be extended for ISO 26262 compliance and how it is supported by APP4MC. Where necessary (e.g., concept phase), missing modelling concepts (e.g., error models) have been identified. Other tools (both open source and commercial) that can be used in combination with the APP4MC to support safety activities in the ISO 26262 have also been suggested.

Future work will include the deployment and validation of the design flow in the companies that are part of AMALTHEA4public. In addition, we aim to strengthen the interface between systems and software engineering by refining the design steps that regard the exchange of information between these levels. Issues of traceability and cross-company information exchange will also be regarded.

We proposed extensions of the platform either through provision of own tools or recommendation of tools compatible with APP4MC to support the additional design steps. However, the benefit of using other external tools needs to be analysed, especially concerning our safety extensions for which commercial tools exist that allow ISO 26262 compliant design in some of the defined steps. But even commercial tools do not allow to follow our design flow in all aspects, so we have to investigate which design steps are supported by external tools, and how they can get integrated with APP4MC. Even if some tools offer interfaces via OSLC, there is still the need for rich traceability between different tools to support the exchange of information between different companies as well as change management. This leads to the implementation of tool adapters and traceability tools across the whole AMALTHEA toolchain.

References

1. Amalthea Project. http://www.amalthea-project.org/. Online; Accessed 16 Mar 2007
2. Amalthea4Public Project. D1.1: Analysis of Necessary Design Steps. Technical report, ITEA (2015). https://itea3.org/project/workpackage/document/download/2347/13017-AMALTHEA4public-WP-1-D11:AnalysisofNecessary DesignSteps.pdf
3. Amalthea4Public Project. D4.1: Gap analysis against ISO 26262. Technical report, ITEA (2015). https://itea3.org/project/workpackage/document/download/2232/13017-AMALTHEA4public-WP-4-13017-AMALTHEA4public-WP-4-d41Gap analysisagainstISO26262.pdf
4. Born, M., Favaro, J., Kath, O., Application of ISO DIS 26262 in practice. In: 1st Workshop on Critical Automotive Applications: Robustness & Safety, pp. 3–6. ACM (2010)
5. Braun, P., Broy, M., Houdek, F., Kirchmayr, M., Müuller, M., Penzenstadler, B., Pohl, K., Weyer, T.: Guiding requirements engineering for software-intensive embedded systems in the automotive industry. Comput. Sci. Res. Dev. **9**(1), 21–43 (2014)
6. Cuenot, P., Peikenkamp, T., Wenzel, T., Khalil, M., Rudolph, A., Lucas, J., Voget, S., Ross, H., Eckel, A., Biendl, E., Adler, N., Otten, S., Buch, S.: Methodology and application rules documentation. Technical report, ITEA (2014). https://itea3.org/project/workpackage/document/download/1629/10039-SAFE-WP-6-SAFED6b.pdf
7. Gallina, B., Kashiyarandi, S., Martin, H., Bramberger, R.: Modeling a safety- and automotive-oriented process line to enable reuse and flexible process derivation. In: COMPSACW, pp. 504–509, July 2014
8. Hamann, R., Sauler, J., Kriso, S., Grote, W., Mössinger, J.: Application of ISO 26262 in distributed development ISO 26262 in reality. Technical report, SAE Technical Paper (2009)
9. Henderson-Sellers, B., Ralyté, J.: Situational method engineering: State-of-the-art review. J. Univ. Comput. Sci. **16**(3), 424–478 (2010)
10. Höttger, R., Krawczyk, L., Igel, B.: Model-based automotive partitioning and mapping for embedded multicore systems. Int. J. Comput. Control, Quantum Inf. Eng. **9**(1), 268–274 (2015)
11. Krawczyk, L., Kamsties, E.: Hardware models for automated partitioning and mapping in multi-core systems using mathematical algorithms. Int. J. Comput. **12**(4), 340–347 (2014)
12. Parkinson, P.: Safety, security and multicore. In: Dale, C., Anderson, T. (eds.) Advances in Systems Safety, pp. 215–232. Springer, London (2011)
13. Ternité, T.: Process lines: a product line approach designed for process model development. In: SEAA 2009, pp. 173–180. IEEE (2009)
14. Wolff, C., Krawczyk, L., et al.: Amalthea - tailoring tools to projects in automotive software development. In: IDAACS, vol. 2, pp. 515–520, September 2015

Evaluating a GUI Development Tool for Internet of Things and Android

Björn A. Johnsson$^{(\boxtimes)}$, Martin Höst, and Boris Magnusson

Department of Computer Science, Lund University, Lund, Sweden
{bjorn_a.johnsson,martin.host,boris.magnusson}@cs.lth.se

Abstract. In the emerging field of Internet of Things (IoT), where computerized devices are combined in creative new ways, there is a need to create Graphical User Interfaces (GUIs) for the systems being built, e.g. in the form of Android "apps". This is generally a complicated, time consuming task. We report from a controlled experiment that evaluates a new approach for building GUIs that aims to make it easier for more people to build quality GUIs. A tool supporting the new approach (GPE) was compared to Android Studio (AS), the industry standard for Android development. Our data analysis shows that GPE is more effective than AS when performing certain tasks, with no measurable degrade in the quality of the produced GUIs. We conclude that non-Android developers and Android developers alike should consider using GPE rather than AS when building Android GUIs for PalCom based IoT systems.

1 Introduction

In this paper we report from a controlled experiment that compares two tools supporting different approaches for building Graphical User Interfaces (GUIs) for Android "apps". The purpose is to evaluate the efficiency of a novel approach to GUI construction supported by the new tool. We compare it to Android Studio [1], the industry standard for Android development, in the context of the Internet of Things (IoT) framework PalCom [9,12,15].

In the emerging field of IoT, our computerized devices are being combined in creative new ways. Many IoT technologies aim to support end-users in combining and configuring their own devices into useful systems, a sentiment which we share. However, from what we have seen for PalCom, it is still mostly developers that create these types of systems. Although ubiquitous systems typically work silently in the background [16], doing what we have instructed them to do, there is often a need to control them in different ways, hence the need for GUIs. The tool we evaluate in this paper aims to make it easier for more people to build quality GUIs. Our technology is platform independent – the created GUIs can be interpreted on any platform. By comparing to an Android specific alternative, we highlight the relative efficiency of our tool for that platform. In projects that use PalCom, these findings should prove useful to developers and project managers

© Springer International Publishing AG 2016
P. Abrahamsson et al. (Eds.): PROFES 2016, LNCS 10027, pp. 181–197, 2016.
DOI: 10.1007/978-3-319-49094-6_12

when deciding on which tool to use for GUI creation – directly if the target platform is Android and indicatively for other platforms.

With an expected increase in adoption of end-user composition of IoT systems, we recognize the need for end-users to tailor GUIs for controlling the systems they build. With this in mind, we designed our approach to not require program code to be written – it could eventually be used by non-programmers.

2 Background

The PalCom framework [9,12,15] provides a unique approach to building IoT systems. PalCom supports a model based on commands for communicating between services hosted on devices, rather than the commonly used model based on communicating byte streams between endpoints e.g. TCP/IP. By supporting this higher level view on communication, PalCom facilitates discovery on both the device and service levels. Automatic routing between devices on heterogeneous networks for both discovery information and commands between services is also supported. Services are put together to form systems with *assemblies*, a mechanism which can bridge functionality between otherwise incompatible services, e.g. from different manufacturers. This is enabled by the meta-level information in the protocol that all services implement, which includes specification of the commands the service can send and receive, and a natural language description. This information also enables a PalCom "browser" to facilitate a mode of direct interaction with services through a crude GUI created from interpreting the meta information.

The GUI language PML [5] provides additional information that is used to render GUIs for PalCom services that are more intuitive and aesthetically pleasing than the ones automatically generated by interpreting the meta information alone. It also facilitates the construction of GUIs that mix commands from more than one service. The Graphical PML Editor (GPE) enables users to interactively build GUIs for PalCom services [6]. It produces platform independent GUI descriptions that can be interpreted on any platform. Since the editor interprets the meta information, the user can start from services and their commands and represent service input commands as e.g. buttons and service output commands as e.g. text boxes. In other words, the user starts by identifying what she wants to do, after which she gets suggestions for graphical components that can achieve that functionality. Because this approach puts focus on presenting functionality in a GUI rather than attaching functionality to manually added components, there is no need for programming.

Alternative technologies include Android Studio [1], which provides a graphical editor in which a GUI can be composed out of graphical components that are placed on a canvas. Their properties (size, color, etc.) can be edited to fit the user's needs. Other examples of such tools are often found as part of Integrated Development Environments (IDEs) such as Swing GUI Builder in NetBeans, Interface Builder in Xcode, or Qt Creator. These tools allow the user to create the code that make up the resulting GUI without explicit coding, thus speeding up development – a notion which we adapted in our own solution. Unlike our solution however, in similar tools the user still needs to implement GUI behavior, typically by writing "glue code" linking the graphical components to the functionality e.g. in a local model or by triggering some communication. The requirement to provide this code makes it impossible for a non-programmer to construct GUIs.

3   Related Work

Although the use of a graphical editor simplifies the construction of GUIs, they are still complicated to develop in general and require experienced developers. Already in [13] an attempt was made to simplify the design of GUIs in C, by developing a simplified toolkit. It was found that college juniors could use it within less than three hours. In [7] an adaptive interface is introduced and evaluated. The results highlight the importance of developing simplified development tools, as in line with this research. Furthermore, in [10] the authors state that GUIs can be made easier and more economical to create by reducing the amount of code that has to be written. We therefore see the result of completely eliminating programming from GUI development as an important step in making the GUI creation process more efficient and more inclusive of end-users.

End-user composition is a well covered area of research. In e.g. [3,11] the authors present systems that enable end-users to compose systems based on everyday metaphors. This research is on the same level as PalCom assemblies, with no support for GUIs. The idea of a GUI language based around a component/service architecture like PalCom is not entirely novel; the languages presented in e.g. [2,8] share many similarities with PML. However, most of these types of languages are not augmented with a graphical editor, and haven't solved the many challenges of development efficiency and end-user composition. Our research relates to classical User Interface Management Systems (UIMSs) in that the underlying functionality of our apps – PalCom services – is clearly separated from the GUI [14]. It is this concept that allows us to eliminate the need to write program code.

4   Experiment Planning

4.1   Goals

The object of study for our experiment is the new approach to GUI development provided by PML through the Graphical PML Editor (GPE). The purpose is to evaluate the performance of the new development approach in relation to the traditional one offered in Android Studio (AS), i.e. the industry standard for developing Android applications. During the evaluation, the quality focus is on the efficiency – in terms of subject productivity – of the tested tools (approaches). Productivity is measured as the mean number of time units per experiment task solved. We perform the evaluation from the perspective of us as researchers, to determine if the subjectively experienced performance gains of the new approach are statistically significant. The subjects of the experiment are engineering students at Lund University (Sect. 4.2). The subjects solve GUI development tasks in the context of a problem created specifically for this experiment (Sect. 4.4). The goal of the experiment is summarized as follows:

> Analyze *the approach to GUI development of PML (through GPE)*
> for the purpose of *evaluation*
> with respect to *efficiency (subject productivity)*
> from the point of view of *the researchers*
> in the context of *software developers solving GUI development tasks for a designed problem.*

Based on the goal, we consider the following research questions:

RQ1 Which tool is most efficient?
RQ2 Is the quality of produced solutions the same for both tools?
RQ3 What are the users' impressions from using the tools?

4.2   Participants

For our experiment, we are interested in investigating what effects the treatments have on the productivity of software developers. We therefore select our subjects from the population of engineering students at Lund University that have gotten good grades in programming courses. Even though interest in the experiment was high, it proved difficult to find a session date that matched everyone's schedule. Because of this, we had to expand on the number of sessions considered. We also had to broaden the type of students that we invited. Students registered interest in an online form (Sect. 4.3). Invitations were sent by email in three waves to:

1. members of Code@LTH[1], and typical 3rd year Computer Science and Engineering (CSE) students with good grades.
2. typical 2nd year CSE students with good grades.
3. engineering students, typically 2nd year, with an interest for Computer Science courses, good grades, and experience with Android Studio.

As a last measure in response to the lack of registered applicants with Android development experience, we also invited staff from our department; two volunteered and were assigned to the AS treatment. Because of how invitations recipients were selected, we know all subjects had a common base of programming knowledge. All applicants that registered were included in the experiment, to a total of 24 subjects. Any applicant that reported previous experience with Android Studio (12 in total) was selected for that treatment. The remaining 12 were assigned to the GPE treatment.

The subjects committed to a half-day of experimentation time by registering interest for participation. In doing so, they gave consent for the experiment

---

[1] Student driven recreational programming community, http://www.codeatlth.org.

administrators to handle their data in a confidential manner. The subjects were paid (on the level of lab assistants) to participate in the experiment. To avoid non-serious applicants, no concrete figure was specified in the invitation, we only mentioned a "symbolic" monetary compensation.

4.3 Experimental Material

To register interest for participating in our experiment, subjects were instructed to fill out an online form. The form included questions to collect name and contact information, which of several dates they could attend, previous programming knowledge (multiple choice, four levels), and whether they would consider using their own computers during the experiment.

The functionality needed to complete the experiment tasks (Sect. 4.4) was provided to the subjects on a virtual machine acting as server. The server was represented as a PalCom device hosting four services: PATIENTSERVICE, LOGINSERVICE, ASSESSMENTSERVICE, and CHECKLISTSERVICE. The services handle identification and information about (fictive) staff and patients, and medical records for patients. Each participants was issued a printed compendium including general experiment instructions, the description for a warmup task (Sect. 4.4), and the specifications for the four PalCom services. Subjects in the AS group were instructed to run Android Studio version 2.1.x when solving the tasks. In the GPE group, the Graphical PML Editor was used instead. Both groups tested their solutions on Android tablets from Sony, model Xperia Tablet Z2 (SGP521), running Android version 6.0.1. This was at the time the most up-to-date (major) release. The PML description interpreter (renderer) for Android was installed on the tablets of the GPE group. Digital experimental material was handed out on USB flash drives containing: copy of compendium (PDF); Graphical PML Editor (GPE group only); source files for 0th iteration (Sect. 4.4); PalCom browser, for exploring the server; and a time tracker software (Sect. 4.7).

To capture the subjects' impressions of the experimental material and the applied treatments, a second online form was digitally distributed at the end of the experiment sessions. Questions included: whether sufficient information was provided to complete the tasks; whether they would consider using their tool; how confident they were in the correctness of their solutions; general comments and comments on individual task; and whether they would like to take part of the results of the experiment, i.e. this paper.

4.4 Tasks

One "warmup" task and eight proper tasks were prepared for the experiment. The purpose of the warmup task was to allow participants to get acquainted with their tool; development time was not recorded. The subjects started working from a small *0th iteration*, i.e. a base application with minimal graphical design and functionality implemented. The tasks were performed in order, each adding or changing functionality and/or design from the previous tasks. The tasks were

Table 1. Functional requirements of task 3; includes requirements from tasks 1 and 2.

ID No.	Description
Application	
A.1	Login screen is opened upon application startup
Login Screen	
L.1	Text box for password entry hides its content e.g. as asterisks
L.2	Text boxes for username and password entry are cleared upon successful login
L.3	Main screen is opened upon successful login
L.4	List of patients is requested from server upon successful login
Main Screen	
M.1	No patient is selected after opening (successful login)
M.2	Patient selection list shows patient names only (no IDs)
M.3	Selecting a patient causes its information to be display
M.4	Selecting no patient clears the patient information section
M.5	Full name of logged in staff member is displayed
M.6	Logout button opens Login screen

designed to mimic the evolution of software in real world development scenarios. For the experiment problem, we drew inspiration from the results of the itACiH [4] project, where an Android application to support nurses in Hospital Based Home Care (HBHC) was developed. No natural order of increasing difficulty per task was planned. Instead, tasks were allowed to organically evolve the application. However, we strived to have the tasks cover a wide range of typical GUI development duties (e.g. adding new screens) and graphical components (dropdown lists, popup dialogs, etc.). Task descriptions were presented in both text – primarily describing functional requirements – and images – mockups of the screens, describing graphical requirements.

The tasks will not be listed in full because the page limitation of this paper does not allow it. They can be made available (in Swedish) upon request. Table 1 lists the functional requirements of task 3, which build upon the those of tasks 1 and 2. After having completed the warmup task, the app allows users to enter a patient's ID into a text box and press a button to request that patient's information from the server; the reply is promptly displayed in the GUI. We summarize the descriptions of the three subsequent tasks as follows:

Task 1 The patient selection mechanism is replaced; the user selects patients by name from a drop-down list populated by content received from the server. *Requirements*: M.2, M.3, M.4.

Task 2 A simple login screen is added. The content of two text boxes (username/password) is sent to the server for authentication when a button is pressed. On positive server reply, the main screen is opened. *Requirements*: A.1, L.1, L.2, L.3, L.4, M.1.

Task 3 The currently logged in user's name, a product logotype and a logout button is added to the main screen. *Requirements*: M.5, M.6.

4.5 Parameters and Hypotheses

The experiment has a single independent variable: GUI Development Approach (GDA). This is measured on a nominal scale by categorization based on tool as either 'GPE' for the Graphical PML Editor or 'AS' for Android Studio. We also identify the following variables:

- Experience of Android development (AXP) is measured on an ordinal scale by introducing a classification with four classes based on prior experience: no prior experience, casually tested tools or novice amateur developer, educated and/or advanced amateur developer, professional.
- General programming experience (GXP) is measured on a scale that is analogous to that of AXP.

The experiment factor is GDA, which has two treatments. GXP is used to verify subject selection, and AXP is used to determine treatment assignment (Sect. 4.2). The dependent variables for the experiment are:

- *Tool efficiency*, measured on a ratio scale as mean development time (μ_T) per task, in minutes.
- *Quality of produced solutions*, measured on a ratio scale as the mean number of specification deviations (μ_D) for a set of tasks. The deviations are unweighted, i.e. all deviations are considered equal in terms of severity. Two types of deviations are considered: functional and graphical.
- *Experiment impressions*, measured on an ordinal scale (1–5) as the mean value of the answers (μ_A) to two questions: (1) *"Would you consider using [tool] to develop Android apps in the context of PalCom systems?"*, and (2) *"How confident are you that your submissions are compliant with specification?"*.

Our primary dependent variable is μ_T, with μ_D and μ_A serving as variables to strengthen conclusions drawn from μ_T.

We formulate three hypotheses based on our research questions. Informally, we hypothesize that the mean development time of the GPE group will be less than that of the AS group (RQ1). Regarding solution quality we do not expect that any treatment will outperform the other (RQ2). Likewise, we expect both groups to consider using their tool, and for the confidence in solution quality to be comparable (RQ3). Formally, we define $A = \{1, 2, \ldots, 8\}$ as the set of all experiment tasks. Then, for all $a \in A'$ for some $A' \subset A$

$$H_{01} : \mu_T(\text{'GPE'}, a) = \mu_T(\text{'AS'}, a)$$
$$H_{a1} : \mu_T(\text{'GPE'}, a) < \mu_T(\text{'AS'}, a) \tag{1}$$

where $\mu_T(t, a)$ refers to the mean development time of task a for treatment $t \in T$ with $T = \{\text{'AS'}, \text{'GPE'}\}$. Furthermore, for all $d \in D$ and some $a \in A$

$$H_{02} : \mu_D(\text{'GPE'}, d, a) = \mu_D(\text{'AS'}, d, a)$$
$$H_{a2} : \mu_D(\text{'GPE'}, d, a) \neq \mu_D(\text{'AS'}, d, a) \tag{2}$$

where $\mu_D(t, d, a)$ refers to the mean number of specification deviations of type d for task a and treatment $t \in T$. $D = \{F, G\}$ refers to functional and graphical deviations respectively. Finally, for all $q \in \{1, 2\}$

$$H_{03} : \mu_A(\text{'GPE'}, q) = \mu_A(\text{'AS'}, q)$$
$$H_{a3} : \mu_A(\text{'GPE'}, q) \neq \mu_A(\text{'AS'}, q) \tag{3}$$

where $\mu_A(t, q)$ refers to the mean value of the answer to question q for the group with treatment $t \in T$.

4.6   Design

The experiment design for the stated hypotheses is of the standard type "one factor with two treatments" [17]. The factor is GDA and its treatments are GPE and AS. Our main hypothesis (hypothesis 1) states that development time will be lower for treatment GPE than AS. We have two auxiliary hypothesis (hyp. 2 and 3) to strengthen the validity of hypothesis 1. The dependent variables 'tool efficiency' and 'solution quality' are measured on ratio scales and are tested with (non-parametric) Mann-Whitney-Wilcoxon (MWW) tests in R. We favor MWW tests over t-tests since we cannot assume that the measured data will follow the normal distribution. The 'experiment impressions' variable is measured on an ordinal scale and is also tested with MWW tests.

4.7   Procedure

Data was collected across 6 distinct experiment sessions, over a period of 6 weeks. 4 sessions included participants for both treatments, and 2 covered only the AS treatment. Each session was preceded by a registration phase, and succeeded by a followup phase.

Before attending an experiment session, the subjects had to register. The registration form served a double purpose: it was used to collect data regarding programming knowledge, i.e. independent variables AXP and GXP. The data was recorded in spreadsheets.

All sessions were scheduled for an afternoon. After an initial hour of introduction and training, the participants worked independently on solving tasks for the remaining three hours. This time restriction was not firmly enforced; the subjects were granted additional time to finish started tasks. The sessions were monitored, and were held in seminar rooms at our department. Upon arrival, subjects were assigned a desk where equipment and documents had been laid out.

The introductory part of the sessions included an overview of the experiment (goals, etc.), an introduction to our technologies (PalCom, PML), training, and information about practical matters. The GPE group, having never used the Graphical PML Editor before, got approximately 20 min of training for the tool. Additionally, the warmup task was considered part of the training; the subjects were allowed to ask any questions during this task. For the subsequent tasks 1–8, a judgment call on the part of the experiment instructor(s) was done on whether to answer the question, or refer to the manual. In general, only questions resulting from technical/practical problems with the tool were answered. The AS group was expected to have previous experience with their tool; no training was provided. Instead, the participants were given a "tour" of the 0th iteration's Android Studio project while the GPE group was receiving training. Intricacies regarding the project's connection to the PalCom world were discussed. They were encouraged to ask questions about this during the warmup task.

During the active phase of the sessions, participants were responsible for recording development times for individual tasks (data for dependent variable μ_T). A custom built time tracker tool was provided for this purpose. The tool ensured task ordering by making the task descriptions available only after the preceding tasks had been completed. Before proceeding to a new task, the time tracker prompted (mandatory) the subjects to upload the files for their current solution (data for dependent variable μ_D). The subjects could "pause" a task in the tool's GUI, e.g. when going to the bathroom. The severity of forgetting to "unpause" was emphasized, and features of the tool were implemented to minimize this risk. The development time data and solution files were collected on USB flash drives at the end of each session.

No restrictions on material was made during the experiment sessions. Subjects had free access to the internet.

After the conclusion of the active phase of the sessions, experiment impressions were collected in an online form. The data (dependent variable μ_A) was recorded in a spreadsheet. The participants were encouraged to fill out the form immediately following the experiment session, in order for the experience to still be fresh in their minds. They were allowed to be anonymous.

4.8   Analysis Procedure

To analyze development time (μ_T) we extracted the data collected by the time tracker, which was stored on USB flash drives (one per subject) in JSON format. The data was loaded into an custom Java program, outputting a comma-separated values (CSV) file containing for each subject: subject ID, and start/stop/total times per task. We processed this file in R. Data for the AS group was divided into tiers based on subject performance in task 1. Hypothesis 1 was tested with Mann-Whitney-Wilcoxon (MWW) tests for the different groups and tiers, and for individual tasks depending on data availability.

We analyzed the quality of submitted solutions (μ_D) by extracting the solution data that was stored on USB flash drives by the time tracker tool. For the AS group, this data consisted of Android Studio projects that could be loaded

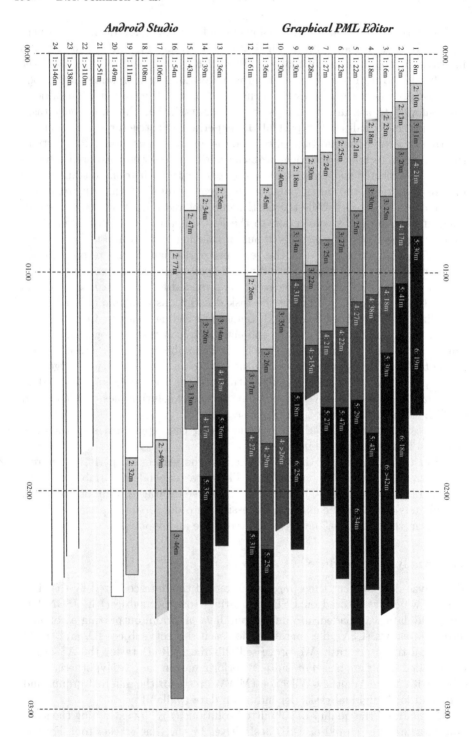

Fig. 1. Development times sorted by task 1, excluding warmup and pauses. Unfinished tasks are slanted where the experiment ended.

into Android Studio to allow for installation and review on an Android tablet. For the GPE group, the extracted files were PML descriptions (XML files) that could be installed, interpreted and reviewed on an Android tablet. Solutions from all subjects in the GPE group were reviewed, but we only considered the top performing AS tier. We reviewed the solutions for the highest numbered task that all subjects in this selection had completed. Review results, per subject, were manually recorded in a spreadsheet. Functional requirements (Table 1) were recorded as either 'passed' or 'failed'. Deviations from the graphical design (screen mockups) were counted by visual comparison. Standard graphical deviations were identified, but ultimately the comparison was made on case-by-case basis, relying on the judgment of the reviewer (one person). The data from the spreadsheet was downloaded as a CSV file and processed in R. We tested hypothesis 2 with MWW tests for the different groups and the identified highest numbered task.

The results of the post-experiment survey were stored in a spreadsheet and were used to analyze participant experiment impressions (μ_A). We downloaded the data as a CSV file and processed it in R. As before, we included the data from all subjects in the GPE group, but only the data from the top performing AS tier. Hypothesis 3 was tested with MWW tests for the different groups and the two questions related to μ_A.

5   Analysis

5.1   Data Set Preparation

At the end of the experiments, some participants mistakenly submitted the solution for the task they were working on. As these solution were at best partially complete, their end-times are not valid. Before processing the JSON files of these subjects, the erroneous end-times were manually removed. Furthermore, to avoid clutter in the graphics (Fig. 1), unfinished tasks that the subjects had worked on for less than 15 min were also removed.

In the post-experiment survey form, subjects were allowed to identify themselves by text. Some subjects wrote their names, while others entered their assigned subject ID. Before downloading the data from the sheet where the results were recorded, all entries were mapped to subject ID to enable proper analysis.

5.2   Descriptive Statistics and Hypothesis Testing

Figure 1 gives an overview of the development times per task for all participants, from all experiment sessions. The participants are sorted based on the development time for task 1. The GPE group consists of subjects 1–12. For the AS group, we group participants into three tiers based on performance:

Top tier completed the first task in less than 60 min (subjects 13–16).
Middle tier completed the first task in more than 60 min (subjects 17–20).

Table 2. Top tier: One-sided MWW test, AS>GPE, for development time.

a	$\mu_T('AS', a)$	$\mu_T('GPE', a)$	p-value
1	43.0	26.0	0.0105
2	48.5	24.4	0.0090
3	24.8	23.1	0.5725

Bottom tier failed to complete the first task (subjects 21–24).

The results from the bottom tier cannot be analysed, and are discarded. We proceed to analyze GPE vs. AS for the middle tier and GPE vs. AS for the top tier separately.

For the middle tier, we analyze development time for task 1: $\mu_T('AS', 1) = 118.5$ min. For the GPE group we get $\mu_T('GPE', 1) = 26.0$ min. Comparing the groups using a one-sided Mann-Whitney-Wilcoxon (MWW) test, assuming AS>GPE, we get a p-value of 0.0021. The null hypothesis H_{01} is rejected for the middle tier with $A' = \{1\}$, i.e. for task 1.

For the top tier we analyze development time, task solution quality, and the values of the answered survey questions. We start by analyzing development times for tasks 1–3; the results for tasks 4–6 cannot be analysed due to a lack of data points in the top tier AS group. The results of comparing the groups using a one-sided MWW test, assuming AS>GPE, are reported in Table 2. The box plot in Fig. 2 shows the data being analysed. We reject the null hypothesis H_{01} for the top tier and $A' = \{1, 2\}$, but not for $A' = \{3\}$.

Next, we analyze the data produced from reviewing the submitted task solutions. We reviewed the solutions for task 3 – the highest numbered task solved by all subjects in both the GPE group and the top tier AS group. The results of comparing the counts of functional (F) specification deviations using a two-sided MWW test are reported in Table 3. R refers to all requirements listed in Table 1 ('ID No.'). For the top tier AS group $4/4$ solutions satisfied requirement M.1,

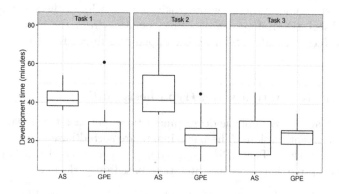

Fig. 2. Box plot of top tier development time data for tasks 1, 2 and 3.

Table 3. Top tier: Two-sided MWW test for functional specification deviations.

Requirements	$\mu_D(\text{'AS'}, F, 3)$	$\mu_D(\text{'GPE'}, F, 3)$	p-value
$R = \langle\text{Table 1}\rangle$	0.250	1.08	0.0201
$R' = R\backslash\{\text{M.1}\}$	0.250	0.166	0.7883

Table 4. Top tier: Two-sided MWW test for answers to survey questions.

q	Description	$\mu_A(\text{'AS'}, q)$	$\mu_A(\text{'GPE'}, q)$	p-value
1	*Would consider using tool*	4.8	4.2	0.163
2	*Confidence in submissions*	4.2	3.8	0.140

while only $^1/_{12}$ solutions from the GPE group did the same. We refer to Sect. 6.1 for a discussion, and run the test again with R' defined as all requirements of R except for M.1. Analyzing the data for the number of graphical (G) specification deviations we find that $\mu_D(\text{'AS'}, G, 3) = 1.75$ and $\mu_D(\text{'GPE'}, G, 3) = 2.08$. Comparing the groups using a two-sided MWW test we get a p-value of 0.8521. We cannot reject the null hypothesis H_{02} for the top tier for either $p = F$ or $p = G$ when $a = 3$ and when considering R' rather than R.

Finally, we analyze the data collected from the participant survey at the end of experiment sessions. 100 % of the participants answered the survey. Table 4 compares the answers of the top tier AS group and the GPE group using a two-sided MWW test. The two questions are described in Sect. 4.5. Both were answered on an ordinal scale of $[1, 5]$. We calculate mean values to provide a sense of how the subjects answered. We cannot reject the null hypothesis H_{03} for the top tier for either question 1 or 2.

6   Discussion

6.1   Evaluation of Results and Implications

Based on informal interviews with the participants of the AS group, we concluded that the scale in the registration form for classifying AXP was unsuccessful. Some subjects were too modest, registering in a lower category than appropriate, while others misinterpreted the classification and mistakenly put themselves in a higher category than appropriate. Because of this, we grouped subjects in the AS group based on their performance during the experiment. Three tiers were identified. We discarded the data of the bottom tier, as we considered their level of AXP to be too low, and hence not applicable for our experiment.

We perceive the middle tier subjects as good programmers with limited AXP. Their results are hence indicative of what happens if good non-Android developers are to create Android applications. This has relevance in practice: after a PalCom system has been created, typically some form of GUI has to be created to interact with it, not uncommonly on Android devices. As hypothesized, the mean development time for the middle AS tier was longer than for the GPE group: 118.5 vs. 26.0 min for task 1. Hence, we reject H_{01} for the middle tier and task 1. In the choice between GPE and AS, the results tell us that non-Android developers should use GPE rather than AS when creating GUIs for PalCom systems.

The subjects of the top AS tier are perceived as good programmers with a fair amount of AXP. Their results are interpreted as the expected outcome of using average Android developers to create Android applications. The mean development time for the top AS tier was, for tasks 1 and 2, longer than for the GPE group: 43.0 vs. 26.0 min and 48.5 vs. 24.4 min, respectively. Hence, we reject H_{01} for the top tier and tasks 1 and 2. For task 3, however, we cannot reject the null hypothesis. From the description of task 3, we observe that the task had a clear focus on graphical design: changing screen title, adding a logo, etc. As opposed to tasks 1 and 2, few functional matters were covered. The novelty of GPE is to change how functionality is specified, thus eliminating the need for glue code. Hence, we argue that it is reasonable for a task where little glue code would have to be written in AS to not be significantly faster to develop in GPE. It appears that even Android developers can benefit from using GPE rather than AS when creating GUIs for PalCom systems.

Analyzing the quality of the solutions for task 3 from the top tier AS and GPE groups, we found no difference in terms of graphical specification deviations: we could *not* reject H_{02} for graphical deviations and task 3. However, it appears that the GPE group deviated more from the functional specification. Looking at the data, we found that almost all GPE subjects failed to satisfy requirement M.1 (Table 1). This cannot be a coincidence, and we do not believe that so many subjects would deliberately submit faulty solutions, hoping we would not notice the infraction. Instead, we believe that the subjects simply missed the error since it is intricate to test and hence easy to miss. The reason that no AS subject failed to satisfy the same requirement is that no additional technical effort (development time) was needed on their part; AS guarantees by default that requirement M.1 is satisfied. We therefore think it is relevant to test for functional deviations again, excluding M.1. In doing so, we could not reject H_{02} for functional deviations and task 3. In practice, it could be argued that the GPE group has produced solutions with no difference in quality compared to the top tier AS group, in less time.

For experiment impressions, we found no differences between the groups, as hypothesized. We could not reject H_{03} for either question. The results tell us that both groups would consider using their tool and that the subject have confidence in their submitted solutions. The latter fits well with our analysis of solution quality. The former is interesting, as the subjects of the GPE group had an agreeable experience (mean 4.2 on a 1–5 scale) using our tool.

6.2   Threats to Validity

Here we discuss threats to the validity [17] of the experiment and findings.

Instrumentation: As mentioned earlier, the scale in the registration form for classifying AXP was unsuccessful due to bad instrumentation. We should have made clearer categories to choose from. This was solved in analysis by dividing the subject of the AS group into three tiers. Since the tasks were created specifically for the experiment, low quality in descriptions could have affected results for one or both treatments. However, in the post-experiment survey, subjects in both treatment groups reported that they had adequate information to solve the tasks.

History: Originally, the experiment was planned for just two sessions on consecutive days to minimize the effect of external factors such as environment and student schedule. To attract enough subjects, we opted for more sessions over a longer period of time. Although not formally analyzed, no single session stands out in terms of inferior results as a consequence of experiment date. We considered varying times of day as a possible threat, and hence scheduled all the sessions in the afternoon.

Compensatory Rivalry: In all communication with subjects (invitations, experiment introduction, etc.) we deliberately expressed ourselves in the most neutral way possible about both treatments, while at the same time not hiding the purpose of the experiment. We wanted to avoid having either group feel like the underdog, which could have affected outcome.

Group Stress: We identified a possible threat in that faster subjects could have a stressful effect on slower subjects, causing more error to be made and obstructing progress. To minimize this effect, we distributed task digitally, one-by-one. Handing out all tasks in the beginning of the experiment was considered, but that could have compromised task ordering, e.g. by subjects accidentally skipping a task.

Interaction of Selection and Treatments: Having subjects that are not representative of the population we want to generalize for is a threat to external validity. The context of this experiment are software developers. While our subjects – students – are not yet fully trained industrial developers, we believe that our subject selection process has ensured enough programming experience for a valid generalization.

Professionals: We cannot claim that we drafted the best possible Android developers for our experiment, not even in the top tier. If we had hired trained Android consultants, the development times of the AS group would probably have been shorter. However, similar logic can be applied to the GPE group: had we spent more than 20 min training the subject we would have gotten shorter development times, even more so had we drafted experienced GPE developers. Therefore, we believe that our comparative analysis is valid. It is however a challenge to identify representative subjects in an experiment like this.

Interaction of Setting and Treatment: A threat when using "toy" problems is that the experimental material might not be representative of industrial standard. We handled this threat by designing the experiment tasks to mimic a typical industry development scenario (Sect. 4.4). The idea was to represent the most general use cases in order to not favor one treatment over the other. We ensured a valid setting by comparing GPE to the most up-to-date version of the market leading tool for Android development (AS).

Reliability of Measures: Since subjects self-monitored development time, there is a certain level of unreliability in the collected data. One possible threat was that the subjects would forget to "unpause" the time tracker tool, thus corrupting the data. We took measures to prevent this in the software, and more than once per session emphasized the severity of forgetting to unpause. Experiment instructors also checked in with participants periodically during the experiments. No incidents were reported or observed. Another threat is subjects deliberately pausing the time tracker to improve their recorded time. However, we do not see what their motivation for doing so would be as the results are anonymous, and again, the sessions were monitored by the experiment instructors.

7   Conclusions

Our analysis shows that for good programmers with limited experience of using AS, the gains in terms of user productivity are significant when using GPE instead of AS. For programmers with a fair amount of experience of using AS the gains are not as pronounced, but still present. The size of the gain also depends on the type of task being solved – GPE is more effective when performing certain tasks, but analysis is inconclusive for others. We found no statistical difference between the treatments in terms of the quality of the solutions produced during the experiment. Furthermore, we found that the GPE group would consider using our tool in the given context. We conclude that in the choice between GPE and AS, non-Android developers and Android developers alike should consider using GPE rather than AS when creating Android GUIs for PalCom systems. In practice, this is relevant because typically when a developer creates a PalCom system, a GUI – not uncommonly for Android – has to be produced as well.

With a basis for how GPE performs against the industry standard tool when used by programmers, in future research we are interested in seeing how GPE performs when used by non-programmers in comparison to programmers. This could be investigated in an experiment similar to this, although the functionality domain would have to be adjusted to be relevant to non-programmers. One such domain could be home automation.

Acknowledgements. We thank Gunnar Weibull, M.Sc., for his work on implementing the Graphical PML Editor and for agreeing to train experiment participants in how to use the tool. We also thank Mia Månsson, M.Sc., for being an enthusiastic first user of the tool and for providing valuable insights on how to improve it. Furthermore, we thank all experiments subjects for taking the time to participate in our experiment. This research was founded by the Swedish research fund VINNOVA through its program on *Challenge Driven Innovation*, and by FORTE on a grant for *Application Support in Healthcare* (LUC3).

References

1. Android Studio: The official IDE for Android (2016). https://developer.android. com/studio/index.html
2. Bishop, J.: Multi-platform user interface construction: a challenge for software engineering-in-the-small. In: Proceedings of the 28th International Conference on Software Engineering, pp. 751–760. ACM (2006)
3. Humble, J., Crabtree, A., Hemmings, T., Åkesson, K.-P., Koleva, B., Rodden, T., Hansson, P.: "Playing with the bits" user-configuration of ubiquitous domestic environments. In: Dey, A.K., Schmidt, A., McCarthy, J.F. (eds.) UbiComp 2003. LNCS, vol. 2864, pp. 256–263. Springer, Heidelberg (2003). doi:10.1007/ 978-3-540-39653-6_20
4. Johnsson, B.A., Magnusson, B.: Supporting collaborative healthcare using PalCom - the itACiH system. In: 2016 IEEE International Conference on Pervasive Computing and Communication Workshops (PerCom Workshops), pp. 1–6. IEEE, March 2016
5. Johnsson, B.A.: PalCom meets the end-user: enabling interaction with PalCom-based systems. Licentiate Thesis **2014**(2), 1–89 (2014). Lund University
6. Johnsson, B.A., Weibull, G.: End-user composition of graphical user interfaces for PalCom systems. Procedia Comput. Sci. **94**, 224–231 (2016)
7. Kalverkamp, M., Gorldt, C.: IoT service development via adaptive interfaces: improving utilization of cyber-physical systems by competence based user interfaces. In: 2014 International ICE Conference on Engineering, Technology and Innovation (ICE), pp. 1–8, June 2014
8. Luyten, K., Vandervelpen, C., Coninx, K.: Migratable user interface descriptions in component-based development. In: Forbrig, P., Limbourg, Q., Vanderdonckt, J., Urban, B. (eds.) DSV-IS 2002. LNCS, vol. 2545, pp. 44–58. Springer, Heidelberg (2002). doi:10.1007/3-540-36235-5_4
9. Magnusson, B., Johnsson, B.A.: Some like it hot: automating an electric kettle using PalCom. In: Proceedings of the 2013 ACM Conference on Pervasive and Ubiquitous Computing Adjunct Publication, pp. 63–66. ACM (2013)
10. Myers, B.A.: User interface software tools. ACM Trans. Comput. Hum. Interact. (TOCHI) **2**(1), 64–103 (1995)
11. Newman, M.W.: Now we're cooking: recipes for end-user service composition in the digital home. In: CHI 2006 Workshop: IT@Home (2006)
12. Nordahl, M., Magnusson, B.: A lightweight data interchange format for internet of things with applications in the PalCom middleware framework. J. Ambient Intell. Humanized Comput. **7**(4), 523–532 (2016)
13. Pausch, R., Conway, M., Deline, R.: Lessons learned from SUIT, the simple user interface toolkit. ACM Trans. Inf. Syst. **10**(4), 320–344 (1992)
14. Rosenberg, J., Hill, R., Miller, J., Schulert, A., Shewmake, D.: UIMSs: threat or menace?. In: Proceedings of the SIGCHI Conference on Human Factors in Computing Systems, pp. 197–200. ACM (1988)
15. Svensson Fors, D., Magnusson, B., Gestegård Robertz, S., Hedin, G., Nilsson-Nyman, E.: Ad-hoc composition of pervasive services in the PalCom architecture. In: Proceedings of the 2009 International Conference on Pervasive Services, pp. 83–92. ACM (2009)
16. Weiser, M.: The computer for the 21st century. Sci. Am. **265**(3), 94–104 (1991)
17. Wohlin, C., Runeson, P., Höst, M., Ohlsson, M.C., Regnell, B., Wesslén, A.: Experimentation in Software Engineering. Springer Science & Business Media, Heidelberg (2012)

Application of GQM$^+$Strategies in a Multi-industry State-Owned Company

An Experience Report

Gustavo López[✉], Brenda Aymerich, Diana Garbanzo, and Alexia Pacheco

Research Center for Communication and Information Technologies (CITIC),
University of Costa Rica, San José, Costa Rica
{gustavo.lopez_h,brenda.aymerich,diana.garbanzo,
alexia.pacheco}@ucr.ac.cr

Abstract. Technological applications have an increasingly important role in most companies. Investment in Information Technologies (IT) is also growing in most of them. The need to align IT-related goals with the company's strategic goals becomes imperative. GQM$^+$Strategies is an approach to align organizational goals, strategies, and measurements at different levels of an organization. This paper describes experiences learned from a GQM$^+$Strategies implementation at a large multi-industry state-owned company. The implementation was conducted by an academic research team joined by representatives of the company. Results showed an improved alignment and integration of different goals. Moreover, a holistic goal visualization was achieved, even though the company works in two different industries. As a state-owned company, external pressures force continuous planning. Sometimes, inadvertently designing those plans is the only goal achieved (i.e., plans are never executed). Using GQM$^+$Strategies, the research team leveraged the separation of goals and strategies, allowing identification of redundancies and replicated efforts across the company. The implementation of the GQM$^+$Strategies approach in such a complex context was very valuable. However, it also required a large amount of effort from the researchers and company representatives.

Keywords: GQM$^+$Strategies · Goal-oriented measurement · Strategic alignment · Software process improvement · IT strategy · Experience report

1 Introduction

GQM$^+$Strategies is a measurement approach that extends the GQM paradigm [1, 2], it promotes the creation of measurement programs that ensure alignment between goals in different levels of a company.

This paper describes experiences gathered while applying GQM$^+$Strategies in a complex context (i.e., a large multi-industry state-owned company). The company has an intrinsically hierarchical structure. Moreover, industry segregation promoted a silo mentality within the company.

© Springer International Publishing AG 2016
P. Abrahamsson et al. (Eds.): PROFES 2016, LNCS 10027, pp. 198–214, 2016.
DOI: 10.1007/978-3-319-49094-6_13

The implementation of GQM⁺Strategies in this context was triggered by a Software Process Improvement (SPI) initiative in the company's IT department. This department serves both industries and an administrative and finance management. Moreover, it is in charge of promoting IT related controls and standards.

The main benefits of GQM⁺Strategies and similar approaches are: an explicit description of goals, strategies, context factors and metrics that allow the organizational alignment; a transparent instrument to improve communication both within the organization and to third parties; and measurement data that allows information-based decision-making [3].

This research has two goals: one industry-related and one academic. The industry-related goal was to align the different levels of a large multi-industry state-owned company and to help this company in their SPI efforts. The academic goal was to assess the applicability of GQM⁺Strategies in such a complex context.

GQM⁺Strategies demonstrated that several efforts within the company were replicated and some goals were promoted by both industries in which the company operates. Moreover, the alignment allowed to reduce segregation and provided a holistic vision of the company's IT roadmap. Senior management saw potential on the GQM⁺Strategies Grid. They started to call it the **company's value map**.

The rest of the paper is structured as follows. Section 2 introduces the theoretical background, delving into GQM⁺Strategies definition and similar experience reports of case studies (i.e., related work). Section 3 describes our implementation of GQM⁺Strategies including: Application context, research approach, execution and results. Section 4 describes the main lessons learned in this research. Section 5 describes similar experience reports and compares those experiences with the ones described on this paper. Finally, Sect. 6 presents some final remarks.

2   Background

2.1   GQM⁺Strategies

Goal-Question-Metric plus Strategies approach (GQM⁺Strategies® [4, 5]) was defined as an extension of the GQM paradigm [1, 2]. GQM is a measurement system that sets rules for interpretation of measurement data in three levels: Conceptual, operational and quantitative. The GQM process identifies goals, derives questions and specifies metrics [1].

GQM⁺Strategies proposes the alignment of the traditional GQM paradigm with organizational goals in three levels: Business, software and project. Moreover, GQM⁺Strategies describes an iterative process to achieve organizational goals alignment through measurement [3] and proposes that constant updates are necessary to reflect organizational, departmental or team goal changes [6]. Figure 1 shows the phases of GQM⁺Strategies and its sub-activities.

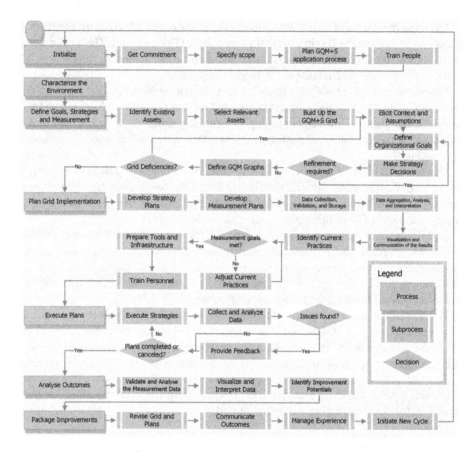

Fig. 1. GQM⁺Strategies flow diagram. Based on phases reported on [3]

GQM⁺Strategies recommends the use of a Grid that links goals to strategies, questions, and metrics, easing communication of common goals in the organization. The Grid facilitates traceability of goal-related data and integration of the measurement program across different levels within the organization [7, 8].

GQM⁺Strategies considers context factors and assumptions that are made during the implementation of measurement programs. Therefore, it allows inspection of erroneous assumptions or context changes over time. GQM⁺Strategies helps organizations to define what, why and how to measure, and interpret those measurements [6].

3   GQM⁺Strategies Implementation

3.1   Context

The company in which GQM⁺Strategies was implemented has several distinct characteristics: (1) It is a large organization (more than 15.000 employees on the payroll), (2) has more than 60 years of existence, (3) it is a multi-industry company, and (4) it is a state-owned company. Furthermore, one of the industries in which the company operates recently transitioned from a monopoly to a competitive environment. Figure 2 shows a simplified company organigram.

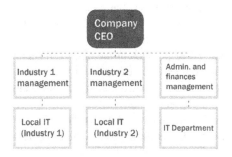

Fig. 2. Company organigram

Figure 3 illustrates the organization within the IT department. The IT department is part of the administrative and finance management, there are also two managements at the same level, one for each industry in which the company operates.

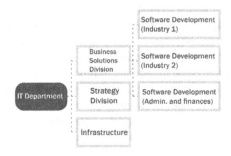

Fig. 3. Organization of the IT department

Industries 1 and 2 have different dynamics, one is a very volatile (i.e., requirement change rates are very high), the other is very structured and passive. The IT department is in charge of IT across the company. However, each management has its local IT (self-funded) therefore a silo mentality has been established (i.e., departments or groups within an organization do not want to share resources (e.g., information, knowledge, funding, among others) with other individuals in the same organization.

The traditional approach towards measurement in the organization has been balanced scorecards [9] and Key Performance Indicators (KPI). Therefore, concepts such as learning and growth, business process, customer or financial perspective, and strategy mapping are deeply rooted in the company.

3.2   Research Approach

The GQM⁺Strategies implementation reported in this paper was performed collaboratively between the University of Costa Rica research team and the company representatives. The research team comprised twelve members: Four PhDs, one PhD-student researcher, three MSc (one researcher and two industry practitioners), and four BSc, during a two-year period (i.e., approximately four at any given time). The company representatives comprised: Three permanent members (all seniors at the organization). The main positions of the company representatives were: Company's IT department manager, IT department's strategy division manager, and another strategy division member. However, the application of GQM⁺Strategies incorporated the vision of over 12 people working in the IT department and its divisions.

GQM⁺Strategies implementation started from senior management's desire of implementing a software factory (i.e., commitment to long-term, integrated efforts to enhance software operations [10]). The research team performed a diagnosis focused on: The company's organizational scheme, software development culture and processes, human resources and technology used in the development process and other regulations.

The diagnosis was implemented through interviews (15 interviews/71 people), site visits (5 visits) and an online survey (281 participants). All these activities were carried with people from the IT department and the local ITs (Fig. 2). From the diagnosis 44 findings were reported. Findings can be categorized as: General, business vision, requirement management, quality assurance, release management, change management and configuration, project management, architecture, support, outsourcing management, IT governance, technology, people, and culture.

In several of these findings the measurement process is mentioned as a requirement before addressing the issues reported (i.e., measurement process must be implemented before fixing the problem), in order to ensure improvement and measure progress. This situation was crucial to boost GQM⁺Strategies implementation in the organization and convince senior management that a measurement approach that also aligns business goals would be very beneficial for the IT department and the company.

3.3   GQM⁺Strategies Execution and Results

The application of GQM⁺Strategies consisted mainly of a set of planning meetings with the company representatives. In the next subsections we will describe how we approached each phase of GQM⁺Strategies in the context of this implementation, the main results and difficulties found along the way.

Initialize

According to [3], required inputs for this phase include a motivational talk and tutorial. We conducted three sessions of motivational talks (due to the number of people that participated). In these sessions, the IT department manager and the company's training manager introduced the planned efforts. Three cases were presented to motivate participants: A former software engineer at Google talked about working culture, a former software testing engineer at Microsoft Corp talked about the importance of high quality software products and a former software developer at Costa Rica's Central Bank talked about software improvement processes in public institutions.

Commitment was a given, since the process originated from the organization. Moreover, the IT department manager was fully involved at this stage. A schedule of activities was prepared and the budget was calculated. At this stage training people is a task that should be executed. However, only two work sessions were conducted due to representatives' insufficient time. Table 1 shows the training sessions, their coverage and dates.

Table 1. Joint events for sensitization and training, all sessions were conducted in 2015

Timeline	Purpose	Elicited Information	Challenges
28 Jul	Project Kickoff	Project goals	
28 Jul	Introduction to metrics, goal oriented measurement, and GQM+Strategies		
25 Aug	Detailes GQM+Strategies presentation		Questions regarding GQM+Strategies applicability emerged

The original GQM$^+$Strategies scope was the IT department, leaving out the local ITs. However, once the process started, provided documentations included IT-related goals of the company's three managements (See Fig. 2).

Characterize the Environment

In this phase, while assessing the applicability of GQM$^+$Strategies, we discovered that IT department's strategy division head compared the approach with balanced scorecards (due to their focus on measurement), this was a difficult to overcome problem, because balanced scorecards have been used for many years and their promotors did not want to change the way measurements were executed.

Since our application contexts is a public state-owned company, they are asked to provide detailed documentation of goals and investments. Therefore, there was a high availability of organizational structure, process, goals, and future plans documentation. At a certain point there was too much documentation. Later on, we will discuss on how plans for each management had duplications and ambiguities that made the GQM $^+$Strategies refinement process very difficult.

Define Goals, Strategies and Measurement

We asked the company representatives to provide information regarding current goals, plans and measurements. Delivered documentation included: Current measurements for the business operative plan, 2016 IT plan, IT strategic framework (2015-2018) at company level, IT strategic framework for the administration and finance management (2015), IT strategic framework for the Industry 1 management (2014-2018), IT strategic framework for the Industry 2 management (2016), and IT Strategic framework, general strategic documentation (2014-2018), proposed metric for ITIL (2011), IT government statute, and the administration and finance management strategy (2015-2018).

The research team read and interpreted all the provided documentation and extracted IT-related goals. Figure 4 provides a structural overview of the GQM$^+$Strategies Grid derived from the documental revision. Due to confidentiality reasons of the case company, the complete list of goals and strategies are not mentioned.

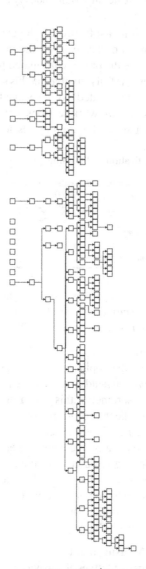

Fig. 4. Structural overview of the GQM⁺Strategies grid (first version)

In the first version of the GQM⁺Strategies Grid, no difference was made between goals and strategies, everything was considered a goal since there were no further details on how the statements were going to be achieved.

A change in mental models was required to understand the GQM⁺Strategies proposal and differentiate between goals and strategies. This effort was very valuable to assess the implementability of many proposed goals in the organization.

In order to move from the first version of the GQM⁺Strategies Grid (Fig. 4) to the final version (Fig. 5), refinement events were carried with company representatives.

They were asked to assess the Grid's vision according with the scope of the implementation and the reviewed documents.

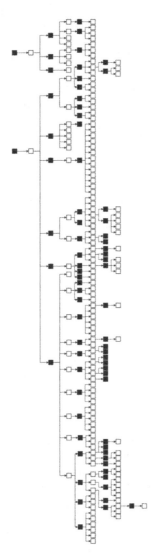

Fig. 5. Structural overview of the GQM⁺Strategies grid (final version)

In Fig. 4, the left most boxes represent the company's strategic goals. They were considered and incorporated in the Grid because one of the documents stated that the goal of IT in the company was to support all the company's strategic goals.

Figure 4 contains twelve company strategic goals (non IT-related), seven high level goals (IT-related), and 193 lower level goals. Some of these goals were similar from each other. Nonetheless, the research team decided to keep them all, in order to provide evidence of the duplicated goals found across documents.

The first refinement session was conducted with the version of the GQM⁺Strategies Grid created from the goal extraction of the documentation. In this first refinement session, both the director of the IT department's strategy division and a senior employee of that division participated. The GQM⁺Strategies grid was introduced and they started to define changes that should be incorporated.

Table 2 shows the GQM⁺Strategies Grid refinement sessions conducted during this GQM⁺Strategies implementation. After each refinement session a new version of the GQM⁺Strategies Grid was generated and used in the next refinement session. This did not occur in the sessions conducted on November 11, all these sessions were conducted with the same version of the grid and a set of changes was prepared to be incorporated after these three sessions.

Table 2. GQM⁺Strategies Grid refinement events carried during 2015

Timeline	Departament(Based on Figure 3)	Participant role
28 oct	Strategy Division	Director
28 oct	Strategy Division	Senior employee
3 nov	Business Solutions Division / Software Development (Industry 1)	Director
5 nov	IT Department	Director / manager
11 nov	Business Solutions Division / Software Development (Admin and finances)	Director
11 nov	Strategy Division	Senior employee
11 nov	Business Solutions Division / Software Development(Industry 2)	Senior employee
18 nov	Business Solutions Division	Director

Even though the research team tried enforced the company representatives to make strategy decisions that would allow later strategy execution, this was not possible. In the context of a large state-owned company, individuals are not used to make decisions alone.

Once the GQM⁺Strategies Grid was ready (i.e., all apparent goals were included), the IT plan for 2016 was released and approved by the board of the company (i.e., it was engraved in stone). This document was facilitated to the research team in early 2016; therefore, the GQM⁺Strategies Grid was reviewed and refined. Again, no difference was found between goals and strategies in the IT plan. A session was conducted to identify how the IT plan and the GQM⁺Strategies Grid could be aligned and the representative's answer was that the Grid was the one that required to be changed, because the IT plan was approved by the company's board of directors.

The defined solution was to implement a mapping tool (initially an Excel document) to translate IT plan language into goals and strategies and incorporate them in the GQM ⁺Strategies Grid. At this point, the GQM⁺Strategies Grid was transferred to be used internally in the company.

Plan Grid Implementation

In this phase, the research team decided to adapt an iterative approach toward improvement [11]. An improvement backlog was developed based on the GQM⁺Strategies Grid strategies, and an iterative improvement process began. In order to assure that measurements are aligned between them, the research team proposed measures for each goal incorporated in the GQM⁺Strategies Grid final version.

The GQM⁺Strategies Grid showed in Fig. 5 is the Grid in its current state. The Grid contains two (non IT-related) company strategic goals that are directly mapped with nine IT-related high level goals. Sixty-two low level goals were finally incorporated into the GQM⁺Strategies Grid. Furthermore, 149 strategies were linked with those goals. The analyze outcomes and package improvement phases of GQM⁺Strategies are still to be implemented after the strategy execution and measurement implementation.

In the next section, we describe some lessons learned of this GQM⁺Strategies implementation. We acknowledge that GQM⁺Strategies is not a novel approach (i.e., it has more than 6 years being applied); however, we did not found evidence (published in academic literature) of the application of this approach in such a complex context: Large multi-industry state-owned company. Therefore, we believe that the insights gathered from this experience could be beneficial for further implementations and researches.

4   Lessons Learned

The context in which GQM⁺Strategies was implemented had traditionally used balanced scorecards as the main measurement approach. Some issues were found in the implementation of balanced scorecards that reduced their value for the organization:

- Metrics were created to be centralized and generalizable. Lower levels of the company were not given the change to develop their own measurements.

By applying GQM⁺Strategies, we did not only allow lower levels to design measurements, but also to incorporate their goals into the GQM⁺Strategies Grid.

- The company worked with silo mentality, from managements to working departments, all areas work separately and do not share information. There was an entrenched lack of information integration.

By reviewing documentation provided by all management offices and both the IT department and local ITs, we took a step forward towards data integration in the company. GQM⁺Strategies, and specially the Grid provided so much value in the eyes of the strategy division director that he started calling it the company's value map.

- Balanced scorecards were developed in different levels of the organization; however, they were not fully integrated.

As we mentioned, information was not integrated horizontally. Furthermore, the measurement process carried did not provide a vertical integration. Therefore, lower level measurements were not always proper to assess higher level goals. In some cases balanced scorecards used different indicators to measure similar things in different levels of the organization.

Delving into the GQM⁺Strategies implementation, we also faced some challenges and we learned some lessons while dealing with those challenges:

- A flexible tool to manage the GQM⁺Strategies Grid

We developed the visual representation of the GQM⁺Strategies grid using Microsoft's Visio. In cases in which the grid is small, there are no major challenges to manage changes. However, in a Grid with over 200 components, changes were difficult to deal with.

A flexible tool designed for business and information management purposes (instead of a diagramming tool) would have been very beneficial for the process. During the implementation of GQM⁺Strategies, the company in which the approach was implemented bought a tool called MindManager, the first activity they performed as soon as the grid was delivered, was to change it from Visio to MindManager due to the flexibility it provided. We acknowledge that our use of Microsoft's Visio was not the best, since we used a basic diagram, however, the use of a specialized tool made the process much easier.

- During the implementation of GQM⁺Strategies, a clear segmentation between the research team and the company representatives was made. The first version of the GQM⁺Strategies Grid was created by the research team by reviewing documentation. This approach was beneficial to avoid bias in the Grid; however, it also increased the cost and time required to finalize the first version of the GQM⁺Strategies Grid.

By creating the Grid from an outsider perspective, the research team was capable of identifying a large number of goals in the reviewed documentation. All these goals were incorporated in the first version of the GQM⁺Strategies Grid. However, once this version was ready to be assessed, we suffered from lack of participant identification and commitment in the refinement sessions. Moreover, we believe that they did not understand the process.

Through training and iterations in the refinement process, this issue was overcome. However, the costs increased. If the company representatives had participated in the process since the beginning this issue would not have appeared, but the unbiased perspective could not have been achieved.

- An automation tool could have been used to keep track of changes

During this implementation we used manual changelogs (to keep track of changes in the grid). A better tool to manage the GQM⁺Strategies Grid could have provided the mechanisms to automate tracking changes and avoid the costs of manually tracking them.

- The company is undertaking a change process. However, deep changes in the organizational structure of the company destabilize these efforts. We faced problems to maintain sponsorship during GQM⁺Strategies execution. The director of the IT department strategy division changed during the implementation. The new director saw potential in the results of the process and promoted it. This could have been the other way around, and sponsorship could have been lost.

The GQM⁺Strategies Grid allowed us to clearly distinguish the organizational changes over time. Excess of documents over the years were proof of those changes. It is hard to assess if GQM⁺Strategies should be implemented while changes so deep are occurring in a company. Furthermore, cultural characteristics were against the incorporation of practices that make visible information within the organization. Therefore, we faced resistance from some employees.

In order to face some of the main issues found during our GQM$^+$Strategies implementation we used some mechanisms including: A changelog to keep track of changes between refinement sessions. This was necessary due to the complexity of the GQM $^+$Strategies Grid initial version.

The changelog is composed of all the changes that arise during the refinement session. The choices of changes proposed to the participants were: Merge, eliminate, modify and create. Merge was used to unify two or more goals attending the same issue or executing similar tasks. Eliminate was available to discard goals that were not considered IT-related. Modify was used to adjust the original texts to either goal or strategy syntax. Create was used when a strategy was devised and it had no associated goal (i.e., the goal was created based on the strategy).

All this was conducted to obtain the first stable version of the GQM$^+$Strategies Grid, after the refinement sessions. However, we also see fit to use the changelog as further reference. For instance, once a goal is achieved, it might be changed or discarded from the GQM$^+$Strategies Grid, without trace of it ever being there. We believe that changelogs or version control might be implemented to provide the company with a memory of its goals.

To implement this proposal, the definition proposed by Münch et al. [12] might be used to characterize each goal, denoting the changes it has undergone: New goal, discarded goal, unchanged goal, revised goal, split goals, merged goal, established goal and linked goal.

The IT plan provided by the company for this GQM$^+$Strategies implementation considers goals to have different maturity levels, including: Foundation establishment, positioning and consolidation/operation. These phases can be mapped to the GQM $^+$Strategies Grid as it changes over time.

The changelog allowed us to effectively track and document the changes made after a refinement session. Also, we used them as a reference before we started a new refinement session. To show to the interviewee the evolution of the Grid and the most recent modifications.

Finally, as it was expected, visualizing such a large GQM$^+$Strategies Grid was almost impossible. Navigation between goals was also a difficult task. Figure 6 shows the final version of the developed GQM$^+$Strategies Grid.

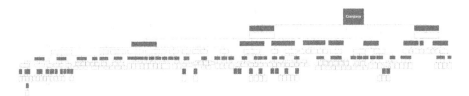

Fig. 6. GQM$^+$Strategies grid traditional visualization

As it is evident, the traditional hierarchical visualization of the GQM$^+$Strategies Grid does not work with so many goals and strategies. It is difficult to understand the context of each goal and navigate between them. We created a poster version of the grid (Fig. 7), dividing each branch at the higher IT-related goals. A highlighted section of the poster shows the highest level relationships. This visualization was very helpful for the company representatives, easing navigation and overall understanding of the GQM +Strategies results.

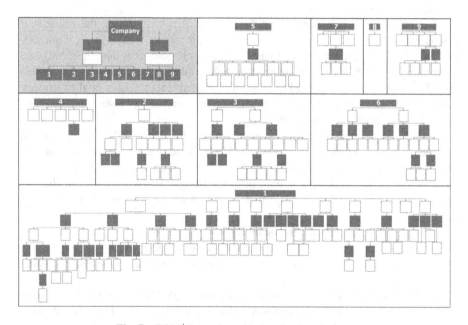

Fig. 7. GQM+Strategies grid visualized as a poster

5   Discussion and Similar Experience Reports

Several experience reports and case studies have been reported in literature addressing the implementation of GQM+Strategies in different contexts. This section describes some of them, their similarities and differences with the experience described in this paper.

In 2010, Mandić et al. [13] proposed an approach to assess GQM+Strategies' practical value and applied it in a Finnish ICT company. Authors concluded that GQM +Strategies had practical value for the company. However, authors only assessed a small department in the company. In this paper, only one department was assessed. Nonetheless, this department serves the whole company and shares goals three different managerial offices.

Also in 2010, Sarcia [14] reported that in order to apply GQM+Strategies in non-software development domains in required to be generalized (i.e., converted into a context free approach). Author assessed the application of GQM+Strategies in a military training domain in Italy. This work was an ongoing experience and no further details were found in literature. Even though the experience described in this paper was gathered from the application of GQM⁺Strategies in an IT Department, one of the industries in which the company works is not related to software development. Some of the high level goals (for this industry) had nothing to do with software development. Therefore, this experiences support the finding that GQM⁺Strategies is applicable and introduces business value in non-software development domains.

In 2011, Kaneko et al. [15] presented results and experiences from applying the GQM ⁺Strategies approach at the Japan Aerospace Exploration Agency's software research department. The efforts were joined with IESE's experts. Three top-level goals are reported; 20 lower level goals are also identifiable in their GQM⁺Strategies Grid. Reported lessons learned include: (1) Reuse of previously developed measurement models is important to reduce efforts and (2) GQM⁺Strategies Grid can contribute to prioritize high level goals by assessing which ones are more feasible. In this experience, consultants had to force a separation between the previously used measurement model and GQM⁺Strategies, because management started to fall back into their traditional measurement practices, and this was considered a threat for GQM⁺Strategies implementation and the SPI initiative as a whole.

Also during 2011, Trendowicz, Heidrich, and Shintani [16], reported lessons learned from a GQM⁺Strategies implementation at the Japanese Information-technology Promotion Agency. Authors present an interesting perspective on how GQM⁺Strategies allows project evaluation regarding their contribution towards higher-level goals, and how clear rationale can be applied for rejecting or approving project proposals based on their contribution. To assess this perspective, the implementation of GQM⁺Strategies should be ingrained in the company and its practices. An evaluation of this contribution in the context of application presented in this paper will require more time and further analysis.

In 2013, Münch et al. [17] reported experiences on a five-month application of GQM ⁺Strategies in an industrial company. Main lessons learned reported include: (1) The necessity of company representatives to have knowledge of GQM⁺Strategies and how to apply it, (2) find a suitable entry point for the approach implementation is crucial. In this case, the efforts presented in this paper are very similar to the ones described by Münch et al. [17]. However, the experience time period was larger due to the complexity of the company and the amount of information available that had to be revised. Moreover, the entry point was a key aspect to boost GQM⁺Strategies implementation. The sponsorship of senior management and participation of representatives with the proper knowledge enhanced sped up the GQM⁺Strategies implementation.

In 2013 Basili, Lampasona, and Ramírez [18], describe an overview of the application of GQM⁺Strategies in ECOPETROL (oil and gas industry). Their main goals were for alignment and formalization of goals, providing strategies with visibility, and defining operational measurement and interpretation of goals. Authors point the effort required to implement GQM⁺Strategies (i.e., the GQM⁺Strategies Grid requires the collaboration of several people representing different levels of the organization and is a non-trivial mental activity). This experience report is very similar to the one conducted at ECOPETRO. Different perspectives were incorporated, not only due to consultant request but also because the company representatives advised that other perspectives should be considered to create the GQM⁺Strategies Grid.

In 2014, Petersen et al. [19] proposed an elicitation instrument to gather stakeholder perspectives and incorporate it into the GQM⁺Strategies approach. In their paper, authors explain the case study performed at Ericsson AB (Telecommunications industry). We tried to apply this elicitation instrument; however, it was too structured for the first implementation of GQM⁺Strategies. This is the most similar case to the one presented in this paper, due to industry similarity. However, Petersen et al. [19], do not delve in the specific results of the implementations. Therefore, a comparison is difficult to conduct.

In this section we presented experience reports, case studies of GQM⁺Strategies conducted from 2010 to 2014. Those reports were compared with the one described in this paper.

6   Conclusions

In this paper we presented our experiences of applying the GQM⁺Strategies approach in a large multi-industry state-owned company. The application was triggered by an improvement initiative to implement a software factory.

GQM⁺Strategies was implemented by a research team jointly with company representatives. The approach was followed as proposed in [3]. The research team managed the process and company representatives worked as stakeholders.

The GQM⁺Strategies Grid was firstly derived from a documental review of the company's information. Over 10 large (100 page or more) documents were reviewed and goals or action plans were extracted. With the list of goals, the research team conducted a process to unify them in one single representation. The first version of the GQM⁺Strategies Grid did not differentiate between goals and strategies.

Following a proposal to operationalize GQM⁺Strategies [19], we conducted refinement sessions. In each refinement session one company representative's vision was incorporated, and doubts emerged from the process were revised and solved. The research team implemented a changelog to keep track of changes in order to modify the Grid and use an improved version in the next refinement session. We observed the following key benefits and advantages of applying GQM⁺Strategies in such a complex context:

- GQM⁺Strategies helped the company to get a complete vision of their goals and provided them with a tool to visualize those goals integrally.
- The approach implementation made visible the benefits provided by operative and low level tasks both to immediately above goals and to the company's objectives.
- As a state-owned company, they suffer external pressures to plan their activities. Such pressures sometimes force them to plan in advance for several years. GQM⁺Strategies provided a tool to enforce alignment between plans (goals) and to define strategies to achieve those goals. Moreover, it allowed the identification of redundancies and replicated efforts.
- As a multi-industry company, they adopted a silo mentality. GQM⁺Strategies promoted the unification of the IT department goals for both industries and the administrative and finance management. Therefore, the segregation was reduced.

Moreover, the research team specifically recorded which industry or management proposed the goals allowing the IT department to prioritize goals that have impact into more than one management.

One of the key lessons from our application GQM⁺Strategies is that goal very difficult and institutions that first try to implement the approach do not distinguish between goals and strategies. In general, the GQM⁺Strategies approach was very valuable in the context in which it was applied. However, the efforts invested were large. We expect for the results to have an impact as large as the effort invested to implement it.

One of the key lessons gathered from this effort was the help that GQM⁺Strategies implementation provided to visualize redundant goals within the company. This visibility allowed the research team to point out deficiencies in the budged investment and the company representatives to convince internal management that a change was necessary to avoid unnecessary expenses. Even though this is not a direct benefit from GQM⁺Strategies researchers could not achieved this result without following this approach.

Acknowledgments. This work was partially supported by CITIC at University of Costa Rica. Grant No. 834-B4-412. We would also like to thank all the consultants that participated in this research, including but not limited to: Dr. Marcelo Jenkins (current minister of Science and Technology of Costa Rica), Dra. Alexandra Martínez, Dr. Carlos Castro, Mag. Mauricio Arroyo, Mag. Marcela Chacón, and Mag. Francisco Cocozza.

References

1. Basili, V.R.: Software Modeling and Measurement: The Goal/Question/Metric Paradigm, Maryland, USA (1992)
2. Basili, V.R., Caldiera, G., Rombach, H.D.: The goal question metric approach. In: Encyclopedia of Software Engineering. Wiley Publishing, Inc. (1994)
3. Basili, V.R., Trendowicz, A., Kowalczyk, M., Heidrich, J., Seaman, C., Lindvall, M., Munch, J.: Aligning Organizations Through Measurement - The GQM⁺Strategies Approach. Springer, Switzerland (2014)
4. Fraunhofer USA Inc.: Fraunhofer Center for Experimental Software Engineering. http://www.fc-md.umd.edu/
5. Fraunhofer-Gesellschaft: Fraunhofer Institute for Experimental Software Engineering. http://www.iese.fraunhofer.de/en.html
6. Janes, A., Succi, G.: The GQM⁺Strategies approach. In: Lean Software Development in Action, pp. 151–170. Springer, Heidelberg (2014)
7. Mandic, V., Basili, V.R., Oivo, M., Harjumaa, L., Markkula, J.: Utilizing GQM⁺Strategies for an organization-wide earned value analysis. In: EUROMICRO-SEAA, pp. 255–258. IEEE Computer Society (2010)
8. Basili, V.R., Lindvall, M., Regardie, M., Seaman, C., Heidrich, J., Rombach, D., Trendowicz, A., Münch, J., Rombach, D., Trendowicz, A.: Linking software development and business strategy through measurement. Comput. (Long Beach Calif.) **43**, 57–65 (2010)
9. Kaplan, R.S.: Conceptual foundations of the balanced scorecard. In: Handbooks of Management Accounting Research, Vol. 3, pp. 1253–1269 (2008)

10. Aaen, I., Botcher, P., Mathiassen, L.: The software factory: contributions and illusions. In: Proceedings of the Twentieth Information Systems Research Seminar in Scandinavia, pp. 736–750. Euro-Arab Management School (1997)

11. Cohn, M.: Succeeding with Agile: Software Development Using Scrum. Addison-Wesley Professional, Reading (2009)

12. Münch, J., Fagerholm, F., Kettunen, P., Pagels, M., Partanen, J.: The effects of GQM +Strategies on organizational alignment. In: DASMA Software Metric Congress (2013)

13. Mandić, V., Harjumaa, L., Markkula, J., Oivo, M.: Early empirical assessment of the practical value of GQM+Strategies. In: Münch, J., Yang, Y., Schäfer, W. (eds.) ICSP 2010. LNCS, vol. 6195, pp. 14–25. Springer, Heidelberg (2010). doi:10.1007/978-3-642-14347-2_3

14. Sarcia, S.A.: Is GQM+Strategies really applicable as is to non-software development domains? In: ACM-IEEE International Symposium on Empirical Software Engineering and Measurement, pp. 1–4 (2010)

15. Kaneko, T., Katahira, M., Miyamoto, Y., Kowalczyk, M.: Application of GQM+Strategies® in the Japanese space industry. In: International Conference on Software Process and Product Measurement, pp. 221–226. IEEE Computer Society (2011)

16. Trendowicz, A., Heidrich, J., Shintani, K.: Aligning software projects with business objectives. In: International Conference on Software Process and Product Measurement, pp. 142–150. IEEE Computer Society (2011)

17. Munch, J., Fagerholm, F., Kettunen, P., Pagels, M., Partanen, J.: Experiences and insights from applying GQM+Strategies in a systems product development organisation. In: Euromicro Conference Series on Software Engineering and Advanced Applications, pp. 70–77 (2013)

18. Basili, V., Lampasona, C., Ocampo Ramírez, A.E.: Aligning corporate and IT goals and strategies in the oil and gas industry. In: Heidrich, J., Oivo, M., Jedlitschka, A., Baldassarre, M.T. (eds.) PROFES 2013. LNCS, vol. 7983, pp. 184–198. Springer, Heidelberg (2013). doi: 10.1007/978-3-642-39259-7_16

19. Petersen, K., Gencel, C., Asghari, N., Betz, S.: An elicitation instrument for operationalising GQM+Strategies (GQM+S-EI). Empir. Softw. Eng. 20(4), 968–1005 (2015)

Verification and Validation

Is Mutation Testing Ready to Be Adopted Industry-Wide?

Jakub Možucha and Bruno Rossi$^{(\boxtimes)}$

Faculty of Informatics, Masaryk University, Brno, Czech Republic
{jmozucha,brossi}@mail.muni.cz

Abstract. Mutation Testing has a long research history as a way to improve the quality of software tests. However, it has not yet reached wide consensus for industry-wide adoption, mainly due to missing clear benefits and computational complexity for the application to large systems. In this paper, we investigate the current state of mutation testing support for Java Virtual Machine (JVM) environments. By running an experimental evaluation, we found out that while default configurations are unbearable for larger projects, using strategies such as selective operators, second order mutation and multi-threading can increase the applicability of the approach. However, there is a trade-off in terms of quality of the achieved results of the mutation analysis process that needs to be taken into account.

Keywords: Software mutation testing · Experimentation · Equivalent mutants · Selective mutation operators · Cost-reduction strategies

1 Introduction

Large amount of resources are wasted yearly due to bugs introduced in software systems, making the testing process one of the critical phases of software development [2]. A recent research reported the cost of software debugging up to a yearly $312 Billion, with developers utilizing 50 % of their allocated time to find and fix software bugs [1]. Software Engineering is for long time striving to find ways to reduce such inefficiencies, with the constant challenge to build more robust software. Mutation Testing is one such ways, representing a powerful technique to evaluate and improve the quality of software tests written by developers [7,14].

The main idea behind Mutation testing is to create many modified copies of the original program called *mutants* — each mutant with a single variation from the original program. All mutants are then tested by test suites to get the percentage of mutants failing the tests. It has been proven that mutation testing can bring several benefits to complement the applied testing practices, e.g. for test cases prioritization [6].

However, mutation testing has been often reported to struggle to be introduced in to real-world industrial contexts [8,11,15]. So why is mutation testing

© Springer International Publishing AG 2016
P. Abrahamsson et al. (Eds.): PROFES 2016, LNCS 10027, pp. 217–232, 2016.
DOI: 10.1007/978-3-319-49094-6_14

not widely adopted within industry? According to Madeyski et al. [9], mainly due to (a) performance reasons, (b) the equivalent mutants problem — syntactically but not semantically equal mutants — and (c) missing integration tools. In our view, the biggest drawback of mutation testing — its great computational costs — prevented until recently to include mutation testing into the development cycle of most companies. This resulted in development of many techniques to reduce the costs of mutation testing. Furthermore, another perceived drawback might be that the advantages of running mutation testing might not be fully clear as opposed to other simpler testing approaches.

Problem. The applicability of Mutation Testing to real-world project is far from reaching consensus [4,8,9,11,15]. While it seems that improvements have been done in tools integration, performance and equivalent mutants concerns still remain the most relevant issues, and call for further analyses.

Contribution. We report on an experiment addressed at understanding the current performance of Mutation Testing in Java Virtual Machine (JVM) environments, based on our previous experience on empirical studies [16] and the needs for more industry-academia cooperation [3]. With the collaboration of an industrial partner, we are in particular looking at different strategies that can reduce runtime overhead of Mutation Testing. Among the results, we provide indications about selective operators efficiency for Mutation Testing and their impact on performance. Practitioners can gain more insights about the performance / quality trade-offs in running mutation testing by evaluating several cost reduction strategies on a typical set of projects. Such information can be relevant for the integration in their own software development process. Furthermore, we make available the experimental package for replications.

The paper is structured as follows. Section 2 reports about the background on mutation testing. In Sect. 3, we refer about the experimental evaluation, describing the experimental design, choices made, results, and threats to validity. Section 4 provides related works that evaluated mutation testing in an experimental setting. Section 5 provides the discussions and Sect. 6 the conclusions.

2   Mutation Testing Background

Mutation Testing has undergone several decades of extensive research. First formed and published by DeMillo et al. in a 1971's seminal paper [5], Mutation Testing was introduced as a technique that can help programmers to improve the tests quality significantly. The core of Mutation Analysis is creating and killing mutants. Each mutant is a copy of original source code modified (*mutated*) with a single change (*mutation*). These mutations are done based on set of predefined syntactic rules called *mutation operators*. Traditional mutation operators consist of statement deletions (e.g. removing a `break` in a loop), statement modifications (e.g. replacing a `while` with `do-while`), Boolean expression modification (e.g. switching a `!=` logical operator to `==`), or variables/constants replacements. These mutation operators can be considered to be traditional mutation operators and are mostly language independent. There are also language-dependent mutation operators that are used to mutate language-specific constructs, taking into account aspects such as encapsulation, inheritance and polymorphism.

Tests are then executed on the mutants and the failure of mutants is expected. When the tests fail, the mutant is considered killed and no further tests are needed to be run using this mutant. For example, the original Java code in Algorithm 1 is mutated using a mutation operator, which replaces == with != and produces the mutant in Algorithm 2.

Algorithm 1. Original Code	**Algorithm 2.** Mutated Code

if *(a == b)* **then**
    // do something
else
    // do something
	if *(a != b)* **then**
	    // do something
	else
	    // do something

If any mutant does not cause the tests to fail, it is considered live. This can have two meanings: that the tests are not sensitive enough to catch the modified code or that this mutant is equivalent. An *equivalent mutant* is syntactically different from the original, but its semantics are the same and therefore it is impossible for tests to detect them. The final indication of tests quality is *mutation score*, that is the percentage of non-equivalent mutants killed by the test data or in other terms, the number of killed mutants over the number of *non-equivalent* mutants generated.

A test data is considered mutation-adequate [12] if its mutation score is 100 %. The higher mutation score is, the more faults were discovered — therefore the better the test process. This process leads to iterative improvement of testing, moreover, inspecting live mutants can lead to discovery and resolution of other source code issues. The most serious problem with equivalent mutants is the distortion of the mutation score: software tools include them in the computation, as their accurate detection is undecidable and can only be performed by manual inspection [9].

Mutation testing is a powerful technique, but has great computational costs. In fact, these costs have prevented mutation testing to be used in a practical way for many years, despite the relatively long history of mutation testing related research. In general, these are the most expensive phases:

1. **Mutant Generation** – aside from great computational costs, also the memory consumption is considerably high in this phase. Mutation operators have to be applied on the original code and mutants have to be stored;
2. **Mutant Compilation** – phase in which the generated mutants have to be compiled. This phase can be very costly for larger programs;
3. **Execution of tests** – for every mutant, the tests have to be executed until they are not killed. Most costly are live mutants, because every test has to be run on them;

There are several approaches that have been proposed to reduce the equivalent mutation problem ([9] provides an extensive review in the area).

At the same time, the problem is very often linked to performance optimization, as less equivalent mutants generated lead to a reduction in the three phases of mutant generation, mutant compilation, and tests execution. For this reason, various cost reducing strategies were developed.

In this paper we look into several of these strategies and their applicability to improve the performance for industrial applicability. A first strategy is the *Selective Mutation* technique — the idea is to use only the mutation operators that produce statistically less equivalent mutants than others. This approach allows to reduce not only equivalent mutants, but also to improve the performance. The aim of Selective Mutation is to achieve maximum coverage by generating the least number of mutants. Complexity reduction of mutants generation is from quadratic ($O(Refs*Vars)$) to linear ($O(Refs)$) [13], while retaining much of effectiveness of non-selective mutation.

Another strategy we adopt in the current paper is *Higher Order Mutation (HOM)*. Taking into account the original mutants we discussed so far as First Order Mutants (FOMs), the technique creates mutants with more than a single mutation, referred as higher order mutants as combination of several FOMs [6]. We look in particular at four different algorithms (*Last2First, DifferentOperators, ClosePair* and *RandomMix*) implemented in Judy [9,10] to combine FOMs into Second Order Mutants (SOMs) — in which two mutants are combined:

- *Last2First* – the first mutant in the list of FOMs is combined with the last mutant in the list, the second mutant with next to last and so on;
- *DifferentOperators* – only FOMs generated by different mutation operators are combined;
- *ClosePair* – two neighboring FOMs from the list are combined;
- *RandomMix* – any two mutants from the FOMs are combined;

All these strategies use a list of first order mutants (FOM) and should generate at least 50 % less mutants, with impact on the final mutation score [9].

3   Experimental Evaluation

We designed an exploratory experiment aimed at getting insights about the current applicability of mutation testing in industrial context (summary of the overall process, Fig. 1). We run in parallel a literature review (1) and an exploratory analysis about the usage of the tools for Mutation Testing (5). The selection of the tools for the experimentation (2), as well as the experimental units (3) were done based on the criteria of the company. We designed the research questions (6) and created the experimental design (7) based on the results from the exploratory analysis, taking both into account the company's needs and theoretical constraints and aspects worth investigation from theory. Experiments were then run (8) and results provided to the industrial partners for knowledge transfer and identification of future works. Based on an exploratory pre-experiment phase, we set the following research questions:

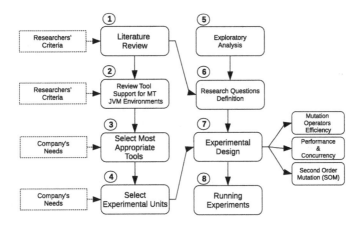

Fig. 1. Research process workflow

- **RQ1.** What is the performance of Mutation Testing by taking into account standard configurations (i.e. no selective operators and no mutation strategy)?
- **RQ2.** What is the impact of Selective Operators on Mutation Testing efficiency & performance?
- **RQ3.** What is the impact of Second Order Mutation strategies on Mutation Testing efficiency & performance?

Given the selection of the tools for mutation testing supported by the industrial partner, we looked specifically at three areas of experiments according to the three research questions set:

EXP1. Mutation Operators Efficiency Experiments. Looking at the selection of the most efficient mutation operators that then be evaluated in the performance experiments;

EXP2. Performance Experiments & Concurrency Experiments. Looking at the single-thread and multi-threading performance of the tools with standard configurations and according to different selective operator strategies;

EXP3. SOM Experiments. Evaluating the impact of different Second Order mutation strategies (*Last2First, DifferentOperators, ClosePair, RandomMix*).

We run an initial review of the tools available for mutation testing in JVM environments, omitting experimental tools. We overall considered seven tools: MuJava, PITest, Javalanche, Judy, Jumble, Jester, MAJOR, that we compared according to several characteristics (Table 1). To speed-up the mutation generation process, it is now a standard the support of byte-code mutation — mutants are applied at the byte code level. The industrial partner involved in the experimentation considered PITest and Judy more relevant for a series of reasons, in particular the availability of plugins and general easiness of integration, as well as the open source license and support for Java 8. Both software were used to run the experiments.

Table 1. JVM mutation testing tools

	MuJava	PITest	Javalanche	Judy	Jumble	Jester	MAJOR
State	active	active	–	active	active	–	active
License	Apache 2.0	Apache 2.0	LGPL	BSD	GPL	open	?
Java vers.	7	5 – 8	5, 6	6 – 8	6 –8	6	7
Unit test. framework	jUnit4	jUnit4, TestNG6	jUnit4	jUnit4	jUnit4	jUnit3	jUnit4
Production tools	GUI, Eclipse	3rd part. plugins	Eclipse plugin	Cmd	Cmd	Cmd	Ant
Automated class/test selection	Only classes	Yes	Yes	Yes	Only tests	Yes	Yes
Mutation Operators	method class	method	method concurr	meth. class	meth	meth	method self-def.
Byte-code mutation	Yes	Yes	Yes	Yes	Yes	–	Yes

For experimentation, we used as experimental projects libraries suggested by the industrial partner (Table 2): various Apache Commons projects and the JodaTime library. The selection was done so that the chosen projects contain possibly the most different distribution of size types, tests duration and test coverage. However, we couldn't include larger projects due to the high complexity of running mutation tests. From an initial list, we had to discard other projects that had either no tests (Apache Commons Daemon) or in which test cases were failing with either PITest or Judy (Apache Commons Compression, BeanUtils).

We included in Table 2 Mutation Size, a metric that can give indication of the complexity of the mutation process. While previous research has proved that the number of mutants is proportional to the number of variable references times the number of data objects *(O(Refs * Vars))* [12]. However, it is uneasy to determine the number of variable references for such large projects. Taking into account that modern mutation testing tools are creating mutants and running tests based on code coverage, Mutation Size is computed as coverage times size of project, as a measure of the complexity of the mutation testing process $MS = coverage * KLOC$.

3.1   Experimental Procedure

The first set of experiments was done with both tools using their default settings. The only modification was the configuration to the same number of threads, as Judy runs by default in parallel, while PITest uses only one thread.

After experiments with default settings, the experiments on mutation operators efficiency were done for each tool. The aim of these tests was to reduce the number of active operators selecting only the most efficient operators — the ones that produce mutants that are not so easy-to-kill.

After the selection of mutation operators, another set of performance tests was done using only the the selected operators. Concurrency tests were done on various number of used threads, comparing time and memory usage (PITest).

Table 2. Projects considered for the experimental evaluation. NCL = Number of Classes, KLOC = Lines of Code (thousands), NTCL = Number of Test Classes, TKLOC = Test Lines of Code (thousands), TT = Test Time, CC = Code Coverage, MS = Mutation Size

Project	Ver.	NCL	KLOC	NTCL	TK-LOC	TT	CC	MS
Apache Commons Chain	1.2	55	9.852	37	7.398	1.17	66.68 %	6.57
Apache Commons CLI	1.3.1	23	6.161	25	5.214	1.39	96.38 %	5.94
Apache Commons Codec	1.10	60	15.869	55	15.042	5.31	95.01 %	15.08
Apache Commons CSV	1.2	11	3.515	15	3.821	1.76	94.00 %	3.30
Apache Commnos DbUtils	1.6	30	7.611	26	4.453	1.36	57.71 %	4.39
Apache Commons Digester	3.2	168	23.125	101	14.220	2.31	72.49 %	16.76
Apache Commons Lang	1.2	133	68.684	148	55.467	16.51	93.80 %	64.43
Apache Commons Validator	3.4	62	16.516	77	14.117	3.42	77.61 %	12.82
Joda Time	1.5.0	166	70.593	158	72.423	5.02	90.18 %	63.66

Second Order strategies were then evaluated in terms of time performance and mutation score (Judy).

All tests were run remotely on 4 x Intel Xeon 3.35 GHz CPUs, 16 GB RAM. Every test result is an average of at least 10 iterations, with code coverage computed using the Cobertura tool. The iterations of tests were launched using simple bash scripts, which also automated renaming and moving of output files into specified folders. Every run of tests was launched under a modified version of the open-source memusg.sh[1] program, which measures the average and peak memory usage of all processes invoked by the current terminal session and sub-sessions[2]. The versions of the two tools used were PITest 1.1.9 and Judy 2 (release from 13.5.2015).

Initial Performance Evaluation. The initial evaluation was run with default settings using one thread with default operators (Table 3). By default Judy has active all 56 mutation operators, while PITest 7 out of 16. Missing values in the table indicate a failure to complete the testing process.

Looking at the time performance in relation with mutation size (MS), introduced in the previous section to characterize the projects, we found a positive correlation (Spearman's Rank-Order, 0.85, p=0.0037, two-tailed). The experiments showed that with one exception, PITest is always faster to generate mutants than Judy, which generated more mutants. Similarly, when comparing how many mutants per second were generated, PITest generated mutants faster than Judy. In our experiments, Judy was not able to finish mutation analysis for larger projects (in particular Lang and Joda Time, that have the highest Mutation Size among the considered projects). When comparing time per number of mutants, Judy is generally faster for all tested projects using the default settings

---

[1] https://gist.github.com/netj/526585.

[2] the experimental package is available at https://goo.gl/5GPdQv.

tests. When considering the tested projects metrics, Judy is faster for smaller projects. However, for bigger projects or for projects with higher line coverage or longer tests run, the performance is rapidly lower.

Comparing average memory consumption, the same pattern applies as for comparison of tests duration. Judy consumes less memory for very small projects, but PITest shows better results for medium and bigger projects. Similarly, the peak of memory consumption is normally lower for Judy, but for big or better covered projects, the memory usage peak for Judy is a lot higher than for PITest.

Table 3. Run-time performance - default settings one thread - values in () are by using selective operators.

Project	Gen.Time (sec)		Total Time (sec)		Peak Memory (MB)	
	PITest	Judy	PITest	Judy	PITest	Judy
Commons Chain	1.1 (1.4)	3.18 (2.0)	33.5 (30.2)	5.67 (2.6)	956 (1587)	302 (240)
Commons CLI	1.3 (1.4)	12.8 (6.3)	45.8 (42.4)	228.5 (46.9)	1764 (1743)	4505 (3677)
Commons Codec	5.7 (6.2)	— (28.3)	247.6 (278.9)	— (2225.5)	3028 (3061)	— (4055)
Commons CSV	1.9 (1.6)	2.5 (1.4)	48.1 (44.1)	10.5 (4)	1648 (1654)	900 (351)
Commons DbUtils	1.6 (1.0)	6.2 (47.7)	34.2 (12)	45.6 (78.7)	784 (399)	1441 (4653)
Commons Digester	3.9 (3.0)	13.6 (8.2)	258.8 (120.1)	38.7 (20.2)	2678 (2540)	1509 (2071)
Commons Lang	21.1 (20.3)	— (—)	943.6 (907.9)	— (—)	3825 (3600)	— (—)
Commons Validator	3.5 (3.5)	13.9 (5.1)	207.9 (148.2)	135.5 (29.7)	1309 (1365)	1638 (609)
Joda Time	28.3 (28.3)	— (—)	638.8 (546)	— (—)	3857 (4267)	— (—)

> *Time required for Mutation Testing is positively correlated with Mutation Size (LOCS*Coverage). It can be used as initial measure of complexity. Missing tests or tests failures (for analysis tool) hinder the possibility to apply MT.*

Mutation Operators Efficiency Results. The procedure of selection of the most efficient operators needs some further clarification. The strong mutation operators are those whose mutants are not easy to be killed. It would be very difficult to create tests that would kill 100 % of selective mutants. Therefore, we adopted a different approach by defining some thresholds to define the selective operators:

1. Run tests on all projects with all stable mutation operators (stable operators — not causing unrecoverable crashes during mutation);
2. Find most the populous (generating the highest number of mutants) mutation operators;
3. Exclude the operator if:
   - Mutation score of mutants created by the operators is higher than the average mutation score on all the tested projects;
   - The mutation operator belongs to the most populous operators and the score of mutants created is higher than the average of 80 % for all the tested projects;

Table 4. Efficiency of PITest operators

Operator	#Mut	%>avg	Operator	#Mut	%>avg
INLINE_CONSTS	12455	56	VOID_METHOD_CALLS (D)	2653	33
NEGATE_CONDITIONALS (D)	11087	100	INCREMENTS (D)	1128	100
RETURN_VALS (D)	10457	89	INVERT_NEGS	71	100
REMOVE_CONDITIONALS_EQ_IF	8335	100	REMOVE_CONDITIONALS_EQ_ELSE		
MATH (D)	3457	78	NON_VOID_METHOD_CALLS		
REMOVE_CONDITIONALS_ORD_ELSE	2752	89	CONSTRUCTOR_CALLS		
CONDITIONALS_BOUNDARY (D)	2752	22	EXPERIMENTAL_MEMBER_VARIABLE		
REMOVE_CONDITIONALS_ORD_IF	2752	67	EXPERIMENTAL_SWITCH		

Table 5. Efficiency of Judy operators

Oper.	#Mut	%>avg	Oper.	#Mut	%>avg	Oper.	#Mut	%>avg	Op.	#Mut	%>avg
JIR_Ifgt	1957	86	AIR_Mul	502	86	PNC	132	0	EOA	14	14
JIR_Iflt	1924	86	JTD	383	57	EOC	116	57	ISI	12	0
JIR_Ifle	1862	14	PRV	370	67	SIR_Ushr	98	100	JDC	12	60
JIR_Ifge	1823	86	AIR_Sub	368	86	SIR_Shl	96	100	FBD	10	50
JIR_Ifne	1575	100	EGE	269	43	JID	91	100	SCR	6	100
EAM	1391	29	PLD	259	0	SIR_Shr	76	0	IOR	5	33
JIR_Ifeq	1134	100	AIR_Add	211	67	LIR_And	58	100	CCD	0	0
OAC	1051	71	LIR_LeftO	187	100	EMM	56	25	CST	0	0
JIR_Ifnull	717	100	LIR_Right	187	100	CCE	33	71	ORV	0	0
AIR_LeftO	529	86	PPD	178	0	ISD	33	100	OMR	605	0
JTI	529	71	LIR_Xor	171	100	CLR	25	67	OMD	358	0
AIR_Div	525	100	IPC	165	57	DUL	23	60	IOD	206	0
AIR_Rem	510	100	LIR_Or	145	100	LSF	23	40	IOP	7	0
AIR_Right	509	86	SIR_LeftO	135	100	REV	23	40	CSR	4	0

Non-excluded operators were considered selective operators and were active for the selective mutation performance tests. Tables 4 and 5 are sorted by the most populous operators from all projects (# Mut) with indication of the percentage of mutation score of the operator being higher than average mutation score ($\% > avg$)[3]. The *(D)* at the end of some operator names for PITest means that the operator is active by default. The red-painted operators are unstable ones, yellow are excluded operators and green are the selected operators for the Selective Operators experiments. The Judy operators that generated many mutants from which none were killed were considered as unstable ones.

Out of the total 16 PITest mutation operators, 5 were selected for selective mutation including the most populous operator INLINE_CONSTS, causing that the total number of generated mutants during selective mutation was almost the same as during the mutation using default PITest operators. For selective mutation using Judy, 28 out of 56 mutation operators were selected and the number of generated mutants was reduced significantly.

---

[3] description of operators can be found at http://pitest.org/quickstart/mutators/ and http://mutationtesting.org/judy/documentation/.

The selected operators can be used to evaluate the number of mutated classes vs the mutation score (Fig. 2a,b). The % of mutated classes refers to the number of mutated classes over the total projects' classes. The comparison of mutation score showed that the mutation score of PITest selective mutation is always lower than mutation score of default operators. This can mean that default operators are either too easy-to-be-killed, or that selected operators produced more equivalent mutants. Comparing selective vs non-selective strategies for mutation score by running a Wilcoxon Signed-Rank Test showed significant differences ($p = 0.0012 < 0.05$, two-tailed, $N = 15$).

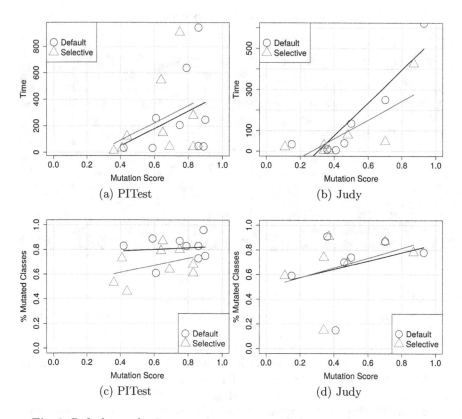

Fig. 2. Default vs selective mutation per mutated classes and mutation score

The total time of mutation analysis showed the real advantage of selective mutation also for PITest tests ((Fig. 2c,d and Table 3). Except of one tested project, all other were done faster using selective mutation. Comparing selective vs non-selective strategies by running a Wilcoxon Signed-Rank Test showed significant differences ($p = 0.0096 < 0.05$, two-tailed, N=16) in duration time. To note also that selective operators allowed Judy to provide results on the Apache Commons Codec project (with mutation size of 15.08).

EXP1. Using Selective Operators can bring benefits in terms of runtime performance, however, at the expense of lower mutation score. Selective Operators can also help in running Mutation Testing on some projects.

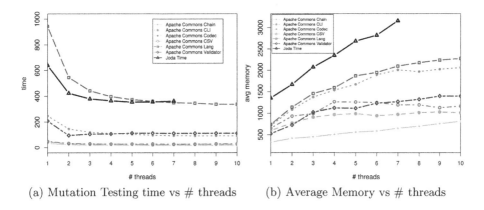

(a) Mutation Testing time vs # threads   (b) Average Memory vs # threads

Fig. 3. Concurrency experiments results

Performance and Concurrency Results. The results of the concurrency experiments showed that using two or three threads can result in considerable reduction of time compared to memory consumption increase (Fig. 3). The average memory consumption is rising for all testing projects almost linearly (fitted regression up to 7 threads, $avgmem=660.42+148.55*\#threads$, adj $R^2=0.22$), while time reduction is less than linear with the number of threads (fitted regression up to 7 threads, $time=262.81-21.71*\#threads$, adj $R^2=0.20$).

Looking at the combined effect of decrease in time and increase in memory consumption, we considered $\Delta time$ vs $\Delta avgmemory$ (Fig. 4). In this case, time reduces less than linearly than the increase in memory (fitted regression up to 7 threads, $time=13.61-0.2656*avgmem$, adj $R^2=0.45$), so using more threads might increase consistently memory usage without larger benefits on time reduction.

EXP2. Up to 2–3 threads can bring high benefits in terms of runtime performance. Change in average memory consumption grows more than linearly compared to reduction in performance when increasing the number of threads.

SOM Experiments Results. We next looked at the *Higher Order Mutation Testing* strategy for the Judy project, in particular the four different algorithms (*Last2First DifferentOperators, ClosePair* and *RandomMix*) to combine first order mutants (FOMs) into second order mutants (SOMs) implemented in Judy [9,10]. Also in this case, we were interested in performance changes and quality of mutation score. In running the experiment, we noticed that the number

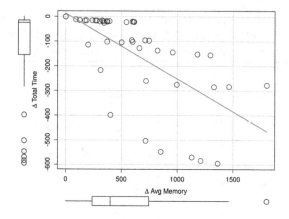

Fig. 4. Delta time vs delta average memory

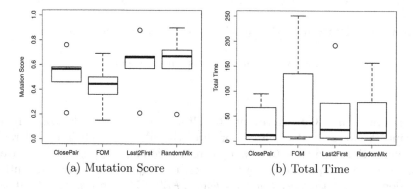

(a) Mutation Score   (b) Total Time

Fig. 5. Application of different SOM strategies vs FOM

of generated mutants was reduced at least by 50 % for some of the strategies and projects. Mutation score for all SOM strategies was higher than for FOM (Fig. 5a), while total time was generally lower for the three strategies in comparison with FOM (Fig. 5b). Running a Friedman non-parametric test for the differences across groups yielded significant results (0.05, two-tailed) for generated mutants ($p = 0.0089$), mutation score ($p = 0.0031$), and total time ($p = 0.0009$). However, like mentioned, the improvement of mutation score might be due to the inclusion of less equivalent mutants by applying such strategies.

When comparing individual SOM strategies, the *ClosePair* strategy gave the lowest mutation score, while *Last2First* and *RandomMix* produced very similar results for most of tested projects. This can be caused by the fact that neighboring mutants from the list of FOMs combined same type of mutants and the highest number of equivalent SOM mutants were generated using this strategy.

> *EXP3. SOM strategies improve the results in terms of mutation score and in terms of generated mutants, having positive benefits on the performance. However, manual inspection is needed to understand how many equivalent mutants are generated.*

Threats to Validity. We have several threats to validity to report [17].

For *internal validity*, measurements performed were averaged over several runs to reduce the impact of external concurring for resources. One of the main issues is the reliability of mutation score as quality indicator. The score always includes equivalent mutants as the automated detection is undecidable [9], and the only way to discover them is by manual inspection — unfeasible for larger projects. In fact, two projects with the same mutation score might be quite different depending on the number of equivalent mutants. We also used thresholds for the definition of the selective operators, and some sensitivity analysis can be more appropriate to define the best ranges.

Related to *external validity*, we cannot ensure that results generalize to other projects. However, we selected 9 heterogeneous projects in terms of size, code coverage. More insights will be given by testing on even larger software projects of industrial partners. Furthermore, the package of the current experiments will be available to increase external validity by means of replications.

For *conclusion validity*, we applied several statistical tests and simple linear regression in different parts of the experiment. We always used the non-parametric version of the tests, without normality distribution assumption, and we believe to have met other assumptions (type of variables, relationships among measurements) to apply each test.

4   Related Works

There are several related works about experimental evaluations of tools for automated mutation testing in JVM environments.

One of the first experimental evaluations [13] was done on the mutation operators of the Mothra project omitting two, four and six of the most populous mutation operators. The test cases killed 100 % of mutants generated by selective mutation. These test cases were then run on non-selective mutants. These test cases killed almost 100 % percent of mutants. Out of 22 mutation operators used by Mothra, 5 were key operators that provide almost the same coverage as non-selective mutation [14].

Madeyski et al. provided an experimental evaluation comparing the performance of generating mutants between Judy and MuJava on various Apache Commons libraries [10]. From the experiments, Judy was able to generate at least ten time more mutants per second as MuJava.

In 2011, the applicability of mutation testing was examined in Nica et al. [11]. The selected tools were MuJava, Jumble and Javalanche, focusing on the performance of generating mutants. The only tool able to generate mutants was MuJava generating about 123 class-level mutants and 30,947 method level mutants in approx. 6 hours. Jumble and Javalanche showed configuration difficulties and low performance. The main conclusion was that mutation testing was too slow to be used in real world software projects.

In 2013, Delahaye et al. compared Javalanche, Judy, Jumble, MAJOR and PITest on several sample projects [4]. The results showed that Jumble, MAJOR and PITest were able to finish the analysis for every project, while Judy generated the highest number of mutants and Javalanche the lowest number of mutants. The research indicated that mutation testing tools still need a lot of improvements to be usable in real world projects.

In 2015, Rani et al. compared MuJava, Judy, Jumble, Jester and PITest in an experimental evaluation [15]. The experiments were run on set of short programs (17-111 LOC). The research showed that all the tools produced almost the same average mutation scores except of PITest, which produced 25 % higher score than the rest of the tools. One of the conclusions was that a new mutation system for Java should be created, with faster generation and execution of mutants.

In 2016 Klischies et al. run an experimentation considering PITest on several Apache Commons projects. As metric for the experiments authors use the inverse of mutation score, as an indication of the goodness of the mutation operator set. They overall considered Mutation Testing applicable to real world projects with a low number of equivalent mutants, inspected manually, on the set of projects that were considered. However, strong concerns remained for the applicability to larger projects and in case code coverage within projects is too low, making the whole mutation analysis less effective [8].

Our work is different from the aforementioned set of related works as we focus on the selection of the best mutation operators and mutation strategies for improvements in performance on a set of medium sized projects. We can directly compare the SOM experiments results with Madeyski et al. [9], getting the same results in terms of increase of mutation score and performance improvement.

5   Discussion

There are several findings about the application of Mutation Testing that we put forward in the current paper. The general performance of Mutation Testing is impacted by Mutation Size, that is the size of the project and the code coverage level (*RQ1*). When taking into account the applicability of Mutation Testing, is appropriate to consider Mutation Size (LOCs size and code coverage) as an indication of the time required. This can be a good indicator to use by analogy for the application to other projects. A good strategy for the application of Mutation Testing is, in fact, to first increase code coverage to good levels, as having lower code coverage levels cannot tell much about the quality of tests. Clearly, larger coverage impacts on the execution of the tests, while mutant generation and mutant compilations stay the same. Taking into account multiple threads, time reduction decreases less than linearly with the increase of memory consumption. Mutation Testing can be optimized by looking at points in which parallelization does not bring enough incremental benefits. For the set of projects considered, 2–3 threads are effective numbers for performance / memory resources optimization.

Identifying the most efficient operators and applying *selective operators* improves the results in terms of runtime performance at the expense of lower mutation score and lower number of mutated classes (*RQ2*). This is a strategy that can be applied to extend the applicability of Mutation Testing to allow to run the approach to wider set of projects. In the selective strategy we looked at the efficiency of the operators in terms of killed mutants, but other approaches may look at the operators that generate more mutants. Based on the results, we believe that this set of strategies can help to apply Mutation Testing within industrial contexts, as default configurations can lead to a larger overhead in running the process. However, practitioners would need to fine-tune the Mutation Testing environments according to the specific projects needs. We included a list of selected operators efficiency based on the overall set of projects, that can give indications for application to other projects.

We looked at the impact of *Second Order Mutation* to recombine *First Order Mutants* and reduce in this way the number of mutants *RQ3*. All different substrategies considered (*Last2First DifferentOperators, ClosePair, RandomMix*) improve in terms of time required to run mutation testing, with higher mutation score than considering the initial mutants. However, while improvements in time are due to the lower number of generated mutants, mutation score can be influenced by equivalent mutants, as such manual inspection would be suggested to look for the effect on each considered project.

6 Conclusion

Mutation Testing is still an evolving testing methodology that can bring great benefits to software development. With increasing computational resources, it can reach wider adoption within industry, aiding to build more robust software. However, there are still aspects that hinder its usage, namely the computational complexity, equivalent mutants and possible lack of integration tools [9].

In this paper, we looked at the current support of Mutation Testing in JVM environments, with an experimental evaluation based on industrial partner's needs. We focused on various aspects of performance, evaluating different strategies that can be applied to reduce the time needed for mutation analysis. We evaluated how *selective operators* and *second order mutants* can be beneficial for the mutation testing process, allowing to reduce runtime overhead. Based on the results, we believe that Mutation Testing is mature enough to be more widely adopted. In our case, the experimental results have been useful for knowledge transfer in an industrial cooperation, with future works aimed at exploring the experimented approaches on the company's source code repositories.

Acknowledgments. We are grateful to the developers of both PITest and Judy for feedback provided in the usage of the tools. In case of Judy, the SOM experiments have been possible with a newer version provided by the developers.

References

1. CJBS Insight: Cambridge university study states software bugs cost economy $312 billion per year. http://insight.jbs.cam.ac.uk/2013/financial-content-cambridge-university-study-states-software-bugs-cost-economy-312-billion-per-year/
2. Crispin, L., Gregory, J.: Agile Testing: A Practical Guide for Testers and Agile Teams. Pearson Education, Boston (2009)
3. Dedík, V., Rossi, B.: Automated bug triaging in an industrial context. In: 42nd EUROMICRO Conference on Software Engineering and Advanced Applications, pp. 363–367. IEEE (2016)
4. Delahaye, M., Du Bousquet, L.: A comparison of mutation analysis tools for Java. In: 13th International Conference on Quality Software (QSIC), pp. 187–195. IEEE (2013)
5. DeMillo, R.A., Lipton, R.J., Sayward, F.G.: Hints on test data selection: help for the practicing programmer. Comput. **11**(4), 34–41 (1978)
6. Jia, Y., Harman, M.: Higher order mutation testing. Inf. Softw. Technol. **51**(10), 1379–1393 (2009)
7. Jia, Y., Harman, M.: An analysis and survey of the development of mutation testing. IEEE Trans. Softw. Eng. **37**(5), 649–678 (2011)
8. Klischies, D., Fögen, K.: An analysis of current mutation testing techniques applied to real world examples. In: Full-scale Software Engineering/Current Trends in Release Engineering, p. 13 (2016)
9. Madeyski, L., Orzeszyna, W., Torkar, R., Jozala, M.: Overcoming the equivalent mutant problem: a systematic literature review and a comparative experiment of second order mutation. IEEE Trans. Softw. Eng. **40**(1), 23–42 (2014)
10. Madeyski, L., Radyk, N.: Judy-a mutation testing tool for Java. IET Softw. **4**(1), 32–42 (2010)
11. Nica, S., Ramler, R., Wotawa, F.: Is mutation testing scalable for real-world software projects. In: VALID Third International Conference on Advances in System Testing and Validation Lifecycle, Barcelona, Spain (2011)
12. Offutt, A.J., Lee, A., Rothermel, G., Untch, R.H., Zapf, C.: An experimental determination of sufficient mutant operators. ACM Trans. Softw. Eng. Methodol. **5**(2), 99–118 (1996)
13. Offutt, A.J., Rothermel, G., Zapf, C.: An experimental evaluation of selective mutation. In: Proceedings of the 15th International Conference on Software Engineering ICSE 1993, pp. 100–107. IEEE Computer Society Press, Los Alamitos (1993)
14. Offutt, A.J., Untch, R.H.: Mutation 2000: uniting the orthogonal. In: Wong, W.E. (ed.) Mutation Testing for the New Century, pp. 34–44. Kluwer Academic Publishers, Norwell (2001)
15. Rani, S., Suri, B., Khatri, S.K.: Experimental comparison of automated mutation testing tools for Java. In: 2015 4th International Conference on Reliability, Infocom Technologies and Optimization (ICRITO), pp. 1–6. IEEE (2015)
16. Roy, N.K.S., Rossi, B.: Towards an improvement of bug severity classification. In: 40th EUROMICRO Conference on Software Engineering and Advanced Applications, pp. 269–276. IEEE (2014)
17. Wohlin, C., Runeson, P., Höst, M., Ohlsson, M.C., Regnell, B., Wesslén, A.: Experimentation in Software Engineering. Springer, Heidelberg (2012)

An Effective Verification Strategy for Testing Distributed Automotive Embedded Software Functions: A Case Study

Annapurna Chunduri[1(✉)], Robert Feldt[1], and Mikael Adenmark[2]

[1] Department of Software Engineering, Blekinge Tekniska Högskola,
SE-371 79 Karlskrona, Sweden
anuchunduri11@gmail.com, robert.feldt@bth.se
[2] Department of Systems and Integration Test, Scania AB,
SE-151 87 Södertälje, Sweden
mikael.adenmark@scania.com

Abstract. Integration testing of automotive embedded software functions that are distributed across several Electronic Control Unit (ECU) system software modules is a complex and challenging task in today's automotive industry. They neither have infinite resources, nor have the time to carry out exhaustive testing of these functions. On the other hand, the traditional approach of implementing an ad-hoc selection of test scenarios based on the testers' experience typically leads to both test gaps and test redundancies. Here, we address this challenge by proposing a verification strategy that enhances the process in order to identify and mitigate such gaps and redundancies in automotive system software testing. This helps increase test coverage by taking more data-driven decisions for integration testing of the functions. The strategy was developed in a case study at a Swedish automotive company that involved multiple data collection steps. After static validation of the proposed strategy it was evaluated on one distributed automotive software function, the Fuel Level Display, and found to be both feasible and effective.

Keywords: Verification strategy · Distributed automotive embedded software · Test coverage · Test process improvement · Case study

1 Introduction

The automotive industry has been significantly affected by the industrial software revolution over the past decade. The share and importance of software within a vehicle is growing steadily. Early on it was anticipated that 90 % of all future automotive innovations will be driven by software [10] and since then it has become clear that the industry is increasingly software-centric.

An automotive vehicle consists of Electronic Control Unit (ECU) systems, which are essentially embedded microcontrollers with corresponding software components. These ECU systems interact in order to execute the desired functionality in the vehicle like controlling the engine and operating air bags.

© Springer International Publishing AG 2016
P. Abrahamsson et al. (Eds.): PROFES 2016, LNCS 10027, pp. 233–248, 2016.
DOI: 10.1007/978-3-319-49094-6_15

In the past, each single ECU system had a single dedicated function. Hence, execution of a function required the software within only one of the ECU systems to execute independently. Nowadays, the functions are being designed to be realized through the interaction among different sub-functions and ECU systems via multiple Control Area Networks (CANs) [11]. Such cross-functionality i.e., a function distributed across multiple ECU systems and consequently across several system software modules is a common and complex phenomenon in today's automobile vehicles.

In the automotive industry, the standard V-model is most widely used for the engineering processes of embedded system software development. A typical V-model implemented by Scania [1], a major manufacturer of commercial heavy vehicles in the European automotive industry, can be seen in Fig. 1. Similarly, across the automotive industry, testing of the embedded system software functions occurs at different test levels. Here, the term 'test level' is used to indicate the test focus. *"Each test level describes an area of test responsibility"* [1]. For instance, at the system test level, for each individual ECU system of the vehicle, the software modules are mounted on the corresponding ECU system hardware like the engine and the gearbox and tested independently. At the vehicle integration test level, the software modules corresponding to all the ECU systems which make up the vehicle are tested together in their actual operational vehicle environment. The testing across the test levels is performed either as Hardware in the Loop (HIL) testing, where individual ECU systems or the entire vehicle is executed under simulated environments [12], or using real ECU systems or vehicles. The exact number of test levels and terminology used to describe each test level may differ from one automotive company to another. But what remains the fundamental similarity in the concept of testing is that, at each test level, the test strategy adopted aims to address and test the system software behavior at a different level of abstraction and provides a different degree of coverage of the object under test [21].

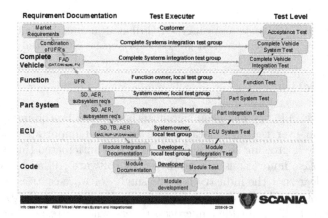

Fig. 1. The V-model implemented at Scania [1] to test their distributed embedded software functions

The distributed nature of functions across several embedded system software modules makes integration testing of the automotive system software a complex and challenging task [17]. Exhaustive integration testing of the distributed functions using the numerous variants across the software modules is not feasible since the automotive industry neither has infinite resources nor has the time to carry out such exhaustive testing [3]. On the other hand, going by the traditional approach of implementing an ad-hoc selection of test scenarios based on the testers experience typically leads to both test gaps and test redundancies across the test levels [8]. Hence, there is a pressing need for a feasible and effective verification strategy for integration testing of the distributed automotive embedded software functions that would help improve test coverage while reducing test redundancies and test gaps across the test levels. A review of research in test, verification, and validation in the automotive domain has revealed that research focusing on studying such challenges of high-level integration testing of the distributed automotive embedded software functions like in [11, 27], is limited. More over, research proposing and validating strategies and solutions to cope with such critical integration test challenges, like in [3], has been found to be sparse.

2   Research Design

The research was conducted in association with Scania, a major manufacturer of commercial heavy vehicles in the European automotive industry. This section provides an overview of the research design. It is based on the guidelines for conducting and reporting case study research in [20].

2.1   Research Questions

The goal of the research was to initially identify the challenges in automotive system software testing of the distributed functions. Thereafter, the research aimed to propose and evaluate a verification strategy which was based on addressing a suitable subset of the identified challenges. Here, the evaluation of the proposed strategy was in terms of its effectiveness and feasibility. Initially, the strategy was evaluated based on static comparitive analysis using scientific literature knowledge and industry expert opinion. Thereafter, the strategy was evaluated based on its implementation on a legacy distributed automotive software function- Fuel Level Display. Hence, in addition to having a realistic real world setting where the proposed strategy was studied, the analysis has been extended towards investigating the perceived effectiveness and feasibility of the proposed strategy based on static data collected from industry experts and scientific literature.

Based on the above mentioned aims of the study, the research questions (RQ) formulated are as follows.

RQ1: What are the major challenges with the current approach to test distributed software functions across test levels at the automotive case company?
RQ2: What is the feasibility and effectiveness of implementation of the proposed

process enhancement based verification strategy according to (a) scientific literature knowledge, (b) industry expert opinion and (c) Historic data in a real world setting?

2.2   Case Selection

Scania was chosen to be a suitable case for conducting the research and answering the research questions. Scania is present in more than 100 countries and has been successfully running for 250 years with over 45,000 employees. It represents a real world setting of an automotive industry that is facing software-related challenges in several fronts including the area of integration testing which is the focus of the current research. Hence, this single-case study has been deemed appropriate due to its *representitive* nature [31] of the automotive industry companies that are effected by the advent of software in the field of integration testing.

2.3   Data Collection Procedure

One of the data collection methods was through conducting interviews of different practitioners involved in the software testing activities at the case company. A non-probabilistic judgement based sampling technique [14] was employed for selection of interview subjects. Practitioners who were involved in, and had adequate knowledge and experience in testing were chosen. The identified practitioners included a total of 13 test engineers from different departments with varied experience belonging to 3 categories based on test levels, which are, System Test Engineers, Function Test Engineers, and Lab and Vehicle Integration Test Engineers. The interviews conducted were face-to-face, semi-structured interviews with open-ended and close-ended questions. Apart from interviews, data from relevant artifacts in databases and archived documents in the form of test reports, test results, test cases, function requirements specification and function architecture design documents among others have been used as alternative sources of data to achieve data triangulation [20].

2.4   Data Analysis Procedure

The data collection methods facilitated collection of both qualitative (predominant) and quantitative data through interviews, archived documents and databases. Strauss and Corbin's Grounded Theory (GT) approach [26], a commonly used method that facilitates the analysis of qualitative and quantitative data was employed to answer the research questions. The three steps of coding process - open coding, axial coding and selective coding- were performed. The theory so generated was confirmed through the hypothesis confirmation method of triangulation. In addition to data traingulation, user-group triangulation [30] based on selection of interview subjects from multiple categories and multiple subjects from each category, and evaluator traingulation [30] based on reviewing the results obtained with several researchers working within similar areas of research was employed. Hence, the final output of data analysis presents results that are both grounded and supported by a body of evidence.

2.5   Validity Procedure

The proposed strategy addresses process-based challenges. The validity of the strategy was evalutated based on its *effectiveness* of obtaining the desired results and its *feasibility* for implementation with optimum cost and effort. To assess these aspects of the strategy, a static comparitive analysis of the process-enhacement approach proposed in this strategy with alternative process enhancement approaches was performed. This analysis was based on scientific literature knowledge and industry expert opinion. Here, scientific literature knowledge was captured by conducting a literature review as per the guidelines presented in [19]. To capture industry expert opinions, six practitioners from Scania with vast experience and high knowledge in the relevant areas were carefully chosen. The evaluation study was conducted based on an assesment of the *cost*, in terms of time and people effort in implementing the strategy, *certainty of Return on Investment (ROI)* in terms of the likelihood that the implementation of the strategy would bring the desired results, and *value of the ROI* in terms of the extent to which the results obtained on implementing the strategy solve the challenges at hand. There after, historic data pertaining to testing a distributed automotive software function - Fuel Level Display across the different test levels for three test rounds spread over three months was collected. This historic data was then used to implement the proposed strategy and analyse the results to assess its feasibility and effectiveness in a real world setting.

3   Challenges in Automotive System Software Testing

The challenges, in the form of issues, pertaining to the approach implemented to test distributed automotive software functions across the test levels at the case company have been summarized and presented in Table 1 to answer research question RQ1. It was identified that the challenges found through the case study were similar to the challenges presented in exisiting scientific literature [11,27]. The study of the interdependent relationships that exist among the identified issues helped establish that there is a very intricate relationship that can be represented through a multi-way dependency among the identified set of people, process and technology issues. For instance, let us consider the complex relationship between one identified set of people, process and technology issues presented in Fig. 2. Hence, it was inferred from the results obtained on performing several steps of data analysis that, an intricate set of people, process and technology issues formed the source for the fundamental issues for integration testing of the distributed software functions at the case company.

A further study of the areas of people, process and technology and the relationships that exist between the issues within these areas in the current context was performed. It was then identified based on literature [18] and on case study results (refer to Fig. 2), that process issues lie at the core of the three identified issue areas. Technology is adopted to fit the process established, and people knowledge and effort is built around the process. Hence, addressing the process

Table 1. Identified challenges in the form of issues with current approach to test distributed embedded software functions at Scania

SNo	Issue category	Description of issues
1	People Issues	Ambiguity of test role at function test level and a lack of bigger picture of function test effort distribution across test levels
		Lack of appropriate means to share knowledge pertaining to test results across the test levels
2	Process Issues	Incomplete, vague and untestable higher level function requirements specification
		Variant-focused testing is highly dependent on each individual tester's knowledge with lack of means to handle function variants through simplistic representation
		Lack of adequate traceability across requirements and test results of the different test levels
3	Technology Issues	Lack of tool support to assist in test management, requirements management and change management
		Complexity of having test artifacts (test results, test reports, test cases, etc.) and function and system requirements spread across multiple locations with limited interoperability
4	Fundamental Test Issues	No comprehensive function test coverage information across test levels
		Ambiguous and inaccurate test reports generated at vehicle integration test level
		Lack of test report generation at the function test level
		Lack of appropriate means to identify where or whether redundant testing and risky test gaps are present across the test levels

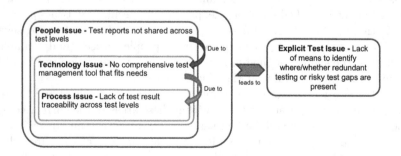

Fig. 2. An instance of the identified people, process and technology issue relationship

issues was deduced to be suitable to help pave the way for studying and addressing the people and technology issues that persist around the established process. Thus, the verification strategy proposed in this research aims to address the process issues in order to resolve the fundamental test issues identified in the approach for testing distributed embedded software functions at the automotive case company.

4 Process Enhancement Based Verification Strategy

The verification strategy proposes to enhance the function requirements specification by implementing a semi-formal scenario-based modelling that provides a means to capture complete and testable requirements with adequate function variant information. Thereafter, the strategy proposes to adopt a multi-level reuse concept of combining test results from the system, function and vehicle integration test levels by establishing appropriate traceability across the requirements and among the test results. Here, test levels with a focus on requirements-based test coverage have been considered to be within the scope. The obtained comprehensive test coverage information can then be used to identify test gaps and test redundancies and take more data-driven decisions to enhance integration testing and thereby improve test coverage of the distributed software functions.

4.1 Steps for Implementation of the Verification Strategy

The steps for implementation of the proposed verification strategy are presented in Fig. 3. A brief description of these steps is discussed below.

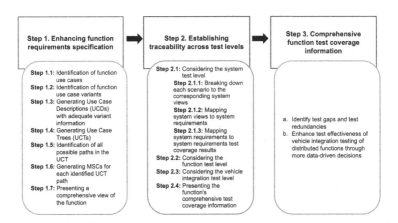

Fig. 3. Steps for implementation of proposed process enhancement based verification strategy

STEP 1. Enhancing Function Requirements Specification

The first step deals with adopting a semi-formal scenario-based modelling of the distributed software function requirements. It initially involves the identification of function use cases and use case variants. Here, each use case of a function describes one of its unique behaviour and use case variants are all possible contexts in which the function use case takes a different sequence of actions to execute the same behaviour described by the use case. For example, let us consider the function Fuel Level Display, for which two use cases are activation and deactivation of the feature of displaying low fuel level warning on the Instrument Cluster (display component) of the vehicle, when the activation and deactivation conditions are met. Here, for one of the use cases- activation of low fuel level warning- its variants can be identified to be all those contexts in which different steps are executed to reach the same outcome of displaying low fuel level warning when activation conditions are met. This here would mean that if activation of low fuel level warning is executed differently in vehicles with liquid engine and in vehicles with gas engine, then the use case variants include vehicles with liquid engine and vehicles with gas engine.

The next step is to generate a Use Case Description (UCD) for each use case of the function and a Use Case Tree (UCT) for each function. A UCD is a step-by-step description of the interaction between the participating systems required to execute the use case in its operational environment, written in structured natural language. There are several different templates proposed in literature for generating UCDs. One such template is presented by Somé [25] which is the inspiration for the current template proposed. The template is tailored and enhanced to be fit the automotive industry. A UCT is a graphical tree-structure representation of all possible paths containing unique combination of steps from the UCD for the execution of the use case.

Thereafter, all possible UCT paths, termed 'scenarios', are to be identified and corresponding Message Sequence Charts (MSCs) [25] are to be generated such that

(a) Nodes common to all variants are covered at least once for each variant, and
(b) Nodes specific to a particular variant are covered at least once for that variant.

Here, a scenario is one single sequence of interaction between the involved systems to execute a use case of the function. Adequate notes should be used within the MSCs to capture the important information of the UCD within the scenario models to enhance their understandability. This representation can hence be used to provide a comprehensive view of the function as a set of complete and testable function requirement scenarios with adequate variant information.

STEP 2. Establishing Traceability across Test Levels

This step deals with establishing traceability to obtain comprehensive test coverage information for the functions across the System, Function and Vehicle Integration test levels.

Initially, the system test level is taken into consideration. Here, there is a need to establish traces between the function scenarios involving multiple ECU systems and system level requirements of each involved ECU system. There after, the system level requirements test coverage pertaining to the mapped requirements are to be captured against the function scenarios. This provides an understanding of how much of the function is tested at the system test level across all the relevant systems. To establish traces between the function scenario and system level requirements, each function scenario is taken and broken down to the system view. Thus, each scenario has a corresponding set of system views of all the systems that contribute to its realisation. Here, each system view represents a set of all relevant input and output combinations pertaining to that system's role in the scenario.

The next sub-step is to consider the function test level. The test focus at this level is on testing the overall function requirements. Therefore, the test results should be mapped to the corresponding scenarios. Here, the scenarios and their expected outcomes represent the function requirements that are to be tested.

The last sub-step is to consider the vehicle integration test level. At this test level the test focus is on interface communication across the systems involved in the execution of the function scenarios. Therefore, at this test level, similar to the function test level, the test results are to be mapped against the function scenarios. Finally, as a result of implementation of this step, the obtained comprehensive function test coverage information across test levels is to be presented.

STEP 3. Comprehensive Function Test Coverage Information
The comprehensive function test coverage information so obtained can then be used within the last step of the strategy to identify risky test gaps, avoidable test redundancies and make a more data-driven decision during integration testing of the distributed embedded software functions to enhance their test coverage.

5   Validation Results and Discussion

The results of the study to validate the *feasibility* and *effectiveness* of the proposed verification strategy to answer research question RQ2 are presented and discussed in this section.

5.1   Scientific Literature and Industry Expert Opinion

As presented in Sect. 4, the proposed strategy is a semi-formal process enhancement approach (Approach 2) to solving the fundamental issues in integration testing of the distributed software functions. Hence, a static comparitive analysis to its alternatives - informal and formal process enhancement approaches (Approaches 1 and 3) was conducted to validate its relative feasibility and effectiveness. For the three alternative process enhancement approaches, the cost, the certainty of ROI and the value of the ROI was assessed using a relative ordinal scale of Highest(H), Medium(M) and Least(L). The results so obtained are presented in Table 2.

Table 2. Comprehensive results of comparative analysis of alternative process enhancement approaches

Approach	Estimation based on Scientific Literature			Estimation based on Industry Expert Opinion		
	Cost	Certainty of ROI	Value of ROI	Cost	Certainty of ROI	Value of ROI
(1)	L	M	L	L	H	L
(2)	M	II	M	M	M	H
(3)	H	L	H	H	L	M

It has been identified based on scientific literature knowledge that, informal approaches using natural language for the concerned process enhancement areas (refer to Table 1) present ease of adoption and lack of need of any special skills which implies low cost of implementation [9]. Yet, such natural language textual requirements and requirements based testing, irrespective of the level of abstraction of the system or software, have been found in ample of cases to still be prone to misinterpretation, ambiguity, inconsistencies and inaccuracy [5]. Moreover, it has been found through experience and reported in literature that in the automotive industry, textual natural language requirements and requirements based testing are *"only part of the game"* [29]. The industry identifies the need for the textual requirements at each level to be supported with adequate ways to capture, model and present various other complex attributes of the industry and thereby facilitate enhanced testing. A similar opinion has been found to prevail among the industry experts interviewed. It is evident that majority of them believe the ROI on such an investment will relatively add least value to the industry in terms of solving the test process issues at hand.

While formal methods have been found to be one of the best options for model based requirements specification, testing and aligning these two disciplines for safety critical systems like the systems within automotive industry [4], it has also been found to be difficult for practitioners to implement. It requires high experience in representing requirements in mathematical and logical notations [5,22]. This makes it is a highly cost-intensive solution. Such is also the opinion of the experts interviewed, who believe that formal approaches might lead to relatively highest cost of implementation with least certainty of ROI.

On the other hand, focusing on semi-formal methods through use cases and scenarios as a means to model and test the functional behaviour of a software or a system has been found to have their own challenges like the challenge of generating executable test cases for enhancing efficiency of testing [2]. But exploring semi-formal Model Based Testing (MBT) methods and addressing the challenges within it has been found to generate solutions that are more cost effective and scalable as compared to the formal MBT methods. This makes it an interesting area of research with high focus from the industry for whom cost effectiveness and feasibility of solutions are critical [4]. A similar estimation of relatively high value of implementing this approach has been found to be the opinion of industry experts. While it might cost the industry considerable time and effort for its implementation, majority believe it is a relatively most feasible approach that will likely produce relatively most effective results.

5.2 Historic Data

The strategy was implemented for Fuel Level Display function which is distributed across six systems, with two function variants and six function scenarios. The comprehensive function test coverage information across the test levels was captured for three test rounds (refer to Fig. 4). This helped identify the following:

- It was evident that most of the test effort across the test levels was focused on liquid engine trucks. This exposes the risky test gap in testing the function adequately across test levels for its implementation in gas engine variant.
- There is redundant testing of the main function scenarios (SCN), SCN1 and SCN5, at the function and vehicle integration test levels. On obtaining comprehensive function test coverage information across test levels, such redundancies can be avoided by ensuring the function and vehicle integration test levels cover different scenarios of the function.
- On analysing the system level function test coverage information, it was identified that most of the test gaps at the system level lie in three of the six systems involved.
- With this data, any change can be traced from the system it is pertaining to, to the appropriate function scenarios that it effects. This reduces the effort in analyzing the change impact at the vehicle integration test level.

Besides successfully obtaining the desired results, two critical gaps which have the capability to potentially hamper the effectiveness of the strategy were also identified. These include missing system-level requirements and missing test reports at the function test level. Another critical result obtained was the identification of a potential error in the function design for one of its variant which was unnoticed previously. This opens up the interesting possibility to more extensively study the

Use Case Variant	Function Scenario (SCN)	TW1602			TW1606			TW1610		
		System Test Level	Function Test Level	Integration Test Level	System Test Level	Function Test Level	Integration Test Level	System Test Level	Function Test Level	Integration Test Level
Liquid	SCN1	61.11%	100%	100%	77.78%	100%	100%	72.22%	100%	100%
	SCN2	57.89%	Not Tested	Not Tested	73.68%	Not Tested	Not Tested	73.68%	Not Tested	Not Tested
	SCN3	50%	Not Tested	Not Tested	71.42%	Not Tested	Not Tested	64.28%	Not Tested	Not Tested
	SCN5	52.94%	100%	100%	76.47%	100%	100%	52.94%	100%	100%
	SCN6	40%	Not Tested	Not Tested	50%	Not Tested	Not Tested	50%	Not Tested	Not Tested
Gas	SCN1	53.33%	Not Tested	100%	46.67%	Not Tested	100%	40%	Not Tested	100%
	SCN4	26.67%	Not Tested	Not Tested	46.67%	Not Tested	Not Tested	46.67%	Not Tested	Not Tested
	SCN5	43.75%	Not Tested	Not Tested	75%	Not Tested	Not Tested	50%	Not Tested	Not Tested
	SCN6	40%	Not Tested	Not Tested	50%	Not Tested	Not Tested	50%	Not Tested	Not Tested

Fig. 4. Comprehensive Fuel Level Display function scenario test coverage across the test levels for three test rounds

effectiveness of the proposed strategy for enhancement of distributed embedded software function design through scenario-based requirements specification.

While the implementation of the strategy in a real world setting helped study its practical feasibility and effectiveness, it also helped identify that its efficiency will likely reach its highest potential with the incorporation of suitable tool support and right people knowledge at steps of the strategy where maximum effort in terms of time and cost was invested. These steps include manual generation of the function scenario models and gathering information spread across multiple data sources to establish the desired traces across the test levels. Hence, these aspects that account to maximum effort in implementation present areas where the efficiency of the strategy can most likely be further enhanced. The current study therefore sets the process focused platform for moving towards a comprehensive solution for the issues with the current approach to test distributed embedded software functions in the automotive industry.

5.3   Threats to Validity

Refering to Runeson et al. [20], a description of the validity threats, along with the counter measures adopted to reduce them to the best of the researchers' ability are presented in this section.

Construct Validity. Construct validity deals with whether the operational measures studied accurately represent what is being investigated. In the conducted research, one construct validity threat was a possibility of designing interview questions for the case study which may be misinterpreted by the interviewees and lead to collecting irrelevant data. This risk was controlled by reviewing and revising the interview questionnaire and by performing simultaneous data collection and data analysis so the questionnaire can be readjusted if deemed necessary. Moreover, traingulation methods were employed to ensure the validity of what was being studied.

Repeatability and Reliability. Repeatability deals with whether the research conducted is repeatable, hence making it reliable. There was a risk that the case study conducted will not be adequately documented to make it repeatable. This risk was controlled by using the case study protocol to design and well document the research. Moreover, the actions undertaken throughout the research were reviewed and discussed among the researchers. Such auditing has been found to help mitigate this risk [31].

Internal Validity. Internal validity deals with how causal relationships are examined and relevant conclusions are drawn. In the conducted research, there is a possible risk of poor data analysis leading to incorrect conclusions. This risk was countered by discussing the results in length among the researchers and other senior practitioners at the case company. Moreover, the results of data analysis were backed with adequate literature support to validate the conclusions drawn. However, there still exists a possible internal validity threat that exists in this research due to the consideration of limited test data for drawing conclusions from the implementation of the proposed strategy. This threat can be reduced further by focusing future work on studying the results of implementation of the verification strategy on more extensive test data spread across several test rounds.

External Validity/Generalisability. External validity deals with the extent to which the findings can be generalized. Since the research was conducted within a single automotive company, the findings may not hold in other cases. This risk was reduced to a great extent by explaining in sufficient detail the context within which the study was conducted in Sect. 2.2. Another major external validity threat lies in the implementation of the proposed strategy for only one distributed embedded software function. These threats exist and can be mitigated by focusing future work on implementating the strategy to a larger number of more complex distributed functions and studying its feasibility and effectiveness within other automotive companies.

6   Related Work

Modelling requirements for verification is not a new concept. It has been adopted for various verification activities, most popularly for testing and is termed MBT. MBT has been found to help significantly enhance the testing process [4]. A semi-formal approach, based on the use of scenarios for modelling requirements within MBT is being increasingly studied in literature [2,15,28]. A large part of the research that focuses on using such semi-formal model-based approach to aligning requirements specification and testing through traceability has been found to involve proposing solutions but little research focus is on evaluating and validating these proposed solutions [4].

Tsai et al. in [28] explore scenario-based traceability in order to select test cases for impact analysis and regression testing of changes. The authors propose the use of scenarios in regression testing of system software function changes for reduced test effort through improved impact analysis. While fundamentally it is similar to the work in the current research in terms of exploring scenarios for improved testing, it differs in aspects where the current research aims to capture scenarios and propose their suitability in reducing test gaps and test redundancies and improving test effort distribution across multiple test levels of the automotive industry V-model.

Nebut et al. in [15] present work on deriving function tests from use cases in the form of test scenarios through test objectives. The major focus of the presented research, similar to [28], is on the automation of the process of using scenario-based requirements specification and testing. Where as, in the current research, the focus is on studying and validating the effectiveness of using scenarios for testing and traceability in the automotive industry.

Within the context of embedded system software, specifically in the automotive industry, most previous related work in MBT and subsequent study on traceability and alignment of the disciplines of requirements specification and testing is based on formal methods [13,24]. While some studies focus on the concept of test scenarios as a means of managing the requirements of the increasingly complex automotive embedded software, they take a formalized approach to the generation and use of test scenarios like in [7].

Moreover, most of the testing focus through such formal modelling methods is concentrated at the system integration and lower test levels of the automotive V-model [23]. While some apply their approaches to distributed functions at the vehicle integration test level like in [24], focus on this area in general is limited. MBT at the vehicle integration test level of the automotive test process and more specifically a semi-formal scenario-based MBT with established traces to lower-level system requirements and testing is unknown today but with great potential for improvement [6]. Such a multi-level reuse of test effort has been recognized for test effort reduction during test case generation [16]. Within the current thesis research, this concept of multi-level reuse is dealt with a broader perspective of reducing test effort by providing a means to take more data-driven decisions to improve test coverage by identifying and mitigating test redundancies and test gaps. Such comprehensive test strategies to cope with the complex aspects of the automotive software testing process like [3], are limited for integration testing of the distributed software functions.

7   Summary and Conclusion

With the advent of software for the realization of several functions of a vehicle, there has been and continues to be several challenges that the automotive industry faces to which it was unfamiliar a few decades ago [10,12,29]. One such identified facet of the software-related challenges is in the area of system software testing [11,27]. The automotive embedded software functions are increasingly distributed in nature, implying that the software modules for the realization of the functions are distributed across several ECU systems of the vehicle. This adds to the complexity of integration testing of the distributed software functions [27]. Research focusing on studying the challenges in integration testing of the distributed software functions [11,27] and possible effective and feasible strategies to tackle these challenges [3] within the automotive industry is limited. Hence, the current research contributes to the area of integration testing of distributed automotive embedded software functions.

The scenario-based function requirements specification proposed as part of the process enhancement based verification strategy in this research has been found to provide an effective and feasible means to capture test-driven requirements in the form of function scenarios. This was found to make them suitable for establishing the desired traceability. Thereafter, the stategy proposed in this research presents a manner in which the requirements and testing data across test levels can be comprehensively tied together to aid in effectively performing the integration testing of the distributed embedded software functions within the automotive industry. Implementation of the proposed strategy in a real world setting has given promising results. The broad concept of multi-level reuse of test results across the test levels of the automotive V-model was found to provide an effective and feasible means of capturing comprehensive test coverage information pertaining to the distributed software functions. Consequently, it has been identified that there is a critical link between requirements and testing that needs to be established across all test levels for implementing the multi-level reuse concept. Such traceability links provide a means to assess the effectiveness of the current approach to test the distributed software functions by identifying and mitigating test redundancies and test gaps across the test levels. It hence helps take more data-driven decisions for integration testing of the distributed software functions and thereby enhance function test coverage.

References

1. Adenmark, M.: Scania Test Levels, Scania Internal Document (REST08012) (2008)
2. Arnold, D., Corriveau, J.P., Shi, W.: Modeling and validating requirements using executable contracts and scenarios. In: Proceedings of the 8th ACIS International Conference on Software Engineering Research, Management and Applications (SERA), pp. 311–320. IEEE (2010)
3. Barhate, S.S.: Effective test strategy for testing automotive software. In: International Conference on Industrial Instrumentation and Control (ICIC), pp. 645–649. IEEE (2015)
4. Barmi, Z.A., Ebrahimi, A.H., Feldt, R.: Alignment of requirements specification and testing: a systematic mapping study. In: Proceedings of the 4th IEEE International Conference on Software Testing, Verification and Validation Workshops (ICSTW), pp. 476–485 (2011)
5. Von der Beeck, M., Margaria, T., Steffen, B.: A formal requirements engineering method for specification, synthesis, and verification. In: Proceedings of the 8th Conference on Software Engineering Environments, pp. 131–144. IEEE (1997)
6. Bringmann, E., Kramer, A.: Model-based testing of automotive systems. In: 1st IEEE International Conference on Software Testing, Verification, and Validation, pp. 485–493 (2008)
7. Conrad, M., Fey, I., Sadeghipour, S.: Systematic model-based testing of embedded automotive software. Electronic Notes Theor. Comput. Sci. 111, 13–26 (2005)
8. Dhadyalla, G., Kumari, N., Snell, T.: Combinatorial testing for an automotive hybrid electric vehicle control system: a case study. In: IEEE 7th International Conference on Software Testing, Verification and Validation Workshops (ICSTW), pp. 51–57. IEEE (2014)
9. Ferrari, A., dell'Orletta, F., Spagnolo, G.O., Gnesi, S.: Measuring and improving the completeness of natural language requirements. In: Salinesi, C., Weerd, I. (eds.) REFSQ 2014. LNCS, vol. 8396, pp. 23–38. Springer, Heidelberg (2014). doi:10.1007/978-3-319-05843-6_3
10. Grimm, K.: Software technology in an automotive company: major challenges. In: Proceedings of the 25th International Conference on Software Engineering, pp. 498–503. IEEE Computer Society (2003)
11. Kasoju, A., Petersen, K., Mäntylä, M.V.: Analyzing an automotive testing process with evidence-based software engineering. Inf. Softw. Technol. 55(7), 1237–1259 (2013)
12. Broy, M.: Challenges in automotive software engineering. In: Proceedings of the 28th International Conference on Software Engineering, pp. 33–42. ACM (2006)

13. Marinescu, R., Saadatmand, M., Bucaioni, A., Seceleanu, C., Pettersson, P.: A model-based testing framework for automotive embedded systems. In: Proceedings of the 40th EUROMICRO Conference on Software Engineering and Advanced Applications (SEAA), pp. 38–47. IEEE (2014)
14. Marshall, M.N.: Sampling for qualitative research. Family Pract. 13(6), 522–526 (1996)
15. Nebut, C., Fleurey, F., Le Traon, Y., Jezequel, J.M.: Automatic test generation: a use case driven approach. IEEE Trans. Softw. Eng. 32(3), 140–155 (2006)
16. Perez, A.M., Kaiser, S.: Integrating test levels for embedded systems. In: Proceedings of the Testing: Academic and Industrial Conference - Practice and Research Techniques (TAIC PART), pp. 184–193. IEEE, September 2009
17. Praprotnik, O., Gartner, M., Zauner, M., Horauer, M.: A test suite for system tests of distributed automotive electronics. In: 2nd International Conference on Advances in Circuits, Electronics and Micro-electronics (CENICS), pp. 67–70. IEEE (2009)
18. Radeka, K.: The toyota product development system: integrating people, process and technology by James M. Morgan and Jeffrey K. Liker. J. Prod. Innov. Manage 24(3), 276–278 (2007)
19. Rowley, J., Slack, F.: Conducting a literature review. Manage. Res. News 27(6), 31–39 (2004)
20. Runeson, P., Höst, M.: Guidelines for conducting and reporting case study research in software engineering. Empir. Softw. Eng. 14(2), 131–164 (2008)
21. Saglietti, F.: Testing for dependable embedded software. In: 36th EUROMICRO Conference on Software Engineering and Advanced Applications (SEAA), pp. 409–416. IEEE (2010)
22. Shah, U.S., Jinwala, D.C.: Resolving ambiguities in natural language software requirements: a comprehensive survey. ACM SIGSOFT Softw. Eng. Notes 40(5), 1–7 (2015)
23. Shokry, H., Hinchey, M.: Model-based verification of embedded software. IEEE Comput. 42(4), 53–59 (2009)
24. Siegl, S., Hielscher, K.S., German, R., Berger, C.: Formal specification and systematic model-driven testing of embedded automotive systems. In: Proceedings of the Europe Conference & Exhibition on Design, Automation & Test (DATE), pp. 1–6. IEEE (2011)
25. Somé, S.S.: Supporting use case based requirements engineering. Inf. Softw. Technol. 48(1), 43–58 (2006)
26. Strauss, A., Corbin, J.: Basics of Qualitative Research: Grounded Theory Procedures and Techniques. Sage Publications, Beverly Hills (1990)
27. Sundmark, D., Petersen, K., Larsson, S.: An exploratory case study of testing in an automotive electrical system release process. In: 6th IEEE International Symposium on Industrial Embedded Systems (SIES), pp. 166–175. IEEE (2011)
28. Tsai, W.T., Bai, X., Paul, R., Yu, L.: Scenario-based functional regression testing. In: Proceedings of the 25th Annual International Computer Software and Applications Conference (COMPSAC), pp. 496–501. IEEE (2001)
29. Weber, M., Weisbrod, J.: Requirements engineering in automotive development - Experiences and challenges. In: Proceedings of the IEEE Joint International Conference on Requirements Engineering, pp. 331–340 (2002)
30. Wilson, C.E.: Triangulation: the explicit use of multiple methods, measures, and approaches for determining core issues in product development. Interactions 13(6), 46–47 (2006)
31. Yin, R.K.: Case Study Research: Design and Methods. Sage Publications (2013)

Problems and Solutions in Mobile Application Testing

Triin Samuel and Dietmar Pfahl[✉]

Institute of Computer Science, University of Tartu, Tartu, Estonia
{triin.samuel,dietmar.pfahl}@ut.ee

Abstract. In recent years the amount of literature published about mobile application testing has significantly grown. However, it is unclear to what degree stated problems and proposed solutions are relevant to industry. To shed light on this issue, we conducted a literature survey to provide an overview of what current scientific literature considers problems and potential solutions in mobile application testing, and how often proposed solutions were reportedly evaluated in industry. Then we conducted a case study involving six software companies in Estonia to find out which of the problems are considered relevant by professionals, and which of the proposed solutions are considered novel and applicable. In total, we identified 49 potential problems or challenges in the mobile application testing domain and 39 potential solutions, some of which were implemented software tools while others were just theoretical concepts. Although some of the solutions were reportedly applied in practice, in most cases the literature did not give much information on the actual usage in industry of the proposed solutions. The case study revealed that while the relevance of each identified problem was highly variable from one company to another, there are some key problems that are generally considered vital both by research and industry. Regarding solution proposals, it turned out they are often described too much on the conceptual level or are too unrelated to the most urgent test-related problems of our case companies to be of interest to them.

1 Introduction

In the recent years, mobile devices have grown from futile entertainment gadgets to popular and ever-present media with a wide range of uses from social applications to business, medicine and others. This has brought the importance of testing mobile applications into highlight. As mentioned by various researchers [1–4] mobile applications have some unique qualities that demand new or modified testing approaches to ensure effectiveness and efficiency. Accordingly, the number of scientific papers written about mobile application testing is steadily increasing. However, it is uncertain whether the proposed solutions are usable in industry and whether the problems mentioned in industry are actually relevant in real mobile application development and testing. In order to find answers to these questions, we decided to carry out a literature survey and followed by a case study to assess the practical relevance of the information collected from literature. The exact research questions are as follows:

© Springer International Publishing AG 2016
P. Abrahamsson et al. (Eds.): PROFES 2016, LNCS 10027, pp. 249–267, 2016.
DOI: 10.1007/978-3-319-49094-6_16

- RQ1: What are the problems specific to testing of mobile applications as opposed to conventional applications, according to scientific literature?
- RQ2: What are the solutions (methods, tools) proposed by literature, if any?
- RQ3: According to literature, to what extent are these solutions used in industry?
- RQ4: Does industry consider the solutions proposed in the literature as relevant?
- RQ5: Does industry consider the solutions proposed in the literature as useful?

The rest of this paper is structured as follows. After a brief overview of the topic given in Sect. 2, the methodology is introduced in Sect. 3. Section 4 covers the results of the literature survey presenting answers to research questions RQ1 to RQ3. More specifically, it presents what scientific literature considers being problems in mobile application testing, which solutions are proposed, and how much the solutions are used in industry. Section 5 discusses the results of interviews conducted within six companies in order to evaluate how relevant industry considers the problems and solutions mentioned in literature. This addresses research questions RQ4 and RQ5. Section 6 provides a brief discussion of the limitations of the literature survey and case study. The paper ends with a summary of the results and conclusions.

2 Background

The first device that could be considered a smartphone was IBM Simon [5] released in 1994. Smartphones as we know them today started gaining mainstream popularity only in year 2007 when the first iPhone was released [6]. Since then, smartphone sales have skyrocketed [7]. What initially were thought to be just enhanced phones and entertainment devices have now developed into a wide range of different devices capable of performing business tasks, simplifying everyday life and enabling users to be continually connected to their work, social circles and service providers [1, 8]. Mobile devices are challenging conventional computers [9]. Consequently, the criticality of mobile applications has significantly increased [1, 3]. This has forced developers to focus more on the quality of their applications.

Testing of mobile applications incorporates many of the problems inherent to software testing in general. However, mobile devices also have qualities that differentiate them from conventional computers and therefore create testing challenges that are either unique to or more relevant in the case of mobile applications.

The three dominating mobile operating systems (OS) are Android, iOS and Windows Phone. According to net market share [10], Android was the most popular OS in the first quarter of 2016 with a 60 % market share. iOS followed with 32 %. Windows Phone was third with 3 %, followed by Java ME having 2 %.

Android is a free open-source operating system based on the Linux kernel and was released by Google in 2008. Android applications are normally developed in Java, compiled to Java bytecode and then to Dalvik bytecode to be run on Dalvik virtual ma-chine (DVM), with most of the code interpreted during runtime. From version 5.0, DVM has been replaced by Android Runtime (ART) that compiles the application to machine code during installation. Therefore, even though Android applications are commonly developed in Java, they cannot be run on Java Virtual Machine.

The second most popular operating system is iOS, a proprietary, closed source operating system released by Apple in 2007. The iOS operating system can be used only on Apple devices. Applications for iOS are normally developed either in Swift or Objective-C. The core of iOS is based on Darwin, a Unix operating system also used for Apple OS X, and Cocoa Touch is used for the user interface.

Windows Phone (previously Windows Mobile, now Windows 10 Mobile) is a proprietary closed-source operating system developed by Microsoft and released in 2010. Applications for Windows mobile devices can be developed in various languages like C#, .NET, C++ and HTML5. The latest mobile operating system from Microsoft was released as Windows 10 Mobile, reflecting Microsoft's intention to essentially merge the desktop and mobile versions of Windows [11] so that same apps could be run on both of them.

3 Methodology

In this section, we describe our research methods, i.e., how we conducted our literature survey and case study. We used the guidelines provided in [12, 13] as an orientation but didn't follow all of them to the letter.

3.1 Literature Survey

In order to get familiar with the literature, we first conducted an informal search in the ACM Digital Library. We searched for articles related to problems in mobile application testing published in 2007 or later because that was the year when the first iPhone, as well as the first alpha version of Android was released. Since we did not use any additional filtering, we got an excessive amount of results which we ordered based on relevance. We skimmed through the most relevant search results and manually chose 26 articles that seemed relevant to the question in hand by title.

Through reading the initial papers, we learned some additional keywords and search criteria that could be used. We also noticed that most of the results were conference papers and papers that mentioned problems usually also discussed solutions to them. We then conducted a second, more formal and structured search for journal articles. Since some relevant papers might not be indexed by the ACM Digital Library, we conducted the second search in the following four databases:

- ACM Digital Library
- SpringerLink (Computer science)
- Scopus (Computer science)
- ScienceDirect (Computer science)

We applied the following inclusion criteria:

- Only journal articles
- Published 2007 or later
- Full-text is available in the database

We applied the following exclusion criteria:

- Papers that were mainly about hardware-related, low-level communication or network issues, as opposed to end-user mobile applications.
- Papers to which we do not have full text access rights.
- Articles that do not analyse or make new contributions to the testing process itself; for example, if the paper was about developing a non-testing-related mobile application and at the end it was tested just to prove that the application works, then the article is not really about testing, even though it features it.
- Papers that are about mobile web application testing. Since web applications run in a browser or in a browser-like program, they don't inherit many of the challenges that native mobile applications have and are often more similar to web applications meant for desktop devices than to native mobile applications [14].
- Testing techniques that are not meant for consumer-oriented mobile applications.

The exact search queries can be found in Appendix I of [15]. The second, formal, search yielded 374 results, 355 of which were unique. Out of these, 84 were left after manual filtering based on the title. Therefore, the total set of abstracts to read was 26 + 84 = 110. Based on the abstract, 57 papers were discarded, which results in a set of 53 papers to read. While reading we discarded two papers because one had low relevance and one was superseded by another more recent publication. This left us with 50 publications.

Extracting Problems and Solutions. For each of the selected publications, we highlighted problems and solutions mentioned. If a solution was proposed in the paper, we assigned an approximate category to it and wrote the most important keywords concerning the solution to the front page. After reading all publications, we went through all the highlighted parts concerning RQ1 and wrote out all the found problems. Researchers rarely used the word 'problem', but often highlighted 'challenges' to justify the necessity of the solution they were going to propose. Offering a solution clearly shows that they considered the 'challenge' something that needed to be solved, so we counted these as problems. Some problems were also collected from general discussion parts of the papers.

After extracting a list of problems, we went through the papers again to write summaries of the proposed solutions (RQ2). The solutions were based mostly on the highlighted parts and the keywords we had written on the papers while reading, but details often needed to be clarified from other parts of the paper.

Assessing Whether Proposed Solutions were Evaluated in Industry. After we had extracted the list of solutions from the selected papers, we analysed the papers once again with the goal to find evidence that proposed solutions had actually been evaluated or applied in industry (RQ3).

3.2   Case Study

Selection of Industry Professionals. We compiled a set of 23 potentially relevant companies based on a Google search and our existing knowledge about software companies in Estonia. Then we explored web sites of the companies and selected those which fulfilled the following criteria:

- Operate in Estonia
- Deal with testing of native mobile applications. If a company develops native mobile applications, then we assumed that testing is done unless the home page hints that it is outsourced
- Are not a one-person company
- Seem professional enough to pay attention to the testing process

This restricted the list to seven companies, which we contacted. Five of the contacted companies replied and were willing to participate. In addition to these, one of the chosen companies put us in contact with a very suitable, but less known company that we were not aware of, which also agreed to participate. This resulted in a total of 6 companies to interview. We then asked our contacts to suggest interviewees involved in testing native mobile applications. In two cases we used pre-existing in-company contacts to find a suitable person in the company to interview.

Participating Companies. The following companies were selected:

- Fob Solutions: a mobile-oriented quality assurance company that on the side also provides development of web and native mobile applications. Fob Solutions has about 20 testers and some developers who work with Android, iOS and Windows Phone. We talked to the head of quality assurance.
- Testlio: a company that provides a community-based testing service. Testlio manages the testing process and prepares everything necessary, but actual testing is performed by a network of approximately 200 freelance testers who are not employees of Testlio. Testlio works with Android, iOS, Windows Phone and to a lesser degree BlackBerry. In Testlio testing is performed manually and the company doesn't diagnose the found problems. The company does have its own platform to facilitate testing but it mostly has management functionalities, not test running or generation. We interviewed a QA manager that we knew prior to the interview.
- TestDevLab: a quality assurance company that in addition to the more common testing services also provides battery, penetration and data usage testing. About 50 people are involved in Android, iOS and Windows Phone applications testing in TestDevLab. TestDevLab QA engineers are not oriented to a certain platform, therefore my interviewee had worked with different platforms (web, iOS, Android) in different projects. TestDevLab owns a test automation tool called Apimation[1]. The company has its headquarter in Latvia but it is common for their employees to

---

[1] https://apimation.com.

temporarily move to where the client is located. Therefore, we got a chance to talk to one of their QA engineers who lives in Estonia.

- Wazombi: a company focused on providing end-to-end solutions where everything from electrical engineering to UI design is done in one house. Wazombi works with Android and iOS, but as learned from the interview, most of their Android applications are not Java-based. Instead, Xamarin and C# are used. Xamarin also constitutes the only test generation tool mentioned by case study participants. Since the company is more oriented on development, it has only one person specifically assigned to mobile application testing, whom we interviewed.

- MoonCascade: a company that mainly provides mobile, responsive web and back-end development. From mobile platforms, Android, iOS and Windows Phone are used. There are four people working at mobile application testing. Some testing frameworks like Appium and Selendroid are used for test running. We interviewed the lead of the quality assurance team.

- Mobi Lab: a mobile application design and development company, formerly a part of current parent company Mobi Solutions. They work with Android, iOS and Windows Phone. We interviewed the only dedicated tester, but developers are also responsible for testing the applications that they are making.

Producing a Problem-Solution Matrix. Explaining every solution proposed in the literature to our interviewees would have resulted in unrealistically long and inefficient interviews. Therefore, we planned to only present solutions to problems that interviewees previously identified as being highly relevant to them. Since we did not have any information about the perceived relevance of each problem prior to the interview, it was not possible to choose the set of solutions to explain beforehand. We needed a mapping of problems and solutions that we could use during the interview to choose which solutions to explain.

In order to find out which problems a given solution solves, we used the knowledge of the solutions that we had gained from reading the papers, as well as the problems and challenges that researchers presented as justifications for their solution. For each problem-solution combination there were 4 options:

- 'Y' - a proposed solution significantly contributes to solving the given problem
- 'Partly' - partly solves the problem
- 'Maybe' - might be useful, but more information is needed to know
- Blank - a proposed solution does not address this problem

This resulted in the problem-solution matrix described in Sect. 5. Having this matrix handy allowed us to present exactly those solutions that were related to the most urgent problems highlighted by the interviewee, no matter which problem that was.

The Interview Process. The interview structure was as follows:

1. We introduced the research problem and collected some general information about the company. This information included the number of employees involved in testing mobile applications, whether the company is oriented at testing or development, mobile platforms the company works with, and experience with using or

developing automated solutions for mobile application testing. In addition to this, before showing the list of problems acquired from literature, we asked whether the interviewee sees any notable challenges in mobile application testing.

2. We presented the list of testing problems found from literature and asked the interviewee to rate the relevance of each problem for their actual mobile application testing. The answers were given on a multiple choice scale that also included options for "N/A" and "Already solved". The questionnaire can be found in Appendix II of [15].

3. We looked at those problems the interviewee considered important (marked as "Definitely") and used the Problem-Solution mapping presented in Sect. 5 to extract the set of corresponding solutions proposed in literature. Thereafter, we introduced these solution ideas to the professional and asked which of them seem potentially useful in practice. Since the respondents were only interested in practically applicable solutions and time was scarce, we omitted articles that were very general or too theoretical.

The time planned for each interview was 1.5 h. The first interview part took about 10 min while the duration of the second part was dependent on how fast the interviewee filled out the questionnaire, averaging at about 30 min. Duration of the third part was affected by how many problems the interviewee considered relevant in the questionnaire. Two respondents filled out the questionnaire very fast, which resulted in these interviews taking only 1 h. One interview was extended to 2 h because there were many potentially relevant solutions to present and discuss.

4   Results from the Literature Survey

The results from the literature survey were used to answer research questions RQ1-3:

- RQ1: What are the problems specific to testing of mobile applications as opposed to conventional applications, according to scientific literature?
- RQ2: What are the solutions (methods, tools) proposed by literature, if any?
- RQ3: According to literature, to what extent are these solutions used in industry?

4.1   Findings Related to RQ1

In this sub-section, we give an overview of problems and challenges (in the following subsumed under the term 'problems') that are specific to or especially relevant in the testing of mobile applications (cf. Table 1). We grouped problems according to their core causes. In reality, however, each problem can have more than one cause and, thus, the grouping shown in Table 1 should be taken as an approximation made in an effort to simplify reading. A detailed description of each problem can be found in [15]. In total 49 problems were identified.

Table 1. List of identified problems grouped by core cause

Core cause	Problems with references
Fragmentation (large variety of platforms with different operating systems, hardware, storage, and screen sizes)	P1 [3, 18, 20, 22–25] - P2 [1] - P3 [23, 26] - P4 [27, 28] - P5 [23] - P6 [22, 26] - P7 [22]
External software dependencies	P8 [1, 29] - P9 [30] - P10 [31]
Frequent external communication	P11 [1, 9, 16, 19] - P12 [19, 24, 29, 31–35] - P13 [1, 23, 24, 36] - P14 [1, 37] - P15 [38] - P16 [9, 21, 28, 32] - P17 [9, 39] - P18 [39] - P19 [39]
Variable users and usage contexts	P20 [40, 41] - P21 [21, 42] - P22 [21, 28, 43–45] - P23 [26] - P24 [35, 43] - P25 [21, 43, 46] - P26 [33, 45] - P27 [43]
Fast evolution	P28 [16, 32] - P29 [18, 21, 22, 47] - P30 [9, 46]
Limited resources	P31 [24, 35] - P32 [35] - P33 [1] - P34 [46]
Novelty	P35 [32, 41, 48–50] - P36 [21, 32, 46, 51] - P37 [36] - P38 [41, 51] - P39 [9, 21, 32, 43, 52]
Limitations related to platform implementation.	P40 [23, 29, 39, 48] - P41 [48] - P42 [19, 53] - P43 [54] - P44 [1, 24] - P45 [55] - P46 [32, 56] - P47 [35]
Other problems	P48 [9, 16] - P49 [9]

4.2   Findings Related to RQ2

In this sub-section, we present the tools and methods proposed in the literature for solving the problems described in the previous sub-section (cf. Table 2). The solutions

Table 2. List of identified solutions grouped by type

Type	Solutions with references
Theoretical	S1 [4] - S2 [21] - S3 [27] - S4 [47] -S5 [33] -S6 [57] - S7 [23]
General tools & methods	S8 [35] - S9 [17] - S10 [29] - S11 [31, 34, 48] - S12 [50] - S13 [26]
GUI-based testing	S14 [52, 58] - S15 [16, 59]
Record-and-replay	S16 [56]
Model-based	S17 [40] - S18 [30]
Model-learning	S19 [55, 60] - S20 [61] - S21 [24]
Search-based	S22 [61–64]
Performance testing	S23 [36]
Reliability testing	S24 [38] - S25 [19] - S26 [39]
Compatibility	S27 [22] - S28 [20] - S29 [18]
Usability and user testing	S30 [65] - S31 [32] - S32 [54] - S33 [28] - S34 [46] - S35 [45]
Security testing	S36 [37] - S37 [66] - S38 [25] - S39 [49]

are grouped by type. A detailed description of each solution can be found in [15]. In total, 39 solutions were identified.

4.3   Findings Related to RQ3

In this sub-section, we discuss to what extent proposed solutions (methods and tools) have reportedly been used in industry.

Most of the solutions listed in Sect. 4.2 were evaluated either on one or a few applications familiar to the researchers or on a more representative set of applications acquired from app stores. However, in both cases the evaluation was performed by the researchers themselves, usually in a controlled environment. Only one paper explicitly mentioned that their proposed solution was used in a company, i.e. Swisscom (S13). Also some proposed tools were evaluated on published apps (S16, S19, S21, S25, S37, S39) and one was partly tested on apps currently under development (S39).

However, publications were (co-)authored by individuals with a company affiliation. This applies to S1 (both authors affiliated with Microsoft), S5 (both authors affiliated with Nokia Research Center), S6 (one of the authors affiliated with Fujitsu Laboratories), S8 (all authors affiliated with Microsoft Research), S10 & S11 (one of the authors affiliated with NASA Ames Research Center), S25 (three out of four authors affiliated with Microsoft Research), S29 (first author is one of the founders of the TestDroid testing platform), S30 (one of the two authors affiliated with Ericsson Research), S35 (one of the authors affiliated with Telecom Italia). Even though in these cases it was not mentioned in the paper whether the proposed solution was evaluated in industry, it is highly probable that some of them are used in the companies to which (some of) the authors are affiliated. It is worth noting, however, that most of the affiliations are with research units within large corporations. Therefore, results reported in the related papers might not have been applied in the business units of these companies, and they might not be suitable for problems in the in the rest of the industry, i.e. in small and mid-sized companies.

5   Results from the Case Study

The results from the case study were used to answer research questions RQ4-5:

- RQ4: Does industry consider the solutions proposed in the literature as relevant?
- RQ5: Does industry consider the solutions proposed in the literature as useful?

In order to make the interviews conducted during the case study more efficient, we developed a problem-solution mapping based on the results from the literature survey. For easier viewing, we made the original file available on Dropbox[2]. Note that the columns in grey indicate solutions that were not presented in detail to the interviewees because they related to problems that were not of high priority for the interviewees.

---

[2] https://www.dropbox.com/s/ia8vgjr7a8ppxkr/Problem-solution%20matrix.ods?dl=0.

5.1   Findings Related to RQ4

Five of the six interviewed companies said that fragmentation was a significant problem in mobile application testing even before seeing the list of problems proposed in the literature. Testlio was the only company that didn't consider fragmentation as a significant problem because their community-based approach already ensures a high number of different platform, OS version, device, and screen size combinations. The interviewee from Testlio mentioned two challenges in mobile application testing. Firstly, there is a lack of fine-grained tools that testers could use to record GUI interactions leading to a fault. The ideal approach would be able to capture videos, screenshots with click positions and have better logs than the current approaches. The second problem was applications that need to be tested in very specific geographical locations, especially on iOS where location information is more difficult to mock than on Android.

The questionnaire answers provided by all of the participating companies are listed in Table 3. Questions corresponding to each question number can be found in Appendix II of [15]. Basically, interviewees were asked to tell for each problem P1 to P49 mentioned in the literature whether it is also a problem for them. The answer choices were: 'Definitely' – 'Maybe' – 'Probably not' – 'Definitely not', plus the answer options 'n/a' (not applicable) and 'Solved' (in case the problem existed but has been solved in the meanwhile). The first column shows the problem ID together with an indicator representing the relevance of the problem for the case companies. The symbol '++' indicates that at least four companies found the problem relevant (at least four times 'Definitely'), '+' indicates that two or three companies found the problem relevant (two or three times 'Definitely'), and '−' indicates that no company felt strongly that the problem is relevant (none of the companies stated 'Definitely').

The responses from the three companies that mainly focus on testing are displayed on the left while companies whose main area of business is mobile application development are displayed in the right half of Table 3.

The surveyed companies didn't agree on the relevance of any of the listed problems. However, some patterns can be pointed out. 18 of 49 listed problems were not considered relevant by all case companies. For example, testing inter-application communications (P14) and more sophisticated testing techniques like simulating external dependencies (P10), automatic page-load detection (P40) and ensuring completely clean application restart (P43) were never mentioned to be definitely relevant. None of the companies considered the lack of testing methods, tools or theory a significant problem (P33–P35, P37). Modelling applications before testing was not popular and some companies mentioned that testing on all devices is not needed because a set of supported devices is chosen before development. It can be argued that this practice of choosing a set of supported devices itself shows that testing an application on all potentially suitable devices is too difficult, expensive or time-consuming.

Some problems not considered highly relevant by companies mainly focusing on development were still considered potentially problematic by testing companies. These included acquiring a mental model of a complex application (P9), the unpredictability of external dependencies during testing (P12), ignoring unexpected user behavior

Table 3. Relevance of problems to our case companies

Problem	Testing companies			Development companies		
	Fob Solutions	Testlio	TestDevLab	Wazombi	MoonCascade	Mobi Lab
P1 ++	Definitely	Solved	Definitely	Maybe	Definitely	Definitely
P2 +	Solved	N/A	Probably not	Definitely	Definitely	Maybe
P3 +	Definitely	N/A	Definitely not	Maybe	N/A	Definitely
P4	Maybe	Solved	Definitely not	Definitely	Probably not	Definitely not
P5 +	Maybe	Solved	Definitely	Definitely not	Maybe	Definitely
P6 ++	Definitely	Solved	Definitely	Definitely not	Definitely	Definitely
P7 +	Definitely not	N/A	Definitely not	Solved	Definitely	Definitely
P8 +	Definitely not	Definitely	Definitely	Probably not	Definitely	Probably not
P9	Probably not	Maybe	Definitely	Definitely not	Definitely not	Definitely not
P10 −	Maybe	Maybe	Probably not	Maybe	Probably not	Definitely not
P11	Probably not	N/A	Definitely	Solved	Maybe	Probably not
P12 +	Definitely	Maybe	Definitely	Probably not	Probably not	Definitely not
P13 +	Definitely not	N/A	Definitely	Solved	Definitely	Definitely
P14 −	Probably not	Maybe	Probably not	Probably not	Maybe	Definitely not
P15 −	Maybe	Solved	Definitely not	Definitely not	Probably not	Definitely not
P16 +	N/A	Definitely	Probably not	Definitely not	Maybe	Definitely
P17 −	Maybe	Maybe	Maybe	Definitely not	Maybe	Definitely not
P18	Probably not	N/A	Definitely	Maybe	Maybe	Definitely not
P19 +	Probably not	N/A	Definitely not	Probably not	Definitely	Definitely
P20 +	Definitely	Definitely	Probably not	Probably not	Definitely	Maybe
P21 +	Maybe	Definitely	Definitely	Solved	Probably not	Maybe
P22	Maybe	Maybe	Definitely not	Solved	Definitely	Probably not
P23 +	Definitely	N/A	Definitely not	Definitely	Definitely	Maybe
P24	Maybe	Solved	Probably not	Probably not	Definitely	Probably not
P25	Probably not	Definitely	Definitely not	Probably not	Maybe	Probably not
P26	Probably not	Definitely	Probably not	Definitely not	Probably not	Definitely not
P27 +	Definitely	Definitely	Maybe	Probably not	Definitely	Definitely not
P28 +	Definitely	Maybe	Definitely	Probably not	Probably not	Definitely not
P29 −	Probably not	N/A	Maybe	Maybe	Maybe	Maybe
P30 −	Probably not	N/A	Maybe	Definitely not	Definitely not	Definitely not
P31	Maybe	Maybe	Maybe	Maybe	Definitely	Definitely not
P32	Definitely not	Maybe	Definitely	Definitely not	Probably not	Definitely not
P33 −	Probably not	N/A	Definitely not	Solved	Probably not	Definitely not
P34 −	Probably not	Maybe	Definitely not	Solved	Maybe	Definitely not
P35 −	Maybe	N/A	Definitely not	Definitely not	Probably not	Definitely not
P36 −	Solved	Maybe	Probably not	Solved	Solved	Definitely not
P37 −	Solved	Maybe	Probably not	Probably not	Solved	Definitely not
P38 +	N/A	N/A	Definitely	Definitely	Definitely not	N/A
P39 −	N/A	N/A	N/A	N/A	N/A	Probably not
P40 −	Probably not	N/A	Definitely not	Definitely not	Probably not	Probably not
P41 −	Solved	Maybe	Definitely not	Solved	Solved	Solved
P42 +	N/A	N/A	Definitely	Definitely not	Definitely	Probably not
P43 −	Probably not	Probably not	Definitely not	Definitely not	Solved	Solved
P44	Solved	Definitely	Definitely not	Solved	Solved	Solved
P45 −	N/A	N/A	N/A	Solved	Solved	Probably not
P46 −	Definitely not	Probably not	Definitely not	Probably not	Maybe	Definitely not
P47 −	Definitely not	Maybe	Probably not	Solved	Solved	Probably not
P48	N/A	Definitely	Probably not	Maybe	Probably not	Definitely not
P49 +	N/A	Maybe	Definitely not	Definitely	Definitely	Definitely not

(P15), users' variable mobile device usage experience (P21), insufficient OS failure logging (P30) and the usability and accessibility aspects of complex input mechanisms (P32). We suppose that testing companies do testing more thoroughly or are just more aware of their testing processes. In addition to this, if testing is performed by developers or at least in the same company, then the people doing the testing probably have a better overview of how the application is intended to function.

Since Testlio was the only company that actively uses a community-based testing approach as opposed to just testing in-house, different problems are sometimes considered relevant by them. Notably, fragmentation (P1) and the large number of test devices to buy (P6) that were considered problems by most companies are not a problem for Testlio because their testers use personal devices for testing. On the other hand, they are subject to some challenges that are not relevant for any other companies. For example, since their testers are working remotely, they need more advanced UI recording tools (P44) than companies that perform testing locally. The large number of test devices (P6) is also not a problem for Wazombi who mainly provides end-to-end services that include both hardware and software development.

The lack of design principles (P36) was considered already solved by guidelines provided by mobile operating systems and cross-platform principles were not considered necessary. The problem of not being able to modify a mobile application after installing (P41) was considered solved by either automatic updates provided by app stores or specialized software that can be embedded into applications for A/B testing. The fact that testing is expected to be faster for mobile applications was not considered a big obstacle because mobile applications on average were said to contain less functionality than desktop applications.

5.2   Findings Related to RQ5

In this sub-section we present the results regarding the extent to which industry professionals interviewed in our case study consider the solutions provided in literature potentially useful in practice (cf. Table 4).

11 solutions were presented to industry professionals based on the problems that they considered relevant. None of the solutions were uniformly accepted by the companies, although solution S26 (An approach for amplifying exception handling code) was considered useful by all the companies that found it applicable.

Solution S8 (MobiBug) was presented to all companies. Respondents from Testlio, TestDevLab and Mobi Lab considered it potentially useful. Wazombi commented that since even devices of the same model don't function completely identically, a model that assumes they do might be inaccurate. MoonCascade said that nowadays OS built-in logging is already more fine-grained than stated in the article and 3rd party libraries for monitoring fault configurations exist, there-fore this solution already exists.

None of the interviewees considered solution S9 (iTest) a useful innovation. Some mentioned that a solution of this kind already exists. Others were skeptical of whether this approach would work well because people rarely give any feedback when things work (Mobi Lab) and it is difficult to ensure a full variety of user profiles in registered testers (Testlio). One company expressed that the success of this approach highly depends on the tester incentive mechanism. Therefore, the technical solution alone does not bring much value.

Solution S10 (Symbolic execution of Android apps) was presented to two companies. TestDevLab considered it potentially useful while Wazombi said the solution would not applicable for them because it can only handle applications written in Java.

Solution S11 (JPF-Android) is not applicable to Wazombi whose applications are not Java-based. TestDevLab was hesitant about whether this would work and MoonCascade said the tool would be useful if it could emulate drivers of all kinds of sensors and developers manage to keep the tool up to date with new OS versions.

Most of the companies liked the concept of solution S16 (VALERA) and thought it would be useful. Wazombi was more skeptical due to the fact that VALERA does not record memory operations.

Solution S21 (Tool with 2 approaches for automated model-based testing) was only presented to the Testlio representative who found it useful.

Solution S23 (Unit-testing performance) was presented to Mobi Lab and TestDevLab. Mobi Lab found it useful while the latter commented that the duration of method execution can depend on things outside the developer's control, e.g. network conditions, therefore duration of execution cannot be accredited to just performance.

TestDevLab considered solution S25 (VanarSena) useful. Mobi Lab said that it is already used for Windows Phone applications.

Solution S26 (Approach for amplifying exception-handling code) was presented to 4 companies. For Wazombi, this solution wasn't applicable due to being Java-based, but the others considered it useful.

Regarding solution S28 (Knowledge base for compatibility testing) Mobi Lab thought it could work and Wazombi said it could work partly, for API version based problems. MoonCascade was skeptical about how an appropriate level of granularity could be set for recording results – if every combination of application version, device, OS version, etc. would be recorded separately then very few queries would get a reply from the database while in other cases there is a high probability of over-generalization. TestDevLab said that a solution like this is probably already integrated to some testing software.

Solution S29 (TestDroid) was not very well-received. Sob Solutions and Mobi Lab said that this solution already exists. TestDroid itself is available online and is not the only cloud-based testing platform. Testlio said that in principle the approach is plausible while TestDevLab thought it might be useful only for small teams that do not have access to an extensive set of test devices. MoonCascade was also of the opinion that for companies of significant size, it is better to have their own set of devices as cloud-based solutions are expensive, unreliable and do not have support for various test styles and frameworks.

In total, there were only 3 solutions that were considered relevant by all companies to which they were presented and who found them applicable, i.e. S10 (2 companies), S21 (1 company), and S26 (3 out of 4 companies). None of the respondents considered S9 a good solution and most were skeptical about S28 and S29.

Upon hearing the solution concepts, many interviewees expressed that the general concept of the solution is familiar to them or already exists. However, they had not marked the corresponding problems as 'Solved' in the questionnaire part of the interview. This implies that the concepts they already knew either do not fully solve the proposed problem or the professionals have not thought about using this concept to solve the given problem. The latter is compatible with our general observation that companies seem to consider the new challenges of mobile application testing inevitable and thus do not think about the possibility to eliminate them with the help of new methods and tools. In that sense, help from the scientific community could actually help if they were considered more seriously.

Several proposed solutions were considered to be either too theoretical, general or relating to problems that were already solved by the case companies. The latter point can to some degree attributed to the fact that we included articles published from 2007, i.e. almost 10 years ago, in the literature study. However, the two least supported solution concepts, TestDroid and iTest, were published in 2014 and 2012, respectively. Therefore, either the field of mobile application testing is developing so fast that only papers published less than two years ago provide practical value for companies or research is sometimes detached from the current problems in industry.

Another observation was that additional attention could be paid to the fact that companies use different tools for developing and testing mobile applications. For example, not all Android applications are developed in Java and cloud-testing platforms would be more useful if they supported different testing frameworks.

6 Discussion of Limitations

In the following, we summarize the limitations of our literature survey and case study.

6.1 Limitations of the Literature Survey

The literature study was performed by one person (the first author) within a limited amount of time (four weeks). Due to this resource limitation a systematic literature study following the guidelines defined in [12] to the letter was not viable. Therefore, it is possible that some relevant papers were either not found or filtered out incorrectly when applying the defined search strings and inclusion/exclusion criteria. Also, there was not enough time for conducting a thorough quality assessment of the included papers. Additionally, since the information was extracted from papers by just one person and without previously specifying what constitutes a problem or solution, the analysis is bound to be somewhat subjective, although we tried to mitigate this problem by having another person (the second author) review the results of the paper identification and selection. The limitation applies to the linking of problems to their potential solutions in the problem-solution matrix. Lastly, since papers from 2007 to 2016 were used in the study, it is possible that some of the problems mentioned in the literature have been solved and thus the problems have become obsolete. Also, Android was significantly more represented than other platforms in the set of found papers and therefore many of the found problems and solutions concern mobile applications on the Android platform.

Table 4. Relevance of solutions

Solution	Company					
	Fob Solutions	Testlio	Wazombi	TestDevLab	MoonCascade	Mobi Lab
S8	No	Yes	No	Yes	Exists	Yes
S9	Exists	Partly	No	No	Exists	No
S10			n/a	Yes		
S11			n/a	Maybe	Maybe	
S16		Yes	No	Yes	Yes	Yes
S21		Yes				
S23				No		Yes
S25				Yes		Exists
S26			n/a	Yes	Yes	Yes
S28			Partly	Exists	No	Yes
S29	Exists	Yes		Partly	No	Exists

6.2 Limitations of the Case Study

In our case study, we used [13] as a guideline but due to time and resource constraints, we didn't follow all recommendations to the letter. While both testing and development oriented companies in Estonia were included in the study, the initial list of companies was compiled mostly opportunistically, i.e. where the first author had some previous knowledge and (in some cases) personal contacts. Therefore, it is likely that the participants of this study are not fully representative for all companies in Estonia doing mobile application testing. During the interviews, participants were asked to assess the potential suitability of some solutions proposed in literature. Since it would be unreasonable to expect participants to read the relevant scientific articles, we shortly explained each solution concept that the interviewees were asked to assess on the spot. As a result, our personal bias and the quality of our explanations might have had an effect on the perceived usefulness of the solutions. Due to time constraints not all potential solutions were presented. In each case, the decision of which solutions to present was made based on the prioritization of problems and using the problem-solution matrix. This creates the possibility that the set of solutions proposed to the case companies might not have been complete.

7 Summary and Conclusion

We conducted a two-staged study involving a literature survey and a case study to find answers to five research questions concerning challenges and solutions of mobile application testing as seen by researchers and industry.

In the attempt to answer RQ1 and RQ2, 49 problems and 39 potential solutions were extracted in our literature survey. These lists answer research question 1 and 2, respectively. For RQ3, the result is less clear. Even though only one paper specified that the proposed solution is already used in industry, it is likely that some of the others are as well, considering that many authors were associated with companies active in the industry. Therefore, it can be said that the solutions are used in industry, but the extent of this usage cannot be adequately determined just based on scientific litera-ture. For RQ4, none of the problems mentioned in literature were considered uniform-ly relevant by all industry professionals. However, most companies considered frag-mentation a serious problem and usually mentioned it before being handed the ques-tionnaire. Many of the problems mentioned in literature were not considered im-portant by our case companies. Regarding RQ5, many of the solutions proposed in literature were too general, too little evaluated, or too little related to the most relevant problems, to be explained to and discussed with the professionals in sufficient detail. And of those that were presented and discussed, only a subset was uniformly consid-ered useful while others were said to already exist (i.e., are already implemented) or have significant shortcomings (and thus would not be considered for implementation).

In conclusion, research literature is addressing some problems that are considered very important by our case companies. However, there seems to be room for making research more useful for industry since many of the currently proposed solutions are considered as too much conceptual and too little practical by professionals.

Acknowledgements. We would like to thank Fob Solutions, Testlio, Mobi Lab, Wazombi, TestDevLab and MoonCascade. This research was supported by the Estonian Research Council.

References

1. Muccini, H., Di Francesco, A., Esposito, P.: Software testing of mobile applications: challenges and future research directions. In: Proceedings of AST 2012, Piscataway, NJ, USA (2012)
2. Paul, S.: Role of mobile handhelds in redefining how we work, live and experience the world around us: some challenges and opportunities. In: Proceedings of SIGCOMM 2010, New Delhi, India (2010)
3. Wasserman, A.I.: Software engineering issues for mobile application development. In: Software Engineering Issues for Mobile Application Development, Santa Fe, New Mexico, USA (2010)
4. Santos, A., Correia, I.: Mobile testing in software industry using agile: challenges and opportunities. In: Proceedings of ICST 2015, Graz, Austria (2015)
5. N. T., Did you know what was the first smartphone ever? PhoneArena, 31 July 2014. http://www.phonearena.com/news/Did-you-know-what-was-the-first-smartphone-ever_id58842. Accessed 10 May 2016
6. Apple Inc., Apple Reinvents the Phone with iPhone. http://www.apple.com/pr/library/2007/01/09Apple-Reinvents-the-Phone-with-iPhone.html. Accessed 12 May 2016
7. Statista Inc., Number of smartphones sold to end users worldwide from 2007 to 2015 (in million units). http://www.statista.com/statistics/263437/global-smartphone-sales-to-end-users-since-2007/. Accessed 14 May 2016
8. Martinie, C., Palanque, P.: Design, development and evaluation challenges for future mobile user interfaces in safety-critical contexts. In: Proceedings of the 2015 Workshop on Future Mobile User Interfaces, Florence, Italy (2015)

9. Corral, L., Sillitti, A., Succi, G.: Software assurance practices for mobile applications. Computing **97**(10), 1001–1022 (2015)

10. Net Applications, Mobile/Tablet Operating System Market Share January–March 2016. https://www.netmarketshare.com/operating-system-market-share.aspx?qprid=8&qpcustomd=1&qpsp=68&qpnp=1&qptimeframe=Q&qpmr=10&qpdt=0&qpct=3. Accessed 12 May 2016

11. Albanesius, C.: Nadella Raises Eyebrows With Plans to 'Streamline' Windows, PC Magazine, 23 July 2014. http://www.pcmag.com/article2/0,2817,2461253,00.asp. Accessed 13 May 2016

12. Kitchenham, B.A., Charters, S.: Guidelines for performing systematic literature reviews in software engineering. Technical report EBSE-2007-01, School of Computer Science and Mathematics, Keele University (2007)

13. Runeson, P., Höst, M.: Guidelines for conducting and reporting case study research in software engineering. Empirical Softw. Eng. **14**(2), 131–164 (2009)

14. Charland, A., Leroux, B.: Mobile application development: web vs. native. Commun. ACM **54**(5), 49–53 (2011)

15. Samuel, T.: Problems and solutions in mobile application testing, MSc thesis, University of Tartu, Estonia (2016). https://comserv.cs.ut.ee/ati_thesis/datasheet.php?id=54422&year=2016

16. Zhifang, L., Bin, L., Xiaopeng, G.: Test automation on mobile device. In: Proceedings of the 5th Workshop on Automation of Software Test, Cape Town, South Africa (2010)

17. Yan, M., Sun, H., Liu, X.: ITest: testing software with mobile crowdsourcing. In: Proceedings of CrowdSoft 2014, Hong Kong, China (2014)

18. Kaasila, J., Ferreira, D., Kostakos, V., Ojala, T.: Testdroid: automated remote UI testing on android. In: Proceedings of 11th International Conference on Mobile and Ubiquitous Multimedia, Ulm, Germany (2012)

19. Ravindranath, L., Nath, S., Padhye, J., Balakrishnan, H.: Automatic and scalable fault detection for mobile applications. In: Proceeidngs of MobiSys 2014, Bretton Woods, New Hampshire, USA (2014)

20. Ham, H., Park, Y.: Designing knowledge base mobile application compatibility test system for android fragmentation. Intl. J. Softw. Eng. Appl. **8**(1), 303–314 (2014)

21. Tang, L., Yu, Z., Zhou, X., Wang, H., Becker, C.: Supporting rapid design and evaluation of pervasive applications: challenges and solutions. Pers. Ubiquit. Comput. **15**(3), 253–269 (2011)

22. Galindo, J.A., Turner, H., Benavides, D., White, J.: Testing variability-intensive systems using automated analysis: an application to Android. Softw. Qual. J. **42**(2), 365–405 (2014)

23. Baride, S., Dutta, K.: A cloud based software testing paradigm for mobile applications. SIGSOFT Softw. Eng. Notes **36**(3), 1–4 (2011)

24. Azim, T., Neamtiu, I.: Targeted and depth-first exploration for systematic testing of Android apps. ACM SIGPLAN Not. **48**(10), 641–660 (2013)

25. Arzt, S., Rasthofer, S., Fritz, C., Bodden, E., Bartel, A., Klein, J., Le Traon, Y., Octeau, D., McDaniel, P.: FLOWDROID: precise context, flow, field, object-sensitive and lifecycle-aware taint analysis for Android apps. ACM SIGPLAN Notes **49**(6), 259–269 (2014)

26. Haller, K.: Mobile testing. SIGSOFT Softw. Eng. Notes **38**(6), 1–8 (2013)

27. Bastien, J.C.: Usability testing: a review of some methodological and technical aspects of the method. Intl. J. Med. Inf. **79**(4), e18–e23 (2010)

28. Ma, X., Yan, B., Chen, G., Zhang, C., Huang, K., Drury, J., Wang, L.: Design and implementation of a toolkit for usability testing of mobile apps. Mob. Netw. Appl. **18**(1), 81–97 (2013)

29. Mirzaei, N., Malek, S., Pasareanu, C.S., Esfahani, N., Mahmood, R.: Testing Android apps through symbolic execution. SIGSOFT Softw. Eng. Notes **37**(6), 1–5 (2012)
30. Kim, H.-K.: Hybrid model based testing for mobile applications. Intl. J. Softw. Eng. Appl. **7** (3), 223–238 (2013)
31. van der Merwe, H., Tkachuk, O., van der Merwe, B., Visser, W.: Generation of library models for verification of android applications. SIGSOFT Softw. Eng. Notes **40**(1), 1–5 (2015)
32. Hussain, A., Hashim, N., Nordin, N., Tahir, H.: A metric-based evaluation model for applications on mobile phones. J. Inf. Commun. Technol. **12**(1), 55–71 (2013)
33. Koivisto, E.M.I., Suomela, R.: Using prototypes in early pervasive game development. In: Proceedings of ACM SIGGRAPH Symposium on Video Games, San Diego, California, USA (2007)
34. van der Merwe, H., Tkachuk, O., Nel, S., van der Merwe, B., Visser, W.: Environment modeling using runtime values for JPF-Android. SIGSOFT Softw. Eng. Notes **40**(6), 1–5 (2015)
35. Agarwal, S., Mahajan, R., Zheng, A., Bahl, V.: Diagnosing mobile applications in the wild. In: Proceedings of ACM SIGCOMM Workshop on Hot Topics in Networks, Monterey, California (2010)
36. Kim, H., Choi, B., Yoon, S.: Performance testing based on test-driven development for mobile applications. In: Proceedings of ICUIMC 2009, Suwon, South Korea, (2009)
37. Ceccato, M., Avancini, A.: Security testing of the communication among Android applications. In: Proceedings of AST 2013, San Francisco, CA, USA (2013)
38. Adamsen, C.Q., Mezzetti, G., Moller, A.: Systematic execution of android test suites in adverse conditions. In: Proceedings of ISSTA 2015, Baltimore, MD, USA (2015)
39. Zhang, P., Elbaum, S.: Amplifying tests to validate exception handling code: an extended study in the mobile application domain. ACM Trans. Softw. Eng. Methodol. **23**(4), 32:1–32:28 (2014)
40. De Cleva Farto, G., Endo, A.: Evaluating the model-based testing approach in the context of mobile applications. Electron. Notes Theor. Comput. Sci. **314**, 3–21 (2015)
41. Zapata, B.C., Fernandez-Aleman, J.L., Idri, A., Toval, A.: Empirical studies on usability of mHealth apps: a systematic literature review. J. Med. Syst. **39**(2), 1–19 (2015)
42. Diewald, S., Geilhof, B., Siegrist, M., Lindemann, P., Koelle, M., Halle, M., Kranz, M.: Mobile AgeCI: potential challenges in the development and evaluation of mobile applications for elderly people. In: Computer Aided Systems Theory – EUROCAST 2015, Las Palmas, Spain (2015)
43. Oulasvirta, A.: Rethinking experimental designs for field evaluations. IEEE Pervasive Comput. **11**(4), 60–67 (2012)
44. Biel, B., Grill, T., Gruhn, V.: Exploring the benefits of the combination of a software architecture analysis and a usability evaluation of a mobile application. J. Syst. Softw. **83** (11), 2031–2044 (2010)
45. Rapp, A., Cena, F., Gena, C., Marcengo, A., Console, L.: Using game mechanics for field evaluation of prototype social applications: a novel methodology. Behav. Inf. Technol. **35** (3), 184–195 (2015)
46. Billi, M., Burzagli, L., Catarci, T., Santucci, G., Bertini, E., Gabbanini, F., Palchetti, E.: A unified methodology for the evaluation of accessibility and usability of mobile applications. Univ. Access Inf. Soc. **9**(4), 337–356 (2010)
47. Nascimento, L.H.D., Machado, P.D.: An experimental evaluation of approaches to feature testing in the mobile phone applications domain. In: Proceedings of DOSTA 2007: in Conjunction with the 6th ESEC/FSE Joint Meeting, Dubrovnik, Croatia (2007)

48. van der Merwe, H., van der Merwe, B., Visser, W.: Verifying android applications using Java pathfinder. SIGSOFT Softw. Eng. Notes **37**(6), 1–5 (2012)

49. Salva, S., Zafimiharisoa, S.R.: APSET, an Android aPplication SEcurity Testing tool for detecting intent-based vulnerabilities. Intl. J. Softw. Tools Technol. Transfer **17**, 201–221 (2015)

50. Aranha, E., Borba, P.: Estimating manual test execution effort and capacity based on execution points. Intl. J. Comput. Appl. **31**(3), 167–172 (2009)

51. Serra, L.C., Carvalho, L.P., Ferreira, L.P., Vaz, J.B.S., Freire, A.P.: Accessibility evaluation of e-government mobile applications in Brazil. Procedia Comp. Sci. **37**, 348–357 (2015)

52. Morgado, I.C., Paiva, A.C.R.: Test patterns for android mobile applications. In: Proceedings of the 20th European Conference on Pattern Languages of Programs, Kaufbeuren, Germany (2015)

53. Wang, X.S., Balasubramanian, A., Krishnamurthy, A., Wetherall, D.: Demystifying page load performance with WProf. In: Proceedings of the 10th USENIX Conference on Networked Systems Design and Implementation, Lombard, IL (2013)

54. Hutflesz, P., Holzmann, C.: Multivariate testing of native mobile applications. In: Proceedings of MoMM 2014, Kaohsiung, Taiwan (2014)

55. Choi, W., Necula, G., Sen, K.: Guided GUI testing of Android apps with minimal restart and approximate learning. ACM SIGPLAN Not. **48**(10), 623–639 (2013)

56. Hu, Y., Azim, T., Neamtiu, I.: Versatile yet lightweight record-and-replay for Android. In: Proceedings of 2015 ACM SIGPLAN International Conference on Object-Oriented Programming, Systems, Languages, and Applications, vol. 50(10), pp. 349–366 (2015)

57. Gao, J., Tsai, W.-T., Paul, R., Bai, X., Uehara, T.: Mobile testing-as-a-service (MTaaS) - infrastructures, issues, solutions and needs. In: Proceedings of 2014 IEEE 15th International Symposium on High-Assurance Systems Engineering, Miami, Fl., USA (2014)

58. Costa, P., Paiva, A.C.R., Nabuco, M.: Pattern based GUI testing for mobile applications. In: 9th International Conference on the Quality of Information and Communications, Guimaraes, Portugal (2014)

59. Bo, J., Xiang, L., Xiaopeng, G.: MobileTest: a tool supporting automatic black box test for software on smart mobile devices. In: Proceedings of AST 2007, Washington, DC, USA (2007)

60. Google, Performance focus. http://developer.android.com/about/versions/lollipop.html#Perf. Accessed 8 Apr 2016

61. Amalfitano, D., Fasolino, A.R., Tramontana, P., Ta, B.D., Memon, A.M.: MobiGUITAR: automated model-based testing of mobile apps. IEEE Softw. **32**(5), 53–59 (2015)

62. Amalfitano, D., Amatucci, N., Fasolino, A.R., Tramontana, P.: AGRippin: a novel search based testing technique for android applications. In: Proceedings of 3rd International Workshop on Software Development Lifecycle for Mobile, Bergamo, Italy (2015)

63. Amalfitano, D., Amatucci, N., Fasolino, A.R., Tramontana, P., Kowalczyk, E., Memon, A. M.: Exploiting the saturation effect in automatic random testing of android applications. In: Proceedings of the 2nd ACM International Conference on Mobile Software Engineering and Systems, Florence, Italy (2015)

64. Amalfitano, D., Fasolino, A.R., Tramontana, P., De Carmine, S., Memon, A.M.: Using GUI ripping for automated testing of android applications. In: Proceedings of ASE 2012, Essen, Germany (2012)

65. Bergvall-Kareborn, B., Larsson, S.: A case study of real-world testing. In: Proceedings of the 7th International Conference on Mobile and Ubiquitous Multimedia, Umeå, Sweden (2008)

66. Guo, C., Xu, J., Yang, H., Zeng, Y., Xing, S.: An automated testing approach for inter-application security in android. In: Proceedings of AST 2014, Hyderabad, India (2014)

Cost-Benefit Analysis of Using Dependency Knowledge at Integration Testing

Sahar Tahvili[1,2]($\boxtimes$), Markus Bohlin[1]($\boxtimes$), Mehrdad Saadatmand[1,2],
Stig Larsson[1], Wasif Afzal[2], and Daniel Sundmark[2]

[1] SICS Swedish ICT, Västerås, Sweden
{sahart,markus.bohlin,mehrdad,stig.larsson}@sics.se
[2] Mälardalen University, Västerås, Sweden
{wasif.afzal,daniel.sundmark}@mdh.se

Abstract. In software system development, testing can take considerable time and resources, and there are numerous examples in the literature of how to improve the testing process. In particular, methods for selection and prioritization of test cases can play a critical role in efficient use of testing resources. This paper focuses on the problem of selection and ordering of integration-level test cases. Integration testing is performed to evaluate the correctness of several units in composition. Further, for reasons of both effectiveness and safety, many embedded systems are still tested manually. To this end, we propose a process, supported by an online decision support system, for ordering and selection of test cases based on the test result of previously executed test cases. To analyze the economic efficiency of such a system, a customized return on investment (ROI) metric tailored for system integration testing is introduced. Using data collected from the development process of a large-scale safety-critical embedded system, we perform Monte Carlo simulations to evaluate the expected ROI of three variants of the proposed new process. The results show that our proposed decision support system is beneficial in terms of ROI at system integration testing and thus qualifies as an important element in improving the integration testing process.

Keywords: Process improvement · Software testing · Decision support system · Integration testing · Test case selection · Prioritization · Optimization · Return on investment

1 Introduction

The software testing process is typically performed at various integration levels, such as unit, integration, system and acceptance level testing. At all levels, software testing suffers from time and budget limitations. Improving the testing process is thus essential from both product quality and economic perspectives. Towards this goal, application of more efficient testing techniques as well as automating different steps of the testing process (e.g., test case generation, test execution etc.) can be considered. For test execution, the decision of which test

© Springer International Publishing AG 2016
P. Abrahamsson et al. (Eds.): PROFES 2016, LNCS 10027, pp. 268–284, 2016.
DOI: 10.1007/978-3-319-49094-6_17

cases to select and the order in which they are executed can play an important role in improving test efficiency. In our previous work [1], we introduced a technique based on dependencies between test cases and their execution results at runtime. The technique dynamically selects test cases to execute by avoiding redundant test cases. In our technique, identified dependencies among test cases give partial information on the verdict of a test case from the verdict of another one. In this paper, we present a cost-benefit analysis and a return on investment (ROI) evaluation of the dependency-based test selection proposed in [1]. The analysis is conducted by means of a case study of the integration testing process in a large organization developing embedded software for trains. In particular, we analyze various costs that are required to introduce our decision support system (DSS) and compare these costs to the achieved cost reductions enabled by its application. To improve the robustness of the analysis, stochastic simulation of tens of thousands possible outcomes have been performed. In summary, the paper makes the following contributions:

- A high-level cost estimation model, based on Monte-Carlo simulation, for the evaluation of integration test-case prioritization with test-case dependencies. The model is generic and can be used to analyze integration testing for a wide range of systems that exhibit test case dependencies.
- An application of the cost estimation model in an industrial case study at Bombardier Transportation (BT) where three alternatives for process improvement are compared to the baseline test execution order.
- A sensitivity analysis for the model parameter values in the case study. Through the analysis, various scenarios have been identified where the application of the proposed DSS can be deemed as either cost beneficial or not.

The remainder of this paper is structured as follows. Section 2 presents the background while Sect. 3 provides a description of the DSS for test case prioritization. Section 4 describes a generic economic model. Section 5 provides a case study of a safety-critical train control management subsystem, and gives a comparison with the currently used test case execution order. In Sect. 6, the results and limitations are discussed and finally Sect. 7 concludes the paper.

2   Background

Numerous techniques for test case selection and prioritization have been proposed in the last decade [2–4]. Most of the proposed techniques for ordering test cases are offline, meaning that the order is decided before execution while the current execution results do not play a part in prioritizing or selecting test cases to execute. Furthermore, only few of these techniques are multi-objective whereby a reasonable trade-off is reached among multiple, potentially competing, criteria. The number of test cases that are required for testing a system depends on several factors, including the size of the system under test and its complexity. Executing a large number of test cases can be expensive in terms of effort and wall-clock time. Moreover, selecting too few test cases for execution might leave a large number of faults undiscovered. The mentioned limiting factors (allocated budget and time constraints) emphasize the importance of test case prioritization in order to identify test cases that enable earlier detection of faults while respecting such constraints. While this has been the target of test selection and prioritization research for a long time, it is surprising how only few approaches actually take into account the specifics of integration testing, such as dependency information between test cases.

Exploiting dependencies in test cases have recently received much attention (See e.g., [5,6]) but not for test cases written in natural language, which is the only available format of test cases in our context. Furthermore, little research has been done in the context of embedded system development in real, industrial context, where integration of subsystems is one of the most difficult and fault-prone task. Lastly, managing the complexity of integration testing requires *online* decision support for test professionals as well as trading between multiple criteria; incorporating such aspects in a tool or a framework is lacking in current research.

The cost of quality is typically broken down into two components: conformance and nonconformance costs [7]. The conformance costs are prevention and appraisal costs. Prevention costs include money invested in activities such as training, requirements and code reviews. Appraisal costs include money spent on testing such as test planning, test case development and test case execution. The non-conformance costs include internal and external failures. The cost of internal failure include cost of test case failure and the cost of bug fixing. The cost of external failure include cost incurred when a customer finds a failure [8]. This division of cost of quality is also a basis for some well-known quality cost models such as Prevention-Appraisal-Failure (PAF) model [9] and Crosby's model [10]. While general in nature, such quality cost models have been used for finding cost of software quality too, see e.g., [11–13]. Software testing is one important determinant of software quality and smart software managers consider the cost incurred in test related activities (i.e., appraisal cost) as an investment in quality [8]. However, very few economic cost models of software testing exist, especially metrics for calculating the return on testing investment are not well-researched. It is also not clear how the existing software test process improvement approaches [14] cater for software testing economics. One reason for this lack of attention of economics in software quality in general is given by Wagner [15]. According to him, empirical knowledge in the area is hampered by difficulties in cost data gathering from companies since it is considered as sensitive. Nikolik [16] proposes a set of test case based economic metrics such as test case cost, test case value and return on testing investment. A test cost model to compare regression test strategies is presented by Leung and White [17]. They distinguish between two cost types: direct and indirect costs. Direct costs include time for all those activities that a tester performs. This includes system analysis cost, test selection cost, test execution cost and result analysis cost. Indirect costs include test tool development cost, test management cost and cost of storing test-related information. A test cost model inspired by PAF model is also presented by Black [18] while several cost factors for ROI calculation for automated test tools are given in other studies [19–21]. Some other related work is done by Felderer et al. [22,23] where they develop a generic decision support procedure for model-based testing in an industrial project and compare estimated costs and benefits throughout all phases of the test process.

3   Decision Support System for Test Case Prioritization

In this section we outline our proposed DSS, which prioritizes and selects integration test cases based on analysis of test case dependencies. Although not the focus of this paper, the DSS is also capable of performing multi-criteria decision analysis. The details of the approach can be found in [1]. In essence, the DSS provides an optimized order for execution of test cases by taking into account the execution result of a test case, its dependency relations and various test case properties. The steps performed in the DSS can be categorized into an offline and online phase: The offline phase produces an order for execution of test cases based on different test case properties (e.g., fault detection probability, execution time, cost, requirement coverage, etc.) while in the online phase, the pass or fail verdict of executed test cases is taken into account in order to identify and exclude upcoming test cases based on knowledge of dependencies between executed and scheduled test cases. The following definition of result dependency for integration test cases, first introduced in [1], constitute the basis of the dependency-based prioritization considered in this paper:

Definition. For two test cases A and B, B is *dependent* on A if, from the failure of A, it can be inferred that B will also fail.

In industrial practice, such dependencies may exist e.g., whenever a subsystem uses the result of another subsystem. During testing, the dependency may manifest whenever a test case B, dependent on test case A, is scheduled for execution before a component, tested by A, has been fully and adequately implemented and tested. By delaying the execution of B until A has passed, we ensure that the prerequisites for testing B are met. For instance, if the power system in a train fails to work, the lighting and air conditioning systems will not function either.

3.1   Architecture and Process of DSS

In this section, we give the basic architecture and process for the decision support system [1]. We use the term 'decision support system' to emphasize that it can be instantiated in contexts similar to ours, i.e., test cases written in natural language, meant for testing of integration of subsystems in embedded system development.

In Fig. 1, we describe the steps of the semi-automated decision support system for optimizing integration test selection. New test cases are continuously collected in a *test pool* (1) as they are developed. The test cases are initially not ordered and are candidates for prioritization. As a preparation for the prioritization of the test cases, the values for a selected set of *criteria need to be determined*

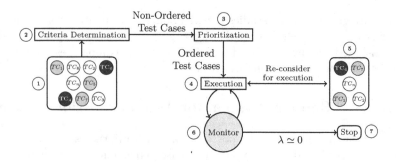

Fig. 1. Architecture of the proposed online DSS.

(2) for the new test cases. To *prioritize* among the test cases, the DSS expects the use of a multi-criteria decision making technique (3, prioritization) [24]. Once prioritized, the test cases are in this step *executed* (preferably) according to the recommended order (4). The result of executing each test case could either be *Pass* or *Fail*. We have previously in [1] shown that by detecting the dependency between test cases, we are able to avoid the redundant executions. When a test case fails during the execution, all its dependent test cases should be disabled for execution. The failed test cases from the previous step enter a queue for troubleshooting. The failed test cases will be *reconsidered for execution* once the reason of their failure is resolved (5). The results of each test are *monitored* (6) to enable (re-)evaluation of the *executability condition* (see [1]) of the test cases that are dependent on it. This will determine if the dependent test case should be selected for execution or not. Furthermore, the completeness of the testing process will be monitored through the metric *fault failure rate* (see [25]), denoted by λ in Fig. 1. This metric is the proportion of the failed test cases to the total number of executed test cases. The goal is to reach successful execution of maximum test cases to be able to finish the current test execution cycle. The current test execution cycle will *stop* (7) once the fault failure rate becomes 0. The steps in the DSS are performed in the integration phase for each iteration/release of the system. This will ensure that the relevant test are executed in a suitable sequence, and that the tests resources are used in an optimal way.

4   Economic Model

In this section we describe an economic model for the cost-benefit analysis of a software integration testing process where test cases are delayed until their execution requirements are fulfilled. The model is independent on the specific multi-criteria decision making technique used and of the specific system under test.

The purpose of the economic model is to adequately capture the costs and benefits which are directly related to the adoption of a DSS-supported testing process aiding in the prioritization of test cases. In industry, it is common that time and cost estimates for software development processes only exist as estimates or averages, if at all. Finally, for an analysis to be useful in practice, the analysis model should be reasonably lightweight and contain only the absolutely necessary parameters. Using the proposed economic model, a stochastic ROI analysis can then be obtained by Monte Carlo simulation. A stochastic analysis avoids the sensitivity of traditional ROI analyses by considering a large number of possible parameter values, thereby offsetting some of the disadvantages in being forced to use less reliable parameter value estimates.

In this paper, we use a cost model with the following parameters:

1. A one-time fixed DSS implementation cost, corresponding to a fixed-price contract negotiated beforehand,
2. Variable costs for DSS training, on a per person-days of DSS usage basis,
3. Variable costs for DSS maintenance, on a per person-days of DSS usage basis,
4. Variable costs for (a) DSS data collection, (b) test planning, on a per test-case basis, and
5. Variable costs for (a) test-case execution (per executed test-case) and (b) troubleshooting (per failed test case).

We make the following simplifying assumptions on the testing process to be analyzed:

(a) A test case is executed at most once in each release cycle,
(b) If a test case fails, it is delayed until the next release cycle,
(c) Reliability of an already implemented and properly maintained system grows according to a simplified Goel-Okumoto model [26], and
(d) Test execution and troubleshooting effort is independent of each other and between test cases.

In the model, we only include the costs and benefits which are affected by using the DSS, and hence, do not need to consider other efforts such as the effort of testing for test cases that pass or that fail for other reasons than dependency. The following cost model is used for the approach in each release cycle t:

$$C_t = C_t^{\text{I}} + d_t \cdot \left(C_t^{\text{T}} + C_t^{\text{M}}\right) + n_t \cdot \left(C_t^{\text{D}} + C_t^{\text{P}}\right) + \gamma_t \cdot \lambda_t \cdot n_t \cdot \left(C_t^{\text{E}} + C_t^{\text{B}}\right), \quad (1)$$

where C^{I} is the implementation cost, d_t is the number of person-days in t, C^{T} is the training cost, C^{M} is the maintenance cost, n_t is the number of test cases, C^{D} is the data collection cost, C^{P} is the test order planning cost, including possible preprocessing, test case data input, DSS runtime, post-processing and test case prioritization output, λ_t is the fraction of failed test cases in the release cycle, γ_t is the fraction of test cases that failed due to a fail-based-on-fail dependency (out of the failed test cases), C^{E} is the average test execution cost, and C^{B} is the average troubleshooting cost. The last term, $\gamma_t \cdot \lambda_t \cdot n_t \cdot \left(C_t^{\text{E}} + C_t^{\text{B}}\right)$, calculates the cost for unnecessarily running test cases which will surely fail due to dependencies. This is the only runtime cost we need to consider when comparing a DSS-supported process and the baseline process without DSS support, as the other costs for running test cases will remain the same.

Over the course of time, the maintenance cost for a deployed system with a small number of adaptations will be approximately proportional to the failure intensity of the system. In this paper, we therefore assume that the DSS software reliability grows according to a simplified Goel-Okumoto model (see [26]), i.e., that the failure intensity decrease exponentially as $\lambda(d) = \lambda_0 e^{-\sigma d}$, where $\lambda(d)$ is the failure intensity at time d, λ_0 is the initial failure intensity, and σ is the rate of reduction. Further, for any release cycle t, each test case belonging to t is assumed to be tested exactly once within t. It is therefore logical to assume that there is no decrease in the test case failure rate during any single release cycle. Under these assumptions, the expected maintenance cost in release cycle t can be calculated as follows.

$$C_t^{\mathrm{M}} = C_0^{\mathrm{M}} \cdot D_t \cdot \mathrm{e}^{-\sigma D_t}, \qquad (2)$$

where C_0^{M} is the initial maintenance cost and $D_t = \sum_{i=1}^{t} d_i$ is the total project duration at release cycle t, where d_i is the duration of a single cycle i.

Apart from the implementation cost C^{I}, there are other unrelated infrastructure costs which are not affected by the process change and can therefore be disregarded from. Likewise, full staff costs are not included, as the team size remains constant, and we instead focus on measuring the savings in work effort cost from a change in process. In the model in Eq. (1), the savings of a process change taking test case dependencies into account can be measured as a difference in costs, under the assumption that all other costs are equal. As each integration test case is normally executed once in each release cycle, after each cycle there is a set of failed test cases that needs to be retested in the next cycle. In this paper, we are interested in estimating the economic benefits of delaying test cases whose testability depend on the correctness of other parts of the system. In other words, we are interested in estimating the number of test cases which fail solely due to dependencies. For these test cases, we can save executing and troubleshooting efforts. If $\gamma_t \cdot \lambda_t$ number of the test cases fail due to dependencies, then, from Eq. (1), we have that by delaying the execution of such test cases, the saving (i.e. benefit) of changing the process can be at most:

$$B_t = \gamma_t \cdot \lambda_t \cdot n_t \left(C_t^{\mathrm{E}} + C_t^{\mathrm{B}} \right). \qquad (3)$$

The estimate is an upper bound as in reality we may not be able to capture all dependencies in our analysis. Further, there is a possibility that the analysis falsely identifies dependencies which do not exist. The effect of delaying the corresponding test cases to the next phase is to delay the project slightly; however, this effect is likely small and we therefore disregard from it in this paper.

4.1   Return on Investment Analysis

A Return on Investment (ROI) analysis represents a widely used approach for measuring and evaluating the value of a new process and product technology [27]. In this study we consider all costs directly related to the process change to be part of the investment cost. If we also assume that the sets of test cases to execute for all release cycles are disjoint, we can calculate the total costs and benefits by adding the costs and benefits for each release cycle. We use the following ROI model based on the net present value of future cash flows until time T and an interest rate r.

$$R_t = \frac{\sum_{t=0}^{T} B_t / (1 + r)^t}{\sum_{t=0}^{T} C_t / (1 + r)^t} - 1 \qquad (4)$$

We assume that the implementation cost is paid upfront, so that $C_t^I = 0$ when $t \geq 1$, and that there are no other benefits or costs at time $t = 0$. In other words, $B_0 = 0, C_0 = C_0^I$ and, consequently, $R_0 = -1$. The interest rate r is used to discount future cash flows, and is typically the weighted average cost of capital for the firm, i.e., the minimum rate of return that investors expect to provide the needed capital.

5   Case Study

In order to analyze the economic feasibility of our approach, we carried out a case study at Bombardier Transportation (BT) in Sweden, inspired by the guidelines of Runeson and Höst [28] and specifically the way guidelines are followed in the paper by Engström et al. [4]. We investigated the software/hardware integration testing process for the train control management subsystem (TCMS) in the Trenitalia Frecciarossa 1000, a non-articulated high-speed trainset. The process aims to identify faults at the interface of software and hardware. The case study spanned six releases of 13 major and 46 minor function groups of the TCMS during a time period of 2.5 y, which involved in total 12 developers and testers for a total testing time of 4440 h. The testing process is divided into different levels of integration, following a variation of the conventional V-model. The integration tests are performed manually in both a simulated environment and in a lab in the presence of different equipment such as motors, gearboxes and related electronics. The testing for each release have a specific focus, and therefore, there are only minor overlaps between the test cases in different releases. Each test case has a specification in free-text form, and contain information (managed using IBM Rational DOORS) on the (1) test result, (2) execution date and time, (3) tester ID, and (4) testing level.

The test result is one of the following: (a) Failed, (i.e., all steps in the test case failed), (b) Not Run, (i.e., the test case could be not executed), (c) Partly Pass, (i.e., some of the steps in the test case passed, but not all), and (d) Pass (i.e., all steps in the test case passed).

According to the test policy in effect, all failed test cases (including "Not Run" and "Partly Pass" test cases) should be retested in the next release. Furthermore, each of these initiates a troubleshooting process that incurs cost and effort. In the rest of this paper, we therefore use the term *failed* to mean any test verdict except "Pass". The objective of the case study is to analyze the improvement potential for the integration testing process at BT from decreasing the number of unsuccessful test executions using knowledge of test-case dependencies. The chosen method is to estimate the economic effect on BT in the form of earned ROI using Monte-Carlo simulation. We answer the following research question in this case study:

RQ: What is the economic effect of introducing a DSS for reducing the number of unsuccessful integration test executions based on dependency knowledge?

The data collection for the case study was done through both expert judgment, inspection of documentation and a series of semi-structured interviews. The initial parameter value estimates for C^I, C^T and C^M were made by the author team, as it was judged that the members of the team, having deployed several decision support systems in the past (see e.g. [29,30]), possessed the necessary experience for this evaluation. Likewise, C^P was estimated by the research team through multiple meetings and re-evaluations. The documentation consists of the test case specification and verdict records in DOORS. In particular, the fault failure rate (λ) was calculated directly by counting the corresponding test case reports, and the fraction of dependent test cases (γ) was estimated through manual inspection of the comments in the same set of reports. Finally, a series of semi-structured interviews were conducted to both estimate the parameter values for the testing process itself, and to cross-validate the full set of parameter values already identified. The interview series were made with two testers (T1 & T2), a developer (D), a technical project leader (PL), a department manager (DM) and an independent researcher (R) in verification and validation. The composition and main purpose of the interviews are shown in Table 1. The final parameter values can be found later in this paper in Tables 2 and 3.

5.1   Test Case Execution Results

To estimate the number of result dependencies between test cases, we performed a preliminary analysis of the results for 4578 test cases. The analysis was based on an early discussion with testing experts, in which test result patterns that

Table 1. Series of interviews to establish parameter values

#	T1	T2	D	PL	DM	R	Main purpose
1	×						Estimate C^D from dependency questionnaire.
2, 3	×	×	×				Identify criteria for dependencies. Validate C^D.
4		×					Validate dependencies.
5, 6	×	×	×	×			Validate number of dependencies (γ). Estimate C^E.
7			×				Estimate C^B.
8			×	×			Validate C^E, C^B, C^I, C^T, C^M and C^P.
9			×	×	×		Validate C^I, C^T and C^M.

Table 2. Quantitative numbers on various collected parameters per release. Note that the γ rate is reported as a fraction of the fault failure rate (λ).

Parameter	Release number						
	1	2	3	4	5	6	Total
Working Days (d)	62	89	168	65	127	44	555
Test cases (n)	321	1465	630	419	1458	285	4578
Fault failure rate (λ)	0.545	0.327	0.460	0.513	0.346	0.246	0.379
Fail based on fail. rate (γ)	0.411	0.267	0.393	0.753	0.630	0.457	0.475

were likely to indicate a dependency were identified. The patterns have previously been independently cross-validated on a smaller set of 12 test cases by other test experts at BT (see [1]). We classified the test results using the same patterns, resulting in 823 possible dependency failures out of 1734 failed test cases, resulting in a total estimate of $\gamma \approx 0.476$. In the semi-structured interviews, two testers independently estimated that approximately 45 % of the failed test cases were caused by dependencies, which is close to our estimate. Table 2 shows the full results for the six release cycles.

5.2 DSS Alternatives Under Study

We analyzed three different DSS variants, which all prioritize the test cases by aligning them with the identified dependencies but vary in the amount of automation they offer. The goal was to identify the tool-supported process change which is most cost-effective (as measured by the ROI metric) within a reasonable time horizon. The following DSS variants were considered:

- **Manual version:** prioritization and selection of test cases in the level of integration testing manually. In this version, a questionnaire on the time for test execution, troubleshooting and set of dependencies to other test cases, is sent to the testing experts. To be manageable for an individual, the questionnaire is partitioned into smaller parts according to the subsystem breakdown. To increase precision and decrease recall, it is preferable that several experts answers the same questionnaire; however, the exact number should be decided based on the experience level of the testers. One of the commercially and publicly available toolboxes for multi-criteria decision analysis (such as FAHP or TOPSIS) are then used for prioritization of test cases. Data is fed manually into and out of the DSS, and a spreadsheet is used to filter, prioritize and keep track of the runtime test case pool.
- **Prototype version:** Dependencies are collected as in the manual version. However, the DSS is custom-made to read the input in a suitable format, automatically prioritize, filter and keep track of the runtime test case pool, and can output a testing protocol outline, suitable for the manual integration testing process.

– **Automated version:** in addition to the prototype version, the DSS detects the dependencies automatically by utilizing a publically-available toolbox (such as Parser [31]). The criteria determination step (in Fig. 1) would be applied on the test cases by utilizing some learning algorithms (for example a counting algorithm for calculating the number of test steps in a test case for estimating the execution time for a test case).

As explained earlier in Sect. 4, we divide the total cost needed for software testing into fixed (one-time cost) and variable cost. The fixed cost includes the DSS cost for three versions which includes implementation, maintenance and training costs.

The variable cost contains execution cost and also troubleshooting cost for the failed test cases. The variable cost changes in proportion to the number of executed test cases and the number of failed test cases per project.

5.3   ROI Analysis Using Monte-Carlo Simulation

The three version of the DSS were evaluated on the six release cycles described before. As many other mathematical methods, ROI analyses are sensitive to small changes in the input parameter values. As an effect, the calculated ROI can fluctuate depending on the varying time estimates. For this reason we chose to both evaluate the ROI model above using Monte Carlo simulation, as detailed below, and to perform sensitivity analysis by varying the expected value of some of the time estimates, as detailed in the results section. The parameters for the three versions are shown in Table 3.

The focus on initial analysis means that estimation efforts should be kept low. For this reason, a single-parameter Rayleigh distribution, which is the basis in the Putnam model (see [32,33]), was chosen for the distribution of effort for software testing and implementation tasks. Test-case failures were sampled from a Poisson distribution.

Table 3. DSS-specific model parameters and distributions

Param.	Comment	Distr.	Distribution param.		
			Manual	Semi	Auto
γ_t	Failed TC rate	Constant	*See* Table 2.		
λ_t	Failed dep. TC rate	Poisson	*See* Table 2.		
C^E	TC execution time, per TC	Rayleigh	2	2	2
C^B	TC troubleshooting time, per TC	Rayleigh	4	4	4
C^I	Total implementation time	Rayleigh	120	825	1650
C^T	Training time, per year	Rayleigh	540	360	360
C^M	Maintenance time, per year	Rayleigh	40	165	330
C^D	DSS data collection time, per TC	Rayleigh	69.2	69.2	0.00
C^P	DSS run time, per TC	Rayleigh	32.3	5.37	0.00

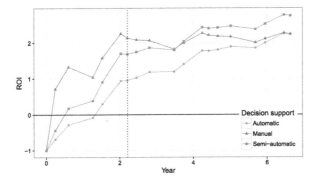

Fig. 2. Expected ROI for the three DSS versions. The vertical dotted line indicate the end of the six release cycles; later cycles are simulated using repeated data.

The three different DSS versions were simulated by sampling 100 000 values for each data point using the parameters in Tables 2 and 3. The mean cumulative results are shown in Fig. 2 for the studied project at BT. In the experiments, utilizing all three versions of DSS resulted in a positive ROI at the end of the six release cycles. Moreover, the maximum value of ROI was found for the manual DSS version, where the maintenance and implementation costs are low as compared to the other versions. By evaluating in total three identical projects in sequence, thereby simulating one team of developers working on three larger projects over the course of almost seven years, it can be noted that the prototype tool is the most promising from an expected ROI perspective. The initial implementation effort and the continued maintenance costs of the automatic version makes it less promising even after seven years of deployment.

5.4   Sensitivity Analysis

To increase the validity of the study, we also performed a sensitivity analysis by varying key parameters. In particular, the ROI analysis is sensitive to changes in the fixed and variable costs for the DSS. For this purpose, we varied the implementation costs, i.e., the fixed up-front cost for the DSS variant, and the maintenance costs, i.e., a critical part of the variable costs. The evaluation was performed using the same parameters as in the previous section, with the exception that the time horizon was fixed to the six development cycles in the case study project, with a duration of approximately 2.2 calendar years. The results of the experiments are shown in Fig. 3. Each data point shows the mean result of 100 000 Monte-carol simulations, each consisting of six release cycles.

As can be seen, when increasing the implementation cost, the relationship between the three variants are the same. The manual variant is profitable even up to an implementation cost factor of 16. If the implementation factor is below 0.5, the prototype tool is the most profitable. It is worth noting that going to the left from the normative case, the ROI of the manual variant changes little, which is due to the fact that the implementation costs for the manual variant is small

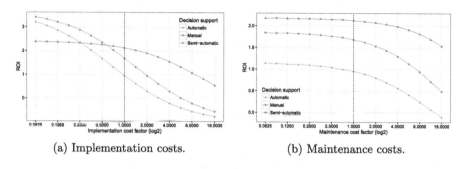

(a) Implementation costs.   (b) Maintenance costs.

Fig. 3. Sensitivity analysis results for DSS costs.

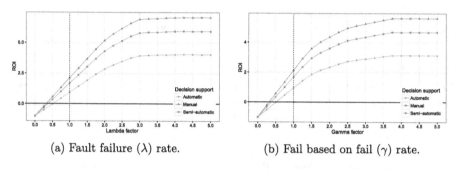

(a) Fault failure (λ) rate.   (b) Fail based on fail (γ) rate.

Fig. 4. Sensitivity analysis results when varying test case failure rates (λ and γ).

compared to the other variants. There is no change in the relationship between the variants when varying the maintenance costs by equal factors (Fig. 3b). Further, changing the cost factor of any single variant by less than 8 still maintains this relationship.

Figure 4 shows the results from varying λ, the fault failure rate, and γ, the fail-based-on-fail rate, using a coefficient between 0.0 and 5.0 individually for each release cycle. As can be seen, for both λ and γ the average ROI is above zero when the coefficient is above 0.5, corresponding to average rates of 0.189 and 0.237, respectively. Further, it can be observed that, for the 6 release cycles, the relationship between the three DSS variants are the same for all coefficients. The tailing-off effect which can be observed for higher coefficients occurs because for each individual release cycle, there is a natural upper limit of 1.0 for both rates, which is enforced after sampling.

6   Discussion and Threats to Validity

In this paper, we have analysed the cost-benefit of utilizing a dependency-based DSS in integration-level testing. It is clear that our results are based on simulation and it will be more convincing to do a similar investigation on real data from an actual project. This is one of our future goals with this direction of research.

Our simulation results indicate that a DSS that considers dependencies in prioritizing test cases for integration level testing may be economically beneficial, but that the extent to which the method should be automated highly depends on the characteristics of the context in which the DSS should be introduced. It should be noted that prioritization based on test dependencies is just one way to reduce effort of integration testing, and the DSS is not inherently limited to dependency-based prioritization. There are a number of other techniques to reduce effort such as system design planning and scheduling implementation. In fact, prioritization of the systems and sub-systems under test can reduce the degree of dependency between test cases. Another point to consider is earlier fault detection [34] which can be enabled by prioritization based on fault detection probability. It should further be noted that the costs in our model, as well as the calculated values of ROI are based on estimates. Consequently, the experimental uncertainty is inherent in the study design. We have tried to mitigate this uncertainty by dividing the costs into smaller units. For example, design cost and implementation cost for a test case are considered as two separated costs. By further defining the execution cost as a separate cost in our cost model, we account for the fact that a test case can be designed and created one time, but can be executed more than one time. We also separate the staff (testers and developers) cost between test case implementation and execution cost. In addition, the gathered data from BT is another source of uncertainty. As discussed in Sect. 5.4, by performing various sensitivity analyses we have identified and evaluated how different factors can impact the cost-benefit and ROI of the application of the DSS. In terms of validity threats, in the economic model, we assume that if test case A fails then running B (which depends on A) after A yields no additional information. This assumption could be invalid in other systems, where execution and failure result of test case B could still provide additional information, which in turn may affect the results of the analysis. Similarly, there are other assumptions related to our work (see Sect. 4), which can be invalid in the real world. Further, in our study we detect dependencies between test cases from test result reports to measure the percentage of fail-based-fail in the analyzed project. Considering the fact that the identification of dependencies by testers to some extent is subjective, other studies using other subjects may result in differences in dependency identification, and estimated gains from the DSS could thus be affected.

7 Conclusion and Future Work

In this paper, we introduced and assessed cost and benefits of applying a decision support system (DSS) for reducing the efforts at integration level testing. We identified the cost factors relevant in integration testing and provided a cost estimation model for calculation of return on investment based on which we evaluated where the use of our proposed DSS will be economically beneficial and result in cost reductions. The proposed decision support system has been applied to an industrial case study of a safety-critical train control subsystem and a brief analysis of the result was given. The results of the BT case study indicate that utilizing the proposed DSS can reduce test execution efforts and achieve a positive value for ROI for a system of that size and complexity, where higher test execution efficiency was enabled by identifying and avoiding test redundancies based on their dependencies. Moreover, by applying the proposed DSS, we can detect the hidden faults in the system under test earlier and fault failure rate increases with time, as we have demonstrated in [24]. The ROI of the proposed DSS increases in situations where the number of test cases is large, the system under test is complex consisting of dependent modules and subsystems, and there exist additional limitations, such as budget, deadline, etc. The level of ROI depend on various cost factors, such as the cost for implementing and maintaining the tool, personnel training, execution time of the decision making algorithms, total number, size and execution time of test cases. This leads also to the conclusion that for a system which is small in the sense that the number of test cases is very small and there are no extra limitations for performing testing activities, a high ROI value may not be achieved by using the DSS.

Acknowledgements. This work was supported by VINNOVA grant 2014-03397 through the IMPRINT project and the Swedish Knowledge Foundation (KKS) grant 20130085 through the TOCSYC project and the ITS-EASY industrial research school. Special thanks to Johan Zetterqvist, Ola Sellin and Mahdi Sarabi at Bombardier Transportation, Västerås-Sweden.

References

1. Tahvili, S., Saadatmand, M., Larsson, S., Afzal, W., Bohlin, M., Sudmark, D., Dynamic integration test selection based on test case dependencies. In: The 11th Workshop on Testing: Academia-Industry Collaboration, Practice and Research Techniques (TAIC PART) (2016)
2. Yoo, S., Harman, M., Regression testing minimization, selection, prioritization: a survey. Softw. Test. Verification Reliab. **22**(2), 67–120 (2012)
3. Catal, C., Mishra, D., Test case prioritization: A systematic mapping study. Soft. Qual. Journal, 2013
4. Engström, E., Runeson, P., Ljung, A.: Improving regression testing transparency and efficiency with history-based prioritization-an industrial case study, pp. 367–376 (2011)
5. Bell, J.: Detecting, isolating, and enforcing dependencies among and within test cases. In: 22nd International Symposium on Foundations of Software Engineering (2014)
6. Zhang, S., Jalali, D., Wuttke, J., Mucslu, K., Lam, W., Ernst, M., Notkin, D.: Empirically revisiting the test independence assumption. In: International Symposium on Software Testing and Analysis (2014)
7. Campanella, J.: Principles of quality costs: principles, implementation and use. ASQ Quality Press (1999)
8. Black, R.: What it managers should know about testing: How to analyze the return on the testing investment (2004)

9. British Standards Institution. Guide to the economics of quality. Proc. cost model. B.S. (Series). BSI (1992)
10. Crosby, P.: Quality is free: the art of making quality certain. Penguin (1980)
11. Slaughter, S., Harter, D., Krishnan, M.: Evaluating the cost of software quality. Commun. ACM **41**(8), 67–73 (1998)
12. Krasner, H.: Using the cost of quality approach for software. Crosstalk J. Def. Softw. Eng. **11**, 6–11 (1998)
13. Boehm, B., Huang, L., Jain, A., Madachy, R.: The R.O.I of software dependability: The iDAVE model. IEEE Softw. **21**(3), 54–61 (2004)
14. Afzal, W., Alone, S., Glocksien, K., Torkar, R.: Software test process improvement approaches: a systematic literature review and an industrial case study. J. Syst. Softw. **111**, 1–33 (2016)
15. Wagner. S. Software product quality control. Springer, 2013
16. Nikolik, B.: Software quality assurance economics. Info. Softw. Technol
17. Leung, H., White, L.: A cost model to compare regression test strategies. In: Proceedings of the 1991 Conference on Software Maintenance (1991)
18. Black, R.: Managing the Testing Process: Practical Tools and Techniques for Managing Hardware and Software Testing. Wiley Publishing (2009)
19. Münch, S., Brandstetter, P., Clevermann, K., Kieckhoefel, O., Reiner Schäfer, E.: The return on investment of test automation. Pharmaceutical Eng
20. Hayduk, B.: Maximizing ROI and Avoiding the Pitfalls of Test Automation. Real-Time Technology Solutions Inc. (2009)
21. Hoffman, D.: Cost benefits analysis of test automation. Software Quality Methods LLC (1999)
22. Mohacsi, S., Felderer, M., Beer, A.: Estimating the cost, benefit of model-based testing: a decision support procedure for the application of model-based testing in industry. In: Proceedings of the 2015 41st Euromicro Conference on Software Engineering and Advanced Applications, SEAA '15 (2015)
23. Felderer, M., Beer, A.: Estimating the return on investment of defect taxonomy supported system testing in industrial projects. In: Proceedings of the 2012 38th Euromicro Conference on Software Engineering and Advanced Applications, SEAA '12 (2012)
24. Tahvili, S., Afzal, W., Saadatmand, M., Bohlin, M., Sundmark, D., Larsson, S.: Towards earlier fault detection by value-driven prioritization of test cases using ftopsis. In: Proceedings of the 13th International Conference on Information Technology: New Generations (2016)
25. Debroy, V., Wong, W.: On the estimation of adequate test set size using fault failure rates. J. Syst. Softw. **84**, 587–602 (2011)
26. Musa, J., Okumoto, K.: A logarithmic poisson execution time model for software reliability measurement. In: Proceedings of the 7th International Conference on Software engineering
27. Rico, D.: ROI of Software Process Improvement. J Ross Publishing (2004)
28. Runeson, P., Höst, M., Rainer, A., Regnell, R.: Case Study Research in Software Engineering. WILEY (2012)
29. Bohlin, M., Wärja, M.: Maintenance optimization with duration-dependent costs. Ann. Oper. Res. **224**(1), 1–23 (2015)
30. Bohlin, M., Holst, A., Ekman, J., Sellin, O., Lindström, B., Larsen, S.: Statistical anomaly detection for train fleets. In: Proceedings of the 21st Innovative Applications of Artificial Intelligence Conference (2012)

31. Marneffe, M., Manning, C.: Stanford typed dependencies manual. Technical report, Stanford University (2008)
32. Putnam, L.A.: general empirical solution to the macro software sizing, estimating problem. IEEE Trans. Softw. Eng. 4(4), 345 (1978)
33. Putnam, L.: A macro estimating methodology for software development (1976)
34. Hunt, B., Abolfotouh, T., Carpenter, J., Gioia, R.: Software test costs and ROI issues. University Lecture (2014)

Using Surveys and Web-Scraping to Select Tools for Software Testing Consultancy

Päivi Raulamo-Jurvanen[1(✉)], Kari Kakkonen[2], and Mika Mäntylä[1]

[1] M3S (M-Group), ITEE University of Oulu, Oulu, Finland
{paivi.raulamo-jurvanen,mika.mantyla}@oulu.fi
[2] Knowit Oy, Helsinki, Finland
kari.kakkonen@knowit.fi

Abstract. We analyzed findings from data collected utilizing surveys and Web-scraping, to support Knowit Oy, a software testing consultation company, in the process of selecting the right tools for software testing & test automation. We conducted two surveys (2013 & 2016) among (mostly Finnish) software professionals to acquire criteria and a list of tools used for software testing in industry. Considering all our data sources Selenium was the most popular pure tool, while Robot Framework was the most referenced tool (latter survey). According to the surveys Jenkins and Sikuli have the highest increase in popularity (or familiarity). Top referred criteria for selection were usability, functionality, maintainability and available support for a tool. While Knowit considers it best to utilize traditional surveys, Web-scraping is seen as cost effective support for such instruments. To get comprehensive picture and to gain knowledge of the tools in markets multiple sources should be used.

Keywords: Test automation · Software testing tool · Software test automation tool · Tool support · Selection criteria

1 Introduction

Software test automation is tool-oriented domain and integral to frequent testing as part of continuous delivery and rapid releases. A recent online survey reported test automation to be a key factor with software quality and R&D cost saving from the viewpoint of management [19]. In another recent survey by ISTQB [5] test automation was ranked as the main area of improvement opportunities in testing activities. In addition to that, test tool/automation consultation was ranked as the service most required from external providers. The results from a survey by Capgemini, Sogeti and HP (the World Quality Report, WQR 2015-2016) [1] highlight that investing in test automation is a must to keep up with the ever increasing demand for velocity. The findings claimed that 40 % of the respondents (IT leaders of mobile technologies) reported lack of right tools for their testing activities. Overall, these sources highlight the importance of test automation which cannot succeed without proper tools.

Selecting tools for software testing is a difficult practical problem as there are numerous software testing tools available. The exact number of tools is unknown as

© Springer International Publishing AG 2016
P. Abrahamsson et al. (Eds.): PROFES 2016, LNCS 10027, pp. 285–300, 2016.
DOI: 10.1007/978-3-319-49094-6_18

what constitutes as a test tool is difficult to define, e.g. many people use Excel to manage test cases. The high number of tools is well reflected for example in the web-site listing tools for pair-wise testing <http://www.pairwise.org/tools.asp>, a technique to generate minimum number of test cases covering all combinations of two test inputs. The web-site has listed 41 tools for pair-wise testing, aka combinatorial testing, alone. Given the number of tools available only for this test input generation technique, we can estimate that there has to be hundreds, if not thousands, of testing tools available.

In this paper, we study the knowledge acquisition phase of the test tool selection process within a consulting company (Knowit Oy). This is our initial work on test automation tool selection and thus we provide only initial answers to following Research Questions: (RQ1) *Why is selecting tools important for Knowit?* (RQ2) *What is the most popular software test tool nowadays, in comparison to year 2013?* (RQ3) *How does Web-scraping compare with traditional surveys?* (RQ4) *What criteria people find important when selecting tools for software testing or test automation?*

2 Prior Work

Test automation consultants Graham and Fewster [2] have studied experiences of test automation with industrial cases over a long period of time. They emphasized that "there is no such thing as the perfect tool, but there are many tools that would be adequate for a given situation", it is the preferences that drive the decisions. They claim that the tool must be appropriate for a job. A tool may be inadequate in some context but suitable in another and several tools may have to be used to accomplish the goals [2].

An online survey published in March 2016 [19] focused on the tools used in test automation, in companies of less and more than 100 employees. The findings from a total of 644 software professionals indicated organizations to use more than a single test automation solution, open source tools being popular, especially in smaller organizations. The amount of tools is thought to be high due to reasons like application complexity, multiple platforms or lack of required functionalities. The study anticipated possible disappearance of commercial tools in favor of open source tools in the near future. The most used tools were, in the order of preference, for smaller size organizations: Selenium (42 %), internal tools (20 %), Junit (12 %), Android SKD (8 %), Appium (7 %), JMeter (3 %), Watir (3 %), Pytest (3 %) and Selendroid (2 %). For larger organizations the tools most used were: Selenium (29 %), internal tools (24 %), Junit (12 %), Appium (8 %), Microsoft (8 %, in general), QTP (7 %), Selendroid (5 %), TestComplete (5 %) and JMeter (2 %) [19].

Past work on software testing tool selection in general by Poston and Sexton [13] perceived systematic data collection method, preferably with forms or checklists, to be the secret for selecting appropriate testing tools. Although several surveys of software testing have been conducted, e.g. [3, 8, 9, 15], those typically do not cover the actual tools used. There are however studies that focus on a few specific tools e.g. comparing TestComplete and QTP on characteristics [7], acknowledging the need for evaluation of tools [12], comparing Selenium, QTP and TestComplete (eventually concluding the best tool being QTP) [6] or comparing a few web-service tools [4].

To summarize, according to the authors' best knowledge peer-reviewed literature is missing surveys that would focus on the tools by actually naming them. Tools are essential for our trade. Academics need tools for teaching and practitioners for their business. Often tools are listed in requirements of job ads making tool knowledge essential for students graduating from universities.

3 Case Context and the Problem (RQ1)

In this section, we first describe the context of our work and the particular problem we are trying to solve. We use a checklist by Petersen and Wohlin [11] to describe our context in Table 1. Evidence-based software engineering can exploit the context description if that is done as completely and accurately as possible for the targeted object of study. Next, we describe the problem with an informal question answer format.

- *Why is selecting tools important for Knowit?* A software development and testing project success is built on people, processes and tools. It is important to be able to recommend and help to choose a set of tools that is effective and efficient in tasks and fit the context in question.
- *Why are tool surveys conducted?* Test tools get more visibility in the industry. Surveys provide understanding about tools on the rise and tools on the decline. There are excellent newcomers to the tool scene, there are changes in product portfolios and features of existing tools sets. Identifying tools gaining market share at a given time helps to steer for the next good tool.
- *What is to be gained by surveys for tool selection?* Tool selection surveys collect and distribute the collective information from people who have invested time in choosing and using a tool. Such knowledge can make the tool comparison and selection process more efficient.
- *What does tool selection mean to the business?* The business of the customer or end user of software development process gains efficiency and effectiveness using the tool. A suitable test automation tool will impact the project velocity positively (enabling e.g. faster time to market). The efficiency provided by two different tools can be significant. For the business of a consultancy company, the tool selection is an essential part of the service offering, a must-have service although a minor one if calculated in turnover. More importantly, the consultancy company wants to provide tools bringing the best efficiency. In the end, both consultancy and customer always share the same common goal of customer business success.
- *What are the experienced difficulties?* Typical challenge is the willingness of unenlightened stakeholders to use a good tool for a purpose other than the tool was originally designed for. That may prevent achievement of the expected results for the tool adoption. Another difficulty is comparison of tools that are similar on paper, e.g. "test management" tools, some of which work on cloud and some with native client. In such case it is essential to understand the really important characteristics of the tools.

Table 1. Case context with the framework by [11]

Object of study	Tool selection and process acquiring related knowledge.
Product	Service offering provided by the software testing consultancy company.
People	Technology consultants, Customer consultants, Tool owner in the customer organization.
Practices, tools & techniques	Partner discussions and information, trade fairs, cross-customer recommendation.
Processes	Software development, Software Testing, Training & Deployment. Technology, Partner, Portfolio and Project management.

4   Research Methods

This section describes research methods used for gathering knowledge about the testing tools.

4.1   Surveys

We present results of two different surveys that collected information about test tool usage, mainly in Finnish software industry. A survey can be thought as a vehicle to harness the "wisdom of the crowds" for tool selection process. The concept embodies the idea of collective opinion (or intelligence), that under the right circumstances a group can be smarter than a single individual [14].

The first tool survey, Survey 1, was conducted in 2013 (as a thesis work for Master degree of Business Informatics at Metropolia) by Knowit employee Minna Tiitinen with Kari Kakkonen as a tutor [16]. This survey offers historical perspective on how Knowit has utilized surveys. The survey was distributed in public email list of Finnish professional testing society (TestausOSY) and also to the partners of Knowit, receiving 107 answers.

In 2016, University of Oulu and Knowit jointly conducted a tool survey, Survey 2, to find out (1) the criteria people used (or preferred) for tool selection and (2) tools that were used by software industry. The survey was targeted to software professionals and links to the questionnaires were provided in Facebook, LinkedIn and Twitter to selected groups (mainly Finnish software testing related groups) and sent to email lists of Finnish professional testing society (TestausOSY) by the partner organization, Knowit. The total of 58 answers had a clear bias in favor of Finnish respondents (51).

The questionnaires for the two surveys were rather different of nature; first, by the number of questions and second, by the design of the questions. The questionnaire for Survey 1 included 61 questions in total (9 questions for the background information about the respondents and 52 questions for the tools). For Survey 2, the total number of questions was only 8 (5 and 3 questions for background information and tools, respectively). Survey 1 provided multiple choice questions with predefined lists of tools (and an option to add tools), the criteria for the predefined lists of tools being ISTQB tool classification and (biased) commonness of the tools. For Survey 2, the intention was not to steer respondents' opinions or tool choices by providing free text fields only. The original questionnaires are available for Survey 1 as Appendix 1 (pg. 113) in [16] and for Survey 2 from http://goo.gl/MjPFCr.

4.2 Web-Scraping

Since surveys in general require effort to create, administer and respond and may suffer from low response rates and respondent bias, we utilized Web-scraping that could support or even possibly substitute surveys. Web-scraping is an approach to fetch content from the internet, a technique to access web-pages and extract a structured view of the required data [10]. However, there are both legal and ethical issues involved in this matter, e.g. the Terms of Service (ToS) for any service may clearly prohibit data scraping from the website or the usage of scraped data may violate a website owner's copyrights. Sometimes a service may provide a public API to access some data, the quality and quantity of which may be lower than (or not as up-to-date as) data acquired by disruptive web scraping. (Some services may offer free services for limited access and require a paid fee for more frequent or massive usage).

We utilized Web-scraping to collect wider views of the Top 15 tools of Survey 2. Data collected included number of Wikipedia page views, number of Google hits (using a particular search string), number of StackOverflow questions and view counts for those, and number of Twitter tweets (see Tables 3 and 4 – please note, rows in both tables are sorted by column "Rank" of Table 4). The time period used for the searches was intentionally set on three months (January 1st – March 31st 2016) to provide some variation and recent body to the content. The data was collected on April 20th and 21st 2016.

Wikipedia is web-based encyclopedia with openly editable content, the English version of which alone contains over 5 million articles. To get the trends of (user created) page views for Wikipedia articles (available in en.wikipedia) we utilized the Pageview API[1] in RStudio/R (required R packages 'httr' and 'jsonlite').

Google Search is claimed to be the most used web search engine on the WWW. ToS of Google strictly deny any access to their services via "using a method other than the interface and the instructions that we provide"[2]. Thus, the Google hits were collected manually using Firefox browser and search string "<toolname> and 'software testing' and tool".

For StackOverflow questions the data was fetched from StackExchange Data Explorer[3] (open source tool) using the provided SQL-query editor. StackExchange data explorer provides libraries of "high-quality questions and answers" and allows to fetch and download data from different sites, of which StackOverflow, language independent site for programmers, is one. The actual data fetched from StackExchange included title

---

[1] https://wikitech.wikimedia.org/wiki/Analytics/PageviewAPI.
[2] https://www.google.com/intl/en/policies/terms/?fg=1.
[3] http://data.stackexchange.com/.

of the question, number of views and creation date for each question (not the full body of the posts).

Twitter is a popular, online social networking service to communicate via short 140-character messages ("tweets"). The existing Twitter API has limitations to fetching tweets (e.g. for the time period or tweets per day). Thus, an open source project GetOldTweets-java (v1.2.0), written by Henrique Jefferson[4], was utilized, allowing to get the tweets for the tools for the defined observation period. The names of the tools were used as hashtags when searching for the posted tweets.

5   Results

First, the results of Survey 1 are summarized only (as from 2013). Then the results of Survey 2 are presented and contrasted with those of Survey 1. Finally, the results from Web-scraping are presented.

5.1   Survey 1

The results of the Survey 1 (107 respondents) showed that agile processes and tools adapted to them were on the rise. Most companies seemed to use both commercial (88 %) and open source tools (60 %), and even proprietary tools (48 %). Unsurprisingly, open source tools dominated in small companies and commercial tools in large companies. The different ways how tools were acquired in companies of different size are shown in Table 2.

Table 2. Types of tools & Company sizes (Survey 1)

	1–10	11–50	51–100	101–500	501–1000	Over 1000	Sum	%
Bought	1	5	4	22	14	46	92	40
Open source	1	5	5	12	6	27	56	24
Proprietary tools	2	2	2	13	7	24	50	22
Cloud service	0	2	2	3	2	6	15	7
Rented	0	0	1	3	1	5	10	4
Other	0	1	2	2	1	1	7	3

In general, in overall analysis of all tools, HP and Atlassian were the most popular commercial vendors (having tools for different testing activities) while Selenium and Robot Framework were the most popular open source tools. For different test activities, mostly tools were used for test execution, test case and defect management and reporting. Excel was widely used on the side of the more sophisticated tools. The test execution tools used in the Survey 1 are shown in Fig. 1. The most popular test execution tool was Selenium with 45 % of the respondents using it. QTP (nowadays replaced by UFT) and Robot Framework seemed almost level while the rest of the tools were used by a small

---

[4] https://github.com/Jefferson-Henrique/GetOldTweets-java/.

number of respondents only. (A category not shown in the figure was "Other" (21 %) which included tools referenced just once by respondents to the option "Other" for the question of test execution tools).

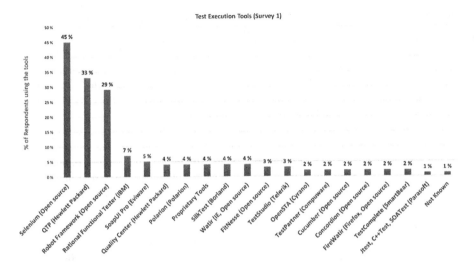

Fig. 1. Test execution tools used (Survey 1)

Some of the actions taken based on the results of the survey emphasized the need (1) to gain tool expertise in choosing tools (not just take the first one) and (2) to look more into the most popular tools in the survey. At the time the survey highlighted the unanticipated importance of Quality Center (HP). Today, the distribution of tools offered by Knowit to the customers has slightly changed (i.e. somewhat more Atlassian & Robot Framework (Knowit is one of the founding members of Robot Framework Foundation) and somewhat less HP). However, tool changes are quite expensive investments into learning, migrating data etc., let alone the actual tool selection and implementation. Thus, tool choices are only questioned every 3–4 years or so. One has to use a tool for some time to gain benefits of it. Also, as tool integration provides extra efficiencies, intent has been increased to integrate commercial and open source tools. The percentages of the adoption of the tools in Survey 1, as a comparison to the Top 15 tools of Survey 2, are listed in Table 3 (column "2013 Survey, Usage %").

5.2 Survey 2

Regarding the expertise of the respondents (58), the average years in software industry was 15.88 (median 15), while maximum years was 43 and minimum 3. Thus, the group of respondents was rather mature in years spent in software industry. The number of those having been in software industry for ten years or more was 47 (82 %).

Criteria (RQ4)

The respondents were requested to describe important criteria when selecting a tool for software testing or software test automation. They were requested to describe in their own words what matters in general (e.g. regardless of technique, testing area or tool), what would be good to know, or take into account in advance. The respondents were expected to provide short, accurate descriptions of the features or characteristics they value in such tools. The question was intentionally left open: *"What are important criteria when selecting a tool for Software Testing/Test Automation? (E.g. What features or characteristics do you value in a tool? Or in your opinion, what would be good to know in advance or matters to you in general?)"*. The fundamental purpose of the question was to collect data as a basis for further studies.

We assume that general requirements for software testing tools (e.g. costs, possible licensing model or developer support, to mention a few) are rather similar (even globally) despite physical location. It is notable that some criteria are always more important to some users than to others and not all criteria work for all even though we can observe general trends. Each and every software project is unique and must choose the criteria and how to apply those in their context.

The criteria were coded in NVivo, first by qualitative coding by topics appearing in the responses, i.e. open coding and axial coding. Later we mapped our codes to the ISO/IEC 25010 quality model[5]. As software testing tools are software too, ISO/IEC 25010 quality model can be used to represent the desired characteristics proposed by our respondents. However, we added "Support" and "Costs" to the categories since those were not included in the model and our respondents frequently brought up those topics. The references to the categories from the quality model are shown in Fig. 2.

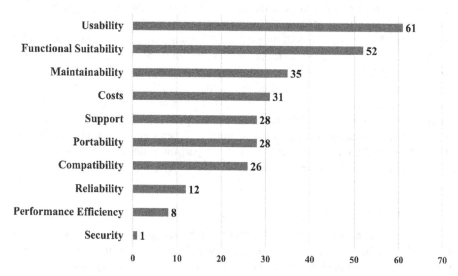

Fig. 2. Survey 2 Criteria categorized using ISO25010 and with "Support" and "Cost" categories

---

[5] http://iso25000.com/index.php/en/iso-25000-standards/iso-25010.

Clearly the issue valued by the respondents was "Usability" with references to "Operability" (43), "Learnability" (13), "User Interface Aesthetics" (3), "Accessibility" (1) and "Appropriateness Recognizability" (1). "Functional Suitability" had references to "Functional Appropriateness" (24), "Functional Correctness" (17) and "Functional Completeness" (11). "Maintainability" included references to "Modifiability" (20), "Modularity" (8), "Reusability" (5) and "Analyzability" (2). None of the respondents referenced the sub-category of "Testability" which seems rather natural.

"Portability" was referenced as "Installability" (18) and "Adaptability" (10), but none of the respondents referenced "Replaceability". "Compatibility" with sub-categories "Co-existence" (6) and "Interoperability" (20), however, this issue about compatibility (with tools/systems/platform/integration) is somewhat ambiguous since respondents were not always specific with their wording. "Reliability" included "Maturity" (8), "Fault Tolerance" (3) and "Availability" (1). "Performance efficiency" had reference to "Time Behavior" (4), "Resource Utilization" (3) and "Capacity" (1). For "Security", there was one reference for "Integrity".

"Support" was added with sub-categories "General Tool Support" (12), "Popularity" (9), "Future of the Tool" (6, we interpreted that the future is mainly of interest because support and new versions of the tool are needed in the future) and "Vendor Independence" (1). For "Costs" there were references for "Price" (11), "License model" (11), "Acquisition costs" (3), "Operating Costs" (3) and "Free" (3).

Open Source software becoming more common may have an impact on the concern for price or costs in general. However, when respondents were referring to "Open Source software" (or "open source interfaces") we interpreted those to refer to licensing model although we were not certain whether they were referring to importance of related costs, licensing model or modifiability of the software, or all of those. Adoption of a software testing or software test automation tool is expected to be a sustainable investment. Since adoption of free tools brings on additional costs, mostly resource related, there are expectations for a lifetime and development of those tools.

"Usability" and "Functional Suitability" of a tool were of high importance. The respondents valued maintainability, i.e. ability to configure or modify the tool according to their needs. "Support" was a topic of its own in the responses. The respondents seemed to prefer tools that were mature, i.e. had been adopted by fellow professionals already for some period of time and had support available in various software forums, e.g. StackOverflow.

Tools Used by the Respondents

The question querying about the tools used resulted in 164 different tools. The question for tools was intentionally open, not to give bias in favor of any tool: *"List tools for Software Testing/Software Test Automation you have been using yourself or tools which have been utilized in your organization. (For non-public, self-made tools you may write "Inhouse tool for doing X")"*. The number of tools, considered as identifiable software testing or test automation tools, was 133 (excluding tools e.g. like Excel, Word, WinSCP, PuTTY or Cygwin).

Table 3. Top 15 tools of Survey 2 (#1): Usage % (figures for Survey 1, (2013) included for reference), Wikipedia page views & Google Hits (rankings for columns included)

Tool	Vendor	2016 Survey Usage %	2013 Survey Usage %	Wikipedia PageViews	Google GoogleHits
Python	Open Source SW	9[8]	---	547245[1]	453000[1]
Selenium	Open Source SW	47[2]	45	112851[3]	428000[2]
Jenkins	Open Source SW	26[3]	---	118621[2]	134000[12]
TFS	Microsoft	5[10]	---	80620[5]	164000[11]
Junit	Open Source SW	12[7]	27	28872[7]	257000[8]
UFT & QTP **	Hewlett-Packard	19[4]	32	34640[6]	414000[4]
Jira	Atlassian	17[5]	54	97178[4]	340000[5]
Quality Center	Hewlett-Packard	17[5]	54	27089[8]	274000[6]
SoapUI	Open Source SW	19[4]	5	24264[10]	187000[10]
jMeter	Open Source SW	14[6]	24	15932[11]	260000[7]
Appium	Open Source SW	9[8]	---	3[14]	64500[13]
ALM	Hewlett-Packard	7[9]	---	24656[9]	212000[9]
Robot Framework	Open Source SW	69[1]	29	11186[12]	14500[15]
FitNesse	Open Source SW	5[10]	3	7670[13]	424000[3]
Sikuli	Open Source SW	14[6]	---	0[15]	32900[14]

To support the goals of the partner organization of having up-to-date sales offering of the most popular testing tools, we analyzed the top 15 tools based on the number of responses. The list of Top 15 tools includes different types and range of tools. The top four referenced tools are all open source tools and only five of the Top 15 tools were commercial. Open source tools seemed popular among the respondents of this survey, too. Nearly 70 % of the respondents (column "2016 Survey, Usage %", Table 3) had

Table 4. Top 15 tools of Survey 2 (#2): StackOverflow questions & view counts, average views per question, Twitter tweets, total sum of rankings and ranking

Tool	StackOverflow Questions	StackOverflow ViewCount	StackOverflow Views / Qs	Twitter Tweets	Total Sum	Rank
Python	42149[1]	2132602[1]	50,6[4]	63664[1]	17	1
Selenium	2765[2]	144305[2]	52,2[3]	2290[4]	18	2
Jenkins	1504[3]	67632[3]	45,0[12]	2049[5]	40	3
TFS	738[5]	41143[4]	55,7[2]	1972[6]	43	4
Junit	753[4]	36381[5]	48,3[8]	419[9]	48	5
UFT & QTP **	44[11]	2091[11]	47,5[9]	1123[8]	53	6
Jira	195[8]	7449[10]	38,2[14]	1388[7]	53	6
Quality Center	15[15]	733[15]	48,9[7]	8924[2]	58	7
SoapUI	191[9]	9483[8]	49,6[6]	105[12]	59	8
jMeter	496[6]	19379[7]	39,1[13]	385[10]	60	9
Appium	356[7]	20315[6]	57,1[1]	296[11]	60	9
ALM	32[12]	1453[12]	45,4[11]	2298[3]	65	10
Robot Framework	154[10]	7703[9]	50,0[5]	40[14]	66	11
FitNesse	27[14]	824[14]	30,5[15]	56[13]	82	12
Sikuli	30[13]	1367[13]	45,6[10]	13[15]	86	13

some experience with the most used tool, Robot Framework. The respondents were mainly from Finland, thus the popularity (of familiarity) of Robot Framework in comparison to other tools in understandable. Interestingly, the Top 5 tools within included tools for different purposes, e.g. for acceptance testing (Robot Framework), web application testing (Selenium), continuous integration (Jenkins) and cross-platform functional testing (UFT/QTP & SoapUI). Tables 3 and 4 show the details of the Top 15 tools and related data.

Contrasting Survey 2 with Survey 1 (RQ2)

Looking at the new results, (although two surveys were somewhat different of nature) it seems that the market has partially changed and partially stayed the same over the three years. The same tools seem to dominate, with just slight changes in market share (e.g. Robot Framework & Selenium). One could see somewhat more mobile-suitable tools, e.g. Appium, in the results as an expected development. In particular, Jenkins (continuous build and test management tool) and Sikuli (visual GUI testing tool) have appeared as new tools in comparison to Survey 1. Both surveys indicated a strong preference for using supportive tools (e.g. Office tools). According to Survey 1 those tools were mainly used for reporting and documentation purposes. Thus, it is unsurprising that reporting features were also listed as one of the important supportive features for test automation in Survey 2.

In both surveys, we also requested the respondents to describe important criteria when selecting a tool (for software testing or test automation). Qualitative coding of the criteria of Survey 2 indicated two clearly important categories, the possibility to modify the tool (to the needs of the organization) and usability of the tool. The respondents seemed to value features such as (in the order of preference) ease and intuitiveness of use, compatibility of the tool with the existing system, applicability (to tasks, methods and processes), reporting features as well as price. Cost related issues were not the topmost interest for the respondents of Survey 2 (although related to the concept of open source tools).

In Survey 1 the functionalities reported to affect the acquisition of software testing tools the most were (in the order of preference) price, ease of use, functionality, management and compatibility with other applications. The differences in conducting the surveys may affect the results (e.g. possibly having options to choose from vs. free text questions as in Survey 1 & 2, respectively).

The Top 15 list of tools from Survey 2 has not yet affected the preferences of Knowit, but it supports their strategy by substantiating the general evidence of the rising trend of open source tools in the market. For example, the company has already adopted Jenkins as part of their offering despite the fact that it did not appear in the 2013 survey. From a viewpoint of a consulting company, tailored sets of tools are required to serve different types of needs of customers. The results from both surveys, in general, seem to correlate with the tools used by the wide customer-base (mainly Finnish companies) of Knowit.

5.3   Web-Scraping of Top 15 Tools

From the data, see Tables 3 and 4, it seems that Python was clearly the tool being most "popular" considering any indicator. This is understandable: Python appeared about 25 years ago, thus the tool is expected to have far more software enthusiasts than any other tool in the list. We are aware Python is not a pure software testing tool, but mainly a programming language, supporting many testing related activities.

Surprisingly, the differences in the number of hits for the search terms were not as diverse among the tools as the case with Wikipedia page views. (Four tools having most hits shared the same level in hundreds of thousands). As a disclaimer, the hits were not analyzed any further to reveal whether those links were actually truly relevant to the original search terms or not. In fact, a hit is a request to a webserver for a file. Since Web pages may contain several files and images, loading a web page does not always equal to one [18]. Thus, it is claimed that a hit is an inaccurate measure of popularity or traffic of a website, page views providing a more accurate measure [17]. All Top 15 tools but two, Sikuli & Appium, had an article (in English) in Wikipedia. UFT shared an article with QTP (QTP being deprecated and replaced by UFT).

The commercial tools seem to have a trend of having less questions in StackOverflow than open source (free) tools. That may be due to a fact that commercial software vendors often provide dedicated customer services for their paying customers in need of help. With open source tools, people rely on the help of their fellow colleagues or forums of software professionals (or software enthusiasts). Also, the user manuals (e.g. online services) for commercial tools may be of higher quality and richer content than those for open source tools (if manuals exist). Interestingly, the differences in the average numbers of view counts per question for tools are not that big. Also, there seems to be a difference between posted tweets for commercial and open source tools compared with the number of StackOverflow questions. The five commercial tools are among the top eight tools for the number of tweets. However, the tweets may, due to the nature of the Twitter – list of short messages, possibly connected with hashtag(s), contain totally irrelevant content. Furthermore, since the length of a tweet is limited the tweets with "valid" content are not expected to include comprehensive discussions or descriptions but rather opinions or short comments like user tips, promotions, job advertisements or release notes.

Contrasting Web-scarping method with Surveys (RQ3)

Utilizing information in the web by different searches has for long been an important method for finding information about tools for Knowit. For a few decades there have been many websites collecting "the most used tools" or "the best tools" for the help of others looking for such tools. However, these are often rather biased geographically (e.g. US-based perspective only) and do not really show how common some tool is.

Web-scraping provides a rather quick way to acquire large amounts of data in comparison to surveys. However, selection of relevant sources for data can be difficult as well as finding the suitable methods to process and analyze the data, in order to provide useful or meaningful information. As experienced in this study, the Top 15 tools are quite different by characteristics and purpose. Thus, the popularity or familiarity of the tools, based on data from Survey 2, are not expected to be comparable, as such. Utilizing

Web-scraping as a big-data style approach, as presented in this paper, gives some of the power of surveys into utilizing the web as a source for information. This makes the popularity of tools more evident. Still, surveys are irreplaceable in giving voice to the people themselves, especially in specific market sectors and contexts – and Web-scraping should be considered only as a good add-on source to surveys.

Contrasting Web-scraping results with Survey (RQ3)

Robot Framework was the most popular tool referenced by the respondents of Survey 2, however, just third but last (among the Top 15 tools) according to the ranking based on the results from Web-scraping (see Tables 3 and 4). Please note, the total ranking is counted from all ranked columns, taking account the number of references in Survey 2, Wikipedia page views, Google hits, StackOverflow questions, view count of those and average number of views per question as well as Twitter tweets. Popularity of Selenium and Jenkins was evident in the results of both Web-scraping and Survey 2 (although the latter was not referenced in Survey 1). Surprisingly, TFS seems to be widely adopted (based on the number of Wikipedia page views, StackOverflow questions, view count of those and even tweets) although that was not the case in Survey 2 (or Survey 1).

Popularity, as being widely adopted, is difficult to generalize from data from a survey since such results are always biased by the size and the origin of the sample, like in the case of Robot Framework. Web-scraping provides a wider, quantitative perspective to the tool scene. However, in our surveys the background information about respondents serves as anchor for positioning the results to more concrete contexts.

6 Discussion

Our data could not confirm the growth of the number of the internal tools in relation to open source frameworks, as reported by [19]. Only about 7 % of the respondents of Survey 2 reported having been using an inhouse tool for some specific purpose. (It may also be that those tools have not been reported accurately or have not been considered as tools related to software testing). Interestingly, the most popular tool, Selenium, reported by [19] was the second most popular in our survey, after Robot Framework (particularly popular in Finland due to its origin). Four and five out of nine different tools reported for small and large size organizations (respectively) were also in the list of Top 15 tools in our Survey 2 [19]. However, the order of the tools was otherwise differing.

When considering popularity or familiarity of software testing or test automation tools, sources like StackOverflow or social media like Twitter are actually rather good sources of information. On the other hand, comparing commercial and open source tools that way does not seem very appropriate since most likely majority of questions or problems faced with commercial tools may have been handled via official (private) customer support channels, not via developer forums. Also, groups of software professionals may have formed self-sufficient support networks within their organizations only.

As with criteria provided by the respondents, ease of use, compatibility and applicability of the tools are important. Some software professionals may have been using some tool for years, may be well familiar with functionalities, pros and cons of such tools, but not aware of existing or new tools that could actually be more suitable (or supportive) for their purposes (e.g. considering costs or effectiveness). Some commercial tools provide a period of free trial but companies may not have the resources to share for trying out different choices or combinations of compatible tools. This is where the wisdom of the crowds could be applied to.

6.1   Limitations

There are several limitations affecting this study. Firstly, the surveys were targeted to (mainly Finnish) selected groups of software professionals, thus the two sets of respondents were rather small and expected to be biased (although experienced based on work history). Secondly, the list of tools analyzed is based on experiences of those small groups of respondents. The tools were not only related to software testing or software test automation but also more general and supportive for the process. Thirdly, comparison of popularity or familiarity of such tools brought up issues like commercialism and concept of open source software, different characteristics and purposes for the tools, different contexts for utilizing those tools and compatibility, just to mention a few. Furthermore, the surveys were not identical as the first survey used a list of preselected tool options while the latter survey was implemented as open text-fields. The question that remains is whether some less used tools are left out if only the main tools are mentioned (e.g. a tool set of a typical project may include 10–20 tools).

7   Conclusions and Future Work

In this paper, we make three contributions. First, we describe the test tool selection problem in a software testing consultancy. Having the right tools is critical for testing consultants when they offer suitable services for their clients (RQ1). Second, we presented results of two surveys conducted in 2016 and 2013 (the responses mainly from Finland). Surveys are a good source of professional knowledge that can be applied, within the limits of a known context, as such. We found that among our respondents' the tools which have gained popularity are Robot Framework, Jenkins, and Sikuli while Selenium has maintained its high popularity (RQ2). Third, we present Web-scraping as a method that may provide additional quantitative (or qualitative) support for the tool selection process (RQ3).

According to our results, from both surveys and Web-scraping, the tools that ranked the most popular (based on the references of 2016 and metrics from Web-scraping, Tables 3 and 4) were Python, Selenium, Jenkins, TFS and Junit (in that particular order). Python was included in the list of Top 15 tools since many of the respondents of Survey 2 had listed it as an important instrument for test automation and thus is clearly of interest in global scale, too.

Results provided by the respondents regarding important criteria for tool selection were surprisingly alike (RQ4). However, when mapping our open coded criteria results to the ISO/IEC 25010 quality model, there were two evident categories that could not be directly mapped to the model, namely "Support" and "Costs". "Support" (including "General Tool Support", "Popularity", "Future of the Tool" and "Vendor Independence") or "Costs" (including "Price", "License model", "Acquisition costs", "Operating costs" or "Free") are in fact characteristics that may be critical in providing value to stated and implied needs of stakeholders.

The results highlight that local preferences may differ from global preferences (considering e.g. Robot Framework), but some tools like Selenium and Junit stand out as popular tools based on our surveys and Web-scraping as well as [19]. Web-scraping is seen as cost effective support for traditional surveys. Utilizing multiple sources enables getting a comprehensive picture of the tools in markets.

As future work, based on this study, another survey is planned to be conducted applying acquired criteria for related tools. The idea is to support the process of selecting the right tools by acquiring and comparing software professionals' knowledge or perceptions of characteristics of selected tools.

Acknowledgments. Our thanks to all respondents for their contribution to this survey.

References

1. Capgemini Consulting: World Quality Report 2015–2016. (2015). https://www.capgemini.com/thought-leadership/world-quality-report-2015-16
2. Fewster, M., Graham, D.: Software Test Automation: Effective Use of Test Execution Tools. ACM Press/Addison-Wesley Publishing Co (1999)
3. Garousi, V., Zhi, J.: A survey of software testing practices in Canada. J. Syst. Softw. **86**(5), 1354–1376 (2013)
4. Hussain, S., Wang, Z., Toure, I. K., Diop, A.: Web service testing tools: A comparative study. arXiv preprint arXiv:1306.4063 (2013)
5. ISTQB (International Software Testing Qualifications Board): ISTQB® Worldwide Software Testing Practices Report 2015–2016 (2016). http://www.istqb.org/references/surveys/istqb-worldwide-software-testing-practices-report.html
6. Kaur, H., Gupta, G.: Comparative study of automated testing tools: selenium, quick test professional and testcomplete. Int. J. Eng. Res. Appl. **3**(5), 1739–1743 (2013)
7. Kaur, M., Kumari, R.: Comparative study of automated testing tools: testcomplete and quicktest pro. Int. J. Comput. Appl. **24**(1), 1–7 (2011)
8. Michael, J.B., Bossuyt, B.J., Snyder, B.B.: Metrics for measuring the effectiveness of software-testing tools. In: 13th International Symposium on Software Reliability Engineering, pp. 117–128. IEEE (2003)
9. Ng, S., Murnane, T., Reed, K., Grant, D., Chen, T.: A preliminary survey on software testing practices in Australia. In: 2004 Australian Software Engineering Conference, pp. 116–125. IEEE (2004)
10. Pan, A., Raposo, J., Álvarez, M., Hidalgo, J., Viña, Á.: Semi-automatic wrapper generation for commercial web sources. In: Rolland, C., Brinkkemper, S., Saeki, M. (eds.). IFIP, vol. 103, pp. 265–283. Springer, Heidelberg (2002). doi:10.1007/978-0-387-35614-3_16
11. Petersen, K., Wohlin, C.: Context in industrial software engineering research. In: 3rd International Symposium on Empirical Software Engineering and Measurement, pp. 401–404. IEEE (2009)

12. Portillo-Rodríguez, J., Vizcaíno, A., Piattini, M., Beecham, S.: Tools used in global software engineering: a systematic mapping review. Inf. Softw. Technol. **54**(7), 663–685 (2012)
13. Poston, R.M., Sexton, M.P.: Evaluating and selecting testing tools. Software **9**(3), 33–42, IEEE (1992)
14. Surowiecki, J.: The Wisdom of Crowds. Anchor, New York (2005)
15. Tassey, G.: The economic impacts of inadequate infrastructure for software testing. National Institute of Standards and Technology, RTI Project, 7007.011 (2002)
16. Tiitinen, M., Kakkonen, K.: Software Testing Tools Research in Finland, Knowit Oy (2013). http://www.knowit.fi/Documents/Testausty%C3%B6kalututkimus_Posteri_A3_Tiitinen_V11_ENG.pdf
17. Wikipedia Page view. https://en.wikipedia.org/wiki/Page_view
18. Wikipedia article traffic. https://en.wikipedia.org/wiki/Wikipedia_article_traffic
19. Yehezkel, S.: Test Automation Survey (2016). http://blog.testproject.io/2016/03/16/test-automation-survey-2016/

On the Need for a New Generation of Code Review Tools

Tobias Baum$^{(\boxtimes)}$ and Kurt Schneider

FG Software Engineering, Leibniz Universität Hannover, Hannover, Germany
{tobias.baum,kurt.schneider}@inf.uni-hannover.de

Abstract. Tool support for change-based code review is gaining widespread acceptance in the industry. This indicates that the current generation of tools is well-aligned to current code review practices. Nevertheless, we believe that further improvements in code review tooling can lead to increased review efficiency and effectiveness. In this paper, we combine results from a qualitative study and results from the literature to substantiate this claim. We derive promising improvement areas and provide an overview of existing research in these areas. A common attribute of these improvements is that they trade flexibility for reviewer support. As flexibility is one of the main characteristics of the current generation of code review tools in Hedberg's classification of review tool generations, we regard these coming tools as part of a new generation of code review tools.

Keywords: Code reviews · Code inspections and walkthroughs · Tool support

1 Introduction

Code review is a well-established method of software quality assurance. In recent years, change-based review has become the dominant style of code review in industry [5,24]. Its main characteristics are the use of code changes performed in a unit of work, e.g. a user story, to determine the scope of the review, and the replacement of management intervention through conventions or rules for many decisions [5]. Change-based review is supported by tools, in some cases specialized code review tools, in other cases general-purpose tools like "diff". Looking at their widespread adoption, these tools seem to address the current needs of the industry. Nevertheless, we believe there is still room for improvement, not least because these tools do not fully incorporate existing research results. The purpose of this article is to derive and collect promising ideas to improve code review effectiveness and efficiency through code review tools in the context of industrial software development. This is done from the point of view of researchers developing these tools and based on results published in the literature and on interviews with software development professionals. This article can be used to guide and direct future research as well as tool development efforts.

© Springer International Publishing AG 2016
P. Abrahamsson et al. (Eds.): PROFES 2016, LNCS 10027, pp. 301–308, 2016.
DOI: 10.1007/978-3-319-49094-6_19

2 Methodology

The style of this article is largely deductive. We extract well-founded hypotheses from existing research and combine them to derive and evaluate improvement opportunities for industrial code review. While there are notable differences between classic Fagan Inspection and modern change-based code review, many important aspects are similar [5,24]. We therefore also include results from research on classic inspections as evidence, as long as we believe them to be applicable. Further experiments could be conducted to ascertain these assumptions. A limitation of this part of our analysis is that we did not perform a systematic literature review (SLR) in the narrow sense of the term. An SLR could have further reduced the risk to miss relevant publications.

We recently performed a study based on semi-structured interviews with 24 software professionals from 19 companies [5,6]. To some extent, these interviews concerned the way in which reviewers work and which problems they perceive. These interviews form the second pillar of our argumentation, in addition to the literature. All interviews were recorded and later transcribed. Most interviews were conducted by the first author. Some interviews were performed by another researcher to reduce the risk of bias. Our sample has a focus on small and medium standard software development companies and in-house IT departments from Germany, but we included contrasting cases for all main factors. The interviewees are mostly software developers and team or project leads, as the development teams were responsible for code reviews in the sampled cases. The interviews were conducted between September 2014 and May 2015. Further methodological details on the interviews can be found in our related articles [5,6]. The main study [6] followed "Grounded Theory" methodology, but the results presented in the current article are not a grounded theory. We cite many statements from the interviews as examples for certain points. The subscripts at these citations denote the interviewee ID from [6].

To assess the current state of code review tools, we combined information from our interviews and from the websites of the respective tools. To a limited degree, we also executed and tried some of the tools.

3   What Do We Know About Code Reviews?

A lot of research has been done on code reviews and inspections, and still many questions could not be answered conclusively. But some results are relatively well supported and a subset of these will form the foundation of our discussion:

The first such result concerns which factors have a major and which only a minor influence on the effectiveness and efficiency of reviews. When analyzing experimental data, Porter et al. "found that [reviewers, authors, and code units] were responsible for much more variation in defect detection than was process structure", and they "conclude that better defect detection techniques, not better process structures, are the key to improving inspection effectiveness." [21]. A similar conclusion is reached by Sauer et al., who identify "individuals' task expertise as the primary driver of review performance" based on theoretical considerations. Correlations between the (inspection) expertise of the reviewer and the number of found defects have also been reported by Rigby [23] and by Biffl and Halling [8], just to name a few. We conclude that the major factors influencing code review effectiveness and efficiency are the reviewer, its relation to the artifact under review and the way in which it performs the checking.

The second important result is about the role of understanding the artifact under review. In their study based on interviews with developers at Microsoft, Bacchelli and Bird found that "[m]any interviewees eventually acknowledged that understanding is their main challenge when doing code reviews" [2], which confirmed earlier results from Tao et al. [26]. Further support for a positive correlation between code understanding and review effectiveness comes from experiments by Dunsmore, Roper and Wood [12]. Our interview results fully support these findings, e.g.: "I have to understand what the other developer thought at that time. And for that you look very closely at the code, and then things that should or could be done better somehow come up automatically" $_3$.

4   The Problem of Large Changes

In our interviews, we asked about problems hampering review effectiveness. One of the most common themes was the difficulty to understand and review large changesets: "Smaller commits are generally not a problem. But these monster commits are always ... not liked very much by the reviewers." $_5$ "What sometimes impedes me is when the ticket is just too big." $_7$ "When you have such a big pile to review the motivation is not very high and you probably don't approach the review with the needed quality in mind." $_{12}$

The conclusion that large changesets are problematic can also be derived from other research results: There is evidence that the review effectiveness greatly decreases when the review rate (checked lines of code/time for checking) is outside the optimal interval (see e.g. [15]). There is also evidence that concentration and therefore review effectiveness fades after some time of reviewing [19,22]. Combining these values leads to an upper limit on the maximal size of an artifact that can be reviewed effectively in a single session.

Given the problems with the review of large changes, many teams resort to the frequent review of small changes [23]. Up to a certain point, this is a good thing to do, but there are also arguments in favor of larger changes and reviews: The change under review should be self-contained, it should fulfill certain quality criteria before central check-in (at least to be compilable) and reviewing very small changes can lead to high overhead and duplicate work [26]. So instead of forcing every change to be very small, we argue to make the review of larger changes more effective and let changes stay at their "smallest natural size".

5   Tool Support to the Rescue

We substantiated in the previous sections that to increase the effectiveness and efficiency of code reviews for defect detection, we should focus on the reviewer

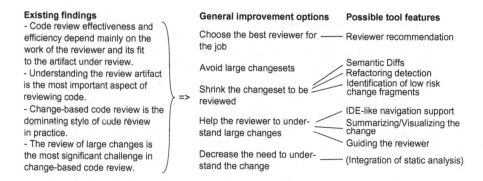

Fig. 1. Overview of argumentation and tool features

and how to help her/him understand large code changes better. We believe that improved tool support provides a lot of opportunities in this regard, and will give examples in the following subsections. Additionally, an overview of our argumentation is shown in Fig. 1. The subsections correspond to the most important influencing factors, deduced from the results mentioned so far:

- Choose the best reviewer for the job (Sect. 5.1)
- Shrink the size of the changeset that has to be reviewed (Sect. 5.2)
- Help the reviewer to understand large changesets (Sect. 5.3)
- Decrease the need to understand the change (Sect. 5.4)

5.1 Reviewer Recommendation

In recent years, there have been a number of studies on "reviewer recommendation", i.e. on finding the best reviewer(s) for a given change (e.g. [3,29]). While this promises a large effect in theory, there are several problems reducing the benefit, especially in smaller teams. The most obvious is that in a small team, it is often fairly easy to see who is a good reviewer for a change, so that computer support does not provide large gains. In some other cases, the reviewer for a certain module is fixed [5], so there is no choice at all. Additionally, always choosing the best reviewer can lead to a high review load for experienced developers, and a high workload has a negative impact on review quality [7]. Therefore reviewer recommendation has to move from determining local optima for every single review to a more global optimization of reviewer assignment.

5.2 Reducing Changeset Size

Given large changesets with singular changes of varying relevance for the review goals, reviewers try to manually pick the relevant subset. This is seen as hard and error-prone: "After some time you get a feeling which files are relevant and which are not, but it's hard to filter them out. And when I don't look at them there might be some change in there that was relevant, anyway. That's problematic." $_8$

An important special case is systematic changes, especially rename and move refactorings. This special case has been studied for example by Thangthumachit, Hayashi and Saeki [28] and Ge [14]. For the more general case, Kawrykow and Robillard [18] developed a method to identify "non-essential" differences. Zhang et al. [30] describe the tool "Critics" to help in inspecting systematic changes using generic templates. Tao and Kim [27] propose an approach to partition composite code changes. Further research could provide a better foundation to decide which changes are low-risk, and it could look into the distinction between change fragments that are error-prone and need to be checked in detail and change fragments that only need to be read to help understanding. Another research avenue is to include more data, such as test coverage information, to assess review relevance. Nevertheless, much could already be gained by bringing the promising existing results into wider use.

5.3   Support for Understanding the Change

A theme that occurred throughout our interviews is that large changes are best reviewed with the search and hyperlinking support of an IDE (e.g. "I think reviewing code purely in'Crucible' only works for trivialities. Because naturally many features are missing that you have in an IDE." $_2$). This improvement has already made its way into some widely used review tools, either by making IDE-like support available in a browser (e.g. "Upsource"[1]) or by making the review tool available as an IDE plugin (e.g. "AgileReview"[2] or "EGerrit"[3]).

Many of our interviewees try to get a high-level understanding of the change at the start of the review ("at first an overview because otherwise the problem is that you loose sight of the interrelation of the changes" $_{10}$). The current support for this activity is very limited, consisting mainly of the overview of the commit messages of the singular commits belonging to the change. There is relatively little research on visualizing and summarizing code changes for better understanding: McNair, German and Weber-Jahnke propose an approach to visualize change-sets [20], as do Gomez, Ducasse and D'Hondt [16]. In addition, several textual summarization techniques have been proposed (e.g. [9]). A related technique that can help to summarize the contents of a change is "change untangling" [4,11,27]. We believe that more research on these topics is needed to make change visualization effectively usable by reviewers.

After having an overview of the changes, the reviewer needs to step through the change's details in some order. Many reviewers try to find an order that helps their understanding, but often fall back to the order presented by their review tool: "The problem is you sometimes get lost and don't find a good starting point." $_{10}$ "If you don't have that, you just step through the files in the commit one after another ..." $_{10}$. A similar finding resulted from a study by Dunsmore, Roper and Wood where participants suggested "ordering of code" to improve

---

[1] https://www.jetbrains.com/upsource/.

[2] http://www.agilereview.org.

[3] https://www.eclipse.org/egerrit/.

inspections [13]. Guiding the reviewer as proposed here shares some similarities with the reading techniques studied intensively for inspections [1,10]. The main difference is that these reading techniques try to change the way the reviewer works, while the proposed guiding moves some cognitive load from the human reviewer to the tool. In addition, most reading techniques proposed so far are not intended to be used with changesets, so that research opportunities abound in this area.

5.4   Decrease the Need for Code Understanding

From a theoretical point of view, reducing the need to understand the code is another possibility to solve the stated problem. Essentially this is a question of efficiency: Is in-depth code review the most efficient way to find a certain defect type or are there more efficient ways, e.g. static code analysis or testing? [15,25] As long as there are practically relevant defect types for which in-depth code review is most efficient, understanding the code will still be needed. And when there will be no such defect types anymore, for example after a breakthrough in static analysis research, code review in its current form will not be needed any longer for defect detection. Therefore, we won't discuss this topic further in this article.

6   A New Generation of Code Review Tools

About a decade ago, Henrik Hedberg proposed a classification of software inspection/review tools into generations [17]. He concluded that the coming fifth generation should provide flexibility with regard to the supported documents and processes and that they should comprehensively include existing research results. This prediction has come true (with limitations): Current review tools like "Gerrit"[4], "Crucible"[5] or "Collaborator"[6] are flexible and commonly support the review of any kind of text file. In the preceding sections, we derived opportunities to reach a higher level of review effectiveness. For most of them, a reification from the review of changes in text files to the review of changes in source code has to take place. Flexibility is traded for better reviewer support to some degree. This leads us to expect the rise of the sixth generation of code review tools, the generation of "cognitive support review tools".

7   Summary

We collected four findings on code review we regard as well established: (1) Code review effectiveness and efficiency depend to a large degree on the reviewer, its style of work and its fit to the artifact under review. (2) Understanding the review artifact is the most important aspect of reviewing code. (3) Review in

---

[4] https://www.gerritcodereview.com.
[5] https://www.atlassian.com/software/crucible.
[6] https://smartbear.com/product/collaborator/.

industry is commonly done change-based. (4) The review of large changes is the most significant challenge in code review. Based on these assumptions we derived leverage points to improve review effectiveness and efficiency through tool support. For each of these points, we surveyed existing research and state open research questions. In our own work, we currently look into some of these research questions. We believe there is an abundance of open questions for other researchers to join us in our efforts to lay the foundation for the generation of "cognitive support review tools".

References

1. Aurum, A., Petersson, H., Wohlin, C.: State-of-the-art: software inspections after 25 years. Softw. Test. Verification Reliab. **12**(3), 133–154 (2002)
2. Bacchelli, A., Bird, C.: Expectations, outcomes, and challenges of modern code review. In: Proceedings of the 2013 International Conference on Software Engineering, pp. 712–721. IEEE Press (2013)
3. Balachandran, V.: Reducing human effort and improving quality in peer code reviews using automatic static analysis and reviewer recommendation. In: Proceedings of the 2013 International Conference on Software Engineering. IEEE Press (2013)
4. Barnett, M., Bird, C., Brunet, J., Lahiri, S.K.: Helping developers help themselves: automatic decomposition of code review changesets. In: Proceedings of the 2015 International Conference on Software Engineering. IEEE Press (2015)
5. Baum, T., Liskin, O., Niklas, K., Schneider, K.: A faceted classification scheme for change-based industrial code review processes. In: 2016 IEEE International Conference on Software Quality, Reliability and Security (QRS). IEEE (2016)
6. Baum, T., Liskin, O., Niklas, K., Schneider, K.: Factors influencing code review processes in industry. In: Proceedings of the ACM SIGSOFT 24th International Symposium on the Foundations of Software Engineering. ACM (2016)
7. Baysal, O., Kononenko, O., Holmes, R., Godfrey, M.W.: Investigating technical and non-technical factors influencing modern code review. Empir. Softw. Eng. **21**(3), 932–959 (2016). doi:10.1007/s10664-015-9366-8
8. Biffl, S., Halling, M.: Investigating the influence of inspector capability factors with four inspection techniques on inspection performance. In: Eighth IEEE Symposium on Software Metrics, 2002, Proceedings, pp. 107–117. IEEE (2002)
9. Buse, R.P., Weimer, W.R.: Automatically documenting program changes. In: Proceedings of the IEEE/ACM international conference on Automated software engineering, pp. 33–42. ACM (2010)
10. Denger, C., Ciolkowski, M., Lanubile, F.: Investigating the active guidance factor in reading techniques for defect detection. In: International Symposium on Empirical Software Engineering, 2004, Proceedings, pp. 219–228. IEEE (2004)
11. Dias, M., Bacchelli, A., Gousios, G., Cassou, D., Ducasse, S.: Untangling fine-grained code changes. In: 2015 IEEE 22nd International Conference on Software Analysis, Evolution and Reengineering, pp. 341–350. IEEE (2015)
12. Dunsmore, A., Roper, M., Wood, M.: The role of comprehension in software inspection. J. Syst. Softw. **52**(2), 121–129 (2000)
13. Dunsmore, A., Roper, M., Wood, M.: Systematic object-oriented inspection - an empirical study. In: Proceedings of the 23rd International Conference on Software Engineering, pp. 135–144. IEEE Computer Society (2001)

14. Ge, X.: Improving tool support for software developers through refactoring detection. Ph.D. thesis, North Carolina State University (2014)
15. Gilb, T., Graham, D.: Software Inspection. Addison-Wesley, Wokingham (1993)
16. Gómez, V.U., Ducasse, S., D'Hondt, T.: Visually characterizing source code changes. Sci. Comput. Program. **98**, 376–393 (2015)
17. Hedberg, H.: Introducing the next generation of software inspection tools. In: Bomarius, F., Iida, H. (eds.) PROFES 2004. LNCS, vol. 3009, pp. 234–247. Springer, Heidelberg (2004). doi:10.1007/978-3-540-24659-6_17
18. Kawrykow, D., Robillard, M.P.: Non-essential changes in version histories. In: Proceedings of the 33rd International Conference on Software Engineering, pp. 351–360. ACM (2011)
19. Laitenberger, O., Leszak, M., Stoll, D., El Emam, K.: Quantitative modeling of software reviews in an industrial setting. In: Sixth International, Software Metrics Symposium, 1999, Proceedings, pp. 312–322. IEEE (1999)
20. McNair, A., German, D.M., Weber-Jahnke, J.: Visualizing software architecture evolution using change-sets. In: 14th Working Conference on Reverse Engineering, 2007, WCRE 2007, pp. 130–139. IEEE (2007)
21. Porter, A., Siy, H., Mockus, A., Votta, L.: Understanding the sources of variation in software inspections. ACM Trans. Softw. Eng. Methodol. (TOSEM) **7**(1), 41–79 (1998)
22. Raz, T., Yaung, A.T.: Factors affecting design inspection effectiveness in software development. Inf. Softw. Technol. **39**(4), 297–305 (1997)
23. Rigby, P.C.: Understanding open source software peer review: review processes, parameters and statistical models, and underlying behaviours and mechanisms. Ph.D. thesis, University of Victoria (2011)
24. Rigby, P.C., Bird, C.: Convergent contemporary software peer review practices. In: Proceedings of the 2013 9th Joint Meeting on Foundations of Software Engineering, pp. 202–212. ACM (2013)
25. Roper, M., Wood, M., Miller, J.: An empirical evaluation of defect detection techniques. Inf. Softw. Technol. **39**(11), 763–775 (1997)
26. Tao, Y., Dang, Y., Xie, T., Zhang, D., Kim, S.: How do software engineers understand code changes? an exploratory study in industry. In: Proceedings of the ACM SIGSOFT 20th International Symposium on the Foundations of Software Engineering. ACM (2012)
27. Tao, Y., Kim, S.: Partitioning composite code changes to facilitate code review. In: 2015 IEEE/ACM 12th Working Conference on Mining Software Repositories (MSR), pp. 180–190. IEEE (2015)
28. Thangthumachit, S., Hayashi, S., Saeki, M.: Understanding source code differences by separating refactoring effects. In: 2011 18th Asia Pacific Software Engineering Conference (APSEC), pp. 339–347. IEEE (2011)
29. Thongtanunam, P., Tantithamthavorn, C., Kula, R.G., Yoshida, N., Iida, H., Matsumoto, K.-I.: Who should review my code? a file location-based code-reviewer recommendation approach for modern code review. In: 2015 IEEE 22nd International Conference on Software Analysis, Evolution and Reengineering (SANER) (2015)
30. Zhang, T., Song, M., Pinedo, J., Kim, M.: Interactive code review for systematic changes. In: Proceedings of 37th IEEE/ACM International Conference on Software Engineering. IEEE (2015)

Process Improvement

GQM⁺Strategies and IDEAL: A Combination of Approaches to Achieve Continuous SPI

An Experience Report in a Large Multi-industry State-Owned Company

Gustavo López[✉], Alexia Pacheco, Francisco Cocozza, Diana Garbanzo,
Brenda Aymerich, and Gabriela Marín

Universidad de Costa Rica, San José, Costa Rica
{gustavo.lopez_h,alexia.pacheco,francisco.cocozzagarro,
diana.garbanzo,brenda.aymerich,gabriela.marin}@ucr.ac.cr

Abstract. GQM⁺Strategies is an approach that aligns the business goals at each level of an organization to strategies and assesses the achievement of goals. The IDEAL model is an organizational improvement model. In this paper, we present our experiences applying the IDEAL model and GQM⁺Strategies to conduct continuous software process improvement (SPI) and establish a measurement program in a large multi-industry state-owned company. Our goal is to provide evidence of the use of these methods and models in such complex scenarios. The motivation for this paper was the lack of "from the trenches" perspectives on SPI in this kind of contexts. The main challenges faced during the experiences reported in this paper include: rigid control structures used to manage and monitor IT investment, inadequate or incomplete use of other measurement methods, and lack of continuous improvement culture (due to many years in a monopolistic industry). Moreover, we present ways in which we combined GQM⁺Strategies and the IDEAL model to deploy a continuous process improvement program in a context of limited resources and serious business threats, and to convince the company employees of the need for process improvement.

Keywords: Software engineering · Software process improvement · IDEAL model · GQM⁺Strategies · Measurement · Large multi-industry state-owned company · Experience report

1 Introduction

Software Process Improvement (SPI) is a complex and expensive task. SPI becomes even harder to implement when the company in which is going to be applied is either non software-driven or managers have not realized that it is in fact a software-driven company.

Nowadays, most companies are software-driven because productivity, time-to-market, and time-to-decide are the most critical differentiators in competitive industries.

© Springer International Publishing AG 2016
P. Abrahamsson et al. (Eds.): PROFES 2016, LNCS 10027, pp. 311–326, 2016.
DOI: 10.1007/978-3-319-49094-6_20

Software processes have a large impact not only on the organizations following them, but also on the products being developed [1]. Moreover, the impact of process change can range from outstanding to chaotic for the companies undertaking SPI initiatives.

Traditionally, small and medium sized enterprises (SME) have worried about fast return of investment (RoI), and large companies have worried about large RoI. However, the volatility in most industries is forcing a change in these perspectives [2].

In this paper, we present an experience report in which a SPI initiative is undertaken in a large multi-industry company. Two major characteristics of this company are that it is a state-owned company and that one of the industries in which it performs recently moved from a monopolistic industry to a competitive one. Furthermore, this company is part of a larger corporation.

One challenge of implementing a SPI program in this context is the fact that the company investment in software development is high; however, most of the investment goes to third parties providing services or products (e.g., outsourcing, solution and infrastructure providers). Another complication is that, since it is a state-owned company, rigid control structures are used to manage and monitor incomes and expenses.

However, the largest challenge is that the fact of being in a competitive environment is only starting to sink in the company employees' minds. Moreover, old monopolistic practices became instantly obsolete when the market opened for competition. To comply with regulations, to invest efficiently in SPI and to speed up the employee adoption of new practices, we combined a systematic approach for SPI (i.e., IDEAL model (henceforth IDEAL)) and a goal alignment method (i.e., GQM$^+$Strategies).

In order to become a high performance company, goals must be understood, stratified by levels and linked to one another [3, 4]. We applied GQM$^+$Strategies to try to achieve this goal. We applied IDEAL to comply with internal and external regulations (e.g., audits, comptroller reviews, and even internal questionings).

This paper presents the efforts of an academic research team jointly with company representatives to execute a SPI in a complex company. The goal of this research is to assess the applicability of IDEAL and GQM$^+$Strategies combined to conduct a SPI effort. This combination was necessary due to the necessity of explicitly stating the SPI plan.

Even though GQM$^+$Strategies is based on a method for SPI [5], it is focused on measurement and goal alignment. The use of Balanced Scorecards [6, 7] is an established practice in the company. Therefore, using other performance management tool (as managers originally saw GQM$^+$Strategies) to drive SPI was not conceptually correct, as it would be contradictory with traditional practices.

This rest of the paper is structured as follows: Sect. 2 presents theoretical background; Sect. 3 delves in the application context in which we implemented GQM$^+$Strategies and IDEAL, Sect. 4 presents the different ways in which we saw fit to combine GQM$^+$Strategies and IDEAL, Sect. 5 describes the main results of our experiences. In Sect. 6 we discuss our experiences and detail lessons learned. Finally, Sect. 7 presents our final considerations.

2   Theoretical Background

2.1   GQM+Strategies

GQM+Strategies is a measurement approach that helps align the goals and strategies of an organization. A goal is a description of a status in which the organization wants to be in the future. A strategy defines the actions that the organization will carry to achieve such status [5].

The core of GQM+Strategies is based on the fact that goals must be measurable in order to assess if they are accomplished or not. Strategies are defined considering context factors and organizational assumptions that could affect their outcome [5].

GQM+Strategies requires interpretation models that would help managerial level decision-makers to understand the measurement results. GQM+Strategies consists of 6 phases [5, 8]:

- **Initialize.** In this phase is intended to assure commitment and resources for applying GQM+Strategies. Moreover, the responsibilities are defined and involved people are trained to understand the approach. The application process is planned and the scope is defined.
- **Characterize the Environment.** The context is key in the application of GQM +Strategies, therefore, this stage is intended to characterize the organization in order to understand the "best" approach to achieve goal alignment.
- **Define Goals, Strategies, and Measurement.** GQM+Strategies main tool is the GQM+Strategies Grid. The grid is an instrument that shows the organization goals and their relation. Moreover, the goals are linked with strategies across different units. The goals also have a measurement model for evaluating goal attainment, and guidelines for interpreting the measurement data. The grid is a live tool (i.e., it changes according to the organization's reality).
- **Plan Grid Implementation.** In this phase, plans are prepared for implementing, measuring and deploying the strategies described in the grid. At this point, specific processes must be executed to implement the strategies defined in the GQM+Strategies Grid (i.e., GQM+Strategies does not propose methods to implement the strategies).
- **Execute Plans.** In this phase, strategies are implemented and measured according to the plans. Plan execution triggers a cycle within itself, therefore, the plan should have been design to assess the execution in order to continue the implementation of strategies across the organization. GQM+Strategies proposes the implementation of strategies in small units at first, to validate and assess their adequacy.
- **Analyze Outcomes.** The idea of analyzing the outcomes of the plan execution phase lies in the assessment of either a serious problem or a successful deployment of the strategy addressed.
- **Package Improvements.** The final phase of GQM+Strategies is designed to learn from the process, and modify the grid according to the lessons learned. Moreover, the authors of GQM+Strategies state that this phase must communicate the outcomes to provide visibility and to initiate a new cycle.

2.2 The IDEAL Model

The IDEAL model is defined as "A life cycle approach for process improvement" [9, 10]. It was developed by the Software Engineering Institute (SEI) at Carnegie Mellon University. IDEAL offers guidelines for the selection, implementation and evaluation of software processes and methods in an organization. Moreover, it provides strategies to understand when the process improvement might be required. IDEAL consists of 5 phases and a total of fourteen activities, which address the specific requirements of one complete cycle of the model. Each phase is composed of several activities.

- **Initiating.** This is the starting point of IDEAL once the stimulus for improvement is evident; the main infrastructure is established, as well as roles, responsibilities, and high level goals. Moreover, this phase sets the context and sponsorship for the improvement. The main product of this phase is a plan to guide the process improvement through the organization. IDEAL has some key groups that lead or execute tasks. In the initiating phase, the Management Steering Group (MSG) and the software engineering process group (SEPG) are defined and conformed.
- **Diagnosing.** This phase sets the baselines for the process improvement. It is aimed to identify the infrastructure, characterize current practices and define improvement recommendations. It's a high level diagnosis of the organization's vision, business plans and current process maturity. The recommendations that arise from this activity provide the basis for an action plan draft.
- **Establishing.** In this phase the organization prioritizes the improvement activities, based on the diagnosis findings, difficulty of implementing the improvements, and other factors. With the improvements prioritized, the plans are created and measurable goals are defined, these goals must be aligned with the ones established in the initiating phase. Monitoring metrics are defined, and the resources required to perform the work are committed. In this phase the technical working groups (TWGs) that will execute the improvement are defined.
- **Acting.** This is the execution phase; solutions to address the areas for improvements are created, piloted, and deployed throughout the organization. This phase has two main purposes: assess the organization's readiness to adopt the new practices, and document the experiences gathered from the pilot implementations of the improvements, in order to ease the institutionalization. After assessing the success of the improvement, it is planned and executed, and the installation is tracked.
- **Leveraging.** The final phase is conducted to learn from the experiences and to determine if the goals have been met. Moreover, this phase is crucial to improve the actions that will be executed in further IDEAL cycles. An evaluation of the strategy, methods and infrastructure is conducted.

This section theoretically described GQM[+]Strategies and IDEAL. These methods were selected to be implemented in a large multi-industry state-owned company. Even though authors consider important the comparison of these approaches with related works, lack of space to deliver a proper comparison left this part of the work out of this research paper. Next section describes the application context.

3   Application Context

The experiences reported in this paper are the result of a SPI application in a large multi-industry state-owned company. Moreover, this company is part of a state-owned corporation. The company has more than 15.000 employees on the payroll. It is multi-industry working in the communications and electricity generation contexts. One of which recently transitioned from a monopoly to a competitive environment. The company is state-owned (i.e., part of the budget is managed by the government).

Figure 1 shows the SPI scope within the main corporation. Even though the SPI is only being applied in only one of the companies, it is expected for the investment to be replicable in all other companies. The main reason for this is that most of the investment comes from public funds.

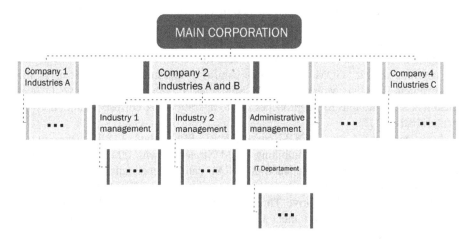

Fig. 1. SPI scope within the corporation (ellipsis represent further levels; dark boxes represent the main scope of the SPI application reported in this paper)

The SPI initiative comes from the IT Department of Company 2. This IT Department provides services for all three management departments within the company; however, it is under the supervision of the administrative management.

Industries 1 and 2 have fairly different dynamics, the most important being that one still works in a monopolistic context and the other recently opened to competition. Furthermore, the main corporation and all its companies have rigorous controls because they are state-owned, and lack process change experiences.

Even though, the necessity to adapt to the new competition rules and to reduce expenses drove the company to conduct a SPI program, IDEAL was used to conduct it systematically, and to comply with regulations and controls. One of the company's goals is to become a high performance enterprise, and improve its internal capabilities to reduce the need for third parties.

We realized that in order to boost the SPI progress, visibility and transparency of investment was required. Moreover, goal alignment was necessary to help managers and employees to dimension the impact of the SPI. To achieve this goal GQM

+Strategies was a perfect fit. However, the first obstacle for GQM+Strategies was the entrenched use of the Balanced Scorecard.

It is not that balanced scorecard is not an appropriate performance management framework, but when applied without clear goals and other additional controls are used, it can easily become a pitfall for the organization applying it [11].

In an effort to visualize the SPI impact, we conducted GQM+Strategies as a process improvement and understood the alignments and possible benefits in the combination of the two approaches (i.e., GQM+Strategies and IDEAL).

4   Combining GQM+Strategies and IDEAL

GQM+Strategies and IDEAL are methods proposed by recognized authors in the software engineering field. The first is a method that provides concepts and phases to link goals and strategies across an organization using a measurement based approach [8], the second a continuous SPI model [9, 10].

GQM+Strategies developers explicitly state the relation between GQM+Strategies and continuous SPI: "GQM+Strategies is helpful to measure the contribution of the improvement initiative. Moreover, GQM+Strategies could be used to improve the goal alignment of continuous SPI approaches and to operationalize corresponding improvement initiatives" [5].

It is clear that the core of GQM+Strategies is a SPI method [12]. However, in our experiences we believe that combining GQM+Strategies with other (not necessarily measurement-driven) SPI model such as IDEAL can be beneficial. For instance, in a state-owned company that already has measurement models, GQM+Strategies could not be used to drive a SPI initiative. Therefore, combining it with IDEAL provide a good fit to assure measurement alignment and convince management that the SPI is being driven in a formal way.

IDEAL is being applied to create a company level program for software process improvement. IDEAL was selected due to its success in several contexts [13–15], and recommendations of expert consultants. The following sections describe the ways in which we combined GQM+Strategies and IDEAL to support the SPI program.

4.1   Base Application of IDEAL and GQM+Strategies as the Method for Measurement Process Improvement

In the context of a SPI application in a large company, we decided to address SPI with IDEAL as our main guide. Therefore, we executed the Initiating phase. The stimulus for improvement was primarily due to the industry competition, and the ever changing requirements in the software development areas of the company.

The sponsorship was clearly defined since members of the corporation requested the involvement of an academic team to enhance their probabilities of succeeding in the implementation of the SPI.

The Diagnosing phase started, interviews, observations and surveys were applied both at tactical and managerial levels of the IT department (Fig. 1). This resulted in a list of over 30 improvement opportunities to be addressed. The diagnosis was based on four dimensions: people, technology, process and culture.

Findings and recommendations were prioritized and the three most important improvement opportunities were selected to be addressed in the first iteration of the Establishing phase. Plans to incorporate agile software development practices, DevOps [16, 17] and improve measurement were developed. Both in agile software development and DevOps, further diagnosis was required in order to establish a concrete implementation plan. On the other hand, software metrics was already being addressed. In parallel, academics and employees of the corporation were working in the application of GQM⁺Strategies. Figure 2 shows how the introduction of GQM⁺Strategies was implemented as a part of the IDEAL model.

Fig. 2. Application of GQM⁺Strategies as the framework to implement measurement process improvement within the IDEAL model

After this stage, we realized the possibilities in which GQM⁺Strategies and IDEAL could be combined to provide systematic SPIs and goal alignment through the company at the same time.

The process concluded at IDEAL's acting phase with a retrospective session for leveraging and the GQM⁺Strategies implementation continued (i.e., in our implementation of IDEAL and GQM⁺Strategies, we concluded the IDEAL cycle and maintained the GQM⁺Strategies cycle specifically for the measurements process improvement and goal alignment).

It is important to mention that one of the a priori decisions was to improve the measurement process. However, the sponsors of the SPI originally, did not want to invest in the implementation of GQM⁺Strategies. Once they realized the results of the GQM⁺Strategies Grid implementation, and the amount of duplicated effort in similar goals across the organization, their perspectives changed.

This approach to combine IDEAL and GQM⁺Strategies is valuable since the application of GQM⁺Strategies assures that all improvements will be aligned with organizational and business goals, and the application of IDEAL makes sure that the improvements are performed in a systematic and well documented way, easing the institutionalization of the successful improvements at company level, and possibly, at corporation level.

4.2 GQM⁺Strategies Results as Inputs for IDEAL's Initiating, Establishing, Diagnosing and Leveraging Phases

To execute IDEAL's initiating phase, the organization requires identifying personnel that would launch the improvement. Moreover, the business critical needs need to be fully understood [10]. Assuming that the organization is already applying GQM+Strategies, that input will be available, since the discovery of qualified personnel to improve processes is also a requirement for GQM+Strategies and the business goals will be aligned with lower level goals that can be addressed in the SPI program.

IDEAL's diagnosing phase requires the organization's vision, business plan, and SPI goals to be synergistic [10]. This is also one of the main results of applying GQM⁺Strategies. In order to establish process baselines in the diagnosing phase, GQM⁺Strategies metrics could be used to lighten baseline implementation.

Table 1 shows how the results of GQM⁺Strategies phases match IDEAL phase inputs, reducing the effort required to implement IDEAL.

Table 1. Match between GQM⁺Strategies results and IDEAL inputs

GQM+Strategies phase	IDEAL phase inputs
Initialize, Characterize the environment	Initiating and diagnosing phases can use the gathered information to define the baselines.
Define Goals, Strategies, and Measurement	Goal alignment can be used to prioritize SPI efforts.
Plan Grid Implementation	The Grid implementation is actually the Establishing phase of IDEAL, in this phase the improvements are planned and progress measurement is defined.
Execute Plans	This is directly mapped with IDEAL`s action phase. However, in order to be consistent with the SPI program, IDEAL is used to execute GQM+Strategies plans (see Section 4.3).
Analyze Outcomes and Package Improvements	This is directly mapped with IDEAL`s Leveraging phase.

The effort of applying GQM+Strategies to gain only these advantages will not be beneficial. However, in a context like the one we are working in, with GQM+Strategies being used to align organizational goals and define progress measurement strategies, and IDEAL to guide other SPI initiatives, the results of GQM+Strategies are really beneficial to reduce the work required for the IDEAL model execution.

The efforts executing GQM⁺Strategies were very useful to drive the SPI program, from the goal prioritization, to SPI progress measurement. Furthermore, the GQM ⁺Strategies Grid, can be used to track and identify SPI impact within the organization.

Figure 3 illustrates how we combined GQM⁺Strategies outputs to boost IDEAL's execution.

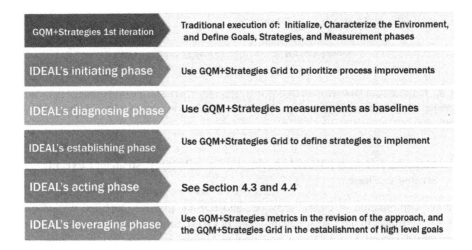

Fig. 3. Illustration of how we used GQM⁺Strategies results to boost IDEAL implementation in processes other than measurement

4.3 GQM⁺Strategies Metrics as Measuring Inputs for IDEAL's Action Phase

The proper application of GQM⁺Strategies requires an effort in defining GQM graphs including measurement goals, questions, metrics, and interpretation models. IDEAL creators propose a similar approach, distributed in the Establishing and Acting phases. In our GQM⁺Strategies application we found a large amount of goals, and an external contractor suggested metrics for each one of them. This approach helped us to define how the Action phase of IDEAL was going to be measured.

It is clear that the metric proposals will require refinement, based on the execution plans for the Action phase. However, metrics were proposed following experiences and case studies reported in literature, good measurement practices or standards. Therefore, they can be a helpful guide to measure SPI progress.

Currently, two improvements are being conducted: Implementing agile practices in the software development process and implementing DevOps culture. However, none of them have reached IDEAL's acting phase. Therefore, this proposal needs to be assessed in order to measure the real value of having a generic metric proposal while implementing IDEAL. Figure 4 illustrates how we propose to use GQM⁺Strategies metrics in specific tasks within IDEAL's acting phase.

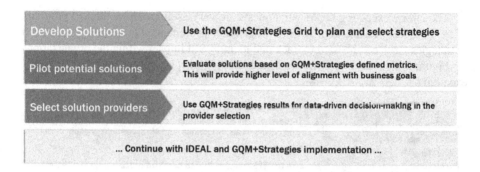

Develop Solutions	Use the GQM+Strategies Grid to plan and select strategies
Pilot potential solutions	Evaluate solutions based on GQM+Strategies defined metrics. This will provide higher level of alignment with business goals
Select solution providers	Use GQM+Strategies results for data-driven decision-making in the provider selection
	... Continue with IDEAL and GQM+Strategies implementation ...

Fig. 4. Illustration of how we used GQM⁺Strategies results to boost IDEAL's acting phase (this figure has a higher granularity than Figs. 2 and 3 as it provides insights for tasks within the acting phase)

4.4 Mapping Between IDEAL's Acting Phase and GQM⁺Strategies Execute Strategies Phase

The last combination of GQM⁺Strategies and IDEAL that we identified was to use IDEAL's artifacts in the Execute Plans phase of GQM⁺Strategies. In GQM⁺Strategies, plans are designed to implement and deploy "improvements" through a series of projects, in order to achieve a GQM⁺Strategies Grid goal. These improvements are assessed and replicated in the organization.

In our context, the approach proposed by GQM⁺Strategies authors is too lightweight (i.e., people within the organization could question the rigor of the process). Therefore, using IDEAL to execute GQM⁺Strategies strategies can provide the necessary documentation to demonstrate the process flow and progress. Even though the final assessment would be provided by the changes in the metric established for the goal that wants to be achieved. The process is as important as the results in order to allow replication in the organization.

Since we defined that IDEAL would be the guide for process improvement beforehand, we did not implement GQM⁺Strategies execute strategies phase. However, we considered that this approach will also be beneficial if these two methods are combined.

5 Results

The main result of the IDEAL model application was the documentation of the SPI program efforts. It is important to mention that we adapted the instruments proposed by the authors or the model in order to lighten them just enough to allow agility while complying with the regulations.

Other important result of applying IDEAL was the establishment of the MSG and SEPG (i.e., IDEAL's permanent work forces [9]), because these groups of people have enough credentials for decision making regarding the SPI and have influence on the budget assignment.

GQM⁺Strategies Grid was a valuable instrument to assess the efforts proposed in a large company. However, the efforts required to execute the initialize, characterize the environment, and the define goals, strategies, and measurement phases was very high. These high costs are a reflection of a segmented company with duplicated goals at management levels.

Figure 5 shows the GQM⁺Strategies Grid structure result of the first GQM⁺Strategies iteration and of the review of a large number of assets within the company. In Fig. 5, dark boxes represent goals and white boxes represent strategies for those goals. The GQM⁺Strategies Grid contains 79 goals and more than 150 strategies.

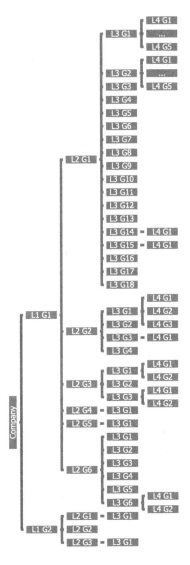

Fig. 5. GQM+Strategies grid. This Figure illustrates the complexity of goals in the company.

One of the most important tasks of the GQM⁺Strategies application was to identify duplicated goals or strategies. Those duplicates were unified in the GQM⁺Strategies Grid, however, the process allowed us to identify which managements were planning on implementing which improvements.

As it was mentioned, other important result of GQM⁺Strategies was the definition of generic metrics for each goal. These metrics are a valuable asset to assess the improvements once they start.

6 Discussion

As we showed in previous section, the combination of GQM⁺Strategies and IDEAL is a good fit for this project context. Even though we know that regulatory policies must be changed, in order to allow agility, this change should be gradual and we found a good tool in IDEAL to start this change.

GQM⁺Strategies is also a great method, especially in these multi-industry contexts. The use of the GQM⁺Strategies Grid provided great visibility of the efforts performed in the SPI program.

The following sections describe the experiences, lessons learned of the combination of GQM⁺Strategies and IDEAL. Moreover, we describe the unsolved problems, work in progress and future work.

6.1 Experiences and Lessons Learned

We believe that IDEAL is a very structured way to conduct SPI programs. Since the context in which SPI is being conducted is used to the application rigorous methods IDEAL is a fit. IDEAL only provides a model to conduct the improvements and does not suggest ways to implement them; therefore, it must be combined with other methods to assure acceptance within the organization.

In a similar way GQM⁺Strategies is a very structured way to align goals within the organization and to define metrics. However, it does not provide insights on the way in which strategies should be executed to achieve those goals. Therefore, it must be combined with other models to attain the organization's regulations (i.e., execute strategies in a structured way).

We know that these regulations are somehow obsolete. In a world in which software processes are becoming more and more agile every day, the necessity of ordered prescriptive processes is lower and lower. Since the context is a state-owned company that is used to perform task in certain ways, the combination of this GQM⁺Strategies and IDEAL is a great match.

In the beginning or our SPI, we suffered from managerial absence and lack of commitment. After gaining confidence with senior management, we suffered from exhausted middle managers that did not want to free resources from their daily tasks to participate in the SPI process. This problem was solved with the change of managers and the participation of new resources specifically selected by the new managers to drive the SPI process.

The application of GQM+Strategies and the creation of the GQM+Strategies Grid allowed us to regulate manager's enthusiasm and help them realize the amount of low level goals defined in the organization. The largest version of the GQM+Strategies Grid contained more than 79 different goals and over 150 strategies associate to those goals. Therefore, when the IDEAL application began, they were able to estimate the amount of effort required to execute a process improvement initiative and the possible impacts of those processes for the organization.

On the other hand, we assessed a large amount of documentation. In some of the documents a lightweight Capability Maturity Model Integration (CMMI) appraisal was conducted and the "ideal" maturity level pre-established by the organization was 5 (i.e., optimized). By applying GQM+Strategies identification and selection of existing assets, we recognized these unrealistic expectations and were able to discuss them with middle and senior management before implementing any improvement.

Other challenge that was faced during the first iteration of the SPI was finding the "right" time to execute the improvements. Middle managers were too busy with their daily tasks and the improvements were stalled. In order to avoid obsolescence of action plans, we decided not to continue the SPI until the sponsorship changed, and efforts to change managerial perspectives were made. Finally, with the change of managers, the sponsorship arrived and the process continued. This could not have been possible without the application of IDEAL guiding the SPI. We would have realized the lack of middle managerial support when the improvement was going to be deployed rather than at the beginning of the process. To avoid resource and time waste, we invested the stall time to proceed with GQM+Strategies application.

As for the measurement, we realized that, due to lack of a better measurement infrastructure, the metrics were calculated using surrogate measures. Moreover, communication problems avoided the proper use of gathered information in the decision-making process. Some of these issues still persist, and we are working on solving them.

Other problem identified by applying GQM+Strategies and IDEAL was the lack of an outsourcing governance program (i.e., standardized outsourcing practices). This issue was identified while applying GQM+Strategies and helped us to include some governance aspects during the IDEAL execution and helped the company to recognize the business risks inherent to lack of outsourcing management standards.

Even though it might be considered a current agile trend, iterative SPI allowed us to demonstrate progress in short periods of time. Moreover, by holding retrospectives we endorsed continuous improvement of the SPI definition and implementation.

One of the best ways to provide visibility to a SPI program is by actually improving. However, process selection based on priorities is required for large scale impact. The big bang approach is rejected in our application context. We know that current SPI program expectations will take several years to be met. However, to increase productivity some changes can be quick fixes. For instance, moving to agile outsourcing contracts [18] and training inside employees to work with contractors in this way.

Finally, our SPI program is aligned with technical training courses and two graduate programs: one on software development and the other on management information systems. These linked programs are expected to help employees understand the new processes, concepts, techniques and problem domains.

6.2 Unsolved Problems and Work in Progress

One problem that rose from the application of GQM⁺Strategies was that, since the method has not been widely adopted in the company, other efforts performed to define goals and strategies were not aligned with the GQM⁺Strategies Grid. For instance, the latest IT Department plan was released and misalignments with the GQM⁺Strategies Grid were found. This issue was fixed by iterating over the GQM⁺Strategies Grid definition to include new goals and strategies. However, these efforts and its costs could have been mitigated if the methods and information were unified.

Other unresolved problem is the change in control structures. IDEAL's documentation would help to provide new models to control agile projects; however, auditors, comptrollers, and other actors need to change their perspectives towards agile practices for the SPI program to work. This issue is directly linked with the company's culture.

Other pending task is to adopt and boost a continuous improvement culture. In our context, this task has become difficult, because some of the employees still have practices aligned with non-competitive markets. We expect to change the culture using the lead by example approach. This change is required in order to be able to meet the company's needs and business goals. Moreover, a bottom up approach can be used to demonstrate senior management that SPI can really increase RoI and transform their vision and willingness to support and launch a long term continuous SPI program.

We have already defined some improvements by working with the management steering group, software engineering process group, and technical working groups. However, a pending task is planning how to get other employees to accept these new processes and participate in other improvements.

In our context, the MSG was matched with other committee that was already in place when the SPI began. Nonetheless, the participants of this board have traditional practices, and do not match the agility requirements neither for IDEAL nor for GQM⁺Strategies. Therefore, effort should be placed to change these practices.

One of the major difficulties that we have faced is that the company has very structured controls and hierarchical interaction approaches, therefore, some employees have aversion to be held responsible for some tasks. We know that in order for the SPI program to be successful, everyone should be held responsible for the improvements.

7   Conclusion

In this paper we presented our experiences applying the IDEAL model and GQM⁺Strategies to conduct continuous software process improvement and establish a measurement program in a large multi-industry state-owned company. Also, we suggested several ways in which IDEAL and GQM⁺Strategies can be used to complement each other.

We were forced to use a systematic approach for SPI, because state-owned companies have rigorous controls over resource investment and are accustomed to use heavy methodologies in most of their processes. However, we expect to change or adapt IDEAL, once a continuous improvement culture becomes part of the company.

We believe that the experience presented in this paper could be beneficial for other endeavors in the application of GQM⁺Strategies that face organizational resistance. We conducted a parallel effort of GQM⁺Strategies and IDEAL up to the point in which we could convince the company representatives that IDEAL was a formality. If the SPI is conducted in a measurement driven way, the formality is not necessary as the progress can be measured by results rather than documents generated. However, the application of IDEAL is not trivial. Therefore, a significant investment was covered while these efforts were conducted in a parallel way.

The use of GQM⁺Strategies was crucial to provide the goal alignment required to implement a SPI program. We believe that, if it was not for the effort invested in constructing the GQM⁺Strategies Grid, we would not even found half of the already proposed strategies to improve processes in the company. Even performing the IDEAL's diagnosing phase in a strict and deep way would not provide the assets that GQM ⁺Strategies did.

We are still working on timing. In order to improve processes and pilot solutions, internal resources are required. However, the company's culture is still too rigid to free the necessary resources to implement improvements. We are working in two specific process improvements: agile development and DevOps; nevertheless, these efforts are not sufficiently strong to produce the impact expected.

We present these experiences because there is a lack of "from the trenches" perspective on SPI in this kind of contexts, and we hope for these experiences to be useful for other researchers or companies implementing SPI programs.

Acknowledgment. This work was partially supported by Research Center for Communication and Information Technologies (CITIC) at University of Costa Rica. Grant No. 834-B4-412. We would also like to thank all the consultants that participated in this research including but not limited to: Dr. Marcelo Jenkins (current minister of Science and Technology of Costa Rica), Dra. Alexandra Martínez, Dr. Carlos Castro, Mag. Mauricio Arroyo, and Mag. Marcela Chacón.

References

1. Alagarsamy, K., Justus, S., Iyakutti, K.: Implementation specification for software process improvement supportive knowledge management tool. IET Softw. **2**, 123–133 (2008)
2. Clarke, P., O'Connor, R.V.: The Influence of SPI on business success in software SMEs. J. Syst. Softw. **85**, 2356–2367 (2012)
3. Pfeffer, J.: Seven practices of successful organizations. Calif. Manage. Rev. **40**, 96–124 (1998)
4. Muda, A.L., Fook, C.Y., Noordin, N.M.: The relationship between learning culture and high performance and productivity culture with job satisfaction: a study among employees in one public organization in Sarawak, Malaysia. In: Fook, Y.C., Sidhu, K.G., Narasuman, S., Fong, L.L., Abdul Rahman, B.S. (eds.) 7th International Conference on University Learning and Teaching (InCULT 2014), Proceedings: Educate to Innovate, pp. 17–25. Springer, Singapore (2016)
5. Basili, V.R., Trendowicz, A., Kowalczyk, M., Heidrich, J., Seaman, C., Lindvall, M., Munch, J.: Aligning Organizations Through Measurement - The GQM⁺Strategies Approach. Springer, Switzerland (2014)
6. Kaplan, R.S., Norton, D.P.: The balanced scorecard - measures that drive performance. Harv. Bus. Rev. **70**(1), 71–79 (1992)

7. Kaplan, R.S.: Conceptual foundations of the balanced scorecard. In: Handbooks of Management Accounting Research, Vol. 3, pp. 1253–1269 (2008)

8. Basili, V.R., Lindvall, M., Regardie, M., Seaman, C., Heidrich, J., Rombach, D., Trendowicz, A., Münch, J., Rombach, D., Trendowicz, A.: Linking software development and business strategy through measurement. Comput. (Long. Beach. Calif.) **43**, 57–65 (2010)

9. Mcfeeley, B.: IDEAL: a user's guide for software process improvement, Pittsburgh, Pennsylvania, USA (1996)

10. Giemba, J., Myers, C.: The IDEAL model: a practical guide for improvement. Bridg. Softw. Eng. Inst., **23**(3) (1997)

11. Fink, A., Marr, B., Siebe, A., Kuhle, J.: The future scorecard: combining external and internal scenarios to create strategic foresight. Manag. Decis. **43**, 360–381 (2005)

12. Basili, V., Caldiera, G., Rombach, H.D.: Experience factory. In: Encyclopedia of Software Engineering. John Wiley & Sons, Inc. (2002)

13. Casey, V., Richardson, I.: A practical application of the IDEAL model. In: Oivo, M., Komi-Sirviö, S. (eds.) Product Focused Software Process Improvement, pp. 172–184. Springer, Heidelberg (2002)

14. Klendauer, R., Hoffmann, A., Leimeister, J.M., Berkovich, M., Krcmar, H.: Using the IDEAL software process improvement model for the implementation of Automotive SPICE. In: Cooperative and Human Aspects of Software Engineering, pp. 66–72. IEEE (2012)

15. Pino, F.J., García, F., Piattini, M.: Software process improvement in small and medium software enterprises: a systematic review. Softw. Qual. J. **16**, 237–261 (2008)

16. Swartout, P.: Continuous Delivery and DevOps: A Quickstart guide. Packt Publishing, Birmingham (2014)

17. Verona, J.: Practical DevOps. Packt Publishing, Birmingham (2016)

18. Larman, C., Vodde, B.: Practices for Scaling Lean & Agile Development: Large, Multisite, and Offshore Product Development with Large-Scale Scrum. Addison-Wesley Professional, Reading (2010)

On the Role of Software Quality Management in Software Process Improvement

Jan Wiedemann Jacobsen[1], Marco Kuhrmann[1(✉)], Jürgen Münch[2],
Philipp Diebold[3], and Michael Felderer[4]

[1] The Mærsk Mc-Kinney Møller Institute,
University of Southern Denmark, Odense, Denmark
janwj12@student.sdu.dk, kuhrmann@mmmi.sdu.dk
[2] Herman Hollerith Center, Reutlingen University, Böblingen, Germany
juergen.muench@reutlingen-university.de
[3] Fraunhofer Institute for Experimental Software Engineering,
Kaiserslautern, Germany
philipp.diebold@iese.fraunhofer.de
[4] Institute of Computer Science, University of Innsbruck, Innsbruck, Austria
michael.felderer@uibk.ac.at

Abstract. Software Process Improvement (SPI) programs have been implemented, inter alia, to improve quality and speed of software development. SPI addresses many aspects ranging from individual developer skills to entire organizations. It comprises, for instance, the optimization of specific activities in the software lifecycle as well as the creation of organizational awareness and project culture. In the course of conducting a systematic mapping study on the state-of-the-art in SPI from a general perspective, we observed Software Quality Management (SQM) being of certain relevance in SPI programs. In this paper, we provide a detailed investigation of those papers from the overall systematic mapping study that were classified as addressing SPI in the context of SQM (including testing). From the main study's result set, 92 papers were selected for an in-depth systematic review to study the contributions and to develop an initial picture of how these topics are addressed in SPI. Our findings show a fairly pragmatic contribution set in which different solutions are proposed, discussed, and evaluated. Among others, our findings indicate a certain reluctance towards standard quality or (test) maturity models and a strong focus on custom review, testing, and documentation techniques, whereas a set of five selected improvement measures is almost equally addressed.

Keywords: Software process improvement · Software quality management · Software test · Systematic mapping study · Systematic literature review

1 Introduction

To organize software development companies look for *Software Process Improvement* (SPI; [19]) allowing them to analyze and to continuously improve their

© Springer International Publishing AG 2016
P. Abrahamsson et al. (Eds.): PROFES 2016, LNCS 10027, pp. 327–343, 2016.
DOI: 10.1007/978-3-319-49094-6_21

development approaches. In the course of conducting a systematic mapping study [24], SPI was mentioned a diverse field: many SPI facets are studied, several hundreds of custom SPI approaches were proposed, e.g., to address weaknesses of standard approaches like CMMI [34], SPI success factors are collected and analyzed, and new trends such as SPI employing agility as improvement principle are addressed. SPI thereby aims at improving companies' competitiveness and is considered important regardless of a company's size [16].

Besides accelerated development procedures, the quality of the software products developed is another important criterion (cf. Bennett and Weinberg [4], who found bug fixing cost increasing by magnitudes in later lifecycle phases). Therefore, improving the quality of software and determining the economic value [14], notably for small and very small companies [28] is of certain relevance. For those companies, emphasizing quality is crucial, as software testing is a strenuous and expensive process [5] consuming up to 50 % of the total development costs [17]. Therefore, improving the quality management and, in particular, the software test activities provide a perfect starting point for improving the software process and hence product quality.

Problem Statement and Objective. SPI programs have been implemented to improve product quality and speed of software development and have shown impact [2]. Also, software quality assurance techniques play an important role to guarantee and improve quality. Yet, the role of software quality assurance and SQM in SPI programs has not explicitly been investigated so far. The objective of this research is therefore to analyze the literature to characterize the role of SQM in SPI.

Contribution. This paper provides an overview of the study population on SPI with a special focus on SQM and shows how these studies are evaluated. It presents the software quality assurance techniques and improvement measures addressed in SPI. Our findings show indication that SPI in the context of SQM is equally focussed on software testing as well as on complementing (support) activities including reviews and documentation techniques. Furthermore, our findings show a trend towards utilizing individual testing approaches rather than implementing/following standards.

Context: A Systematic Mapping Study on SPI. This study is grounded in a comprehensive systematic mapping study on the state of SPI of which the findings where published in [24] (to which we refer to as the *main study*). Outcomes of this study show SPI being an actively researched topic, yet lacking theories and models. Instead, the field of SPI is shaped by a constant rate of approx. 10–12 new SPI models per year. These trends observed were used to form topic clusters of which one cluster addresses *Software Quality Management and Software Test*. The study at hand investigates this particular cluster in more detail utilizing a systematic review (cf. Sect. 3).

Outline. The remainder of the paper is organized as follows: Sect. 2 discusses related work. In Sect. 3, we describe our research approach, before we present the results of our study in Sect. 4. We provide a discussion on the results in Sect. 5 and conclude the paper in Sect. 6.

2 Related Work

In (general) SPI, different topics are researched in secondary studies. For instance, Monteiro and Oliveira [31], Bayona-Oré [3], and Dybå [7] study SPI success factors, while Helgesson et al. [15] and van Wangenheim et al. [36] review maturity models, and Hull et al. [18] review different assessment models. These exemplarily mentioned studies show that the SPI community has started the search for generalizable knowledge. Yet, the mentioned studies address more general SPI issues.

The study at hand is the first literature study explicitly dedicated to the role of *Software Quality Management* (SQM) and *Test Process Improvement* (TPI) in SPI. It is, however, related to other reviews and secondary studies in SPI, TPI, and the improvement of other analytical and constructive software quality aspects. For instance, regarding TPI, Afzal et al. [1] provide a systematic review, which identified 18 approaches and their characteristics, and an industrial case study on two prominent approaches, i.e., TPI Next and TMMi. Authors found that many of the test process improvement approaches do not provide sufficient information nor do the approaches include assessment instruments. A systematic review by Garcia et al. [10] identified 23 test process models, many of them adapted from TMMi and TPI. Reviews and comparisons of TPI models are also covered by a number of industrial white papers (so-called "grey literature", e.g., [21,27]), which points to the practical relevance of this field. At the more general level of analytical verification and validation processes, Farooq and Dumke [9] discuss research directions for the improvement of verification and validation processes. Authors identify research challenges concerning quantitative management, improvement of existing approaches, approaches for emerging development environments as well as empirical investigation of success factors and tool selection. Regarding constructive software quality aspects, several systematic reviews (e.g., for software documentation [39]) are available, but reviews discussing these quality aspects in relation to SPI are missing so far.

All these representatively selected studies address specific topics, yet, they do not contribute to a more general perspective on SPI in the context of SQM. The paper at hand thus fills a gap in literature by collecting and analyzing publications that emphasize SPI in the SQM context and, therefore, also lays the foundation to direct future research in this field in SPI research.

3 Research Design

This study is an in-depth analysis of a data subset identified in a systematic mapping study [24]. In this section, we present the research design including research questions, data collection and analysis procedures, as well as considerations on the study's validity. Our research approach for the present study follows the procedures applied in [25]; an in-depth analysis of SPI in Global Software Engineering.

3.1 Research Questions

In the course of analyzing the selected papers on SQM, this study aims to answer the following research questions:

RQ 1 *What is the study population on SPI with a special focus on SQM?* This research question aims at capturing the field of SPI from the perspective of quality management and test. It also helps positioning the sub-study to the main study.

RQ 2 *Which software quality assurance techniques and improvement measures are addressed in SPI?* Based on 58 new metadata attributes, this research question aims at determining the different quality assurance techniques and improvement measures addressed by SPI.

RQ 3 *How are studies on SQM in SPI evaluated?* This research question is concerned with the determination of the impact of the investigated studies, in particular, to determine the rigor and relevance [20] of the result set.

3.2 Data Collection Procedures

Being a study on a data subset (see also [25]), in this study, we had no need for an explicit and self-contained data collection. Input data was obtained from the main study's result set [24], which we refer to as the study's *raw data*. The selection of the data of interest in the raw data was carried out by selecting all publications from the raw data having the attributes "Quality Management" and/or "Test" set (Fig. 3), which initially results in 96 publications. The resulting subset (to which we refer to as the *study data*) was then copied to an own spreadsheet. To improve the reliability of the data analysis, two external researchers joined the team. Finally, two researchers carried out the data selection and cleaning procedures and the initial data analysis, one researcher was concerned with the definition of the extended metadata set and the data classification and analysis, and the two remaining researchers took over quality assurance tasks.

Having the study data available, in the course of downloading all selected papers, an initial quality assurance was performed. This quality assurance led to the exclusion of four papers (reasons: misclassification, violation of language constraints). Those papers' metadata was updated, such that they will be returned to the main study (Sect. 6). Eventually, **92** papers remained in the cleaned study dataset, which where then analyzed as described in Sect. 3.3.

3.3   Analysis Procedure

As "preparatory" study with the purpose of getting the big picture, the main study was conducted as a systematic mapping study following the guidelines as proposed by Petersen et al. [32]. The present study however aims to deliver more insights and details and, thus, is carried out also using the systematic review instrument as described by Kitchenham and Charters [23]. In particular, during the paper download and quality assurance, the initial metadata set (40 attributes, Fig. 3) was revisited and, if necessary, updated. Furthermore, with calling in an external researcher (an expert in quality management and testing), the set of metadata was substantially extended by 58 extra attributes in nine new metadata categories (see Fig. 4).

During the analysis, each paper was inspected by two researchers, who checked (and if necessary revised) the initial values of the metadata, provided an initial assignment of values to the new attributes, and developed a paper summary of 2–3 sentences. Finally, to evaluate the papers regarding their rigor and relevance, we applied the model proposed by Ivarsson and Gorschek [20] to complete the picture. These steps were iteratively double-checked by a third researcher, and finally independently checked by the two researchers concerned with (general) quality assurance. The analysis as such utilizes descriptive statistics (e.g., charts and tables), whereas we mainly rely on bubble-charts and heat maps.

3.4   Validity Procedures

To improve the validity of the results, we applied the following measures: First, we called in two external researchers and formed two teams. Team 1 (3 persons) conducted the data analysis, while team 2 (2 persons) was taking over the quality assurance. Second, in the data analysis phase, team 1 re-applied the procedures of the main study [24], i.e., all papers were re-inspected to check the correct assignment and to complete the assignment of the 40 metadata attributes. Third, in the inspection, the assignment of the attributes (40: main study, 58: new, scoped), and the evaluation according to the rigor-relevance model [20] were carried out using the *systematic review* instrument [23] using the full text of the study-relevant papers.

4   Study Results

In this section, we present the results of the study. We start with an overview of the study population, before we present the results of the analyses structured according to the research questions in Sects. 4.1, 4.2 and 4.3. Section 5 presents an integrated discussion of the results obtained from the study.

In total, 92 papers remained in the study data set for inspection. Figure 1 provides an overview of the publication frequency in the study timeframe. In general, in the result set, we see about 3 and 4 papers on the topic of interest

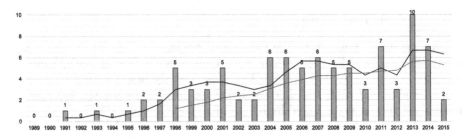

Fig. 1. Number of publications on SPI with a focus on software quality management and/or testing ($n = 92$). The graph includes two trend lines to visualize the long-term development of the field (calculation basis: mean, 3-year (black) and 10-year (red) period), which show periodical waves, but also a continuously growing general interest. (Color figure online)

published per year, but Fig. 1 also shows a first big jump in 1998 (from there on, the average publication frequency is 5+ papers per year). In subsequent sections, we provide further details and analyze them in relation to the trend observed.

4.1   RQ1: General Study Population

In this section, we first give an overview of the general study dataset using the instruments from the main study [24] to allow for comparability. Figure 2 provides an integrated overview of the study dataset according to the classification using the standard schemas (*research type facet* (RTF) according to Wieringa et al. [37]) and *contribution type facet* (CTF) according to Petersen et al. [32]).

Figure 2 shows the studied publications forming two CTF-clusters. In particular, SPI with a special emphasis on software quality management and software test is mainly reported as *framework* or as *lessons learned*, whereas the framework-classified papers usually propose solutions and the lessons learned emerge from experience and evaluation research. Furthermore, a considerable share of the *lessons learned* papers are classified as *philosophical papers*, i.e., secondary studies or discussion/comparison papers. In line with the findings from the main study [24], models and theories are in the minority or missing. Another (unexpected) finding is the small number (only 2 out of 92 papers) of tool-related publications. However, although tools are underrepresented in the "formal" literature, in [11], authors argue that more tool-related material can be found in the "grey literature". Insofar, the chart from Fig. 2 can be considered consistent with the findings from [11].

Figure 3 shows the classification of the study dataset using the metadata system introduced in [24]. Regarding the *process* dimension, the study dataset shows a strong focus on general improvement and custom models. Furthermore, standard SPI and maturity models (CMMI and ISO/IEC 15504) are addressed, but we can also see a certain focus on general measurement (and assessment) activities. Regarding the *context* dimension, in the lifecycle phases, only project management is significantly represented showing the close relation of project-

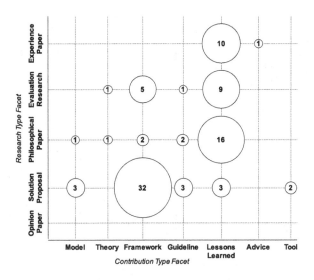

Fig. 2. Classification of the study dataset according to the RTF and CTF schemas.

and quality management. Other lifecycle phases are scarcely addressed, which suggests the publications from the dataset being narrowly scoped. Concerning the *application domain*, the classification does not highlight any favorite, i.e., SQM and testing are considered relevant in all application domains. Finally, regarding the *company size and scale* group, publications address companies of all sizes. Furthermore, globally distributed development is also addressed by the study dataset. Figure 3 shows the studied field mostly researched in a practical manner, i.e., case study research is found the most frequently used instrument. The figure shows that a number of multi-case or longitudinal studies are available (which is above the general tendency observed in the main study), yet, still, replication research is absent.

4.2 RQ2: Improvement Measures and Quality Assurance Techniques

To investigate which improvement measures and quality assurance techniques are addressed by the study dataset, we extended the metadata system from [24] and defined 58 new attributes for classifying the papers under study. We added "Quality Management and Testing" as new dimension, and we refined this dimension into nine groups (Fig. 4). For space limitations, in the following, we provide the big picture in Fig. 4, but focus on the groups "Improvement Measures" and "Quality Assurance Techniques". The big picture in Fig. 4 shows the groups *test activity*, *non-functional testing*, and *level of testing* well covered. Furthermore, the dataset provides rich information regarding the groups *improvement measures* and *quality assurance techniques*. However, especially regarding test maturity models (or "standardized" testing approaches in general),

The following table (Fig. 3) is organized into three dimensions with sub-groups. Columns: Total, then years 1989–2015.

Dimension / Group	Attribute	Total	89	90	91	92	93	94	95	96	97	98	99	00	01	02	03	04	05	06	07	08	09	10	11	12	13	14	15
Process / Publication Objective	Agile / Lean	19																1	2		1		2	2	2	2	1	5	1
	Process Simulation	3										1		1					1										
	Process Line/Patterns	1																1											
	Product Line/Management	1																1											
	Success Factors	17				1				1		1			2		1	1		1	2	2		1			2	1	1
	Custom Model	56		1			1	1		2	3	1	3		2	3	5	3	4	3	3	2	4	3	7	4	1
	General Improvement	31			1			1	2	4	1	1	3		1	2	2	2	1	1	3		3		2		1
Process / Assessment and Ass. Models	CMMI	59			1		1	1	2	4	3	2	3	2	2	5	4	2	1	3	2	1	4	1	9	4	2
	ISO/IEC 15504	30			1		1	1	1	1	3	1	1	1		5	2		2	1		2	1		6		1
	General Measurement	37		1		1		1	1		1	1	1	1		2	1		3	3	3	2	1	4	2	3	3	1
Process / (Quasi-) Standards (and Techniques)	Six Sigma	4														1									1		1	1
	Bootstrap	13									1	2		2	1		2	1						1		1	1	1
	CompetiSoft	2																			1					1	
	Continuous Improvement	6											1				1					1	1	2			
	PSP/TSP	7											1			1	2	1		1						1
	ISO/IEC 29110	1																							1	
	ISO/IEC 12207	6																		1	1				1	1	2
Study Type and Method	Survey/Interview	16							1			1	1	1			1	1					2		2	3	
	Single Case-Study	33						1		2	1	1	1	1	2	3	3	1	3	1	2		2	2	3	3	1
	Multi-Case/Long. Study	24				1			1	2	3		3			1	2	1	3	2	2	1	1	1
	Replication Study	0																										
	SLR/SMS	7															1		2		1	2	1
	Grounded Theory	4																1			1		1		1
Context / Life Cycle Phases	Project Management	33							1		4	2	1	1	2	1	4	3	2	1	2		2		3	3
	Quality Management	89		1		1		1	2	2	5	3	3	5	2	2	6	6	5	6	5	2	7	2	9	7	2
	Requirements Engineering	10									1	2		1	1	1		1	1				1	1
	Architecture	4										1		1	1		1							
	Implementation	3									1						1						1
	Test	37							1		2	1		2	1	1	2	2	2	1	2	2	3	3	2	6	4
Context / Company Size and Scale	VSE/SME	22				1			1		1	1			2	1	1	2	2	1	1	3
	Other Company Size	31				1		1		2	4		1	2	1	2	2	2	2	1	4	1		3	1
	GSE	22				1		1	1				3	2	1	2	2	1	2		1	2		2	1
Context / Application Domain	Embedded Systems	12											1		1		2	2	1			1	1	2	1
	Telecommunications	12					1	1					1	1	1	1	1		1			1	1	1
	Medical Devices	4													1			1					1
	Automotive	4														2	1						1
	Mission-critical Defense	5						1	1											1	1		1
	Business IS	3												1	1		1
	Web/Mobile/Cloud	6											1			1	1		1		1	1
	Skills and Education	1						1

Fig. 3. Overview of the different standard metadata attributes addressed over time. The darker the color, the more papers in a year have this attribute assigned, whereas one paper can have multiple attributes assigned. (Color figure online)

the dataset provides only little information, which indicates to a confirmation of the observed trend from [24] regarding the reluctance towards standardization— also for quality management and testing (and as initially found in [26]).

Regarding the groups "Improvement Measures" and "Quality Assurance Techniques", in the data, we see a fairly balanced distribution, i.e., a variety of topics is equally researched. The only remarkable outlier is the attribute *software infrastructure*. Favorites regarding the *improvement measures* are the improvement of defect handling (50 mentions), cost and time optimization (54 and 56 mentions). Regarding the *quality assurance techniques*, review (62), as well as testing and documentation (60 mentions each) are the most frequently mentioned ones. Subsequent sections provide further details for the aforementioned two "favorite" groups.

Group		Attribute	Total	1989	1990	1991	1992	1993	1994	1995	1996	1997	1998	1999	2000	2001	2002	2003	2004	2005	2006	2007	2008	2009	2010	2011	2012	2013	2014	2015
Quality Management and Testing	Level of Testing	Unit Testing	29			1				1			2			1		2	3	2	2	2	1	2		2	1	4	3	
		Integration Testing	14			1							2				1	1								1	2	1	2	2
		System Testing	22			1				1			1			1	1		1	2	2	2			1	2	2	3	2	
		Regression Testing	8										1						1		1					1	1		2	1
		Other	33			1			1	1			3			2	1	1	1	2	3	2	2	1	2	2	2	2	3	3
	Non-Functional Testing	Performance	4			1							1								1								1	
		Security	2			1							1																	
		Usability	8			1												1			1		1			2	1	1		
		Other	15			1							1			1		1	2		1	1		1		2		3	1	
	Test Activity	Test Planning	19										1				1		1	2	1	2	2	1		3	1	3	1	
		Test Design	10			1														1	1			1		1	1	1	3	
		Test Automation	8																3	1		1						3		
		Test Execution	8										1						1							1	2	3		
		Test Evaluation	7																	1	1			1		1	1	1	1	
		Other	23						1				1					1		1	1	2	2	3	2	3	1	4	1	
	Test Maturity Model	TPI	6													1				1						1	1	2		
		TPI Next	2																							1		1		
		TMM	4														1				1					2				
		TMMi	4																					1				3		
		Test SPICE	3																					1				2		
		Tmap	1																							1				
		Tmap Next	0																											
		TMi	0																											
		Other	7													1				1			2			1	1		1	
	Methods for TPI	Maturity Model	2					1															1							
		Metrics	5								1		1							1			1			1				
		Control Theory	0																											
		Simulation	0																											
		Other	5																1		1	1				2				
	Testing Artifacts	Test plan	11										1				1		1	1	1			1	1			2	2	
		Test requirement	1																									1		
		Test code	2																1									1		
		Test data	1																				1							
		Test model	1																			1								
		Test report	2																			1						1		
		Test architecture	1																			1								
		Test Metrics	6														1				2					1		2		
		Other	11													1	1			1		2		2	1	2	1		
	Test Role	Tester	14															1	1	2	1	2	2	1		1		2	1	
		Test manager	8																	1	1	3				1	1	1		
		Test engineer	4													1	1		1										1	
		Other	21				1			1	1	1				2	1		1		3	1	2		3	2	1	2		
	Improvement Measure	Quality Criteria	47	1			1	1			5	1	2		4		2	3	2	2	2	2	3	1		4	1	3	5	2
		Defects	50	1				1	2		3	2			2			1	2	4	5	2	2	3	3	3	3	6	4	1
		Risk	23					1			2	1						1	2		2	1	1	1	1	1		6	3	
		Cost	54	1				1	1		4	2	3		2	1	2	6	3	2	2	3	3	2		3	1	5	6	
		Time	56	1				1		1	1	5	3		1	3	1	3	4	4	3	3	3	2	2	2	2	6	7	1
		Other	48	1				1	1		3	3	2		2	1	1	3	3	2	4	3	2	1		5	1	4	5	
	Quality Assurance Technique	Review	62	1				1	1	1	4	2	2		3	1	2	3	3	3	5	3	5	2		4	3	7	5	1
		Static Analysis	23					1			1				1		1	1	1		2	2				4	2	4	2	1
		Testing	60	1				1	1		4	2			1	2	1	2	4	3	4	3	4	3		3	1	8	6	2
		Verification	34					1	1			2	1		2	1		1	2	1	3	1	1	1		3	1	7	4	1
		Documentation	60	1				1	1	1	4	2	3		3	1	2	4	3	2	3	2	4	2		4	2	9	4	2
		Guidelines	46	1				1	1	2	3	1	2		1	1		3	2	1	3	3				3	1	6	5	2
		Software Infrastructure	2																	1			1							
		Traceability	15								2	1						1	1	1			1			1	2		1	
		Training	43	1				1	2	2	1	2	2		2	1	2	3	3	1		3	4	1		1	1	6	3	1
		Other	25	1						1		2			1	1		1	4		2	1	1	1		2	1	3	2	

Fig. 4. Overview of the 58 new metadata attributes addressed over time. The darker the color, the more papers in a year have this attribute assigned, whereas one paper can have multiple attributes assigned. (Color figure online)

4.3 RQ3: Evaluation of Software Quality Management and Software Testing

In this section, we limit our analysis to the groups *improvement measures* and *quality assurance techniques*. As a first step, we review the study methods applied to the papers reporting knowledge in the groups of interest. In the second step, the publications contributing to the groups of interest are evaluated according to the rigor-relevance model [20] to allow for rating the (general) impact of the different topics.

	Study Type	Improvement Measure						Quality Assurance Technique									
		Quality Criteria	Defects	Risk	Cost	Time	Other	Review	Static Analysis	Testing	Verification	Documentation	Guidelines	Software Infrastructure	Traceability	Training	Other
Study Type	Survey / Interviews	7	6	7	9	10	8	9	3	9	5	7	9		1	5	3
	Single Case-Study	17	21	6	22	20	19	27	12	25	16	26	16	1	8	20	11
	Multi-Case/Long. Study	10	13	7	13	16	10	14	3	16	4	15	10		3	10	5
	Replication Study																
	SLR/SMS	5	3	1	4	4	4	3	1	3	2	3	6		1	1	1
	Grounded Theory	3	1	1	3	3	3	3	1	3	1	2	2			1	

Fig. 5. Overview study types applied to the groups *improvement measures* and *quality assurance techniques*. (Color figure online)

Methods Applied. Figure 5 provides a heat map summarizing the study types applied to investigate the different topics. The overview shows that SPI in the context of SQM is a fairly practically researched field. The majority of the papers assessed combine different research methods, whereas case study research is the most used approach—quite often in a mixed-method approach and also implementing a multi-case or longitudinal study approach (for term definitions, see Wohlin et al. [38]). A remarkable insight is the absence of replication research. Secondary studies and research based on Grounded Theory is present in the study data set, yet the action research approach prevails. Regarding the topic clusters, from the data, we see the cluster "Improvement Measures" fully covered, whereas in the cluster "Quality Assurance Technique" the topics *software infrastructure, traceability, training,* and *other* are only partially covered.

Evaluation of Rigor and Relevance. In the second step, we evaluate the papers within the groups of interest for their rigor and relevance according to [20]. In the overall dataset, 58 out of 92 papers are rated highly relevant (4 points), and of those, 37 papers are rated of high to very high rigor (2–3 points). In the following, we break-down our analysis to the groups "Improvement Measures" (Fig. 6) and "Quality Assurance Techniques" (Fig. 7). In Sect. 5, we use the following presentation to direct the detailed discussion.

Figure 6 visualizes the six topics within the group "Improvement Measures" and shows that the topics of favor in these groups are (general) *quality criteria, defects, cost,* and *time.* Research addressing the improvement of risk management is, so far, underrepresented and of less rigor and relevance. Remarkable, the majority of the papers in the aforementioned four categories is considered highly relevant (score 4).

Regarding the group "Quality Assurance Techniques", Fig. 7 shows the following topics of relevance: *review, testing, documentation, guideline,* and *training.* The groups *guideline* and *training* comply with an expectation when coming from the 'pure' SPI perspective—a focus on methods, their documentation (as guideline) and training. Among the more 'applicable' techniques, *review, testing,* and (test) *documentation* show a clear focus of the study data, whereas the

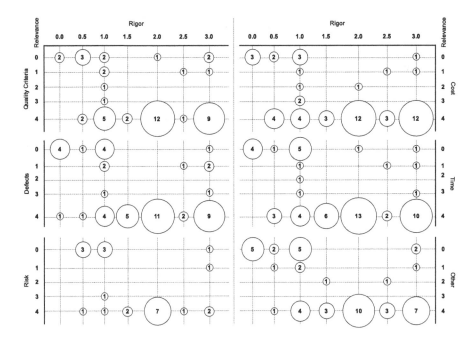

Fig. 6. Classification of the study dataset (attributes from "Improvement Measures") according to the rigor-relevance model.

techniques *static analysis* and *verification* are not that present in the data. More "sophisticated" topics, such as *traceability* and *software infrastructures* are (yet) not well represented in the study data.

5 Study Summary and Discussion

To provide a in-depth discussion, we ranked the highest rated papers regarding their coverage of improvement measures and quality assurance techniques (Figs. 6 and 7; both based on the classification according to the rigor-relevance model). Table 1 summarizes these papers for the two categories "Improvement Measure" and "Quality Assurance Technique", whereas we only provide a subset for the in-depth discussion. In particular, we select the papers [8,14,22,29] as sample from the study data set, as we found those papers represented in both categories.

Elliot et al. [8] document a methodology for implementing a software quality management system (SQMS). Table 1 shows the method proposed addressing quality management in general thus covering a number of attributes (in particular *documentation*, *guideline*, and *training*; *reviews* and (general) *testing* were mentioned as concrete techniques to, inter alia, better address different quality criteria, especially in the "system use" section). Key factors for the successful

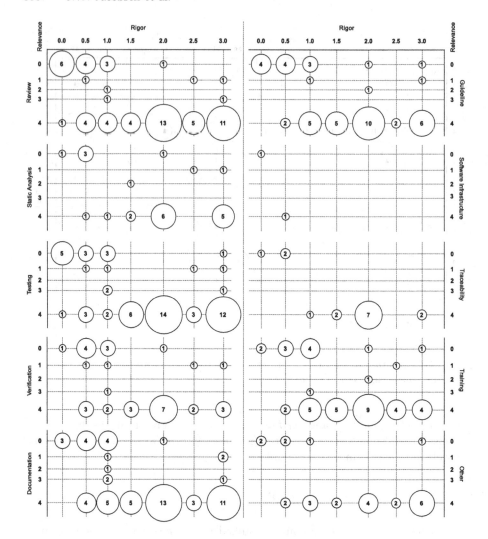

Fig. 7. Classification of the study dataset (attributes from "Quality Assurance Techniques") according to the rigor-relevance model.

implementation of the SQMS were staff training and treating users like customers, which was also required for a cultural change within the organization.

Harter et al. [14] present a framework for assessing the economic value of SPI and quality over the software lifecycle. The effects to be measured are defined based on the number of defects (development quality: defects found prior customer testing; conformance quality: defects found in customer testing prior acceptance)—similar measures are defined for development effort and cycle time, and support costs. Therefore, in [14], authors mainly address the attributes *defects*, *cost*, and *time* to conclude the economic value of SPI (Table 1).

Table 1. Overview of the highest rated papers according to the rigor-relevance model in the categories Improvement Measure and Quality Assurance Technique.

Impr. Measure	Paper	QA Technique	Paper
Quality Criteria	[8, 13, 14, 22, 29, 30, 33]	Review	[8, 14, 22, 29, 35]
Defects	[12–14, 22, 29, 30]	Static Analysis	[6, 35]
Risk	[12, 30]	Testing	[6, 8, 14, 22, 29, 35]
Cost	[8, 12–14, 22, 29, 30, 33]	Verification	[22, 35]
Time	[8, 12–14, 22, 29, 30, 33]	Documentation	[6, 8, 14, 22, 29, 35]
		Guideline	[8, 14, 22]
		Software Infrastructure	—
		Traceability	[6, 22]
		Training	[6, 8, 35]
Other	[8, 12, 13, 30, 33]	Other	[6, 8, 22, 35]

Eventually, authors found that higher quality is associated with reduced cycle times and development effort, and that savings accrue due to reduced rework and, moreover, that support activity savings outweigh development savings. Harter et al. conclude that future research efforts should focus on how SPI strategies affect support activities.

Kasoju et al. [22] use evidence-based software engineering (EBSE) to help an organization improve its testing process (domain: automotive software). They use an in-depth investigation of automotive test processes using a mixed-method approach including case study research, systematic reviews and value stream analysis/mapping. For eight analyzed projects, authors collect information regarding the test approaches, project/system kind and size, and the development approach used (Table 1; mainly attributes *cost, time, testing, verification*). In interview sessions, among other things, authors found interviewees stating a lack of a clear test process, which can be applied to any project lifecycle. Only 3 out of 8 studied projects follow a defined process (which indicates to the mainly individual and non-standardized process selection as already found in [26]; moreover, authors found that a basic testing strategy is actually defined, yet not implemented by most of the teams, which is also consistent with our previous findings from [26]). Eventually, in [22], authors conclude strengths found for automotive software testing, such as work in small agile teams, implementing agile (communication) practices, or different approaches like exploratory testing. However, authors also mention that these findings also depend on project/team size, i.e., teams of different size might go for different solution, e.g., comprehensive test case management tools are considered more valuable for larger teams. Nevertheless, authors found process issues problematic for teams of any size (consistent with [16]), e.g., lacking unified testing process, unawareness of the process, or different process-related constrains like available time windows. Finally, authors identified seven wastes, which were mapped to the testing process to drive process improvement.

Li et al. [29] describe how agile processes affect software quality, software defects and defect fixing efficiency (Table 1; mainly attributes *defects*, *testing*, *time*). A major finding is that a significant reduction of defect densities or changes of defect profiles could not be found after Scrum was used. Yet, due to the iterative development approach, the development was considered more efficiently (e.g., fewer surprises, better control over the quality, and better schedule adherence). However, on the downside, authors also mention that Scrum puts more stress and time pressure on the developers (which could make them more reluctant towards performing tasks relevant for later maintenance). In a nut-shell, authors conclude that the actual development approach is less important than iterative development and early testing (in their study, authors showed that about half of the (critical) defects was identified and fixed early thus reducing the risk of finding bugs late).

Summarizing the big picture obtained (Fig. 4) and the exemplarily selected papers (Table 1), we conclude: first, testing as such is not that massively represented in the study data as expected. For this, we argue that there is specialized (grey) literature on test process improvement (TPI), which is not properly linked to SPI—a phenomenon that we already observed for GSE [25]. In particular, so far, we did not found detailed data, e.g., regarding the actual impact of switching to an alternative test approach. On the other hand, we found indication for individual and project-specific test approach selection (even in highly-regulated domains; [22]), which confirms a finding we made in [26]. Second, so far, we found improving the quality focussing on reducing the number of defects. In [22,29], the authors found a lack of unified (standardized) testing approaches [22], and that the actual development approach (agile or traditional) seemingly not affects the defect densities or defect profiles. Harter et al. [14] suggest putting more effort in improving support activities. It therefore remains as a question for future work whether an SPI program with a "broader" perspective is more beneficial then optimizing a "technical" test method.

Threats to Validity. In the following, we evaluate our findings and critically review our study regarding the threats to validity. As a literature study, this study suffers from potential incompleteness of the search results and a general publication bias. Beyond this general threat to validity, we have to particularly discuss the internal and external validity. The *internal validity* could be biased by personal ratings of the researchers. To address this risk, we continued and refined our study [24], which follows a proven procedure that utilizes different tools and researcher triangulation to support dataset cleaning, study selection, and classification. The internal validity is also affected by the limited data collection, in particular, no new data was collected, and data analyzed is derived from the main study that serves as an umbrella. Calling in extra researchers to analyze and/or confirm decisions therefore further increases internal validity. The *external validity* is threatened by missing knowledge about the generalizability of the results. Furthermore, this study "inherits" several limitations regarding the external validity by relying on the main study's raw data only. Consequently, this study also inherits the main study's scope thus having certain limitations regarding the generalizability. Nevertheless, to increase the external validity, further independently conducted studies are required to confirm our findings.

6 Conclusion

The paper at hand provides an in-depth investigation of how software quality management (SQM) is treated in software process improvement (SPI). Based on a systematic mapping study [24], we selected all papers from the main study's dataset that address the topics SQM and software testing. In total, in this study, we inspected 92 papers.

Our findings show indication that SPI in the context of SQM is equally focussed on software testing as well as on complementing (or support) activities including reviews and documentation techniques. Furthermore, our findings show a trend in SPI towards utilizing individual testing approaches rather than implementing/following standards. A detailed discussion of four exemplarily selected papers reveals that the actual software process is less relevant than a smart arrangement of test activities (early testing) and an interactive implementation of the development process [29]. Furthermore, Harter et al. [14] suggest putting more effort on supporting activities rather than optimizing (isolated) technical tasks.

Limitations. Our study is limited by the context of the main study [24], yet showed some overlap and similar trends as obtained in other independently conducted studies, such as [11,26]. In total, only 92 papers were selected for analysis and, therefore, this study cannot claim to have delivered a generalizable set of conclusions. A major limitation is the use of a given dataset only without an extra topic-specific literature search, which potentially limits the reliability of the data. An extension and a complementing search, however, is subject to future research.

Future Work. This paper provides the first analysis iteration of the 92 papers selected thus barely scratching the surface. Future work therefore includes further detailed analyses of the study data. Furthermore, as being a study on a data subset, in future iterations, the data analyzed will be (re-)integrated with the main study's data to improve the overall data quality and reliability of the data.

References

1. Afzal, W., Alone, S., Glocksien, K., Torkar, R.: Software test process improvement approaches: a systematic literature review and an industrial case study. J. Syst. Softw. **111**, 1–33 (2016)
2. Ashrafi, N.: The impact of software process improvement on quality: in theory and practice. Inf. Manag. **40**(7), 677–690 (2003)
3. Bayona-Oré, S., Calvo-Manzano, J., Cuevas, G., San-Feliu, T.: Critical success factors taxonomy for software process deployment. Software Qual. J. **22**(1), 21–48 (2014)

4. Bennett, T., Wennberg, P.: Eliminating embedded software defects prior to integration test. CROSSTALK J. Defense Softw. Eng., pp. 13–18 (2005)
5. Bertolino, A., Marchetti, E.: A brief essay on software testing. In: Software Engineering: Development Process, 3rd edn., vol. 1, pp. 393–411 (2005)
6. Damian, D., Zowghi, D., Vaidyanathasamy, L., Pal, Y.: An industrial case study of immediate benefits of requirements engineering process improvement at the australian center for unisys software. Empirical Softw. Eng. **9**(1), 45–75 (2004)
7. Dybå, T.: An instrument for measuring the key factors of success in software process improvement. Empirical Softw. Eng. **5**(4), 357–390 (2000)
8. Elliott, M., Dawson, R., Edwards, J.: An evolutionary cultural-change approach to successful software process improvement. Software Qual. J. **17**(2), 189–202 (2009)
9. Farooq, A., Dumke, R.R.: Research directions in verification & validation process improvement. ACM SIGSOFT Softw. Eng. Notes **32**(4), 3 (2007)
10. Garcia, C., Dávila, A., Pessoa, M.: Test process models: systematic literature review. In: Mitasiunas, A., Rout, T., O'Connor, R.V., Dorling, A. (eds.) Software Process Improvement and Capability Determination, pp. 84–93. Springer, Heidelberg (2014)
11. Garousi, V., Felderer, M., Mäntylä, M.V.: The need for multivocal literature reviews in software engineering: complementing systematic literature reviews with grey literature. In: Proceedings of the 20th International Conference on Evaluation and Assessment in Software Engineering, EASE 2016, pp. 26:1–26:6. ACM, New York (2016)
12. Camargo, K.G., Ferrari, F.C., Fabbri, S.C.P.F.: Identifying a subset of TMMi practices to establish a streamlined software testing process. In: Brazilian Symposium on Software Engineering, SBES, pp. 137–146. IEEE (2013)
13. Green, G.C., Hevner, A.R., Collins, R.W.: The impacts of quality and productivity perceptions on the use of software process improvement innovations. Inf. Softw. Technol. **47**(8), 543–553 (2005)
14. Harter, D.E., Krishnan, M.S., Slaughter, S.A.: The life cycle effects of software process improvement: a longitudinal analysis. In: Proceedings of the International Conference on Information Systems, ICIS, Atlanta, GA, USA, pp. 346–351. Association for Information Systems (1998)
15. Helgesson, Y.Y.L., Höst, M., Weyns, K.: A review of methods for evaluation of maturity models for process improvement. J. Softw. Evol. Process **24**(4), 436–454 (2012)
16. Horvat, R.V., Rozman, I., Györkös, J.: Managing the complexity of SPI in small companies. Softw. Process Improv. Pract. **5**(1), 45–54 (2000)
17. Huang, L., Boehm, B.: How much software quality investment is enough: a value-based approach. IEEE Softw. **23**(5), 88–95 (2006)
18. Hull, M., Taylor, P., Hanna, J., Millar, R.: Software development processes - an assessment. Inf. Softw. Technol. **44**(1), 1–12 (2002)
19. Humphrey, W.S.: Managing the Software Process. Addison Wesley, Boston (1989)
20. Ivarsson, M., Gorschek, T.: A method for evaluating rigor and industrial relevance of technology evaluations. Empirical Softw. Eng. **16**(3), 365–395 (2011)
21. Karthikeyan, S., Rao, S.: Adopting the right software test maturity assessment model. Technical report, Cognizant (2014)
22. Kasoju, A., Petersen, K., Mäntylä, M.V.: Analyzing an automotive testing process with evidence-based software engineering. Inf. Softw. Technol. **55**(7), 1237–1259 (2013)

23. Kitchenham,B., Charters, S.: Guidelines for performing systematic literature reviews in software engineering. Technical Report EBSE-2007-01, Keele University (2007)
24. Kuhrmann, M., Diebold, P., Münch, J.: Software process improvement: a systematic mapping study on the state of the art. PeerJ Comput. Sci. **2**(1), 1–38 (2016)
25. Kuhrmann, M., Diebold, P., Münch, J., Tell, P.: How does software process improvement address global software engineering? In: International Conference on Global Software Engineering, ICGSE, pp. 89–98. IEEE (2016)
26. Kuhrmann, M., Fernández, D.M.: Systematic software development: a state of the practice report from Germany. In: International Conference on Global Software Engineering, ICGSE, pp. 51–60. IEEE (2015)
27. Kumar, P.: Test process improvement - evaluation of available models. Technical report, Maveric (2012)
28. Larrucea, X., O'Connor, R.V., Colomo-Palacios, R., Laporte, C.Y.: Software process improvement in very small organizations. IEEE Softw. **33**(2), 85–89 (2016)
29. Li, J., Moe, N.B., Dybå, T.: Transition from a plan-driven process to scrum: a longitudinal case study on software quality. In: Proceedings of the 2010 ACM-IEEE International Symposium on Empirical Software Engineering and Measurement, ESEM 2010, pp. 13:1–13:10. ACM, New York (2010)
30. McGarry, F., Burke, S., Decker, B.: Measuring the impacts individual process maturity attributes have on software products. In: Proceedings of Fifth International on Software Metrics Symposium, Metrics 1998, pp. 52–60. IEEE (1998)
31. Monteiro, L.F.S., de Oliveira, K.M.: Defining a catalog of indicators to support process performance analysis. J. Softw. Maintenance Evol. Res. Pract. **23**(6), 395–422 (2011)
32. Petersen, K., Feldt, R., Mujtaba, S., Mattson, M.: Systematic mapping studies in software engineering. In: International Conference on Evaluation and Assessment in Software Engineering, EASE, pp. 68–77. ACM (2008)
33. Pino, F.J., García, F., Piattini, M.: Software process improvement in small and medium software enterprises: a systematic review. Software Qual. J. **16**(2), 237–261 (2008)
34. Staples, M., Niazi, M., Jeffery, R., Abrahams, A., Byatt, P., Murphy, R.: An exploratory study of why organizations do not adopt CMMI. J. Syst. Softw. **80**(6), 883–895 (2007)
35. Sylemez, M., Tarhan, A.: Using process enactment data analysis to support orthogonal defect classification for software process improvement. In: International Conference on Software Process and Product Measurement, IWSM-MENSURA, pp. 120–125, October 2013
36. von Wangenheim, C.G., Hauck, J.C.R., Salviano, C.F., von Wangenheim, A.: Systematic literature review of software process capability/maturity models. In: International Conference on Software Process Improvement and Capability Determination-SPICE (2010)
37. Wieringa, R., Maiden, N., Mead, N., Rolland, C.: Requirements engineering paper classification and evaluation criteria: a proposal and a discussion. Requirements Eng. **11**(1), 102–107 (2005)
38. Wohlin, C., Runeson, P., Höst, M., Ohlsson, M.C., Regnell, B., Wesslén, A.: Experimentation in Software Engineering. Springer, Heidelberg (2012)
39. Zhi, J., Garousi-Yusifoğlu, V., Sun, B., Garousi, G., Shahnewaz, S., Ruhe, G.: Cost, benefits and quality of software development documentation: a systematic mapping. J. Syst. Softw. **99**, 175–198 (2015)

Transitioning Towards Continuous Experimentation in a Large Software Product and Service Development Organisation – A Case Study

Sezin Gizem Yaman[1](✉), Fabian Fagerholm[1], Myriam Munezero[1], Jürgen Münch[1,2], Mika Aaltola[3], Christina Palmu[3], and Tomi Männistö[1]

[1] Department of Computer Science, University of Helsinki,
P.O. Box 68, 00014 Helsinki, Finland
{sezin.yaman,fabian.fagerholm,myriam.munezero,
jurgen.munch,tomi.mannisto}@helsinki.fi
[2] Reutlingen University, Danziger Straße 6, 71034 Böblingen, Germany
juergen.muench@reutlingen-university.de
[3] Ericsson, Hirsalantie 11, 02420 Jorvas, Finland
{mika.aaltola,christina.palmu}@ericsson.fi

Abstract. *Context:* Companies need capabilities to evaluate the customer value of software-intensive products and services. One way of systematically acquiring data on customer value is running continuous experiments as part of the overall development process. *Objective:* This paper investigates the first steps of transitioning towards continuous experimentation in a large company, including the challenges faced. *Method:* We conduct a single-case study using participant observation, interviews, and qualitative analysis of the collected data. *Results:* Results show that continuous experimentation was well received by the practitioners and practising experimentation helped them to enhance understanding of their product value and user needs. Although the complexities of a large multi-stakeholder business-to-business (B2B) environment presented several challenges such as inaccessible users, it was possible to address impediments and integrate an experiment in an ongoing development project. *Conclusion:* Developing the capability for continuous experimentation in large organisations is a learning process which can be supported by a systematic introduction approach with the guidance of experts. We gained experience by introducing the approach on a small scale in a large organisation, and one of the major steps for future work is to understand how this can be scaled up to the whole development organisation.

Keywords: Continuous experimentation · Experiment-driven software development · Product management · Lean startup · Customer development · Customer involvement · Organisational transition · Agile software development · Case study

© Springer International Publishing AG 2016
P. Abrahamsson et al. (Eds.): PROFES 2016, LNCS 10027, pp. 344–359, 2016.
DOI: 10.1007/978-3-319-49094-6_22

1   Introduction

Continuous experimentation is a software development approach where research and development (R&D) activities are driven by constantly conducting experiments with product value [1–3]. Customers and users are involved in the decision-making process as experiment subjects, providing data by interacting with experiment materials, such as the software features being developed or related design artefacts. Product value is tested by observing actual behaviour rather than relying on secondary sources, opinions, or assumptions.

Although several approaches to experiment-driven software development have been proposed (e.g. [1,2,4]), guidance is lacking on how development teams in large organisations with complex business partnership networks can adopt them. In this paper, we investigate the introduction of continuous experimentation in a large software development organisation in a B2B domain. We observe different roles, means of communication, and integration with the overall development process. Furthermore, we investigate how customers and users are accessed and involved. We collect observed challenges and lessons learned that arise when the teams attempt to perform experiments to support decision-making. More specifically, we seek to answer the following research question:

RQ: How can a large software development organisation transition towards continuous experimentation in a B2B domain?

In order to address the research question, we conducted a single-case study in which we observed and participated in the introduction of continuous experimentation in a large company. Two teams, a development and a UX team, collaborated to select a target for experimentation and to design and implement an experiment to help make a focused product decision. Through the case study, we uncovered some of the critical factors that may support or impede the transition.

The rest of this paper is structured as follows. Section 2 presents the background and related work relevant to this study. Section 3 describes the research approach, including the context in which the case study was conducted, and the data collection and analysis methods. The design and execution details of an experiment conducted by the case company are detailed in Sect. 4. The transition process towards continuous experimentation is outlined in Sect. 5. The findings are discussed and the research question is addressed in Sect. 6. Section 7 concludes the paper and highlights potential future work.

2   Background and Related Work

Considering product value as a first-class concept in software development was proposed in value-based software engineering (VBSE) [5]. VBSE asserts that instead of treating software engineering as value-neutral, its major artefacts and activities should be analysed to assess what value they provide to customers and users, and use knowledge of that value in decision-making. Value has also been considered in agile software development [6,7] and in approaches to product development and entrepreneurship such as Lean Startup [8], Customer Development [9], and Lean Analytics [10]. A body of literature is emerging in software research that addresses this and related topics. In this section, we review a selection from this set of related work.

To survive and compete in today's fast-changing development environments, organisations have to develop, release, and learn from their software products and services quickly [11]. Hence, many software companies have adopted or are adopting agile practices, which champion flexibility, efficiency, and speed in developing software [6]. Nevertheless, Holmström Olsson et al. [12] suggest that the application of agile methods in software R&D activities is only one stage on the maturation path of companies' software engineering practices. At the final stage of the model – R&D as an experiment system – development is based on rapid experiments that utilise instant customer feedback and product usage data to identify customer needs.

The experiment-driven stage of software product and service development not only allows for quick delivery of value to customers but also helps companies make decisions based on customer or user data rather than opinions [1–3,13]. Through experiments, organisations can gain evidence about which features customers actually want, thus helping them to avoid developing features that are not valuable to customers [4]. As Bosch [14] states, "the faster the organisation learns about the customer and the real-world operation of the system, the more value it will provide."

Continuous experimentation may take different forms in different environments. Rissanen and Münch [3] list a number of customer-related challenges that continuous experimentation faces in B2B domains. For instance, customers may have to be informed in advance and sign a written agreement to participate in experiments. End users are not always the customers of the organisation, but they can be a customer's customer. Pro-active lead customers might have to be involved in the experiment design process, but may be challenging to acquire. Also, it may not be possible to interrupt the daily work of users in order to involve them in experiment tasks.

Thus, how to integrate experimentation in the software product development cycle is still a key question. Fagerholm et al. [2] propose the RIGHT model for continuous experimentation. The model consists of a process model and an architectural model. In the process model, assumptions are first identified, experiments are designed to test them, experiment materials (such as minimum viable features) are built, the experiment is executed, and analysis results are then used to support product development decision-making. The decision may be to fully develop and deploy a feature or to pivot if the experiment indicates that the feature is unsuccessful. The architectural model outlines additional infrastructure that is required to carry out such experiments continuously, in parallel, and at scale. In this study, we are guided by the fundamentals of the RIGHT model in the introduction of continuous experimentation.

3   Research Approach

This study follows a holistic single-case study approach [15] in order to gain deeper understanding of how development teams in a large organisation adopt continuous experimentation. Additionally, the study has elements of action research, in that the researchers were actively involved with the process being studied [16]. The unit of analysis is the process of transitioning towards continuous experimentation. We observe only the start of the transition, but consider this unit of analysis to be bounded by an identifiable starting point, and potentially ending in either non-adoption or adoption to different degrees. The transition process may be considered to concern several parts of the organisation, but our observation is limited to one unit concerned with product development. The data collection phase took place over a three-month period in autumn 2015.

3.1   Case Context

The company involved in the case study is a global corporation specialising in providing communication technology and services. The organisation is highly distributed, with globally allocated development teams. This study is conducted in the context of a connectivity management and billing service platform that the company develops for telecom operators and their enterprise customers. This platform includes a management portal, used by operator users, which is the focus of this study.

Figure 1 illustrates the parties and their location in the B2B network, revealing a multi-layer structure of stakeholders. The platform development project involves 11 teams, with around 70 people, who are distributed over multiple locations globally. The unit of observation in this study is one software development team and one UX team located in Finland, who are working on the aforementioned management portal.

The teams are incrementally developing a new version of the portal, which includes modernising the visual design and functionality. While the purpose is to keep the current set of functionality, enhancements to user workflows can be made if this does not impede the delivery schedule.

At the time of the study, the two teams were tasked with implementing an activity log inside the portal which would provide information about mobile subscription events, such as when a SIM card is registered on the network, a data transfer occurs, or an SMS is sent. The activity log is used by operator users to troubleshoot problems with enterprise subscriptions. A typical scenario would involve troubleshooting during a support call. The activity log was chosen for this study both because it was the teams' next assignment, and because there were open questions regarding its design.

3.2   Research Process

The study was conducted in an iterative fashion, with company representatives evaluating decision points, executing the experiment, collecting and analysing

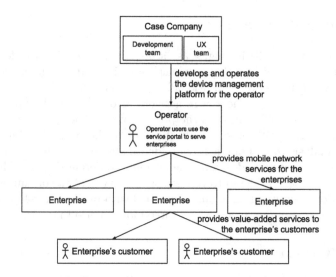

Fig. 1. The case company and other actors in the B2B network formed around the platform. For clarity, only one operator is shown, although there are multiple operators.

the experiment data, and with researchers observing the process, analysing the collected research data, and proposing alternative decision paths. An initial meeting was held where the principles of continuous experimentation and the RIGHT model [1,2] were explained to development and UX teams and product owners. After reaching a positive decision from the company, the joint collaboration proceeded. Multiple meetings were held, both online and face to face, to (1) understand the case context, (2) explore and select an experiment target, (3) identify assumptions related to that target, (4) develop a hypothesis and experiment design, (5) discuss operational details regarding experiment execution, (6) analyse experiment data, (7) draw conclusions based on the analysis and (8) plan the next steps. Between meetings, materials from previous iterations were analysed and developed to support subsequent decisions and actions.

This study uses materials produced in and for the meetings as well as other primary data sources, which include participant observation, transcripts of audio recordings of face-to-face meetings, minutes and notes of meetings (both at the customer site and online, including weekly online status meetings), open-ended semi-structured interviews, email communication and background material from the company. In total, there were three on-site and eight remote meetings. The accumulated material was analysed using thematic analysis [16,17]. The data was first extracted and analysed to form initial themes. These were then cross-checked against the gathered materials and refined into final themes which are presented and discussed in Sect. 5.

4   Designing and Executing the Experiment

As our aim was to observe the introduction of continuous experimentation in a company, we conducted an actual experiment round with a real product, i.e., the activity log described in Sect. 3.1. Here, we did not seek to reach a valid and generalisable result in the scientific sense, but rather to obtain enough evidence to support a technical decision. In this section, we describe the process of designing and executing the experiment.

The experiment was planned by a technical coach from the development team, two people from the UX team, and three researchers. The first decision to be made was to select a target for the experiment by analysing the feature requirements for the activity log. Behaviour-driven development (BDD) stories [18] were developed and analysed during the study in order to better understand the user requirements associated with the activity log.

In total, seven BDD stories pertaining to the activity log were analysed. With each BDD story, underlying assumptions regarding user needs and behaviour were identified. From the identified assumptions, hypotheses to be tested were formed. Subsequently, proposals of experimental designs to validate the hypotheses were drafted. From these, the development and UX teams selected one design proposal to be the experiment target, which was then elaborated into a more complete experiment design.

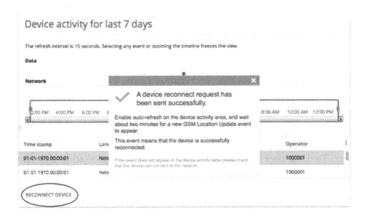

Fig. 2. Mockup of activity log with "reconnect" button indicated and feedback message displayed.

The selected experiment tested options for a feedback message that is displayed after operator users click on a "reconnect" button in the activity log (see Fig. 2). The reconnect button sends a request to the mobile network, asking it to flush the current SIM card registration, which means the mobile device must reconnect in order to resume normal operation. This action can be used to recover from certain error conditions. As the mobile network provides no feedback on the request, the reconnect status cannot be accurately displayed to users in the activity log. This might lead to a situation where a user clicks the button several times to no avail. Thus a good feedback message would inform a user on the current state of the system as well as what to do next, while a bad feedback message would result in increased load on the network, delays in problem resolution, worse experience for all users involved, and potential costs associated with these negative effects.

A series of user interface mockups with feedback messages were created for the experiment. These were first piloted with the product owner and updated based on the feedback given. After the update, the experiment was run with test subjects. Two runs of the experiment were conducted as illustrated in Table 1. In the first run, the experimenters realised that there were flaws in the mockups and feedback messages – they were unclear and misleading to the test subjects. Additionally, the experimenters had difficulties determining whether a user succeeded according to the criteria outlined in the hypothesis (see Table 1). Hence, the mockups and feedback messages were updated and the experiment was rerun. In the second run, the original reconnect feedback message was also included. In both of the runs, the order of the message candidates was balanced so that each message appeared at least once and the order changed for each test subject in order to avoid the risk of a learning effect biasing the results.

From the data analysis of the second run, one feedback message (message 6 in Table 2) had the highest score, on criterion 1, which was prioritised by the teams. It also scored well on the other criteria. Message 6 was thus selected for inclusion in the next product release. The results also revealed that the original message (message 7) performed poorest on all three criteria.

5   Transitioning Towards Continuous Experimentation

In the process of planning, designing, executing, and analysing the experiment, a number of observations and inferences were made regarding the transition towards continuous experimentation both from practitioners' and researchers' points of view. In this section, we present these findings under the themes that were deduced from our data analysis.

5.1   Initial Circumstances

Prior to the decision to proceed with experiment-driven software development, we observed an initial interest towards continuous experimentation among company representatives, but also concerns as the adoption process started in the middle of development with an evolving product. The product owner wanted to limit risks while practising with the new approach. This raised some important questions: is it possible to start at the team level and with small-scale experiments in order to gain experience before scaling up to multiple teams, higher in the organisation, and experiment targets that have a larger impact on the

Table 1. Experiment details for the first and second experiment run.

BDD story	As an activity log user, I want to flush network memory for a subscription so that I can be sure that there is no mismatched information and next I can see when the device connects to the network	
	First run	**Second run**
Hypothesis	We believe that with the right feedback message, users should be able to tell: (1) what the state of the device connection is and (2) what the next action is. In order to validate this, users will be shown a set of feedback messages and will be asked to provide answers to the above two criteria. The message with the most "yes" answers for each criterion will be the best message and will be selected	We believe that with the right feedback message, users are able to tell: (1) what the next action to take is, (2) what the state of device connection is, and (3) what to do if the device does not connect to the network. In order to validate this, users will be shown a set of feedback messages and will be asked to provide answers to the above three criteria. The message with the most "yes" answers for each criterion, especially criterion 1, will be the best message and will be selected
Minimum viable feature	Five mockups (PowerPoint) with different feedback messages	Seven mockups (PowerPoint) with different feedback messages
Test subjects	Three internal company employees invited by the experimenters based on availability	Seven internal company employees invited by the experimenters based on availability
Experimenters	One person from development team and one from UX team	One person from development team, one from UX team and an additional observer from the UX team (present only in some sessions)
Collected data	Yes or no scores for each test subject according to each hypothesis criterion, experimenters' observations of test subjects during the experimentation, and unstructured interview notes	
Duration (total)	60 min	120 min
Data analysis	Experimenter judgement (yes or no) scores on each criterion for each feedback message candidate were summed. The sums were used to rank the feedback messages to identify the best message	

system being developed? Moreover, existing release deadlines dictated the target and scale of the experiment, as well as the resources that could be allocated to it.

Table 2. Scores for each feedback message with the winning message highlighted. Each test subject was exposed to seven message candidates and was scored by two experimenters. Criterion 1 had double the weight when choosing the winner. (Note: There was a data entry error for message 5 where one test subject's scores on criterion 2 and 3 were not recorded. However, this does not impact the result of the experiment.)

Feedback message candidate	Criterion 1 (weight: 2×)		Criterion 2 (weight: 1×)		Criterion 3 (weight: 1×)	
	Yes	No	Yes	No	Yes	No
1	7	7	7	7	4	10
2	9	5	10	4	3	11
3	5	9	8	6	2	12
4	5	9	10	4	2	12
5	7	7	8	4	6	6
6	13	1	11	3	4	10
7	4	10	5	9	3	11

5.2 Starting with Small Teams

We observed that beginning with small teams who are interested did facilitate the introduction of a new way of working in the large case organisation. The development team consisted of four developers and the UX team consisted of two persons. Each team had an active person, a "champion", who took the lead in conducting the experiment and communicating the approach to other team members.

While it was possible to get a quick, low-risk start by beginning with small, motivated teams, we observed challenges which might impact scaling of continuous experimentation. For instance, we observed that organisational factors influenced the ease at which experimentation targets could be identified. The necessary product requirements were not always available at the team level. We furthermore observed that limitations in the teams' area of influence affected the experimentation activities. For instance, the decision to involve real users in conducting the experimentation required approval from different management levels and extra consideration since most of the customers were abroad. Also, dependencies on other teams and release management decisions meant that product changes based on the experiment result could not be immediately integrated into the next release, but into the succeeding one.

5.3 Small-Scale Experiments

From the time that BDD stories were developed to the analysis of the results, while the experiment planning process took approximately one month, executing the experiment only took a couple of hours (see Table 1). Nevertheless, the aim was to initiate the experimentation activity and to learn how to experiment, i.e., to "experiment with experimentation" as the technical coach put it. He also added that "[It's better to] start experimenting with something small. [...] It's more important to start now. Practice will make it perfect."

As continuous experimentation is a way to achieve customer and user involvement, user access was a discussion point during the experiment planning stage. The decision to use internal test subjects was mostly a question of time and effort as noted by the UX designer: "It would be really time consuming to contact our actual customers, write emails and explain what this [experiment] is about. [The whole] idea of experimentation is quite new to our customers so [there are] kind of political reasons why in the first place we did not contact our customers. It was so agile to do it in-house and we did it so fast with our workmates. [...] We wanted to learn about the continuous experimentation approach and it would be easier to practice it in-house for the beginning". The technical coach also added that "there is a limit to how much you can e.g., interview the customers before you provide something [concrete]". The team members were aware of the drawbacks of using internal test subjects, but deemed it more important to get started with the first cycle than spending time on accessing users. "Of course we thought of how much [more benefit could be gained by experimenting] with actual customers. But then, this experimentation is about the UX part, [...] and we did not see that we would get much more benefit if we had waited weeks to get real customer input." (Technical coach).

5.4 Identifying an Experimentation Target

We observed that it was not straightforward to identify an experimentation target. In particular, options tended to be more technical than value-based. During planning, it emerged that there was no clear understanding on some of the platform features, and user requirements were not directly available in written form. Instead, we deduced them from other materials, such as user journeys and personas obtained from user research, and mockups from prototypes, all developed in the beginning of the project. We had numerous discussions with the teams to clarify the purpose of the activity log and its different functions. Finally, BDD stories were developed and utilised to identify assumptions behind the user requirements, and the experiment was derived from those assumptions.

5.5 Designing and Executing the Experiment

The experiment was run with internal company employees. Even though the case company had done a pilot study with a product owner to revise the experiment design, they easily recognised during the first experiment run with test subjects that additional planning was essential. Test feedback messages were unclear and scoring criteria specified in the hypothesis were not explicit enough for experimenters to reach an agreement. Therefore, better background information and clearer instructions for the subjects were developed before running a second round of the experiment. The hypothesis was also revised and clearer tasks for the experimenters were defined. Although some effort should be spent on improving the design and execution, we found that it had to be balanced with available resources. Small-scale experiments especially meant that effort should not be expended beyond what is required to get a sufficient result: "over-planning [improving the experiment beyond a certain point] would be pointless", according to the technical coach.

5.6 Collaborating with Experts

Expertise was provided by the five researchers involved in the introduction of the continuous experimentation approach. Support for the transition was particularly provided during the planning and execution of the experiments.

At the beginning of the study, the teams and other company representatives had to spend time introducing the product and its context to the experts. However, they stated that it was beneficial to have expert facilitators guiding the transition and providing support and guidance when they needed it. In this case, some mistakes were avoided through expert opinion. For instance, during the execution stage, guidance was provided on how to achieve more valid results and avoid introducing bias during the experiment – e.g. avoiding leading the users by keeping discussions between experimenters and test subjects minimal, and ensuring that there were at least two experimenters.

5.7 Persistence

Continuous experimentation may be easy to understand in principle, but actually starting it in a real, large B2B organisation required persistence. The final experiment design was reached after a number of attempts. The pilot run and two rounds of actual experiment runs were required to obtain data for the final analysis. The teams indicated that when starting, one should not dwell on temporary failures. Better to "fix the experiment [the] best way you can and run it again. You can learn so much with each experiment." (Technical coach)

Moreover, the teams were willing to include experimentation in some of their standard procedures. They decided to build a wiki library where all experimentation details and learnings would be stored so that the information can be reused when necessary and help guide other teams who want to practice the approach. Also, the champions in the teams were persistent in documenting each step of the process, which helped communication internally and with experts. Thus, some of the prerequisites of scaling the approach to cover a larger portion of the organisation are in place.

Table 3 summarises the challenges faced when transitioning towards experimentation together with observed mitigation strategies under each of the six themes presented in Sects. 5.1, 5.2, 5.3, 5.4, 5.5, 5.6 and 5.7.

6 Discussion

Transitioning towards continuous experimentation is a learning process, at the core of which is the development of the organisational capability to identify

Table 3. Identified challenges and mitigation strategies.

Theme	Challenges	Mitigation strategies
Initial circumstances	– Evolving product, existing plans, deadlines – Limited resources – Need to limit risks	– Allocate only few resources to begin with – Choose a small scope for the initial experiment
Starting with small teams and small-scale experiments	– Higher level product information might not be visible at the team level – The team's area of influence may be limited – Inaccessibility of real users – Experimentation activities may not be initiated because of prior commitments	– Involve people from different teams in brainstorming and planning the experiment together – Utilise resources that are more accessible, e.g. internal company employees – Good to have champions in teams pioneering the transition
Identifying an experimentation target	– Difficult to select the features to start experimenting with – Identified experiment targets may be on a mostly technical level	– Utilising existing product-related materials helps identify experiments, e.g., BDD stories – Having discussions with team members and experts – Carefully analyse the feature to be experimented on to identify user needs and assumptions
Designing and executing the experiment	– The lack of experimenter experience can lead to biases being introduced in the design and execution of experiments – Effort and time for planning needs to be allocated for running a valid experiment	– Piloting and rerunning the experiment helps to enhance the experiment design, and reach more valid results – Seek expert advice to avoid potential biases in the experiment – Overplanning should be avoided; when starting, the important thing is to learn
Collaborating with experts	– Effort is needed for introducing the product and the context to the experts	– Experts can help avoid mistakes in experiment design and execution; the effort to introduce may pay off – Introduction may be sped up by using materials that are already needed in development, such as user stories and requirements expressed as, e.g., BDD stories
Persistence	– First experimentations can be seen as effortful and non-efficient	– Keep practising, learning will increase efficiency – Experiment designs and guidelines for executing experiments can be gathered and reused, reducing future effort

assumptions, test them in experiments, and support development decisions based on the evidence. However, many other factors play a role in the transition both on the team and organisational levels. In this section, we address the research question and compare the study findings with related work.

How can a large software development organisation transition towards continuous experimentation in a B2B domain?

Based on the findings from the case study data analysis, we identified circumstances and activities that can be taken to enable the transition towards continuous experimentation. Even though there might be initial circumstances that constrain the transition, we observed that initiating the transition is possible by starting with small teams and small-scale experiments. In order to lower the barriers to starting, experiment targets can be identified from existing materials. Collaboration with experts can be used for guidance and support but team effort is still needed in planning, designing and executing experiments. At this stage, learning about experimentation is the most important thing. Later, it is essential to find ways to sustain the process, making it continuous, and scaling it to cover a larger part of the development organisation.

6.1   Challenges and Lessons Learned

The biggest benefit gained by the teams was that they learned to perform experimentation in a more systematic way, which will help them to better understand what their customers want and take the right steps in increasing user satisfaction and reduce support costs. Doing experimentation also helped the teams gain new insights and better understanding of their ongoing work. In addition, based on the teams' experiences, they realised that "experimentation made it clear to the team that there is no need to debate between opinions and assumptions as you can quickly test them with an experiment." (Technical coach)

Information about user needs, e.g. requirements, is needed to identify assumptions. In this case, BDD stories proved to be useful for this purpose, but other forms may be possible, as well. The experimentation activity needs to be integrated with the overall development process. Once integrated, the effort put in planning experiments could diminish. In this case, planning the study and the experiment took around a month each, since they included establishing the collaboration between the experts and the teams from the organisation, getting to know the context, and identifying assumptions in the product. On the other hand, running the experiment itself took only hours.

Several challenges arose because of the complex B2B environment. For instance, the path from the development organisation to users through the B2B network was long and involved many organisations. For this reason, end users could not be included in experiments with reasonable effort, a finding that is in line with Rissanen and Münch's [3] observations. Other approaches to get experiment data were needed in order to compensate this challenge. In this case, internal test subjects were an economical way to start developing the capability for continuous experimentation, and made it possible to even gain some decision support for a small product decision although the set of subjects was limited.

Some barriers faced were a result of timing. The process started in the middle of development with an evolving product. Existing release deadlines influenced the resources available, as well as the target and scale of the experiment. The selected product feature to be experimented on was quite small and the experiment was more about optimisation rather than validating a complete feature. However, when the purpose is to practise experimentation, this is not a critical issue, but it must be understood that experiment results might not be the most beneficial or target the most value-creating features in the beginning.

In general, it was difficult to design an experiment that would actually test the value of a feature. This would have entailed determining whether the feature is necessary or suitable for accomplishing a given task that has already been found to fulfil a user need. There are multiple possible reasons for why designing a value-related experiment was difficult, and the long chain from development to user was one of them. It was unclear what the value of different features was and for whom. Also, the long chain meant more uncertainty about how a feature contributes to value. A feature may fulfil a need indirectly, and mapping the chain was not possible in this study.

Another challenge was that it was difficult to design a behavioural experiment task, meaning a task that would test whether a feature contributes to a behaviour change. This would have been necessary in order to determine whether the feature contributes to a user need, since it is through behaviour that the need is fulfilled. In this study, the experiment relied on subjects telling what they would do rather than observing whether they carried out certain actions or not. Part of the reason was the effort and cost of setting up required experiment materials. Observing behaviour requires interactive materials that allow the user to express the behaviour to be observed. Lack of such materials may be a barrier when initiating the transition towards continuous experimentation.

Furthermore, it was observed that the scale of experiments can be adjusted operationally so that little or no development effort is required, for example by using PowerPoint mockups as in this case. On the other hand, conducting small-scale experiments is part of a tradeoff between smoothing the path towards continuous experimentation and reaching the level where experiments directly target customer value.

6.2   Threats to Validity

Researchers' expectancy bias might be a threat in this study. Researchers might interpret the collected data in such a way that it fulfils their expectations. In order to mitigate this threat, participants from the case company were involved in the study data analysis stage and participant validation was used in order to verify the study results.

Researcher triangulation was used to address construct and external validity in terms of accuracy checking. Two researchers first conducted the initial study data analysis, then reviewed the analysis process with a third researcher and later, all five researchers reviewed the results along with discussion sessions. This ensured that the study results would not rely on interpretations of single researchers only.

In terms of generalisability, we are interested in whether the results of this study would be applicable to other software development organisations transitioning towards continuous experimentation. The characteristics of the case company, such as its size, structure, customers, business domain, the scale of the experiment, the product, and other contextual factors may limit the transferability of the results presented in this paper. It is not yet clear how such transfers can be made. Due to the novelty of the field and early maturity of experimentation in the company, there is not much evidence available to support transferring the results. We hope our findings will contribute to the knowledge about transition to continuous experimentation when combined with further research.

7   Conclusion

We conducted a holistic single-case study in a large, global telecom company operating in a B2B environment. We introduced an approach to continuous experimentation in the case company. Two company teams and five researchers conducted a single experiment cycle with internal test subjects. The experiment results allowed the company to make a product development decision which improved the usability of a part of their product. By participating in the activity, we observed the first steps of a transition towards continuous experimentation.

We found that the approach was easy for practitioners to understand and reception was favourable in general. The experiment activity highlighted important questions about the product under development and how it could best serve users. The collaboration between the UX and development teams was also enhanced, as expertise from both was required to plan and execute the experiment. Starting with small teams and experiments with a tightly limited scope allowed a fast start and a short, one-month cycle time from design to results.

We also found several challenges that may hinder the adoption of an experiment-based approach and limit its benefits in the initiating phase. Our study shows that it may be difficult to find an experiment target due to information about user needs and goals being scattered in a large B2B organisation. This makes it difficult to identify the assumptions that should be tested in experiments. It may also be difficult to reach the level where experiments directly address product value rather than optimising usability. Involving users directly in experiments was difficult in this B2B case, and may come with additional cost, but would also make experiments more valid and relevant. Designing experiments around assumptions about the user behaviours that are related to value creation should result in experiments with more impact. This remains a difficult challenge which warrants further research. More research is also needed on how to integrate continuous experimentation with the overall organisation and how this affects culture, architectures, methods, processes, management, and staffing in contemporary organisations.

References

1. Fagerholm, F., Guinea, A.S., Mäenpää, H., Münch, J.: Building blocks for continuous experimentation. In: Proceedings of the 1st International Workshop on Rapid Continuous Software Engineering, RCoSE 2014, pp. 26–35. ACM, New York (2014)
2. Fagerholm, F., Guinea, A.S., Mäenpää, H., Münch, J.: The RIGHT model for Continuous Experimentation. J. Syst. Softw. (2016, in press). doi:10.1016/j.jss.2016.03.034.
3. Rissanen, O., Münch, J.: Continuous experimentation in the B2B domain: a case study. In: Proceedings of the Second International Workshop on Rapid Continuous Software Engineering, RCoSE 2015, Piscataway, NJ, USA, pp. 12–18. IEEE Press (2015)
4. Holmström Olsson, H., Bosch, J.: The HYPEX model: from opinions to data-driven software development. In: Bosch, J. (ed.) Continuous Software Engineering, pp. 155–164. Springer, Cham (2014)
5. Boehm, B., Huang, L.G.: Value-based software engineering: a case study. Computer 36(3), 33–41 (2003)
6. Highsmith, J., Cockburn, A.: Agile software development: the business of innovation. Computer 34(9), 120–127 (2001)
7. Cockburn, A., Highsmith, J.: Agile software development, the people factor. Computer 34(11), 131–133 (2001)
8. Ries, E.: The Lean Startup: How Today's Entrepreneurs Use Continuous Innovation to Create Radically Successful Businesses. Crown Business, Houston (2011)
9. Blank, S.: The Four Steps to the Epiphany: Successful Strategies for Products That Win, 2nd edn. K&S Ranch, Pescadero (2013)
10. Croll, A., Yoskowitz, B.: Lean Analytics: Use Data to Build a Better Startup Faster. O'Reilly Media, Sebastopol (2013)
11. Tichy, M., Bosch, J., Goedicke, M., Fitzgerald, B.: 2nd International Workshop on Rapid Continuous Software Engineering (RCoSE 2015). In: Proceedings of the 37th International Conference on Software Engineering, vol. 2, pp. 993–994. IEEE Press (2015)
12. Holmström Olsson, H., Alahyari, H., Bosch, J.: Climbing the "Stairway to Heaven" - a mulitiple-case study exploring barriers in the transition from agile development towards continuous deployment of software. In: 2012 38th Euromicro Conference on Software Engineering and Advanced Applications, pp. 392–399 (2012)
13. Yaman, S.G., Sauvola, T., Riungu-Kalliosaari, L., Hokkanen, L., Kuvaja, P., Oivo, M., Männistö, T.: Customer involvement in continuous deployment: a systematic literature review. In: Daneva, M., Pastor, O. (eds.) REFSQ 2016. LNCS, vol. 9619, pp. 249–265. Springer, Heidelberg (2016). doi:10.1007/978-3-319-30282-9_18
14. Bosch, J.: Building products as innovation experiment systems. In: Cusumano, M.A., Iyer, B., Venkatraman, N. (eds.) ICSOB 2012. LNBIP, vol. 114, pp. 27–39. Springer, Heidelberg (2012). doi:10.1007/978-3-642-30746-1_3
15. Yin, R.: Case Study Research: Design and Methods, 4th edn. SAGE Publications, Inc., Thousand Oaks (2009)
16. Robson, C.: Real World Research. Wiley, Chichester (2011)
17. Braun, V., Clarke, V.: Using thematic analysis in psychology. Qual. Res. Psychol. 3(2), 77–101 (2006)
18. North, D.: Introducing BDD. Better Software., March 2006

Why Do We Do Software Process Improvement?

Study on Commonly Used Goals in Practice

Anna Schmitt[✉] and Philipp Diebold

Fraunhofer Institute for Experimental Software Engineering IESE,
Fraunhofer-Platz 1, 67663 Kaiserslautern, Germany
{anna.schmitt,philipp.diebold}@iese.fraunhofer.de

Abstract. Every company tries to improve its overall business, especially in the fast and reacting world of software. For these improvement activities, the development process is a major aspect. Our goal was the elicitation of common improvement goals that are considered for improving the development process. For collecting the common improvement goals, we used a mixture of methods. We started with existing literature and results of a survey. Further, we extended both by a set of workshops with industrial partners. Besides the common aspects of time, cost, and quality, some new goals, such as participation and democratization, appeared. These results lead to a more practitioner-oriented field of process improvement, since we are aware of common practical improvement goals.

Keywords: Development processes · Software process improvement · Improvement goals · Reasoning

1 Introduction and Motivation

Software process improvement (SPI) methods, such as CMMI or SPICE, deal with the continuous improvement of existing development processes and are an important aspect of software engineering [1, 2]. Nonetheless, SPI projects are hardly ever initiated for their own sake [3]. Instead, process improvement initiatives are generally triggered by organizational or project-specific improvement goals. And here, we lack insight into which organizational improvement goals are actually driving SPI initiatives in practice and of these, which are the most important?

One aspect that has been researched thoroughly is SPI success factors [1], which are only partially related to the improvement goals. In this study, we want to shed light on the state-of-the-practice in setting SPI goals. That is, we want to identify those goals that are typically considered when improving the software development process. Although we investigate a wide variety of software domains, special emphasis has been placed on web domains, business processing, and tool development in small and medium-sized enterprises (SMEs).

© Springer International Publishing AG 2016
P. Abrahamsson et al. (Eds.): PROFES 2016, LNCS 10027, pp. 360–367, 2016.
DOI: 10.1007/978-3-319-49094-6_23

The remainder of this paper is structured as follows: After this introduction, we briefly discuss some related work on improvement goals (Sect. 2). Section 3 contains our approach of how we collected the resulting improvement goals of Sect. 4.

2 Related Work

Software process improvement often relies on assessments and the use of reference models, such as CMMI for Development [4] or SPICE (ISO15504) [5]. These approaches only incorporate SPI goals implicitly by aiming for capability or maturity levels that are loosely coupled with high-level improvement goals (e.g., "GP2.2 - plan the process" or "GP2.5 - train people").

However, there is some existing work on goal-based SPI: Diebold and Zehler [6] introduce an Agile Capability Analysis that uses different improvement goals and applies GQM [7] and GQM+Strategies [8] approaches. This work also incorporates ISO 25010: Systems and software Quality Requirements and Evaluation (SQuaRE) - System and software quality models [9], which are used as sub-goals for product quality.

Along with these very process-specific aspects, there are goal-based software engineering approaches in specific fields such as requirements engineering (RE) [10] and testing [11]. These approaches focus on project and product improvement goals and do not consider process and organizational ones.

3 Data Collection Approach

First of all, we used the input that was directly connected with our work ([6, 9] presented in Sect. 2) as initial idea. (1) Out of this input, we put three examples on a poster to collect further ideas at the OOP2016 conference (www.oop-konferenz.de). We ended with 26 possible improvement goals, collected by the conference participants and other exhibitors. (2) Afterwards, these items were discussed, sorted, and categorized in a workshop with partners from academia and practice.

For further refinement and extension, we (from academic viewpoint) (3) conducted three independent workshops with different industrial partners, all SMEs. These workshops were guided by one of the authors and performed in an open way. We asked generic questions regarding the improvement goals. We collected the data from all workshop-participants (from 2 to 5 participants) on sticky-notes. In this collecting process different roles took part, e.g. management, project leaders, and developers. The notes were discussed, grouped, and consolidated together with all participants. After the workshops, we integrated these results into a mind map that visualized the previous results.

To come up with final results, we conducted a further workshop with practitioners and academics to discuss the final mind map in detail. The results that were concluded in this meeting will be presented in the following section.

4   Result: Current Improvement Goals

We visualized the different improvement goals in a mind map including different levels of abstraction due to their level of granularity. The highest level of the mind map (Fig. 1), level 1, shows the initially established improvement goals *customer involvement, time-to-market, quality,* and *organizational democratization.*

Fig. 1. Improvement goals

On level 2, the respective improvement goals from level 1 are refined. Therefore, **customer involvement** is divided into *customer participation, customer satisfaction/ acceptance, (intermediate) product-transparency, budget-transparency,* and *project-transparency.* **Organizational democratization** is clustered into the following three sub-goals: *internal knowledge management* (technical as well as nontechnical), *personnel motivation,* and *project democratization.* **Quality** is composed of *innovative solutions, conceptual quality, technical quality, testability/acceptance criteria,* and *user experience.* Finally, **time-to-market** has four sub areas: *automation, competence focusing, resource management,* and *time-transparency.* All improvement goals on level 2 will be described in the following sub-sections.

4.1   Customer Involvement

Objective is the integration of the customer in the early phases of the product development process. This is to receive early and regular feedback regarding the customer's expectations. It is addressed by the sub-goals *customer participation* and *customer satisfaction/acceptance.* Furthermore, giving stakeholder transparency on the development increases comprehension of the product and business process. This conveys the feeling of being involved in every step and is addressed by *budget-transparency* and *project-transparency.*

Customer participation: For a high customer involvement in the development process, an appropriate qualitative and quantitative feedback is needed. Additionally, predefined deadlines with defined commitments to assess the intermediate product results helps increasing the involvement. To reach respectable feedback, receiving real user feedback in an adequate quantity is important.

Customer satisfaction/acceptance: Understanding customers is a prerequisite to reach their satisfaction/acceptance. This includes personal aspects and, especially, the expectations of the customer. Misinterpretations of expectations can be created by either the customer by, e.g. being uncertain about the desired result, or by the contractor by misunderstanding the customers' wishes. The objective is to reach a common understanding concerning the desired output and to build up a common vocabulary regarding the timed collaboration und functioning.

Budget transparency: Before gaining this goal, an initial (and later continuous) effort estimation is needed and presented openly. Furthermore, the up-to-date information needs to be accessible anytime. The idea is to improve the cost estimation to decrease number of adaptions. Additionally, a good, regular, and truthful communication regarding time and progress is pursued.

Project transparency: To enable a good project transparency, a close and regular documentation of the project work needs to be implemented in the company (work package, problems, problem solutions, etc.). Additionally, every employee and customer must have an overview over the ongoing projects. Further aspect is the increase of understanding the system, e.g. by clearer and detailed requirements, clarification of expectations, clear/understandable definition of the work packages, and transformation of customer wishes into concrete realizable tasks. Moreover, tracking of progress needs to be enabled, so the status quo can be presented to the stakeholders. Another important sub-goal is the contract management, in particular, the tender preparation and project approval. Project approval enables the customer to recognize, which products will be contemporarily available on the market. Besides, the customer and the market competitors are comprehensible shown, which effort (e.g. budget, duration, and employees) is required to produce the end-product.

4.2 Organizational Democratization

Democratization of the organization tends to uniform, equal (working) conditions and rights of co-determination of all employees within the company. It is clustered into: *internal knowledge management*, *employee motivation*, and *project-democratization*.

Internal knowledge management: It is focused on technical as wells as on organization knowledge management, that is divided into: elimination of bottlenecks, better documentation, knowledge transfer, exchange of experience, better communication within and across teams, and increase of understanding the system (incl. interfaces). Possible bottlenecks need to be prevented, existing bottlenecks need to be eliminated, e.g. competition, cultural differences, distribution within and of team. Better documentation refers to documentation of change requests to prove anytime: "What shall be proved when and how, and what has been changed in fact." The exchange of experience focusses on information distribution across all stakeholders and preparation of project learning. Combined with them, a better communication within and across the team is addressed. This is achieved as all employees are informed about time, progress, and budget status of every project. The technical knowledge management should increase the understanding of the system, including its interfaces. This increase shall be ensured by an appropriate tool support at the beginning (e.g. Jira for ticketing) and by avoiding repeating mistakes.

Employee motivation: The aspired improvement goals are: acceptance of the course of action by the personnel, pleasure at work, satisfaction within the team/staff/company, increasing creativity, assumption of responsibility by all personnel, credibility concerning successful implementation, recruiting of new personnel by increasing attractiveness of the company, and qualification (e.g. training opportunities). Attracting the aspects pleasure at work, satisfaction within the team/staff/company, increasing creativity, assumption of responsibility by all personnel, and credibility concerning successful implementation boost employee motivation by creating an overall feeling of togetherness, being successful, and being appreciated. Recruiting new staff increase motivation by established employee by, on the one hand, getting new insights and ideas, and, on the other hand, defending the acquired position. Acceptance of the course of action leads to the identification with the company values, vision, and working methods.

Project-democratization: Derived from the high-level organizational democratization, flat hierarchies, simplification of the communication and escalation paths, discussions about project content, multi-project-management, uniformity of processes, and/or filing by a close documentation need to be achieved and improved. This assures uniform conditions regarding the collaboration of every single (team) employee. Additionally, it improves the overall productivity.

4.3 Quality

One workshop resulted in a deeper clustering of the goal "quality". The companies explicitly addressed and discussed the sub-goals *innovative solutions, conceptual quality, technical quality, testability/acceptance criteria, user experience,* and *documentation.*

Innovative Solutions: One way to increase the process and, thus, the resulting product quality is the creation of more innovative solution within the products. It leads to a competitive advantage on the product market. This is because of creating attractive products, the customers get convinced of their (innovative) unique quality.

Conceptual and technical quality: In particular, both quality aspects were discussed elaborately due to their high importance. *Conceptual quality* refers to compatibility, maintainability and portability of the system or the software. In contrast, the *technical quality* focuses on the quality aspects of the ISO25010. These aspects contain functionality, performance, usability, reliability, and security of single technical parts of the products. They improve software architecture, prototyping, technical up-to-dateness as well as the balance between individual/customized and standard software.

Testability/acceptance criteria: A further possibility is the implementation of a more efficient testability/more efficient acceptance criteria. This results in a faster testing process. It enables a higher amount of iterations with different scope and, thus, a faster commercialization of a high-value product.

User experience: This goal focuses on the involvement of the user experience as it is propagated by the ISO25010 [9] with its "quality in use". Similar to [6], it shows the importance of the different quality aspects of the ISO, whereas the customers (especially in information systems) focus on user experience. User experience increases by fast recovering, evaluating, and implementing.

Documentation: Documentation is part of software development. Thus, it is an important ingredient for quality. The quality of documentation depends on different aspects, namely amount, availability, maintenance, and granularity of the documents.

4.4   Time-to-Market

Time-to-market aims at bringing products to the market fast for a competitive advantage regarding the price policy. It contains the time from a vague idea through the development and test phase up to the real market launch. Time-to-market is divided into *competence focusing*, *resource management*, and *time transparency*.

Competence focusing: First of all, competence focusing needs to be implemented and lived. Time and effort available shall fully be used in exactly these fields of work, which represent the core competencies of the company. Therefore, core competencies need to be identified. Afterwards, dealing with these within teams and organization must be learned.

Resource management: Resource management needs to be optimized for not wasting time, effort, and resources. It refers to a project specific planning, adaption, and application of resources. Thus, a project specific capacity needs to be carried out as well as a balance between projects, products and customers (e.g. regular customer vs. new customer).

Time transparency: Time management/time transparency might be the most important factor to fulfill the time-to-market. It is addressed and fulfilled by the following two sub-goals: (1) Adhere to internal and external deadlines. (2) Communicate delays within the project plan (e.g. inclusion of the time buffer while doing time-critical tasks) in a transparent, calm, and objective way. Furthermore, including sufficient time buffer for changes that need be done besides the daily business is necessary.

5   Threats to Validity

The aim of this study was not to come up with a complete model. The exploratory focus was on having first ideas of existing improvement goals in practice. Thus, we are aware that conducting a collection on a conference (with mainly German companies) and conducting workshops with only three industrial partners might be a low number. Therefore, we performed the workshop with different roles of partners to get different views and increase the number results. Furthermore, the three workshops were structured in the same way. Also, they were performed by the same persons for a better comparability and integrability.

6   Conclusions and Future Work

This paper presents the collection approach of improvement goals behind SPI as well as the results from practitioners' perspective. We identified four main goals, customer involvement, organizational democratization, quality, and time-to-market, refined into sub-goals. These sub-goals were collected together with different companies based on their individual challenges. All results represent common improvement goals derived from problems or challenges of SMEs. These results show that companies have similar improvement potential on the high-level goals, but very individual and specific detailed goals. These improvement goals simplify working on goal-specific SPI approaches that address practical issues.

Nonetheless, we are aware of the threats to validity of our results. Thus, we are collecting further input on this topic, e.g. with our project webpage (www.prokob.info) or specific events. Another aspect of future work is the creation of an SPI-approach similar to the application scenario in [6] for addressing the different company goals.

The elaborated results help practitioners comparing and baselining their company. They have the possibility to identify commonalities and differences of other enterprises with respect to their improvement goals. Such that they can identify missing improvement goals. On this basis, practitioners consider, whether it is beneficial and useful including these goals in SPI.

Acknowledgments. This research is being funded by the German Ministry of Education and Research (BMBF 01IS15038). We thank all the participants of the OOP-conference, and workshops. Finally, we were happy to receive feedback of Thomas Zehler on this paper.

References

1. Münch, J., Armbrust, O., Kowalczyk, M., Soto, M.: Software Process Definition and Management. Springer, Heidelberg (2012)
2. Kuhrmann, M., Diebold, P., Münch, J.: Software process improvement: a systematic mapping study on the state of the art. PeerJ. Comput. Sci. **2**, e62 (2016)
3. Austen, R., Hall, T.: Key success factors for implementing software process improvement: a maturity-based analysis. JSS **62**(2), 71–84 (2002)

4. SEI: CMMI for Development (CMMI-DEV), Version 1.3 (2010)
5. International Organization for Standardization. ISO/IEC 15504:2012 – Information technology – Process assessment (SPICE) (2012)
6. Diebold, P., Zehler, T.: The agile practice impact model – ideas, model, and application scenario. In: ICSSP 2015. ACM (2015)
7. Van Solingen, R., Basili, V., Caldiera, G., Rombach, H.D.: Goal Question Metric (GQM) Approach. Encyclopedia of Software Engineering. Wiley, Hoboken (2002)
8. Basili, V., Trendowicz, A., Kowalczyk, M., Heidrich, J., Seaman, C., Münch, J., Rombach, D.: Aligning Organization Through Measurement – The GQM+Strategies Approach. Springer, Heidelberg (2014)
9. International Organization for Standardization: ISO/IEC 25010: 2011 – Systems and Software Engineering—Systems and Software Quality Requirements and Evaluation (SQuaRE)— System and Software Quality Models (2011)
10. van Lamsweerde, A.: Goal-oriented requirements engineering: a guided tour. In: RE 2016, pp. 249–262. IEEE Press (2001)
11. Nguyen, D., Perini, A., Tonella, P.: A goal-oriented software testing methodology. In: Luck, M., Padgham, L. (eds.) AOSE 2007. LNCS, vol. 4951, pp. 58–72. Springer, Heidelberg (2008). doi:10.1007/978-3-540-79488-2_5

Developing Processes to Increase Technical Debt Visibility and Manageability – An Action Research Study in Industry

Jesse Yli-Huumo[1(✉)], Andrey Maglyas[1], Kari Smolander[2],
Johan Haller[3], and Hannu Törnroos[4]

[1] Lappeenranta University of Technology, Lappeenranta, Finland
jesse.yli-huumo@aalto.fi, maglyas@gmail.com
[2] Aalto University, Espoo, Finland
kari.smolander@aalto.fi
[3] Tieto Sweden AB, Stockholm, Sweden
johan.haller@tieto.com
[4] Tieto Oyj, Helsinki, Finland
hannu.tornroos@tieto.fi

Abstract. The knowledge about technical debt and its management has increased in recent years. The interest of academia and industry has generated many viewpoints on technical debt. Technical debt management consists of technical and organizational aspects, which make it a challenge in software development. To increase technical debt visibility and manageability, new processes must be developed and thoroughly empirically tested for their applicability. In this paper, we use the action research methodology to design processes for identification, documentation, and prioritization of technical debt. Our partner in this research is a large Nordic IT company Tieto, currently in a need for new ways to improve their technical debt management. The results include a set of processes and templates that were successfully used to identify and document technical debt. The identified technical debt items were later prioritized based on evaluation by Tieto employees. Tieto was able to create a prioritized technical debt backlog, which is now used for reduction activities to create a healthy and sustainable product for the future.

Keywords: Technical debt · Technical debt management · Software process improvement · Action research

1 Introduction

Technical debt refers to a situation in software development where shortcuts and/or workarounds are used in technical decisions to gain time-to-market [1]. The benefit of taking technical debt is an earlier and faster release, which can lead to customer satisfaction and other economic advantages [2]. However, the drawback is the '*debt*' that is left in the system. In the long-term, shortcuts and workarounds will turn to unnecessary complexity (*interest*) in the source code and architecture. Complexities in software can become hard to fix and change, which may cause decrease in software

© Springer International Publishing AG 2016
P. Abrahamsson et al. (Eds.): PROFES 2016, LNCS 10027, pp. 368–378, 2016.
DOI: 10.1007/978-3-319-49094-6_24

quality and productivity of the development team [3]. Therefore, technical debt can be a major problem for a software development company.

While shortcuts and workarounds can be seen as intentional decisions to speed up release cycles, or to circumvent a complex part of the code, unintentional technical debt occurs without immediate awareness [4]. Unintentional technical debt is introduced to software, for example, by inexperienced developers or legacy software. An inexperienced developer can create technical debt unintentionally with non-optimal solution. Old legacy software can consist of obsolete or non-optimal technology and solutions from past decades, which may require a rewrite or replacement.

Technical debt management refers to activities that are used to manage and reduce both intentional and unintentional technical debt with various approaches, practices and tools [5]. Technical debt management not only includes technical development activities but also organizational ones, such as communication and decision-making.

This study is made in cooperation with one of the largest IT companies in Scandinavia, Tieto. Tieto's Capital Market product unit is currently planning new processes for their technical debt management. The goal of the study is to develop new processes for technical debt identification, documentation, and prioritization. The outcome of this study includes new processes to increase the visibility and manageability of technical debt, which can be used in the future for better decision-making.

This paper is limited to studying technical debt that has already been acquired previously, and does not take in consideration the management activities related to decision-making process of acquiring new technical debt.

2 Background

Processes for technical debt management have been studied and suggested in the literature. Li et al. [5] gathered in a mapping study relevant research on technical debt management. The study showed that technical debt management can be divided into following activities: (1) *identification,* (2) *measurement,* (3) *prioritization,* (4) *prevention,* (5) *monitoring,* (6) *repayment,* (7) *representation/documentation,* and (8) *communication* [5]. Li et al. [5] also state that currently there is a lack of empirical evidence about technical debt management. In this study, we are mainly focusing on three out of the eight management activities. Our goal is to use processes for *representation/ documentation, identification,* and *prioritization* of already incurred technical debt to provide empirical evidence with a real case company.

Technical debt representation/documentation has been studied and suggested in literature with specific lists and templates as an approach to store technical debt issues [6, 7]. A backlog or a list should increase technical debt visibility and manageability. When technical debt is properly documented, it is easier to start other technical debt management activities, because it is visible to the company.

Before a technical debt issue can be documented, it has to be identified. Identification of smaller technical debt issues from the source code is possible with specific tools [8]. However, technical debt is not always only related to issues in the source code [9]. Technical debt in software architecture and design is a larger challenge [5, 9].

The identification of architectural technical debt with tools is difficult and often the only solution is to use human knowledge and examination [9].

The prioritization of technical debt is difficult, because some technical debt might be important to fix for business reasons, while other for technical reasons. Some models and methods have been developed for prioritization. Seaman et al. [10] suggested four approaches for technical debt decision-making: *simple cost-benefit analysis, analytic hierarchical process, portfolio management model, and options*. These approaches have been used also in other domains, such as finance [10]. They support evaluating the tradeoffs between proposed enhancements, corrective maintenance, and the payment of technical debt items [10]. Schmid [11] developed a formal model based on providing several well-defined approximations, which can be used for technical debt prioritization. In addition, some papers have used quality attributes from ISO 9126 as an evaluation to technical debt [12–14].

Overall, there exists a variety of different ideas for technical debt documentation, identification and prioritization. However, most of them are focused on one specific activity only. Studies that approach the whole process from identification to repaying technical debt are rare. Therefore, we collaborate with a real software company to find and develop processes, including technical debt identification, documentation, and prioritization. We take inspiration from a study conducted by Li et al. [7] that had a similar goal. Their approach was to identify architectural technical debt based on architecture decisions and change scenarios [7]. Our approach extends this by expanding the technical debt evaluation and prioritization processes. Our goal is to create more reasoning possibilities in decision-making, which is required especially in organizational aspects of technical debt management.

3   Research Methodology

Action research was selected as a research methodology for this study. Action research combines theory and practice [15]. Action research is an iterative process involving researchers and practitioners acting together on a particular cycle of activities, including problem diagnosis, action intervention, and reflective learning [15]. Action research is especially relevant in situations where participation and organizational change processes are necessary [16]. It attempts to provide practical value to the client organization while simultaneously contributing to the acquisition of new theoretical knowledge [17]. The action research cycle [18] consists of three stages: (1) a pre-step - *to understand context and purpose*; (2) six main steps - *to gather, feedback and analyze data, and to plan, implement and evaluate action*; (3) a meta-step - *to monitor*.

The rationale for using action research as a research methodology is the nature of this study. The company in this study had a goal to improve their technical debt management. The research group in this study had previous experience on working with various companies and cases related to technical debt and its management. Therefore, action research, as an approach where both the company and the research group work together to understand the problem and develop a solution, was especially fit for the purpose.

The selected product line in this research is a financial system used in the capital market industry by multiple customers around Nordics. The product is one of the three main products provided by Tieto and it has a long development history including source code from over 20 years ago. The product and development team have faced both technological changes and organizational changes during their lifetime. Now the main objective of Tieto's Capital Market product unit is to migrate to new technology with the aim to replace and rewrite old one, to improve quality and productivity, while still serving all of its customers.

The objective of the study was to increase technical debt visibility and manageability by improving processes related to identification, documentation and prioritization. Therefore, we set up the following research questions to address the problem:

RQ1: How to improve technical debt identification and documentation? The limitations of the tools currently available for technical debt identification can be seen as a big challenge. The identification of architectural technical debt with tools is very difficult. Therefore, most if not all technical debt identifications have to be done with manual code and architecture inspection, where developer or architect examines the system and the source code for possible issues. Our goal is to observe how technical debt is currently identified in practice and how it is documented afterwards. The objective is to identify possible improvements to these current processes, and test them in practice.

RQ2: What factors should be taken in consideration when prioritizing technical debt? The decisions related to technical debt can be sometimes made based on hunches without any specific model or method to follow. Business owners might prioritize issues that give direct value to customers, while technical people might put value more on software quality and sustainability. Understanding both business and technical effects of technical debt repayment can help technical debt evaluation and improve the prioritization process for safer decisions. We will observe the processes of technical debt evaluation and prioritization in practice with the aim to improve technical debt evaluation and prioritization.

4 Action Research Process

The action research process used in this study is presented in Fig. 1. This research can be divided into five main activities and outcomes.

The first step of the research process is *interviews,* where researcher interviews people related to the product line or company to understand the current issues related to technical debt and its management. We conducted seven semi-structured interviews with the average of 45 min. We recorded, transcribed and analyzed all the interviews. In the analysis of the interviews, we identified major issues. First, we did not find any systematic process for technical debt identification, evaluation or prioritization. This led to a technical debt communication gap between the development team and project managers. Knowledge of technical debt seemed to be tacit personal knowledge rather than explicitly stored in a common list. Secondly, we noticed that the developers and architects had much knowledge about the current issues regarding technical debt, but

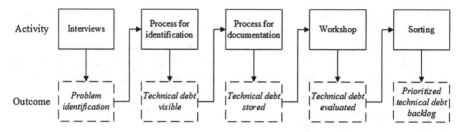

Fig. 1. The research process

there was not any systematic way to document it. Thirdly, when there were technical debt issues in discussion, the decision-making was mostly done based on hunches, rather than evaluating and prioritizing them first. The outcome of this step is a *problem identification*, which helps to understand the problem in current processes within a company.

The second step is to develop a *process for identification*. In our case, the identification was conducted by gathering the data from previous knowledge and history of people related to the product. The members of the product line used ten weeks to search and identify technical debt issues. The reason for manual inspection was that the company did not have any specific tools in use to identify technical debt. The outcome of this step is the increase of *technical debt visibility*, which helps to understand the overall technical debt view.

The third step is to develop a *process for documentation*. We decided to introduce a simple process to document all technical debt issues to a single technical debt backlog. The idea was to use backlog as an aid to make technical debt more visible to everyone in the product line. We used a similar template (Table 1) to Guo and Seaman [6] to collect all technical debt items. The template was sent to nine members of the product line that was later returned back to the managers. The managers then combined all the reported issues and created the technical debt backlog. The outcome of this step is getting *technical debt stored*.

The result of documentation process was technical debt backlog that consisted 47 identified technical debt issues. For categorization we used 15 different technical debt types identified by Alves et al. [19] in a mapping study. The majority of identified technical debt (33/47 issues) was related to issues in *design, architecture, code*, and a new category called *legacy* debt. Other types of technical debt (14/47) *requirements,*

Table 1. Template for technical debt documentation

Technical Debt ID	Technical debt identification number
Date/Reporter	Reporting date/Reporter name
Technical Debt Name	Name of identified technical debt
Description	Description of identified technical debt
Alternatives	Explanation of possible alternative solutions
Rationale	Reasons to fix technical debt

test, test automation, and process debt were associated more to activities outside product implementation.

The fourth step is to organize a *workshop*. We developed a process to prioritize technical debt issues with a simple technical debt evaluation and prioritization template (Table 2). This template was used when all the technical debt issues were collected to the backlog. In the workshop, the participants would evaluate each identified technical debt issue based on the five questions to create a prioritization. The outcome of this step is getting *technical debt evaluated.*

The research group also analyzed the returned evaluation templates based on each question to understand how technical debt was being evaluated.

We identified three different **benefit** categories: *technical, economic,* and *organizational benefits.* Technical benefits include improvements in software *quality,* software *maintainability,* software *reusability,* software *performance,* software *testability,* and software *deployment.* Organizational benefits include better software *deployment,* development team *productivity,* organizational *communicability,* and future *adaptability.* Economic benefits include *economic value* and *customer satisfaction.*

We identified three different **risk** categories: *economic, technical,* and *organizational risk.* Economic risks include *cost, time effort, testing effort,* and *customer satisfaction.* Organizational risks include *management* and *competence.* In addition, technical risks like *system breakdown* and *instability* are critical to companies.

For **reasons**, we identified three different categories: *intentional decision, unintentional cause,* and *organizational cause.* Intentional reasons were often related to *time constraints, lack of resources,* and *business driven development.* Unintentional causes were *legacy product* and *lack of knowledge.* For organizational causes, *software processes* and *lack of management* were the main reasons for technical debt.

We identified two types of **solutions** for technical debt: *technical* and *organizational solutions.* Technical solutions were *refactoring, redesigning, rewriting, architectural analysis,* and *increased testing.* Organizational solutions were *new processes* and *new management plan/strategy.*

The fifth step of the research process is *sorting.* When there is an evaluation for each technical debt item, it is easier to sort the issues out based on their importance. The last outcome of the process is *prioritized technical debt backlog.* The majority of the issues (27/47) were prioritized at the lowest priorities 5 or 4, which shows that most technical debt was not considered dangerous now. There were total of 14 issues rated as the highest priorities at level 1 or 2. There were three level 1 issues related to *legacy*

Table 2. Technical debt evaluation template

#	Question
1	What are the benefits of fixing this issue? (Business value, quality, productivity, less bugs etc.)
2	Are there any risks in fixing this issue? (Expensive, breaks the system etc.)
3	Why was this issue done previously like that?
4	How to fix this issue and what resources the fix would require?
5	From scale 1 – 5, how important would you rank this issue to be dealt with? (1 – most important, 5 – not so important)

debt, which can be explained by Tieto's current goals to migrate to a new technology to replace and rewrite old technology. Interestingly, the priorities also show that most of the technical debt related to *design, architecture,* and *code debt* were prioritized as 4 or 5, while *test, test automation,* and *process debt* were rated higher. However, it is important to notice that number of technical debt issues in *design, architecture,* and *code* is much higher than other types of debts, which might explain the difference.

The outcome of this action research cycle was a prioritized technical debt backlog that can be now used to add more development tasks related to technical debt reduction. For example, Tieto managers expressed that the backlog would be used in the future by Tieto to reduce technical debt in small iterations. Tieto managers also mentioned that this same process would be applied in future to other product lines.

5   Discussion

RQ1: How to improve technical debt identification and documentation? Our study made technical debt identification and documentation possible with simple practices that make technical debt more visible and manageable. These similar practices have been already suggested in other literature [6, 7]. However, the problem is not the practices themselves, but the fact that changing or adding new practices in companies is always a challenge and takes time [20]. In our case, we had a company that was motivated to improve and change these practices. We started some new practices with templates and processes that gathered previously identified technical debt from the minds of architects and developers to a specific backlog designed only for technical debt.

Technical debt identification is a challenge in software development. Identification of smaller technical debt issues happening in single code lines can be done with static code analysis tools and often it can be fixed by single developers. However, larger issues in architecture and structure are often unreachable with tools [9, 21] and require technical knowledge and competence [22], and discussion on an organizational level. In our case, the people in the product line did not use any tools to find and identify technical debt. Instead, the technical debt was identified based on previous experience and history with the product. The experience with the product of workshop participants shows that the people responsible for identification had extensive knowledge of the product development history and high competence to build software. We used this fact to our advantage, since we did not have to guide developers and architects to investigate product history, because the knowledge was already acquired during the development years. This helped to identify existing technical debt and document it based on our recommendations.

An interesting perspective on identified and documented technical debt and is the variety of types of technical debts. The large variety of technical debt types shows that when talking about technical debt, it is not only related to issues in design or code. Instead, like in our case, the same phenomena of shortcuts and bad solutions happen in other parts of software product development as well. To some development teams, technical debt might include only issues happening in the source code and design, while to some other teams, like in Tieto it might also include issues like those in testing and processes. We argue that technical debt management is successful when a company sets a clear standard to what is technical debt in their context and start to manage technical debt based on that standard. However, in academia, there is a need to create a common understanding for technical debt.

RQ2: What factors should be taken in consideration when prioritizing technical debt? The prioritization in this study was based on evaluation of *benefits, risks, reasons, and solutions* of technical debt. Using these factors to evaluate each technical debt issue could be a good beginning for companies that are trying to improve their technical debt management. However, these factors are not always measureable with a numeric value. The *interest* in technical debt that accumulates larger if not repaid, it is difficult to estimate [23]. Therefore, rather than trying to measure exact values, technical debt could be easier to understand from management perspective, if evaluated based on factors related to it.

Companies should evaluate each technical debt issue on the basis of how fixing the issue can benefit both company and software, such as improved quality, and how does this quality improvement affect other factors such as maintainability, performance or customer satisfaction. One challenge and risk of technical debt is that it often requires competence to fix or change existing solutions. When developers are changing very old parts of the code, it is not always certain that it will go as planned and it can be a huge risk that needs to be evaluated before.

Understanding the reasons behind technical debt can help to understand bigger underlying problems with technical debt. For example, a single technical debt issue in one smaller feature can be caused by some larger architectural issue. Instead of just fixing one single technical debt issue with the most economical value, it might be possible that another major technical debt item can be actually more beneficial to fix in a long term. Sometimes the solution might only require small refactoring, while sometimes it might need a full rewrite of that certain part of the code. Therefore, it is important to evaluate how much resources and effort does fixing technical debt require. Understanding the solution can enable a better evaluation, whether the time required for fixing is worth compared to its benefit.

We believe that technical debt prioritization should be done based on evaluation rather than measurement. The combination of the presented factors can be used as a simple way to create basic prioritizations, which can help companies to make decisions with more rationality. The decision-making may improve when development teams and management communicate and understand the benefits and risks in each technical debt issue, accompanied with knowledge on the reasons and solutions for technical debt.

Study limitations. *The first limitation* to this study is the generalization of the results. It is not certain that this process is usable in other companies. In our case, most of the involved people had many years of experience with the product. This helped the identification stage, since the people from the product line had already extensive knowledge about the issues in the product. *The second limitation* is that we conducted only one round of this action research. Conducting more rounds might change some results in the priorities and numbers of technical debt issues, but we believe it would not have any changes to the actual processes that were used in this study. *The third limitation* is that the used process only takes in consideration already occurred technical debt, and does not include management processes for a situation, where a decision has to be made for a new technical debt case. This makes the developed management process limited to only already occurred technical debt.

6 Conclusions

We used the action research process [18] together with a large IT company Tieto to find and develop processes for technical debt identification, documentation, and prioritization to increase technical debt visibility and manageability. The action research process consisted several interviews and meetings with the company representatives and an organized technical debt workshop to improve processes in the company. The outcome of the research was a set of templates and processes to identify, document, and prioritize technical debt. These templates and processes were used successfully at Tieto to transition from a situation where knowledge of technical debt was not explicitly documented, to a situation where a specifically prioritized technical debt backlog was available to reduce technical debt. Tieto's Capital Market product unit is now using this new technical debt backlog to increase technical debt visibility and manageability. Since the results with the developed process were considered successful by both the research group and the company, the same process will be expanded to other product lines in Tieto. The main challenges and lessons learned can be summarized as following:

- Technical debt can be brought visible with simple practices and processes in a company that does not have a priori knowledge on technical debt management.
- Identification of larger scale technical debt, such as architecture and design, with tools is a challenge that needs to be addressed and improved in future research.
- Technical debt documentation can be done with simple templates, but requires motivation and resources from software organization.
- Technical debt prioritization based on measurements is difficult, and therefore rougher evaluations based on e.g. benefits and risks through opinions can be seen easier to start with.

References

1. Cunningham, W.: The WyCash Portfolio Management System, Experience Report (1992)
2. Yli-Huumo, J., Maglyas, A., Smolander, K.: The sources and approaches to management of technical debt: a case study of two product lines in a middle-size finnish software company. In: Jedlitschka, A., Kuvaja, P., Kuhrmann, M., Männistö, T., Münch, J., Raatikainen, M. (eds.) PROFES 2014. LNCS, vol. 8892, pp. 93–107. Springer, Heidelberg (2014). doi:10.1007/978-3-319-13835-0_7

3. Yli-Huumo, J., Maglyas, A., Smolander, K.: The benefits and consequences of workarounds in software development projects. In: Fernandes, J.M., Machado, R.J., Wnuk, K. (eds.) ICSOB 2015. LNBIP, vol. 210, pp. 1–16. Springer, Heidelberg (2015). doi:10.1007/978-3-319-19593-3_1
4. McConnell, S.: Technical Debt-10x Software Development | Construx, 1 November 2007. http://www.construx.com/10x_Software_Development/Technical_Debt/. Accessed 25 March 2014
5. Li, Z., Avgeriou, P., Liang, P.: A systematic mapping study on technical debt and its management. J. Syst. Softw. **101**, 193–220 (2015)
6. Guo, Y., Seaman, C.: A portfolio approach to technical debt management. In: Proceedings of the 2nd Workshop on Managing Technical Debt, New York, NY, USA, pp. 31–34 (2011)
7. Li, Z., Liang, P., Avgeriou, P.: Architectural technical debt identification based on architecture decisions and change scenarios. In: Proceedings of the 12th Working IEEE/IFIP Conference on Software Architecture, WICSA (2015)
8. Zazworka, N., Vetro', A., Izurieta, C., Wong, S., Cai, Y., Seaman, C., Shull, F.: Comparing four approaches for technical debt identification. Softw. Qual. J. **22**(3), 403–426 (2013)
9. Kruchten, P., Nord, R.L., Ozkaya, I.: Technical debt: from metaphor to theory and practice. IEEE Softw. **29**(6), 18–21 (2012)
10. Seaman, C., Guo, Y., Zazworka, N., Shull, F., Izurieta, C., Cai, Y., Vetro, A.: Using technical debt data in decision making: potential decision approaches. In: 2012 Third International Workshop on Managing Technical Debt (MTD), pp. 45–48 (2012)
11. Schmid, K.: A formal approach to technical debt decision making. In: Proceedings of the 9th International ACM Sigsoft Conference on Quality of Software Architectures, New York, NY, USA, pp. 153–162 (2013)
12. Curtis, B., Sappidi, J., Szynkarski, A.: Estimating the size, cost, and types of technical debt. In: Proceedings of the Third International Workshop on Managing Technical Debt, Piscataway, NJ, USA, pp. 49–53 (2012)
13. Theodoropoulos, T., Hofberg, M., Kern, D.: Technical debt from the stakeholder perspective. In: Proceedings of the 2nd Workshop on Managing Technical Debt, New York, NY, USA, pp. 43–46 (2011)
14. Letouzey, J.-L.: The SQALE method for evaluating technical debt. In: Proceedings of the Third International Workshop on Managing Technical Debt, Piscataway, NJ, USA, pp. 31–36 (2012)
15. Avison, D.E., Lau, F., Myers, M.D., Nielsen, P.A.: Action research. Commun. ACM **42**(1), 94–97 (1999)
16. Baskerville, R.L., Wood-Harper, A.T.: A critical perspective on action research as a method for information systems research. J. Inf. Technol. **11**(3), 235–246 (1996)
17. Sjoberg, D.I.K., Dyba, T., Jorgensen, M.: The future of empirical methods in software engineering research. In: 2007 Future of Software Engineering, Washington, DC, USA, pp. 358–378 (2007)
18. Coughlan, P., Coghlan, D.: Action research for operations management. Int. J. Oper. Prod. Manag. **22**(2), 220–240 (2002)
19. Alves, N.S.R., Mendes, T.S., de Mendonça, M.G., Spínola, R.O., Shull, F., Seaman, C.: Identification and management of technical debt: a systematic mapping study. Inf. Softw. Technol. **70**, 100–121 (2016)
20. Dyba, T.: An empirical investigation of the key factors for success in software process improvement. IEEE Trans. Softw. Eng. **31**(5), 410–424 (2005)

21. Zazworka, N., Spínola, R.O., Vetro', A., Shull, F., Seaman, C.: A case study on effectively identifying technical debt. In: Proceedings of the 17th International Conference on Evaluation and Assessment in Software Engineering, New York, NY, USA, pp. 42–47 (2013)
22. Robillard, P.N.: The role of knowledge in software development. Commun. ACM **42**(1), 87–92 (1999)
23. Falessi, D., Shaw, M.A., Shull, F., Mullen, K., Keymind, M.S.: Practical considerations, challenges, and requirements of tool-support for managing technical debt. In: 2013 4th International Workshop on Managing Technical Debt (MTD), pp. 16–19 (2013)

Applying Social Network Analysis and Centrality Measures to Improve Information Flow Analysis

Stephan Kiesling[1(✉)], Jil Klünder[1], Diana Fischer[2], Kurt Schneider[1], and Kai Fischbach[2]

[1] Software Engineering Group, Leibniz Universität Hannover, Hannover, Germany
{stephan.kiesling,jil.kluender,
kurt.schneider}@inf.uni-hannover.de
[2] University of Bamberg, Bamberg, Germany
{diana.fischer,kai.fischbach}@uni-bamberg.de

Abstract. In software development projects, documents are very important for sharing requirements and other information among employees. However, information can be transported in different ways. Conversations, meetings, workshops and emails convey and impart information as well. Especially large companies struggle in dealing with unclear and incorrect information flows. These information flows can be improved by means of information flow analysis and flow patterns. One technique to analyze information flows is the FLOW method. It supports visualization and analysis of information flows to detect lacks and anomalies and thereby improves information flows. An analyst gathers information transported in the company. Afterwards, information flows are visualized and analyzed based on patterns and personal experience. Nevertheless, analysis based on individual knowledge is error-prone. Hence, we improve the FLOW method with the help of social network analysis applying centrality measures to the FLOW method and to support the FLOW analyst.

1 Introduction

Documents play a major role in process-driven software development companies. They share requirements and other information among team members. However, information is also transferred through other channels like conversations, meetings or workshops. Agile methods, becoming more and more established these days, prefer direct information communication channels and use less documents. Especially big companies have to cope with unclear and wrong information flows in and between teams. Companies struggle to localize these communication problems. To find the problems, information flows must be analyzed.

Information flow analysis can uncover disruptions in information flows in companies, so that they can be corrected. The first step of the analysis is to determine the flow of information in the company. After that, the flow needs to be visualized and analyzed. The analysis may uncover findings that can be used for information flow improvement.

© Springer International Publishing AG 2016
P. Abrahamsson et al. (Eds.): PROFES 2016, LNCS 10027, pp. 379–386, 2016.
DOI: 10.1007/978-3-319-49094-6_25

There are various possibilities to conduct an information flow analysis. One technique is the FLOW method, which is in focus in this paper [1].

FLOW analysis is a systematic method to visualize, analyze and improve information flow [2]. The FLOW method provides a graphical notation (Fig. 1) as well as an approach to identify and gather information flows. The graphical notation provides two different types of information flows. Non-documented, verbal or informal flows of information are denoted as fluid, whereas solid information flows are always documented. By using this graphical notation, so-called FLOW diagrams can be created. These diagrams represent all information flows and all information stores for a task or process. On the one hand, FLOW diagrams help the FLOW analyst to analyze gathered information flows. On the other hand, they can be used after analysis to present findings to the company the analysis was conducted for.

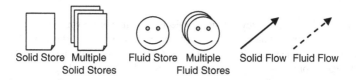

Solid Store   Multiple   Fluid Store   Multiple   Solid Flow   Fluid Flow
              Solid Stores   Fluid Stores

Fig. 1. The basic FLOW notation

The FLOW method consists mainly of three phases: (1) Information flows need to be collected by interviewing appropriate persons. (2) After the elicitation, FLOW diagrams are created by combining partial diagrams from each interviewee into an overall one. (3) Afterwards, the analysis phase starts. The analyst regards the FLOW diagram's structure and looks for bad patterns to decide on improvement recommendations. Moreover, the analyst also compares the depicted information flow with additional information elicited in phase (1) to look for possible contradictions or conflicts.

Mainly the last phase entails several problems. The analysis can be very subjective due to varying personal experiences. The analyst can overlook or misinterpret aspects. He may look into some details more closely and dismiss others only based on a gut feeling.

To reduce the influence of personal experience during analysis, we extend FLOW with methods from social network analysis. We choose centrality measures that are suited for FLOW and use them to compute key indicators for FLOW diagrams. An analyst can use these key indicators as support for his calculations and indicators that point to possible information flow issues. These indicators are specifically intended to support analysis of complex and large FLOW diagrams.

The remaining work is structured as follows. Section 2 presents related work. Section 3 introduces the concepts of the new method. Finally, Sects. 4 and 5 conclude this paper with a discussion and outlook.

2   Related Work

In the following section, we provide an overview of existing research on the relevant topics in this paper.

Modelling and analyzing **information flow** in organizations is motivated by the need to improve the information processes, e.g. by eliminating redundant processes, minimizing the duplication of information, or managing and sharing intra- and inter-organizational information flow [3]. The FLOW method is a method for diagrammatic modelling information flow in teams with the aim to identify critical points which may cause loss of information.

Stapel et al. [2] considered the information flow within different kinds of project teams to detect critical points like lacks of information, a wrong amount of information sharing or gatekeepers who are very central within the network.

Stapel [1] extends this approach by presenting possibilities to analyze the FLOW diagrams which visualize the information flows within the team or business.

In the organizational context, **social network analysis** can help understand how inter- and intra-organizational networks are linked to outcomes and processes [4], such as job exit, team performance, innovation and individual satisfaction (for an overview see, for example, [5]). In addition, social network analysis has been applied to explore the information flow in and between organizations. For example, Braha and Bar-Yam [6] analyzed the information flow structure of intra- and inter-organizational networks in large-scale product development organizations. Friedkin [7] found that the strength of relationships between employees has an impact on intra-organizational information flow. Ryynänen et al. [8] observed the internal information flow network in the project sales process to understand and improve the information flow between the employees.

Information flow networks resulting from the FLOW method are directed networks. Analyzing directed networks requires a distinction between measures for incoming ties and measures for outgoing ties [9]. This is important for the measures, which will be applied in the network analysis in this contribution.

Social network analysis provides a wide range of measures to analyze a network (e.g. [9]). In order to understand and analyze the roles of actors in networks, many studies in social science have relied on centrality measures [6]. Centrality measures help to understand the individual actor's prominence according to the actor's position in the network [10]. We argue that centrality measures are suitable means to analyze the directed flow networks.

3   Improving the FLOW Method

This section gives an overview of our concept to enrich FLOW diagrams with social network analysis by calculating key indicators.

3.1 Selection of Appropriate Centrality Measures

This approach concentrates on the use of centrality measures which help to analyze FLOW networks to simplify the process. Nevertheless, the FLOW analysis cannot be fully automated, since a FLOW network will not include all information – in particular, interpersonal aspects will be hard to visualize. However, there are some centrality measures which help to identify critical points and support the individual analysis. We will focus on embedding five centrality measures in FLOW analysis.

Degree centrality is a local measure counting the number of edges of a node, i.e. the sum of sources (in-degree) and receivers (out-degree) of information. In directed networks, in- and out-degree can be considered as two different values to differentiate between the quantities of incoming and outgoing information [11]. Applied to FLOW analysis, degree centrality measures the frequency and the amount of incoming and outgoing information. Degree centrality is a first indicator for a person being important for information sharing. It identifies central persons who need to share or receive much information. A drop out of one of these central persons can threaten project success since all information passing this person would either be lost or delivered in a longer time.

Closeness centrality measures the average distance of a node to each other node within the network [11]. It can be seen as a measure for the well-positioning of a person within a network [10]. This measure assumes that information originates from all other persons with equal probability and that all information flows along the shortest paths [10]. A low raw closeness score is an indicator for a person being well-positioned to obtain novel information early [10]. Nodes with a short distance to other nodes tend to receive flows sooner, assuming comparable times of information transport between all nodes in the network. Thus, closeness centrality is normally interpreted as the time until arrival of something flowing through a network [12]. Persons with high closeness scores have short distances and hence a high collaboration [13] with other persons and will receive information sooner. In FLOW analysis, these persons are very important for information sharing. Identifying these persons is one of the aims of the FLOW method, since they obtain novel information early. In addition, they bundle much information that can be shared within the network. In some cases, there are tasks referencing to several processes. Furthermore, they bundle information of many processes and hence can transport them to responsive persons. Replacing such persons by farseeing persons with less closeness centrality would go along with a drop in performance.

Betweenness centrality measures how often a node is located on the shortest (i.e. geodesic) paths between two other nodes. Persons are central if they have the potential to mediate the flow of resources or information between other actors [14]. Thus, persons who can mediate the flow of information between other actors are considered as central. This measure identifies persons who are indispensable for information sharing between other persons. Furthermore, regular exits due to holidays, retirement, or termination, can cause problems since it is difficult to replace the respective persons adequately. Therefore, knowing these persons is desirable.

Flow betweenness extends betweenness centrality in two ways: It considers all paths between nodes and not only geodesics, and it is appropriate for graphs and weighted graphs in which larger weights indicate stronger ties between actors. Edge weights are taken to represent the potential for the flow of information between nodes assuming that the constraints for a metric in a mathematical view (except for the symmetry in directed graphs) hold [15]. Applied to FLOW analysis, flow betweenness describes the amount of information, forwarded by a single person by considering all information transported via this specific person. These persons are interesting because they coordinate the process-independent information flow.

As an extension of degree centrality, **eigenvector centrality** defines actors to be central if they have ties to other actors who, in turn, are central themselves [14]. In FLOW analysis, eigenvector centrality identifies persons who are important for information flow since they probably get many information in a short time. Furthermore, they can share their information with other important persons with little effort. These persons themselves can share the information so that the information can spread in a short time.

Each of these centrality measures is an indicator for problems concerning the information flow within a team. Hence, we use them to help the FLOW analyst identify critical points in FLOW networks. Having determined these measures, the FLOW analyst can interpret the network and help the team ensure the right amount of information flow and unburden persons who must not fail.

3.2 Transforming Flow Diagrams to Networks

In order to apply centrality measures to a FLOW diagram, the diagram has to be transformed into a valid network first. The ongoing of this transformation is not trivial, since FLOW diagrams highly resemble networks but differ in some significant aspects. To clarify this, we provide a short introduction to structure of FLOW diagrams and their elements below.

A FLOW diagram consists of information stores, information flows, and FLOW activities.[1] Having a nested structure, a FLOW activity can contain information stores, information flows, and other FLOW activities. To convert the FLOW diagram into a network, information stores and information flows can be mapped directly to nodes and edges of these networks but nested structures need to be dissolved.

As illustrated in Fig. 2, there are three different ways of transforming a FLOW activity. The left side of the figure shows an example of a FLOW diagram containing an activity with a nested structure to be transformed. On the right side of the arrows are all possible alternatives to transform the nested structure of the activity:

1. Directly connecting all incoming and outgoing stores of the activity.
2. Representing the activity through a distinct node connected to all incoming and outgoing stores.
3. Specifying the underlying information flow structure by deciding for each incoming and contained store to which contained or outgoing store it has to be connected. In this case, "A" is defined as an incoming store, "X" and "Y" are defined as contained stores and "B" is defined as an outgoing store.

---

[1] Refer to [16] for a detailed description of the FLOW syntax.

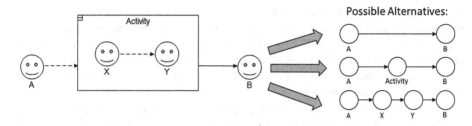

Fig. 2. Three alternatives to represent the same FLOW activity (left) in a network (right)

To transform FLOW activities properly, we have to clarify the purpose of the actual activity first. In the first alternative, store "A" provides information for the activity, which might or might not be processed and changed in the activity. It is obtained by neither "X" nor "Y". "B" receives the possibly changed information. This signifies that an internal way of processing this information is not considered to be relevant for the overall process.

In the second alternative, the activity represents an abstract task or sub-process, which can neither be transformed nor removed. This may occur, if a FLOW diagram contains uncertain information, which could not be elicited during FLOW interviews. For example, "A" and "B" do not know how information is being passed in the activity and "X" and "Y" could not be identified and are thereby obscured for the FLOW analyst.

The third alternative represents a fully unrestricted way of interconnecting incoming and outgoing stores. This case should be used in all cases except alternative 1 and 2. This case can occur if the activity contains a sub-process of the overall modelled process. In this example, "A" provides information for "X", while "Y" provides information for "B".

Only the analyst can decide which alternative of these three above he should apply. He has to decide for each FLOW activity which case is appropriate and which incoming and outgoing information stores have to be selected.

3.3   Calculating Key Indicators

We developed a converter to transform FLOW diagrams from xml files created with our FLOW editor ProFLOW into networks. The transformed network now has to be analyzed by applying centrality measures. For this task, we use UCINET[2] to calculate key indicators based on our centrality measures depicted above. The converted FLOW networks can be imported to UCINET, which calculates the key indicators. This process cannot be done automatically yet because user interaction with UCINET is necessary. After calculation, the determined key indicators are exported by the analyst for further analysis of the FLOW network.

---

[2] UCINET is a common used tool for social network analysis.

4   Discussion

In this section we point out the limitations of our method followed by an interpretation of our findings.

4.1   Limitations and Interpretation

Applying information flow analysis in a software company does not imply to remedy all company's problems, but can improve information flows. Furthermore, findings uncovered through information flow analysis must be accepted by the company and implemented by the employees.

The benefit of information flow analysis depends on the chosen flow analysis method. In our case, we have chosen FLOW to analyze information flows which suited well for the analyses we conducted so far. Applying the FLOW method takes a lot of time and is highly based on personal experience. The approach requires a considerable number of manual steps. One reason is that these steps require a decision from the FLOW analyst that cannot be automated (see Fig. 2). Another reason is the interface between UCINET and our ProFLOW editor. UCINET does not allow automated processes. It is likely that the analysis will become more time-consuming for the analyst but he will gain more insights.

A way to decrease manual steps would be to integrate the converter into the used FLOW editor and relieve the user to switch between applications and to choose the FLOW diagram to convert.

In this contribution we applied centrality measures which can enrich the original FLOW method. Considering the added information (as key indicators) can lead to results that have been overlooked before.

5   Conclusion

This paper describes concepts, methods and tools to improve the analysis of information flows by improving the FLOW method with social network analysis. The approach is to convert FLOW diagrams into networks and to calculate centrality measures for the converted diagrams. These centrality measures support the analysis of structure and meaning of the original FLOW diagram and enables an easier detection of inconsistencies and anomalies in information flows. This improves processes and procedures in the project as well as in the entire software company.

We accomplished our goal to reduce the influence of personal experience on the FLOW method as well as our purpose to uncover more findings in information flows in software companies.

Acknowledgements.   This work was supported by the German Federal Ministry of Education and Research under grant number K3: FKZ 13N13548 (2015-2018) and by the German Research Foundation (DFG) under grant number 263807701 (Project TeamFLOW, 2015-2017).

References

1. Stapel, K.: Informationsflusstheorie der Softwareentwicklung, 1st edn., Univ, Hannover, Dr. Hut, München (2012)
2. Stapel, K., Knauss, E., Schneider, K.: Using FLOW to improve communication of requirements in globally distributed software projects. In: Workshop on Collaboration and Intercultural Issues on Requirements: Communication, Understanding and Softskills (CIRCUS 2009), pp. 5–14 (2009)
3. Durugbo, C., Tiwari, A., Alcock, J.R.: Modelling information flow for organisations: a review of approaches and future challenges. Int. J. Inf. Manag. 33(3), 597–610 (2013)
4. Merrill, J., et al.: Findings from an organizational network analysis to support local public health management. J. Urban Health Bull. N.Y. Acad. Med. 85(4), 572–584 (2008)
5. Borgatti, S.P., Foster, P.C.: The network paradigm in organizational research: a review and typology. J. Manag. 29(6), 991–1013 (2003)
6. Braha, D., Bar-Yam, Y.: Information flow structure in large-scale product development organizational networks. In: Vervest, P., Heck, E., Pau, L.-F., Preiss, K. (eds.) Smart Business Networks, 1st edn., pp. 105–125. Springer, Heidelberg (2005)
7. Friedkin, N.E.: Information flow through strong and weak ties in intraorganizational social networks. Soc. Netw. 3(4), 273–285 (1982)
8. Ryynänen, H., Jalkala, A., Salminen, R.T.: Supplier's internal communication network during the project sales process. Proj. Manag. J. 44(3), 5–20 (2013)
9. Wasserman, S., Faust, K.: Social Network Analysis: Methods and Applications, 1st edn. Cambridge University Press, Cambridge (1994)
10. Borgatti, S.P.: Centrality and network flow. Soc. Netw. 27(1), 55–71 (2005)
11. Freeman, L.C., Roeder, D., Mulholland, R.R.: Centrality in social networks: II. Experimental results. Soc. Netw. 2(2), 119–141 (1979)
12. Borgatti, S.P.: Centrality and AIDS. Connections 18(1), 112–114 (1995)
13. Schneider, K., Liskin, O.: Exploring FLOW distance in project communication. In: 2015 IEEE/ACM 8th International Workshop on Cooperative and Human Aspects of Software Engineering (CHASE), pp. 117–118 (2015)
14. Faust, K.: Centrality in affiliation networks. Soc. Netw. 19(2), 157–191 (1997)
15. Newman, M.J.: A measure of betweenness centrality based on random walks. Soc. Netw. 27(1), 39–54 (2005)
16. Stapel, K., Schneider, K., Lübke, D., Flohr, T.: Improving an industrial reference process by information flow analysis: a case study. In: Münch, J., Abrahamsson, P. (eds.) PROFES 2007. LNCS, vol. 4589, pp. 147–159. Springer, Heidelberg (2007). doi:10.1007/978-3-540-73460-4_15

Design of Project Management Capabilities

Solvita Berzisa[(✉)] and Jānis Grabis

Information Technology Institute, Riga Technical University, Kalku 1, Riga, Latvia
{solvita.berzisa,grabis}@rtu.lv

Abstract. Project management (PM) capabilities define organizational abilities of delivering predictable project results in a changing environment. To increase maturity of the PM capabilities, they need to be formalized, aligned with standards and best practices, measured, controlled and improved. One of capabilities standardization and formalization approaches is to perform capability modelling. This paper proposes to use the Capability Driven Development methodology to model the PM capability models because this methodology allows for representing unique capability delivery context situations and specification of context-aware PM processes. The paper outlines the capability modelling processes and elaborates the capability model for the risk management sub-capability. Potential applications of the capability model are discussed.

Keywords: Project management capability · Capability modelling · CDD methodology · Capability design tool

1 Introduction

An organizational project management (PM) capability enables success of PM in organization and provides processes, technologies and peoples for predictable PM delivery [1]. PM is a process of applying knowledge, skills, methods, techniques and tools to project activities to meet the project requirements [2]. Organizational PM is a framework for aligning PM practice with the organizational strategy by customizing or fitting these practices to organization context and situation [3]. An organization needs to know what specific PM practices, knowledge, skills, tools and techniques are necessary for it to successfully achieve the organization strategy and effective PM [1]. So it is necessary to identify current organizational PM capabilities, required improvements and establish a roadmap to implement these improvements [1].

The Capability Maturity Model [4] evaluates an organizational ability to complete projects successfully and describes practices helping to increase process maturity [5], [6]. However, the maturity level is not the only factor contributing to the project success [7]. Similarly, PMBOK [2] describes project management references processes without considering specific project management situations. Recently, Capability Driven Development (CDD) [8] methodology has been proposed to enable development of organizational capabilities with respect to specific contextual situation. It defines capabilities as ability and capacity that enable an enterprise to achieve a business goal in a certain context. Capability modelling and design ensures formal definition of the PM capability to provide for evaluation of the current PM capability and its improvement options.

© Springer International Publishing AG 2016
P. Abrahamsson et al. (Eds.): PROFES 2016, LNCS 10027, pp. 387–395, 2016.
DOI: 10.1007/978-3-319-49094-6_26

The purpose of this position paper is to present a PM capability model and illustrate a process of transforming traditional reference PM processes into context-aware PM processes suitable for development of context-aware Project Management Information Systems (PMIS). Development of context-aware PMIS as well as analysis, evaluation and improvement of the PM capabilities are the main application areas of the PM capability model. The main contribution of this work is development of building blocks (i.e., PM capability models and patterns) needed for further elaboration of context-aware PMIS. That enables improvement of maturity of the PM processes on the basis of established PM practices.

The rest of the paper is structured as follows: Sect. 2 describes theoretical background about the PM capabilities, capability modelling approach and motivation of the PM capability modelling. Design of the PM capability model is presented in Sect. 3 and application possibilities of models are discussed in Sect. 4. Conclusions and future work are presented at the end of the paper.

2 Theoretical Background and Motivation

The PM capability (described in Sect. 2.1.) is one of digital organization's capabilities that is important for successful project-oriented organizations and is often evaluated during tenders and outsourcing together with technical capabilities [2]. Capability modelling (described in Sect. 2.2.) helps to understand and standardize organization current PM practices and to understand what PM capabilities an organization has. Other benefits of the PM capability modelling are:

- Understanding of factors that affect project and PM in an organization;
- Identification of PM capability gaps preventing fulfilment of the strategy;
- Identification of the PM capabilities maturity level and improvement possibilities based on context situation specific PM practices. Also improvement of quality management in an organization because many of quality management requirements (e.g. ISO 9001) are related to implemented PM practices;
- Helping to understand requirements and to choose PMIS for an organization;
- Helping to understand configuration requirements of PMIS for a particular project;
- Movement towards design and development of the context adaptive PMIS.

2.1 Project Management Capability

The PM capabilities includes peoples, processes and technologies [1]. Effective PM requires the right peoples with right skills [1] and is one of organization challenges to get these peoples. The PM capability focuses to PM processes, but also needs to review related process in project oriented organization – product related and support processes [2]. All processes need to be tailored to organization context situation and standardized, measure, controlled and improved to achieve higher processes capability [1]. From the PM capability perspective, processes of organization project [2], program [9] and portfolio management [10] need to be considered. The third element of the PM capabilities is technologies available to the organization. For example, PMIS that supports implementation of processes and helps people to perform their tasks.

2.2   Capability Modelling Approach

The capabilities are modelled using concepts defined in the capability meta-model [8] (simplified view of main concepts given in Fig. 1). Every capability has goals and achievement of these goals is measured by indicators or KPI. The context (context set, context element range, context element, context element value) defines circumstance affecting capability delivery and also defines context situations in which the capability being able to deliver. The capability delivery is supported by a process. Process variants can be constructed for dealing with specific capability delivery context situations. Patterns are used to support capability design. The patterns provide reusable solutions for capability delivery. They are also characterized by their context, which defines situation when this pattern is applicable.

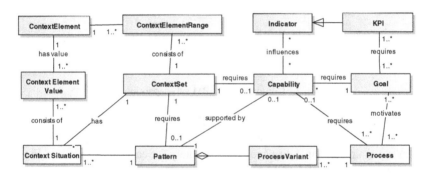

Fig. 1. Main concepts of capability modelling

3   PM Capability Design

According to the CDD methodology, the capability design process can be organized following various pathways [11]. For the PM capability design purposes the capability modelling is organized according the following pathway [12]:

1. Define and name capability;
2. Define the capability goals;
3. Model context - identification of contextual factors affecting the capability;
4. Define main activities of process supporting the capability;
5. Identify process variation - indicate process dependences on context;
6. Specify of capability indicators and KPI;
7. Identification of appropriate patterns in pattern repository and integration in process.

The capability model designed provides a capability overview and an elaboration of one of the sub-capabilities, namely, project risk management capability. The capability model is divided in several sub-models and CDT (Capability Design Tool) [12] is used for modelling.

The **PM capability** consists of interrelated sub-capabilities in different levels: project, program and portfolio (Fig. 2 demonstrates PMI view to PM sub-capabilities based on [2, 9, 10]). There are interrelated and shared elements among the sub-capabilities. Some of the sub-capability have duplicated names in different levels but these capabilities have specific meaning in each level. The main PM capability is "Effective and efficient PM" [1].

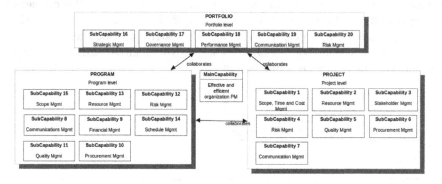

Fig. 2. Composition of PM sub-capabilities

Definition of the **goals** is similar to enterprise modeling [13] but in the case of the PM capability that also has been distributed to different levels. It is possible to define goals for the main PM capability and also separately for each sub-capability. Figure 3 summarizes main goals of the PM capability according to PMI [3]. The main goal and focus of the PM capability is to derive business value from implementation of practices.

Fig. 3. Goals of PM capability based on [3]

The **context situation** of the PM capability depends on such contextual elements as domain, structure of organization (also geographical distribution and location), culture, technologies, human resources, project and other characteristics. The impact of these context elements on project success have been analyzed in several investigations: culture aspects [14]; culture, industry and PM practice/technology [15]. Similarly, as for the goals, the context can be modelled for the main PM capability and also for each sub-capability. The context model helps to identify environment in which the organizational PM capability works. Some example: PM in local project (location in one country) will differ from global project (involved different countries, team distributed in different time zones) or IT and construction PM capabilities also is deliver differently. A fragment of the general PM context model is given in Fig. 4. that includes culture, geographical distribution and project characteristics context elements.

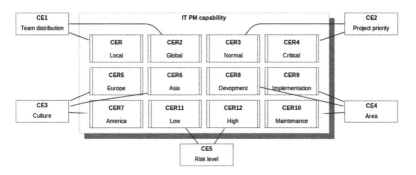

Fig. 4. Fragment of the PM context model

The next step is definition of the capability **delivery process**. This task is performed for each PM sub-capability. The process initially describes base activities what is followed by identification of context dependent variations in the next step. The risk management capability process is considered for demonstration purposes. The reference risk management capability process and sub-processes are summarized in Table 1.

Table 1. Processes of project risk management

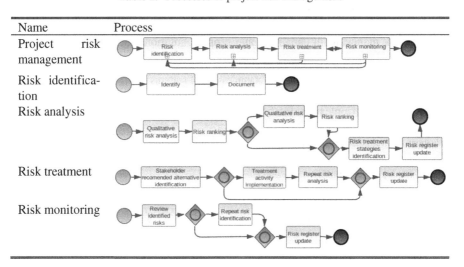

Context situation changes affect the capability delivery process and require **process variations**. The process variants can be viewed as execution scenarios of the delivery process in a specific context situation. The process variations for the context situations define in Fig. 4 are: local Europe software development (this process variant describes the process of managing a software development project in Europe performed by a team located in one country) or global Asia software implementation (software implementation in Asia performed by a globally distributed team). Process variants are identified for each PM sub-capability and can be aggregated in an overall process for the main capability. To identify the process variation can be used systematic analysis of process variation points (process gateway where decision depends on context element value; example of variation point is in Fig. 5.) and it combinations during the process.

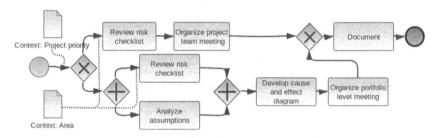

Fig. 5. Updated risk identification process

The **indicators** are used for performance evaluation of the capability delivery. Classical PM capability indicators according to successful project definition [2] are time, quality and budget, and number of satisfied customer and other indicators. At least one indicator is needed to be defined for each PM sub-capability. In the risk management capability example, percentage of occurred unidentified risks is one of the indicators.

During capability design, the **patterns** are used as recommendations or solutions for process execution in a particular context. They are stored in the pattern repository [16]. Some examples of the PM patterns are given in Table 2. These example patterns are related to risk management capability and propose solutions for risk identification in

Table 2. Examples of PM patterns

Pattern problem	Context and other characteristics	Solution
Pattern 1: Risk identification for low priority project	Project priority = *normal* Capability = *project risk Mgmt*	
Pattern 2: Risk identification for critical project	Project priority = *critical* Capability = *project risk Mgmt*	

two context situations – one solution for critical priority projects and other for normal priority. The risk identification process after integration of these patterns is given in Fig. 5. After this update, the risk identification process becomes more elaborated and relies on best practices. Its performance depends of two context elements – area (change basic risk checklist used for review) and risk priority (change processes of risk identification and create process variation point). During pattern identification and integration new process variation points and new process variants can be identified. Figure 5 shows these new context dependent variation points for the risk identification sub-process.

4 Application of PM Capability Models

As mentioned in Sect. 2, there are different benefits of capability design and modelling what can be summarized as two application directions of the developed capability models:

1. Organization PM capability analysis. There are several objectives of this analysis, for example, to analyze problems and to evaluate context that affects the organization PM capabilities; to evaluate capabilities and identify capability gaps; benchmarking against the best practices and identification of improvement possibilities to increase the maturity level of the PM capability; and to evaluate possibilities for attaining new capabilities.
2. PMIS tailoring to support contextual process variability what is discussed in more detail below.

PMIS is a standardized set of automated tools and techniques used in PM for planning, execution, management and closing of the project, as well as for collecting, combining and distributing project information [2]. PMIS is also part of PM capability and its quality impacts the PM capability. PMIS provides a wide range of functions directly supporting PM, as well as tools for its configuration and modification, where configuration is perceived as the most appropriate PMIS setup depending on project situation [17]. Definition of the PMIS configuration requirements must include the following information [17]: data entities used in project; attributes of each data entity; and processes related to the data entities. The capability model specifies the specific project situation by defining context situations. It helps to understand data entities, their attributes and processes.

During the configuration of context-aware PMIS is proposed to separate a core PM system and a context adaptive part. The core PM system implements processes often using packaged PM systems such Jira or Microsoft Project Server. Context specific processes would be setup dynamically depending on the observed context situation. That is to be performed by the context adaptive part according to specifications provides in the capability model. Context data might be static or dynamic and context brokering solutions could be used for retrieving dynamic context data.

5   Summary and Conclusions

This paper introduces the PM capability models and describes PM capability design process and challenges. Design of the PM capabilities helps to document and formalize the PM processes in an organization, understand the context situation in which the organization can ensure predictable project results. Main application directions of the PM capability model are the organization PM capability analysis, and PMIS tailoring to requirements of the organizational PM capabilities.

PM capability modelling is complicated by a number of issues:

1. The PM capability is not one capability but it consists of interrelated sub-capabilities. In this paper, one of the sub-capabilities is elaborated. Each particular organization needs to decide how to organize sub-capabilities because they can be joined and spilled differently. For example, risk/communication management in all level will be one capability or it will be separate for project, program and portfolio level.
2. The PM context varies among sub-capabilities. Each sub-capability might have its own context situation. Context granularity also should be decided upon, for example, location can be identified with continents or country.
3. The PM processes contain many interrelations and cycles. The processes include many variation points and their combinations. Many processes are organization dependent and are related to product delivery and support process details.

Currently developed capability models reported in this paper are derived from PMI standards. That demonstrates that the PM capability models allow adopting existing general practices and standards for modelling of context-aware PM processes. On the other hand, that limits a breath of context situations covered to those envisioned in the PMI standards. Consideration of other PM standards and practices is needed to cover a wider range of context situations and will be tackled in future research activities.

Future work will focus to three directions:

1. Modelling: modelling of different PM sub-capabilities with focus to design of the general PM capability. This general PM capability can be used as a base for design or evaluation of particular organization capability.
2. Development the context-aware PMIS as outlined in Sect. 4: research of possibilities to design the context adaptive PMIS from methodological view and also from PMIS functionality and possibilities to support adaption according to the context changes.
3. Creation of the PM pattern repository: design of the PM pattern repository will ensure collection of PM practices and reusable solutions.

Case studies of the organization PM capabilities and the pattern repository usage and experimental designs of the context-aware PMIS also will be performed.

Acknowledgement. Support for this work was provided by the Riga Technical University through the Scientific Research Project Competition for Young Researchers No. ZP-2016/24.

References

1. PMI: Organizational Project Management Maturity Model (3ed). PMI, Pennsylvania (2013)
2. PMI: A Guide to the Project Management Body of Knowledge (5ed). PMI, Pennsylvania (2014)
3. PMI: Implementing Organizational Project Management: A Practice Guide. PMI, Pennsylvania (2014)
4. Paulk, M.C., Curtis, B., Chrissis, M.B., Weber, C.V.: Capability Maturity Model SM for Software, Version 1.1. Carnegie Mellon University, Pennsylvania (1993)
5. Miklosik, A.: Improving project management performance through capability maturity measurement. Procedia Econ. Financ. **30**, 522–530 (2015)
6. Nenni, E.M., Arnone, V., Boccardelli, P., Napolitano, I.: How to increase the value of the project management maturity model as a business-oriented framework. Int. J. Eng. Bus. Manag. **6**, 1–6 (2014)
7. Lee, L.S., Anderson, R.M.: An exploratory investigation of the antecedents of the IT project management capability. e-Service J. **5**(1), 27–42 (2006)
8. Bērziša, S., Bravos, G., Gonzalez, T.C., Czubayko, U., España, S., Grabis, J., Henkel, M., Jokste, L., Kampars, J., Koç, H., Kuhr, J.-C., Llorca, C., Loucopoulos, P., Pascual, R.J., Pastor, O., Sandkuhl, K., Simic, H., Stirna, J., Valverde, F.G., Zdravkovic, J.: Capability driven development: an approach to designing digital enterprises. Bus. Inf. Syst. Eng. **57**, 15–25 (2015)
9. PMI: The Standard for Program Management (3ed). PMI, Pennsylvania (2013)
10. PMI: The Standard for Portfolio Management (3ed). PMI, Pennsylvania (2013)
11. Koç, H., Sandkuhl, K.: A business process based method for capability modelling. In: Matulevičius, R., Dumas, M. (eds.) BIR 2015. LNBIP, vol. 229, pp. 257–264. Springer, Heidelberg (2015). doi:10.1007/978-3-319-21915-8_17
12. Bērziša, S., España, S., Grabis, J., Henkel, M., Jokste, L., Kampars, J., Koç, H., Sandkuhl, K., Stirna, J., Valverde, F., Zdravkovic, J.: Deliverable 5.2: The Initial Version of Capability Driven Development Methodology, CaaS – Capability as a Service for Digital Enterprises, FP7 project no. 611351 (2015)
13. Sandkuhl, K., Stirna, J., Persson, A., Wibotzki, M.: Enterprise Modeling: Tackling Business Challenges with the 4EM Method. Springer, Heidelberg (2014)
14. Zwikael, O., Shimizu, K., Globerson, S.: Cultural differences in project management capabilities: a field study. Int. J. Proj. Manag. **23**, 454–462 (2005)
15. de Carvalho, M.M., Patah, L.A., de Souza Bido, D.: Project management and its effects on project success: cross-country and cross-industry comparisons. Int. J. Proj. Manag. **33**, 1509–1522 (2015)
16. Stirna, J., Zdravkovic, J., Henkel, M., Kampars, J.: Capability patterns as the enablers for model-based development of business context-aware applications. In: Fleischmann, A., Guédria, W., Heuser, L., Kornyshova, E., Loucopoulos, P., Oberweis, A., Pastor, O., Proper, H.A., Schmidt, W., Schönthaler, F., Stary, C., Vossen, G., Zdravkovic, J. (eds.) Complementary Proceedings of the Workshops TEE, CoBI, and XOC-BPM at IEEE-COBI 2015, pp. 1–12, CEUR-WS.org (2015)
17. Bērziša, S., Grabis, J.: Combining project requirements and knowledge in configuration of project management information systems. In: Caivano, D., Baldassarre, M.T., García, F.O., Genero, M., Mendes, E., Runeson, P., Sillitti, A., Travassos, G.H., Visaggio, G. (eds.) Second Proceedings: Short Papers, Doctoral Symposium and Workshops of the 12th International Conference of Product Focused Software Development and Process Improvement (PROFES 2011), pp. 89–95. ACM, New York (2011)

Speed and Agility in System Engineering

Relationship of DevOps to Agile, Lean and Continuous Deployment

A Multivocal Literature Review Study

Lucy Ellen Lwakatare[(✉)], Pasi Kuvaja, and Markku Oivo

Faculty of Information Technology and Electrical Engineering,
University of Oulu, Oulu, Finland
{lucy.lwakatare,pasi.kuvaja,markku.oivo}@oulu.fi

Abstract. In recent years, the DevOps phenomenon has attaracted interest amongst practitioners and researchers in software engineering, reflecting the greater emphasis on collaboration between development and IT operations. However, despite this growing interest, DevOps is often conflated with agile and continuous deployment approaches of software development. This study compares DevOps with agile, lean and continuous deployment approaches in software development from four perspectives: origin, adoption, implementation and goals. The study also reports on the claimed effects and on the metrics of DevOps used to asses those effects. The research is based on an interpretative analysis of qualitative data from documents describing DevOps and practitioner's responses in a DevOps workshop. Our findings indicate that the DevOps phenomenon originated from continuous deployment as an evolution of agile software development, informed by a lean principles background. It was also concluded that successful adoption of DevOps requires agile software development.

Keywords: DevOps · Agile · Lean · Continuous deployment · Effect

1 Introduction

According to Sharp, Robinson and Woodman [1], the software engineering (SE) field is characterized by rapid change and constant emergence of new paradigms that dominate most research agendas. In recent times, DevOps and the continuous deployment (CD) paradigm have attracted widespread interest among SE practitioners and researchers [2,3]. With the increasing diversity of software development approaches described under the general heading of DevOps, practitioner-led forums have highlighted a lack of clarity around the use of this term, which has become an umbrella for more definitive terms appearing mostly in mobile and web contexts [4]. DevOps is commonly associated with related software development approaches—especially agile, continuous delivery and CD— to the extent that it is often conflated with these terms. While there are some similarities, it remains crucial to differentiate between these concepts in order

© Springer International Publishing AG 2016
P. Abrahamsson et al. (Eds.): PROFES 2016, LNCS 10027, pp. 399–415, 2016.
DOI: 10.1007/978-3-319-49094-6_27

to clarify the contribution and significance of DevOps for both practice and research.

As a blend of the words 'development'and 'operations', DevOps emphasises cross-functional collaboration within and between teams, with the goal of accelerating delivery of software changes [5]. Adoption of DevOps has many benefits; in particular, it enables better collaboration and reduces time to market of new features to production [6]. According to Dingsøyr and Lassenius [3], the leading edge of DevOps is driven by the industry and consultants, with research lagging behind in synthesizing and systematizing knowledge and in testing the many claims made by proponents of the concepts. Among studies emerging to address this concern, DevOps has been compared and contrasted with release engineering practices [5] and roles [7].

As part of a broader goal of improving understanding of the DevOps phenomenon, the present study seeks to clarify the relationship of DevOps to associated software development approaches. Specifically, an interpretative analysis of data collected from online sources and from a workshop with practitioners explores the relationship of DevOps to agile software development, lean software development and CD. The article also reports on the claimed effects of DevOps and on the metrics used to assess those effects. The study addresses the following research questions.

- RQ1. How does DevOps relate to agile, lean and CD?
- RQ2. What are the claimed effects of DevOps, and what metrics can be used to assess those effects?

The rest of the paper is organised as follows. The next section describes the background of DevOps and related work. Section 3 details research method, and the results are presented in Sect. 4.

2   DevOps: Background and Related Work

The essential purpose of DevOps is to align the incentives of all those involved in delivering software, with a particular emphasis on developers, testers and operations personnel [6]. The term has been popularised through a series of DevOps-Days, which started following a presentation by Patrick Debois and Andrew Clay Shafers at the 2008 Agile Conference [8]. This phenomenon, and in particular the definition of DevOps, has been said to lack clarity [4,5]. The first definition that can be considered scientific was proposed by Penners and Dyck [5] in 2015. In 2016 Lwakatare, Kuvaja and Oivo [4] advanced the proposed definition as follows '*a mind-set substantiated by a set of practices to encourage cross-functional collaboration between teams—especially development and IT operations—within a software development organization, in order to operate resilient systems and accelerate delivery of change*'. This enhanced definition was validated by analyzing descriptions of DevOps by practitioners in online documents such as blog posts.

DevOps is often associated (or used interchangeably) with the concepts of agile software development and CD. In their book[1], Bass, Weber and Zhu [9] note that the emphasis on the relationship between DevOps and agile practices is one characterization of DevOps. Refering to IBM's disciplined agile delivery, they describe how DevOps adds to agile practices. According to their account [9], DevOps practices affect and relate to all three phases of IBMs framework: inception, construction and transition. For instance, the construction phase of disciplined agile delivery includes key elements of DevOps practices, which are also agile practices that collectively play an important role in the ability to automate the deployment pipeline [9]. These key elements include code branching management, continuous integration (CI) and CD, whilst automated testing is considered to be incorporated [9]. CD differs from continuous delivery; while the latter aims to keep software in a constantly releasable state [3], CD also automates the final step of delivering software to production as soon as code is checked-in and all automated tests have been successfully passed [2]. CD enables businesses to reduce cycle time so that feedback is quickly obtained from users. In addition, the risk and cost associated with production deployments is reduced and managed, as there is improved visibility in the delivery process itself [6].

Few studies have compared and contrasted DevOps with other areas of established knowledge and practices in SE. Penners and Dyck [5] recognised that the lack of a clear definition of DevOps means that the term is easily confused with or used as a synonym for other terms, such as release engineering. In investigating their differences and relationship, Penners and Dyck [5] found that, as a discipline concerned with establishing and improving the process of delivering high-quality software to customers in a holistic manner, release engineering is broader in scope than DevOps. While not itself a discipline, DevOps stresses the improvement of collaboration between development and operations teams through cultural change in the operation of resilient systems and accelerated delivery of software changes [5]. Kerzazi and Adams [7] compared the main tasks of release and DevOps engineers by analysing online job postings, concluding that the role of a release engineer is broader than that of a DevOps engineer because the former combines the principal activities of DevOps and traditional build engineers. The present study aims to improve understanding of the DevOps phenomenon by comparing and contrasting DevOps with other software development practices, especially agile, lean and CD.

3   Research Method

Adopting a qualitative research approach, data were collected from (1) non-scientific documents, (2) scientific articles and (3) responses from practitioners who participated in a DevOps workshop. Scientific articles were gathered by expanding our previous literature search on DevOps [10] to include recent publications from November 2014 to March 2016. Non-scientific documents were collected using the multivocal literature review (MLR) method [11–13].

---

[1] For more detail, see [9], pp. 12–13.

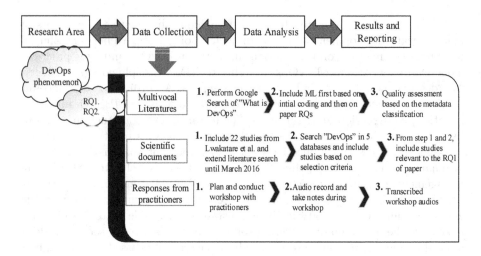

Fig. 1. Research process

The responses of practitioners were obtained during a half-day workshop conducted on 25 April, 2016; the workshop was attended by eleven practitioners from seven companies involved in the Need for Speed (N4S) project[2]. Thematic analysis was used to analyse the collected documents. The research approach is summarised in Fig. 1.

3.1   Data Collection: Non-Scientific Documents

The first part of the data collection process involved non-scientific documents, such as blog posts and trade journals that are collectively known as grey or multivocal literature (ML) [11–13]. ML typically comprises a large collection of readily accessible writings available in a wide variety of forms. Because it contains the views of a diverse set of authors and incorporates different research (or non-research) logics, it is important to have a clear goal prior to ML data collection. Here, the overall research goal of an MLR was to understand how different practitioners variously describe the DevOps phenomenon. The goal of this study—to identify how DevOps relates to agile, lean and CD—emerged from initial coding within that overall goal.

There is no explicit guideline for collecting ML, and it is an acknowledged challenge that the diversity of ML means that it cannot be collected and assessed in the same way as scientific literatures. For this reason, data collection was informed by procedures recommended or adopted by other authors using similar methods, including Ogawa [11], Tom, Aurum and Vidgen [12] and Garousi and Mäntylä [13]. The data collection procedure took account of the following aspects: (1) data sources and search strategy, (2) inclusion and exclusion and (3) quality assessment.

---

[2] http://www.n4s.fi/en/.

– *Data Sources and Search Strategy.* The Google search engine was used to locate ML from the World Wide Web, using the query 'What is DevOps?'. From the retrieved records, links to search results were reviewed page by page, and the outputs of each link were saved in PDF format. This procedure was followed until pages showing job adverts began, at which point the review was stopped. In total, 230 records were gathered for inclusion in the next step.
– *Inclusion and Exclusion.* All 230 documents were imported into NVivo[3] for initial analysis. Inclusion or exclusion of records was simultaneous with initial coding. No pre-defined themes were used; instead, themes were allowed to emerge from the data. The process also involved the classification of records with different attributes, such as author information (e.g. name, role and place of work) and source information (e.g. publication year, forum and link). Following the review of all 230 documents, 201 sources were identified as relevant while 29 were excluded as either duplicates, video links, pointers to catalogues, course adverts, certification adverts or presentation slides. The initial coding identified 'claimed effects'and 'DevOps in relation to agile, lean and CD'as new themes for further analysis; the first of these was found in 66 and the second in 75 of the 201 documents.
– *Quality Assessment.* Quality assessment was performed mostly during the classification of sources by metadata. This process provided information about author and source, as well as the minimum information required to establish credibility.

3.2   Data Collection: Scientific Documents

The second part of the data collection process involved scientific studies, using as a starting point 22 scientific documents already identified in our previous study [10] and adopting a similar approach to identify new scientific documents published after 11 November 2014. Because of the large number of retrieved studies, snowballing was not used. The procedure adopted (both previously and here) involved the following steps.

– The search term 'DevOps' was used to search and retrieve documents published after 11 November 2014 from the following five databases: ACM Digital Library, ISI Web of Science, Science Direct, IEEE Xplore and Scopus. Refinement of publication year for each database yielded a total of 340 documents, distributed as follows: ACM (41), Web of Science (37), Science Direct (72), IEEE Xplore (72) and Scopus (118).
– Similar inclusion criteria were applied to scientific documents; these were (a) relevance to the topic, (b) peer review and (c) publication in a scientific journal or in conference proceedings. Following exclusion during the first stage of 104 duplicates and 55 irrelevant document types, such as glossaries, indexes and prefaces, a total of 181 studies remained. The inclusion criteria were then further applied by reading titles and abstracts for relevance to the topic, as well

---

[3] http://www.qsrinternational.com/what-is-nvivo.

as publication forums (for peer reviews and publication in scientific journals and conference proceedings). On that basis, 87 studies in total were identified and added to the 22 previously selected studies for analysis. For the current study, a fourth criterion was added, including only those publications discussing agile, CD and lean in addition to DevOps. Ultimately, 33 studies were included in the present analysis to address the research questions.

3.3 Data Collection: Practitioners

The last source of data was a workshop conducted with practitioners involved in the N4S project. This is a large national programme that aims to create the foundation for software-intensive Finnish businesses in the digital economy, in which participating companies seek to develop real-time experimental business models and capability for instant value delivery, based on deep customer insights. The workshop sought to identify what DevOps means to practitioners and how they have implemented the approach in practice. Any effects attributed to the use of DevOps and their associated metrics were also explored. The workshop session was organised by researchers from three institutions. Two researchers facilitated the session by posing a question to the practitioners, who then worked in small groups and presented their answers, using flipcharts as communication aids. The presentations and discussions were recorded and subsequently transcribed for analysis.

3.4 Data Analysis

Using thematic analysis, all data from the literature search, MLR[4] and workshop were saved and analysed in NVivo. Thematic analysis is a process for identifying, analysing and reporting data patterns (themes); according to Braun and Clarke [14], this process has six phases. The first phase of thematic analysis, *familiarisation with data*, was conducted in tandem with the second phase, *generating initial codes*. The initial codes were identified inductively from ML documents into categories (themes) related to the initial research objective (describing the DevOps phenomenon). The analysis yielded multiple themes, including the two considered here: (1) DevOps in relation to agile, lean and CD and (2) Claimed impacts of DevOps and metrics. These two themes were also used for deductive coding of scientific articles and responses from practitioners. The third phase of thematic analysis, *searching for themes*, was executed during the second iteration of coding, which involved inductive coding of the above two categories. In addition to thematic coding, some elements of discourse analysis were used specifically in the coding of emerging sub-themes for DevOps in relation to agile, lean and CD practices, focusing on the words that authors used in explaining their understanding of the concept. Discourse analysis is often utilised to understand what people are using language for in a given situation. After completing

---

[4] Link to list of ML: http://tinyurl.com/z3jpu5v.

the second iteration, themes were reviewed for refinement, naming (e.g. adoption, implementation) and subsequent reporting in order to complete the fourth (*reviewing*), fifth (*defining and naming themes*) and sixth (*producing report*) phases of thematic analysis.

4   Findings

This section presents the results of the analysis in respect of the two research questions. Figure 2 shows a comparison of included MLR and scientific articles.

4.1   How DevOps Is Related to Agile, Lean and Continuous Deployment

The analysis showed that authors relate DevOps to agile, lean and CD with respect to four main topics: (1) origin and background, (2) adoption, (3) implementation and (4) goals. Table 1 (at the end of section) summarises these findings.

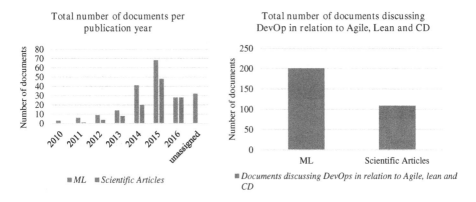

Fig. 2. Publication years and number of included ML and scientific articles.

DevOps and Agile Software Development

1. *Origin and Background.* Most ML items described DevOps as an evolution or extension of agile software development—in particular, of agile principles and values as specified in the Agile Manifesto—with the aim of applying to operations the same values, ideas and practices of agile software development applied by developers. A similar claim was identified in scientific articles [15–19]. In addition, some ML and scientific articles framed DevOps as a type or part of agile software development [20–22].

2. *Adoption.* DevOps has also been related to successful adoption of agile software development. While few ML and scientific documents reported on the latter, those that did so described agile methods as the key factor in using DevOps [23–29]. The arguments fell into two categories. First, agile methods are well established [28], and their emphasis on cooperation among stakeholders helps to formalise similar collaborations between development and operations [18,24]. For this reason, IT organisations applying agile methods will find DevOps familiar and easy to use and work with [25,27]. Second, most of the practices advocated by DevOps are incompatible with the traditional waterfall approach because one of the main goals of DevOps is to deliver new software features frequently and quickly [22,29]. On the other hand, use of agile methods does not in itself amount to adopting DevOps, unless collaboration with operations has been established to address challenges of deploying and operating software in live environment where customers can appreciate the value of software in the same time support continuous flow of work. The latter was evidently an important learning point for practitioners during the workshop; as one practitioner put it,

> *"I think that when we talk about success factors, we want to emphasise people and commitment over technologies. This is a somewhat familiar idea from the agile world, but when you talk about DevOps, many people immediately mention CI and Jenkins and Docker; these are useful tools as well, but I think that the best DevOps achievement was just me and one of the ops guys sitting down and setting up the initial environment together. The most important thing is to get the communication going, and it helps a lot when you have that element of commitment."*

3. *Implementation.* DevOps is also related to the implementation aspect of agile software development, as evidenced by two main points deduced from ML and supported by scientific articles. First, DevOps builds upon agile software development practices, especially continuous integration [22,26,30–33], as well as on existing software development roles in agile methods. Second, DevOps practices enhance existing agile practices and roles by also taking account of operations activities. In this latter regard, rethinking the day-to-day working relationship of the development team with the operations team and using agile principles to guide interactions between the two groups usually helps [17,24]. For instance, one ML source listed improvements to Scrum methodology when using DevOps [34]. Additionally, the following response from a practitioner in a large non-consultancy organisation elaborated on the implementation aspect:

> *"One of the things I came across is learning, and then collaboration. Breaking the silos and enabling communication channels increases the organisations overall competence. Because people are learning and collaborating, youre able to iterate these cycles faster and faster. Even in a big organisation, this enables quite a lot of things, like the ability to break down bureaucracy and silos. In one instance, a big customer*

took a build directly from a CI at the end of the day. Normally, that build should have ended up with the customer after six months because of the bureaucracy chain. As a result, learning happened because somebody took this step and learned that he can take the build directly from the CI and put it in a live system."

However, unlike agile software development, DevOps does not have methodologies such as Scrum and extreme programing. Instead, DevOps embodies a vast and diverse set of practices, from which some patterns can be identified [23] and generically applied under certain conditions, depending on the environment [30].

4. *Goals and Values.* DevOps and agile software development are driven by similar basic goals and values. First, in terms of organisational silos, DevOps tears down the walls between developers and operations, not unlike how agile methods tear down the walls between the development team and the customer, as well as walls within the team. DevOps requires the development team to work closely with the operations team and to understand its needs and priorities in much the same way as agile methods require developers to work with the customer to understand real business needs and priorities and to solve business problems together. Second, DevOps brings more decisions about how the total system is set up and run to the level of the dev-and-ops teams, just as agile methods bring more decisions on how the system needs to work down to development team level. Moreover, when their goals are combined, DevOps and agile software development focus on rapid and incremental releases, gathering feedback quickly and correcting problems [35].

DevOps and Continuous Delivery/Deployment

1. *Origin and Background.* Some ML authors [8,36] have argued that DevOps emerged directly from CD during a presentation given by John Allspaw and Paul Hammond at a Velocity conference in 2009. On that occasion, Allspaw and Hammond showed how Flickr used the DevOps approach to deploy software updates to production multiple times a day [8,36]. CD represents a step forward from continuous integration, and DevOps is required in order to complete such a step [37]. DevOps in context of CD highlights issues and challenges of deploying software updates on continuous basis (and in fast iterations) to production environment whilst also ensure reliable operability of the live environment. When asked why the embedded systems company he worked for had decided to introduce DevOps, one practitioner explained:

"We saw that infra-development separation doesnt work anymore. The mindset has changed a lot in recent years. We need increased transparency and getting things done. We have and are doing continuous integration—CI mostly—but if were going forward from CI, we need to have this DevOps going on."

2. *Adoption.* According to many ML and scientific articles [16,26,33,35,37–43], using DevOps is a necessary and potentially great way to achieve CD.

The split between developers and operations is a major obstacle to fast and frequent software releases; DevOps can bridge the gap by enabling more efficient collaboration [44]. The use of DevOps facilitates continuous software updates in both web and embedded systems domains [45]. However, the use of DevOps in the embedded systems domain raises a number of concerns [26,30,45], including competency challenges related to the use of technologies not traditionally associated with embedded systems, such as cloud systems in cyber-physical and embedded systems [45]. These concerns were also mentioned by two practitioners from a telecommunications company. According to the first, who heads a global efficiency team,

> *"We have many product creation teams; I dont know how they do DevOps in detail, but in general, I know that were not doing very much product development using DevOps principles."*

The second practitioner (from network management) explained the reason for this:

> *"For example, in our product line, were still looking into what it would mean for us as a very large organisation of 2000+ people to move towards DevOps. Were still struggling with CD, even for internal purposes. We have our internal customers to do the network integration and network verification, in which multiple different product lines are delivering multiple different products for integration as one system. So lets say that were struggling with the scale of this work and the multiplicity of different organisations, as well as the different parts of the different organisations and were not even talking about the operator customer yet, at this point in time."*

3. *Implementation.* Both ML and scientific articles agreed that the practices and tools advocated by DevOps help to achieve CD. Some of these practices involve: (1) organisational and cultural changes designed to eliminate the gap between development and operations, (2) automation of deployment process in the deployment pipeline, (3) automation in infrastructure management to ensure reliability, reproducability and programatic operations and, (4) monitoring that ensures reliable operations and feedback [42,44,46–48]. Both sources claimed that CD implementation typically includes a deployment pipeline in which tests and the deployment process are automated [19,35,46]. This deployment pipeline is an automated delivery process involving software changes from version control and software building through multiple stages of testing and deployment until a new software version is delivered to users [49]. The process includes automated monitoring of software quality and performance at multiple stages in order to obtain feedback quickly. Use of a deployment pipeline may mean that developers are responsible for testing, deploying and monitoring software [24].

4. *Goals and Values.* Both DevOps and CD share a background in agile and lean thinking. For that reason, they exhibit the same driving goals and values (i.e. small and quick changes with a focus on the end customer) but from differing perspectives [50]. In particular, CD is much broader than DevOps in the

sense that it's focus on fast, frequent and rapid releases requires incorporating additional changes in software delivery organisation such as business model.

DevOps and Lean Software Development

1. *Origin and Background.* Most of what has been addressed in DevOps is informed by a lean thinking background [26,30]. Lean thinking goes further than agile software development by emphasising that software development does account for the entire IT value stream. In the same way, the DevOps approach seeks to optimize the whole process as required in lean software delivery [26,51].
2. *Adoption.* The Japanese word kaizen, meaning continuous improvement, is often used in the lean software development context [31,52]. A kaizen culture is described as implementing behaviour that continuously shows improvements [31,52]. Applying kaizen thinking results in focused attention on increased feedback and a culture of collaboration between developers and operations [52].
3. *Implementation.* ML and scientific documents related DevOps implementation to lean software development in terms of the product development process flow, encompassing a systems thinking approach (i.e. end-to-end integration of product development processes). In contrast to batch-and-queue thinking, product development flow requires effective teamwork beyond the software development function to effectively and immediately connect the actions of product design, implementation and testing, as well as deployment of product features once requirements are identified [31]. In addition, developers can improve decision making about incremental product improvements by exploiting operations knowledge. This highlights the effective utilisation of a short feedback loop in eliminating waste and moving beyond individual performance to system performance, informed by insights into product quality [38]. An ML author [53] argued for the use of kanban in implementing lean software development, and this sits well with DevOps. This argument finds empirical support in [19,47]. Schneider [19] advocates kanban rather than Scrum because of the potential to work immediately on high priority targets for feature development and particularly on tasks that need to be performed at once when they are occurring e.g. reacting on the basis of insights or anomalies from production.
4. *Goals and Values.* DevOps incorporates lean principles and thinking into the entire IT value stream, which extends development into production.

4.2   DevOps Effects and Metrics

Reflecting the dynamic nature of the DevOps concept, the analysis suggested a wide range of effects and metrics for measuring DevOps success. Table 2 lists some of the frequently claimed effects of DevOps and associated metrics identified in this study. (The list is not exhaustive.) The analysis focused on identifying claimed effects of DevOps from ML and on validating those claims, based on

Table 1. Summary of DevOps in relation to agile, lean and CD findings

DevOps as related to	Results	Source
Agile	Agile software development principles, values and practices are required for successful adoption of DevOps	58 of 75 ML 21 of 33 sci. doc.
CD	DevOps implementation is necessary to enable CD	36 of 75 ML 23 of 33 sci. doc.
Lean	Lean software development principles and practices inform DevOps implementation	22 of 75 ML 9 of 33 sci. doc.

scientific articles and practitioners workshop responses. While there was some evidence of a correlation between different claimed effects, this was not of immediate interest here. Most authors of ML described the effects with reference to the annual State of DevOps survey reports (by Puppet Labs) and the 2015 annual State of DevOps (by Delphix) as supporting evidence. One limitation is that the identified effects were too generic, and it remains difficult to argue that such effects are based entirely on the integration of operations and development.

Most of the claimed effects of DevOps and associated metrics mentioned in ML were also reported in the scientific articles. For instance, Farroha [18] listed advantages of DevOps and key performance indicators that can be used to assess the approachs success in an organisational context. However, only a few studies provided empirical evidence of the claimed effects, such as improved release cycle time [35] in the context of an e-commerce platform and [46] in a project to develop and deliver a system to network service providers. Claims about DevOps effects and metrics similar to those reported in ML were identified from the workshop with practitioners, who were asked to name the most important effect of DevOps in their organisation and how this was measured. Importantly, other factors such as context, customers and type and maturity of the project/product emerged as key considerations in relation to effects and metrics.

5   Discussion and Conclusion

The aim of this study was to explore DevOps in its relationship to agile, lean and CD. Our findings confirm that the DevOps phenomenon originated from CD as an evolution of agile software development and is informed by a lean principles background. While claimed DevOps effects and metrics were also identified here, most lacked sufficient empirical support. These findings invite four conclusions

- Agile software development principles, values and practices are required for successful adoption of DevOps.
- DevOps implementation is necessary to enable CD.
- Lean software development principles and practices inform DevOps implementation
- Effects of DevOps include the ability to release software quickly, frequently and with improved quality. However, the use of popular metrics such as deployment

Table 2. Summary of DevOps Effects and Metrics

	Source		
	ML	Sci. docs	Practi.
Effects			
Fast and more frequent releases/deployments (fast time-to-market, shortened lead time, rapid releases)	58	[18,21,23,30,37,45–47,49]	X
Improved quality and reliability of software product, deployments and infrastructure	25	[18,23,46,51]	X
Increased efficiency through automation	22	[16,35,47,49]	X
Increased innovation and customer experience	18	[18,45]	
Fast recovery time following unexpected events, security flaws etc	16	[18,21,30,48]	X
Increased transparency and collaboration between stakeholders especially developers and operations; Improved employee morale and work culture	15	[19,31,37]	X
Lower chance of product failure once deployed	14		X
Maintainability and scalability of infra, Ops processes	13	[16,23,29,37]	
Cost saving (associated with effective utilization of resources, reduced outages and automation)	13	[16]	X
Frequent operational and user feedback	8	[18,45]	X
Metrics			
Deployment frequency/rate	13	[37,46,51]	X
Mean time to recover	12	[18,21,47]	X
Cycle/Lead Time (Time required to release software to production)	12	[30,46,47,51]	X
Change success/failure rate	11	[47]	
Frequency of production failures/outages	6	[47]	
Customer/business associated metrics (customer satisfaction, conversion rate, sales)	6	[23,47]	X

rate and cycle/lead time are insufficient to determine whether these effects arise from implementation of DevOps or other approaches.

While the supporting empirical evidence was poor, many sources (especially ML) stood over many of the presented claims. The lack of empirical evidence suggests that DevOps is still in its infancy. Additionally, most discussion of DevOps is confined to informal talks, workshops and events in forums outside more formal dissemination channels.

In conclusion, it seems clear that the DevOps concept is often conflated with other concepts, notably agile software development and CD. However, the present study serves to clarify the essential differences between these concepts. Like agile, lean and CD practices, DevOps makes its own significant contribution to SE while also building upon existing knowledge from agile and lean software development. Future DevOps research should be clearer about its unique contribution and about what distinguishes it from and connects it to other established and emerging practices in SE. As empirical studies on DevOps remain relatively rare as compared to broad and mainstream informal discussions on DevOps within the industry, studies of real-world projects can help to test these results and conclusions.

6   Validity and Limitations

This study fulfils the thick-descriptive purpose of qualitative research in explicating the meanings and perspectives constructed by individuals, groups or both in a particular context rather than effectiveness or causal relationships [54]. Three major quality criteria for thick-description qualitative research were addressed here: triangulated and descriptive data, member checking and situating the meaning of data [54].

Triangulation and member checking are crucial techniques for establishing credibility, and three data collection methods were utilised for triangulation. Given the nature of the ML, we did not conduct member checking by sending individual e-mails to ML authors. Instead, we presented and solicited feedback on the initial resultsand especially on the claimed effects and metrics of DevOps as derived from MLto practitioners at the end of the workshop. We acknowledge threats to validity, and that our results are limited (particularly in terms of the relationship of DevOps to agile, lean and CD practices) because there was no member checking. Additionally, as most of the ML sources lacked empirical evidence or rigorous presentation of the authors opinions or experiences, the claims made need to be verified in future empirical evaluations, regardless of our selection criteria. Additionally, we do not contend that the study has examined all relevant material, especially from online sources. However, we believe our choice of materials to be representative. Limitations also arise from the fact that a majority of sources are of low to medium pertinence in discussing the relationship of DevOps to agile, lean and CD practices.

Acknowledgement. This work was supported by TEKES as part of the N4S project of DIMECC (Digital, Internet, Materials and Engineering Co-Creation).

References

1. Sharp, H., Robinson, H., Woodman, M.: Software engineering: community and culture. IEEE Softw. **17**(1), 40–47 (2000)
2. Humble, J., Farley, D.: Continuous Delivery: Reliable Software Releases through Build, Test, and Deployment Automation. Addison-Wesley Professional, Boston (2010)
3. Dingsøyr, T., Lassenius, C.: Emerging themes in agile software development: Introduction to the special section on continuous value delivery. IST **77**, 56–60 (2016)
4. Lwakatare, L.E., Kuvaja, P., Oivo, M.: An exploratory study of DevOps: extending the dimensions of DevOps with practices. In: 11th International Conference on Software Engineering Advances, pp. 91–99. IARIA, Rome (2016)
5. Penners, R., Dyck, A.: Release engineering vs. DevOps-an approach to define both terms. In: Full-Scale Software Engineering, pp. 49–53 (2015)
6. Humble, J., Molesky, J.: Why enterprises must adopt DevOps to enable continuous delivery. Cutter IT J. **24**(8), 6–12 (2011)
7. Kerzazi, N., Adams, B.: Who needs release and DevOps engineers, and why? In: International Workshop on Continuous Software Evolution and Delivery, pp. 77–83. ACM (2016)

8. Wikipedia: DevOps. https://en.wikipedia.org/wiki/DevOps
9. Bass, L., Weber, I., Zhu, L.: DevOps: A Software Architect's Perspective. Addison-Wesley Professional, Old Tappan (2015)
10. Lwakatare, L.E., Kuvaja, P., Oivo, M.: Dimensions of DevOps. In: Lassenius, C., Dingsøyr, T., Paasivaara, M. (eds.) XP 2015. LNBIP, vol. 212, pp. 212–217. Springer, Heidelberg (2015). doi:10.1007/978-3-319-18612-2_19
11. Ogawa, R., Malen, B.: Towards rigor in reviews of multivocal literatures: applying the exploratory case study method. Rev. Educ. Res. **61**(3), 299–305 (1991)
12. Tom, E., Aurum, A., Vidgen, R.: An exploration of technical debt. J. Syst. Softw. **86**(6), 1498–1516 (2013)
13. Garousi, V., Mäntylä, M.V.: When and what to automate in software testing? a multi-vocal literature review. IST **76**, 92–117 (2016)
14. Braun, V., Clarke, V.: Using thematic analysis in psychology. Qualit. Res. Psychol. **3**(2), 77–101 (2006)
15. Guerriero, M., Ciavotta, M., Gibilisco, G., Ardagna, D.: A model-driven DevOps framework for QoS-aware cloud applications. In: 17th International Symposium on Symbolic and Numeric Algorithms for Scientific Computing, pp. 345–351. IEEE (2015)
16. Virmani, M.: Understanding DevOps & bridging the gap from continuous integration to continuous delivery. In: 5th International Conference on the Innovative Computing Technology, pp. 78–82. IEEE (2015)
17. Olszewska, M., Waldén, M.: DevOps meets formal modelling in high-criticality complex systems. In: 1st International Workshop on Quality-Aware DevOps, pp. 7–12. ACM (2015)
18. Farroha, B., Farroha, D.: A framework for managing mission needs, compliance, and trust in the DevOps environment. In: Military Communications Conference, pp. 288–293. IEEE, October 2014
19. Schneider, T.: Achieving cloud scalability with microservices and DevOps in the connected car domain. In: CEUR Workshop Proceedings on Continuous Software Engineering, pp. 138–141. CEUR-WS.org (2016)
20. Walter, J., van Hoorn, A., Koziolek, H., Okanovic, D., Kounev, S.: Asking "What", automating the "How?": the vision of declarative performance engineering. In: 7th International Conference on Performance Engineering, pp. 91–94. ACM (2016)
21. Syed, M.H., Fernandez, E.B.: Cloud ecosystems support for internet of things and DevOps using patterns. In: 1st International Conference on Internet-of-Things Design and Implementation, pp. 301–304. IEEE (2016)
22. Borgenholt, G., Begnum, K., Engelstad, P.: Audition: a DevOps-oriented service optimization and testing framework for cloud environments. In: Conference of Norsk Informatik Konferanse, pp. 146–157 (2013)
23. Cukier, D.: DevOps patterns to scale web applications using cloud services. In: Conference on Systems, Programming, & Applications: Software for Humanity, pp. 143–152 (2013)
24. Spinellis, D.: Being a DevOps developer. IEEE Softw. **33**(3), 4–5 (2016)
25. Deshpande, A.: DevOps an Extension of Agile Methodology How It will Impact QA? (2016). http://www.softwaretestinghelp.com/devops-and-software-testing/
26. Lwakatare, L.E., Karvonen, T., Sauvola, T., Kuvaja, P., Olsson, H.H., Bosch, J., Oivo, M.: Towards DevOps in the embedded systems domain: why is it so hard? In: 49th Hawaii International Conference on System Sciences, pp. 5437–5446. IEEE (2016)
27. Racspace: Building Your DevOps Engine (2015). http://tinyurl.com/htovgd9

28. Staples, M., Zhu, L., Grundy, J.: Continuous validation for data analytics systems. In: 38th International Conference on Software Engineering Companion, pp. 769–772. ACM (2016)
29. Cook, N., Milojicic, D., Talwar, V.: Cloud management. J. Internet Serv. Apps. **3**(1), 67–75 (2012)
30. Ebert, C., Gallardo, G., Hernantes, J., Serrano, N.: DevOps. IEEE Softw. **33**(3), 94–100 (2016)
31. Fitzgerald, B., Stol, K.J.: Continuous software engineering: a roadmap and agenda. J. Syst. Softw., 1–14 (2015)
32. Waller, J., Ehmke, N.C., Hasselbring, W.: Including performance benchmarks into continuous integration to enable DevOps. ACM SIGSOFT Softw. Eng. Not. **40**(2), 1–4 (2015)
33. Zhu, L., Bass, L., Champlin-Scharff, G.: DevOps and its practices. IEEE Softw. **33**(3), 32–34 (2016)
34. Scrum-Alliance: DevOps and Agile: Key Considerations for DevOps and Agile to Coexist for Expedited Delivery (2014). http://tinyurl.com/j9xqxlw
35. Soni, M.: End to end automation on cloud with build pipeline: the case for DevOps in insurance industry, continuous integration, continuous testing, and continuous delivery. In: International Conference on Cloud Computing in Emerging Markets, pp. 85–89. IEEE (2015)
36. A Short History of DevOps (2014). http://rewrite.ca.com/us/articles/devops/a-short-history-of-devops.html
37. Balalaie, A., Heydarnoori, A., Jamshidi, P.: Microservices architecture enables DevOps: migration to a cloud-native architecture. IEEE Softw. **33**(3), 42–52 (2016)
38. Claps, G.G., Berntsson Svensson, R., Aurum, A.: On the journey to continuous deployment: technical and social challenges along the way. IST **57**, 21–31 (2015)
39. Cois, C.A., Yankel, J., Connell, A.: Modern DevOps: optimizing software development through effective system interactions. In: International Professional Communication Conference, pp. 1–7. IEEE (2014)
40. Rodríguez, P., Haghighatkhah, A., Lwakatare, L.E., Teppola, S., Suomalainen, T., Eskeli, J., Karvonen, T., Kuvaja, P., Verner, J.M., Oivo, M.: Continuous deployment of software intensive products and services: a systematic mapping study. J. Syst. Softw. (2016). http://www.sciencedirect.com/science/article/pii/S0164121215002812
41. Wettinger, J., Andrikopoulos, V., Leymann, F.: Automated capturing and systematic usage of DevOps knowledge for cloud applications. In: International Conference on Cloud Engineering, pp. 60–65. IEEE (2015)
42. Wettinger, J., Breitenbucher, U., Leymann, F.: Dyn tail - dynamically tailored deployment engines for cloud applications. In: 8th International Conference on Cloud Computing, pp. 421–428. IEEE (2015)
43. Wettinger, J., Andrikopoulos, V., Leymann, F.: Enabling DevOps collaboration and continuous delivery using diverse application environments. In: OTM 2015. LNCS, vol. 9415, pp. 348–358. Springer International Publishing, Switzerland (2015)
44. Wettinger, J., Breitenbücher, U., Kopp, O., Leymann, F.: Streamlining DevOps automation for cloud applications using TOSCA as standardized metamodel. Future Gener. Comput. Syst. **56**, 317–332 (2016)
45. Axelsson, J.: Architectural allocation alternatives and associated concerns in cyber-physical systems. In: The European Conference on Software Architecture Workshops, pp. 1–6. ACM (2015)

46. Callanan, M., Spillane, A.: DevOps: making it easy to do the right thing. IEEE Softw. **33**(3), 53–59 (2016)
47. Rong, G., Zhang, H., Shao, D.: CMMI guided process improvement for DevOps projects. In: International Workshop on Software and Systems Process, pp. 76–85. ACM (2016)
48. Sun, D., Fu, M., Zhu, L., Li, G., Lu, Q.: Non-intrusive anomaly detection with streaming performance metrics and logs for DevOps in public clouds: a case study in AWS. Trans. Emerg. Topics Comp. **4**(2), 278–289 (2016)
49. Weber, I., Nepal, S., Zhu, L.: Developing dependable and secure cloud applications. IEEE Int. Comp. **20**(3), 74–79 (2016)
50. Coté: DevOps, You Keep Using That Word What Is DevOps? A Discussion And History (2015). https://blog.pivotal.io/podcasts-pivotal/features/devops-you-keep-using-that-word-what-is-devops-a-discussion-and-history
51. Liu, Y., Li, C., Liu, W.: Integrated solution for timely delivery of customer change requests: a case study of using DevOps approach. Int. J. U- & E-Serv., Sci. & Tech. **7**(2), 41–50 (2014)
52. IT-Revolution: DevOps Culture (2012). http://itrevolution.com/devops-culture-part-1/
53. Swift-Kanban: Kanban for DevOps/Continuous Delivery (2016). http://tinyurl.com/gpvra3r
54. Cho, J., Trent, A.: Validity in qualitative research revisited. Qualit. Res. **6**(3), 319–340 (2006)

Agile Practices, Collaboration and Experience

An Empirical Study About the Effect of Experience in Agile Software Development

Martin Kropp[1]([⊠]), Andreas Meier[2]([⊠]), and Robert Biddle[3]([⊠])

[1] University of Applied Sciences and Arts Northwestern Switzerland,
Windisch, Switzerland
martin.kropp@fhnw.ch
[2] Zurich University of Applied Sciences, Winterthur, Switzerland
meea@zhaw.ch
[3] Carleton University, Ottawa, Canada
robert.biddle@carleton.ca

Abstract. Agile Software Development has been around for more than fifteen years and is now widespread. How does experience effect the application of agile methods in organizations and what are the implications on the individual and organizational culture? This paper presents in-depth analysis of the Swiss Agile Study 2014. Switzerland offers an illustrative microcosm of software development, with a range of industry domains and sizes, and well-educated and internationally aware professionals. The study included more than a hundred professionals and managers, contacted through professional and industry associations. The topics addressed included experience with Agile development, motivations for adopting it, barriers perceived, specific practices used, and specific benefits realized. Analysis of the data identified important trends and differences. Agile experience seems to be an important factor, which affects many aspects of practice and workplace culture. More troubling is that it appears stress and overwork may be common among Agile professionals. All these findings illustrate important differences between Agile processes as prescribed, and as actually practiced.

Keywords: Agile · Software process · Collaboration · Organizational culture · Software practices

1 Introduction

After 15 years since the publication of the Agile Manifesto [1], Agile software development has become mainstream. In most recent studies 70 % up to 94 % of the participating companies claim to follow an Agile approach in their software projects [11,15], with Scrum by far the most dominant process identified. These studies report about the distribution and application of Agile practices in companies, and the effects and changes they cause. But as far as we know, there are no studies about if and how the application of Agile methods and practices change

© Springer International Publishing AG 2016
P. Abrahamsson et al. (Eds.): PROFES 2016, LNCS 10027, pp. 416–431, 2016.
DOI: 10.1007/978-3-319-49094-6_28

over time and with experience. Moreover, the Agile landscape has changed. In earlier times, for example, Extreme Programming (XP) advocates often advised novices to learn and apply all XP practices [5,8] whereas more recently, with a greater variety of Agile processes and practices, it has become common for educators and workplaces to make their own selections [6,7] and blend as they see fit. This has meant that there can be a large difference between Agile processes as-prescribed, and as-practiced.

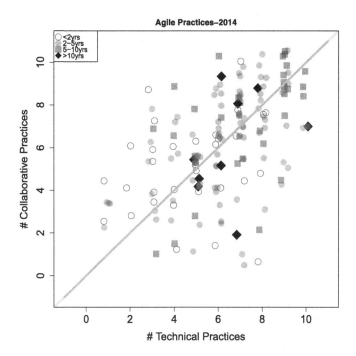

Fig. 1. Number of technical and collaborative practices applied by company.

In this paper we explore the data from the Swiss Agile Study 2014 [11] with respect to the agile experience of the study participants, and in particular we were interested in answering the following questions:

- *RQ1*: Is the usage of Agile practices dependent from the Agile experience of the IT professionals and organizations?
- *RQ2*: Does the application of Agile methods have any influence on the organizational culture of companies and, if so, how does this evolve with experience?
- *RQ3*: What is the influence of Agile on the individual IT professional? Does he work less overtime, has less stress? (as propagated by eXtreme Programming, for example).
- *RQ4*: What improvements are reported by Agile professionals and companies, and are these dependent from their experience?

Our analysis of the data reveals two major issues: The amount of applied Agile practices evolves only slowly with the Agile experience of the companies as indicated in Fig. 1. Second, following an Agile approach over a long time changes the organizational culture in companies.

One indication of the pattern and practices revealed is shown in Fig. 1. For each company surveyed, this shows the relationship of the number of collaborative practices reported to the number of technical practices reported. Points nearer the bottom left show companies reporting few practices, and points near the top right show those reporting many. Points above the diagonal show companies reporting more collaborative practices, whereas those below the diagonal report more technical practices. Each company's experience with Agile is shown by a colored symbol, with the darker colors indicating more experience. There is some variation, but the pattern is evident: in general, more experienced companies report using more practices, and especially more collaborative practices.

Our study data reflects the current state of Agile software development in Switzerland. Since Switzerland offers an illustrative microcosm of software development, with a range of industry domains and sizes, and well-educated and internationally aware professionals, we suggest that this situation might be very similar to other countries. The results of our study show that it takes many years of Agile experience until organizations have adopted the Agile work style. Change to the collaborative practices seems to be especially hard, due to resistance to organizational changes. However, the longer organizations are applying Agile development the more they tend to have a collaboration and cultivation organizational culture. The results also show that it takes many years of Agile experience until Agile development becomes effective; but once Agile has been really adopted it seems to bring improvements across the board. We speculate that if organizations would pro-actively address the organizational change from the beginning, Agile development might become effective much faster and organizations would benefit much earlier.

In the rest of this paper, we will show in detail how the application of the technical and collaborative practices changes with Agile experience, when the major improvements occur, how barriers for further Agile application change, and how the individual professional experiences the transformation to an Agile work style, with all its consequences like personal stress, work life balance, engagement in the project and identification with the work and team. We will discuss the results and their possible consequences for companies introducing Agile approaches.

2   Study Method

The Swiss Agile Study, conducted by the authors, is a biennial Swiss nationwide online survey about the usage of development methods and practices in the IT industry.

It addresses both Agile and non-Agile companies and IT professionals. It comprises a catalog of about 30 questions about applied software development methodology, techniques and practices on technical level, collaborative level and

Table 1. Demographics of participating companies: role, % of participants

Role	%
CEO	29 %
Development manager	14 %
Project manager	8 %
Team leader	7 %
CIO	6 %
CTO	5 %
Senior software developer	5 %
Designer/Architect	2 %
Product manager	1 %
Other	23 %

Table 2. Sizes of the participating companies

Size	%
Micro enterprise (≤ 9)	18 %
Small enterprise (10–49)	29 %
Medium enterprise (50–249)	25 %
Large enterprise ≥ 250)	28 %

value level as outlined elsewhere [10]. The complete study reports are freely available [11]. The latest survey, in 2014, included specific questions concerning the organizational culture in Agile and non-Agile companies according the organizational culture model of William Schneider [12].

101 companies and 128 IT professionals participated in the last survey in 2014. We emailed 1461 companies and about 5000[1] IT professionals in Switzerland. The addresses of the companies and the professionals were delivered from the participating IT associations SwissICT, SWEN and ICTnet, as well as from our own institutional databases. In the company survey we addressed representatives of the company or the development department of a company, i.e. the management level. Table 1 shows the demographics of the company participants. It shows that almost 30 % of the participants were Chief Executive officers. The relatively high number of "others" includes roles like Business Analysts, Business Unit Managers, and CFOs, for example.

Table 2 show the distribution of the sizes of the participating companies following the official categories of the Swiss Federal Statistical Office[2]. The main branches of the companies are IT Services/IT Consulting (40 %), Software Industry/Development (25 %). Medical and Health Care companies and Finance and Insurance companies make 5 % each. The rest are 3 % and below. The responding IT professionals were typically Senior Software Developers (19 %), Software Developers (18 %) and Project Managers (11 %).

---

[1] We do not know the exact number, since these mailings were partially done by the partner associations.

[2] http://www.bfs.admin.ch/bfs/portal/en/index/themen/06/02/blank/key/01/groesse.html.

3   Findings

3.1   Influence

In this section we look at the influences which Agile has on the software development process, i.e. which aspects in software projects and project management got better or worse and how they change over time. The professionals responding to the survey answered the question: "How has Agile software development influenced the following aspects?" To display which Agile influences are strongest, we use co-occurrence grids, as shown in Fig. 2. Each grid shows the occurrences of each influence, and co-occurrences of each pair of influences; this allows us to see which influences are commonly occurring together. The influences are listed on the left and the bottom of each grid. On the diagonal of each grid, the number of professionals answering the question with *improved* or *significantly improved* is shown on the diagonal, with higher numbers shown in shades of blue, and lower numbers in shades of red. At each grid intersection, the co-occurrence of two influences is shown.

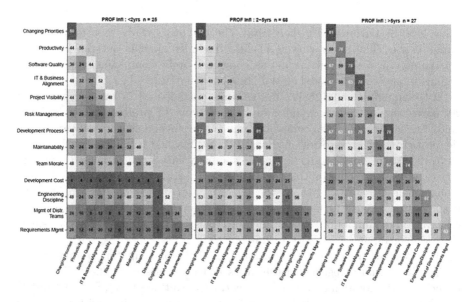

Fig. 2. Agile influence by experience. (Color figure online)

At the left of Fig. 2 are the results for the 25 professionals with less than 2 years Agile experience. The pattern is clear and a bit of a disappointment: Agile has clearly a positive influence on managing changing priorities and, to a lower degree, on team morale, productivity and the development process. The remaining items of the co-occurrence map are mostly red, i.e. those aspects have not improved. In particular, development costs have not improved at all.

Why is this? This is most likely because reducing development cost is not the main objective of an Agile transformation. Instead of reducing development cost, the money is spent on developing more features and better software products. Also note that nobody regarded distributed teams as an influence.

In the middle of Fig. 2 are the results for the 68 professionals with 3 to 5 years Agile experience. With more experience, a notable cluster of positive influences occur. This cluster includes, in decreasing order, responding to changing requirements, development process, team moral, software quality, alignment between IT and business, project visibility, maintainability and engineering discipline. Distributed teams are still not noted as an influence.

At the right of Fig. 2 are the results for the 27 professionals with more than 5 years Agile experience. The pattern is clear: mature teams profit much more of the benefits of Agile. This is reflected in the blue color of the co-occurrence grid. There are only three outliers: development cost, risk management and management of distributed teams. These outliers are a topic for concern and future study.

In summary, the presented data suggests that Agile has a profound positive influence on many aspects of software projects but it takes long time and suggests great effort.

3.2 Agile Practices

In the introduction to this paper we highlighted Fig. 1 showing the number of practices varied with experience, and also the balance between categories of practices: technical and collaborative practices [10]. The practices we enquired about are shown in Table 3. The practices comprise those recommended by eXtreme Programming [4] and by Scrum [13], plus new practices that have come since then like Continuous Delivery, Acceptance Test Driven Development, Behaviour Driven Development. To explore the relationship between experience and practices more closely, we now show which practices are used with which levels of experience.

At the left of Fig. 3 are the results for the 34 professionals with less than 2 years Agile experience. The pattern is clear: at the top in light blue are a number of commonly used technical practices: unit testing, automated builds, coding standards, and continuous integration. Lower down, the use of user stories, daily standups, and task boards are indicated. But otherwise, the grid is predominantly red, showing very little usage of many practices, especially the collaborative practices such as pair programming, collective ownership, retrospectives, and others.

To display which practices were used by each group, we again use co-occurrence grids, as shown in Fig. 3. In the middle of Fig. 3 are the results for the 93 professionals with 2–5 years Agile experience. Here the pattern is somewhat different. The practices used in the grid at the left are now more commonly used, as indicated by the darker shade of blue: both for the technical practices at the top, and the collaborative practices such as user stories and daily standups.

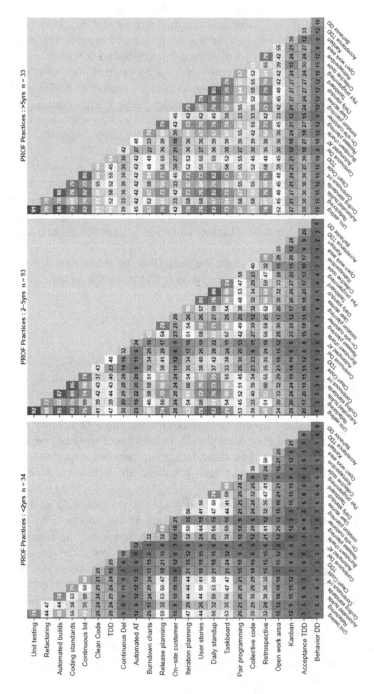

Fig. 3. Agile practices by experience. (Color figure online)

Table 3. Agile practices

Practice	Type
Unit testing	Technical
Refactoring	Technical
Automated builds	Technical
Coding standards	Technical
Continuous integration	Technical
Clean code	Technical
Test Driven Development (TDD)	Technical
Continuous delivery	Technical
Automated acceptance testing	Technical
Burndown charts	Technical
Release planning	Collaborative
On-site customer	Collaborative
Iteration planning	Collaborative
User stories	Collaborative
Daily standup	Collaborative
Taskboard	Collaborative
Pair programming	Collaborative
Collective code ownership	Collaborative
Retrospective	Collaborative
Open work area	Collaborative
Kanban pull system/Limited WIP	Advanced
Acceptance Test Driven Development (ATDD)	Advanced
Behavior Driven Development (BDD)	Advanced

But now there are other practices also indicated. Practices shown include burn-down charts and release planning, retrospectives, and also use of pair programming.

At the right of Fig. 3 are the results for the 33 professionals with more than 5 years of Agile experience. Again, the pattern is different, but continues the same trends. Practices with light usages reported by the other groups are now much more common, and practices such as collective code, test-driven development (TDD), and clean code are strongly indicated.

Overall, the pattern is strikingly clear: professionals with more experience report applying considerably more practices, more consistent use of practices, and more use of related practices. Moreover, while those with less experience report principally technical practices, more experience brings use of more collaborative projects.

3.3   Barriers

Our basic study [11] revealed that the ability to change organizational behavior
was listed as the greatest barrier to adoption of Agile software development in
an organization. We were also interested whether the barriers reported vary with
Agile experience within organizations, and if so, in which direction. Figures 4
and 5 show the relevant data for the IT professionals and companies. The figures
show which three barriers were most important.

The figures reveal that the change within the organization is by far the most
critical issue when companies switch to Agile, especially at the beginning. More
than 50 % of the IT professionals and more than 40 % of the companies ranked
this issue as the greatest barrier. We find it interesting that this issue remains
among the greatest barriers even in companies experienced with Agile methods.
The figures also show that other issues become more important. However the
views of the professionals and the companies differ. Both see customer collaboration becoming an important issue. But while the experienced professionals
rate the lack of skilled personal as critical, the managers of experienced companies suggest the handling of complex projects as the major barrier for further
adoption of the Agile methods.

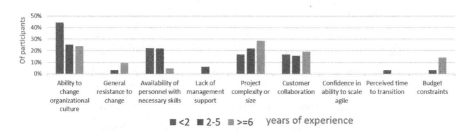

Fig. 4. Barriers by companies

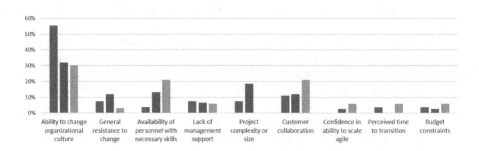

Fig. 5. Barriers by IT professionals (Legend as in Fig. 4)

3.4   Organizational Culture

We examined the organizational culture of the participating companies, applying the organization model of William Schneider. Schneider identifies four different organizational cultures, the control culture, competence culture, collaboration culture and the cultivation culture [12]. To identify culture, we used the questionnaire from Schneider's book [12]. We were using ten out of 20 of William Schneider's questions about which organizational culture the participating companies exhibit. In this approach, the answer to each question identifies which of the four culture categories is indicated, and so the overall response yields four numbers, one for each culture. In our results it was most common for one particular culture to dominate the others by three or four points, and we therefore chose that as the dominant culture. We then evaluated if the organizational culture depends on the Agile experience. Figure 6 shows that, as experienced by IT professional, organizations start with the preference of the traditional control and competence culture, which changes with more Agile experience towards a cultivation and collaboration culture. This seems to imply, that following an Agile approach over a long time changes an organization's culture to collaboration and cultivation culture.

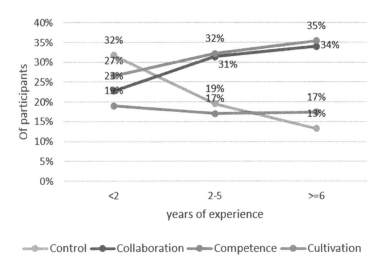

Fig. 6. From a control and competence to a collaboration and cultivation culture.

3.5   My Agile

One section of the survey asked professionals to reflect on their personal experiences with Agile development; we called the section "My Agile". Whereas earlier we had asked about the influences they saw, this set of questions asked about their actual personal experience. We suggested a range of possibilities, and asked whether it applied in their case.

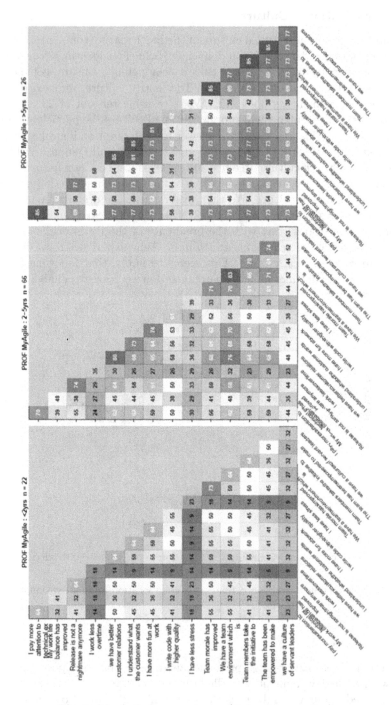

Fig. 7. My Agile by experience. (Color figure online)

The data is illustrated in Fig. 7. We again show co-occurrence grids, and distinguish professionals with less than 2 years, between 2 and 5 years, and more than 5 years. Again, the grids show shades of blue for higher reported factors, and red for those reported less. The patterns and differences are clear.

The grid on the left shows the data for the 22 less experienced professionals. The most reported individual element was team morale, and other common elements reported include technical excellence, release stability, customer relations, more fun, better team environment and initiative. There also are some patterns where several of these factors are reported. The most striking part of the grid, however, are the entries highlighted in red, indicating very few responses. Most prominent were "working less overtime" and "I have less stress". There are also absences shown for team empowerment and servant leadership.

In the grids in the middle (2–5 years) and the right (more than 5 years), we see remarkable changes. In particular far more factors are reported, and the most experienced professionals show many reports of almost all of the elements. However, in both cases, the weakest elements reported are the same as for less experienced professionals.

The progression from less to more experience clearly shows an increasing appreciation of a greater range of advantages, and that seems reasonable. However, the emphatic indications about overtime and stress lack are concerning. In Beck's books about Extreme Programming [3,4], there were specific recommendations about what in the second book was called "sustainable pace". It appears this is not occurring, especially for less experienced professionals, and perhaps even for those with more experience. It is interesting to note that the stress and overtime are happening at the same time that high team moral and fun are both reported, suggesting a mixed picture of positive and negative aspects.

The milder issue raised by the data involves team empowerment and "servant leadership". This concept is emphasized in several Agile processes, including Scrum and XP, neither of which suggests a manager in any traditional sense. This is a long history of approaches to socio-technical teams [14] and self-organizing teams [9], and a wide range of related thought before and since. However, our data suggests this is seen as one of the least common benefits of Agile processes. Further work is necessary to establish why this is so: Are professionals not concerned? Or has it simply not been possible? If, so, what were the circumstances and consequences?

3.6   Quality Control

Figure 2 showed that significant improvements in software quality come rather late. Accordingly, we were also interested if there is a relation between quality control and the late quality improvement, and if quality control is also dependent on Agile experience.

Figure 8 shows the corresponding data for the IT professionals. We focus on the data from the professionals because the quality control measures we explore are at a detail level commonplace to professionals – managers may be unaware of tools at this level.

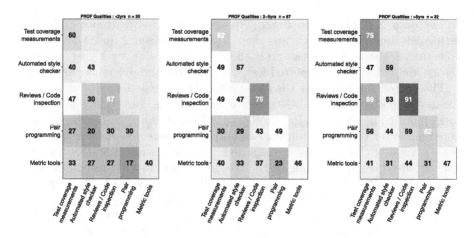

Fig. 8. Agile quality control by experience. (Color figure online)

At the left of Fig. 8 are the results for the 30 professionals with less than 2 years Agile experience. The grid shows that these professionals just start using code coverage and code reviews for quality control as indicated by the light blue color. The application of other measures is low (light red to dark red color). In the middle of Fig. 8 are the results for the 87 professionals with 2–5 years Agile experience. Here the pattern is a little different. The measures used before are now more common (dark blue color) and also the usage of style checker tools has increased. At the right of Fig. 8 are the results for the 32 professionals with more than 5 years of Agile experience. Here the pattern changed significantly. The numbers of the used tools have further increased, and also Pair Programming is now widely applied. Quite striking is the very high application of code reviews (91 %).

Again, the pattern is clear: the usage of quality control tools increases with experience. However, it takes more than five years of Agile experience until the majority of the listed quality control measures are applied by the majority of the professionals.

4   Discussion

Our goal in this paper was to study how Agile methods as-prescribed might differ from Agile methods as-practiced and how Agile evolves with experience in organizations. In the previous sections we have presented our main findings with respect to the research questions formulated in Sect. 1, and we will now attempt to articulate answers to these questions:

Agile and Workplace Culture: One of the issues addressed in the 2014 survey was workplace culture. In particular, the model of Schneider [12] was used, and questions from Schneider's book were included in the survey. The model suggests 4 kinds of workplace: Control, Collaborative, Competence, and Cultivation. We did find that most sets did emphasize one of these, and the responses did align with responses to questions about Agile methods: see Sect. 3.4.

Agile Changes with Experience: Perhaps the most wide-ranging finding from our survey was how the responses to a range of questions related to experience with Agile. In Sect. 3.1 we showed differences in reports of influences of Agile processes, and in Sect. 3.2 we showed how the practices used varied from a few mostly technical practices for beginners, to a wide range of practices for those with more experience. As we outlined in the introduction, in the early days after the Agile Manifesto, it was common to advocate following all the practices, especially for beginners. More recently it has become common for workplaces to choose their particular process, mixing elements from Scrum, XP, and a range of sources. While our results show a clear pattern, we do not know why that pattern emerges, what the implications are, and what, if anything, might be preferred.

Agile Influence for Improvements: In Sect. 3.1 we showed that it takes very long until Agile development becomes effective in Agile organizations showing significant improvements. While there are immediate improvements with handling changing priorities, only in more experienced Agile organizations we see improvements in requirements management, software quality, productivity, and in the engineering discipline. This long-term benefit may be related to the late application of many practices, but it might also reflect the strong resistance to organizational changes, especially when starting with the transformation to Agile. It could be a matter of further research to find out why the improvements come so late, and if it is possible to shorten this path to success, and if so, how it could be done.

Agile is Commonly Stressful: In Sect. 3.5 above, we examined the results from the survey where professionals reported their own reflections. Surprising to us was that the topics least agreed with were all related to stress or overwork. This seemed odd, considering that time-boxed iterations, collaborative environments, and self-management are all Agile practices, and would appear beneficial and lead away from stress. It appears this might not be the case. A potentially important observation is that the professionals also reported that team moral was high. This combination has been suggested before, in the 2007 study of social factors in Agile teams by Whitworth and Biddle [16]. Quotes from that study reflect a kind of characteristic zeal with a dark side: "This isn't a place that you go and hide". Moreover, they point to research by Barker [2] on self-managing teams, entitled "Tightening the Iron Cage: Concertive Control in Self-Managing Teams". That research shows how the strong social control in teams leads to a peculiar kind of stress that is more intense because it is connected to social factors in team commitment. Barker's term "Iron Cage" is a sobering indication that this aspect of Agile processes needs more attention.

Our aim for the survey was to be descriptive, so we must consider threats to external validity, and especially factors that might make our results differ from reality. One such factor is self-selection, and this might lead to more participants with responses they strongly wish to share: these might be positive or negative, and might therefore exaggerate results both ways. Another factor might be uneven response from different workplaces, especially in responses from professionals, where multiple participant might describe the same workplace. This was not possible for the company responses, but there still might be more responses from some industries or areas than others.

When analyzing the data, we noticed that the results from the IT professionals partly differ significantly from those of the managers. This is very obvious in Figs. 4 and 5, in which both groups partially have quite different opinions on the barriers for further adoption of Agile methods. We feel these do not suggest inconsistency, but rather a different perception of their corresponding environments. While management may often have a high-level view on the business, the IT professionals are dealing with everyday detail issues. Another surprising result came up in the response to influence of Agile on various aspects in Fig. 2. While the majority of experienced participants report improvements in requirements management and in handling of changing priorities, and report applying the retrospective practice in Fig. 1, they report no improvements in risk management. We assume that this question has been misunderstood: While there is no explicit "Risk Management" activity foreseen in Agile methods, short iterations, early feedback and retrospective are risk management per-se. So we might have to change this question in future surveys.

5   Conclusions

In this paper we addressed the issue of how Agile software development processes are actually used and viewed, showing how the process as prescribed differs from the process as practiced. We presented data from the 2014 Swiss Agile Survey, with responses from 101 companies and 128 professionals in Switzerland. The survey covered a wide range of topics, from influences of Agile, to practices actually used, barriers perceived, and reflections on personal experience.

Our main findings show several themes. One is that experience with Agile methods is an important factor. More experience is related to a greater number of practices used, greater emphasis on collaboration, and more sustainable workloads. Another finding is that, despite Agile principles such as "sustainable pace" and strict time-boxing of iterations, there are warnings that stress and overload remain a problem, especially for those new to Agile, but sometimes even for experienced professionals. This is despite indications of high team morale.

There are limitations in our survey approach, because of self-selection and of inability to follow up interesting results immediately with questions to probe details and causality. In addition, the granularity in some questions might be improved, for example to better gauge experience on a finer scale.

In future research on this topic, we suggest that questions of causality should be the priority. In particular, it would be interesting to know why some practices appear only with more experience. In particular, practices around customer collaboration are seen as very important, but only arise with more experience. Is it that only then is the importance realized, or are there barriers that prevent it by those with less experience? Also, it would be important to explore causes of stress and overwork. Is it simply enthusiasm stemming from high morale, or perhaps is it lack of familiarity with certain practices?

References

1. Agile Manifesto Signatories. Agile Manifesto (2001). http://agilemanifesto.org
2. Barker, J.R.: Tightening the iron cage: Concertive control in self-managing teams. Adm. Sci. Q. **38**(3), 408–437 (1993)
3. Beck, K.: Extreme Programming Explained: Embrace Change. Addison-Wesley Longman Publishing Co., Inc., Boston (2000)
4. Beck, K., Andres, C.: Extreme Programming Explained: Embrace Change, 2nd edn. Addison-Wesley Professional, Reading (2004)
5. Bergin, J., Caristi, J., Dubinsky, Y., Hazzan, O., Williams, L.: Teaching software development methods: the case of extreme programming. SIGCSE Bull. **36**(1), 448–449 (2004)
6. Diebold, P., Dahlem, M.: Agile practices in practice: a mapping study. In: Proceedings of the 18th International Conference on Evaluation and Assessment in Software Engineering, pp. 30:1–30:10. ACM, New York (2014)
7. Diebold, P., Ostberg, J.-P., Wagner, S., Zendler, U.: What do practitioners vary in using scrum? In: Lassenius, C., Dingsøyr, T., Paasivaara, M. (eds.) XP 2015. LNBIP, vol. 212, pp. 40–51. Springer, Heidelberg (2015). doi:10.1007/978-3-319-18612-2_4
8. Goldman, A., Kon, F., Silva, P.J.S., Yoder, J.W.: Being extreme in the classroom: experiences teaching XP. J. Braz. Comput. Soc. **10**(2), 4–20 (2004). http://www.swissagilestudy.ch/files/2015/05/SwissAgileStudy2014.pdf
9. Hackman, J.R., Oldham, G.R.: Work Redesign. Addison-Wesley, New York (1980)
10. Kropp, M., Meier, A.: Teaching agile software development at university level: values, management, and craftsmanship. In: Software Engineering Education and Training (CSEE&T), pp. 179–188. IEEE, May 2013
11. Kropp, M., Meier, A.: Swiss agile study 2014. Technical report, Swiss Agile Study (2014). http://www.swissagilestudy.ch/files/2015/05/SwissAgileStudy2014.pdf. ISSN: 2296–2476
12. Schneider, W.: The Reengineering Alternative. McGraw-Hill Education, Columbus (2000)
13. Schwaber, K., Beedle, M.: Agile Software Development with Scrum 1st edn. Pearson (2001)
14. Trist, E.L., Bamforth, K.W.: Some social and psychological consequences of the longwall method of coal-getting. Technol. Organ. Innov.: The Early Debates **1**, 79 (2000)
15. VersionOne. 9th state of agile survey. Technical report, VersionOne Inc. (2015)
16. Whitworth, E., Biddle, R.: The social nature of agile teams. In: Proceedings of the AGILE 2007, AGILE 2007, pp. 26–36. IEEE Computer Society, Washington, DC (2007)

A Multiple Case Study on the Architect's Role in Scrum

Matthias Galster[1](✉), Samuil Angelov[2], Marcel Meesters[2], and Philipp Diebold[3]

[1] University of Canterbury, Christchurch, New Zealand
mgalster@ieee.org
[2] Software Engineering, Fontys University of Applied Sciences, Eindhoven, The Netherlands
{s.angelov,m.meesters}@fontys.nl
[3] Fraunhofer Institute for Experimental Software Engineering, Kaiserslautern, Germany
philipp.diebold@iese.fraunhofer.de

Abstract. Context: Previous research investigated how to approach architecting in agile projects (e.g., in terms of processes and practices), but the *role* that architects play in Scrum is still not well understood. Objective: We aim at capturing scenarios of how architects (or those taking on architecture-related tasks) are involved in Scrum. Furthermore, we aim at identifying how those taking on the role of the architect interact with other roles in Scrum. Method: We conducted a multiple case study and interviews with practitioners from six Dutch software organizations. Results: We identified three generic scenarios of architects in Scrum ("internal architect", "external architect", "internal and external architects"). We found that how architects interact with other roles in Scrum heavily depends on the Product Owner role. Conclusions: Some of our results are not in line with recommended practices in the Scrum Guide. Our findings support those who take on architecture-related tasks in preparing for Scrum-like projects.

Keywords: Software architect · Architecture · Agile software development · Scrum

1 Introduction

Software architecture is crucial for software project and product success [1]. However, architecting activities and the role of the software architect are often not explicitly considered in agile software development approaches (e.g., Scrum) [2]. This allows agile teams (a) to consider specifics of individual projects, (b) to not restrict how architecting responsibilities are distributed but to make most use of the expertise, skills and experience of individual team members, and (c) to highlight that every team member is responsible for all activities needed to make the project a success. Previous research investigated how software architecting could be approached in agile development projects, including processes and practices to design and maintain flexible, adaptive, and evolving architectures [3]. For example, it has been acknowledged that in agile projects, an architecture may emerge during a project based on an architecture metaphor and "quick design sessions", rather than being fully designed upfront [4]. Yet, there is currently little attention devoted to the *role* of software architects (i.e., the actor(s) in a

© Springer International Publishing AG 2016
P. Abrahamsson et al. (Eds.): PROFES 2016, LNCS 10027, pp. 432–447, 2016.
DOI: 10.1007/978-3-319-49094-6_29

software development process who perform architecture-related activities) and how this role (and related tasks and capabilities) appears in agile development projects.

The most frequently used agile development framework is Scrum [5]. The Scrum Guide[1] (which describes recommended practices for Scrum) recommends cross-functional team members but does not explicitly consider the role of an architect or any other task-related role (see also the discussion on roles in Scrum in Sect. 2.1). In addition, anecdotal evidence from industry suggests that there is no explicit role of an architect in Scrum [4]. However, as discussed by Abrahamsson et al. [2], it is highly recommended to include an architect role in agile projects: "Software architects are expected to act as facilitators in whole software development projects and as the representatives of a system's overall quality attributes". Even though there is no dedicated role of an architect in many organizations that follow Scrum, certain roles in these organizations create architecture designs and communicate their decisions to development teams [4]. This means that by adopting Scrum, an organization does not suddenly "forget" that there are many different activities to perform (including design and architecture related activities, quality assurance and testing). There must be actors in a Scrum team who perform these activities. Depending on the type of product and maturity/experience/skills of team members, those team members might be more or less influential. However, detailed and systematic insights into the architect's role is currently missing. In this paper, we look beyond agile architecting practices and at investigating the role of architects themselves. This results in the following research goal:

> *Analyse* architect(s) in Scrum *with respect to* their role and interactions with other roles in Scrum *in the context of* an industrial setting *for the purpose of* defining scenarios of how architects operate and interact *from the point of view of* practitioners.

We focus on Scrum because it is the most often used agile development framework [5]. Also, focusing on Scrum helps us scope our study and explicate the applicability of our results. Concrete research questions are formulated in Sect. 3. To achieve the goal of our study, we conducted a case study in industry [6]. This case study involved interviews with practitioners in Scrum projects in six Dutch companies.

The main contribution of this paper is an empirically-grounded model of the architect's role in Scrum projects, including scenarios that describe interactions of architects with other roles in Scrum. These roles and interactions may not be in the Scrum Guide. Furthermore, results help educate and train less experienced (or novice) architects for architecting activities in Scrum by explicating their position and relationships with other actors in the development process. Finally, our findings are a guidance for defining and understanding roles related to architecting in Scrum when setting up new teams or projects.

In Sect. 2, we discuss background and related work. In Sect. 3, we present the case study design. In Sect. 4, we present the results which are discussed in more detail in Sect. 5. The paper ends with conclusions and future work in Sect. 6.

---

[1] http://www.scrumguides.org/scrum-guide.html.

2   Background and Related Work

We first discuss Scrum based on the Scrum Guide, focusing on roles in Scrum. We do not describe Scrum in further detail but refer the reader to literature [7, 8]. We then discuss the role of architects in general. Finally, we highlight related work of architects in agile development.

2.1   Roles in Scrum

The *Scrum Master* takes care of the proper implementation of Scrum and related practices. He/she also helps resolve any impediments the team may face and manages resources (software, hardware, space, time, etc.). Finally, the Scrum Master protects the development team from undesired influences during sprints. The *development team* is self-organizing and cross-functional (i.e., team members allocate tasks to themselves and perform activities as needed) and performs all software development activities, including architectural work if required. The *Product Owner* performs all communications between the team and the stakeholders outside the team (e.g., end users or management). In this sense, the Product Owner shields the team from the external environment. The Product Owner needs to be an expert in the product domain or should at least be able to become an expert quickly. As reported by Friedrichsen [9] and Diebold et al. [10], most Product Owners care only about functional requirements but not about nonfunctional requirements and quality attributes. Typically, Product Owners do not engage in the architecting aspects of a project as they "are often employees of a business department or a different non-IT department" [9].

2.2   Role of the Software Architect

Generally, architects have three main tasks: getting input from outside world (listen to stakeholders, learn about technologies, etc.), architecting (i.e., make architectural decisions to decompose systems, select technologies, decide on architectural patterns and styles, etc.) and providing information (communicate architecture, help stakeholders, etc.) [11]. Activities of architects and required skills center on processes, practices, and technologies. The line between "development" and "architecture" is thin [12]. However, in contrast to architects, developers implement, test and maintain code-related software artifacts, and spend most of their time coding (relative to other types of activities). Developer and architect are not necessarily separate: They are roles (not ranks or positions), i.e., one position can take on more than one role.

2.3   Related Work on the Role of the Architect in Agile Development

Faber describes experiences from architecting and the role of architects in agile projects at a specific company [13]. According to Faber, architects should actively guide but not dominate developers, i.e., architects should accept deviations from original architectural designs if developers request (and justify) it [13]. Martini and Bosch introduce three types of architecture-related roles in large agile organizations (not Scrum-specific): the chief architect (takes high-level architecture decisions and drives other architects and teams), the governance architect (role between teams and chief architect) and the team architect (responsible for architecture in team). These roles interact with different types of teams in large scale projects, i.e., feature teams (responsible for implementing features on the backlog and therefore most similar to "teams" in Scrum), runway teams (responsible for the "architecture feature" and architecture refactoring), architecture teams (groups of architects for different projects), and governance teams (teams of architects and other high-level decision makers). With regards to roles in agile teams, Scott Ambler argues for "architecture owners" in large teams to facilitate architectural decisions on a sub-team[2]. In this sense, architecture owners are similar to a chief architect or governance architect defined by Martini and Bosch. In contrast to Martini and Bosch, our study (a) investigates Scrum in small, medium, and large organizations instead only on large agile organizations in general, and (b) focuses on the role (in terms of tasks and capabilities) of architects that interact with other roles in Scrum and teams, rather than with other roles in an organization in general.

Some frameworks for Scrum at larger scale (e.g., Scrum@Scale[3], The Nexus – Scaled Professional Scrum Framework[4], Large-scale Scrum Framework[5], "Scrum of Scrums"[6]) include high-level architecture-related practices, but do not discuss the role of the architect in the development process. One exception is SAFe (Scaled Agile Framework)[7], which considers a "System Architect/Engineer" at development program level (program level is where teams work on a common enterprise mission). There are also "non-Scrum" agile frameworks, such as the DSDM (Dynamic Systems Development Method)[8] which explicitly include architecture-related roles (e.g., the "technical coordinator" in DSDM designs the system architecture).

In our own previous work, we identified challenges that architects face in Scrum projects [14]. This current study is an extension and focuses on the role that architects play in agile teams and agile development settings, as well as scenarios to describe interactions of architects with other actors in Scrum projects.

3   Research Method

We study architects in Scrum in practice. Furthermore, architects cannot be studied in isolation from their context (e.g., organization, project) and we have little control over all variables (e.g., people, organizational structures). Therefore, we apply case study research. Case studies offer a deeper understanding of the tasks of architects in Scrum projects and the context in which they operate. The research followed guidelines

---

[2] http://www.ambysoft.com/essays/agileRoles.html.
[3] https://www.scruminc.com/scrum-scale-case-modularity/.
[4] https://www.scrum.org/Resources/The-Nexus-Guide.
[5] https://less.works/.
[6] https://www.scruminc.com/scrum-of-scrums/.
[7] http://www.scaledagileframework.com/.
[8] https://www.dsdm.org/resources/dsdm-handbooks/dsdm-atern-handbook-2008.

described by Runeson and Hoest [6] and is described below. Based on the study goal defined in Sect. 1, we defined the following research questions (RQ):

- **RQ1:** *What is the position of the architect in Scrum projects?*
- **RQ2:** *How does the architect interact with other roles in Scrum?*

Case study design: Our study is a multiple case study with six cases (Table 1). Our research is exploratory as we are looking into an unexplored phenomenon [15]. Our unit of analysis is the architect (specifically, tasks and role) in Scrum projects. Our sampling method is purposive sampling (i.e., we investigate organizations that use Scrum; organizations were selected on actual Scrum practices rather than only based on their own claim to use Scrum) augmented with convenience sampling (we selected cases based on their accessibility and availability of interviewees) [16]. Also, studied organizations should be representative rather than in very specific domains. Therefore, we selected six well-known organizations from the Netherlands that use Scrum and have established software development practices (due to confidentiality reasons, we only use case numbers in Table 1).

Table 1. Overview of the case organizations

Case	Domain	Size	Interviewees	(Multi-)national	Reach
1	E-commerce	Medium (<150)	Lead developer	Multi-national	Global
2	Software solutions	Small (~50)	Lead developer	National	Local
3	Finance	Large (~3,500)	Senior architect	National	Local
4	Consultancy	Large (>11,000)	Senior architect	Multi-national	Global
5	Navigation systems	Large (~4,500)	Senior architect, Software architect	Multi-national	Global
6	Appliances	Large (>100,000)	Design owner	Multi-national	Global

Preparation for data collection: Data for each case was collected via semi-structured interviews on-site and follow-up phone calls and e-mails. Interviewees were not only selected based on their job title, but also based on their tasks and capabilities and their involvement in architecting activities. All interviewees held representative roles within their organizations to report on architecture practices, process issues, roles, etc. To answer our research questions, we asked questions about the position and role of the interviewees in development projects and about the tasks which they perform using tasks-descriptions from [11, 17]. For each task, we asked if and how it was performed, if challenges/problems were observed when performing it, what kind of interactions would take place, with which actors, etc. Open questions were used to find out additional information not captured through questions in the interview guideline[9]. We took notes during interviews and each interview was recorded and later transcribed.

Analysis of collected data: The transcripts of recordings were complemented with information from the notes taken during the interview. The full transcripts were then analysed and information was clustered. To cluster data, we used open coding where one code can be assigned to many pieces of text, and one piece of text can be assigned to more than one code [18]. After initial coding, we looked at groups of code phrases and merged them into concepts and related them to the role, position, and interactions of architects. Codes and concepts emerged during the analysis and were not defined up-front. Since data was collected in a case study and is context sensitive, we performed iterative content analysis to make inferences from collected data in its context [19]. Analysing qualitative interview data requires integrating data where different interviewees might have used terms and concepts with different meanings or different terms and concepts to express the same thing. To address this problem, we use reciprocal translation. Furthermore, we checked with interviewees to ensure that our interpretation of data and findings is valid. Data were analysed and discussed by all authors.

4   Study Results

4.1   Overview of Results and Initial Observations

In Table 1, we provide an overview of the cases. "Size" in Table 1 refers to the number of employees, "(Multi-) national" indicates whether an organization has sites/employees in different countries or only in the Netherlands. "Reach" indicates whether an organization targets global or local markets. Below, we provide initial observations for each case with regards to the role of the architect(s).

- In case 1, there is no explicit architect role in the company. Discussions/decisions about the architecture involve the whole Scrum team. The lead developer is the most senior technical person and thus has the final say in an architectural decision.
- In the organization of case 2, one project is usually done by one Scrum team. Each team has a lead developer who is responsible for the architecting activities but the whole team works on the architecture and architecture-relevant tasks.
- In the organization of case 3, a senior architect residing outside the Scrum team elaborates a high-level architecture and explains it to the team leader (who also fulfils the role of the Scrum Master). The architect elaborates the detailed architecture during the project (and if needed evolves the architecture). He supports the team on architectural aspects throughout the project.
- Case 4 is a consultancy company offering specialized architects to clients. Architects reside outside the Scrum teams and provide their services and expertise to various Scrum teams.

---

[9] https://sites.google.com/site/samuilangelov/InterviewQuestions.docx.

- In the organization of case 5, there is a senior software architect who is not part of the Scrum team and another software architect who is part of the Scrum team. Given the scale of the projects, multiple Scrum teams are involved in single projects. Therefore, Scrum is applied integrated in the Scaled Agile Framework (SAFe) with Scrum teams at "Team" level of SAFe and the senior software architect at "Program" level (at which teams work towards an enterprise mission).
- In case 6, an architecture team that is located outside Scrum teams maintains a reference architecture which Scrum teams have to apply. The reference architecture and a prototype implementation is provided to a Scrum team at the beginning of a project. In addition to the architecture team, a system architect outside the Scrum team maintains a requirements specification focusing on legal and regulatory aspects of the software. Furthermore, a Scrum team has a design owner who streamlines the architecting activities within the team and elaborates when necessary detailed designs.

To answer **RQ1** (position of architects in Scrum), we analyzed the data from the interviews and the characteristics of the six cases. We identified the following three general scenarios (these scenarios are described in further detail in Subsects. 4.2–4.4):

- "Internal architect" scenario in case 1 and case 2
- "External architect" scenario in case 3 and case 4
- "Internal and external architect" scenario in case 5 and case 6

We acknowledge that the three scenarios are still high-level and each scenario comes in its own "flavor" depending on the organization (as described in Subsects. 4.2–4.4). Also, these scenarios might not come as a surprise or appear novel. However, in our study, we derived these scenarios from empirically studying industry practice, rather than anecdotal evidence from personal experience. Exploratory studies provide a picture of reality and reality is rarely surprising or controversial [20].

With regards to **RQ2** (interactions of architects with other roles in Scrum), we found that the interactions depend on the positioning of architects in the process and the skills of Product Owners. Just like in "non-agile" projects, the architect in Scrum projects needs to document and communicate the architecture; understand requirements, the overall architecture and its implementation status; and facilitate and offer services to teams [21]. Overall, architects interact with all other types of roles and stakeholders in Scrum projects. We discuss RQ2 and interactions in more detail in the following sections where we introduce the three scenarios found for RQ1.

4.2 "Internal Architect" Scenario

In case 1 and case 2, we found an "internal architect" scenario (Fig. 1) where the architect is part of the development team. Figure 1 shows an aggregation of the interactions from the two cases (i.e., we extracted the commonalities from case 1 and case 2). In Fig. 1, entities within the "Team" indicate roles, rather than individuals.

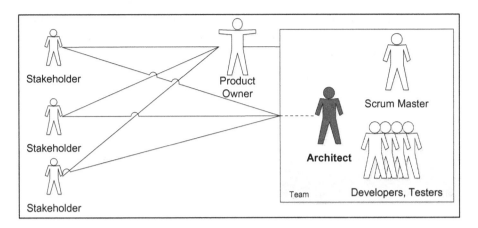

Fig. 1. "Internal architect" scenario

The architect may take multiple roles, e.g., also act as developer and contribute to coding. The architect defines an architecture draft together with the other team members, which is maintained, updated and extended throughout the project. If there is no dedicated architecture expert in the team (as in case 1), the role of the architect can be taken on by the whole team. As an interviewee in case 2 noted, "It is important to regard all members of the Scrum team as equal members. Also engineers with limited work experience can have an important contribution to the team's architecture. In this way, the best comes out of the team, and communication goes much more smoothly".

With regards to interactions (RQ2), we found in case 1 that Product Owners with no architectural knowledge, although being open to architecting activities, cannot facilitate architecture work. "Internal" architects need to directly communicate with external stakeholders about architecture issues which increases their workload and to some degree defeats the purpose of the role of the Product Owner in Scrum. As we found in case 2, Product Owners provide incomplete information to architects and the team. Therefore (and similar to case 1), external stakeholders interact with the team and the architect directly and vice versa (indicated by the dotted line in Fig. 1). Some Product Owners in case 2 take offence from being left out in communications and therefore conflicts between Product Owners and architects may arise. Note that in Fig. 1 the Product Owner may communicate with any team member (including the architect) and we do not illustrate the communication within the team (all team members communicate with each other).

4.3 "External Architect" Scenario

In case 3 and 4, we identified an "external architect" scenario (Fig. 2). Figure 2 shows an aggregation of the interactions from the two cases (i.e., we aggregated case 3 and case 4 into a generic scenario). In this scenario, the architect is not part of the Scrum team and there is also no "internal" architect. The architect elaborates an initial high-level design and presents it to the team. The architect is available during the project to clarify the design, to resolve problems, to adapt or extend the architecture or to make new architectural decisions. The architect also monitors the compliance of the product with the architecture design.

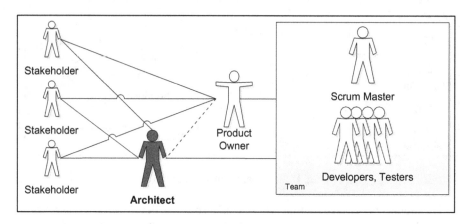

Fig. 2. "External architect" scenario

With regards to RQ2 (interactions), we found in case 3 that architects need to educate project stakeholders outside the team about architecting and the value of architecting. However, due to time constraints of the Product Owner in this case, the architect cannot educate the Product Owner on architecting issues or involve the Product Owner in architectural decisions. Also, since the architect is external to the team and responsible for more than one team, the architect is not always available to the teams and is not always up-to-date on the team's developments. Therefore, the architect involves team leaders to act as a "proxy" to represent the architect to the team. In case 4, similar to case 3, the architect does not communicate with the PO on architectural issues as the PO has no architecting knowledge (dotted line in Fig. 2). In contrast to case 3, in case 4, the architect is available to the team on a more regular basis.

4.4   "Internal and External Architects" Scenario

In case 5 and 6, we identified the "internal and external architects" scenario (Fig. 3 again shows a generalized scenario for case 5 and 6). In this scenario, there is an external and an internal architect. The "internal" architect deals with tasks related to the day-to-day work of the team whereas the "external" architect is concerned with higher level decisions that potentially affect also other teams. In case 6, the external architect is a member of the architecture team and is coupled with the Scrum team.

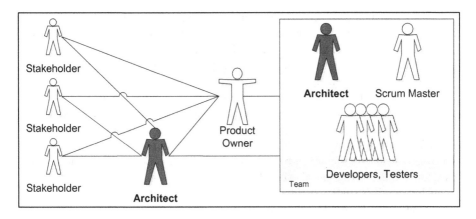

Fig. 3. "Internal and external architects" scenario

With regards to interactions (RQ2), we found that the external architect interacts with external stakeholders and the communication between external architect and team is via the internal architect. In case 5, the external architect is empowered to remove stories from the sprint backlog which the Product Owner did not specify sufficiently, positioning the architect hierarchically higher than the Product Owner. Furthermore, internal architects in different teams are encouraged to communicate between each other on architectural decisions that affect other teams or parts of a project (not depicted in Fig. 3, as this is a specific of case 5). As we found in case 6, there is often a one-directional communication between external architects and external stakeholders. This means that the architects receive input from stakeholders, but do not check back with stakeholders about the quality of their decisions. Furthermore, in case 6, the external architects might not provide sufficient input for the development team during a project, which is crucial in agile projects where architectural decisions may change over time. To mitigate this issue, an external architect temporarily joins the development team at the beginning of a project. In case 6, there is an additional system architect outside the Scrum and architecture teams. The system architect interacts with the team independently from the "external" architect, creating an additional communication channel towards the team and imposing additional documentation requirements on the team.

5   Discussion

5.1   Relation to Existing Literature

The general idea that architects can appear at different positions in agile projects has been discussed by others [22]. Our work goes beyond the general idea and differs in that we derive three *concrete* scenarios for Scrum teams. In this section, we therefore relate architect scenarios and interactions that we identified to existing literature. Furthermore, since we were conducting a qualitative analysis of data, this comparison with literature strengthens the theoretical validity of each scenario found in our study.

- The "internal architect" scenario has similarly been described by Schwaber [8] and Cohn [23]. Others have argued that all team members are involved in architecting activities but no single team member will carry the title or full responsibility of an "architect" [24]. As stated in the agile principles: "The best architectures, requirements, and designs emerge from self-organizing teams"[10]. Friedrichsen [9] also argues that architectural work should be done by "[…] either the whole team, or at least some specifically skilled team members - to share the knowledge across the team". Similarly, Waterman et al. [25] view architectural decisions as a result of the collaboration of the whole team. In contrast to Martini and Bosch who define the team architect as a role taken by a technical leader or experienced developer [26], we found that this role can also be taken by the whole team. Van der Ven and Bosch conclude in their study that an architect role in the team (either shared between all team members or carried by one team member) significantly contributes to successful projects and besides architects, the Product Owner and the development team are also "involved in, and sometimes responsible for, the architecture decision process" [27]. We found that the team is involved in the architecting process but not necessarily the Product Owners due to their lack of understanding of architecting issues.
- In the "external architect" scenario, the architect might work with multiple agile teams and partner with other architects (for example, as a project architecting team or as a member of an architecture board where common architecting practices are agreed and implemented) [13]. As suggested by Faber [13] and Madison [28], an "external" architect focuses on the high-level architecture diagrams, the architectural choices and quality attributes. The architect communicates with external stakeholders and works closely with the Product Owner and with the team to define and evolve the architecture. According to literature, good communication with the Product Owner is vital [13, 28]. However, in our study, we observed insufficient communications with Product Owners due to their lack of architectural knowledge. The "external architect" in our study is similar to the role of the "chief architect" identified by Martini and Bosch. However, "chief architect" implies a formally recognized role to take high-level decisions to drive the rest of architects to support strategic business goals [26]. This might apply to large-scale organizations, but in our case 4 we found that external architects do not necessarily have the role of the chief architect responsible for higher level decisions. This role might exist, but was not found to be interacting with Scrum teams in particular. However, a role similar to the "governance architect" who would be responsible for scalability of agile architecting in a large setting as an intermediate between chief architect and team [29] could be considered the "external" architect in this scenario.
- The "internal and external architects" scenario is similar to the setup discussed by Fowler [17] and Abrahamsson et al. who define two types of architects in agile projects: architects who focus on the big decision, who are facing requirements and act as external coordinators ("architectus reloadus"), and architects who focus on internal team communications, mentoring, troubleshooting and code ("architectus oryzus") [2]. It could also be seen as the setup of a team architect combined with a

---

governance architect discussed by Martini and Bosch [26]. As noted by Abrahamsson et al. [2], the "internal and external architect" setup is mostly valuable in projects developing a "large, challenging, novel system". In the study presented by Babar [30], the two roles are named "solution architect" (performing more management activities) and an "implementation architect" (ensuring the implementation of the user stories and mentoring the developers).

5.2 Implications for Practice and Research

Overall, our study contributes to highlighting different interaction scenarios of those responsible for architecting activities in Scrum. Even though the architect may not be an explicit and formally recognized role, related tasks and capabilities exist in Scrum settings. In this section, we summarize potential scenario-specific and general implications for practice and research:

- In the scenarios that involve external architects (i.e., the "external architect" and the "internal and external architects" scenarios), we noticed that external architects fail to provide sufficient information to external stakeholders about architectural decisions made (cases 5 and 6) and to teams, including "internal" architects (cases 3 and 6). This defeats the purpose of external architects. A possible explanation can be their high and diverse workloads (reported in case 3), geographical distance between a team and external architect (reported in case 5), or external stakeholders who lack an understanding of the value of architecting (cases 3 and 5). Further research is needed to better understand the reasons for external architects not performing some of the activities for which they are responsible.
- In the "external architect" scenario, potential challenges for the architect can be caused by the distance between the architect and the development team. Since there is no "internal" architect, architecturally relevant input from the team may therefore be harder to capture at the beginning of the project. This could cause problems in particular in critical projects. Also, the external architect may not be able to constantly support and mentor the team during the project. Moreover, being an outsider, the architect may face difficulties in convincing the team in the rightfulness of his/her ideas and into following the architectural decisions consistently throughout the project. Architecturally relevant changes requested by the team during a sprint may be harder to address due to the lack of easy access to the architect.
- The "external architect" scenario seems to contradict the idea of a cross-functional team in Scrum and the Scrum paradigm, while the "internal architect" scenario is what the Scrum framework expects and supports. However, in organizations with the "external architect" scenario we found other practices recommended in Scrum. It could be argued that the "external architect" scenarios show that organizations who claim to adopt Scrum might simply be struggling with doing so (e.g., due to unclear responsibilities for architecture-related tasks).
- In the "internal and external architects" scenario, synchronization of ideas and understanding between the external and internal architects may be difficult and even lead to conflicts. This is particularly true where no clear hierarchical structure exists

between external architects, the team (including team architect, Scrum Master) and Product Owner.

- The tasks of the architect in Scrum are similar to the tasks of architects in non-Scrum projects (see general role of the software architect discussed in Sect. 2.2). However, in all cases of our study, we observed that architects in Scrum projects should have certain skills that go beyond "traditional" architecting, such as understanding agile practices, being able to communicate to and convince a Product Owner about their decisions, and being able to fulfill (or delegate) responsibilities of different types of architects as described in the different scenarios. Furthermore, Scrum architects may perform architecting activities differently, e.g., architect smaller parts of the design early on, interacting with a more diverse range of stakeholders, apply specific practices, such as agile modeling as suggested by Scott Ambler[11] (i.e., model and document "just barely good enough" architecture, modeling as part of iteration planning activities, documenting continuously but late, etc.). Identifying architecture skills in agile settings that potentially differ from skills required for "traditional" up-front architecting is a topic for future research.

- We found that the activities of architects were significantly affected by the architectural background, knowledge, and availability of Product Owners. An architecturally un-savvy Product Owner may introduce multiple challenges to an architect. For example, architects may face the need to cope with low priorities of architecturally critical user stories (e.g., stories related to refactoring) prioritized by the Product Owner without understanding the significance of these stories for the product. Also, architects may not involve Product Owners in architecting activities (e.g., in an architecture review to evaluate "the proposed architectural solutions against the architecturally significant requirements" [30]) and communicate their decisions directly to the team and external stakeholders. This seems to contradict common agile principles and definitions of roles in Scrum. According to the Scrum Guide, the Product Owner's "decisions are visible in the content and ordering of the Product Backlog. No one is allowed to tell the Development Team to work from a different set of requirements, and the Development Team isn't allowed to act on what anyone else says". Some of these variations of Scrum in practice have already been discovered [10]. In theory, an architecturally savvy Product Owner could substantially facilitate the work of the architect. The Product Owner could provide a single point of communication for the information provided by external stakeholders, simplifying communications between architects and external stakeholders. This implies that the Product Owner needs to collect and provide architecturally relevant information, communicate architectural decisions to the stakeholders, and even get involved in architecting activities (e.g., architecture reviews). All activities related to "getting input" for architecting and "providing information" to stakeholders that go beyond the team would target the Product Owner rather than the external stakeholders. However, this additional responsibility requires more effort and time from the Product Owner, but also competence in architecting activities. Except for case 5, in all our cases, the Product Owners were not skilled enough to support architects in

---

[11] http://www.agilemodeling.com/.

their activities. Product Owners must be trained to not hamper communication between Product Owner and team due to lacking architecture related knowledge (and thus inability to provide the team with architecture-relevant input from the stakeholders).

- Architects faced challenges with regards to adoption of their architectural decisions in all but one cases. These were mostly due to disagreements with other stakeholders or team members. Related to that Woods reports that "difficulties frequently arise when agile development teams and software architects work together" and proposes general architecture practices that encourage collaborative architecture work in agile development [31]. These issues were not reported for architects only in case 2. This could be because the organization of case 2 follows strictly Scrum practices (advocating team autonomy and team architecting). Again, further studies are needed to understand what Scrum practices affect architecting, interactions between architects and other actors, and in what way.

5.3   Threats to Validity

With regards to *construct validity* (did we measure what is intended), our study is limited since we gathered data only from a limited number of sources. However, we obtained insights from different organizations and projects. Also, we followed semi-structured interviews based on an interview guideline. We included control questions and checked the accuracy of data with the organizations. Also, some findings about Product Owners are based on the perception of those involved in architecting activities. Future work may address how Product Owners see their role in architecting and supporting teams in architecting related activities. With regards to *external validity* (extend to which findings are of interest outside the investigated cases) we acknowledge that we focus on an analytical generalization (i.e., our results are generalizable to other organizations that have similar characteristics as the cases in our case study and use Scrum). The list of scenarios is based on six cases and is insufficient for drawing major conclusions. However, we also compared our findings with other literature to increase theoretical validity. With regards to *reliability* (how data analysis depends on researchers), we recorded interviews and interview data, and reviewed data collection and analysis procedures before conducting the study. Also, the types of scenarios found in organizations could depend on the type of organization and its complexity. Cases 1 and 2 are from small and medium-sized companies, while cases 3, 4, 5, 6 are from large organizations. *Internal validity* is not a concern since our exploratory case study does not make any claims about causal relationships.

6   Conclusions

We performed a case study with six cases involving companies that apply Scrum practices to better understand the role of architects in Scrum projects. The cases were chosen to cover different scenarios of how architects can be involved in Scrum. We identified three scenarios: "internal architect", "external architect" and "internal and external architect". With regards to communication and interactions of architects, we found that architecting activities are significantly impacted by the skills of the Product Owner role in Scrum. In order to improve architectural work in Scrum settings, attention may be paid to educating Product Owners in architectural relevant matters in order to (a) appreciate the value of architecting, and (b) help Product Owners extract architecturally relevant information from stakeholders to support architects in performing their tasks. Some of our findings are not in line with the Scrum Guide, but represent variations in Scrum as presented in [10]. The findings reported in this paper increase architects' awareness (especially of novice architects) about different positions in a Scrum process and interactions with other roles in Scrum. They support architects (or individuals who take on architecture-related tasks) in preparing for participating in Scrum-like projects. Furthermore, our findings support setting up new teams, processes, and projects.

Some future work has already been outlined in the previous section. As further research, we plan to extend the number of cases (covering companies of different sizes and different countries) and provide more general conclusions and a more refined list of roles and interactions. Furthermore, we plan on identifying relevant architecting skills for the different roles in Scrum. Finally, we aim at investigating group dynamics and organization theory to understand the three scenarios and in particular interactions in more detail.

References

1. Bass, L., Clements, P., Kazman, R.: Software Architecture in Practice. Addison-Wesley, Boston (2012)
2. Abrahamsson, P., Babar, M.A., Kruchten, P.: Agility and architecture: can they coexist? IEEE Softw. **27**, 16–22 (2010)
3. Yang, C., Liang, P., Avgeriou, P.: A systematic mapping study on the combination of software architecture and agile development. J. Syst. Softw. **111**, 157–184 (2016)
4. Eloranta, V.-P., Koskimies, K.: Lightweight architecture knowledge management for agile software development. In: Babar, M.A., Brown, A., Mistrik, I. (eds.) Agile Software Architecture. Morgan Kaufmann, Boston (2014)
5. VersionOne Inc.: 9th Annual State of Agile Survey (2015)
6. Runeson, P., Hoest, M.: Guidelines for conducting and reporting case study research in software engineering. Empirical Softw. Eng. **14**, 131–164 (2009)
7. Schwaber, K.: Agile Project Management with Scrum (Developer Best Practices). Microsoft Press (2004)
8. Schwaber, K., Beedle, M.: Agile Software Development with Scrum. Prentice Hall, Upper Saddle River (2002)
9. Friedrichsen, U.: Opportunities, threats, and limitations of emergent architecture. In: Babar, M.A., Brown, A., Mistrik, I. (eds.) Agile Software Architecture, pp. 335–355. Morgan Kaufmann, Boston (2014)
10. Diebold, P., Ostberg, J.-P., Wagner, S., Zendler, U.: What do practitioners vary in using scrum? In: Lassenius, C., Dingsøyr, T., Paasivaara, M. (eds.) XP 2015. LNBIP, vol. 212, pp. 40–51. Springer, Heidelberg (2015). doi:10.1007/978-3-319-18612-2_4
11. Kruchten, P.: What do software architects really do? J. Syst. Softw. **81**, 2413–2416 (2008)
12. Brown, S.: Software Architecture for Developers. Leanpub (2012)
13. Faber, R.: Architects as service providers. IEEE Softw. **27**, 33–40 (2010)

14. Angelov, S., Meesters, M., Galster, M.: Architects in scrum: what challenges do they face? In: 10th European Conference on Software Architecture (ECSA), Copenhagen, Denmark. Springer, Switzerland (2016, in press)
15. Wohlin, C., Runeson, P., Hoest, M., Ohlsson, M., Regnell, B., Wesslen, A.: Experimentation in Software Engineering. Kluwer Academic Publications, Boston (2000)
16. Kitchenham, B., Pfleeger, S.L.: Principles of survey research - Part 5: populations and samples. ACM SIGSOFT Softw. Eng. Notes 27, 17–20 (2002)
17. Fowler, M.: Who needs an architect? IEEE Softw. 20, 2–4 (2003)
18. Miles, M.B., Huberman, A.M.: Qualitative Data Analysis. Sage Publications, Thousand Oaks (1994)
19. Krippendorff, K.: Content Analysis: An Introduction to Its Methodology. Sage Publications, Thousand Oaks (2003)
20. Torchiano, M., Ricca, F.: Six reasons for rejecting an industrial survey paper. In: First International Workshop on Conducting Empirical Studies in Industry (CESI), pp. 1–6. IEEE Computer Society, San Francisco (2013)
21. Babar, M.A., Ihme, T., Pikkarainen, M.: An industrial case of exploiting product line architectures in agile software development. In: 13th International Software Product Line Conference, pp. 171–179. CMU, San Francisco (2009)
22. Rost, D., Weitzel, B., Naab, M., Lenhart, T., Schmitt, H.: Distilling best practices for agile development from architecture methodology. In: Weyns, D., Mirandola, R., Crnkovic, I. (eds.) ECSA 2015. LNCS, vol. 9278, pp. 259–267. Springer, Heidelberg (2015). doi: 10.1007/978-3-319-23727-5_21
23. Cohn, M.: Succeeding with Agile: Software Development Using Scrum. Addison-Wesley, Reading (2009)
24. Beck, K.: Extreme Programming Explained. Addison-Wesley, Boston (1999)
25. Waterman, M., Noble, J., Allan, G.: How much up-front? a grounded theory on agile architecture. In: 37th International Conference on Software Architecture, pp. 347–357. IEEE Computer Society, Florence (2015)
26. Martini, A., Bosch, J.: A multiple case study of continuous architecting in large agile companies: current gaps and the caffea framework. In: 13th Working IEEE/IFIP Conference on Software Architecture (WICSA), pp. 1–10. IEEE, Florence (2016)
27. van der Ven, J.S., Bosch, J.: Architecture decisions: who, how and when? In: Babar, M.A., Brown, A., Mistrik, I. (eds.) Agile Software Architecture, pp. 113–136. Morgan Kaufmann, Boston (2014)
28. Madison, J.: Agile architecture interactions. IEEE Softw. 27, 41–48 (2010)
29. Martini, A., Pareto, L., Bosch, J.: Role of architects in agile organizations. In: Bosch, J. (ed.) Continuous Software Engineering, pp. 39–50. Springer, Berlin (2014)
30. Babar, M.A.: An exploratory study of architectural practices and challenges in using agile software development approaches. In: Joint Working IEEE/IFIP Conference on Software Architecture & European Conference on Software Architecture (WICSA/ECSA), pp. 81–90. IEEE Computer Society, Cambridge (2009)
31. Woods, E.: Aligning architecture work with agile teams. IEEE Softw. 32, 24–26 (2015)

Continuous Integration Applied to Software-Intensive Embedded Systems – Problems and Experiences

Torvald Mårtensson[1](✉), Daniel Ståhl[2], and Jan Bosch[3]

[1] Saab AB, Linköping, Sweden
torvald.martensson@saabgroup.com
[2] Ericsson AB, Linköping, Sweden
daniel.stahl@ericsson.com
[3] Chalmers University of Technology, Gothenburg, Sweden
jan@janbosch.com

Abstract. In this paper we present a summary of factors that must be taken into account when applying continuous integration to software-intensive embedded systems. Experiences are presented from two study cases regarding seven topics: complex user scenarios, compliance to standards, long build times, many technology fields, security aspects, architectural runway and test environments. In the analysis we show how issues within these topics obstruct the organization from working according to the practices of continuous integration. The identified impediments are mapped to a list of continuous integration corner-stones proposed in literature.

Keywords: Software integration · Software testing · Continuous integration · Embedded systems

1 Introduction

Continuous integration is widely promoted as an efficient way of conducting software development. The practice is said to enable that tests can start earlier, that bugs are detected earlier and to increase developer productivity [3, 12].

Martin Fowler's popular article [4] is often referred to as a summary of the practice of continuous integration. Paul Duvall summarizes continuous integration in a similar way into a list of seven corner-stones [3]. The corner-stones (here labelled C1-C7) are presented in Table 1.

Applications of continuous integration and other agile practices on large, complex systems have been presented by Craig Larman and Bas Vodde [7] and Dean Leffingwell [8]. There are also reports describing various experiences from introducing continuous integration practices, often together with other agile practices [2, 6, 9–11]. However, these reports do not describe experiences from applying continuous integration to software-intensive embedded systems (software systems combined with electronic and mechanical systems).

© Springer International Publishing AG 2016
P. Abrahamsson et al. (Eds.): PROFES 2016, LNCS 10027, pp. 448–457, 2016.
DOI: 10.1007/978-3-319-49094-6_30

Table 1. Duvall's seven corner stones of continuous integration

Id	Continuous integration corner stone
C1	All developers run private builds on their own workstations before committing their code to the version control repository to ensure that their changes don't break the integration build
C2	Developers commit their code to a version control repository at least once a day
C3	Integration builds occur several times a day on a separate build machine
C4	100 % of tests must pass for every build
C5	A product is generated that can be functionally tested
C6	Fixing broken builds is of the highest priority
C7	Some developers review reports generated by the build, such as coding standards and dependency analysis reports, to seek areas for improvement

The topic of this paper is an overview and discussion of factors specific for software-intensive embedded systems that could constrain a full adaptation of continuous integration (as defined by Duvall's corner-stones). The authors of this paper have under a long period of time been involved in software development projects for large-scale and complex systems. Through our work in various roles related to integration and testing, we have gained experiences of problems and issues related to the practices of continuous integration.

The main contribution of this paper is a summary of factors that we believe must be taken into account when applying continuous integration to software systems combined with electrical and mechanical systems. Further work could examine solution approaches that can be applied in multiple case-studies.

The remainder of this paper is organized as follows. In the next section the study cases are described. Subsequently in Sect. 3 we present the problems and issues that we have experienced regarding seven topics. In Sect. 4, we present an analysis of how the topics described in Sect. 3 are related to the corner-stones for continuous integration that were presented in Sect. 1. The paper is concluded in Sect. 5 where we summarize those relationships.

2   Case Study Companies

In order to discuss impediments for continuous integration, we will compare experiences from two study cases, which both are companies developing large-scale and complex software for products which also include a significant amount of mechanical and electronical systems.

2.1   Study Case A

Study Case A is a telecommunications company with a wide range of products that serves the B2B market. The products are highly software-intensive, but also include significant electronical and mechanical parts.

Study Case A has an advanced system of automated build and test, which has been implemented to support continuous integration. Build, test and analysis of varying system scope and coverage run both on event basis and on fixed schedules, depending on needs and circumstances. A wide range of physical target systems as well as a multitude of both in-house and commercial simulators are used to execute these tests.

2.2 Study Case B

Study Case B is developing airborne systems and their support systems. The main product is the Gripen fighter aircraft, which has been developed in several variants. Gripen was taken into operational service in 1996. An updated version of the aircraft (Gripen C/D) is currently operated by the air forces in Czech Republic, Hungary, South Africa, Sweden and Thailand. The next major upgrade (Gripen E/F) which will include both major changes in hardware systems (sensors, fuel system, landing gear etc.) and a completely new software architecture.

Continuous integration practices such as automated testing, private builds and integration build servers are applied in development of software for the Gripen computer systems. The software teams commit to a common mainline. Testing is conducted in simulated environments, rigs and test aircraft.

3   Problems and Experiences

In this section we will compare the conditions at Study Case A and Study Case B regarding seven topics (derived from the characteristics of the companies' products). The seven topics are shown in Table 2. In general, our experiences of applying continuous integration practices are positive, but we present challenges related to applications with complex software systems together with mechanical and electronical systems.

Table 2. The seven topics discussed in Sect. 3

Id	Topic title
T1	Complex user scenarios need manual testing
T2	Compliance to standards shifts focus away from working software
T3	Longer build time due to tightly coupled systems
T4	Complete system a secondary concern due to many technology fields
T5	Restricted access to information due to security aspects
T6	End-to-end testing impossible without architectural runway
T7	Test environments often a limited resource with bespoke hardware

3.1   T1: Complex User Scenarios Need Manual Testing

Study Case A is developing communications solutions where systems interact which other systems. The user experience is limited to measurable capabilities such as quality and data transfer speed. Every other aspect of the user experience is linked to the user interface of products that are provided by other companies.

Study Case B on the other hand develops a product where the pilot cockpit is a vital part of the product. The pilot's judgment is critical with regards to whether the presentation and manoeuvring of sensors, weapons and other systems on the displays can support the pilot to fulfil the assigned missions.

Our experience is that usability testing for a product such as the Gripen fighter (Study Case B) is very difficult to discuss in terms of automated testing. Testing with the purpose of checking if for example a symbol is presented after a button is pressed can be automated, but the pilot's judgement when evaluating a complex user scenario is extremely difficult to replace with an automated test case. Our experience is that the challenges of testing which include subjective experiences are clearly valid for Study Case B, but are much less pronounced (if present at all) at Study Case A.

3.2 T2: Compliance to Standards Shifts Focus Away from Working Software

Development of airborne systems follows standards like DO-178B or specifically in Sweden RML-V-5. Development is to a great extent requirement-driven, where high-level requirements are broken down into low-level system requirements. Specific roles are responsible for quality assurance through reviews and audits. The telecom industry also has rules and regulations, but often not to the same extent as avionics software systems.

If evidence that the product is compliant to a standard is at the same importance as the product itself, however, a document review can be seen as time-critical and be given higher priority than software problems. Our experience is that Study Case B (fighter aircraft) to a greater extent than Study Case A (telecom systems) has milestones and project progress connected to audits (on system design or software) or formal documents (a document is issued that is required at a certain stage in the process).

3.3 T3: Longer Build Time Due to Tightly Coupled Systems

The Gripen aircraft (Study Case B) is a highly integrated system which uses rate-monotonic scheduling with a cyclic execution pattern. Both execution within a computer and communication between the central computers are scheduled. Our experience is that when working with a highly integrated (tightly coupled) system, a small delivery to the main track may cause building and linking of a large part of the computer system which implies long build times.

Study Case A's telecom systems have varying degrees of real time characteristics, typically depending on the level of abstraction with regards to the underlying physical interfaces. Similarly, the degree of coupling and ability to modularize also varies. Study Case A has had (where possible) very positive experiences of increasing "integration time" modularity – in other words, building and testing the systems in smaller, independent pieces. This approach is impeded by the tighter coupling of Study Case B.

3.4 T4: Complete System Secondary Concern Due to Many Technology Fields

Development of a product requires knowledge of all technology fields that the product covers. The Gripen aircraft (Study Case B) covers technology fields spanning from for example aerodynamics, engine control and electrical power system to communication system, navigation and mission planning. The telecom products of Study Case A also covers many technology fields, such as network optimization or handling of customer data.

Our experience is that a large number of technology fields fosters silo behaviours. The organization tends to establish tailored ways of working for each system (technology field) and also tends to see it as "our system", and treating the complete system as a secondary concern. This is arguably as a consequence of limited understanding of the unique challenges and requirements governing the many parts of the complete system. Silo mentality in not unique for this scenario, but we find it severely exacerbated when these silos operate in separate engineering disciplines with little or no understanding of one another's unique characteristics or challenges.

3.5 T5: Restricted Access to Information Due to Security Aspects

All companies have to take into account how to protect company confidential information. Almost every company has a strategy for how to avoid information leakage. Another aspect is the ability to protect customer data. That is, to ensure that information about one customer's performance or available functionality is not exposed to other customers. Both Study Case A and Study Case B must make allowances for this.

A third aspect is defence-related security. Defence-related security includes safeguarding of national security and foreign policy objectives for all (military) customers, but also to follow export control regulations for parts or sub-systems supplied by a foreign vendor. US arms regulations demand that it is secured that only specified individuals have access to software included in defence-related items, which increases the difficulty of a common understanding of the product. Export control of US technology (especially arms regulations) is regulated by The International Traffic in Arms Regulations. Our experience is that these regulations are affecting Study Case B (fighter aircraft), but are not relevant for Study Case A (telecom systems).

3.6 T6: End-to-End Testing Impossible Without Architectural Runway

Platforms like .NET or Java Virtual Machine possible for a developer to rapidly produce software that includes both user input/output and communication with other software modules. Embedded systems developed by Study Case A (telecom systems) and Study Case B (fighter aircraft) are not built on a commercially available platform like .NET. Instead, the development of an entirely new product includes a long period of in-house construction of a platform with all infrastructure functions. When you start from a clean slate you give up the luxury of a platform with working infrastructure including for example communication between systems, functional monitoring or data registration.

Dean Leffing well defines the term architectural runway as infrastructure sufficient to allow incorporation of new requirements (new functionality) [8]. Development for bespoke hardware with tight dependencies to the physical interfaces miss out the benefits from a commercially available platform. Consequently, the architectural runway is much longer.

Our experience from both study cases is that at the initial phase of development of a new product (lasting for a significant part of the project) the sub-systems cannot be integrated. Due to this, the product cannot for a long time be functionally tested end-to-end to expose any problems.

3.7 T7: Test Environments Often a Limited Resource with Bespoke Hardware

Development of embedded systems is highly dependent on bespoke hardware, both mechanical and electronical parts. The telecommunication equipment delivered by Study Case A (for example network nodes) often contain specialized internally developed hardware, and is deployable in a large number of variants. The equipment may also coexist with a wide variety of topologies, including equipment developed by Study Case A and/or any competing vendor. The computer system in the Gripen aircraft (Study Case B) is built on internally developed hardware and equipment developed for aeronautical applications. Gripen is designed in different variants, and each variant have sub-variants. Simulators with models of hardware are used by both Study Case A and B, but have limitations regarding for example timing.

When the system is based on bespoke hardware (not running on any standard computer) and hardware is considered expensive or in short supply, the test environments often become a limited resource. Further on, a large number of hardware configurations (caused by customer-specific hardware) increases the test effort needed for every build. Our experience is that both Study Case A and Study Case B are highly dependent on bespoke hardware, with Study Case A having to handle a greater degree of differences in hardware configurations.

4 Analysis

In the previous section we compared the conditions at Study Case A and Study Case B regarding seven topics (T1-T7 in Table 2) related to product characteristics, based on our experiences. In this section we will analyse how this relates to the seven-bullet summary of continuous integration (C1-C7 in Table 1).

4.1 C1: All Developers Run Private Builds

The first corner stone (C1) states that "All developers run private builds on their own workstations before committing their code to the version control repository to ensure that their changes don't break the integration build".

Test environments easily become a limited resource if the system is based on bespoke hardware (T7). We argue that if the developers build and test in a simulated environment, they cannot fully ensure that the exact same test cases will not expose problems during test activities that run on real hardware.

4.2   C2/C3: Commit Code and Build Often

As we find the two corner-stones "Developers commit their code to a version control repository at least once a day" (C2) and "Integration builds occur several times a day on a separate build machine" (C3) related they will be jointly discussed.

Build time is correlated with the size of the code base. If a product can be divided into several parts that are built and linked in parallel as separate binaries, build time can be reduced. If the product is a tightly coupled system, such sectioning is more difficult or even impossible which implicates a longer build time. We argue that a long build- and test-time (T3) reduces the developer's interest in committing to the main track often, and the developers will not commit their code to the repository at least once a day. Kent Beck quite simply states that "if integration took a couple of hours, it would not be possible to work in this style" [1]. If build- and test-time for the integration build (T3) extends to several hours, this severely limits the number of integration builds that can be produced in a day.

4.3   C4: 100 % of Tests Must Pass for Every Build

To use automated tests to support the practices of continuous integration is a far more effective approach than manual testing [3]. We find automated tests to be a prerequisite for the continuous integration of any not-trivial software system.

Testing should include different categories of tests, from unit tests and component tests to functional tests and tests of load/performance and other capabilities. Tests of Human Machine Interaction (HMI) differ from other types of testing, as the purpose of the tests are to check that the usability is considered at least good enough by user representatives. Manual usability tests take longer time to execute and are less predictable than automated tests, which means they cannot be repeated for every integration build (at a build rate of several builds a day or more).

When the system is based on bespoke hardware (not running on any standard computer) and hardware is considered expensive or in short supply, the test environments soon become a limited resource. Further on, a large number of hardware configurations (caused by customer-specific hardware) increases the test effort needed for every build. With a wide range of hardware configurations it is no longer clear what "100 % of tests must pass" actually means – does it mean testing on all valid configurations or a representative subset?

Test environments more easily become a limited resource with bespoke hardware, especially if the product uses many hardware configurations which increases the test effort (and consequently the demand of test environments). A large number of hardware configurations also increases the risk for flaky tests, as there are more test environments to maintain.

We argue that both a product with complex user scenario testing (T1) and many bespoke hardware configurations (T7) can be impediments when trying to adhere to the rule that "100 % of tests must pass for every build".

4.4 C5: A Product Is Generated That Can Be Functionally Tested

Before a first version of all infrastructure for the complete product has been developed, the developers don't have a minimum viable product which then can be incrementally expanded upon. That is, before the architectural runway is established, the product cannot be generated (assembled) and cannot be functionality tested end-to-end (T6).

Another aspect is that is important that all participants have common understanding of the desired functionality of the product. We argue that if the product has a large number of technology fields (T4) and especially if the technology fields are not adjacent, it becomes more difficult to agree on the content and meaning of functionality tests. Security aspects (T5) can also be an impediment, such as when developers are hindered from communicating freely regarding the exact content of the functions they have built. This further increases the difficulty of a common understanding of the product, which also becomes an impediment related to testing the product end-to-end.

4.5 C6: Fixing Broken Builds Is of the Highest Priority

Fixing broken builds fast restores the confidence for a stable and sound main track. If status of the software is undisputed as the full picture of status in the project, it is easy to keep focus on fixing broken builds fast.

"Working software over comprehensive documentation" is one of the values in the agile manifesto, which also fully applies to continuous integration. This might be seen as a value that collides with the principles of development of safety-critical, highly regulated software such as medical devices, nuclear power stations or flight-critical software. This conflict is also discussed by Janet Gregory and Lisa Crispin [5].

Regulated environments typically apply one or several standards that require that the developing organization should "show evidence" of compliance to the standard, which should be done in written documents. We argue that the obligation to show compliance to a standard (T2) can be an impediment in relation to the intention of fixing broken builds as the highest priority.

4.6 C7: Developers Review Reports to Seek Areas for Improvement

The last corner stone states that "Some developers review reports generated by the build, such as coding standards and dependency analysis reports, to seek areas for improvement". We argue in the same way as for corner-stone C5 (Sect. 4.4) that a large number of technology fields (T4) and security aspects (T5) make it more difficult to achieve a common understanding of the product. Only a few people have an overview of the whole product, and in many cases information cannot be shared due to security restrictions. To some extent, this affects how developers review reports on other parts of the product than where they are working themselves.

5 Conclusion

The analysis in the previous section relates the seven topics to the corner stones for continuous integration that were presented in the introduction. The analysis is summarized into the following bullets:

- If the developers run tests in a simulated environment, they cannot fully ensure that the same tests will pass for the integration build that runs on real hardware
- Tightly coupled systems (causing long build- and test-time) implies additional challenges related to frequent deliveries and integration builds several times a day
- A product with complex user scenarios and/or bespoke hardware (especially a large number of hardware configurations) implies that the rule "all tests must pass for every build" must be replaced with other testing approaches
- In a highly regulated environment, "fixing broken builds" must be balanced against other project objectives
- At the initial phase of development of a new product (before the architectural runway is established) the sub-systems cannot be assembled in order to test the system functionally end-to-end and expose any integration problems
- It is more difficult to achieve a common understanding of a product with a large number of technology fields or security aspects, which affects tests and reviews

The relations that were found are summarized in Fig. 1.

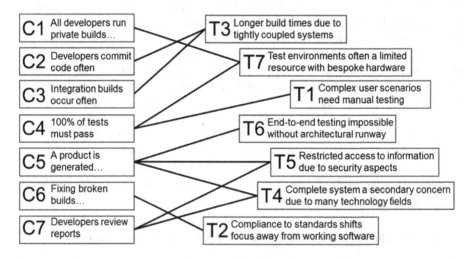

Fig. 1. Relations between corner stones and impediments

We believe that these experiences represent an area of further work of high relevance to large segments of the software industry. Any research promising to mitigate the discussed impediments would be of great value in the embedded software development community.

References

1. Beck, K.: Extreme Programming Explained: Embrace Change. Addison-Wesley Professional, Reading (2004)
2. Downs, J., Hoskins, J., Plimmer, B.: Status communication in agile software teams: a case study. In: Fifth International Conference on Software Engineering Advances, Nice, France (2010)
3. Duvall, P.: Continuous Integration. Addison Wesley, Reading (2007)
4. Fowler, M.: Continuous Integration (2006). http://www.martinfowler.com/articles/continuousIntegration.html
5. Gregory, J., Crispin, L.: More Agile Testing, Chap. 21 ("Agile Testing in Regulated Environments"). Addison Wesley, Reading (2015)
6. Karlström, D.: Introducing extreme programming-an experience report. In: Proceedings of the 3rd International Conference on eXtreme Processing and Agile Processing Software Engineering (XP 2002) (2002)
7. Larman, C., Vodde, B.: Practicies for Scaling Lean & Agile Development. Addison Wesley, Reading (2009)
8. Leffingwell, D.: Agile Software Requirements. Addison Wesley, Reading (2011)
9. Miller, A.: A hundred days of continuous integration. In: Agile 2008 Conference, Toronto, Canada (2008)
10. Roberts, M.: Enterprise continuous integration using binary dependencies. In: Eckstein, J., Baumeister, H. (eds.) XP 2004. LNCS, vol. 3092, pp. 194–201. Springer, Heidelberg (2004). doi:10.1007/978-3-540-24853-8_22
11. Stolberg, S.: Enabling agile testing through continuous integration. In: Agile 2009 Conference, Chicago, IL (2009)
12. Ståhl, D., Bosch, J.: Experienced benefits of continuous integration in industry software product development: a case study. In: The 12th IASTED International Conference on Software Engineering (2013)

Exploring Norms in Agile Software Teams

Viktoria Stray[1(✉)], Tor Erlend Fægri[2], and Nils Brede Moe[2]

[1] University of Oslo, Oslo, Norway
stray@ifi.uio.no
[2] SINTEF, Trondheim, Norway
{tor.e.fegri,nils.b.moe}@sintef.no

Abstract. The majority of software developers work in teams and are thus influenced by team norms. Norms are shared expectations of how to behave and regulate the interaction between team members. Our aim of this study is to gain more knowledge about team norms in software teams and to increase the understanding of how norms influence teamwork in agile software development projects. We conducted a study of norms in four agile teams located in Norway and Malaysia. The analysis of 22 interviews revealed that we could extract a varied set of both injunctive and descriptive norms. Our results suggest that team norms have an important role in enabling team performance.

Keywords: Group norms · Team values · Collaboration · Self-managing teams · Behavioral software engineering

1 Introduction

Teamwork is an integral part of contemporary software practice. Productive collaboration in software teams requires a certain unity in norms. Team norms are emergent, consensual standards that regulate team members behaviors [1]. Productive teamwork carries with it a set of norms such as listening and responding constructively to views expressed by others, giving others the benefit of the doubt, providing support and recognizing the interests and achievements of others [2]. Such norms are important because they promote individual performance, which boosts team performance, and good team performance boosts the performance of the organization. Understanding and influencing team norms is therefore key to building a productive software team [3].

With the emergence of agile development methods, we have also seen a substantial research interest in team-related topics such as communication [4], coordination [5] and self-managing teams [6], to name a few. Despite the increased interest in teamwork and behavioral aspects in software development research, team norms has been largely ignored [7]. This paper seeks to contribute to our understanding of team norms in software development by drawing on studies of norms in other disciplines [8–10]. Our main contribution is the application of team norm categorizations to a case study of four software teams. Not only do we report on particular norms in the software development context, but we also

© Springer International Publishing AG 2016
P. Abrahamsson et al. (Eds.): PROFES 2016, LNCS 10027, pp. 458–467, 2016.
DOI: 10.1007/978-3-319-49094-6_31

hope this contribution will enable more data-driven empirical research in this area in order to improve software processes.

We may think of team norms as shared expectations of how to behave in the team [11]. Norms have the power to partially explain human behavior by expressing our motivation for doing certain actions [8]. Norms are normative in the sense that they associate value to certain patterns of behavior. Norms thereby discriminate between acceptable and unacceptable behaviors of members in a team [12]. Furthermore, norms are a fundamental element of a team's structure and constitute an important vehicle for team members' identification with the team. When team members identify themselves with a team they will more easily commit themselves to team goals [10,12]. One of the most important characteristics of team norms is that they do not exist if they are not shared with others [13]. Norms may promote adaptive and effective behavior because people feel compelled to act in ways that are consistent with the norms. Norms simplify team processes because they make it possible for members to count on certain things being done and other things not being done [12].

A recent study at Google found that some norms, for example the norm that team members speak roughly the same amount, could raise the teams collective intelligence, while other norms could halt the team [3]. A study by Teh et al. suggested that team norms can be adjusted to promote certain behaviors in software teams [14]. In that particular study, group norms were altered using task priming, whereby team members would complete a pilot task under direct guidance to establish new norms. Agile methodologies require a shift from command-and-control management to leadership-and-collaboration [15]. McHugh [16] found that norms influence behavior in agile teams and argue that since traditional bureaucratic controls are often reduced in agile teams, team norms may be even more of importance than in traditional software teams. Further, Moe [17] argue that a software team, in order to become self-managing, needs to change the operating norms within the team, as well as in the wider environment. While developing productive norms are important in co-located software teams, it is even more important in distributed software teams. Sharp and Ryan [18] noted that a crucial element of virtual team design was the establishment of a shared set of norms. They argue that virtual teams benefit from learning to express explicit norms and role expectations to new members.

2   Study Design

The company in which this study was set is an international telecommunications software company with roughly 700 employees. It was selected as a research site because it was part of a large research project on teamwork in agile software teams. We studied two teams located in Norway (Mercury and Mars) and two teams located in Malaysia (Jupiter and Pluto), as shown in Table 1. One of the team members worked in both Mercury and Mars, but identified more strongly with the latter, and therefore we place her in this team in Table 1. All teams had used Scrum with the recommended practices for more than two years.

Table 1. Sample of teams

Team name	Country	Team members	Team members interviewed
Mercury	Norway	9	1 architect, 1 developer, 1 Scrum Master, 1 tester
Mars	Norway	9	3 developers, 2 Scrum Masters, 1 technical writer
Jupiter	Malaysia	10	5 developers, 1 project manager, 1 Product Owner, 1 Scrum Master, 1 tester
Pluto	Malaysia	6	1 architect, 1 developer, 1 team leader

The 22 interviews were semi-structured and the respondents were asked questions regarding teamwork and meetings. The interview guide was based on a teamwork model [19], which covers the following teamwork components: communication, team orientation, team leadership, monitoring, feedback, backup, and coordination. By understanding the teamwork components in each team, it will be possible to understand the patterns of behavior and the influencing norms. Understanding team orientation is of particular interest in this study. Team orientation is defined as [19]: "the attitudes that team members have toward one another and the team task. It reflects acceptance of team norms, level of group cohesiveness, and importance of team membership.".

The average interview duration was 60 min. All the interviews were audiotaped and fully transcribed. The first author also observed the teams in meetings and during daily work. Statements in the interviews regarding daily stand-up meetings have been used in previous work [20], but the information concerning norms was analyzed and reported on for the first time for the study reported in this paper.

The two first authors studied the interview transcripts and observation notes and identified statements that indicated norms - i.e. patterns of behavior. We looked for statements where team members described a behavior as an "unwritten rule" or "how our team does it". All the interviews were coded in NVivo. We decided to use the categorization by Cialdini et al. [8] to understand and analyze two type of norms: *injunctive* and *descriptive* (explained in Sect. 3). We discussed which of the categories the identified norms belonged to, and whether we believed the norms positively or negatively affected team performance. We also considered the framework proposed by Forsyth [1], but found that the categories were not as clear as those of Cialdini et al.

3   Results and Discussion

Upon analyzing our data we identified both injunctive and descriptive norms. Injunctive norms are concerned with what people *ought* to do or *should* do. Such norms describe approved or disapproved behaviors. Descriptive norms are norms of what *most* people do, how they *typically* act, feel, and think in a given situation. Because what is approved behavior (injunctive norms) is often the same as what is typically done (descriptive norms), it is easy to confuse these two types, but they are conceptually and motivationally distinct [8].

3.1 Injunctive Norms

We found that injunctive norms were the easiest type of norm to identify because the interviewees often expressed these as ways people ought to behave. For example, one developer in Jupiter described a norm of how to dress for work: *"We have to wear long pants, and we cannot wear slippers."* In Teams Jupiter and Pluto they had the norm that "the Product Owner (PO) is not allowed to attend retrospective meetings." A third example is that all teams had the injunctive norm: "team members have to be on time for meetings", and they tried to counteract the tendency to violate this norm with concrete sanctions, such as having to pay a fine. While talking about allocation of tasks, one developer from Team Jupiter noted: *"We have specialized roles in order to go in depth in solving problems and to be able to solve tasks faster."* The expected behavior in this team was that team members chose tasks according to specialization. This behavior was positively sanctioned because the team members believed that it made them more productive. This norm suggests that the team prioritized role specialization at the expense of agile teamwork norms such as having backup behavior and knowledge redundancy [5].

Another respondent in Jupiter commented on the autonomy level of the team: *"The thing is, the differences from now and the early days of Scrum is that we have full design rights. Previously we did not."* The reference is here to the positively sanctioned design behavior, i.e. team members are allowed to design. Design is a part of the work that sets direction for the subsequent coding. This is a norm that contributes to team performance since it brings decision-making authority to the level of operational problems.

One developer in Pluto reflected on a negative incident with a team member: *"Someone actually decided to take up a user story without informing us and then told us it was done before the story was even groomed. It is not ok that team members take such decisions without informing the rest of the team."* The injunctive norm here suggests that team members should not pick up user stories without informing the other team members. This kind of behavior is often referred to as decision hijacking [21] and is an example of violation of a norm. The injunctive norm that team members should inform each other is an enabler for effective teamwork because agile team members should make decisions together.

3.2 Descriptive Norms

Descriptive norms are concerned with the behavior that generally occurs, and these norms are predominantly based in implicit assumptions. Hence, in order to identify these norms, we had to supplement the analysis of the interviews with observational data to identify the usual behavior of the team members. For example, when investigating how the burndown chart was updated, one respondent in Team Mars replied: *"In Team Mercury, the team members report and the Scrum Master update it. We have concluded that we do not do it like that. We do it ourselves. Each one of us has the responsibility to update it."* This statement suggests a pattern of behavior that is established in the team. However, we observed that the team members rarely updated the burndown chart. Hence, the descriptive norm in the team was to update the burndown chart rarely, even if the project manager wanted them to update it often.

In Team Jupiter, during planning poker, the team member who estimated the highest or lowest number of hours had to give an explanation of his or hers estimate. This had resulted in a norm that most team members tried to estimate a middle value in order to avoid speaking up and explain their value to the others.

Another observation of a descriptive norm in Team Jupiter was that it was ok to be present in team meetings without paying attention, if the team member said they had something more important to do. For example, some team members coded during planning meetings. A consequence of this norm may be a reduced shared understanding of the work and the teams goals, which negatively affects team performance.

In all of the teams, team members often arrived at work just in time for the daily stand-up meeting, even if company policy stated an earlier time. This illustrates an important aspect of team norms: the informally agreed on guidelines for acceptable behavior in a team may conflict with the organization's expectations of behavior. Team members will then find themselves in a position where they, often unconsciously, choose or negotiate between different norms. In this example, team norms got precedence above organizational norms. This may indicate that the team members identified more strongly with the team than the organization.

3.3 Co-existing Norms

Injunctive and descriptive norms may co-exist in the same behavioral pattern [8]. In the beginning of our data analysis this created some confusion. An example of an injunctive and descriptive norm acting simultaneously is the following statement from a developer: *"When I have a problem, I ask for help immediately, I do not try to sit for days trying to solve the problem myself"*. We often observed that team members asked each other for help, either by going to a person sitting close by or by sharing the problem in the daily stand-up meeting. The behavior of seeking and providing assistance from each other was positively sanctioned in these teams (injunctive norm). At the same time, it was what people usually did (descriptive norm).

Another, more intricate example of co-existing norms is illustrated by the following statement from a manager: *"John is not too harsh on the PO, so the PO would always give him new tasks behind the Scrum Masters back. This is how John approaches stuff, so we can just let him. It is not really wrong by the way, he is just doing his part to improve the product."* It is disapproved (and hence an injunctive norm) to allow the PO to approach team members directly without the Scrum Masters consent. Nevertheless, this often happens (descriptive norm.)

Teams go through a natural process of creating norms to find a comfortable way to operate [12]. They try to operate in such a way that they maximize the chances for success and minimize the chances for failure, and that they also maximize the satisfaction of the team members and minimize interpersonal discomfort [22]. For example, the team as a whole are satisfied when they try not to accept tasks from the PO, but at the same time they accept that some team members solve this type of tasks because it minimizes interpersonal discomfort to let this person say yes. Nevertheless, we believe that the injunctive norm (team members should reject tasks from PO) positively affected team performance, while the acceptance of this being violated (the descriptive norm) negatively affected team performance.

3.4 Psychological Safety

Some norms of communication were described by the interviewees as cultural differences. For example, in Malaysia, one tester noted: *"In Norway, the testers would just go to the developers cubicle and just talk to them whenever there is a problem. In Malaysia, maybe the working culture is different, because most of the time we are communicating through e-mail to have it in black and white."* However, we believe that other factors than culture are also important in explaining norms for communication. Norms of how team members behave towards each other are closely related to the concept of psychological safety, which is a sense of confidence that the team will not embarrass, reject or punish someone for speaking up [23].

We identified several norms that indicated a high degree of psychological safety. For example, in Jupiter, the developers had the norm that they responded positively whenever they were confronted with a bug. One tester explained: *"In my previous job I was afraid that developers would be offended when I filed a bug because basically you are telling them that they have made a mistake. So I had to think a lot of how I would present the bugs I found. But, I do not get that feeling in this team because this team is quite mature. The developers are happy if you find a bug. It makes me feel happy about my job and my team."* This supports the findings in a recent study of norms that stated that productive software teams have norms that fosters a high degree of psychological safety in the team [3].

3.5 Changing Norms

A capacity for learning about norms and how to change them is needed to improve team performance. The results of this study indicate that it is important that teams reflect on the two types of norms associated with how they are operating as a team, and how such norms evolve. Norms are socially developed through interactions among team members. As a consequence, they are not static. An intriguing aspect of norms is that behavior that is found effective can gradually be turned into routine, norm-driven behavior [12,24].

Organizations seek to establish norms in different ways by enforcing process standards, code of conduct etc. Similarly, teams will try to establish norms, for example by agreeing on rules to regulate the team's interaction. One example is the set of rules defined by Team Pluto. Figure 1 is a picture of a working agreement that the team had posted on the wall in the office space. However, agreeing on these rules are not sufficient to designate them as norms, they are merely potential injunctive norms. A rule must also be associated with motivation to behave according to this rule (which, naturally, will most often be the case). Hence, we must find evidence of people's inclination to behave according to a certain pattern of behavior to verify if they are indeed injunctive norms.

By discussing the working agreement in Team Pluto, the team tried to establish their own norms for effective teamwork. Teams that are able to improve their own work methods often achieve a higher level of autonomy than teams that do not make such decisions [11]. One way of changing norms in a conscious manner is by reflection. To enable reflection, agile methods typically establish some form of retrospective meetings. We argue that these should be used as a means to discuss team norms.

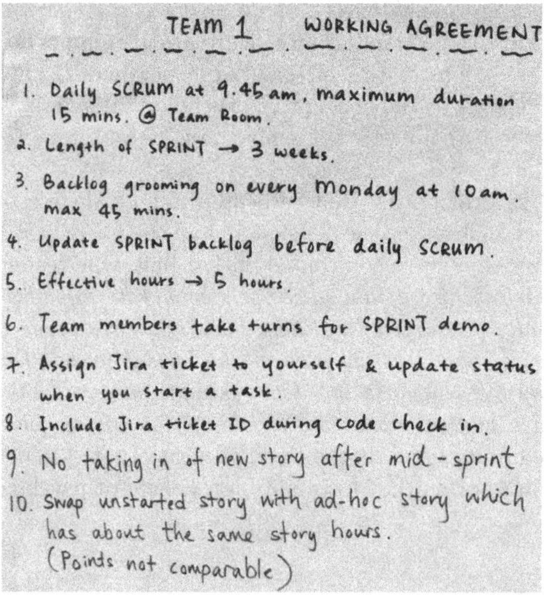

TEAM 1   WORKING AGREEMENT

1. Daily SCRUM at 9.45 am, maximum duration 15 mins. @ Team Room.
2. Length of SPRINT → 3 weeks.
3. Backlog grooming on every Monday at 10 am. max 45 mins.
4. Update SPRINT backlog before daily scrum.
5. Effective hours → 5 hours.
6. Team members take turns for SPRINT demo.
7. Assign Jira ticket to yourself & update status when you start a task.
8. Include Jira ticket ID during code check in.
9. No taking in of new story after mid-sprint
10. Swap unstarted story with ad-hoc story which has about the same story hours. (Points not comparable)

Fig. 1. Working agreement in Team Pluto

In observation of retrospective meetings, we noted several examples of issues related to team norms, for example: (1) How can we make sure people are punctual to grooming meetings? (2) How can we make team members prioritize the retrospective meetings when they are busy preparing for the sprint demo? (3) Should we ban laptops from meetings? and (4) How can we make sure that the burndown chart is updated more often? By discussing these issues, the teams reflected on descriptive norms and tried to establish injunctive norms that would subsequently be adopted as typical. This shows that rituals and ceremonies such as daily stand-up meetings and retrospective meetings may reinforce acceptable behaviors. Discussing the team's own norms is an example of clan-based control. Often, the team will seek to establish sanctions to uphold these injunctive norms [9]. Clan control is a type of control that operates when the behavior in a team is motivated by shared values and norms [25]. Clan control empowers team members in agile software teams [16].

4 Methodological Implications and Future Work

As far as we are aware, this is the first study of norms in agile software teams. Studying norms is a challenging undertaking because most people do not reflect on how norms guide their behavior. Additionally, they may not be aware of which norms that regulate their actions. We have come to understand norms better through our analysis according to the framework by Cialdini et al. [8]. Perhaps symptomatic for many soft topics in software engineering, we need to be vigilant to opportunities for using theory from other disciplines that explain the practice of software development.

While it seems clear to us that norms are an integral aspect of working in a team, they may be difficult to uncover because of their degree of visibility, as shown in Fig. 2. In order to understand norms, researchers have to uncover assumptions. One may start with identifying artifacts and behaviors in the teams to decipher the underlying sources of motivations, such as norms. Our position

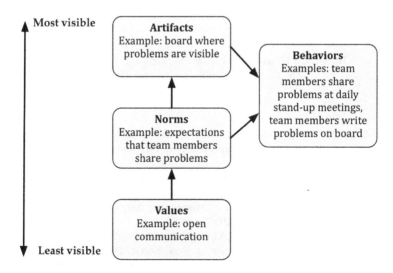

Fig. 2. Visibility of values and norms. Figure adapted from [25], examples from Team Mercury

is that it is not enough to just interview project members to uncover norms, one should supplement this data collection method with field observations to see what people actually do. Research in social psychology can serve as useful examples for future research in software teams [10].

Future research might also explore the concept of team values. Team values guide behavior and decision making in the team and they underlie norms [26,27]. However, team values may be even more difficult to identify because they are even less visible than norms.

5   Conclusion

Productive teams, where team members act in a collaborative manner to achieve project goals, are important for successful software projects. In such teams, team members often exhibit a strong sense of commitment to the team, and members are influenced by shared norms. The purpose of our study was to evaluate the presence of norms in four software teams. The results support the idea that some norms enable team performance, while others hinder. In order to encourage productive team member behaviors, we suggest that teams regularly reflect on both their injunctive norms (what is approved/disapproved behavior) and descriptive norms (what is commonly done). Our contribution can serve as an initial basis to guide and integrate research findings about norms in software teams.

Acknowledgments. We thank Yngve Lindsjørn and Øystein Ingebrigtsen for assisting with data collection. We also thank the participants for sharing their experiences with us. This work was supported by the Smiglo project, which is partly funded by the Research Council of Norway under the grant 235359/O30.

References

1. Forsyth, D.R.: Group Dynamics. Wadsworth, Cengage Learning, Belmont (2010)
2. Katzenbach, J., Smith, D.: The discipline of teams. Harvard Bus. Rev. **71**, 1–11 (1993)
3. Duhigg, C.: What Google Learned From Its Quest to Build the Perfect Team. http://goo.gl/6md7HQ
4. Pikkarainen, M., Haikara, J., Salo, O., Abrahamsson, P., Still, J.: The impact of agile practices on communication in software development. Empir. Softw. Eng. **13**, 303–337 (2008)
5. Moe, N.B., Dingsøyr, T., Dybå, T.: A teamwork model for understanding an agile team: a case study of a scrum project. Inf. Softw. Technol. **52**, 480–491 (2010)
6. Moe, N.B., Dingsøyr, T., Dybå, T.: Overcoming barriers to self-management in software teams. IEEE Softw. **26**, 20–26 (2009)
7. Lenberg, P., Feldt, R., Wallgren, L.G.R.: Behavioral software engineering: a definition and systematic literature review. J. Syst. Softw. **107**, 15–37 (2015)
8. Cialdini, R.B., Reno, R.R., Kallgren, C.A.: A focus theory of normative conduct: recycling the concept of norms to reduce littering in public places. J. Pers. Soc. Psychol. **58**, 1015–1026 (1990)

9. Barker, J.R.: Tightening the iron cage: concertive control in self-managing teams. Adm. Sci. Q. **38**, 408–437 (1993)
10. Terry, D.J., Hogg, M.A.: Group norms and the attitude-behavior relationship: a role for group identification. Pers. Soc. Psychol. Bull. **22**, 776–793 (1996)
11. Levine, J.M., Moreland, R.L.: Progress in small group research. Ann. Rev. Psychol. **41**, 585–634 (1990)
12. Hackman, J.R.: The design of work teams. In: Handbook of Organizational Behavior, pp. 315–342. Prentice-Hall, Englewood Cliffs (1987)
13. Cialdini, R.B., Trost, M.R.: Social influence: social norms, conformity and compliance. In: Handbook of Social Psychology, pp. 151–193. McGraw-Hill, New York (1998)
14. Teh, A., Baniassad, E., Van Rooy, D., Boughton, C.: Social psychology and software teams: establishing task-effective group norms. IEEE Softw. **29**, 53–58 (2012)
15. Nerur, S., Mahapatra, R., Mangalaraj, G.: Challenges of migrating to agile methodologies. Commun. ACM **48**, 72–78 (2005)
16. McHugh, O.: A study of clan control in agile software development teams. Ph.D. thesis, NUI Galway (2011)
17. Moe, N.B.: Key challenges of improving agile teamwork. In: Baumeister, H., Weber, B. (eds.) XP 2013. LNBIP, vol. 149, pp. 76–90. Springer, Heidelberg (2013). doi:10.1007/978-3-642-38314-4_6
18. Sharp, J.H., Ryan, S.D.: A preliminary conceptual model for exploring global agile teams. In: Abrahamsson, P., Baskerville, R., Conboy, K., Fitzgerald, B., Morgan, L., Wang, X. (eds.) XP 2008. LNBIP, vol. 9, pp. 147–160. Springer, Heidelberg (2008). doi:10.1007/978-3-540-68255-4_15
19. Dickinson, T.L., McIntyre, R.M.: A conceptual framework of teamwork measurement. In: Team Performance Assessment and Measurement: Theory, Methods, and Applications, pp. 19–43. Psychology Press, NJ (1997)
20. Stray, V., Sjøberg, D.I.K., Dybå, T.: The daily stand-up meeting: a grounded theory study. J. Syst. Softw. **114**, 101–124 (2016)
21. Aurum, A., Wohlin, C., Porter, A.: Aligning software project decisions: a case study. Intl. J. Softw. Eng. Knowl. Eng. **16**, 795–818 (2006)
22. Feldman, D.C.: The development and enforcement of group norms. Acad. Manage. Rev. **9**, 47–53 (1984)
23. Edmondson, A.C.: Psychological safety and learning behavior in work teams. Adm. Sci. Q. **44**, 350–383 (1999)
24. Benner, M.J., Tushman, M.L.: Exploitation, exploration, and process management: the productivity dilemma revisited. Acad. Manage. Rev. **28**, 238–256 (2003)
25. Kirsch, L.J., Ko, D.-G., Haney, M.H.: Investigating the antecedents of team-based clan control: adding social capital as a predictor. Organ. Sci. **21**, 469–489 (2010)
26. Hogan, S.J., Coote, L.V.: Organizational culture, innovation, and performance: a test of Schein's model. J. Bus. Res. **67**, 1609–1621 (2014)
27. Schein, E.H.: Coming to a new awareness of organizational culture. Sloan Manage. Review. **25**, 3–16 (1984)

Forces that Prevent Agile Adoption in the Automotive Domain

Philipp Hohl[1]([✉]), Jürgen Münch[2,3], Kurt Schneider[4], and Michael Stupperich[1]

[1] Daimler AG, Research and Development, Ulm, Germany
{philipp.hohl,michael.stupperich}@daimler.com
[2] Reutlingen University, Reutlingen, Germany
juergen.muench@reutlingen-university.de
[3] University of Helsinki, Helsinki, Finland
[4] Leibniz Universität Hannover, Hannover, Germany
kurt.schneider@inf.uni-hannover.de

Abstract.
Context: The current transformation of automotive development towards innovation, permanent learning and adapting to changes are directing various foci on the integration of agile methods. Although, there have been efforts to apply agile methods in the automotive domain for many years, a wide-spread adoption has not yet taken place.
Goal: This study aims to gain a better understanding of the forces that prevent the adoption of agile methods.
Method: Survey based on 16 semi-structured interviews from the automotive domain. The results are analyzed by means of thematic coding.
Results: Forces that prevent agile adoption are mainly of organizational, technical and social nature and address inertia, anxiety and context factors. Key challenges in agile adoption are related to transforming organizational structures and culture, achieving faster software release cycles without loss of quality, the importance of software reuse in combination with agile practices, appropriate quality assurance measures, and the collaboration with suppliers and other disciplines such as mechanics.
Conclusion: Significant challenges are imposed by specific characteristics of the automotive domain such as high quality requirements and many interfaces to surrounding rigid and inflexible processes. Several means are identified that promise to overcome these challenges.

Keywords: Software development · Agile methods · Automotive

1 Introduction

The automotive industry is confronted with high-frequent changes due to innovations and new technology. Today, it is a competitive advantage for car manufacturers to develop and distribute high-quality software at a high pace. A promising solution to keep pace with this progress are agile software development methods.

© Springer International Publishing AG 2016
P. Abrahamsson et al. (Eds.): PROFES 2016, LNCS 10027, pp. 468–476, 2016.
DOI: 10.1007/978-3-319-49094-6_32

High quantities with high cost pressure, test and validation under real-time conditions and a high amount of software variants are important characteristics for automotive software development. Safety-critical applications on the one hand and cost pressure on the used hardware on the other hand are encountered in the automotive domain. Furthermore, strict processes for car development have to be considered. Automotive functions must be verified by long term field tests and endurance tests that are enforced by law.

This survey investigates the specifics of agile adoption in the automotive domain. It presents an interview-based qualitative survey that aims to understand today's state of the practice of perceived forces on agile adoption. This work focuses on the agile software development for electronic control units (embedded software) in the automotive domain.

2   Related Work

Since a decade and more, agile software development methods show promising benefits in domains such as mobile or web development. In the beginning, it was not yet clear if agile software development would be applicable to the automotive field. In 2004, Manhart and Schneider [1] "tried to break the ice" for agile embedded development. They summarized existing experiences with agile methods, but emphasized that more knowledge of agile practices is needed. A survey by Kugler Maag CIE [2] in 2015, revealed a non-uniform adoption of agile development in the automotive domain with various and selective adopted agile methods and practices.

A leader in agile adoption is the Original Equipment Manufacturer (OEM) Volvo. Eliasson et al. [3] performed several case studies at Volvo to identify the limitation of agile development in the automotive domain. These studies focus on impacts with respect to software architecture and pointed out cooperation problems with subcontractors. In 2014, Eliasson et al. [4] identified the necessity to reveal possible showstoppers in the earlier phases of projects by means of faster feedback. In addition, they focus on requirements engineering combined with agile practices. Stelzmann et al. [5] analyzed success factors which help projects to become agile. Katumba et al. [6] conducted a case study to identify challenges in software development process related to frequent task switching, individualism, lack of complete knowledge and communication. With this in mind, our study aims at identifying hindering forces on the agile adoption and potential solution approaches.

3   Study Approach

3.1   Research Questions

RQ 1: What are the perceived forces that prevent agile adoption in automotive?

RQ 1.1: What are the habits and inertia that prevent agile adoption?

RQ 1.2: What are the anxiety factors that prevent agile adoption?
RQ 1.3: Which context factors prevent agile adoption?

RQ 2: What are the perceived means to adopt agile in automotive?

3.2   Research Design

The study is based on a qualitative survey. It is designed as an exploratory semi-structured interview. The method provides insights into the examined topic and gives essential information to understand the phenomenon in its real context [7,8]. For a semi-structured interview an interview guide was implemented [9]. The interview guide was structured along a funnel model [8]. Each section begins with open, exploratory ground mapping questions [10]. These questions reveal all topics of interests [11]. In addition, dimension mapping questions are used to focus on interesting topics [11]. The interview guide was tested in a pilot interview and adjusted to the problems which have arisen.

3.3   Data Collection and Analysis

Research Sites and Participants. The interview participants were selected from employees of an OEM and an automotive consultant. The interviewee selection was based on two criteria: First, the interviewee should have a work experience of several years. The length of employment varied from 3 to 20 years, with an average working experience of 16 years. Second, the interviewee should already use agile practices for software development. To get a different point of view on the examined topic, the following participants were selected: Two managers, five process owners, two system architects, six software developers and one automotive consultant for agile development processes. The interviews were conducted by the primary researcher at the interviewees departments from May to June 2016.

Interviews. There were 14 face-to-face interviews as well as a group interview with two participants. Every interview took around one hour. The interview questions were initially defined in English and translated to the native language of the interviewees. In consent with the interviewee, the interview was recorded and transcribed verbatim for detailed analysis. All transcribed interviews notes were managed using the reference management program Citavi.

Analysis. According to the classification of Stol et al. [12], the coding concepts of Straussian Grounded Theory were used. We used the three coding phases of Straussian Grounded Theory: open coding, axial coding, and selective coding [12, 13]. The interpretive process of open coding generates categories and concepts by breaking down the data analytically. The concepts were grouped together and related to their subcategories in the axial coding. In the selective coding the central categories were defined.

Validity Considerations. Validity was threatened by the possibility of misunderstandings between interviewees and the researcher. To minimize this risk, the study goal was explained to the participants prior to the interview. Steps taken to improve the reliability of the interview guide included a review and a pilot test. To reduce researcher bias, the interviews were recorded and transcribed.

4 Results

4.1 Forces on Agile Adoption

We define six categories of forces on agile adoption (cf. Fig. 1). The categorization aims to better understand the different aspects of the transition process from traditional to agile development practices. We distinguish between "trigger", "push" and "pull" as forces that lead to agile adoption. In contrast, we define "inertia", "anxiety", and "context" as forces that prevent the agile adoption. The classification is inspired by the Customer Forces Diagram by Maurya[1] that itself is inspired by the Forces Diagram by Moesta and Spiek from the Jobs-to-be-done framework[2].

A trigger force initiates a change and pushes an individual or an organization towards agile adoption. A push force pushes an individual or an organization towards adopting agile practices based on issues or demands. A pull force come into effect when individuals or organizations are pulled towards agile adoption based on the attractiveness of a future situation.

Inertia forces, such as habits, keep people from trying out something new and hence prevents agile adoption. The anxiety forces are representing fears which could prevent the adoption of agile. Often, uncertainties surrounding new situations cause anxiety. The context forces result from constraints and obstacles in the environment (such as organizational structures or process barriers) and prevent agile adoption. In the following, the preventing forces found in the study are subsequently described and explained using the information from the interview transcripts and the interpretations from coding and analysis.

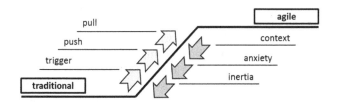

Fig. 1. Agile adoption forces diagram

---

[1] https://leanstack.com/science-of-how-customers-buy/.

[2] http://jobstobedone.org.

4.2   Perceived Forces that Prevent Agile Adoption

Inertia. Most of the interviewees mention that a major problem is the missing understanding of the applicability of agile methods within their context. Some interviewees emphasize that it is not clear for the management how to manage agile development and how to integrate it into their departments. Managers point out that a change of the mind-set is needed to adopt agile, but it is unclear how to achieve this. All interviewees mention that applying agile methods might require more communication effort. 50 % of the interviewees agree that communication effort is manageable in local, small teams but it is difficult to coordinate if the development is distributed.

Anxiety. The developers believe that it is necessary in agile development to give more responsibility to software developers; they mention that the management does not want to give up responsibilities. The managers emphasize that it is unclear how to provide correct estimations on development efforts when applying agile practices. They mention that it is difficult to prioritize features without correct estimations. In addition, the managers mention that they do not want to displease software developers by changing roles and responsibilities. In fact, they fear that annoyed developers might leave the department. The software developers emphasize their biggest fear that customer-relevant defects remain in the delivered software.

Context. Except of two, all interviewees mention that with the current structure of the company too many responsible persons are involved in negotiations about feature implementation. The interviewees state that this slows down the software development and prevents agile adoption. Most of the interviewees consider the high amount of process-dependencies for software development as an impediment for the transition towards agile development. One manager mentions the demand for more employees to maintain and manage the intersection between the agile department and the traditional organization. The processes on the higher system levels are seen as important. At the same time, however, they are considered to prevent and restrict agile development. The software developers emphasize the need to synchronize with fixed freeze dates and hardware-development what is seen as slowing down the process. In addition, one interviewee attributes the longer development time to the increased communication effort during the implementation. The interaction with the purchasing department and suppliers is highlighted by most interviewees as a challenging task. The communication with a supplier is identified to be a problem. Challenges with respect to communication are as well present in the context of globally distributed software development projects.

All interviewees mention the high effort to fulfill compliance and validation. Technical risks and challenges are mentioned by seven interviewees. It is important that the software is validated and of high quality. The developers mention that test and validation departments cannot increase speed due to the necessity of integration and validation in a real car. All interviewees refer to limited capacity in manpower and test systems when it comes to validation. Therefore, it is necessary to reuse software parts in order to reduce certification efforts. Other restrictions which are seen as important for adopting agile are long term field tests and endurance runs that are enforced by law, e.g. summer and winter tests. These tests must be kept at reasonable costs.

4.3   Perceived Means to Adopt Agile

How to Overcome the Inertia? Most of the participants mention that they already use incremental builds to shorten the release cycles. In addition, the interviewees stress that they have implemented approaches to build prototypes independent from the main development. Therefore they introduced auxiliary processes to provide an environment for faster internal releases.

The managers mention that more than 80 % of the software development for selected electronic control units is already transferred to in-house development. One developer emphasizes that in-house development is appropriate if the specification effort for a feature functionality exceeds the development effort. Another interviewee describes a situation in which in-house implementation is not possible. He stresses that the collaboration with the supplier should be a closer collaboration with more coordination and communication.

How to Overcome the Anxiety? The developers mention an increasing software quality at an early stage of the development is allaying their fear of late defects in the software. An increase in learning speed is considered as a mean to increase the odds for delivering high quality software. Other interviewees expect that prototyping might help to create a safe to fail environment that allows a fast feedback about a new function which is under development. In addtition, the risks of late defects can be reduced.

Several interviewees mention that software developers should be granted more responsibility. One manager referes to the one-room principle where different employees from different engineering domains like software, electronics and mechanics are sitting together in one office. He highlights the benefits from interdepartmental cooperation. A mind-set change and redistribution of responsibility is therefore necessary to keep a cooperative atmosphere.

How to Overcome Obstacles Imposed by the Context? All interviewees identified organizational structures in large organizations as a main reason of preventing the adoption of agile practices. They stress that it is almost impossible to change the organization. Three participants mention that although top management is fostering the change towards agile development, this is not the case on all management levels. They recommend reorganization with lower hierarchies.

One interviewee describes how his department embedded agile software development in small agile environments in the organization. He emphasizes that this approach is manageable on a small scale but needs more employees to maintain the intersection with the traditional organization. The interviewee mentions the need for new processes in order to manage the interaction between the traditional organization and the agile environment. Two participants mention that they recruited a consultant to adapt agile practices appropriately to the context of their department.

Several interviewees state that the benefits achieved so far by the use of product line management should not be neglected. Therefore, one participant emphasizes that the level of software reuse should be maintained and extended by the use of simulations that replace unavailable parts during development. Table 1 summarizes the challenges with associated possible solution approaches for the forces that prevent agile adoption.

Table 1. Challenges and Solution approaches

Forces	Challenge	Solution approach
Inertia	Missing understanding of the applicability of agile methods in a specific context	Organize context-specific agile training and coaching
	A change of the mind-set is needed to adopt agile practices	Collaborate with (external) experts
	More communication effort required	Word-of-mouth recommendations and feedback-culture
	Current development process is seen as satisfying	Explain benefits of agile adoption
	Limited acceptance for organizational restructuring	Slow and stepwise integration of agile methods
Anxiety	Management does not want to give up responsibilities	Redefine management role; Software developers should be granted more responsibility
	Unclear how to provide correct estimations on development efforts when applying agile practices	Shorten estimation interval
	Fear that customer-relevant defects remain in the delivered software	Provide a safe to fail environment and prototype development
Context	Rigid and inflexible surrounding processes	Define interface between agile and traditional processes
	Hierarchy in the organization	Transform hierarchies into networks
	Frequent synchronization with suppliers and QA	More in-house software development
	Globally distributed software development	Use of simulations that replace unavailable parts
	Keep benefits from software reuse	Reorganize product line development

5   Discussion and Conclusion

The study presented a state of the practice analysis on agile adoption in the automotive domain. In 2015, Kugler Maag CIE [2] revealed a selectively adoption of agile methods in the automotive domain. In addition, our study identified the forces on the agile adoption. Furthermore, our study associates the findings by Katumba [6] and Eliasson [3,4]. Key challenges in agile adoption are related to transforming organizational structures and culture, achieving faster software release cycles without loss of quality, the importance of software reuse in combination with agile practices, appropriate quality assurance measures and the collaboration with suppliers.

The survey reveals many avenues for further research. Potential directions could be to integrate agile practices into existing product lines in the automotive domain and to identify means for addressing the restrictions of a rather strict surrounding process.

References

1. Manhart, P., Schneider, K.: Breaking the ice for agile development of embedded software: an industry experience report. In: Proceedings of the 26th International Conference on Software Engineering, pp. 378–386, 23–28 May 2004
2. Weber, S.: Agile in Automotive – State of Practice (2015). www.kuglermaag.com/agile2015. Accessed 1 Dec. 2015
3. Eliasson, U., Heldal, R., Pelliccione, P., Lantz, J.: Architecting in the automotive domain: descriptive vs prescriptive architecture. In: Bass, L., Lago, P., Kruchten, P. (eds.) 12th Working IEEE/IFIP Conference on Software Architecture, WICSA, pp. 115–118. IEEE, Piscataway (2015)
4. Eliasson, U., Heldal, R., Lantz, J., Berger, C.: Agile model-driven engineering in mechatronic systems - an industrial case study. In: Dingel, J., Schulte, W., Ramos, I., Abrahão, S., Insfran, E. (eds.) MODELS 2014. LNCS, vol. 8767, pp. 433–449. Springer, Heidelberg (2014). doi:10.1007/978-3-319-11653-2_27
5. Stelzmann, E., Kreiner, C., Spork, G., Messnarz, R., Koenig, F.: Agility meets systems engineering: a catalogue of success factors from industry practice. In: Riel, A., O'Connor, R., Tichkiewitch, S., Messnarz, R. (eds.) EuroSPI 2010. CCIS, vol. 99, pp. 245–256. Springer, Heidelberg (2010). doi:10.1007/978-3-642-15666-3_22
6. Katumba, B., Knauss, E.: Agile development in automotive software development: challenges and opportunities. In: Jedlitschka, A., Kuvaja, P., Kuhrmann, M., Männistö, T., Münch, J., Raatikainen, M. (eds.) PROFES 2014. LNCS, vol. 8892, pp. 33–47. Springer, Heidelberg (2014). doi:10.1007/978-3-319-13835-0_3
7. Dresch, A., Lacerda, D.P., Antunes, J.A.V.: Design Science Research. Springer International Publishing, Cham (2015)
8. Runeson, P., Hst, M.: Guidelines for conducting and reporting case study research in software engineering. Empirical Softw. Eng. 14(2), 131–164 (2009)
9. Bryman, A.: Social Research Methods, 2nd edn. Univ. Press, Oxford (2004)
10. Easterbrook, S., Singer, J., Storey, M.-A., Damian, D.: Selecting empirical methods for software engineering research. In: Shull, F., Singer, J., Sjberg, D.I.K. (eds.) Guide to Advanced Empirical Software Engineering, pp. 285–311. Springer-Verlag, London Limited, London (2008)

11. Ritchie, J. (ed.): Qualitative Research Practice: A Guide for Social Science Students and Researchers. Sage, repr ed., Los Angeles (2011)
12. Stol, K.-J., Ralph, P., Fitzgerald, B.: Grounded theory in software engineering research. In: Dillon, L., Visser, W., Williams, L. (eds.) Proceedings of the 38th International Conference on Software Engineering, pp. 120–131 (2016)
13. Corbin, J., Strauss, A.: Grounded theory research: procedures, canons and evaluative criteria. Qual. Sociol. **13**, 3–21 (1990)

Exploring IoT User Dimensions

A Multi-case Study on User Interactions in 'Internet of Things' Systems

Helena H. Olsson[1(✉)], Jan Bosch[2], and Brian Katumba[1]

[1] Department of Computer Science, Malmö University, Nordenskiöldsgatan 1,
205 06 Malmö, Sweden
{helena.holmstrom.olsson,brian.katumba}@mah.se
[2] Department of Computer Science and Engineering, Chalmers University of Technology,
Hörselgången 11, 412 96 Göteborg, Sweden
jan.bosch@chalmers.se

Abstract. 'Internet of Things' (IoT) systems are fundamentally changing the way in which users interact and perceive technology. In this paper, we focus on two of the numerous dimensions of IoT systems with which the users interact; (1) the IoT user interface and (2) the IoT ecosystem. Based on literature, we develop a model that identifies how data is presented to users and how users interact with the system, and the level at which systems interconnect with, and collects data from, multiple systems. Companies can use the model to assess their systems in order to identify the *current state* of their systems and to identify the *desired state*. Moreover, the model can be used to better understand the steps necessary for *transforming* from one dimension to another in order to develop more advanced IoT systems.

Keywords: Internet of Things · User interface · Ecosystem · User value

1 Introduction

In the 'Hype Cycle for Emerging Technologies', the 'Internet of Things' (IoT) is presented as the new digital business paradigm that will offer fundamentally new ways for service- and value creation [1–3]. With technologies allowing interconnectivity of objects, unobtrusive user interfaces and embedded intelligence, IoT applications will rapidly permeate our everyday lives by transforming the way we interact with information technology and our surrounding environment. Already now, we see examples of how IoT technologies change everyday life. As one example, 'smart cities' is rapidly transforming city planning, construction and infrastructure [4]. Another area that is dramatically changing due to IoT technologies is the area of 'smart homes' [5]. Finally, and as an area that is receiving increasing interest is the area of wellbeing, where IoT applications help people monitor their own health and fitness by collecting data on e.g. number of steps, calories, heart rate and pulse etc. [6].

© Springer International Publishing AG 2016
P. Abrahamsson et al. (Eds.): PROFES 2016, LNCS 10027, pp. 477–484, 2016.
DOI: 10.1007/978-3-319-49094-6_33

IoT systems involve numerous interesting dimensions that challenge existing views on how users interact with these. In this paper, we focus on two of the many dimensions that make IoT systems interesting from a user perspective: (1) the *IoT user interface* and (2) the *IoT ecosystem*. We develop a model in which we define these two dimensions and we explore how they influence user interaction and user value of IoT systems. We evaluate the two dimensions in the model in five case companies, and we outline the typical evolution path that companies take when transitioning towards developing more advanced IoT systems.

2   Background: 'Internet of Things' (IoT)

IoT is the interconnection of uniquely identifiable embedded computing devices within the existing Internet infrastructure [7–9]. The devices collect information through the use of embedded sensors, and data is transferred without human-to-human or human-to-computer interaction. Based on the data that is collected, IoT systems dynamically adjust to the environment and behaviors of which they are part, and allow for increasing opportunities for intelligent identification and monitoring of objects. IoT systems allow many new opportunities in how to present information to users and how to have users interact with the system [10, 11]. Today, users interact not only by touching, pointing and scanning, but also by audio, video and gestures [12], and as recognized in [13–15], the desktop metaphor with windows, icons and pointers is quickly being replaced with smartphone user interfaces and touch screen input. By definition, IoT systems are networks of interconnected objects [16]. The diversity of objects and devices offers endless opportunities for innovation of new products and services [17]. Jim Hunter [18] presents a pyramid in which he outlines the different needs of an IoT system. At the bottom level in the pyramid, basic capabilities such as e.g. connectivity, power, security and network are identified, and that must exist for any IoT system to be useful. At the very top of the pyramid, capabilities that are realized when multiple systems interconnect are identified. These capabilities allow IoT systems to learn about users, to share what they learn with other systems and to predict user behaviors [13, 19].

3   The UDIT Model: 'User Dimension In IoT'

Based on literature, and an explicit interest in the user interface and the ecosystem dimension of IoT systems, we develop the UDIT model: 'User Dimensions In IoT' (Fig. 1). The model focuses on two of the many dimensions of IoT systems: (1) the *IoT user interface* dimension and (2) the *IoT ecosystem* dimension. In our model, the 'IoT user interface' dimension pictures the different formats in which information is presented to users, and the ways in which users interact with the system. The 'IoT ecosystems' dimension pictures the ways in which the system interconnects with external systems. In Fig. 1, we present the model and the definitions of each dimension.

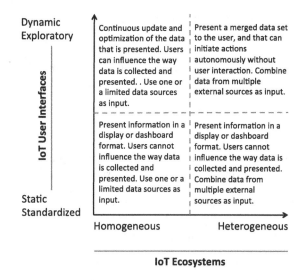

Fig. 1. The UDIT model: 'User Dimensions In IoT'.

4   Method

This paper reports on a five-months multi-case study (August – December 2015) in five companies developing IoT systems. In our study, we adopt an exploratory approach [20–23], in which we develop and evaluate two dimensions of IoT systems. We develop a model in which we picture two dimensions of IoT systems in a two-by-two matrix. A draft of the model was presented to the case companies at a cross-company workshop to get initial feedback on the two dimensions. To further evaluate the model, we met with representatives from the case companies to conduct interviews where we asked them to assess and map one selected system according to the two dimensions in the model. The interviews were exploratory in nature [24]. All interviews were carried out face-to-face and lasted for 1–1.5 h. A problem that has been identified in relation to qualitative research is that different individuals may interpret the same data differently [25]. This problem was addressed by using a 'venting' method, i.e. a process whereby interpretations are discussed with professional colleagues [26, 27]. The case companies are briefly outlined below:

Company A is a supplier of energy and energy related services. For the purpose of this study, we met with the project manager for business innovation with a main responsibility in the areas of smart homes and sustainable cities.

Company B develops mobile phones, tablets, smart wear and associated devices that enhance use and experience of information and communications technology for consumers and businesses. For the purpose of this study, we met with one of the senior research managers for technology research and advanced applications.

Company C offers a wide portfolio of IP-based products and solutions for security and video surveillance. For the purpose of this study, we met with two senior people from the core technology group.

Company D offers mesh network technology with a software package that enables mobile devices to form instant networks. For the purpose of this study, we met with two software developers.

Company E develops monitoring and alarm solutions for homes. For the purpose of this study, we met with three people from the research and development unit.

5   Results

In this section, we summarize our empirical findings by presenting (1) the *current state* of the systems in each company, and (2) the *desired state and transition* towards more advanced IoT systems as identified in each company. Finally, we present the mapping of the systems that was carried out by the interviewees.

Current state: Homogenous and static IoT systems

Company A. The application is a monitoring solution that helps users track and reduce energy consumption. It is used in private households, in larger apartment buildings and in large public buildings. The application uses two main sources of data i.e. an optical reader and a smart plug reader device sensor. Currently, data is collected from a limited number of internal sources, and it is not combined or merged with any external data source.

Company B. The application is an activity tracker application that presents information in the form of 'tiles' via a mobile phone app interface. The different tiles present information such as e.g. running and walking activities, surfing the web, watching a film, sleep patterns, heart rate, pulse etc. Currently, data is collected primarily from a few internal sources, and the company is actively looking into the opportunities to connect to external sources to add user value and experience.

Company C. The product is a surveillance camera that streams video data from surveillance systems at airports and grocery stores etc., and stores it for further analysis. Currently, data is collected from one source, and although functionality such as interconnectivity to other systems can be added, this is not yet done.

Company D. The technology provides connectivity when there are no master nodes and when network infrastructure is poor. Connection of devices is realized by broadcasting and peer-to-peer connection in a mesh network. In providing instant connection to other devices, the system has the opportunity to use data from several external sources.

Company E. The system is a home security and surveillance system that allows the user to keep in contact with the home wherever you are. Through a mobile app, users can switch off the coffee machine, get information about who is at home, switch on the home alarm system, control locks, lights and electronic devices and household appliances. Currently, users cannot influence the mode of presentation and the system does not integrate with external systems.

Desired state: Heterogeneous and dynamic IoT systems

Company A. The primary goal is to have the system connect with other data sources such as e.g. data collected in other households, weather forecast data, and social media. This would increase the opportunities for correlation of data as well as community building among users. Also, the company aims at developing functionality that provides the users with proactive recommendations, and that allow comparisons to other households to stimulate competition among households. The intention is to have an increasingly autonomous system that learns from previous experience and from other systems and that, based on these insights, acts proactive to improve user behaviors.

Company B. The company aims at providing a more dynamic system in which the different tiles base their information on several data sources, and where the presentation of data is continuously updated without any delays. In being a consumer product, the user experience is a key factor. Therefore, the interviewee identifies the ability for users to customize the information, as well as the appearance of the tiles, as critical to increase user value and maintain user experience over time.

Company C. In similar with company A and B, company C views the transition towards a more heterogeneous system as the first and most important step in advancing IoT systems. As an example, a camera in a grocery store could monitor people, but also availability of products, what groceries that need to be refilled and with a connection to the sales system it could issue orderings etc. As such, the system would increase efficiency and productivity and they would help automate manual tasks.

Company D. The company aims at having the technology they provide become a standard for mobile communication so that future mobile devices have the technology as a standard option to connect to the Internet. Also, there is great potential in building applications on top of the network in order to allow dynamic interaction among multiple users, and with an interface that responds dynamically to any change in the network.

Company E. The company aims at having the system connected with other systems in order to provide an integrated user experience. This would allow the company to collect data from several sources, and to combine this data to enhance functionality and increase the value. The company believes that a lot of additional functionality, such as e.g. audio and video, could be added to the product to increase user value.

Mapping of IoT systems: The UDIT model

As part of the interview study, we asked the interviewees to map the system they had selected according to the dimensions in the UDIT model. In Fig. 2 below, we present this mapping. As can be seen, the majority of the systems are placed within the lower left quadrant implying that the user interface dimension is static/standardized, i.e. the systems present information in a 'display' or 'dashboard' format, and that users cannot influence the way data is presented. Also, this quadrant implies that the systems use one or a very limited number of data sources as input.

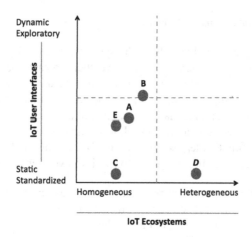

Fig. 2. Mapping of case study IoT systems.

6   Discussion

Based on our interviews, we see that the companies identify the transition towards heterogeneous ecosystems as critical. The main reason for this is the access to multiple data sources that, if connected, could leverage new user value and innovative business opportunities. This will be critical to maintain user interest and value over time. Also, a heterogeneous ecosystem that connects with, and collects data from, multiple sources would allow increasing system automation. Going a step further, heterogeneous ecosystems allow for embedded analytics, logic and distributed intelligence to be shared [18]. In our case companies, the opportunity to have interconnected systems that learn from each other, and that adjust based on input from each other, is seen as the next step towards autonomous systems. With systems that learn from each other, and adjust accordingly, many of today's manual tasks and decisions can be reduced, and based on our research this is equally important regardless of domain.

With regard to the user interface dimension, our study reveals interesting findings in that companies strive for increasingly dynamic user interfaces, while they view exploratory interfaces as less important. Although they all agree on that exploratory interfaces are important for improving user experience, they emphasize that with increasingly intelligent systems user interaction will, and should, be reduced over time [28]. In contrast to the prevailing belief that more options, more interaction and more customization opportunities drive user value, the companies we studied foresee successful IoT systems as systems that over time require less human intervention.

Although the companies we studied target different domains, we identify a number of similarities in relation to what drives the transition towards more advanced IoT systems. All companies view the transition towards heterogeneous ecosystems as driven by the increasing desire for system automation and autonomy. In our study, this is reflected in companies striving for interconnected systems and multi-source data collection as the basis for automation of actions and system-initiated decision-making.

The transition towards dynamic interfaces is driven by the desire to have systems that continuously update and optimize information in order to present accurate recommendations based on real-time data.

7 Conclusion

In this paper, we explore the user interface and the ecosystem dimension of IoT systems. We develop a model that captures these dimensions and we evaluate the model in five case companies. Based on our findings, we conclude that *(1)* companies transition towards heterogeneous ecosystems to increase system automation and autonomy, *(2)* companies transition towards dynamic user interfaces to improve system accuracy and optimization, and *(3)* companies foresee future IoT systems as increasingly autonomous systems for which the desire for user interaction will decrease over time.

References

1. Fenn, J., Raskino, M.: Mastering the Hype Cycle: How to Choose the Right Innovation at the Right Time. Harvard Business Press, Boston (2008)
2. Gartner's 2015 Hype Cycle for Emerging Technologies Identifies the Computing Innovations That Organizations Should Monitor. http://www.gartner.com/newsroom/id/3114217
3. Heather Levy: What's New in Gartner's Hype Cycle for Emerging Technologies (2015). http://www.gartner.com/smarterwithgartner/whats-new-in-gartners-hype-cycle-for-emerging-technologies-2015/
4. Yonezawa, T., Galache, J.A., Gurgen, L., Matranga, I., Maeomichi, H., Shibuya, T.: A citizen-centric approach towards global-scale smart city platform. In: 2015 International Conference on Recent Advances in Internet of Things (RIoT), pp. 1–6 (2015)
5. De Silva, L.C., Morikawa, C., Petra, I.M.: State of the art of smart homes. Eng. Appl. Artif. Intell. **25**, 1313–1321 (2012)
6. Kovatcheva, E., Nikolov, R., Madjarova, M., Chikalanov, A.: Internet of Things for wellbeing – pilot case of a smart health cardio belt. In: Roa Romero, L.M. (ed.) XIII Mediterranean Conference on Medical and Biological Engineering and Computing 2013, pp. 1221–1224. Springer, Switzerland (2014)
7. Miorandi, D., Sicari, S., De Pellegrini, F., Chlamtac, I.: Internet of Things: vision, applications and research challenges. Ad Hoc Netw. **10**, 1497–1516 (2012)
8. Gubbi, J., Buyya, R., Marusic, S., Palaniswami, M.: Internet of Things (IoT): a vision, architectural elements, and future directions. Future Gener. Comput. Syst. **29**, 1645–1660 (2013)
9. Chen, G., Huang, J., Cheng, B., Chen, J.: A social network based approach for IoT device management and service composition. In: 2015 IEEE World Congress on Services (SERVICES), pp. 1–8 (2015)
10. VentureScanner: The State of Internet of Things in Six Visuals. https://medium.com/@VentureScanner/the-state-of-internet-of-things-in-six-visuals-a4b9cda3324c#.qu0y4pk2k
11. Kranz, M., Holleis, P., Schmidt, A.: Embedded interaction: interacting with the Internet of Things. IEEE Internet Comput. **14**, 46–53 (2010)

12. Rukzio, E., Leichtenstern, K., Callaghan, V., Holleis, P., Schmidt, A., Chin, J.: An experimental comparison of physical mobile interaction techniques: touching, pointing and scanning. In: Dourish, P., Friday, A. (eds.) UbiComp 2006. LNCS, vol. 4206, pp. 87–104. Springer, Heidelberg (2006). doi:10.1007/11853565_6
13. Rowland, C., Goodman, E., Charlier, M., Light, A., Lui, A.: Designing Connected Products: UX for the Consumer Internet of Things. O'Reilly Media, Inc., Sebastopol (2015)
14. Gärdenfors, D.: All or nothing? Interfaces for the Internet of Things — The Conference. https://medium.com/the-conference/all-or-nothing-interfaces-for-the-internet-of-things-15b 64bd04ae3#.k2iduusp3
15. Yau, S.S., Buduru, A.B.: Intelligent planning for developing mobile IoT applications using cloud systems. In: 2014 IEEE International Conference on Mobile Services (MS), pp. 55–62 (2014)
16. Evans, D.: The internet of things: how the next evolution of the internet is changing everything. CISCO White Pap. **1**, 14 (2011)
17. Leminen, S., Westerlund, M., Nyström, A.-G.: Living labs as open-innovation networks. Technol. Innov. Manag. Rev. **2** (2012)
18. Hunter, J.: The Hierarchy of IoT "Thing" Needs. http://social.techcrunch.com/2015/09/05/the-hierarchy-of-iot-thing-needs/
19. Liu, Y., Zhou, G.: Key technologies and applications of Internet of Things. In: 2012 Fifth International Conference on Intelligent Computation Technology and Automation (ICICTA), pp. 197–200 (2012)
20. Dubé, L., Paré, G.: Rigor in information systems positivist case research: current practices, trends, and recommendations. MIS Q. **27**, 597–636 (2003)
21. Yin, R.K.: Case Study Research: Design and Methods. Sage Publications, Los Angeles (2009)
22. Benbasat, I., Goldstein, D.K., Mead, M.: The case research strategy in studies of information systems. MIS Q. **11**, 369–386 (1987)
23. Eisenhardt, K.M.: Building theories from case study research. Acad. Manage. Rev. **14**, 532–550 (1989)
24. Kvale, S.: Doing Interviews. SAGE, Los Angeles (2008)
25. Runeson, P., Höst, M.: Guidelines for conducting and reporting case study research in software engineering. Empir. Softw. Eng. **14**, 131–164 (2008)
26. Kaplan, B., Duchon, D.: Combining qualitative and quantitative methods in information systems research: a case study. MIS Q., 571–586 (1988)
27. Goetz, J.P., LeCompte, M.D., et al.: Ethnography and qualitative design in educational research. Academic Press, Orlando (1984)
28. Sarkar, C., Nambi, S.N., Prasad, R.V., Rahim, A.: A scalable distributed architecture towards unifying IoT applications. In: 2014 IEEE World Forum on Internet of Things (WF-IoT), pp. 508–513. IEEE (2014)

Requirements and Quality

An Industrial Case Study on Measuring the Quality of the Requirements Scoping Process

Krzysztof Wnuk[1](✉), Markus Borg[2],
and Sardar Muhammad Sulaman[3]

[1] Software Engineering Research Lab, Department of Software Engineering,
Blekinge Institute of Technology, Karlskrona, Sweden
krzysztof.wnuk@bth.se
[2] SICS Swedish ICT AB, Lund, Sweden
markus.borg@sics.se
[3] Department of Computer Science, Lund University, Lund, Sweden
sardar@cs.lth.se

Abstract. Decision making and requirements scoping occupy central roles in helping to develop products that are demanded by the customers and ensuring company strategies are accurately realized in product scope. Many companies experience continuous and frequent scope changes and fluctuations but struggle to measure the phenomena and correlate the measurement to the quality of the requirements process. We present the results from an exploratory interview study among 22 participants working with requirements management processes at a large company that develops embedded systems for a global market. Our respondents shared their opinions about the current set of requirements management process metrics as well as what additional metrics they envisioned as useful. We present a set of metrics that describe the quality of the requirements scoping process. The findings provide practical insights that can be used as input when introducing new measurement programs for requirements management and decision making.

Keywords: Requirements engineering · Software metrics · Process improvement

1 Introduction

Requirements Management (RM) [4] iteratively integrates the requirements elicitation and analysis results into the project management and development flows. RM also supports managing requirements during the product lifecycle and between the products. Large, globally operating software companies need to manage large quantities of features and requirements that continuously arrive from ever-changing markets [10]. Measuring and optimizing requirements identification, prioritization, definition and implementation processes is, in a market-driven context [10], crucial for achieving and sustaining competitive product growth [5].

© Springer International Publishing AG 2016
P. Abrahamsson et al. (Eds.): PROFES 2016, LNCS 10027, pp. 487–494, 2016.
DOI: 10.1007/978-3-319-49094-6_34

The process of selecting a subset of requirements for implementation within a given project is called scoping. Many software-intensive companies increase the flexibility of decision making by allowing scope fluctuations. Our previous work highlighted that large companies experience frequent scope fluctuations and have limited support in scope management [14]. The resulting late changes increase the need for improved monitoring and management capabilities that can evaluate the adequacy of the selected requirements management process models. Despite that, most published work on requirements measurement focus on the attributes of requirements [2] rather than the requirements management process [1]. Some published process metrics include: (i) how much value a software team delivers in every iteration [3], (ii) the number of requirements awaiting analysis, prioritization or decision, and (iii) the lead time in each state for each user story [7].

In this paper, we present the results from an exploratory interview-based case study with 22 participants working with the requirements management process at a large company that develops embedded systems for a global market. During semi-structured interviews with mostly senior-level practitioners working with requirements gathering, prioritization, scope management, software resource planning and high-level management, we investigated the following two research questions:

RQ1: What are the current scope management process quality metrics used by the case company?

RQ2: What scope management process quality metrics would the practitioners like to implement in the future?

2 Case Company

The case company is a large (5,000 employees) organization active in the telecommunication domain, developing embedded systems for the global consumer market. As the inflow of new requirements is rapid, product management often needs to make unplanned scoping decisions [14]. The company utilizes the Software Product Lines concept [9] where different development projects contribute to an evolving common code base, also called a platform. The total number of features registered in the company's database exceeds 10,000 and is steadily growing as new products are added to the product line, each containing on average 60 to 80 new features and associate up to 20 system requirements per feature. Feature implementation is allocated to approximately 20 to 25 development teams (each team has from 40 to 80 developers).

Features are managed based on a state machine depicted in Fig. 1. When features are created, they are put into an administrative state called New Feature (NF). In the next step, features enter the process and are discussed at the M0 forum. This forum critically reviews if a proposed feature has a sponsor, sufficient business justification and is aligned with the current product and portfolio strategy. Many features are rejected at this stage mainly due to insufficient business justification or unclear definition. Next, a feature is promoted to the M1 state where it is prioritized against other features by scope owners using a one-dimensional prioritization based on business value. A feature could be returned to the M0 state for further refinement.

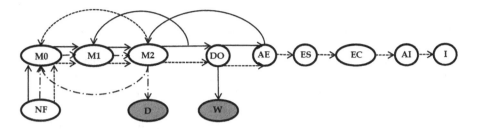

Fig. 1. The example history of three features. The first feature, marked with dashed lines was implemented. The second feature marked with solid arrows was withdrawn. The third feature marked with dashed-dotted arrows was discarded. Also available at [13].

At the next stage, called M2 in Fig. 1, the development resources are consulted and implementation schedules are discussed and agreed upon. Each feature comes to this forum with a target delivery date that is discussed and adjusted depending on the current software development organization load and other responsibilities. Prototypes are used at this stage to provide more accurate effort estimates and possible delivery times. A pipeline tool is used at the M2 stage to control the resources and to schedule delivery of several hundreds of implementation running in parallel. After the M2 state, the development organization takes the main responsibility for the features which are promoted to the: Definition Ongoing (DO), Awaiting Execution (AE), Execution Started (ES), Execution Completed (EC), Awaiting Integration (AI) and Integrated (I). Transitions between any two states are in theory allowed, including backward transitions. However, there is one optimal path without backward transitions through a state machine which is visualized with a dashed line in Fig. 1.

3   Research Methodology

To gain deep understanding and explore different requirements management metrics at the case company, a flexible case study design was chosen [11] with semi-structured interviews as the method for data collection.

We started phase 1 by iteratively developing an interview instrument in collaboration with four practitioners from the case company. Finally, two senior software engineering researchers and two practitioners reviewed the 17 questions and they were grouped into 6 topics: background, business goals, current metrics, desired metrics, visualization, and open innovation. The interview instrument can be accessed online [12]. Note that the results reported in this paper are exclusively related to questions under topics 3 and 4 as well as background questions under topic 1. The remaining topics are covered in a separate publication [15].

In the next step, we selected interview respondents by using a combination of maximum variance and convenience sampling [11] to cover as many views on the requirements management process as possible. Twenty-two respondents participated in the study. Their average experience in working with requirements processes was 6.5 years with the most experienced participant having almost 13 years of experience and the least experienced participant having about 3 years of experience [12].

Prior to the interviews, we sent the questions to the participants to help them understand the scope of the study and prepare for the discussions under the interviews. The first author then interviewed all participants individually, recorded and transcribed the interviews. The transcripts were sent to the interviewees to validate the content, and to enable clarifications where needed.

As the industry partner requested a quick summary of the findings, we concluded the first phase with five senior managers in a seminar. During this seminar, the first author presented preliminary results from an initial analysis of the data. The seminar delivered early tangible outcomes and the discussions at the seminar also acted as a validation, i.e. a sanity check that the direction of our work was promising, and motivated the deeper analysis in phase 2.

Phase 2 involves the four steps of the systematic data collection and analysis. First, the first author divided the transcripts into chunks of text containing a few connected sentences. The second author then repeated the process for 4 of the interviews (21 %), to validated that we had a reasonable level of granularity. The authors compared the chunk sizes, and agreed on simple rules resulting in the creation of a chunk for each relevant proposition (i.e. what is believed, doubted, etc.) expressed in the interviews. The first author then reiterated the remaining chunks to apply the rules.

In the second step, the first and second authors collaboratively analyzed 11 of the interviews (48 %) with the goal of developing a robust coding scheme. The first and second authors then independently coded the remaining 12 interviews (52 %). The authors calculated an inter-rater agreement using Cohen's Kappa [6] on the coding results. We achieved a Kappa score of 0.59, which we interpret as moderate agreement on the coding scheme.

In the third step of phase 2, we analyzed the coded data. The output from the coding step was synthesized by the first and second authors, and reviewed by the third author to provide further validation and observer triangulation. Finally, all authors prepared the manuscript for this research article.

Validity. We discuss validity issues based on the guidelines by Runeson et al. [11]. We attempted to mitigate the *interpretive validity* threats by asking interviewees to check the interview transcripts. Threats to *evaluative validity* are not applicable in this case due to exploratory nature of the study and a lack of evaluative purpose. Threats to *description validity* were addressed by recording the interview sessions and transcribing them. The transcripts were sent back to the interviewees for validation. Threats to *theoretical validity* have a minimal impact on this study due to its explorative nature and therefore a lack of theory, specific hypotheses, or conceptual frameworks to be validated. Moreover, we minimized the bias of unclear questions by iteratively developing the interview guidelines. The questions were formulated in a way to minimize the possibility of imposing a particular answer. We took precautions that the interviewer expressed neutrality when asking the questions and therefore the risks of reflexivity are minimized.

Due to an exploratory nature of this study, exploring to what extent our conceptualizations and conclusions derived from the interviews are correct remains to a certain degree unclear and calls for inspection by other researchers in the field as well as follow-up studies. Since the investigated problem originates from the case company, we can for sure claim that it is an authentic research problem.

We report that both *internal and external generalizability* are strongly limited in this case, mainly due to only one company involved. The paper's exclusive focus on an individual company narrows the applicability of the observations. Nevertheless, we attempted to gather as many perspectives as possible on the studied phenomenon by inviting participants with various roles and experiences from the case company.

4 Results

Table 1 summarizes the 26 scope management process quality metrics identified in the study. Among them, only five metrics are measured and 21 are needed or requested metrics. The five currently used metrics are: the number of backward transitions (Q1) and their reasons (Q2), the software design quality and if the process actually prioritizes the most important features from the portfolio planning (Q4) and customer perspectives (Q5).

The requested metrics include the impact of priorities on the lead-times (Q6 and Q7) as well as the impact of high priority features on low priority features (Q8). The accuracy of estimates and its impact on the efficiency of requirements analysis or definitions (Q9 and Q12) clearly indicate that focusing plainly on speed may not give the desired effects as quality of the work should not be compromised.

Several metrics also describe the features and their nature in terms of testability or complexity, e.g. Q10 and Q11. These metrics should be introduced during the requirements analysis phase and used as extensions to the widely accepted aspects, e.g. correctness, ambiguity or completeness. Q10 and Q11 further detail requirements on system test metrics suggested by Petersen and Wohlin [8].

Metrics Q14 and Q15 focus on how many times or why a feature was sent back in the process due to unclear information. This indicates that some stages of the process may either not do their work rigidly or receive appropriate input from earlier stages - thus delivering requirements of insufficient quality.

Similarly, our respondents would like to measure how many times a feature is moved between the releases (Q13) and why they were moved, which could indicate either: i) issues with accurate release planning or ii) several strategic changes after the release plan is agreed upon. Metric Q13 provides interesting input for the iterative release planning approaches that are based on continuous release re-planning and timely responses to a frequently changing market situation. The number of release changes could be correlated with how many times previously set delivery dates are altered (Q25).

Two requested metrics focus on the "waste" generated by analyzing unimplemented features (Q18 and Q19) while one metric (Q20) focuses on the effort saved on unimplemented features or software definitions in relation to the previous (waterfall) way of working. Two other requested metrics correlate the defined scope with the overall product strategy (Q24) or increased sales from successful products (Q23).

Table 1. Elicited metrics. Respondents are coded with Greek alphabet letters.

ID	Metric definition	Mentioned or need for/respondent
Q1	How many times a feature is sent backwards in the process	Measured, ZETA
Q2	Why features are sent backwards in the process from the M2 forum	Measured, RHO
Q3	The quality of the software design and the associated user interaction features	Measured, TAU
Q4	The overlap or potential discrepancies between the early product definitions from the portfolio planning and the product scope at the TG Commit	Measured, SIGMA, ETA
Q5	Priority levels of highly requested features by various stakeholders	Measured, KAPPA
Q6	The correlation between the priorities set and the time needed to implement the features or the time needed for definition or implementation	Need for, GAMMA, LAMBDA
Q7	The frequency of priority changes in relation to the dev. performance	Need for, PI
Q8	How new-coming highly-prioritized features impact low-priority features (e.g. low-prioritized get delayed)	Need for, RHO
Q9	The accuracy of the estimates in relation to the efficiency of the process	Need for, ZETA
Q10	The testability of the "vertical features" (features involving several technical areas) and their impact on various technical areas	Need for, THETA
Q11	The complexity of the features that are sent to the definition (cf. DO in Fig. 1) in terms of their impact on other organizations	Need for, THETA
Q12	The quality of feature definitions and estimates	Need for, KAPPA
Q13	How many times features are moved between the releases and why	Need for, BETA, ETA, KAPPA, MY
Q14	How many times (and why) the features are send back from the M1 to the M0 forum	Need for, ALFA and CHI
Q15	How many times (and why respondent CHI) features are send back from M2 to M1 forum (respondents JOTA and LAMBDA)	Need for, CHI, JOTA, LAMBDA
Q16	How many time a feature is resubmitted at the M0 forum due to unclear information or quality issues	Need for, LAMBDA
Q17	The reasons why features are send back from the M0 forum to redefinitions	Need for, RHO
Q18	How much "waste" the process is producing (analyzed but unimplemented features, e.g. how many features are withdrawn at each stage)	Need for, PHI, CHI
Q19	The "waste of the scope" after the features are promoted to the definition	Need for, KSI
Q20	The effort saved on unimplemented features or software definitions in relation to the previous (waterfall) way of working	Need for, PHI
Q21	The stability of the scope after the customer acceptance test	Need for, KAPPA, NY
Q22	How many changes to the OSS code each feature requires and when to share these changes with the open source community	Need for, PI
Q23	If the planned scope later implemented in the products is meeting the set sales and customer satisfaction business targets	Need for, ETA
Q24	To what degree the features that are created in the process reflect the overall strategy of the company	Need for, PI
Q25	How many times previously set delivery dates altered (caused by e.g. resource shortages or changed priorities)	Need for, ETA
Q26	The percentage of effort put on legacy work	Need for, CHI

Finally, the amount of changes in the open source code each feature requires (Q22) in combination with the percentage of effort put on legacy work while developing new features (Q26) can bring interesting insights regarding the selected sourcing strategy and also suggestions about the amount of open source code in the product.

5 Implications and Conclusions

Our study delivers several implications for research and practice. Firstly, the fact that we elicited 26 quality metrics is a clear indication that it is challenging to come up with an accurate set of metrics to capture the important aspects the requirements management process. Secondly, the fact that 21 identified (required) quality metrics were collected brings a possible interpretation that more focus should be directed towards complementing efficiency metrics with quality metrics. For example, quickly delivering features with minimal process waste is highly desired, as long as these features will provide value to the end customers and positively realize product strategies, see for example metrics Q23 and Q24.

Thirdly, requirements prioritization for agile development should go beyond popular one-dimensional priority or urgency lists and be correlated with measures that take the holistic perspective on prioritization (see e.g. metrics Q5, Q6 and Q8) and integrate it with product and portfolio planning.

Fourthly, measuring lead-times and delays on the interface between the requirements and development organizations appears to be equally important as measuring the requirements process lead-times. Additional significant factor is to measure backward transitions and understand why they happen (see metrics Q1, Q2, Q14, Q16 and Q17) or transitions between the releases (Q13). Fifthly, measuring the number of features in each state should be complemented with the derived measures of the ratios between the features in two states. This provides useful indications for rapid identification of process bottlenecks.

In future work, we plan to create a conceptual model of measuring and tracking potential waste in requirements management and decision making processes. Moreover, we plan to conduct additional case studies at other companies that record the information during their requirements management processes. Such empirical studies would help us in expanding our knowledge about the applicability of our model.

Acknowledgements. This work is supported by the IKNOWDM project from the Knowledge Foundation in Sweden (20150033).

References

1. Ambriola, V., Gervasi, V.: Process metrics for requirements analysis. In: Conradi, R. (ed.) EWSPT 2000. LNCS, vol. 1780, pp. 90–95. Springer, Heidelberg (2000). doi:10.1007/BFb0095017
2. Costello, R.J., Liu, D.-B.: Metrics for requirements engineering. J. Syst. Softw. **29**(1), 39–63 (1995)

3. Feyh, M., Petersen, K.: Lean software development measures and indicators - a systematic mapping study. In: Fitzgerald, B., Conboy, Kieran, Power, K., Valerdi, R., Morgan, L., Stol, K.-J. (eds.) LESS 2013. LNBIP, vol. 167, pp. 32–47. Springer, Heidelberg (2013). doi:10. 1007/978-3-642-44930-7_3

4. Hood, C., Wiedemann, S., Fichtinger, S., Pautz, U.: Requirements Management: The Interface Between Requirements Development and All Other Systems Engineering Processes. Springer, Heidelberg (2007)

5. Höst, M., Regnell, B., Natt och Dag, J., Nedstam, J., Nyberg, C.: Exploring bottlenecks in market-driven requirements management processes with discrete event simulation. J. Syst. Softw. **59**(3), 323–332 (2001)

6. Landis, J.R., Koch, G.G.: The measurement of observer agreement for categorical data. Biometrics **33**, 159–174 (1977)

7. Mujtaba, S., Feldt, R., Petersen, K.: Waste and lead time reduction in a software product customization process with value stream maps. In: 21st Australian Software Engineering Conference (ASWEC), pp. 139–148 (2010)

8. Petersen, K., Wohlin, C.: Measuring the flow in lean software development. Softw. Pract. Exp. **41**, 975–996 (2010)

9. Pohl, K., Böckle, G., van der Linden, F.J.: Software Product Line Engineering: Foundations, Principles and Techniques. Springer, New York (2005)

10. Regnell, B., Svensson, R.B., Wnuk, K.: Can we beat the complexity of very large-scale requirements engineering? In: Paech, B., Rolland, C. (eds.) REFSQ 2008. LNCS, vol. 5025, pp. 123–128. Springer, Heidelberg (2008). doi:10.1007/978-3-540-69062-7_11

11. Runeson, P., Höst, M., Rainer, A., Regnell, B.: Case Study Research in Software Engineering Guidelines and Examples. John Wiley & Sons, Hoboken (2012)

12. The interview instrument can be accessed at http://serg.cs.lth.se/fileadmin/serg/ InterviewQuestions.pdf

13. Wnuk, K., Gorschek, T., Callele, D., Karlsson, E.-A., Regnell, B., Ahlin, E.: Supporting scope tracking and visualization for very large-scale requirements engineering-utilizing FSC +, decision patterns, and atomic decision visualizations. IEEE Trans. Softw. Eng. **42**, 47–74 (2016)

14. Wnuk, K., Regnell, B., Karlsson, L.: What happened to our features? Visualization and understanding of scope change dynamics in a large-scale industrial setting. In: 17th IEEE International Requirements Engineering Conference, RE 2009, pp. 89–98 (2009)

15. Wnuk, K., Pfahl, D., Callele, D., Karlsson, E.A.: How can open source software development help requirements management gain the potential of open innovation: an exploratory study. In: ACM-IEEE International Symposium on Empirical Software Engineering and Measurement (ESEM), pp. 271–279 (2012)

Quality Rule Violations in SharePoint Applications: An Empirical Study in Industry

Apostolos Ampatzoglou[1(✉)], Paris Avgeriou[1], Thom Koenders[2], Pascal van Alphen[2], and Ioannis Stamelos[3]

[1] Department of Computer Science, University of Groningen, Groningen, Netherlands
apostolos.ampatzoglou@gmail.com, paris@cs.rug.nl
[2] SharePoint Department, Capgemini Netherlands, Utrecht, Netherlands
thomkoenders@gmail.com, pascal.van.alphen@capgemini.com
[3] Department of Computer Science, Aristotle University, Thessaloniki, Greece
stamelos@csd.auth.gr

Abstract. In this paper, we focus on source code quality assessment for Share-Point applications, which is a powerful framework for developing software by combining imperative and declarative programming. In particular, we present an industrial case study conducted in a software consulting/development company in Netherlands, which aimed at: identifying the most common SharePoint quality rule violations and their severity. The results indicate that the most frequent rule violations are identified in the JavaScript part of the applications, and that the most severe ones are related to correctness, security and deployment. The aforementioned results can be exploited by both researchers and practitioners, in terms of future research directions, and to inform the quality assurance process.

Keywords: Quality assessment · Defect prediction · Sharepoint

1   Introduction

Although some organizations have such unique business processes that urge for custom-made software solutions, in most cases, business processes are fairly typical; therefore, their needs can be accommodated using more standardized solutions (e.g., by reusing existing commercial-off-the-self—COTS software). This has led to a shift from developing custom-made solutions to standardized solutions that are based on modular development. A prominent way to develop such solutions is SharePoint, in which standardized COTS are combined to offer the required functionality. These standardized modules can be configured to target and facilitate the specific needs of diverse organizations. The configuration of such solutions can be performed by using a declarative programming language (e.g., XML). Furthermore, SharePoint can be extended with custom modules and code, so as to provide functionality that is not found in the offered COTS. This way, solutions can be created by combining standardized off-the-self components and organization-specific modules (developed using an imperative language—e.g., C#).

Similarly to conventional software development maintainability of SharePoint applications is of paramount importance, since maintenance of a software system is

© Springer International Publishing AG 2016
P. Abrahamsson et al. (Eds.): PROFES 2016, LNCS 10027, pp. 495–505, 2016.
DOI: 10.1007/978-3-319-49094-6_35

considered as the most effort-intensive part of the software development lifecycle [11], urging organizations to increase maintainability to reduce the overall maintenance expenditures [1]. In this paper we study a particular aspect of maintainability, namely source code quality. Source code quality has been assessed in many ways in the literature: through software metrics [2], number of defects [10], number of vulnerabilities [3], etc. Focusing on the number of vulnerabilities (also known as quality rule violations) has certain benefits: (a) they are more easily interpreted compared to metrics, since they are targeting specific lines of code and the way to resolve them is simple; and (b) they can be handled at a pre-deployment phase (in contrast to defects), thus they do not reach the attention of the customer/end-user. A common practice for identifying such rule violations is code reviews [6], which can be performed manually (*code inspection*), or with tool-support (*tool-assisted code review*). The latter enables not only distributed reviewing, but also improves both the quality and the quantity of reviews [7].

The goal of this paper is to investigate the source code quality of SharePoint applications, through tool-assisted code reviews. Specifically, we aim at investigating which rules: (a) are more frequently violated; and (b) are the most severe ones depending on certain characteristics. The identification of the most frequently violated rules can provide insights into what are the most common "programming mistakes". Among those, special attention should be given to the rules that are most severe, as well as those that are more probable to lead to defects, as the number of defects is crucial for the success of a software system. To achieve this goal, we performed am industrial case study, based on the guidelines provided by Runeson et al. [9] (more details in Sect. 3).

2   Related Work

In this section we present research efforts that can be characterized as related work to our study. We note that, to the best of our knowledge, there are no available studies in SharePoint quality assessment. Therefore, we present related work that uses rule violations as a means for quality assessment. Quality rule violations have been extensively investigated as indicators of quality in the software engineering literature. For example, Misra and Bhavsar [8] have explored rule violations as indicators for correctness, and Zaman et al. [12] have explored them as indicators for security and performance. When using rule violations to quantify quality, it is a common practice to classify them into categories. Zaman et al. [12] classified rule violations according to their effect on specific QAs (e.g., security and performance). Therefore, to evaluate software projects with respect to their quality, one can perform static analysis by collecting the number of violated rules. One of the most established tools that is used for this purpose is FindBugs. FindBugs is capable of detecting vulnerabilities in software by using bug patterns [4], divided into five categories (in total 246 bug patterns) that can be mapped to: correctness, performance, and security. In this study, since FindBugs is not applicable for SharePoint applications, we used SPCAF (see Data Collection and Analysis in Sect. 3). Other tools that perform such analysis are PMD and CPPcheck.

3 Case Study Design

Objectives and Research Questions: The goal of the study is described using the Goal-Question-Metric (GQM) approach, as follows: *"analyze* quality rule violations for SharePoint applications *for the purpose* of evaluation, *with respect to* their (a) frequency of occurrence, and (b) severity according to certain characteristics, *from the viewpoint of* software engineers, *in the context of* SharePoint application development". Based to the aforementioned goal, we derived two research questions that guide the design and reporting of the case study.

RQ₁: What are the most frequently violated rules in SharePoint applications?

This research question aims at identifying the rules that are most frequently violated in real-world SharePoint applications. Existing tools for SharePoint quality assurance are capable of assessing approximately 400 predefined quality rules, so we will explore which ones are more frequent. In addition, we investigate the frequency of rules at different levels of criticality (e.g., warning, error, critical error, etc.)

RQ₂: What is the severity of SharePoint rule violations?

SharePoint quality rules can be classified based on several characteristics (e.g., some rules are related to correctness). Before specific defects can be detected, it is important to determine what kinds of rules are more severe, (difficult to identify or critical). Therefore, this research question is focused on the orientation of preventive maintenance activities (i.e., the ones that aim at identifying and correcting latent faults in the software product before they become effective faults [11]).

Case Selection: This study involves different cases for each research question. For RQ_1, as cases we used three projects developed at Capgemini. The three projects have been selected so as to belong to a different production stage (ranging from 'under development' to 'production-ready' versions). The projects are referenced as Project-A, Project-B, and Project-C for confidentiality reasons. Project-A was developed internally by Capgemini. At the time of the analysis, the project was still in its early stages of development. Project-B was developed by an external organization and Capgemini was managing the code-base. At the time of the analysis, this code-base was ready for use in a production environment according to the external organization that was responsible for the development. Finally, Project-C had been developed internally by Capgemini. At the time of the analysis, the code-base was being used in a production environment. Concerning RQ_2, we conducted a supervised survey with SharePoint experts, so as to investigate the relationship of quality rules and defects. The term supervised survey [5] refers to the process during which an interview takes place, but with a specific data collection instrument (questionnaire) with mostly closed questions that the responded would be able to complete without any guidance. Nevertheless, in supervised surveys the researcher is in the same place as the subjects to provide possible clarifications. The questionnaire has been given to 10 SharePoint experts of Capgemini Netherlands.

Data Collection and Analysis: The case study has been performed within *Capgemini*, which is an international corporation primarily focused on providing IT services, which is present in over 40 countries with more than 180,000 employees. At this point, concerning SharePoint solutions, the quality assurance process is in a research stage. Therefore, this project was of great interest to the company.

Used Tool—Code quality analysis for SharePoint is still in its infancy. An initial research on the state-of-practice on this topic, unveiled that there is only one tool that is in front of competition, namely SPCAF[1]. SharePoint Code Analysis Framework (SPCAF) is a commercial set of four tools, specialized for SharePoint applications, each one focused on different aspects of code quality in SharePoint. From these tools, since we are interested in identifying rule violations, we used only SPCop, which validates both the imperative and declarative code. The tool is offered with several predefined rule sets, each set consisting of a certain group of rules (e.g., the "All Rules" set includes all of the rules[2]). If a violation of one of the rules is encountered, the occurrence is added to the rule violations report. The rule violations are listed using the title of the rule that is violated and the location (file and line number), where the violation was discovered. For the purpose of our study, we used the predefined set of analysis rules (i.e., those that would be selected without any tool customization), to increase replicability of the study, and mitigate researcher bias (which would be raised if any selection was made by the authors). The rules that we used in our case study identify quality rule violations of the following categories: correctness (cor), supportability (sup), deployment (dep), security (sec), design (des), best practices (pra), memory (mem), naming (nam), localization (loc), and JavaScript (jsh).

Data Collection Instruments from Experts—The outcome of using certain constructs in SharePoint can be difficult to predict, because some aspects are hard to assess, unless they have been previously encountered. Therefore, we decided to collect knowledge from experts to fill in these uncertainties, and in addition to validate the information and conclusions. We elicit data from experts using one questionnaire, aiming at answering RQ_2. The *questionnaire* consisted of five questions, each inquiring about the severity of a certain SharePoint rule type, and an initial one aiming at understanding which part of SharePoint code is more defect prone.

[q1]   SharePoint projects are built using two types of code. The first type being the imperative code, which is the C# code. The second type being the declarative code, which is the XML code. Which of these types of code do you consider more prone to produce defects (*Imperative code, Declarative code*, or *Equal*)?

[q2]   The absence of referenced resources will most probably be followed by rule violations. A missing resource should be easily detectable. From this perspective, how severe do you consider this kind of rule violations ("*Not severe at all considering it is easily detectable*", "*Moderately severe, it may be easy to detect, but that does not make the rule less important*", or "*Highly severe, it is important such a rule violation is detected and solved as soon as possible*")?

[q3]   On the contrary, having too many resources might also result in rule violations. In some cases SharePoint deploys prohibited assemblies, e.g. "ssocli.dll", or

---

[1]   http://www.spcaf.com.

[2]   **Rules are available in** https://docs.spcaf.com/v6/SPCAF_PAGE_QUALITY.html.

includes the same assembly in different configuration files. How severe do you consider this (*the options are the same as q2*)?

[q4]   In the XML configuration files, a lot of required attributes have to be defined. Not filling in these required attributes might result in rule violations. How would you value assistance on this kind of violations ("*Very important, I consider these rules to be severe*", "*Moderately important, assistance would help me solve these rule violations faster*", or "*Do not need assistance, these rule violations are easy enough to solve on my own*")?

[q5]   A possible aspect of security related rule violations is that they may not be as detectable as other violations, since security-related rules do not have to cause crashes, but result in unwanted behavior that is more difficult to discover. These rule violations might pose a big threat. How do you value security related rule violations that produce this unwanted behavior ("*Highly severe, any assistance in this field would be highly helpful since these rule violations are hard to detect*", "*Moderately severe, this kind of rule violations are uncommon*", or "*Not severe, these kind of rule violations are no problem at all*")?

[q6]   The previous questions have covered the following kinds of rule violations: (a) Missing resources, (b) Having too many resources, (c) Missing attributes in XML, and (d) Security issues. Are there categories of rule violations that have not been covered by the previous questions? If so, what types of rules do you feel are not represented (*This is an open-ended question*)?

Data Analysis: The research questions have been answered by using descriptive statistics. In particular we have used frequency tables, and bar charts for all questions. For RQ_2, in case subjects provided some qualitative data, we tried to analyze and synthesize their answers using semantic analysis. Nevertheless, this process was very simple due to the low number of responses and the similarity of answers.

4   Results

In this section we present the results of our data analysis, organized by research question. Implications to researchers and practitioners are provided in the discussions section (see Sect. 5). Figure 1 presents the number of violations identified in each project. From the figure, we can observe that the three studied projects are different, providing broad and representative data. Additionally, regardless of the maturity of the code-base, the tool was able, in all three cases, to provide valuable data on how to improve the source code quality.

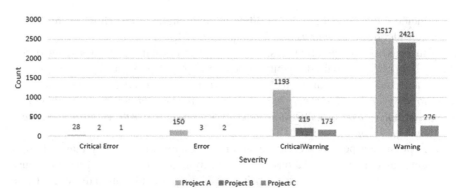

Fig. 1. Demographics on Rule Violations Criticality

Rule Violations Frequency: In Table 1, we present the most frequent rule violations in the three examined projects. In particular, in Table 1 we present the category, the criticality, the name, and the occurrence frequency of the most recurrent rule violations. We note that each rule has a single criticality, regardless of the context in which it is used.

Table 1. Most Frequent Rule Violations.

Category	Criticality	Name	Frequency
loc	W	Use resources for localizable attributes	1642
jsh	W	Use curly braces around blocks	745
jsh	W	Use correct === and ! ==	700
jsh	W	Declare variable before it is used	430
jsh	W	Avoid trailing whitespaces	379
jsh	W	Do not exceed max length of a line in code	324
sec	CW	Avoid usage of "RunWithElevatedPrivileges"	196
jsh	W	Remove unused variables	189
nam	W	Files / Folders should contain the name of the parent solution	146
sec	CW	Avoid setting "AllowUnsafe Updates" on SPWeb	142

From Table 1, two observations can be made: (a) *jsh* is the category, in which the most frequent rule violations can be identified, and (b) the top-10 most frequent rule violations are *Warnings or Critical Warnings*. The first column of the table shows that six out of the ten most recurring rule violations are found in the JavaScript (jsh) category. This means that *an important percentage of the identified rule violations is found in the JavaScript code*. However, this does not necessarily mean that violating these rules has a negative impact on the external behavior of the system, since some of these rules focus only on code conventions. Nevertheless, it still is interesting to take such an observation into account, when optimizing and improving code quality. Additionally, two out of the ten most frequent rule violations are critical warnings, while the remaining eight are warnings. Therefore, *there are no errors in the first positions of the rule violation frequency table*. By inspecting the complete list of rule violations (omitted from this manuscript due to space limitations), it becomes apparent that the first twenty-two rule violations are either critical warnings or warnings.

Table 2. Most Frequent Errors caused by Rule Violations

Category	Criticality	Name	Frequency
cor	E	Define attribute 'ID' in FieldRef in correct casing	50
dep	E	Do not deploy assembly multiple times	28
cor	E	Declare required attributes in schema of ListTemplate	27
dep	E	Do not deploy assembly with DEBUG mode	24
cor	CE	Define unique value for 'Id' in CustomAction	22
dep	E	Do not deploy TemplateFile multiple times	10
sup	CE	Do not access SharePoint API via reflection	6
sup	E	Do not read ConnectionString from SPContent-Database	6
cor	E	Declare required attribute in CustomAction	4
cor	E	Declare required attributes in SiteDefinition	4

By inspecting the top-10 most encountered errors (see Table 2), one can highlight the following:

- **The number of occurrences of the ten most occurring critical errors and errors is relatively low**, especially when compared to the amount of occurrences of the ten most frequently occurring rule violations. However, each of these errors has a higher potential to cause system crashes or unexpected behavior. Therefore, the information that is provided by these reports can be considered valuable, since they directly provide information on aspects that require immediate attention.
- The other aspect that is different between the ten most frequently occurring rule violations and the ten most recurring errors are the categories of the violations. The list of top-10 most frequently occurring rule violations was dominated by the Java-Script (front-end) category, whereas **the top-10 most recurring errors is identified in the SharePoint backbone categories** (i.e., correctness and deployment). A possible explanation for this is that rules of the JavaScript category rule violations cannot have a large negative influence on the system, but rather result in user interface

problems, while SharePoint backbone categories, can potentially have a huge impact on the ability of the system to function as intended.

Severity of Rule Violations: In this section we discuss the level of severity of rule violations, organized by the six questions included in our questionnaire. The first question was designed to determine what type of code, (i.e., imperative or declarative), *was considered most prone to result in defects* (related to Correctness). The results obtained based on experts opinion suggest that 10 % of the participants considers imperative code and declarative code equally prone to defects. The remaining 90 % chose the imperative or the declarative code options nearly the same amount of times, consisting an indecisive difference. Therefore, both types of code are considered equally prone to result in defects. In addition to the quantitative results, we have encountered some qualitative results as well: One developer stated that coding in C#, and XML was mostly used to facilitate communication between websites. A second developer pointed to code written with XSL, which is a form of declarative language, as the most defect prone parts of the code. The third comment stated that XML is more sensitive to syntax related mistakes, and that these small mistakes may have big consequences. However, these are supposed to be easier to fix, leaving choice on the multiple choice part to the imperative option. Finally, the fourth comment stated that XML is more error prone, but the impact on the systems' defects and performance is significantly less.

The second question was designed to *determine the severity of leaving out referenced resources*, the emphasis being on the influence, since this rule violation should be relatively easy to detect (related to Deployment). Only 20 % of the participants considered the potential to result in defects to be highly severe. On top of that, 60 % considered the potential to result in defects to be moderately severe. Overall, this means that a total of 80 % considered the potential for defects at least moderately severe. This is a good indication that this aspect of SharePoint has to be monitored when analyzing the code quality. The third question was designed to *determine the negative influence of adding too many assemblies*, i.e. prohibited assemblies or including the same assembly twice (related to Deployment). Out of the 80 % of the participants that chose one of the multiple choice answers, only 10 % considered the defect not severe. Therefore, it was concluded that this kind of rule violation in SharePoint will be considered moderately severe meaning this kind of rule violations will be monitored when analyzing the code quality. After initial research into the SPCAF tool, it soon became clear that it offered good detection and assistance on *missing required attributes in the XML configuration files*. The fourth question was designed to explore *the severity of this kind of defects*, to determine its impact on the number of times the system present unexpected behavior, and to ascertain the importance of this rule. 40 % of the participants considered the assistance very important, since they considered potential defects that can result from this rule violation. 30 % considered the assistance moderately important, mainly because it allowed them to solve the problematic code faster. Only 20 % of the participants stated that they did not find the assistance valuable. In conclusion, the severity of this type of rules will be regarded as highly severe since 70 % considered it at least moderately important and 40 % considered it as very important.

Even though Security related vulnerabilities might not have a huge impact on the behavior of the software, possible rule violations may have an even bigger impact on the system. Software carrying security related vulnerabilities may appear to function as intended, but would malfunction in the security area, e.g., it may provide entrance to users to parts that should not be accessible. The fifth question is designed to *determine how valuable the experts consider detection and assistance in the security area*. The results suggested that 70 % of the participants considered the potential of rule violations to result in defects, highly severe, and that assistance on this type of defects is highly appreciated. The remaining 30 % of the participants consider the rule violations moderately severe (since they are uncommon). Finally, the sixth question aimed to *provide the experts with the ability to name types of rules that were not discussed* in the first five questions. This way, the types of rules that were not yet represented, could still be brought forward. The additional types of vulnerabilities were: (a) Memory violations, e.g. disposing all sorts of instances or memory leaks; (b) Performance related violations, e.g. endless loops or other inefficient code; (c) Common coding mistakes, e.g. wrong syntax or improper use of variables; (d) Not using unique identification of components; and (e) Inconsistency of developed code. This new insight posed a valuable addition to the types of rules that were already considered in the code quality analysis.

5   Discussion

The results of this study can be considered as a starting point for code quality analysis in SharePoint applications, which is a rather understudied research field. The obtained results can be useful to both researchers and practitioners:

- (researchers) The relation of some SPCAF rules to defects remains uncertain. These rules require further investigation.
- (researchers) This research effort was exploratory since it was based on expert opinion and descriptive statistics. More explanatory research is required.
- (researchers) Evolution analysis with data analytics can be performed, to confirm the relationship between the existence of defects and specific rule violations.
- (practitioners) The majority (approx. 67 %) of the predefined rules offered by SPCAF is associated to defects. Therefore SPCAF can consist a good starting point for tool-assisted code reviews.
- (practitioners) Most rule violations are related to the client-side of the application, but these rules are not that sever. Correctness, deployment, and security rule violations should be prioritized.

6   Threats to Validity

In this section we present potential threats to validity for our study following the guidelines proposed by Runeson et al. [9]. According to Runeson et al., there are four types of threats to validity: construct, reliability, external and internal validity threats. In this study internal validity will not be considered, since causal relations are not in the scope of this study. Concerning *construct validity*, we have identified one possible threat, i.e., the fact that we assessed the quality of the code, based on the suggestions of a single tool. Although this threat is important, a discussion with practitioners suggested that 2 out of 3 rule violations, identified by the tool, are considered vital by practitioners. In addition to that, no other tools for SharePoint applications quality assurance exist, to the best of our knowledge. To mitigate threats to *reliability*, we presented in detail the case study design, and we have not parameterized the used tools, to ensure that our results are reproducible and comparable to future replications. Concerning *external validity*, we need to underline that the obtained results cannot be generalized to all SharePoint projects and that the use of a different tool for code reviews, might have led to different results. Nevertheless, the diversity of the examined projects ensures some heterogeneity in the cases.

7   Conclusions

This study aimed at exploring the quality assessment processes in SharePoint application development, through tool-assisted code reviews. The results of the study suggested that the majority of the rule violations can potentially lead to defects, and that they exist in all stages of software, regardless of their positioning in the software development life-cycle. As expected, the number of critical errors and errors are eliminated in production ready software. In addition, the most frequently occurring rule violations are warnings that exist in the JavaScript part of the applications, whereas the more severe errors (i.e., correctness, deployment, and security) are more probable to appear in the imperative parts of SharePoint applications.

References

1. Ampatzoglou, A., Ampatzoglou, A., Chatzigeorgiou, A., Avgeriou, P.: The financial aspect of managing technical debt: a systematic literature review. Inf. Softw. Technol. **64**(8), 52–73 (2015). Elsevier
2. Charalampidou, S., Ampatzoglou, A., Avgeriou, P.: Size and cohesion metrics as indicators of the long method bad smell: an empirical study. In: 11th International Conference on Predictive Models and Data Analytics in Software Engineering (PROMISE 2015). ACM, Beijing, October 2015
3. Feitosa, D., Ampatzoglou, A., Avgeriou, A., Nakagawa E.Y.: Investigating quality trade-offs in open source critical embedded systems. In: 11th International Conference on the Quality of Software Architectures (QoSA 2015). ACM, Canada, May 2015
4. Hovemeyer, D., Pugh, W.: Finding bugs is easy. ACM SIGPLAN Not. **39**(12), 92–106 (2004)
5. Kitchenham, B., Pfleeger, S.L.: Principles of survey research part 2: designing a survey. ACM Spec. Interest Group Softw. **27**(1), 18–20 (2002)
6. McConnell S.C.: Code Complete: A Practical Handbook of Software Construction. Microsoft Press, Redmond (2004)
7. Meyer, B.: Design and code reviews in the age of the internet. ACM Commun. **51**(9), 66–71 (2008)
8. Misra, S.C., Bhavsar, V.C.: Relationships between selected software measures and latent bug-density: guidelines for improving quality. In: Kumar, V., Gavrilova, Marina, L., Tan, C.J.K., L'Ecuyer, P. (eds.) ICCSA 2003. LNCS, vol. 2667, pp. 724–732. Springer, Heidelberg (2003). doi:10.1007/3-540-44839-X_76

9. Runeson, P., Höst, M., Rainer, A., Regnell, B.: Case Study Research in Software Engineering: Guidelines and Examples. John Wiley and Sons, Inc. (2012)
10. Vokac, M.: Defect frequency and design patterns: an empirical study of industrial code. IEEE Trans. Softw. Eng. **30**(12), 904–917 (2004)
11. Van Vliet, H.: Software Engineering: Principles and Practice. Wiley & Sons, New York (2008)
12. Zaman, S., Adams, B., Hassan, A.E.: Security versus performance bugs. In: 8th Working Conference on Mining Software Repositories (MSR 2011), pp. 93–102 (2011)

Quality Assurance of Requirements Artifacts in Practice: A Case Study and a Process Proposal

Henning Femmer[1(✉)], Benedikt Hauptmann[1], Sebastian Eder[1], and Dagmar Moser[2]

[1] Technische Universität München, Munich, Germany
{femmer,hauptmab,eders}@in.tum.de
[2] Munich Re, Munich, Germany
dmoser@munichre.com

Abstract. Requirements artifacts build the basis for various software engineering activities, such as development, testing or effort estimations. As such, the quality of requirements artifacts impacts the efficiency and effectiveness of these activities. Consequently, requirements artifacts should be subject to quality assurance (QA).

Unfortunately, QA of requirements artifacts struggles in practice. We contribute a first industrial case study, in which we found that the main problems in QA for requirements artifacts were a missing common *quality understanding*, the low *feedback speed*, low *efficiency* in the QA process, and, consequently, the lack of creating a *sustaining* QA processes.

Based on these results, we furthermore contribute a process for requirements artifact QA that is designed to address these problems. We discuss feasibility and impact of the process with industry, who acknowledge its potential to increase efficiency and to provide a more sustaining QA process in practice.

Keywords: Requirements Engineering · Artifacts · Quality Assurance

1   Introduction

Requirements artifacts (such as use cases) are central entities for software projects: Based on these artifacts, developers build the system, test managers set up a test-strategy, etc. Consequently, it is widely accepted that quality defects in requirements artifacts can cause expensive consequences in downstream software development activities [1]. We supported the evidence of negative consequences of requirements quality defects also through experiments, e.g. for the impact of passive voice on understanding in [2].

But how can we detect these quality defects to remove them before they propagate with the aforementioned negative consequences? As analytical quality assurance techniques, Fagan inspections [3] or perspective-based reading have

© Springer International Publishing AG 2016
P. Abrahamsson et al. (Eds.): PROFES 2016, LNCS 10027, pp. 506–516, 2016.
DOI: 10.1007/978-3-319-49094-6_36

shown a high effectiveness for detecting quality defects in various empirical studies (summarized in [4]). However, based on our experience in industry, we argue that, in practice such heavy-weight processes are (at most) only applied at the beginning of a project, if at all. After a while, projects neglect quality assurance (QA) more and more, until QA is performed just in an ad-hoc instead of continuous fashion, depending on the available resources in the projects. While requirements engineers in a recent study by Mendez and Wagner [5] name various quality defects, e.g. incomplete, hidden, inconsistent, or underspecified requirements, as well as their expensive consequences, the question remains: Which are the concrete issues that engineers face during requirements engineering artifact QA (in the following short: *requirements QA*)?

To understand these problems, we report on an first exploratory case study, in which we analyze the situation at Munich Re, one of the largest reinsurance companies world-wide, to understand the individual challenges of requirements engineers in practice. Based on the outcomes, we develop a process that aims at controlling these challenges to enable a sustaining QA process for RE artifacts.

Problem Statement: We lack knowledge on the challenges of real-world requirements QA processes, and efficient processes in requirements (artifact) QA.

Contributions: This paper contributes an analysis of the challenges of requirements QA processes in a case study and a proposal for a more efficient QA process for RE artifacts.

2   A Case Study on Requirements QA in Practice

To gain first insights into the state of the practice as well as the main problems that requirements engineers face, we performed an exploratory case study with three cases in the context of one company.

2.1   Research Questions

We concentrated on the following research questions:

RQ 1: How is quality understood?
RQ 2: What is the status quo of quality and QA of requirements artifacts?
RQ 3: What are the main problems for QA of requirements artifacts?

2.2   Case and Subject Description

To get practically relevant outcomes, we performed our study in the context of industrial software projects within Munich Re. Munich Re has about 45,000 employees in reinsurance and primary insurance worldwide. For their business, they develop and maintain a variety of individual software systems. The produced systems often involve many stakeholders across the globe, and software systems are often run by changing, distributed teams over a long period of time. Therefore, good requirements engineering (RE) and RE artifacts are very important to the company.

We performed three interviews with in total five requirements and system engineers of Munich Re. The engineers we interviewed are responsible for three different, globally running business information systems. Each of the systems is up to seven years old and under active development and maintenance. In the projects, requirements are typically documented in form of use case descriptions, business rules and change requests documented in Microsoft Word.

2.3 Data Collection and Analysis

To answer RQ 1 to RQ 3, we collected qualitative data through semi-structured interviews. Upfront, we created an interview guideline in which we discussed four aspects of the current project of the participants.

Each interview took about 60 min and covered different aspects of the project's requirements QA. After the interviews, we openly classified our notes. Afterwards, we summarized the results and compared the results across the different interviewees. To increase the validity of our interpretation, the results were presented and discussed in the company at various different levels, including requirements engineers from projects, RE methodologists and department heads.

2.4 Results of the Case Study

In the following, we report on the results, structured through the aspects *understanding of quality*, *status quo*, and *challenges*.

RQ 1: Understanding of Quality in RE

We first discussed with requirements engineers what they understood by *good* requirements artifacts. We asked them to describe what high or low quality in RE means for them.

We found that all projects strongly agreed on the importance of requirements artifact quality, such as the quality of use cases. When asked about what quality meant for the requirements engineers, they described quality in two different forms, as summarized in Table 1. While in the former understanding, engineers broke down quality into properties of artifacts, in the latter, engineers described it in terms of what the requirements engineer wants to use it for (activity-based quality; cf. also our work in [6]).

Interpretation: We observed that the criteria can be split up into properties of artifacts and properties of activities to be performed with the artifacts effectively and efficiently (quality-in-use). Nevertheless, these two views are strongly related: The rationale of most of the aspects of the former category is that certain activities of the latter can be executed. For example, the artifact should have no implicit knowledge, to enable an efficient understanding, and thereby to enable an efficient switch to new suppliers.

Table 1. Two views on quality

Quality as properties of artifacts:	Quality-in-use: Artifacts enable...
– Artifact is correct/valid	– Estimate the testing and development effort
– Artifact is clearly traced to tests	
– Artifact contains no implicit knowledge	– Implement a requested change
– Artifact is up to date	– Keep an overview of the system and its requirements
– Artifact has appropriate level of abstraction	
	– Find a certain information of the business process
– Artifact is well-structured	
– Artifact is using only un-ambiguous phrases and grammatical constructs (e.g. active instead of passive voice)	– Understand the system / compensate for team fluctuation
	– Switch the development team to a new supplier

Result: In summary, the requirements engineers were aware of or even advocating the importance of requirements artifact quality. There was no unique view on quality, instead it could be seen from both the properties of the artifacts, as well as quality-in-use perspective. Together, these views holistically form the understanding of quality in the projects.

RQ 2: Status Quo of Quality and Requirements QA

As a second research question, we analyzed the status quo of the cases regarding quality assurance in RE.

There was no systematic process for requirements QA in the cases we have seen. Two of the projects used to have a requirements QA process at the beginning of the project. However, after a while, the processes decayed.

As a consequence, two of the projects explained that they are aware that their requirements artifacts might not be up-to-date. They stated their dissatisfaction with this situation, and explained the reasons (see next section). The requirements engineer of the third project claimed that the project's requirements artifacts were of *"relatively high quality"* (*"up-to-date"*, *"well-maintained"*). She said she takes care of this aspect, since these artifacts are vital for her to keep an overview. However, also she did not have a systematic process for requirements quality in place; instead, requirements QA was performed ad-hoc.

Interpretation: In all three projects there was no systematic requirements QA in place. In some, there used to be a process, which was abandoned for the reasons that we will explain in RQ 3. Regarding the impact of the missing requirements QA, we had mixed responses.

Result: In summary, in these cases, requirements QA is done irregularly. The resulting quality was, by the engineer's own admissions, strongly varying.

RQ 3: Requirements QA Challenges

From the first results, we understood that the requirements engineers were willing to create good artifacts, they had a varying understanding of what *good artifacts* meant in their domain (see RQ 1). However, afterwards, we discovered that there were no systematic processes (anymore) to analytically ensure that the RE artifacts were of high quality (see RQ 2). The reason for this partially lays in the process in which the company aims to focus on high quality of the product instead of requirements and documentation. In addition, they explained various challenges that hinder systematic analytical requirements QA:

Problem 1: *QA is time consuming and expensive.* In practice, requirements QA mostly means manual reviews. These reviews are time-consuming activities since they require various coordinated actions by various stakeholders: review goal definitions, review participant selection, participant coordination, participant review execution, collection of results, discussion of results, and finally, a check whether all changes were executed correctly.

Problem 2: *Synchronous QA meetings are inefficient.* Synchronizing for QA, i.e. having a group of people coming together for a review, was considered inefficient. Scrolling through the text together, and discussing typos, ambiguity or other aspects in the group was perceived unnecessary, especially if the group is large.

Problem 3: *QA processes have long feedback loops.* The company's software development process is built around short iterations (usually two-weeks). One engineer said that a full-blown review, as they performed in the beginning of the project, would take too long to fit into one iteration[1].

Problem 4: *QA initiatives decay over time.* Maybe as a consequence of Problem 1–3, amplified by project pressure, after a while, the existing QA processes decay and things are done in a cowboy-fashion, as we also see in the answers to RQ 2.

Problem 5: *Quality of requirements artifacts decays over time.* Maybe also as a consequence of Problem 4, participants state that the quality of artifacts gets worse over time, especially in terms of being outdated. This makes the artifact less and less usable, since stakeholders, such as testers or developers cannot rely on it. This again will deteriorate the quality, starting a vicious circle.

---

[1] In a presentation after the study, another engineer reported that for a review it usually took multiple weeks until the original author received feedback. The person mentioned that after she received feedback, she herself, although being the original author, needed some time to understand the content again.

Problem 6: *QA processes lack support for the maintenance phase.* All analyzed cases were in maintenance phase, meaning, that applied changes not always introduce new use cases. Instead, sometimes just passages of existing use cases are changed. Since reviewing the whole use cases was considered unnecessary, no QA was performed instead. On the long run, this obviously leads to unreviewed changes and decay of quality (see also Problem 4).

Problem 7: *No support for introducing QA in the middle of a project.* Lastly, the question was raised whether it made sense to start improving all use cases now. Sometimes, the authors of the original artifacts have left the team. Therefore, a QA initiative now would probably reveal many different findings, overwhelm the inspectors, and leave the question where to start with cleaning up. This is again related to Problem 4 and 6.

Problem 8: *Quality definition varies.* In addition to the aforementioned, explicitly stated problems, RQ 1 shows another problem, unmentioned by the requirements engineers: The understanding of requirements engineers strongly varies from project to project.

Interpretation: We can group these problems into four categories: First, the main challenges lay in the time-consuming QA review activities. Manual reviewing is an expensive activity that does not immediately pay back. Second, engineers express their discontent with the long feedback cycles, which (a) constraints the development process and (b) creates additional effort, since authors must re-read the texts again. Third, probably since QA is not the primary responsibility of requirements engineers, many projects face difficulties sustaining the QA process. Fourth, quality definition varies. This is not necessarily a problem, since different projects may require different quality definitions. However, there should be systematization or control behind the varying quality definitions.

Many of these problems are linked to each other (e.g. one problem is the consequence of another). For example, as stated in the introduction, it is a common assumption in the processes community that decay of QA processes leads to quality decay. Many of these challenges are unavoidable facts. There is no free lunch and QA will always cost resources. Although most challenges are common-sense, listing them as constraints helps to improve the process by trying to limit the effect and hassle of each individual factor.

Result: The case revealed eight main problems, which can be summarized into *time-consuming QA*, *long feedback cycles*, *lack of sustaining the process*, and a *varying understanding of quality*.

2.5   Proposals for Sustaining Requirements QA

Based on the aforementioned problems, we developed a set of principles that target these problems and foster a sustaining QA process for requirements arti-

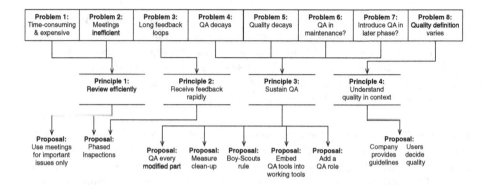

Fig. 1. Problems, principles and proposals

facts (see Fig. 1). Each principle is supported by one or more process proposals. The proposals transfer various concepts from QA of source code or project management to RE.

2.6   A Step-by-Step Process for Requirements QA

We suggest to combine the various principles and proposals into step-by-step QA process. We assume that the process is applied either in the beginning of a project or in the middle of a development process (see Problem 7). The process is applied continuously, for each change in the requirements. We furthermore assume the existence of tool support in terms of automatic feedback. For possibilities and limitations of such a tool, see e.g. AQUSA [7] or our own [8,9]. Lastly, we assume the existence of a QA system that supervises the process itself. Figure 2 illustrates the complete process.

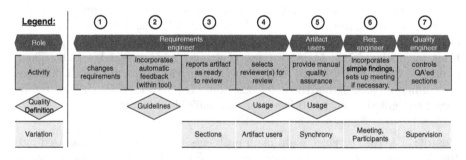

Fig. 2. A proposal for a quality assurance process with roles, activities, quality definitions and variation points, based on proposals of Fig. 1

3   Discussion in Practice

As a next step, we need to understand whether the proposed process is applicable and benefitial in practice. As a first step in this direction, we discussed the proposed process in terms of feasibility, impact, and effort with one of the leading requirements engineers of the company.

Feasibility: First, we wanted to find out whether the expert thought the approach was feasible in practice. The expert answered this question in the affirmative. She stated, however, that besides the QA process itself, an additional aspect is the *integration into concrete development processes* in the projects. Her company strongly advocates short iterations and often development and testing is performed in parallel to requirements engineering, hence, the question remains when to conduct the QA.

Benefits: Second, we iterated through the problems of RQ 3, as described in Sect. 2.4, and asked whether the expert thought these problems could be addressed by the process. She stated that in general, she saw the potential for this. However, it also much depends individual people and projects at hand, so further studies are necessary.

Required Effort: Third, we asked about the required effort for such a process in comparison to the status quo. She named various cost items, which she estimated to be relevant: In general, the most relevant cost item are still the *manual reviews*. She suggested that if the users of the artifacts execute the review (as proposed in the process), these efforts could be reduced. She argued that these users, e.g. the testers, have to read and work with the requirements anyways. Costs for manual reviews include furthermore *organizational costs* for synchronous reviews. In addition, writing *protocols for reviews* was considered costly, both for reporting findings from the reviewer to the requirements engineers, but also reporting changed sections from the requirements engineer to the reviewer after the review comments have been incorporated. All aspects strongly depend on the appropriate *tool support*. Consequently, the success of the proposed process depends to some extent how it is integrated in a QA tool. This result supports similar conclusions in the domain of code quality, as reported by other researchers [10,11].

Summary: Altogether, the effort depends on the concrete integration into the project, the participating individuals, and the tool support. In future work, when evaluating the process in practice, these factors should be analyzed in detail.

Threats to Validity. Regarding internal validity, recording and interpretation of the interview is subject to confirmation bias and similar subjectivity. Therefore, two researchers took notes independently and compared the notes afterwards.

In addition, we validated our results and conclusions through presentation in various meetings with the company. Furthermore, we distributed a first draft of this paper in the company. Participants acknowledged the validity of the results.

The external validity of the results contains two levels. Regarding the representativeness of results for the whole company, we performed data source triangulation through three cases. These interviews provided a coherent view on this matter. In addition, in discussions at the company, various senior engineers reported that, according to their own experience and perception, these results were representative for this company. Yet on a more general level, future work must analyze whether the same results hold for other companies and processes.

4   Related Work

Various authors have published in the related fields of QA for source code, as well as QA for requirements.

Our paper is related to the area of requirements engineering process improvement. A recent systematic mapping study by Mendez et al. found *"very few exploratory papers"* [12] in this area.

Various techniques in related work provide pieces for the puzzle. The probably best-known method in reviewing are Fagan inspections [13]. Other technique are perspective based reading (c.f. [4]), which includes, just as we do, the concept of the stakeholder viewpoint, as well as ad-hoc, checklist-based, scenario-based, pattern-based or defect-based reviews [14]. The last piece in the puzzle are phased inspections, as proposed by Knight and Myers [15]. In their paper, Knight and Myers discuss the combination of automatic and manual approaches and discuss the consequences. In this early work, they also discuss application in requirements engineering, but mainly focus on code.

However, these methods do not put the small pieces together. In our opinion, the work that most holistically combines different approaches was written by Katasonov and Sakkinen [14]. In conclusion, our process proposal extends this classification through various aspects. Based on the problems that we phased in QA in practice, we extend the framework of Katasonov and Sakkinen in Fig. 3.

Salger [16] provides an analysis of what he argues to be the five main challenges in reviews, based on related work. We detail his results through an empirical analysis from the perspective of industrial requirements engineers. The results overlap only partly. Nevertheless, the gap indicates that RE research must carefully coordinate research topics with practitioners to gain traction in industry.

Discussion: In contrast to previous works, we approach the topic holistically (suggesting a complete process instead of only parts) and inductively, i.e. through an exploratory, empirical investigation in a certain context and a derivation of a process from this context. We extend the work by Katasonov and Sakkinen [14] through additional variables in Fig. 3.

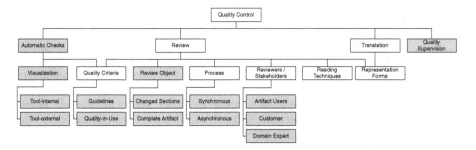

Fig. 3. Our process within the framework of Katasonov and Sakkinen [14]. We highlight added aspects in light-blue. (Color figure online)

5 Conclusion and Future Work

In the presented paper, we interviewed requirements engineers in a case study to gain first insights into the challenges of requirements QA in practice. The study shows that quality assurance is a time-consuming and difficult endeavor that can quickly decay. Based on the interviews, we argue that the key lies in the efficiency of the process. We suggest various tools, most prominently automatic guideline and quality checks, to increase efficiency. In summary, we consider our process a pragmatic QA process. This means that on the one hand the process provides strict guidelines. On the other hand, the process aims to avoid the inefficiency of heavy-weight processes by optimizing cost drivers. As a very first step towards evaluation, we discuss the process with an expert from industry, giving us a first indication that the process could be applied in practice and, to some extent, provide the required improvements.

There are some aspects that should be studied in future work. First, we reported on two different perspectives on requirements quality. Future work could analyze how they are related and intertwined. In addition, we executed the case study on three projects, but only in one context. Future work should extend this to different domains and compare the resulting challenges. We also proposed a process that seems fit in our context. We integrated this to an existing framework by Katasonov and Sakkinen, and compared our results to those by Salger. Future work could extend our approach and propose different solutions that are more fit in other domains. Lastly, future work is required in the form of experiments and longitudinal studies to evaluate whether the proposed process can indeed prevent the decay on the long run.

Acknowledgments. The authors thank Daniel Méndez Fernández, Dominik Holling, and Jakob Mund for their reviews on drafts of this paper. We furthermore want to thank the participants of Munich Re, for their support of the study. This work was performed within the project Q-Effekt; it was funded by the German Federal Ministry of Education and Research (BMBF) under grant no. 01IS15003 A-B. The authors assume responsibility for the content.

References

1. Broy, M.: Requirements engineering as a key to holistic software quality. In: ISCIS 2006 (2006)
2. Femmer, H., Kucera, J., Vetrò, A.: On the impact of passive voice requirements on domain modelling. In: ESEM (2014)
3. Fagan, M.E.: Design and code inspections to reduce errors in program development. In: Broy, M., Denert, E. (eds.) Pioneers and Their Contributions to Software Engineering, pp. 301–334. Springer, Heidelberg (2002). doi:10.1007/978-3-642-48354-7_13
4. Shull, F., Rus, I., Basili, V.: How perspective-based reading can improve requirements inspections. IEEE Comput. 33(7), 73–79 (2000)
5. Méndez Fernández, D., Wagner, S.: Naming the pain in requirements engineering: a design for a global family of surveys and first results from Germany. In: IST (2014)
6. Femmer, H., Mund, J., Méndez Fernández, D.: It's the activities, stupid! a new perspective on RE quality. In: RET (2015)
7. Lucassen, G., Dalpiaz, F., Brinkkemper, S., van der Werf, J.: Forging high-quality user stories: towards a discipline for agile requirements. In: RE Conference (2015)
8. Femmer, H., Méndez Fernández, D., Juergens, E., Klose, M., Zimmer, I., Zimmer, J.: Rapid requirements checks with requirements smells: two case studies. In: RCoSE (2014)
9. Femmer, H., Fernández, D.M., Wagner, S., Eder, S.: Rapid quality assurance with requirements smells. J. Syst. Softw. (2016)
10. Deissenboeck, F., Juergens, E., Hummel, B., Wagner, S., Mas y Parareda, B., Pizka, M.: Tool support for continuous quality control. IEEE Softw. 25(5), 60–67 (2008)
11. Steidl, D., Deissenboeck, F., Poehlmann, M., Heinke, R., Uhink-Mergenthaler, B.: Continuous software quality control in practice. In: ICSE (2014)
12. Méndez Fernández, D., Ognawala, S., Wagner, S., Daneva, M.: Where do we stand in requirements engineering improvement today? First results from a mapping study. In: ESEM (2014)
13. Fagan, M.: Design and code inspections to reduce errors in program development. IBM Syst. J. 15(3), 182–211 (1976)
14. Katasonov, A., Sakkinen, M.: Requirements quality control: a unifying framework. RE 11(1), 42–57 (2005)
15. Knight, J.C., Myers, E.A.: An improved inspection technique. Commun. ACM 36(11), 51–61 (1993)
16. Salger, F.: Requirements reviews revisited - residual challenges and open research questions. In: RE Conference (2013)

Commodity Eats Innovation for Breakfast: A Model for Differentiating Feature Realization

Aleksander Fabijan[1(✉)], Helena Holmström Olsson[1], and Jan Bosch[2]

[1] Faculty of Technology and Society, Malmö University, Nordenskiöldsgatan 1,
211 19 Malmö, Sweden
{Aleksander.Fabijan,Helena.Holmstrom.Olsson}@mah.se
[2] Department of Computer Science and Engineering,
Chalmers University of Technology, Hörselgången 11,
412 96 Göteborg, Sweden
Jan.Bosch@chalmers.se

Abstract. Once supporting the electrical and mechanical functionality, software today became the main competitive advantage in products. However, in the companies that we study, the way in which software features are developed still reflects the traditional 'requirements over the wall' approach. As a consequence, individual departments prioritize what they believe is the most important and are unable to identify which features are regularly used – 'flow', there to be bought – 'wow', differentiating and that add value to customers, or which are regarded commodity. In this paper, and based on case study research in three large software-intensive companies, we (1) provide empirical evidence that companies do not distinguish between different types of features, which causes poor allocation of R&D efforts and suppresses innovation, and (2) develop a model in which we depict the activities for differentiating and working with different types of features and stakeholders.

Keywords: Customer feedback · Innovation · Commodity · Wow feature · Flow feature · Duty feature · Checkbox feature

1 Introduction

The amount of software in products is rapidly increasing. At first, software functionality was predominately required in order to support tangible electrical, hardware and mechanical solutions without delivering any other perceptible value for the customers [1]. Today, software functionality is rapidly becoming the main competitive advantage of the product, and what delivers value to the customers [2]. However, the way in which software features are being developed, and how they are prioritized is still a challenge for most organizations. Often, and due to immaturity and lack of experience in software development, companies treat software features similarly to electronics or mechanics components, with the risk of being unable to identify what features are differentiating and that add value to customers, and what features are regarded commodity by customers. As a consequence individual departments continue to prioritize

© Springer International Publishing AG 2016
P. Abrahamsson et al. (Eds.): PROFES 2016, LNCS 10027, pp. 517–525, 2016.
DOI: 10.1007/978-3-319-49094-6_37

what they find the most important and miss the opportunities to minimize and share the investments into commodity features [3, 4].

In this paper, we identify that the lack of distinguishing between different types of features is the primary reason for inefficient resource allocation that, in the end, make innovation initiatives suffer.

The contribution of the paper is twofold. First, we give guidelines on how to distinguish between different types of features that are being developed and we provide empirical evidence on the challenges and implications involved in this. Second, we present a conceptual model to guide practitioners in prioritizing the development activities for each of the feature types. With this model, companies can develop only the amount of feature that is required for commoditized functionality and, on the other hand, maximize their investments in innovative features.

2 Background

In most companies, customer feedback is collected on a frequent basis in order to learn about how customers use products, what features they appreciate and what functionality they would like to see in new products [5–8]. The number of requests and ideas that originate from this feedback often outnumbers available engineering resources and prevents companies from realizing all of them [9]. To help practitioners control the information overload originating from customer feedback, Knauss et al. [10] propose a feedback-centric requirements approach, together with a tool that elicits the most important information. Recently, Johansson et al. [11] stressed the importance of complementing the qualitative customer feedback with quantitative input by showing its implications on the product managers prioritization decisions. Moreover, and in order to further develop only those requirements that will deliver the most business value, various prioritization techniques have been introduced in requirement engineering and product development literature [12–16]. However, these do not consider market factors such as the availability of the features being assessed in competitors' products [17]. Also, very little is known on how to prioritize the development activities for different types of features.

To recognize the importance of distinguishing between different types of functionality from a complexity point of view, Bosch [18] developed the 'Three Layer Product Model'. The model provides a high-level understanding of the three different layers of features, i.e. commodity, differentiating and innovative, however, does not give guidance on how to distinguish between the different types, neither which activities to invest into for each of them. The model distinguishes between three types of functionality layers, i.e. *commoditized functionality* (functionality necessary for system operation that customers take for granted), *differentiating functionality* (the functionality that differentiates the product from its competitors) and *Innovation functionality* (functionality providing significant value).

3 Research Method

This case study [19] research builds on an ongoing work with three case companies (see Table 1 below) involved in large-scale development of software products. It was conducted between August–December 2015.

3.1 Data Collection and Data Analysis

First, we conducted a workshop at each of the companies. Second, we conducted twenty-two interviews that lasted one hour. During analysis, the workshop notes,

Table 1. Description of the companies and the representatives.

Company and their domain	Representatives
Company A is a provider of telecommunication systems and equipment, communications networks and multimedia solutions for mobile and fixed network operators. The company has several sites and for the purpose of this study, we collaborated with representatives from one company site. The participants marked with an asterisk (*) attended the workshop and were not available for a follow up-interview	1 Product Owner 1 Product Manager 2 System Managers 2 Software Engineer 1 Release Manager 1 Area Prod. Mng.* 1 Lean Coach* 1 Section Mng.*
Company B is a software company specializing in navigational information, operations management and optimization solutions. All the participants attended the workshop and were interviewed	1 Product Owner 1 System Architect 1 UX Designer 1 Service Manager
Company C is a manufacturer and supplier of transport solutions, construction technology and vehicles for commercial use. All the participants that attended the workshop were interviewed. In addition, one sales manager and one technology specialist wished to join the project at a later stage, and were interviewed	1 Product Owner 2 Product Strategists 2 UX Managers 2 Function Owners 1 Feature Coord. 1 Sales Manager 2 Technology Spec.

interview transcriptions and graphical illustrations were used when coding the data. The data collected were analyzed following the conventional qualitative content analysis approach [20] where we derived the codes directly from the text data.

To improve the study's construct validity, we conducted semi-structured interviews at the workshops with representatives working in several different roles and companies. Since these companies represent the current state of large-scale software development of embedded systems industry, we believe that the results can be generalized to other large-scale software development companies.

4 Findings

4.1 Feature Realization: Current State of Feature Differentiation

Features that are being developed are handed over from one development stage to another, together with their requirements and priorities. The differentiation strategy is unclear to the practitioners developing the features (see e.g. Table 2).

Table 2. The current State of Feature Differentiation.

Current State	Description	Quote
Vague differentiating strategy	Practitioners struggle to know if the feature is innovative and requires e.g. direct investment, or commodity and can be covered from e.g. running maintenance budget	*"Should we go into Maintenance budget? Or should it go to investment budget and we prioritize there?"*, – Product Strategist from Company C
Dev. investment level does not vary	Based on the interview data, we do not see a significant difference in defining the investment level allocated to the feature	*"There is a lot of functionality that we probably would not need to focus on."* – Technology Specialist from Company C
Feature prioritization processes is in favor of commodity	Prioritizing innovative features is suppressed with numerous commodity efforts that are needed to satisfy the standards and follow the competitors instead of accurately understanding what adds value to the stakeholders	*"Customer could be more involved in prioritization that we do in pre-development. Is this feature more important that the other one?"* – Product Owner from Company B

4.2 Differentiating Features: Challenges and Implications

The current state advocates a situation where features are not differentiated in the strategy between being innovative, differentiating or commodity and, as a consequence, development activities do not differ between the features. Based on our interviews, we see that there are a number of challenges associated with this situation. We present the challenges in Table 3 below.

Due to an unclear differentiating strategy, our case companies experience a number of implications during the development process of a feature. We summarize them in Table 4 below.

Table 3. The challenges with differentiating features.

Challenge	Description	Quote
Understanding the stakeholder and purpose of the feature	The way in how feedback is being collected is rather ad-hoc and it depends on the stage of the feature and not on the	*"We want to understand what the customer wants to have and also truly, what do they need."* – Product Manager from Company A
Incomprehensible high-level directives	Identifying whether a feature is commodity, differentiating or innovative, and investing into activities needed for each type is left to the practitioners developing the feature	*"Functionality is software basically and the features are more subjective opinions and things that we can't really... it is hard to collect data."* – Function owner from Company C
Commodity functionality is internally considered to be innovative	Companies do not learn from customers fast enough and, occasionally, consider and invest in development activities for features they believe are innovative	*"Those are the things that worries us the most. All of us, since it is so hard, you need to gamble a bit. If it turns out that you are wrong, then you are behind."* – Product Manager from Company A

Table 4. The implications of feature realization.

Implication	Description	Quote
Uniform stakeholder impression	Individuals in our case companies typically find it difficult to identify and truly understand the stakeholder and their needs that the feature is being developed for	*"If you are sitting in a team...you see that this is the most important thing we need to do."* – Product Manager from Company A
Arbitrary investments in development activities	Companies risk to invest extensively in development activities that are not required for a certain type of feature	*"We tend to focus on,...on the wrong things. We need to look at the benefit for their customers."* – Product Manager from Company A
Commodity suppresses innovation	As a consequence, features that are expected to be innovative do not get to be prioritized. Instead, and in a rush to keep the pace, our case companies study close competitors and analyze their most promising features	*"In our organization is really hard to sew everything together, to make it work. That requires funding that is almost nonexistent."* – Software engineer from Company A
Projecting competitors current state is the norm	Companies base themselves on competition right now instead of where it will be in the future	*"We do also our own tests of competitors....We measure are we on track or not."* – Product Strategist from Company C

5   The Feature Differentiation Model

In response to the empirical data from our case companies, combined with the findings and the implications that we presented above, we expand the 3LPM model to a new dimension and present our model for feature differentiation in the following section. The contribution of our model is twofold. First, we provide four different categories of features and their characteristics in order to give practitioners an ability to better differentiate features early in the development cycle. Second, and as a guidance for practitioners after classifying a feature, we provide a summary of development activities for every type of feature. Practitioners can use the guidance in prioritizing the development activities for the features that they are developing. With this model, companies can develop only the amount of feature that is required for commoditized functionality and, on the other hand, free the resources to maximize their investments in innovative features that will deliver the most value.

5.1   Differentiating Characteristics of New Feature Development

Our model advocates an approach in which four fundamentally different types of features are being developed. We name them "duty", "wow", "checkbox" and "flow" types of features. With "duty", we label the type of features that are needed in the products due to a policy or regulation requirement. "Checkbox" features are the features that companies need to provide in order to be on par with the competition that provides similar functionality. With "wow", we label the differentiating features that are the deciding factor for buying a product. Finally, and with "flow", we label the features in the product that are regularly used. We depict the four types of features on Fig. 1, where we place each of the types in relation to the 3LPM commodity-differentiating-innovative categorization.

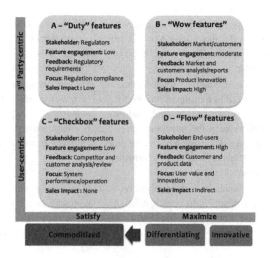

Fig. 1. The Feature Differentiation Model.

On the horizontal axis, we indicate the development extent for the features, ranging from "Satisfy" to "Maximize". On the vertical axis, however, we indicate the distinction between primarily "User-centric" and "3rd party-centric" features. By this, we divide between features that are primarily being developed for users of the product (hence "User-centric") and other, 3rd parties-centric features, which are not directly used by the users. And to help practitioners categorize a feature on these axis, we distinguish between five characteristic points; *the stakeholder* (e.g. the requestor of the feature), *feature engagement* (e.g. the expected level of feature usage), the source of the feedback (e.g. the stakeholder generating the most feedback), *the focus of the feature* (e.g. is the feature indenting to minimally satisfy a known need, or to innovate in a new area?) and its *impact on driving sales* (is it a feature focusing on the customer paying for the product?).

5.2   The Development Process

For each of the four feature types, we suggest how to set the extent of the feature that should be developed. Here, the extent of the feature can be either defined once (constant) or dynamically adjusted during development and operation (*floating* - alternates, *following* - follows the competitors *or open* - no limitation). Next, the sources that contain the information required to set the development extent need to be defined, together with the techniques that make it possible for the practitioners to collect relevant customer feedback. Next, we suggest the most important R&D activities. They are followed by the activities that do not deliver value for that type and should be avoided. Finally, we suggest how to set the deployment frequency. We summarize the most important differences between each approach in Fig. 2.

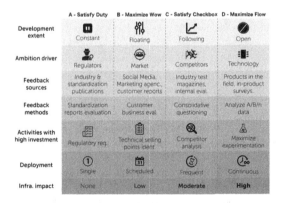

Fig. 2. The summary of the 4 different development approaches.

6 Discussion

Multi-disciplinary teams involved in the development of a software product are increasingly using customer feedback to develop and improve their products and features. Both qualitative techniques [5, 6, 8] and quantitative techniques [7, 8] are used to collect customer feedback and product data. Previous research shows that the number of requests and ideas that originate from this feedback often outnumbers available engineering resources [9]. And with increasing amount of ideas, prioritizing development resources and identifying which features to develop to what extent is a crucial step in new feature development process. Bosch [18] recognized the importance of dividing functionality between commodity, differentiating and innovative. However, and as shown in our empirical findings, companies still struggle with this and, consequently, invest into development activities that do not deliver value to the stakeholders. Innovative features are suppressed by commodity.

To address the concerns above, we develop the Feature Differentiation model, where we illustrate how development activities depend on the type of the feature being developed with respect to characteristics. The model helps companies to (1) differentiate between the four types of the features, and (2) prioritize the necessary development activities.

7 Conclusion

In this paper, and based on case study research in three large software-intensive companies, we (1) provide empirical evidence that companies do not distinguish between different types of features, i.e. they don't know what is innovation, differentiation or commodity, which is the main problem that causes poor allocation of R&D efforts and suppresses innovation. We (2) develop a model in which we depict the activities for differentiating and working with different types of features.

References

1. Boehm, B.: Value-based software engineering: reinventing. SIGSOFT Softw. Eng. Notes **28**, 3 (2003)
2. Khurum, M., Gorschek, T., Wilson, M.: The software value map- an exhaustive collection of value aspects for the development of software intensive products. J. Softw. Evol. Process. **25**, 711–741 (2013)
3. Lindgren, E., Münch, J.: Software development as an experiment system: a qualitative survey on the state of the practice. In: Lassenius, C., Dingsøyr, T., Paasivaara, M. (eds.) XP 2015. LNBIP, vol. 212, pp. 117–128. Springer, Heidelberg (2015). doi:10.1007/978-3-319-18612-2_10
4. Olsson, H.H., Bosch, J.: Towards continuous customer validation: a conceptual model for combining qualitative customer feedback with quantitative customer observation. In: Fernandes, João M., Machado, Ricardo J., Wnuk, K. (eds.) ICSOB 2015. LNBIP, vol. 210, pp. 154–166. Springer, Heidelberg (2015). doi:10.1007/978-3-319-19593-3_13

5. Fabijan, A., Olsson, H.H., Bosch, J.: Customer feedback and data collection techniques in software R&D: a literature review. In: Software Business, ICSOB 2015. pp. 139–153, Braga, Portugal (2015)
6. Williams, L., Cockburn, A.: Introduction: Agile Software Development: Its About Feedback and Change (2003)
7. Holmström Olsson, H., Bosch, J.: Towards data-driven product development: a multiple case study on post-deployment data usage in software-intensive embedded systems. In: Fitzgerald, B., Conboy, K., Power, K., Valerdi, R., Morgan, L., Stol, K.-J. (eds.) LESS 2013. LNBIP, vol. 167, pp. 152–164. Springer, Heidelberg (2013). doi:10.1007/978-3-642-44930-7_10
8. Bosch-Sijtsema, P., Bosch, J.: User involvement throughout the innovation process in high-tech industries. J. Prod. Innov. Manag. **32**, 1–36 (2014)
9. Bebensee, T., Weerd, I., Brinkkemper, S.: Binary priority list for prioritizing software requirements. In: Wieringa, R., Persson, A. (eds.) REFSQ 2010. LNCS, vol. 6182, pp. 67–78. Springer, Heidelberg (2010). doi:10.1007/978-3-642-14192-8_8
10. Knauss, E., Lubke, D., Meyer, S.: Feedback-driven requirements engineering: the heuristic requirements assistant. In: 2009 IEEE 31st International Conference on Software Engineering, pp. 587–590. IEEE (2009)
11. Johansson, E., Bergdahl, D., Bosch, J., Holmström Olsson, H.: Requirement prioritization with quantitative data - a case study. In: Abrahamsson, P., Corral, L., Oivo, M., Russo, B. (eds.) PROFES 2015. LNCS, vol. 9459, pp. 89–104. Springer, Heidelberg (2015). doi:10.1007/978-3-319-26844-6_7
12. Kano, N., Seraku, N., Takahashi, F., Tsuji, S.: Attractive quality and must-be quality. J. Japanese Soc. Qual. Control. **14**, 39–48 (1984)
13. Wiegers, K.E.: Automating requirements management. Softw. Dev. **7**, 1–5 (1999)
14. Karlsson, L., Thelin, T., Regnell, B., Berander, P., Wohlin, C.: Pair-wise comparisons versus planning game partitioning-experiments on requirements prioritisation techniques. Empir. Softw. Eng. **12**, 3–33 (2007)
15. Leffingwell, D., Widrig, D.: Managing Software Requirements: A Unified Approach, pp. 10, 491. Addison-Wesley Longman Publ. Co., Inc., Boston (1999)
16. Karlsson, J., Ryan, K.: A cost-value approach for prioritizing requirements. IEEE Softw. **14**, 67–74 (1997)
17. Kakar, A.K.: Of the user, by the user, for the user: engaging users in information systems product. In: SAIS 2014 Proceedings (2014)
18. Bosch, J.: Achieving simplicity with the three-layer product model. Computer (Long. Beach. Calif) **46**, 34–39 (2013)
19. Runeson, P., Höst, M.: Guidelines for conducting and reporting case study research in software engineering. Empir. Softw. Eng. **14**, 131–164 (2008)
20. Hsieh, H.-F., Shannon, S.E.: Three approaches to qualitative content analysis. Qual. Health Res. **15**, 1277–1288 (2005)

Process and Repository Mining

PROMOTE: A Process Mining Tool for Embedded System Development

Arttu Leppäkoski$^{(\boxtimes)}$ and Timo D. Hämäläinen

Tampere University of Technology, Tampere, Finland
arttu.leppakoski@student.tut.fi, timo.d.hamalainen@tut.fi

Abstract. Embedded system development workflow is complex, often poorly modelled, and thus difficult to optimize. We propose a new process mining tool PROMOTE as the first step of the flow improvement. The tool includes an event log analyzer and web user interface. PROMOTE has been tested in four real industrial projects, and in an open source SW project. We exposed several bottlenecks otherwise undiscovered, which proved the need and feasibility of PROMOTE. It will be deployed in production in a big embedded system company in 2017.

Keywords: Process mining · Embedded system development · Workflow · Business process modeling · Optimization · Web interface · Event log

1 Introduction

Embedded systems have become very complex requiring increasing efforts in safety critical SW development. Unexpected changes e.g. in HW sourcing can cause significant changes. The projects use hundreds of design tools, thousands of configuration files, and millions of the source code lines [1]. A change in a tool can drastically affect the tasks, ordering and scheduling.

According to a survey [2], an average project duration was 12.4 months and 57 % finished "late or canceled". The biggest technology challenge was "managing the design complexity" [2]. Desagent Oy and TUT performed a similar survey for 102 Finnish companies in 2013. The potential to improve the design efficiency was 30–50 % for 87 % of the answers. Only 3 % mentioned their process is formally modeled. 65 % uses office documentation. Practically none explicitly measure the efficiency of the development process. The reason is that the workflow is very complex and e.g. vulnerable to tool changes. The bottlenecks may remain hidden and nobody knows the overall efficiency. The tools, such as Issue and Bug Tracking, Version Control System (VCS), Continuous Integration (CI), Test Management and Code Review are widely used and lots of documentation is produced. Thus, the developers dislike any extra tasks for workflow modelling. To overcome this, we use process mining to examine tool event logs and then automatically construct the workflow model [3].

Several tools are available for process mining [4, 5]. ProM is excellent, but we also required outstanding visualization for non-expert users. Many process mining reports

© Springer International Publishing AG 2016
P. Abrahamsson et al. (Eds.): PROFES 2016, LNCS 10027, pp. 529–538, 2016.
DOI: 10.1007/978-3-319-49094-6_38

exist of the systems themselves [6, 7], but none of the development process. Some studies focus in SW development [8–10]. In [11], visualizations were utilized to illustrate events in the issue management system. We have utilized the basic mining techniques found in the related work also in our tool.

We have examined real logs in a large Finnish engineering and service company and from an open source SW project [12]. It soon turned out that current process mining tools were too focused on business domains, for which reason we propose a new tool, PROMOTE (PROcess Mining tOol for embedded sysTem dEvelopment). The goal is to bring a consolidated and transparent view to embedded systems development process from the information scattered around log files. The aimed users are project stakeholders.

The key contributions in this paper are (1) usage of process mining in embedded system development in a real industrial case, (2) new intuitive tool for it, and (3) analysis of the case studies as proof-of-concept.

This paper is organized as follows. Section 2 introduces the proposed PROMOTE tool, and Sect. 3 describes its user interface. Section 4 focuses on the evaluation of the log data and Sect. 5 concludes the paper with ideas for future work.

2   PROMOTE Core Architecture

Figure 1 depicts the overall architecture. PROMOTE captures event logs from other systems using the other tool interfaces available. Event logs are stored into database and then processed and converted into a common format using conversion scripts. Converted event logs are visualized and shared using WebUI, which is aimed to product stakeholders.

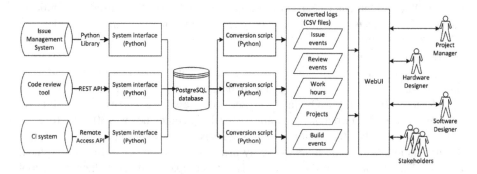

Fig. 1. General architecture

PROMOTE consists of several interface and conversion scripts which are implemented in Python. Systems to be analyzed are specified using a configuration script, which stores their information (name, type, URI etc.) into a dedicated database. Capturing and conversion is executed automatically without any user interaction. Event log data is stored into PostgreSQL database, which allows analysis to be executed in incremental steps without need to retrieve all event logs for each analysis. Database data is processed and stored into CSV and JSON file formats which are accessible by the

WebUI. Processed data is stored into several files using categories such as *Issue events*, and *Review events*.

Three specific challenges were identified in event log handling. The first one is coherency of timestamps across the systems, since otherwise the differences can cause misleading analysis results. All timestamps were converted to Coordinated Universal Time (UTC) and events without timestamp were discarded.

The second challenge is multiple usernames for same person in different systems. This matter was solved by creating a special algorithm for detecting which usernames belong to single user. Individual users are detected by comparing usernames, full names and email addresses. The third challenge was to determine and extract the relevant information from the event logs and to process that information into usable form. This requires external system specific knowledge and was manually included to the event log analysis.

PROMOTE can capture the whole development workflow by linking events between different systems. The links used are e.g. issue IDs and VCS commit hash tags. Figure 2 illustrates how the event log data is processed to capture the whole development workflow. The Event log handler (middle) analyses event logs (left) and generates the process model (right). Typically issue IDs used in the issue management system (e.g. Task-23) is used to identify events in other systems as well. For example VCS commit is linked to an implementation task by adding an issue ID to a comment or code review is linked to an issue ID or a VCS commit. After the links have been captured, the process model is generated by arranging events into a temporal order and by calculating the amount of transitions.

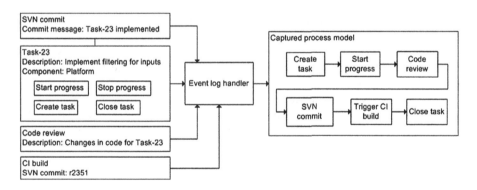

Fig. 2. Capturing of the workflow

The typical size of a capturing script is 150–400 lines of Python code. Several libraries were created for handling user detection, process modeling, and timestamp conversions. Currently PROMOTE includes a total of 4530 lines of Python code and supports the following systems: GIT, Subversion, Review Board, Jenkins, Redmine, SourceForge, Jira, and VersionOne.

3   PROMOTE WebUI

The existing process mining tools are often used by analysis experts, for which reason they are not easy to use by normal users. PROMOTE WebUI aims at changing this and visualize the results for any project member. WebUI includes a hierarchy of views starting from the overall status and digs into details as the user desires. The WebUI is based on the HTML KickStart framework [13], which allows adding new views rapidly. Each visualization view has been designed for universal usage and implemented with the d3.js Javascript library that supports CSV and JSON files [14].

The start view, shown in Fig. 3, contains a list of analyzed systems and the status summary with a word cloud from the most frequent words.

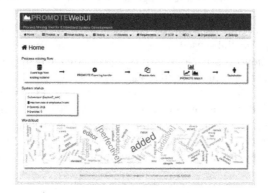

Fig. 3. PROMOTE WebUI start page

Figure 4 lists all the available views. Highest tree level includes categories distinctive for the embedded system development. Second level views were selected to present the most important information related to each category. Scatterplot view is similar to the Dotted chart analysis available in ProM [4] but other views are created based on the systems and processes available for the embedded system development. We present the most important views in more detail in the following. For brevity, we also discuss analysis findings from the industrial studies at the same context.

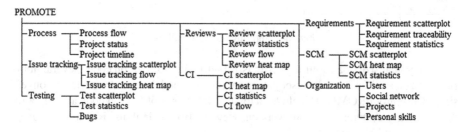

Fig. 4. PROMOTE WebUI views

Project status is intended for showing an overall project status and it can be displayed in large info screens.

Process flow graph shows information about traces between events in one or multiple systems. It shows how different systems are linked to each other and reveals the actual workflow. In addition, the graph is used to analyze how the actual and planned workflow differs. WebUI includes a process flow graph for the whole development process or a single system. Figure 5 depicts the process flow of Kactus2 including creation and closing of Redmine issues and SVN commits. Amount of transitions is shown on top of each transition.

Fig. 5. Process flow example from Kactus2. (Color figure online)

Analysis of industrial CI system revealed that build pipelines were not utilized at all. In practice, builds are triggered by VCS commits or by predefined schedule, and a single commit can cause several builds to be executed in parallel. Pipelines should be used to ensure that most important builds are executed first and build failures are detected as early as possible.

Scatterplot provides a way to investigate events in a temporal and logical manner. It is intended to everyone to analyze their own behavior. The vertical axis contains task IDs and the horizontal axis the timeline. Each task can include several events such as *Create issue, Assign*, and *Close issue*. Each type of event is painted in individual color. Issue filtering helps finding causalities. WebUI includes scatterplots for the following categories: Issue tracking, Testing, Reviews, Requirements, VCS, and CI.

Figure 6 depicts the review events for over 1200 reviews in industrial projects using Review Board. Several anomalies were discovered. For example, Review Board is not used in the same way in all projects. Some reviewers mostly add comments instead of opening defects, while some only open defects. A common guideline is clearly needed. Occasionally the time between opening and closing of the review is quite long. In most of the cases the review has ended but forgotten to be closed. Thus, the review looks to have taken even several months. It could also be seen that the review was left open on purpose and defects were fixed later. However, open defects may cause other problems. Most of the reviews are completed within few days and reviews are rarely reopened. Interestingly quite many reviews are discarded because the review had become obsolete or the review had been created incorrectly.

Timeline collects all events in the embedded system development project to provide a one glance overview. Timeline is mainly intended for the project managers to analyze overlapping tasks and compare planned and realized schedule. Timeline for an industrial development project is shown in Fig. 7. Timeline includes VCS tags (vertical lines), VCS commits (brown dots), VCS merge commits (purple dots), CI builds (grey dots),

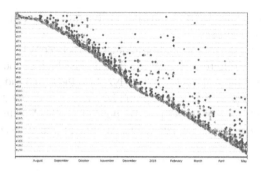

Fig. 6. Scatterplot for review events from an industrial study.

tasks (green horizontal lines), scrum stories (red horizontal lines), reviews (purple horizontal lines) and scrum sprints (blue boxes on the background).

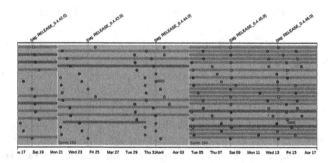

Fig. 7. Project timeline from an industrial study. (Color figure online)

Timelines of the industrial projects show that reviews are not always completed before the sprint ends. Some have taken even three sprints. We suggest to complete in the same sprint so that the scrum story can be closed at the end of the sprint. In addition, reviews should be small enough to take only few days, and time should be allocated for upcoming reviews.

Heat map illustrates usage of the system in question. Darkness of the color indicates the amount of the activities for the current hour. WebUI includes heat maps for following categories: VCS, Issue tracking, CI, and Review. With heat maps it is possible to investigate when the system is accessed most often and when people are working. Target group for the heat maps are project managers and system administrators.

Figure 8 illustrates the usage of VCS in one large industrial project including over 1500 commits during two years. In this case VCS is used quite evenly from Monday to Thursday but on Friday the amount of commits increases heavily. Further analysis indicates that this is most likely caused by the weekly release schedule, which requires that a new SW version must be released on every Friday. This leads into situation that new features are committed into VCS as late as possible, which causes problems in testing that is executed after the release. Thus, developers should commit source codes evenly on every weekday, and the release schedule should be modified so that the weekly release would be done on Wednesday or latest on Thursday.

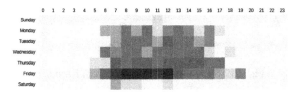

Fig. 8. VCS heat map from an industrial study.

Figure 9 illustrates the usage of CI server. CI heat map and CI process flow indicates that CI server is executing scheduled builds during night. By analyzing the heat map it is recommended that nightly builds should be divided more evenly for the whole night to avoid overloading. In addition, dependency between the amounts of CI builds and VCS commits depicted in Fig. 8 is clearly visible and highlights that events in one system affects other systems. This further advocates for the usage of CI pipelines.

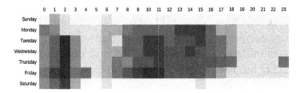

Fig. 9. CI heat map from an industrial study.

Project members graph shows which persons have participated into which project. The graph is used to check who are familiar with certain projects and helps illustrating development organization. In addition, this graph is used to find out which persons are in key roles in the organization.

Social network is used to investigate how users collaborate, who are working together and what kind of hierarchy exists in the organization. In addition, social networks are used to discover roles of the project participants [4].

Target group for the social network graph are project managers, team leaders, human resources, and stakeholders interested in collaboration between persons and teams. Figure 10 illustrates the social network for the Kactus2 project especially for the issue assignment. This particular social network implies that one user has a bigger role than others when assigning tasks. It is notable that most of the assignments are done by the users for themselves which reflects that the issue management should have more attention. Scatterplot indicates that the issues are not prioritized, only categorized using target version. In addition, Fig. 10 shows that one person has much more tasks than other persons, which indicates that workload should be divided more evenly.

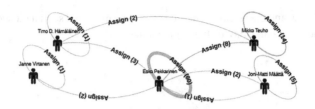

Fig. 10. Social network example from Kactus2.

Analysis of the social network for industrial projects shows that developers tend to use same reviewers for all of their reviews. It would be beneficial to use a bigger group for reviewing source codes to ensure high review quality and coverage. Developers should also include persons from other teams as reviewers. This would help spreading information, knowledge, and practices between developers and teams.

Personal skills view illustrates the skills of the individuals in the form of radar charts. The charts are created for the usage of tools and for programming skills. The results can be used e.g. for identifying if some developer needs training, finding out the best candidate for a new task or to investigate the overall usage of tool. The personal skills view is targeted for the project managers and team leaders, but also for the other project members for self-examination. Figure 11 shows an example of skills in usage of Redmine in the Kactus2 project for a single user (left) and all users (right). It can be seen that Redmine is utilized quite well in the Kactus2 project excluding feature *Add news*, but a single user has used only a portion of all features.

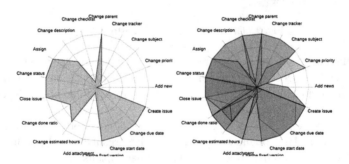

Fig. 11. Redmine skills for single user and for all users from Kactus2.

4 Evaluation

PROMOTE has been piloted in Kactus2 and four industry projects including 15 developers and test specialists. Table 1 lists contents of the latter. Events in the different systems were linked together with issue management IDs and VCS commit IDs. PROMOTE was run on top of 64-bit 2 GHz Ubuntu 14.04 server with 1 GB of RAM and 16 GB of hard-drive space.

Table 1. Systems included into industrial pilot

System	Content of the analysis
7 GIT repositories	7185 commits, 1205 branches
VersionOne (Issue tracking system)	10 projects, 20 epics, 221 backlog items, 606 tasks
Jenkins (CI system)	35 jobs, 2586 builds
Review board	1247 reviews

Kactus2 utilizes the following systems: Subversion (2084 commits), Redmine (255 issues), and SourceForge. Time needed for the capturing and conversion was about 10 min. The conclusion is that Kactus2 is a small and agile project with flexible milestones rather than strictly scheduled and prioritized traditional SW project. In large industrial setups, time for the capturing and conversion is significantly higher. The first execution of the PROMOTE Log handler commonly requires several hours. Follow-up executions are much faster, typically taking 5–10 min, because only the new events needs to be captured. Size of the PostgreSQL database generated in industrial pilot was 5 MB, but can be 100 MB in larger setups.

The user acceptance of PROMOTE has been very good based on about 15 persons test group. The WebUI fulfills the requirements of visualizing and summarizing the information gathered from several sources. It was noticed that compared to related work, PROMOTE's architecture provides faster and more straightforward way to automatically capture and analyze event logs from several sources. In addition, deployment of PROMOTE in new environments has proven to be very easy because of an expandable architecture, simple configuration, and reusable scripts.

5 Conclusions

PROMOTE performed very well in the presented cases, in which usage of tools is extensive, documentation is comprehensive, and traceability between systems has been taken into consideration. PROMOTE will also be tested with less rigorous development setups to disclose even bigger bottlenecks. Implementation of PROMOTE started in 2015, an industry pilot in spring 2016, and later in this year it will be taken into wider use in the pilot company.

In the future, we will model the workflows using YAWL [15, 16] and compare with the models captured by PROMOTE to adjust model accuracy. Implementation of PROMOTE continues by adding support for systems such as Quality Center, and by adding reasoning to automatically find bottlenecks and suggest corrective actions. As a conclusion, PROMOTE is promising even as such and will be immediately deployed in a company, and will be used as the data and process mining part for workflow optimization research.

References

1. Leppäkoski, A., Salminen, E., and Hamalainen, T.D.: Framework for industrial embedded system product development and management. In: 2013 International Symposium on System on Chip (SoC), pp. 1–6, 23–24 October 2013
2. Blaza, D., Wolfe, A.: Embedded Market Study, presentation on Design West, San Jose, Ca, USA, 22–25 April 2013. http://presentations.ubmdesign.com/events/san-jose/2013. [Cited: 4 May 2013]
3. van der Aalst, W., Weijters, T., Maruster, L.: Workflow mining: discovering process models from event logs. IEEE Trans. Knowl. Data Eng. 16(9), 1128–1142 (2004)
4. van der Aalst, W.M.P.: Process Mining: Discovery, Conformance and Enhancement of Business Processes, p. 352. Springer, Heidelberg (2011). ISBN:978-3-642-19344-6
5. Aalst, W., et al.: Process mining manifesto. In: Daniel, F., Barkaoui, K., Dustdar, S. (eds.) BPM 2011. LNBIP, vol. 99, pp. 169–194. Springer, Heidelberg (2012). doi: 10.1007/978-3-642-28108-2_19
6. Heikkinen, E., Hämäläinen, T.D.: LOGDIG log file analyzer for mining expected behavior from log files. Accepted for 14th Symposium on Programming Languages and SW Tools, SPLST 2015, Tampere, Finland, 9–10 October 2015
7. Andrews, J.H., Zhang, Y.: General test result checking with log file analysis. IEEE Trans. SW Eng. 29(7), 634–648 (2003)
8. Poncin, W., Serebrenik, A., van den Brand, M.: Process mining SW repositories. In: 2011 15th European Conference on SW Maintenance and Reengineering (CSMR), pp. 5–14, 1–4 March 2011. ISBN:978-1-61284-259-2
9. Anwar, W.A., Moussa, A.S., Salah, A.: Extracting hidden information and conclusions in SW testing via distributed relational visual mining. In: 2013 17th International Conference on Information Visualisation (IV), pp. 527–531, 16–18 July 2013
10. Rubin, V., Lomazoma, I., van der Aalst, W.M.P.: Agile development with SW process mining. In: ICSSP 2014 (2014)
11. Lehtonen, T., Eloranta, V., Leppänen, M., Isohanni, E.: Visualizations as a basis for agile SW process improvement. In: 20th Asia-Pacific SW Engineering Conference (2013)
12. Tampere University of Technology, Kactus2 (2016). http://funbase.cs.tut.fi. [Cited: 6 June 2016]
13. J. Gatcke: HTML Kickstart HTML Elements Documentation (2016). http://www.99lime.com/elements/. [Cited: 6 June 2016]
14. Bostock, M.: D3.js - Data-Driven Documents (2016). http://d3js.org. [Cited: 6 June 2016]
15. The YAWL Foundation: YAWL (2015). http://www.yawlfoundation.org/. [Cited: 6 June 2016]
16. Adams, M., ter Hofstede, A.H.M., La Rosa, M.: Open source SW for workflow management: the case of YAWL. IEEE SW 28(3), 16–19 (2011). 0740-74

Evaluation of Kano-like Models Defined for Using Data Extracted from Online Sources

Huishi Yin and Dietmar Pfahl[(✉)]

Institute of Computer Science,
University of Tartu, J. Liivi 2, 50409 Tartu, Estonia
{huishi,dietmar.pfahl}@ut.ee

Abstract. The Kano model is a frequently used method to classify user preferences according to their importance, and by doing so support requirements prioritization. To implement the Kano model, a representative set of users must answer for each feature under evaluation a functional and dysfunctional question. Unfortunately, finding and interviewing users is difficult and time-consuming. Thus, the core idea of our proposed approach is to extract automatically opinions about product features from online open sources (e.g., Q & A sites, App reviews, etc.) and to feed them into the Kano questionnaire to prioritize software requirements following the principles of the Kano model. One problem with our proposed approach is how to pair input extracted from the internet into paired answers to the functional dysfunctional questions. This problem arises because the reviews and comments from online sources that we plan to transform into answers to either the functional or dysfunctional question are usually unpaired. Therefore, the aim of this study is to find a method that produces results resembling those of the traditional Kano model although we only retrieve partial information. We propose two Kano-like models, i.e., the Half- and the Deformed-Kano model, for unpaired answers to functional and dysfunctional questions. In order to analyze the performance of the two proposed models as compared to that of the traditional Kano model, we run several simulations with synthetic data. Then we compare the simulation results to see which Kano-like model produces results that are similar to those of the traditional Kano model. The simulation results show that on average both the Half-Kano and Deformed-Kano models on average generate feature categorizations similar to those of the traditional Kano model. However, only the Deformed-Kano model generates the same range of categorizations as the traditional Kano model. The Deformed-Kano can be used as an approximation of the traditional Kano model when the input is unpaired or partly missing.

Keywords: Kano model · Requirement prioritization · Online source

1 Introduction

In software product management, requirement prioritization is often used for determining which candidate requirements of a feature should be included in a software release. Requirements are also prioritized to minimize risk during development so that the most important or low-risk requirements are implemented first [1, 2]. Several

© Springer International Publishing AG 2016
P. Abrahamsson et al. (Eds.): PROFES 2016, LNCS 10027, pp. 539–549, 2016.
DOI: 10.1007/978-3-319-49094-6_39

methods for classifying and prioritizing software requirements exist. The Kano model is one of the best-known and frequently used methods to do this.

The Kano model was developed by Noriaki Kano in the 1980s [3]. It defines the relationship between user satisfaction and product features. Since the Kano model can be used to prioritize user needs as a function of customer satisfaction, it is one of the most popular methods that address customer needs prioritization. The traditional Kano model defines five categories of user needs that have different effects on user satisfaction. Those are O, A, M, I, R[1] [4–8]. Since it is possible to receive contradictory responses from customers, the category Q (Questionable) is also an option.

In the context of a larger research project, we plan to use advanced machine learning and data mining techniques to help us extract systematically user needs from online open sources for complementing traditional sources for the elicitation and prioritization of software requirements. In order to fuel the information generated in this way into requirements prioritization activities, we intend to use the principles of the Kano model to classify user needs according to their importance. In this paper, we do not report on the automatic elicitation and sentiment analysis of user needs voiced in online open sources. In the following we rather focus on how to use the ideas and principles of the Kano model when the information extracted does not correspond to paired answers of the Kano questionnaire.

2   Related Work

Since the 1980s when the Kano model was first introduced, it has become a popular theory used by researchers and business practitioners across many industries. After an extensive review of the literature on the Kano model, Josip and Darko summarized and evaluated five methods, which classify quality features into the categories defined by the Kano model [9], however, in a different way than Noriaki Kano proposed. The methods analyzed were the original Kano model developed by Noriaki Kano [3], the "Penalty reward contrast analysis" (PRCA) originally proposed by Brandt [10], the "Importance grid" developed by IBM [11], the "Qualitative data methods" including CIT (critical incident technique) developed by Herzberg and ACC (analysis of complaints and compliments) used by Cadotte [12], Oliver [13], Friman, and Edvardsson [14], and the "Direct classification" method proposed by Emery and Tian [15]. Among those five methods, only CIT and ACC have the same assumption, i.e. that "quality features can be categorized by comparing how frequently customers mention it in a positive context or a negative context" [9]. However, the reliability of both CIT and ACC methods, as compared to the Kano model, remains questionable when the frequencies with which customers mention features are low. According to Josip and Darko's research, the Kano model and the direct-classification method are the only methods capable of classifying features.

---

[1] O = One-dimensional Quality, A = Attractive Quality, M = Must-be Quality, I = Indifferent Quality, R = Reverse Quality.

Based on the analysis of the related work, we concluded that the traditional Kano model is the best approach to elicit future customers' perceptions regarding a product's features.

3 Research Goal and Method

To apply the Kano model on data extracted from online open sources, we assume that we have already filtered out the sentiment information expressing a person's feeling from online reviews, comments, and questions, and that we have translated the sentiment information into a data set similar to the format of the Kano model. For example, the statement "I dislike X very much!" represents a very negative answer to the functional question, and "I would be very happy if there is no function X." represents a very positive answer to the dysfunctional answer regarding feature X. We put all answers to the functional questions in one "Yes" (Y) vector, and all answers to the dysfunctional questions in one vector "No" (N) vector.

One of the biggest problems we are facing is how to pair the required input to the Kano model without conducting interviews with real people giving answers to both functional and dysfunctional questions. The reviews and comments from an online source are usually unpaired so that we cannot process the data following the traditional Kano model. Because of this, we need to design Kano-like model algorithms for processing unpaired data.

In this paper, we propose two kinds of Kano-like models, i.e., the Half-Kano model and the Deformed-Kano model. The goal of our study is to compare the performance of the Kano-like models with that of the traditional Kano model and to decide which of the two Kano-like models behaves more similar to the traditional Kano model. Our research method uses simulation experiments with synthetic data (see Sect. 5 for details).

4 Kano-like Models

The two Kano-like models we propose differ in the way how they interpret the unpaired answers derived from online open sources. The assumption of the Half-Kano model is that we only have either answers to the functional question or answers to the dysfunctional question. The assumption of the Deformed-Kano model is that answers to the functional and the dysfunctional questions are from the same group of people, even though we lost the links between answers. One output of the traditional Kano model will only contain one specific category to which a feature is classified to. However, in our study, to be able to compare with the output of the Kano-like models, we use the probability of each category that one feature is categorized into instead of the one category to which the feature is most frequently categorized into. For example, if we get five paired answers about one feature, and each paired answer leads to one category, then we have a list of five categories (e.g., M, M, A, M, O). The traditional Kano model output is that this feature is classified to category M. However, in our study, we say the output is that this feature is 60 % classified to category M, 20 % to A, and 20 % to O.

4.1   Half-Kano Model

To implement the Kano-like models on unpaired data, we assume an extreme case, i.e., that each time when we have an interview with our interviewees, we ask only functional questions or only dysfunctional questions relating to one software feature, hence we only get two groups of responses for functional and dysfunctional questions from different interviewees. In this case, we cannot use two responses from different interviewees to classify one person's satisfaction and based on that derive the satisfaction category the software feature belongs to. However, we can implement an algorithm which calculates probabilities with which a software feature would be classified based on the responses for the functional and the dysfunctional questions. Since the data in the Y and the N vectors are not matched, the Half-Kano model is not a traditional Kano model. Nevertheless, we calculate the probabilities following the traditional Kano model. The difference is that in this method, we use each signal value from Y and N vectors to derive a satisfaction category. Figure 1 shows an example of the process of how the Half-Kano model processes the Y and N vectors when the unpaired input is "1" in the Y vector, and "−2" in the N vector. In this case, we can say that with a probability of 40 % this feature should be classified to the M category, with 30 % probability to the I category, and with 10 % probability each to the R, O, and Q categories.

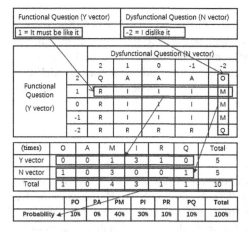

Fig. 1. An example of the process of Half-Kano model (2 = I like it, 1 = It must be like it, 0 = I am neutral, −1 = I can tolerate it, −2 = I dislike it.)

Fig. 2. An example of the process of Deformed-Kano model

The algorithm of probability (P) that vector Y (Functional) and vector N (Dysfunctional) are categorized to the same category (X) can be written as

$$P(cat(Y) = cat(N) = X) = \frac{\sum_{i=1}^{m} F_x cat(Y(i)) + \sum_{j=1}^{n} F_x cat(N(j))}{(m+n) * 5}$$

and

$$F_O cat(Y(i)) = \begin{cases} 1 \ if \ Y(i) = 2 \\ 0 \ if \ Y(i) \in \{-2, -1, 0, 1\} \end{cases} \qquad F_A cat(Y(i)) = \begin{cases} 3 \ if \ Y(i) = 2 \\ 0 \ if \ Y(i) \in \{-2, -1, 0, 1\} \end{cases}$$

$$F_M cat(Y(i)) = \begin{cases} 1 \ if \ Y(i) \in \{-1, 0, 1\} \\ 0 \ if \ Y(i) \in \{-2, 2\} \end{cases} \qquad F_I cat(Y(i)) = \begin{cases} 3 \ if \ Y(i) \in \{-1, 0, 1\} \\ 0 \ if \ Y(i) \in \{-2, 2\} \end{cases}$$

$$F_R cat(Y(i)) = \begin{cases} 4 \ if \ Y(i) = -2 \\ 1 \ if \ Y(i) \in \{-1, 0, 1\} \\ 0 \ if \ Y(i) = 2 \end{cases} \qquad F_Q cat(Y(i)) = \begin{cases} 1 \ if \ Y(i) \in \{-2, 2\} \\ 0 \ if \ Y(i) \in \{-1, 0, 1\} \end{cases}$$

and

$$F_O cat(N(j)) = \begin{cases} 1 \ if \ N(j) = -2 \\ 0 \ if \ N(j) \in \{-1, 0, 1, 2\} \end{cases} \qquad F_A cat(N(j)) = \begin{cases} 1 \ if \ N(j) \in \{-1, 0, 1\} \\ 0 \ if \ N(j) \in \{-2, 2\} \end{cases}$$

$$F_M cat(N(j)) = \begin{cases} 3 \ if \ N(j) = -2 \\ 0 \ if \ N(j) \in \{-1, 0, 1, 2\} \end{cases} \qquad F_I cat(N(j)) = \begin{cases} 3 \ if \ N(j) \in \{-1, 0, 1\} \\ 0 \ if \ N(j) \in \{-2, 2\} \end{cases}$$

$$F_R cat(N(j)) = \begin{cases} 4 \ if \ N(j) = 2 \\ 1 \ if \ N(j) \in \{-1, 0, 1\} \\ 0 \ if \ N(j) = -2 \end{cases} \qquad F_Q cat(N(j)) = \begin{cases} 1 \ if \ N(j) \in \{-2, 2\} \\ 0 \ if \ N(j) \in \{-1, 0, 1\} \end{cases}$$

and F_x is a function that maps the statement X to the set $\{0,1,3,4\}$

$$F_x : X \rightarrow \{0, 1, 3, 4\}$$

where

$$i \in \{1, 2, 3 \ldots m\}$$

$$j \in \{1, 2, 3 \ldots n\}$$

$$X \in \{O, A, M, I, R, Q\}$$

m is the number of values of Y vector
n is the number of values of N vector

4.2   Deformed-Kano Model

In the Deformed-Kano model, we assume that the responses are from the same group of people, but we lost the links between answers to functional and dysfunctional questions.

We sequentially pick a number of the Y vector to combine with each number of the N vector to derive the satisfaction categories, and then we get a list of satisfaction categories. After each value in the Y vector has been combined with all values of the N vector, we calculate the overall proportion of the appearance of each category. Figure 2 shows the example of the process of the Deformed-Kano model when the unpaired input is "2, 1" in Y vector, and "−1, −2" in N vector. The output is that this feature is 25 % classified to category M, 25 % to A, and 25 % to O, and 25 % to I.

The algorithm of probability (P) that vectors Y (Functional) and N (Dysfunctional) are categorized to the same category (X) can be written as

$$P(\text{cat}(Y) = \text{cat}(N) = X) = \frac{\sum_{i=1}^{m}(\sum_{j=1}^{n} x_x(\text{cat}(Y(i)) * \text{cat}(N(j))))}{m * n}$$

and

$$\text{cat}(Y(i)) * \text{cat}(N(j)) = \begin{cases} O \text{ if } Y(i) = 2 \text{ and } N(j) = -2 \\ A \text{ if } Y(i) = 2 \text{ and } N(j) \in \{-1,0,1\} \\ M \text{ if } Y(i) \in \{-1,0,1\} \text{ and } N(j) = -2 \\ I \text{ if } Y(i) \in \{-1,0,1\} \text{ and } N(j) \in \{-1,0,1\} \\ R \text{ if } Y(i) \in \{-2,-1,0,1\} \text{ and } N(j) = 2 \,||\, Y(i) = -2 \text{ and } N(j) \in \{-1,0,1\} \\ Q \text{ if } Y(i) = 2 \text{ and } N(j) = 2 \,||\, Y(i) = -2 \text{ and } N(j) = -2 \end{cases}$$

and x_x is a function that map the statement X to the set {0,1}

$$x_x : X \rightarrow \{0, 1\}$$

where

$$i \in \{1, 2, 3 \ldots m\}$$

$$j \in \{1, 2, 3 \ldots n\}$$

$$X \in \{O, A, M, I, R, Q\}$$

m is the number of values of Y vector
n is the number of values of N vector

5 Simulation Study

Simulation Input: There are 31 possible value sets[2] both in the Y and N vectors. For example, value set ID No.1 indicates that the Y and N vectors only contain elements with value '−2'. Value set ID No.31 indicates that both vectors contain all possible values, i.e., '−2, −1, 0, 1, 2'.

---

[2] $C_5^1 + C_5^2 + C_5^3 + C_5^4 + C_5^5 = 31$.

Simulation Approach: We use the R language to execute the simulation algorithms we proposed in Sects. 4 and 5. We first set the length of Y and N vectors equals to 20, and these 20 numbers are picked from each possible value set to simulate responses of one feature. We combined all 31 possible value sets of Y and N vectors. The total number of possible ways to combine the Y with the N vector value sets is 31 * 31 = 961. In each round simulation, for each combination of value sets of Y and N, we sample data randomly following a chosen distribution, e.g., uniform distribution. Then we run traditional Kano and Kano-like models five times respectively. Next, we calculated the average value of those who have the same value set ID of Y and N vectors and join them together to finally get a table which contains 961 rows and 20 columns (Value set ID of Y and N vectors plus PO, PA, PM, PI, PR, and PQ for the traditional Kano, Half-Kano, and Deformed-Kano model, respectively).

Simulation Hypothesis 1: Deformed-Kano model generates more similar output to the traditional Kano than the Half-Kano model.

We pick the data from one out of 961 rows to show an example of the way to calculate the difference between the traditional Kano model and the Kano-like models. Table 1 shows the way to calculate the difference between traditional Kano and Kano-like models, and the calculation results are shown as well. When we calculate the absolute value of the difference between the two sets of data (Traditional and Half or Traditional and Deformed), the range is 0 to 200 %. Hence, we divide the absolute value by 2 to get the result in the range from 0 to 100 %.

Table 1. An example of the difference between the traditional Kano model and the Kano-like models

	PO	PA	PM	PI	PR	PQ
Traditional (%)	0	20	0	45	25	10
Half (%)	3	15.5	7	40.5	27.5	6.5
Deformed (%)	0	19.5	0	45.5	24.5	10.5
Difference (%)	**Traditional − Half** = $(\|0 - 3\| + \|20 - 15.5\| + \|0 - 7\| + \|45 - 40.5\| + \|25 - 27.5\| + \|10 - 6.5\|) / 2 = 12.5$					
	Traditional − Deformed = $(\|0 - 0\| + \|20 - 19.5\| + \|0 - 0\| + \|45 - 45.5\| + \|25 - 24.5\| + \|10 - 10.5\|) / 2 = 1$					

The lower value of difference represents closer output to traditional Kano model. In the case shown in the Table 1, we can see the Deformed-Kano model's output is closer to the output of the traditional Kano model (difference = 1 %) than the output of the Half-Kano model (difference = 12.5 %).

The ranges and means of the differences between the outputs of the traditional Kano model and the Kano-like models are shown in Table 2. We can see from Table 2 that the range of difference between the traditional and Half-Kano models varies from 10.5 % to 80 %, which is much higher than the range of differences between the traditional and Deformed-Kano models, which is 0 % to 18.74 %. The means show the same trend. 25.99 % between the traditional and Half-Kano models and 4.28 % between the traditional and Deformed-Kano models.

Table 2. The range and means of the difference between the outputs of Traditional Kano model and the Kano-like models

	Traditional-Half (%)	Traditional-Deformed (%)
Ranges	[10.5, 80]	[0, 18.74]
Means	25.99	4.28

To see more clearly the distribution of the differences of outputs between the traditional Kano model and the Kano-like models, we draw 3D and 2D figures. Figures 3 and 4 show that the Deformed-Kano model shows outputs which have lower differences with the outputs of the traditional Kano model.

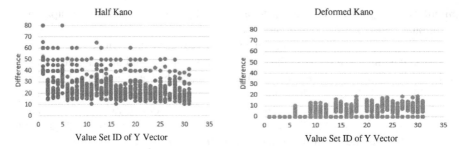

Fig. 3. The projection of the distribution of differences between the traditional Kano and the Kano-like models on Y vector plane

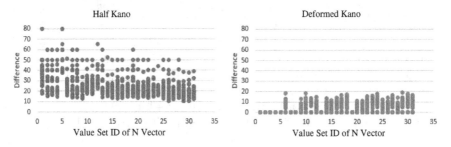

Fig. 4. The projection of the distribution of differences between the traditional Kano and the Kano-like models on N vector plane

Simulation Hypothesis 2: The Deformed-Kano model provides similar outputs as the traditional Kano model.

According to the simulation results, we found that when the input value of the Y vector or the N vector belongs to {−2}, {−1}, {0}, {1}, {2}, {−2, 0}, {−2,1}, {0, 1}, {−2, 0, 1}, the difference always equals zero, which means 477 out of 961 (49.6 %) output combinations of Deformed-Kano and traditional Kano model show no difference.

When the input value of Y vector and N vector does not belong to $\{-2\}$, $\{-1\}$, $\{0\}$, $\{1\}$, $\{2\}$, $\{-2, 0\}$, $\{-2,1\}$, $\{0, 1\}$, $\{-2, 0, 1\}$, the difference will always be more than zero. The simulation results show that 484 out of 961 (50.4%) combinations show differences between the outputs of the traditional Kano and the Deformed-Kano model with a range in 1% to 18%. In addition, the average values are less than 11 %.

6 Threats to Validity

There are several limitations and threats to validity linked to our simulation study. First of all, both Half-Kano and Deformed-Kano models are not fulfilling the requirements of the traditional (interview-based) Kano model, because the input taken from online sources will most of the time not generate paired answers to functional and dysfunctional questions, and the number of answers extracted from online sources will not be balanced. The latter point is particularly limiting our study as comparisons with the traditional Kano model could only be done with sets of balanced data. Thus, we had to restrict our simulation experiments to cases of balanced data. Another limitation is the choice of distributions used in our simulation experiments. Since we have not yet started with extracting real data from online sources, we do not know what empirical distributions of values in the Y and N vectors are realistic. Therefore, we chose a neutral approach and sampled from uniform distributions in our simulation experiments. Finally, we noticed that the relative amount of questionable categorizations might deviate from the typical numbers when using the traditional Kano model. However, since we exclude questionable data from the comparisons between the Kano-like and traditional Kano model, this limitation does not influence our comparison results.

It should be mentioned that the comparison of the Kano-like models used in our simulation study with the traditional Kano model is not based on a single category resulting from the majority of categorizations per interview (in the traditional Kano model) and per vector matching (in the Kano-like models). Instead, we compare the distributions (expressed as probabilities) categorizations per feature. Although this is a deviation from the procedures used by the traditional Kano model, our approach could be considered as giving richer output. Assume, for example, an extreme case where you get 1000 paired answers, with 501 answers leading to category 'M' and 499 answers leading to category 'I'. The output of the traditional Kano model is that this feature should be categorized as "Must be" (M). If only this final categorization is conveyed, one will not know that 49.9 % of the interviewees considered this feature to be "Indifferent" (I).

7 Discussion

It is clear from our simulation study that the Deformed-Kano model produces outputs that are more similar to those of a traditional Kano model than what the Half-Kano model produces.

Although the Deformed-Kano model only partly works like the traditional Kano model, based on our simulation experiments, we found that 49.6 % of its outputs have no difference to the outputs of the traditional Kano model, and for those 50.4 % outputs showing a difference, the differences are very small, with an average of less than 11 %.

Although the Deformed-Kano model does not work exactly like the traditional Kano model, it has several advantages. Firstly, it can handle unpaired and unbalance input (Y and N vectors). Secondly, the ability to process unpaired and unbalanced data but nevertheless producing similar results than the traditional Kano model makes the analysis of user preferences cheaper as all steps can be automated and now costly interviews are needed. Thirdly, it is difficult to guarantee the representativeness of the opinions voiced by a small set of selected interviewees. Using data from online sources has the potential of generating a more complete and thus more realistic input to the analysis of user preferences.

8 Conclusions

According to our simulation experiments, we find that the results of using the Deformed-Kano model are always close to the results of the traditional Kano model. Because of that, we consider the Deformed-Kano model to be a good approximation of the traditional Kano model. Moreover, the Deformed-Kano model can be used even when the input is unbalanced or partly missing. Therefore, we believe that the low cost of using the Deformed-Kano model combined with the possibility to use unbalanced data compensates for the potential lack of paired data when comparing with the traditional Kano model.

Acknowledgement. This research was supported by the Estonian Research Council.

References

1. Lehtola, L., Kauppinen, M., Kujala, S.: Requirements prioritization challenges in practice. In: Bomarius, F., Iida, H. (eds.) PROFES 2004. LNCS, vol. 3009, pp. 497–508. Springer, Heidelberg (2004). doi:10.1007/978-3-540-24659-6_36
2. Berander, P., Andrews, A.: Requirements prioritization. In: Aurum, A., Wohlin, C. (eds.) Engineering and Managing Software Requirements, pp. 69–94. Springer, Heidelberg (2005)
3. Kano, N., Nobuhiku, S., Fumio, T., Shinichi, T.: Attractive quality and must-be quality. J. Jpn. Soc. Qual. Control **14**(2), 39–48 (1984)
4. Berger, C., Blauth, R., Boger, D., Bolster, C., Burchill, G., DuMouchel, W., Timko, M.: Kano's methods for understanding customer-defined quality. Center Qual. Manage. J. **2**(4), 3–35 (1993)
5. Jiao, J.R., Chen, C.H.: Customer requirement management in product development: a review of research issues. Concurrent Eng. **14**(3), 173–185 (2006)
6. Kai, Y.: Voice of the Customer: Capture and Analysis. McGraw-Hill, New York (2007)
7. Sharif Ullah, A.M.M., Tamaki, J.I.: Analysis of Kano-model-based customer needs for product development. Syst. Eng. **14**(2), 154–172 (2011)

8. http://foldingburritos.com/kano-model/. Accessed 15 June 2016
9. Mikulic, J., Prebezac, D.: A critical review of techniques for classifying quality attributes in the Kano model. Managing Serv. Qual. An Intl. J. **21**(1), 46–66 (2011)
10. Brandt, R.D.: A procedure for identifying value-enhancing service components using customer satisfaction survey data. In: Surprenant, C. (ed.) Add Value to Your Service, pp. 61–65. American Marketing Association, Chicago (1987)
11. Vavra, T.G.: Improving Your Measurement of Customer Satisfaction: A Guide to Creating, Conducting, Analyzing, and Reporting Customer Satisfaction Measurement Programs. ASQ Quality Press, Milwaukee (1997)
12. Cadotte, E.R., Turgeon, N.: Dissatisfiers and satisfiers: suggestions from consumer complaints and compliments. J. Consum. Satisfaction Dissatisfaction Complaining Behav. **1**, 74–79 (1988)
13. Oliver, R.L.: Satisfaction: A Behavioral Perspective on the Consumer. McGraw-Hill Series in Marketing Show all Parts in this Series. McGraw-Hill, New York (1997)
14. Friman, M., Edvardsson, B.: A content analysis of complaints and compliments. Managing Serv. Qual. Intl. J. **13**(1), 20–26 (2003)
15. Emery, C.R., Tian, R.G.: Schoolwork as products, professors as customers: a practical teaching approach in business education. J. Educ. Bus. **78**(2), 97–102 (2002)

Log File Analyzing in Intelligent Transportation Systems Development

Esa Heikkinen[✉] and Timo D. Hämäläinen

Department of Pervasive Computing, Tampere University of Technology,
P.O. Box 553, 33101 Tampere, Finland
esa.heikkinen@student.tut.fi, timo.d.hamalainen@tut.fi

Abstract. Intelligent Transportation Systems (ITS) consist of a large number of vehicles and stop monitors, as well as operations management center and servers. Their development can be challenging due to 3rd party black-box components and limited debugging visibility. Our solution is log file analysis. We developed a tool framework called LOGDIG, which differs from related work by supporting also very complex system behaviors discovered by recurrent and backward processing of the log files. The tool was successfully used to find and fix faulty timing of bus stop monitor information in a product called ELMI.

Keywords: Log file analysis · Systems engineering · Data mining · RTPIS · ITS

1 Introduction

This paper presents our experiences in developing an Intelligent Transportation System (ITS) product called ELMI [1]. It included real-time bus tracking and bus stop monitors displaying time of arrival estimates. ELMI is based on proprietary radio network and involves parts from several vendors, which complicates testing on the field. Log file analysis helped us discovering the real vs. expected behavior of the black-box parts, which helped fixing the open ELMI parts. The first log tools were TCL scripts but eventually we ended up with a general purpose tool framework called LOGDIG.

The new contributions in this paper are (i) using feedback from log analysis for continuous system development improvement loops, (ii) using a log generator to create test logs and expand real data for better problem tracking and (iii) using LOGDIG framework to analyze behavior of the case study ELMI.

This paper is organized as follows. Section 2 describes the motivation and related work, and Sect. 3 the log file analysis in ELMI as complex behavior mining. Section 4 presents LOGDIG analyzer with generated data and in Sect. 5 using real case study. The paper is concluded in Sect. 6.

2 Motivation and Related Work

In ELMI, we have applied a continuous development process combining Systems Engineering [2, 3], CRISP-DM [4] data mining process and event-driven development [5, 6]. Figure 1 depicts an overview (A) and a detailed (B) model of our development

© Springer International Publishing AG 2016
P. Abrahamsson et al. (Eds.): PROFES 2016, LNCS 10027, pp. 550–559, 2016.
DOI: 10.1007/978-3-319-49094-6_40

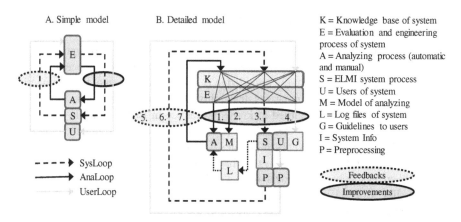

Fig. 1. Models of improvement loops in ELMI continuous development process

process. The knowledge base and the engineering process are out of scope, but we focus on the following loops.

UserLoop is based on end users' feedback that we call bug reports independent of the form. Understanding and reasoning can take much time and is sensitive to misunderstanding, but this is definitely the last source if nothing else is available.

SysLoop is based on an automated monitor and can detect and report misbehavior for a system operator. The report is manually processed and sent to the engineering process. This is less prone to human errors than above. It should be noted that the

Table 1. Feedback features for engineering process

Feature of feedback	UserLoop	SysLoop	AnaLoop
1. Knowledge response time (no delay)	Low	High	Medium
2. Knowledge delivery interval	Low	Medium	Medium
3. Knowledge accurance and probability for understanding	Low	Medium	High
4. Automation	Low	Medium	High
5. No data preprocessing	Low	Medium	High
6. Variety of knowledge	Medium	Low	High
7. Amount of knowledge	Low	Medium	High
8. Analyzing small development time	Medium	High	Low
9. Analyzing complexity	Low	Medium	High
10. Final (physical) behavior observations	High	Low	Low
11. Suitability for engineering process	Low	Medium	High

monitors may not be originally designed for the engineering process at all, which was the case in ELMI.

AnaLoop can automatically and regularly analyze the log files for extracting the expected behavior. Reports are automatically sent to the engineering process. Human errors are not probable, because the knowledge is already in the format the engineering process requires. Table 1 summarizes feasibility of the three feedback loops. The AnaLoop is the best, as we learned to know in practice in ELMI as well.

Our focus is in discovering the realized behavior that appears as an execution trace or sequential interdependent events in log files. Log file analyzers can be divided in two groups. The first group includes analyzers, like Synoptic [7], Invarimint [8] and Daikon [9], which creates behavior models from the log files. The second group includes analyzers, like LFA [10], Texada [11] and CEP type analyzers [5], which have a built-in expected behavior model independent of the log files. The latter only checks if the behaviors in the log files are expected or not. Similar approach is also presented by

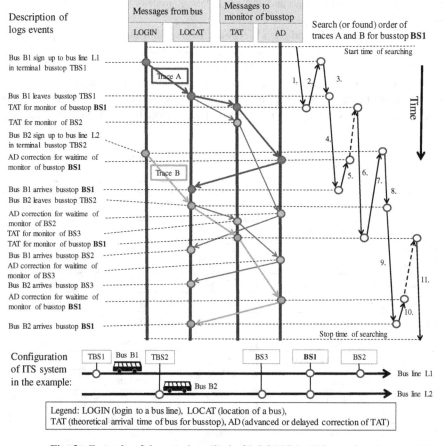

Fig. 2. Example of the search method of LOGDIG in ITS type log data

Maoz [12] that uses model-based traces as runtime models. Batch-job analyzers can be slower, but few on them, like LOGDIG, can perform very complex analysis.

LOGDIG has also a special "versatile searching" feature, which we have not seen in any other scientific analyzer. This means the possibility of backward searching as presented in Fig. 2. Other scientific analyzers seem to read log lines (events) only by a forward way and often row by row all the lines. LOGDIG can read only the selected lines from the log files.

One challenge in log analysis is that the information might not be purposed for error detection but e.g. for business, user or application context. This requires capability to interpret log information. In addition, there can be chains of sequential interdependent events, for which simple statistical methods are not sufficient [13]. This requires state sequence processing. LOGDIG [14] supports this, because it is intended for *expected behavior* mining. We have also proposed a Behavior Mining Language (BML) to support these needs [15]. There are also commercial real-time analyzers, like Apache Spark, but they are out of scope of this paper.

3 Complex Behavior Mining in LOGDIG

Figure 2 depicts an example of the search method of LOGDIG. For brevity we consider the figure self-explaining. This is a typical example of ITS system logs from sources like buses and central computer. The behavior is seen in the following sequential events: (1) a bus has sent *login* (i.e. *start*) to the line, (2) the bus has left the terminal bus stop, (3) the central computer has sent the first waiting time estimation to a bus stop monitor, (4) the central computer has sent the last time estimation to the bus stop monitor and (5) the bus has arrived to the monitor's bus stop. The searching has found two chains of sequential events, which we call traces A and B. Figure 2 also shows how the searching actually works in a versatile way. It is selective, because it rejects non-essential traces, which are shown as grey arrows. It can also go backward, like in arrows 2, 5, 6 and 10.

4 Testing LOGDIG with Generated Log Data

We have used both real and generated log data in testing LOGDIG. We discuss first the latter. To generate the test log files, we have implemented a tool called LogGen that takes static and dynamic properties as parameters. The former is e.g. test area, bus stop areas and bus lines. The latter are e.g. scheduling and speeding of buses, number of buses, number of generated traces and timing of logs. Figure 3 depicts a visualized example of the static properties in our example case, which consists of 4 bus lines, 4 terminal bus stops for direction A in left side of the test area, 3 terminal bus stops for direction B in the right side and 6 bus stop monitors in the edges of the matrix area. The sizes of all areas have been defined as meters. Bus lines are links as between bus stops, e.g. the red bus line goes through A1, M1, M3 and B1 bus stops.

The details of LogGen and LOGDIG are out of scope, but we present two example sets with the help of Fig. 4: Short (A) and complex (B) traces. The log file data is

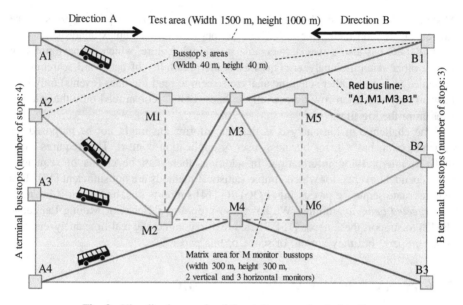

Fig. 3. Visualized example of the static properties in LogGen

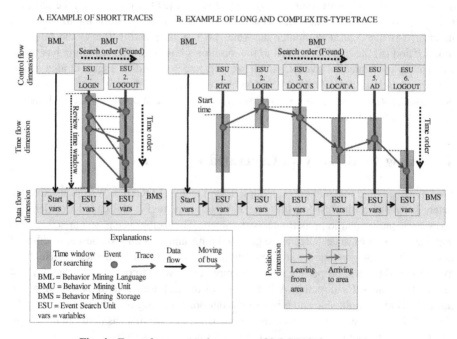

Fig. 4. Example traces and structure of LOGDIG for searching

depicted in the middle of Fig. 4 by the order of lines originally written to them. BMU executes the search of desired events (ESU) specified in the BML language. The results are traces from the log files as explained in the following.

In Example A, we want to search many short traces. The main objective is to measure all lengths of line logging and check if they are too long. To achieve this, LOGDIG (1) searches LOGIN event of a bus, (2) searches LOGOUT event of the bus and (3) checks if the time difference between the events is too long. This is repeated as many times as all LOGIN events has been read in the given review time window. In the example we have four "line logging" traces. The results are output to a Static Behavior Knowledge (SBK) formatted .csv file depicted in Table 2.

Table 2. The SBK file of example A

```
SBK_ID,BUS_ID,LOGIN,LOGOUT,DIFF,STATUS,CNT_OK,CNT_ERROR
1,1,2016-06-21 12:01:00,2016-06-21 12:11:00,600,ERR,0,1
2,2,2016-06-21 12:06:00,2016-06-21 12:15:00,540,OK,1,1
3,3,2016-06-21 12:08:00,2016-06-21 12:13:00,300,OK,2,1
4,1,2016-06-21 12:12:00,2016-06-21 12:17:00,300,OK,3,1
```

In Example B we want to search one complex and long trace. The main objective is to measure the time difference between real arriving and estimated time of a bus to the stop monitor. To achieve this, LOGDIG (1) searches Real Theoretical Arrival Time (RTAT) event of the bus, (2) LOGIN event of the bus, (3) leaving time of the bus from a terminal, (4) arriving time to the bus stop monitor, (5) last Advanced or Delayed (AD) event of the bus, (6) LOGOUT event of the bus and (7) calculates time difference. The results are written to the SBK file.

For brevity and clarity, the examples do not include all the details, like input parameters and adjusting of the time windows during the searching. For example, it is possible to search events only for certain bus or for all buses. A start and a stop time of the time windows typically depends on the results of previous searches. This can be seen as dotted horizontal lines between search states in Fig. 4.

5   Testing LOGDIG with Real Case Study

A severe bus stop monitor problem was discovered in ELMI, in which the arriving bus symbol disappeared too early [16]. The real case is similar to example B in Fig. 4, but with thousands of traces per day. Figure 5 depicts a screenshot of LOGDIG for the first 9 traces from a bus line between 07:00–8:30. The searching time windows are presented as vertical lines, and horizontally the traces with the corresponding colors. We can find there some issues. Trace 4 had problems, because no arriving was found to the stop monitor and the trace shape is different than others. There are maybe missing trace and departure of a bus between traces 4 and 5. Traces 8 and 9 have been almost the same and maybe two buses have been driving one after the other because of the morning rush hours.

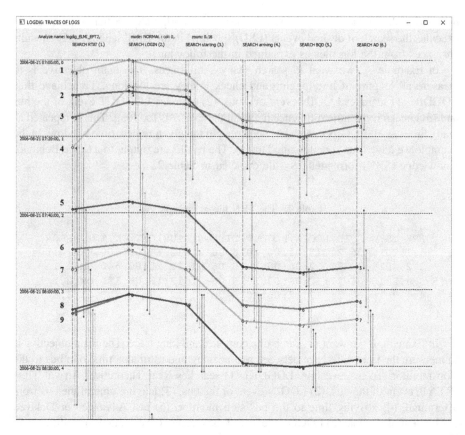

Fig. 5. LOGDIG's screenshot of real traces from ELMI logs

Some of the original data is unfortunately no longer available even if we know how the problem occurred. Thus, we augmented the original data with some generated data to expose the problem. The results are from one bus line (2132) per one day between 03:00–23:00, and we present only the most important results helping to fix the problems. Tables 3 and 4 depicts the minimum, average and maximum errors of the waiting times in five bus monitors (Sign ID). The waiting time errors were divided into 15, 10 and 5 min before arriving to a stop monitor and 0 min when a bus has just arrived to the stop monitor. A positive waiting time error means that the bus has arrived too late, and negative one means the opposite. The most important value is the average error value for 0 min. After fixes to ELMI, it has clearly been improved from 124 to 17 s. Another important result in Fig. 6 is the follow-up list, which lists all "bad" bus lines, buses and stop monitors. This means over 2 min waiting time errors. Figure 6 depicts how the total number of errors has been decreased from 16 (8 + 2 + 6) to 9 (3 + 2 + 4) after improvements. Also the percentage values are much smaller, e.g. in bus line 0021321 it has been decreased from 45,2 % to 2,4 %.

Table 3. Waiting time errors before improvements

Num	Sign ID	D R	L C	TAT-msg Amount	15 minutes min	ave	max	10 minutes min	ave	max	5 minutes min	ave	max	0 minutes min	ave	max
1:	1031	E	1	15	-12	66	308	-12	66	308	-12	71	290	85	131	184
2:	1033	W	1	62	-430	86	634	-434	137	608	-429	107	462	62	133	548
3:	1041	E	1	15	-22	59	278	-22	59	278	-22	60	157	63	129	179
4:	1061	W	1	77	-249	55	441	-145	104	412	-86	116	426	-165	127	540
5:	1071	E	1	12	-23	43	270	-23	43	270	-23	43	270	-23	38	141
ALL				181	-430	66	634	-434	104	608	-429	100	462	-165	124	548

Table 4. Waiting time errors after improvements

Num	Sign ID	D R	L C	TAT-msg Amount	15 minutes min	ave	max	10 minutes min	ave	max	5 minutes min	ave	max	0 minutes min	ave	max
1:	1031	E	1	15	-12	66	308	-12	66	308	-12	51	146	3	15	25
2:	1033	W	1	62	-430	45	543	-501	35	459	-517	0	376	1	22	427
3:	1041	E	1	15	-22	59	278	-22	59	278	-22	20	79	-10	10	29
4:	1061	W	1	77	-249	40	412	-190	30	412	-168	10	369	-246	17	405
5:	1071	E	1	12	-23	43	270	-23	43	270	-23	43	270	-23	10	121
ALL				181	-430	46	543	-501	38	459	-517	13	376	-246	17	427

```
1: BUS,111      =  10 /  20 = 50.0 %          1: BUS,463       =  1 /  24 = 4.2 %
2: BUS,138      =  13 /  25 = 52.0 %          2: BUS,53        =  1 /  29 = 3.4 %
3: BUS,228      =   8 /  18 = 44.4 %          3: BUS,73        =  3 /  39 = 7.7 %
4: BUS,283      =   3 /   6 = 50.0 %
5: BUS,451      =   9 /  20 = 45.0 %          1: LINE,0021321  =  1 /  42 = 2.4 %
6: BUS,463      =  16 /  24 = 66.7 %          2: LINE,0021322  =  4 / 139 = 2.9 %
7: BUS,53       =  16 /  29 = 55.2 %
8: BUS,73       =  20 /  39 = 51.3 %          1: SIGN,1033     =  1 /  62 = 1.6 %
                                              2: SIGN,1061     =  3 /  77 = 3.9 %
1: LINE,0021321 =  19 /  42 = 45.2 %          3: SIGN,1071     =  1 /  12 = 8.3 %
2: LINE,0021322 =  76 / 139 = 54.7 %          4: SIGN,ALLS     =  5 / 181 = 2.8 %

1: SIGN,1031    =   7 /  15 = 46.7 %
2: SIGN,1033    =  33 /  62 = 53.2 %
3: SIGN,1041    =   9 /  15 = 60.0 %
4: SIGN,1061    =  43 /  77 = 55.8 %
5: SIGN,1071    =   3 /  12 = 25.0 %
6: SIGN,ALLS    =  95 / 181 = 52.5 %
```

Fig. 6. Follow-up list errors, Original (left) and Fixed (right).

Figure 7 depicts the variation of waiting time errors from −5 to +8 min by 30 s resolution for all stop monitors. For example, there have been 5 waiting times in 0 min errors and 44 waiting times in +1,5 min errors.

After the improvements the results are clearly better. Almost all (155) waiting time errors are in 0 min and the variance is much smaller. There are still some single problem cases, like one bus arrived 7 min too late to the stop monitor.

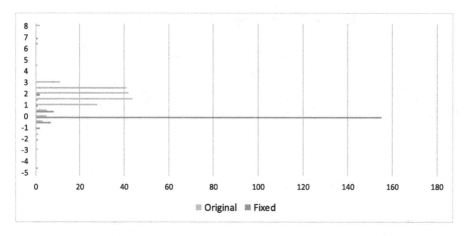

Fig. 7. Histogram of the waiting time errors in 0 min.

6 Conclusions

We have introduced an automatic, general purpose log-file analyzer framework LOGDIG, which was used to improve the ELMI real time passenger information system after the field deployment. To our best knowledge, there is no other such log file analyzer capable of backward and selective searches through the log files, which was required to fix ELMI. LOGDIG also automated many analysis tasks that are usually carried out manually. The results are looped to the systems engineering process every night, so the improvements can be started in the next working day. LOGDIG and the tools are freely available at GitHub [17] as well as the generated test data used in this paper. In the future, we will evaluate the feasibility of commercial log file analyzers and study further generation of representative and generally applicable test logs.

References

1. Aaltonen, J.: Implementation of GPS based real time passenger information system. Licentiate in Technology, Tampere University of Technology, pp. 1–76 (1998)
2. Wasson, C.S.: System Engineering Analysis, Design, and Development: Concepts, Principles, and Practices. John Wiley & Sons (2015)
3. Blanchard, B.S., Fabrycky, W.J., Fabrycky, W.J.: Systems Engineering and Analysis. Prentice Hall, New Jersey (1990)
4. Chapman, P., Clinton, J., Kerber, R., Khabaza, T., Reinartz, T., Shearer, C., Wirth, R.: CRISP-DM 1.0 Step-by-step data mining guide (2000)
5. Luckham, D.: The Power of Events. Addison-Wesley, Reading (2002)
6. Dunkel, J., Fernández, A., Ortiz, R., Ossowski, S.: Event-driven architecture for decision support in traffic management systems. Expert Syst. Appl. 38(6), 6530–6539 (2011)

7. Beschastnikh, I., Abrahamson, J., Brun, Y., Ernst, M.D.: Synoptic: studying logged behavior with inferred models. In: Proceedings of the 19th ACM SIGSOFT Symposium and the 13th European Conference on Foundations of Software Engineering, pp. 448–451. ACM

8. Beschastnikh, I., Brun, Y., Abrahamson, J., Ernst, M.D., Krishnamurthy, A.: Unifying FSM-inference algorithms through declarative specification. In: Proceedings of the 2013 International Conference on Software Engineering, pp. 252–261. IEEE Press (2013)

9. Ernst, M.D., Perkins, J.H., Guo, P.J., McCamant, S., Pacheco, C., Tschantz, M.S., Xiao, C.: The Daikon system for dynamic detection of likely invariants. Sci. Comput. Program. **69**(1), 35–45 (2007)

10. Andrews, J.H., Zhang, Y.: General test result checking with log file analysis. IEEE Trans. Softw. Eng. **29**(7), 634–648 (2003)

11. Lemieux, C., Beschastnikh, I.: Investigating program behavior using the texada LTL specifications miner. In: 2015 30th IEEE/ACM International Conference on Automated Software Engineering (ASE), pp. 870–875. IEEE (2015)

12. Maoz, S.: Using model-based traces as runtime models. Computer **42**(10), 28–36 (2009)

13. Valdman, J.: Log file analysis, Technical report, Department of Computer Science and Engineering, University of West Bohemia in Pilsen (FAV UWB), Czech Republic,, Tech. Rep.DCSE/TR-2001-04, pp. 1–51 (2001)

14. Heikkinen, E., Hämäläinen, T.D.: LOGDIG log file analyzer for mining expected behavior from log files. In: SPLST 2015 14th Symposium on Programming Languages and Software Tools, Tampere, Finland (2015)

15. Heikkinen, E., Hämäläinen, T.D.: Behavior mining language for mining expected behavior from log files. In: IECON The 42nd Annual Conference of IEEE Industrial Electronics Society, Firenze, Italy, Accepted for publication in 24–27 October 2016

16. Pesonen, H., Laine, T., Bäckström, J., Granberg, M., Vehmas, A., Niittymäki, J.: Assessment of impacts and socio-economical profitability of real-time passenger information system (ELMI). FITS Publications 7/2002, Ministry of Transport and Communications, Strafica Ltd., SCC Viatek Ltd., LT-Consultants Ltd., Helsinki (2002) http://virtual.vtt.fi/virtual/proj6/fits/julkaisut/hanke2/fits7.pdf

17. Heikkinen, E.: LOGDIG's source codes and examples, GitHub. https://github.com/ErasRasmuson/LA. (Accessed 1 April 2016)

On the Effectiveness of Vector-Based Approach for Supporting Simultaneous Editing of Software Clones

Sciyu Numata[1], Norihiro Yoshida[2]([⊠]), Eunjong Choi[3], and Katsuro Inoue[1]

[1] Osaka University, 1-5 Yamadaoka, Suita, Osaka 565-0871, Japan
{s-numata,inoue}@ist.osaka-u.ac.jp
[2] Nagoya University, Furo-cho, Chikusa, Nagoya, Aichi 464-8601, Japan
yoshida@ertl.jp
[3] Nara Institute of Science and Technology,
8916-5 Takayama-cho, Ikoma, Nara 630-0192, Japan
choi@is.naist.jp

Abstract. Code clone is one of the factors that makes software maintenance more difficult. Once a developer find a defect in a code fragment, he/she has to inspect the all of the code clones of the code fragment. In this study, we investigated the effectiveness of query-based use of a vector-based clone detection tool for supporting simultaneous fixing of buggy clones in source code and compared it with the query-based use of a token-based clone detection tool CCFinder.

Keywords: Code clone detection tool · Software maintenance · Simultaneous editing

1 Introduction

A code clone is a code fragment that has identical or similar code fragments to it in the source code [10]. So far, a lot of code clone detection techniques have been developed to capture various aspects of source code similarity [7,10,13].

For the detection of syntactically identical or similar code fragments, token-based and tree-based approaches detect identical token sequence and similar syntax tree in source code, respectively [7,10]. These approaches are able to detect useful clones (i.e., code fragments to be merged [5], inconsistent code clones that are suspected to include a bug [9]), but have limitations of false positives [5] (syntactically similar but semantically different code) and false negatives [4] (syntactically different but semantically similar clones). As a more sophisticated approach, a few techniques have been proposed for the detection of only semantically similar clones from source code [7,11,12].

For example, Komondoor and Horwitz proposed an approach to finding isomorphic subgraphs of program dependence graphs (PDGs) in order to find semantic clones from source code [12]. Also, MeCC detects C functions implementing semantically-similar computations based on the similarity of abstract

© Springer International Publishing AG 2016
P. Abrahamsson et al. (Eds.): PROFES 2016, LNCS 10027, pp. 560–567, 2016.
DOI: 10.1007/978-3-319-49094-6_41

memory states between them [11]. Jiang and Su proposed an approach to compare program execution traces via random testing in order to find functionally equivalent code fragments [8]. However, those approaches have limitations. Identifying isomorphic subgraph of PDG is time-consuming as well as identifying abstract memory states of C functions [11], and comparing execution traces require a number of test suites to achieve sufficient level of test coverage. Also, it is difficult for those approaches to be applied to uncompilable source code.

In our previous research [18], we developed a vector-based approach for the lightweight detection of function clones. In our vector-based approach, a feature vector is generated for each function, based on the occurrence of identifiers and reserved keywords, and then clustering of the generated vectors is performed by means of locality-sensitive hashing (LSH) [6]. Finally, clones are detected based on the similarities between each pair of feature vectors. We confirmed the advantages of the vector-based approach over MeCC as follows:

- Detects a number of function clones but also maintains a low false positive rate in comparison to MeCC
- Detect in a shorter time
- Finds a larger number of clone-related defects and bad smells

We introduced the tool based on the vector-based approach to a Japanese multinational IT company and then got feedbacks from practitioners in the company. According to the feedbacks, the practitioners need to know the effectiveness of the vector-based approach for supporting simultaneous fixing of buggy clones. They are mainly motivated to perform query-based use of the vector-based approach. When they find a defect in a function, they would like to give the function as a query to the vector-based approach and then discover clone-related defects from the detected function clones. In our previous research [18], we detected function clones from OSS and then manually confirmed that a large number of the detected function clones included defects and bad smells. However, the effectiveness of query-based use of the vector-based approach is still unknown so far.

In this study, we investigated the effectiveness of query-based use of the vector-based clone detection tool for supporting simultaneous fixing of buggy clones in source code. In the investigation, we used the collection of clone-related defects that was collected by Li and Ernst for the evaluation of a cloned buggy code detector CBCD [14,15].

The remainder of this paper is organized into the following sections. Section 2 details a vector-based approach to detecting code clones. Section 3 describes a method to investigate the effectiveness of query-based use of a clone detection approach. Section 4 explains the investigation result, Sect. 5 reviews related work and finally, Sect. 6 summarizes this study.

2   Vector-Based Approach to Detecting Clones

Figure 1 provides an overview of the vector-based approach. The Vector-based approach takes source code is used as the input, and the output consists of a list

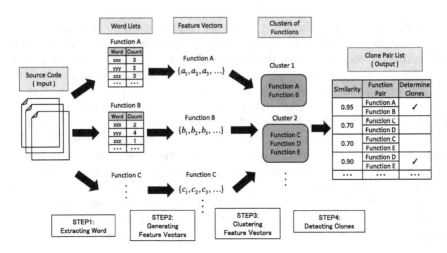

Fig. 1. Overview of the Vector-based approach

of clone pairs (i.e., pairs of function clones that are identical or similar to one another).

Hereafter, we use the term *word* to represent a set of identifiers (e.g., variables and function names) and reserved keywords (e.g., conditional statements and interactive statements).

2.1   STEP1: Extracting Word

In this step, *word*s are extracted from functions in the source code. During this process, if an identifier consists of more than one word, it is divided into different words as follows:

- It is divided using a delimiters such as hyphens or underscores, between words.
- It is split by using a capital letter for each word using CamelCase

2.2   STEP2: Generating Feature Vectors

In this step, feature vectors are generated based on the weights of extracted words from STEP1. For this, we use Term Frequency Inverse Document Frequency(*TF-IDF*) [2], a popular technique, in IR, for weighting each word. Uramoto et al. used *TF-IDF* to weight newspaper articles for the relation of multiple news articles [17]. In this study, we use *TF-IDF* to weight words in the source code.

TF-IDF combines Term Frequency(TF) weights and Inverse Document Frequency(IDF) weights. For example, suppose N_w represents the occurrences of w in a function, and N_{all} represents the total number of occurrences of all words in a function. In addition, *Function* represents the set of all functions in the source code, while *Function_w* represents the set of functions that contain word

w exists. The weighting of w using *TF-IDF* is defined as follows:

$$tf_w = \frac{N_w}{N_{all}} \qquad idf_w = \log \frac{|Function|}{|Function_w|} \qquad tfidf_w = tf_w \times idf_w$$

2.3   STEP3: Clustering Feature Vectors

Clustering is used to identify candidates for clone pairs, and is conducted. prior to clone detection (STEP4) for the sake of time efficiency. In this step, the feature vectors generated in STEP 2 are clustered using Locality-Sensitive Hashing(LSH) [6], which is known to be an efficient nearest neighbor search algorithm.

To cluster feature vectors, in this study we used E^2LSH^1 [1], which implements the LSH algorithm. Given a feature vector as a query, E^2LSH performs clustering of feature vectors approximate to the query from the dataset, based on Euclidean distance. Using a dataset of functions, with each feature vector (function) as a query, a set of similar functions is returned.

2.4   STEP4: Detecting Clones

Clone pairs are detected based on the *cosine similarity* between all of the feature vectors of the clustered feature vectors obtained in STEP 3. *Cosine similarity* identifies similarities between multidimensional vectors. Formally, the *cosine similarity* between two vectors $\boldsymbol{a}$, and $\boldsymbol{b}$ whose dimension is d are determined as follows:

$$sim(\boldsymbol{a}, \boldsymbol{b}) = cos(\boldsymbol{a}, \boldsymbol{b}) = \frac{\sum_{i=1}^{d} a_i b_i}{\sqrt{\sum_{i=1}^{d} a_i^2} \sqrt{\sum_{i=1}^{d} b_i^2}}$$

Cosine similarity takes a value between 0 and 1, because feature values only have positive values, as seen in the formulation of the TF-IDF described in STEP 2. If the *cosine similarity* value between two feature vectors is higher than the threshold, these two vectors are regarded as clone pairs. In this study, we set the threshold at 0.9 to reduce the probability of false positive results.

3   Investigation Method

We investigated the effectiveness of query-based use of the vector-based clone detection tool for supporting simultaneous fixing of buggy clones in source code and compared it with the query-based use of a token-based clone detection tool CCFinder [10]. Please note that we set 10 tokens as minimum length of a token sequence for CCFinder because most clone-related defects in the dataset are 10 tokens or smaller in source code.

As we mentioned in Sect. 1, this research was triggered by the feedbacks from the Japanese multinational IT company. Because this company has used CCFinder for several years, they would like to know the effectiveness comparison of the vector-based approach and CCFinder.

---

[1] http://www.mit.edu/~andoni/LSH/.

Table 1. The numbers of N1, N2, N3 and N4

	Vector-based approach		CCFinder
	Threshold = 0.9	Threshold = 0.5	
N1	11	10	10
N2	22	13	11
N3	4	11	16
N4	1	4	1

3.1   Dataset

For our investigation, we used the dataset of clone-related defects that was collected by Li and Ernst [14,15]. The clone-related defects in the dataset are from
the OSS repositories of Git, Linux kernel and PostgreSQL that are written by
C/C++.

The dataset also includes commit IDs of not only clone-related defects but
also code clones of those defects [14]. Please note that we removed the instances
if a defect and its code clones in the same function because the purpose of this
study is the investigation of effectiveness of query-based use of the vector-based
approach.

3.2   Effectiveness Criteria

We used not only precision/recall and F-measure but also a categorization proposed by Li and Ernst [15]. Li and Ernst proposed the following categorization
for each instance in their dataset of clone-related defects.

- N1: no false positives, no false negatives
- N2: no false positives, some false negatives
- N3: some false positives, no false negatives
- N4: some false positives, some false negatives

After clones of each clone-related defect are detected, each clone detection tool
can be characterized by the numbers of N1, N2, N3 and N4.

Precison/recall and F-score for each approach are calculated from the total
numbers of true positives, detected functions and buggy functions that are
involved in the dataset.

4   Investigation Results

Table 1 shows the numbers of N1, N2, N3 and N4 and Table 2 shows recall,
precision and F-score for each approach.

According the numbers of N2 in Table 1, the vector-based approach with
threshold=0.9 is the most efficient for supporting simultaneous fixing of buggy

Table 2. Recall, Precison and F-score

	Vector-based approach		CCFinder
	Threshold=0.9	Threshold=0.5	
Recall	0.41	0.53	0.53
Precision	0.59	0.11	0.01
F-score	0.48	0.18	0.02

clones because N2 means no false positive. When developers have only a limited time, the vector-based approach with threshold=0.9 is the most suitable.

In terms of the numbers of N3 in Table 1, CCFinder is the highest. For the development of a high-reliability software system, CCFinder is the most suitable because N3 means no false negative.

N1, N2, N3 and N4 take account of the existence of false postives and negatives and do not take account of the numbers of them precisely. On the other hand, Recall/Precision takes account of the numbers of them precisely.

According to Table 2, the precision of CCFinder is extremely low. In several instances of clone-related defects in the dataset, CCFinder detects a large number of false positives (max. 218). This means that CCFinder is unsuitable when developers have only a limited time. The vector-based approach with threshold=0.9 is most suitable when developers have only a limited time according to the precision in Table 2.

In terms of recall, the all of the score are almost same. The vector-based approach with threshold=0.5 and CCFinder are the highest score between them. Since the precision of CCFinder is extremely low, the vector-based approach with threshold=0.5 is more suitable for the development of a high-reliability software system.

5   Related Work

Thus far, various techniques have been proposed for the detection of code clones from source code. For the detection of syntactically identical or similar code fragments, the token-based and tree-based approaches detect identical token sequences and similar syntax trees in the source code, respectively [7,10]. However, these approaches may result in false positives (syntactically similar but semantically different clones) [5] and false negatives (syntactically different but semantically similar clones) [4].

As a more sophisticated approach, a few techniques have been proposed for the detection of only semantically similar clones from the source code [8,11,12]. For example, Komondoor and Horwitz proposed for finding the isomorphic subgraphs of PDGs in order to find the semantic clones from the source code [12]. Additionally, MeCC [11] detects C functions implementing semantically similar computations, based on the similarity of their abstract memory states. Jiang and Su proposed an approach to comparing program execution traces via random testing in order to find functionally equivalent code fragments [8]. The vector-based approach in this paper is inspired by the existing vector-based approach that is proposed by Marcus et al. [16]. Their original approach uses a LSI-based clustering technique to form all clusters of similar entities. LSI-based retrieval is a considerable idea to improve the recall of the vector-based approach in our study. However, we do not use LSI because it leads the increase of the detection time.

Various applications of the detection of code clones from source code have been proposed. For example, several studies have been conducted on the support of clone refactoring using clone detection techniques. Balazinska et al. proposed a code clone classification method for the identification of reengineering opportunities [3]. Higo et al. [5] proposed a set of metrics to represent the difficulty of merging clones detected by the token-based clone detection tool CCFinder [10]. Yoshida et al. proposed an approach for extracting clone clones that are related to each other from the output of CCFinder, and suggesting these be used as a large-scale reengineering opportunity [19]. Combining these approaches with the vector-based approach appears to be a promising solution for achieving the efficient support of clone refactoring.

6   Summary

In this study, we investigated the effectiveness of the query-based use of the vector-based clone detection tool for supporting simultaneous fixing of buggy clones in source code. In the investigation, we used the collection of clone-related defects that was collected by Li and Ernst for the evaluation of a cloned buggy code detector CBCD [14,15].

The summary of the investigation result is as follows:

– The detection result of the vector-based approach with threshold=0.9 is highest precesion.
– The detection results of the vector-based approach with threshold=0.5 and CCFinder are highest recall.
– Since the precision of CCFinder is extremely low, the vector-based approach with threshold=0.5 is more suitable for the development of a high-reliability software system.

Acknowledgments. This work was supported by JSPS KAKENHI Grant Numbers 25220003, 26730036, 15H06344 and 16K16034.

References

1. Andoni, A., Indyk, P.: Near-optimal hashing algorithms for approximate nearest neighbor in high dimensions. CACM **51**(1), 117–122 (2008)
2. Baeza-Yates, R., Ribeiro-Neto, B.: Modern Information Retrieval: The Concepts and Technology behind Search, 2nd edn. (ACM Press Books) Addison-Wesley Professional, Harlow (2011)

3. Balazinska, M., Merlo, E., Dagenais, M., Lague, B., Kontogiannis, K.: Measuring clone based reengineering opportunities. In: Proceedings of METRICS 1999, pp. 292–303 (1999)

4. Deissenboeck, F., Heinemann, L., Hummel, B., Wagner, S.: Challenges of the dynamic detection of functionally similar code fragments. In: Proceedings of CSMR 2012, pp. 299–308 (2012)

5. Higo, Y., Kusumoto, S., Inoue, K.: A metric-based approach to identifying refactoring opportunities for merging code clones in a java software system. J. Softw. Maintenance Evol. **20**(6), 435–461 (2008)

6. Indyk, P., Motwani, R.: Approximate nearest neighbors: towards removing the curse of dimensionality. In: Proceedings of STOC 1998, pp. 604–613 (1998)

7. Jiang, L., Misherghi, G., Su, Z., Glondu, S.: DECKARD: scalable and accurate tree-based detection of code clones. In: Proceedings of ICSE 2007, pp. 96–105 (2007)

8. Jiang, L., Su, Z.: Automatic mining of functionally equivalent code fragments via random testing. In: Proceedings of ISSTA 2009, pp. 81–92 (2009)

9. Jiang, L., Su, Z., Chiu, E.: Context-based detection of clone-related bugs. In: Proceedings of ESEC-FSE 2007, pp. 55–64 (2007)

10. Kamiya, T., Kusumoto, S., Inoue, K.: CCFinder: a multilinguistic token-based code clone detection system for large scale source code. IEEE Trans. Softw. Eng. **28**(7), 654–670 (2002)

11. Kim, H., Jung, Y., Kim, S., Yi, K.: MeCC: memory comparison-based clone detector. In: Proceedings of ICSE 2011, pp. 301–310 (2011)

12. Komondoor, R., Horwitz, S.: Using slicing to identify duplication in source code. In: Proceedings of SAS 2001, pp. 40–56 (2001)

13. Krinke, J.: Identifying similar code with program dependence graphs. In: Proceedings of WCRE 2001, pp. 301–307 (2001)

14. Li, J., Ernst, M.D.: CBCD: Cloned buggy code detector. Technical report UW-CSE-11-05-02, University of Washington Department of Computer Science and Engineering (2011)

15. Li, J., Ernst, M.D.: CBCD: cloned buggy code detector. In: Proceedings of ICSE 2012, pp. 310–320 (2012)

16. Marcus, A., Maletic, J.I.: Identification of high-level concept clones in source code. In: Proceedings of ASE 2001, pp. 107–114 (2001)

17. Uramoto, N., Takeda, K.: A method for relating multiple newspaper articles by using graphs, and its application to webcasting. In: Proceedings of ACL 1998, pp. 1307–1313 (1998)

18. Yamanaka, Y., Choi, E., Yoshida, N., Inoue, K.: A high speed function clone detection based on information retrieval technique. IPSJ J. **55**(10), 2245–2255 (2014). in Japanese

19. Yoshida, N., Higo, Y., Kamiya, T., Kusumoto, S., Inoue, K.: On refactoring support based on code clone dependency relation. In: Proceedings of METRICS 2005, pp. 16:1–16:10 (2005)

Business Value and Benefits

The Developers Dilemma: Perfect Product Development or Fast Business Validation?

Henri Terho[(✉)], Sampo Suonsyrjä, and Kari Systä

Tampere University of Technology, P.O. Box 553, 33101 Tampere, Finland
{henri.terho,sampo.suonsyrja,kari.systa}@tut.fi

Abstract. To find a fast-track to profitability, a startup needs to streamline and speed up two vital processes – developing novel products and finding new markets for their products. These two goals are typically opposed to each other, business development requiring quick iteration and product development requiring focus on quality. This difference in mindsets, where the focus should be on the balance of quality to the business experimentation causes a conflicting environment for the developers to develop products. This problem is aggravated in a startup environment, where the reasons for product failure are not clear, increasing the frustrations felt by the developers. Clear ways to communicate the product goals and even successes between management and developers is needed to create an environment for success. This balancing act between quality and speed to achieve fast product iteration is the developers dilemma.

Keywords: Startups · Software development · Business development · Lean startup · Prototyping · Agile

1 Introduction

The success of a startup, or a potential company looking for a repeatable and scalable business model, is often related to the time it takes for the startup to develop their business model. [4,9] Consequently, the importance of fast iteration cycles is intensified, as the entire business model can be unclear or at least it remains under constant development [3,13].

Mastering this requires optimized techniques and methods for product and customer management [3]. An emerging choice for such a management method is the Lean Startup framework [4,9]. Products are tested through hypothesis driven iterations, where the success of the product is measured by actionable metrics. Moreover, when a product is deemed failed, a pivot is encouraged. As each iteration brings new knowledge, iteration speed is vital – Failing faster means also finding success faster. To meet the requirements of rapid course corrections in the business, i.e. pivoting, the product development process has to adapt to fast iterations [13].

In a startup environment the developers should be constantly aware that the software might become waste and therefore typical quality thinking can become

© Springer International Publishing AG 2016
P. Abrahamsson et al. (Eds.): PROFES 2016, LNCS 10027, pp. 571–579, 2016.
DOI: 10.1007/978-3-319-49094-6_42

difficult. This creates a situation where a software developer is pulled in two directions: should I follow the values of professional software development or work fast to support the constantly changing business directions?

This delicate balancing act between writing good quality software and spending as little resources as possible on a product that could be scrapped creates the *Developers Dilemma* that we explore further in this paper.

2   Background

The Lean Startup method is a popularized collection of best practices from multiple previous entrepreneurship theories such as Creation theory [1] and Bricolage [2]. With it, business development is seen as an iterative process of confirming business hypotheses with minimum viable products (MVPs) [9]. The method consists of iterative cycles of building, measuring, and learning.

Each cycle is typically linked with its own MVP, which is used to test the hypothesis of the current cycle. Based on these tests, the company either stays on the same path, building additional MVPs on top of the data gained from the first, or pivots their business plan to a new trajectory. Startups could even be said to be defined by their pivot making capabilities [12].

An MVP is a version of the product that enables a full turn of the build-measure-learn loop. It should contain the features that realize the unique value proposition of the software solution and little else. The idea is to cut out all non-essential features and leave just the core features of your application and the tools to enable learning [8].

As a software development method, producing MVPs is somewhat similar to prototyping. Prototyping approaches have been developed for situations where the work steps of a project cannot be clearly detailed before execution [10]. Prototyping incorporates many styles, such as iterative, rapid, evolutionary, throwaway incremental and mock up prototyping [7]. Stephen and Bates [11] define the prototype through two common characteristics:

1. The prototype enables a high degree of user evaluation which substantially affects requirements, specifications, or design.
2. The prototype initiates a learning process for users and developers of the system.

The first definition matches the MVP's aspect of user evaluation. The second definition matches the MVP cycle, where the MVP is designed to enable one cycle of the experimentation and produce learning with minimal development effort.

The prototypes can be split into throwaway and evolutionary prototypes. These two types are classified by their intended life cycle. Development based on evolutionary prototypes goes through sequences of re-design, re-implementation and re-evaluation without knowing the complete set of requirements beforehand [7]. Although the exact requirements for further development might be unclear, the implementation choice still matters as large parts of the code will be reused. On the contrary, throwaway prototypes will not be reused.

Comparing these two with MVPs, MVPs cover both aspects and possibilities of prototypes. In MVP development, the key idea is to validate the business case as fast as possible with a minimum set of features. If the experiment fails, the MVP should be thrown away, but in the case of a success it will be used again. However, it is not typically known beforehand if the MVP results in a throwaway prototype or in an evolutionary prototype. Therefore, the developers encounter a dilemma of writing code suitable for either throw-away or evolutionary prototyping.

3   Developers Dilemma

3.1   Environment

Modern software development, especially in a startup business where direction is changed rapidly, challenges the professional mind-set of software developers. These contradicting goals summarize the Developer's dilemma:

- As any professionals, software developers want to create artifacts. However, experimentation and pivoting that are implemented in many startups often lead to abandoning of software that did not receive positive feedback from the users or could not create an attractive business model fast enough.
- One of the main ways of showing your skills as a software developers is to write elegant code. However, when aiming at the minimum viability, developers should not refine their work in terms of quality and functionality to a level that they can be proud of.
- Developers can be used to creating prototypes that are thrown away, but this is not the case if they look at an MVP more as the first version of a final product, i.e. an evolutionary prototype. When such an MVP fails, this can cause a sense of loss for the developers who have poured their talent into the creation of the MVP.
- In the sense that an MVP is actually closer to being a tool for market research than an actual product, developers might spend too much effort on developing features that are ultimately not needed. The stress about features which are not essential is unneeded.

This environment of creating software, where the passion of the software developers might work against the goals of the company is typical in product development and startup environments. It creates a difficult environment to manage and develop software in.

To further elaborate, developers typically want to distinguish prototypes from a real products, but if the operation of the company is based on business experimentation, the choice is not known in advance.

3.2   Organizational View

The developers dilemma is a problem and a strategic question for the whole organization. The disjoint between the quality expectations of the software and the learning that the organization wants to achieve can cause problems.

This problem is illustrated in Fig. 1. The quality of the software and the size of the learning goals are placed on different axes. Typically the more complex the learning objectives, the larger product has to be built. For example, you are assessing solutions to complex networked problems or totally novel technology.

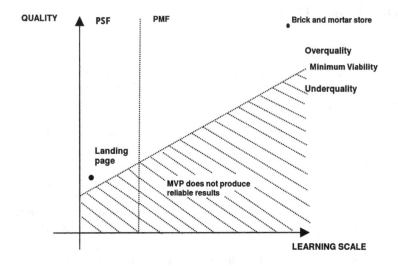

Fig. 1. Quality vs learning scale

The quality of this product has to be above a viable level to produce reliable results. This is illustrated by the Minimum Viability line on the graph. The quality of an MVP above the line is such that it does not interfere in assessing an business hypothesis. To further elaborate, the reason why the customers will not use or buy the MVP is that the they actually do not see it worthy – not because for example that the UI is horrible. Consequently, MVPs that are under the Minimum Viability line do not produce reliable results to the learning goals.

On the other hand, when the learning goals are still small and abstract, such as when an organization is just looking for the initial problem solution fit (PSF), MVPs can be smaller and of worse quality than when looking for product market fit (PMF). This is illustrated by the dotted vertical line.

In this case, we define quality to include not only typical quality attributes, but also the effort level it takes to develop an MVP such as additional features and keeping track of technical debt. So the challenge is to optimize quality as close to the Minimum Viability line as possible to reduce the amount of wasted quality and work. Also the two steps to product validation, PSF and PMF are marked to the chart to show the different phases of validation [4].

Research into the motivations of programmers show that competence, not experiments and financial incentives motivate them. [5] For the developers the way to show talent is to write quality code, so the natural tendency for quality in this is to go up. When such overquality prototypes are thrown away, the efforts of the developer are wasted and it results in frustration for the developers. The goal of the organization would be to make sure that the developers understand the goals of the prototype/MVP. The management has to message to the developers the point in the x-axis for the current product. The developers are then responsible for the positioning in the y-axis.

Some typical first products are positioned on the scale. Landing pages are small products which enable learning on a small scale, but do not require much quality. Typically the goal of the landing page MVP is to just assess the initial PSF. Brick and mortar stores as the first product on the other hand require a huge investment of resources to start and they may result in an immediate failure, if the clientele is not interested in the products of the store. The idea being that initially starting a brick-and-mortar store to asses your initial business hypothesis produces a high quality "product", but is a huge risk.

This positioning on the axes is at the heart of the developers dilemma and how the wanted position in these axes is messaged to the developers. The positioning on both axes is important to the success of the company, but the management typically forgets to take into account the quality tendencies and its psychological effects when deciding the goals.

3.3   Example

The issues that result from the developers dilemma in development can be better shown through an example:

A small startup is investigating their new hypothesis that people want to buy blood pressure measurement services. An MVP to test the validity of the idea is created. This MVP is a small website which enables customers to contact a person to come and measure their blood pressure. For the software development the user story in the backlog would be "As a user I want to fill in my contact details so the company can contact me to measure my blood pressure". In this first iteration, the experiment is to see if people want to even buy these services. The enabling MVP is the website that collects and stores contact information.

After the success of MVP, the company decides to experiment if they can expand the business by changing the contact form to a time reservation system. This way they can allocate personnel more efficiently. To facilitate this, a time reservation website is built as the second MVP.

At the third stage, the company has seen that there is demand for blood pressure measurements and decides to experiment if the people are willing to measure their blood pressure in predesignated locations. To test this, they develop a mobile application with GPS location to show the closest free blood measurement point. The new user story is: "As a user I want to be able to find out the nearest point where I can measure my blood pressure and reserve it." Here the experiment has expanded from a web form to a mobile application.

Again from the angle of the software developer, the development of the mobile application is a new production of a new stand alone application.

On the business development side, the continuous development of the theme progresses and builds upon the results from the previous application, expanding the scope of the project to one direction at a time. This however is not reflected even in the backlog items created. The actual goals of the company are not reflected by the user stories that the development is based upon. To improve upon this, the startup should have a backlog item that shows the goals of the current experiment, e.g. "We as a startup want to know if the customers want to come to our premises for measurement."

This communication problem causes the developers to develop three different projects. First a web application contact form is developed. Next a reservation system is developed and third a separate GPS location application is built. These three separate projects do not have large amounts of overlap and also the two previous versions of the product have now been throwaway prototypes. On top of this, the developer has seen two of his products thrown out as waste.

Even though the company has achieved its goals, this feeling might not have been transferred to the developers. The feeling with the developers might even be that most of their work was wasted, even though it clearly contributed to the company goals. Similarly, if the developers have used huge amount of resources in refining for example the first contact form MVP and its back-end scalability, the organization can leave the developers without proper recognition as their efforts have done in vain in the eyes of the organization.

3.4   Lean Startup Difficulties

One of the most difficult things in the execution of Lean Startup's Build-Measure-Learn cycle is understanding why an MVP actually fails. This assessment of product failures is a critical part of the Developer's Dilemma. The Lean Startup tries to avoid the dilemma, however, by focusing on learning goals, not on development goals.

By developing different types of MVPs, a startup can split their learning goals into appropriately sized fragments. The different types of MVPs have been described e.g. in [9,13]. By sharing the vision of using many of them along the life cycle within the whole organization, we think that the risk of Developer's Dilemma can be mitigated.

However, if the targets of developing an MVP are not made clear for the whole organization (including developers) Lean Startup will not help in resolving the Developer's Dilemma. Therefore, the underlying communications problems and the way developers valuate their own work form the crux of the Developer's Dilemma.

We propose that developers are intrinsically drawn to think that it is the lack of refining, missing features and things such as technical debt that make an MVP fail. If this opinion is given the most value, an unsetting can be created in which an MVP is refined forever or until the organization runs out of funds, but no one really understands (or accepts) why no user actually needs the product.

On the other hand, the development organization can be drawn to think that an idea and the related MVP do not have any business value because the MVP does not succeed straight away at a targeted level. In such a case, the organization might perceive the developed MVP as a perfect artifact to find out if a business problem is worth solving. This, however, is quite often not the case. Rather, MVPs usually need some refining to be able to produce reliable results for learning, if a business problem is actually worth solving. Again, this premature rejection of an MVP can create an unfavorable setting. In such, MVPs are thrown away before they are developed to their minimum viability.

We propose that the difficulty of balancing between these two unfavorable settings, can be a root cause for the Developer's Dilemma. On one hand, the technical development of MVPs that can produce reliable results is required and expected from the software developers. Also the developers naturally tend toward better quality because it is a way for them to show their skills. However, developing MVPs above the quality of minimum viability can be considered waste. Thus, developers need to understand thoroughly the level of quality they are expected to produce. On the other hand, the organization needs to have an amazing competence in chopping down the learning goals to appropriate size experiments. If these two premises do not exist in a case, the setup is ready for example for contradicting opinions on why an MVP fails, i.e. one of the result of the Developer's Dilemma.

3.5   Analysis of the Developer's Dilemma

This conflict between business-driven and technical-driven goals is not new. Similar dilemma exists in most Agile processes since the development should focus on the tasks of the biggest business value. This often leads to compromises in the architecture, and the maintenance of the architecture requires special care in Agile development [6]. In one way, Lean approaches partly amplify this since non-productive work is considered *waste* but by including principles like *build quality in* the Lean community has recognized the importance of professional development.

Many aspects of the developer's dilemma are known but the startup approach amplifies the developer dilemma since the process is driven by the business experiments. As in all organizations, the key element is communication and understanding of common goals. Based on these assumptions we propose several aspects that can be used to identify the developers dilemma:

- *Do the same people develop the software and business aspects of the software?* The easiest way to understand both sides of the problem is to work on both development and management roles. This allows for a larger perspective on the whole company. The management should be transparent and allow for opinions from both sides to be intermixed.
- *Is the software development outsourced?* Outsourcing the software development splits the goals of the company in two. The software company is responsible for delivering software and they have their own goals. The original business is left with just the business goals in mind and can optimize to fulfill

those. For the outsourcing companies, the fulfillment of developer ethos might be easier because the clients bring the problems to them and the company does not have to do validation on those. Even if the product would fail on the business side, the software developers have met their goals.

- *What are the performance indicators that are used to measure the software development?* You get what you measure is an old mantra that still holds true. If the development is only measured in regard to quality or number of tickets completed the development work is separated from the business goals. The measures should be developed in such a way to encompass business and quality indicators.
- *If asked, do management and software development teams have the same goals for the product?* Do they see the same future for it, i.e. still in use after 6 months, profitable. Also what do the developers see as the core targets, optimizing performance, creating products quick? Does management share these goals?
- *How does the company handle the failures of the previous MVP?* Is it taken as a way to learn from failure and do the management and development see it in the same way. Are questions like was the UI good enough handled in the same light as was there a market for the product?

4   Conclusions and Future Work

In this paper, we have analyzed the mismatch and especially the Developers Dilemma between professionalism in software development and the needs of fast business development. Thus this problem is not just limited to lean startup, but also to other environments, where rapid product development is needed.

As as response, we propose a set of questions that can be used to analyze if the developers dilemma is a problem in your company, outlined in Subsect. 3.4. These questions allow for the initial recognition of possible problems between unified goals of the developers and the management. It seems that one core aspect to the developers dilemma might be the usage of different measurements to measure product success on the business development side and the software development side. If these two sides are brought closer together and both sides share a deeper understanding of the project goals the problem can be mitigated.

Although the idea comes from our personal experience and communication with a number of local startups, there is still work to be done in refining and validating the proposed concepts.

As future work, we want to analyze how startups can efficiently recognize the difference between throw-away and evolutionary parts of MVPs to assess the first solution. Similarly, we need to study to which extent the idea of experiments as top-level requirements is already used and how it affects development. Also other ways that companies use to handle failure and waste are of interest. Instructions on how to write and manage such requirements should be developed e.g. with action research methodology. These two methods could be used to help solve the dilemma.

The Developer's Dilemma is a mismatch between the software developer's professional ambitions and the startup's need for fast business experimentation. As not responding to the dilemma can have grave consequences for the company, the dilemma should be alleviated as well as possible to ensure the growth. This is not just a problem for the management, but a challenge for the whole company on how to communicate their core targets.

Acknowledgments. The authors wish to thank Digile's Need4Speed program (http://www.n4s.fi/) funded by the Finnish Funding Agency for Innovation Tekes (http://www.tekes.fi/en/tekes/) for its support for this research.

References

1. Alvarez, S.A., Barney, J.B.: Discovery and creation: alternative theories of entrepreneurial action. Strateg. Entrepreneurship J. **1**(1–2), 11–26 (2007)
2. Baker, T., Nelson, R.E.: Creating something from nothing: resource construction through entrepreneurial bricolage. Adm. Sci. Q. **50**(3), 329–366 (2005)
3. Blank, S.: The Four Steps to the Epiphany. K&S Ranch, Pescadero (2013)
4. Blank, S., Dorf, B.: The Startup Owner's Manual. K&S Ranch, Pescadero (2012)
5. Da Silva, F.Q., França, A.C.C.: Towards understanding the underlying structure of motivational factors for software engineers to guide the definition of motivational programs. J. Syst. Softw. **85**(2), 216–226 (2012)
6. Eloranta, V.P., Koskimies, K.: Aligning architecture knowledge management with scrum. In: Proceedings of the WICSA/ECSA 2012 Companion Volume. pp. 112–115. WICSA/ECSA 2012. ACM, New York (2012). doi:10.1145/2361999.2362023
7. Floyd, C.: A systematic look at prototyping. In: Budde, R., Kuhlenkamp, K., Mathiassen, L., Züllighoven, H. (eds.) Approaches to Prototyping, pp. 1–18. Springer, Heidelberg (1984). doi:10.1007/978-3-642-69796-8_1
8. Maurya, A.: Running lean: iterate from plan A to a plan that works. O'Reilly Media Inc., Sebastopol (2012)
9. Ries, E.: The Lean Startup. Penguin, New York (2011)
10. Sandor, C., Klinker, G.: A rapid prototyping software infrastructure for user interfaces in ubiquitous augmented reality. Pers. Ubiquit. Comput. **9**(3), 169–185 (2005)
11. Stephens, M., Bates, P.: Requirements engineering by prototyping: experiences in development of estimating system. Inf. Softw. Technol. **32**(4), 253–257 (1990)
12. Terho, H., Suonsyrjä, S., Jaaksi, A., Mikkonen, T., Kazman, R., Chen, H.M.: Lean startup meets software product lines: survival of the fittest or letting products bloom? (2015)
13. Terho, H., Suonsyrjä, S., Karisalo, A., Mikkonen, T.: Ways to cross the rubicon: pivoting in software startups. In: Abrahamsson, P., Corral, L., Oivo, M., Russo, B. (eds.) PROFES 2015. LNCS, vol. 9459, pp. 555–568. Springer, Heidelberg (2015). doi:10.1007/978-3-319-26844-6_41

Workshop-Based Corporate Foresight Process: A Case Study

Leila Saari[1(✉)], Tanja Suomalainen[1], Raija Kuusela[1], and Tapio Hämeen-Anttila[2]

[1] VTT Research Centre of Finland, Oulu, Finland
{leila.saari,tanja.suomalainen,raija.kuusela}@vtt.fi
[2] Elisa Appelsiini, Helsinki, Finland
tapio.hameen-anttila@elisa.fi

Abstract. Corporate foresight is a value-creation tool that helps companies survive in a competitive, ever-changing business environment. Foresight can be perceived as a company's capability to commit to continuous environmental scanning and to respond quickly to the discovered market threats and opportunities. Currently, there is scarce literature about foresight application procedures in organizations. This paper presents a single-case study, with a foresight process that was experimented in a real industrial setting. Based solely on a workshop series, this simple and straightforward process used the participants' tacit knowledge and insights as the main data sources. The participants presented different roles and departments of the case company. As a result, two new application areas, My Data and eHealth, were found, and a message to the company's top management was formulated. The future will show how the results will be implemented in the company and what will be their business impact.

Keywords: Corporate foresight · Environmental scanning · Innovation · Insight · Process · Workshop

1 Introduction

The current global business environment is ever changing. Competition is tough; new technologies, innovations, threats, and opportunities emerge continuously. An early identification of discontinuities can prevent companies from loosing ground in competition. Companies have to consider how to survive or to defeat rivals. Many companies have started to prepare better for the future by starting foresight practices. Foresight requires future-oriented awareness and planning that enable businesses to respond quickly to future market threats and opportunities [1].

Software companies have realized that changes in their business environment will occur frequently with increasing speed and may include serious discontinuities. Companies need to be aware of their business environment and be able to adopt or even create radical adjacencies, that is, stepping outside the core and operating in new markets and/ or with novel products [2]. Moqaddamerad [3] defines corporate foresight as an organization's ability to scan the environment constantly and to consider future options.

© Springer International Publishing AG 2016
P. Abrahamsson et al. (Eds.): PROFES 2016, LNCS 10027, pp. 580–589, 2016.
DOI: 10.1007/978-3-319-49094-6_43

Both the overall corporate and specific business strategies should bend to foresight and continuous innovation and hence help the company react to changes in the internal and the external environments. As claimed by Grant [4], a turbulent business environment makes systematic strategic planning more difficult than before. Organizations are affected by both external changes, such as the economy, competition, and political interference, and internal changes, such as management systems, organizational culture, and employee morale [5].

Despite the abundance of current literature on the use of foresight, details of successful methods and the results of foresight activities are scarce [1]. Plenty of foresight tools and methods are available today. However, it is challenging to choose the most suitable ones for an organization. Companies interested in implementing foresight are often unable to identify best practices because these firms conduct foresight activities behind closed doors [1]. Mazurkiewicz et al. [6] also argue that foresight activities do not always lead to successful implementations of their results. Foresight practitioners usually focus on developing methodologies and conducting foresight exercises and have no influence on the implementation of the results [6].

To fill in this gap, a single-case study was conducted at Elisa Appelsiini, one of the leading telecommunications, information and communication technology (ICT), and online service companies in Finland. ICT industry field relies heavily on software engineering as their products and innovations include software. The empirical data was gathered through a series of workshops. The specific research question was formulated as follows: How business opportunities can be discovered by a workshop based foresight process? Thus, this paper's main contributions are its presentation of an uncomplicated, workshop-based foresight process and description of the first experiences in using it. The experiences gained from the case study form the first validation of the process.

This paper is structured as follows: Sect. 2 reviews the current literature on foresight. Section 3 describes the study's research design. Section 4 presents and summarizes the case study's findings. Finally, in Sect. 5, the conclusions are drawn from the research.

2 Related Research

This section briefly describes the characteristics of foresight. Since foresight and innovation are closely related, they are discussed as well. Foresight frameworks, methods, and tools are then presented.

2.1 Setting Scene for Foresight

Foresight involves future-oriented awareness, enabling businesses to respond quickly to future market threats and opportunities. It is useful in managerial planning, where the ever-changing environment makes past data an unreliable basis for future action.

This paper focuses on the foresight of enterprises and corporations. Moqaddamerad [3] defines corporate foresight as an organization's ability to commit to continuous environmental scanning and to implement corrective actions accordingly. Thus, foresight requires exploring new markets, products, and services to ensure the company's long-term survival and success. Likewise, Rohrbeck [7] views corporate foresight as the capability to detect, interpret, and respond to discontinuous changes.

The starting point of foresight includes environmental scanning, which identifies trends, driving forces, change factors, weak signals, and so on, that impact the business environment Thus, foresight enables an enterprise to respond to the changes in the business environment or to actually foresee the coming changes, trends, and discontinuities and prepare for them [3].

In enterprises, strategic planning had previously been solely the concern of the top management. The growing request for transparency in management is gradually increasing the share of staff members who have the possibility to contribute to the foresight or even the strategy of an enterprise. This broader participation has to be organized with suitable tools because face-to-face dialogue is not feasible with a huge group [8]. Foresight is not just a method or a technique but a social activity [9].

Foresight increases the future awareness of an enterprise and helps corporations survive in a competitive business environment in times of continuous changes [3]. At the organizational level, foresight refers to examining possible futures in a range of areas, including technology, politics, and demographics, as well as determining what decisions should be made today to establish the best possible future for the organization [10].

Moqaddamerad [3] argues that companies try to win the innovation race in different ways, such as the integration of foresight into their innovation processes. The purpose of innovation management is to discover creative capabilities, constantly generate new products, renew internal processes, and create a new market opportunities to promise a long-lasting competitive advantage [3].

2.2 Foresight Process

The foresight process presented by Voros [11] was selected as our reference framework because it is widely referred to in the current literature, e.g. [1, 8] and a practical approach, describing the foresight process with questions to be answered. Actually, foresight feeds strategic thinking with the "what if" question [11]. Prior to the process, inputs represent the strategic intelligence that feeds the forthcoming foresight. The foresight process itself has three phases—analysis, interpretation, and prospection. The process outputs bring options to decision making. In a strategy, the question of what will be done will be decided; in action planning, how it will be done will be determined. The three phases of foresight, together with the precondition (inputs) and post condition (outputs), were selected as the starting points of our summary presented in Table 1, which includes other foresight frameworks.

As shown in Table 1, the phases presented by the authors overlap to some extent. The precondition (inputs) is mentioned by Voros [11], Bishop et al. [12], and Popper [8]. According to Voros [11], this phase is needed for information gathering before the actual foresight. Popper's [8] practical approach includes the people's involvement. All the presented foresight processes initially have an observation phase, that is, scanning, monitoring, exploring, or sensing, which Voros [11] refers to as analysis. His second foresight phase is named interpretation, which other authors call forecasting, analysis, or seizing. Prospection, Voros' third foresight phase, is termed visioning, projection, or anticipation by other authors. The post-condition phase—output for strategy—comprises action planning, transformation, renewal, and asset reconfiguration. The options are proposed for decision making, to be included in strategy and action planning.

Table 1. Foresight phases in literature

Voros [11]	Bishop et al. [12]	Keenan et al. [13]	Popper [8]	Teece [14]
Input for foresight	**Framing:** identifying the problem		**Pre-foresight:** setting the overall aspirations **Recruitment:** enrolling key individuals and stakeholders	
Analysis What seems to be happening in the environment?	**Scanning:** understanding the context of the organization	**Monitoring:** recognizing relevant trends	**Generation:** generating prospective knowledge and shared visions in three phases; exploration, analysis, and anticipation	**Sensing:** identifying opportunities and threats (both internal and external)
Interpretation What is really happening? Which changes are meaningful?	**Forecasting:** taking into account future possibilities	**Analysis:** understanding the drivers of change		**Seizing:** creating business models, determining organizational boundaries, adapting the strategy
Prospection What might happen?	**Visioning:** moving from possible to preferred future	**Projection:** anticipating the future		
Output for strategy What might we need to do?	**Planning:** building a pathway to the future **Action:** continuously translating foresight into action	**Transformation:** drawing implications for business	**Action:** committing key players **Renewal:** mixing intelligence and wisdom	**Asset reconfiguration:** aligning tangible and intangible assets

3   Research Design

This section describes the research design of this study. It includes the purpose, methods, and process of the research, as well as the case company description.

3.1 Research Method and Process

This research was built on a single-case study [15]. A case-study approach was decided to gain practical experiences. Järvinen [16] emphasizes the ability of case studies to examine complicated circumstances and in this way, to gather information for the creation of new knowledge. Additionally, the case-study methodology is reported to be well suited for software engineering research as it involves the study of contemporary phenomena in their natural context [17]. This study also follows the participative action research [18] approach, which emphasizes participant collaboration. Action research is an iterative process involving researchers and practitioners acting together on a particular cycle of activities, including problem diagnosis, action intervention, and reflective learning [18].

The research process followed the case-study research design presented by Yin [15]. It consisted of the following three phases: (1) define and design; (2) prepare, collect, and analyze individual case results; and (3) analyze and conclude cross case results. The research process was initiated by conducting a literature review, whose purpose was to provide an understanding of the current state and knowledge relating to the main research area. It is essential to construct a preliminary theory about a study [15]. The development of the preliminary theory helps in defining the appropriate research design and data collection, as well as in generalizing the case study's results.

Another intention of the literature review was to discover gaps and thus focus the research on the most unexplored areas of study, and then to help structure the empirical data collection. Thereafter, the case company was selected, and the data collection protocol was designed. It was decided that the empirical data would be gathered through several workshops, comprising the second phase of the research process. Both the case company and the workshop participants were selected by using purposive sampling [19]. Purposive sampling involves designating a group of people for selection based on some traits that are important for the study. After each workshop, all findings and results were filed and memos were written. Finally after all four workshops were conducted the results were validated with the attendees in a remote session.

3.2 Data Collection and Analysis

The main data collection method used in this case study involved a series of four workshops held at Elisa Appelsiini during the autumn of 2015. The research started with planning meetings with three researchers and four contact persons from Elisa Appelsiini. In these meetings (four in total), the schedule, number, and content of the workshops were drafted, as well as the desired roles of the participants to be invited.

Thereafter, four half-day workshops were organized, with the following main themes: (1) kick-off, (2) analysis, (3) interpretation, and (4) prospection and selection. A total of 13 Elisa Appelsiini employees representing different roles participated, from solutions consultants to directors. There were 13 participants in the first workshop, nine in the second, 11 in the third, and nine in the last one.

In the kick-off workshop, an introduction to foresight was given, including the process description, and various foresight methods and potential tools were presented before agreeing on the title of this process. The second workshop's goal was to gather all trends, threats, discontinuities, and weak signals that might have effects on the company's business. In the third workshop, the findings of the previous workshop were further processed, this time from the viewpoint of potential customers. In the last workshop, the participants prioritized the identified initiatives, evaluated their business opportunities, analyzed the capabilities needed to implement the prioritized initiatives, and formulated their message to the top management.

The workshops were facilitated by three researchers. One of them mastered the process and ensured its smooth progress. The other researchers supported and documented both the process and its intermediate findings, keeping notes and taking pictures. The result slides were created based on the memos, post-it notes, and photos taken during each workshop, and shared with the participants via email before the next workshop.

Finally, a result and feedback session for all initially invited workshop participants was organized. The results were presented, and feedback was requested. The participants honestly evaluated the content of the presentation, gave good feedback, and expressed willingness to continue, either by deepening the same scope or selecting a new perspective.

3.3 Case Company

Elisa Appelsiini is a merger of Elisa and Appelsiini. In 2010, Elisa acquired Appelsiini, which started in 1999 as a small company with just a few employees. Elisa Appelsiini continues to operate as Elisa's affiliated company. Since their fusion, Elisa and Appelsiini have offered a comprehensive service package in Finland, specifically targeting small and medium enterprises. Elisa is a telecommunications, ICT, and online service company serving 2.3 million consumers, including corporate and public sector customers. The firm provides services for communication and entertainment, along with tools for improving organizations' operating methods and productivity.

4   Workshop-Based Foresight Process

The workshop participants were committed and enthusiastic, open to proposing new ideas and thoughts, as well as trying novel methods and tools. First of all, they anticipated that the results would be useful for the company. They were eager to bring the results to the top management and to see the possible impacts of their proposals.

After the introduction in the kickoff workshop, the participants started to discover what should be the scope of this foresight experiment. Through the me-we-all method, it was decided that the title of this process would be "The Business Transformation Initiative of Elisa Appelsiini". At the end of the kick-off workshop, there were high expectations for the results; most of the attendees thought that emerging or radical business opportunities would be found during the process.

The second (analysis) workshop focused on environmental scanning. Usually, this phase builds heavily on external information, including the literature review, bibliometrics, and patent maps. In this case, we wanted to rely on the participants' insights instead of studying reports that others had written. The workshop fostered an open atmosphere to ensure that opposing views would also be expressed. Moreover, some facilitation methods were used to switch the viewpoints of the participants. For example, as we were identifying trends, the political, economic, social, technological, environmental, and legal (PESTEL) classification [19] was shown to enlarge the focus. The identified trends (over 50) were evaluated with a matrix of probability and impact. Four topics were selected for further discussion: My Data, eHealth, morals and ethics in business, and outsourcing/insourcing.

The third (interpretation) workshop started with stakeholder mapping, which identified the case company's various interest groups. After the generic stakeholder map, more detailed studies on customers, partners, and competitors were conducted for both of the selected application areas—My Data and eHealth. These maps were generated for later use when considering potential partners and co-creators of new businesses.

The next step was to create several customer-segment canvases, one for each identified segment. Adopted from the business model canvas [20], this canvas had the customers as the starting point, including their jobs, pains while doing their tasks, and gains if not having the pain. In total, 11 customer-segment canvases were created and classified, with the new–old matrix showing the customer on the vertical axis and the product (or service) on the horizontal axis. According to this evaluation by the participants, most of the identified products were seen as new products for new customers.

The fourth and last workshop wrapped up the previous ones. It started with a matrix (where participants had to move to the spot that described their attitude) with two axes, as follows: "Foresight will have huge/no business impact" and "Afraid of/happy with the organizational change." The matrix generated a vibrant and open discussion, from which the message to the top management was formulated. After the warm-up with the matrix, the opportunities for the selected application areas (My Data and eHealth) were prioritized and further refined. The selected product or service ideas (found via the customer-segment canvases in the third workshop) were analyzed, using the needs, approach, benefits, competition (NABC) analysis developed at the Stanford Research Institute [21].

After the NABC analysis, a short pitch (five-minute talk) was given to clarify the necessity of each product or service. A preliminary architecture was drawn to find out the elements needed to implement the selected ideas. Each identified element was classified by rating it with one to three stars. One star meant that the case company already had the element, two stars signified that the company would develop it, and three stars denoted that the company would buy or develop the element with a partner.

When closing the last workshop, the attendees had high spirits, believing that they had formulated a meaningful proposal to the top management. Feedback was gathered from their answers to open questions and four factors rated on a point scale from 4 to 10[1]. The averages of factors were: facilitator's skills 9.0, the feasibility of the used methods and tools 8.45, the workshop-based foresight process itself 8.76, and the probability of their recommending this process to a peer organization 9.0.

---

[1] General scale in Finnish schools, where 4 = F, fail, 10 = A+, excellent.

Elisa Appelsiini's business development manager concluded, "We are truly satisfied with learning about the foresight process and are eager to begin the adaptation of these practices in our organization. The workshops led by VTT were very professional, combining the academic background with more hands-on methods in the actual workshops. For us, this presented both the necessary framework to understand the big picture and the concrete iterative model to look at the innovation for a competitive edge in our market. We are truly looking forward to the next steps, as well as sharing our experiences along the way."

5   Discussion and Further Work

An uncomplicated workshop-based foresight process was facilitated at Elisa Appelsiini during the autumn of 2015. In the kick-off workshop, the goal of the workshop series was formulated as "the business transformation initiative of Elisa Appelsiini." In the workshops, the initiatives were processed with disruptions, technologies, business models, and customer needs. In the final workshop, the results were crystallized and a message to the management was also formulated.

In this process, the participants' insights were discovered and formulated through various methods and tools. In this regard, all available tools are not easy to adopt and exploit. Their selection and implementation require both knowledge on foresight and experience in facilitation. While facilitating a foresight process, it is important to push the thinking towards new tracks as the process relies on the participants' insights.

The plan was to involve about ten attendees, representing different roles and departments of the case company in each workshop to keep the work intensive. The attendees' roles varied from the director to business development managers and solution consultants. The outcome of this process was the common distillation of the participants' insight. Therefore, the same results would likely not have been found with another group of people.

The single-case study chosen in this research raises the question of the generalizability of the results. Additionally, a single-case study poses the risk of misjudging and exaggerating the research data [22]. This research uses the qualitative approach, which relies much on interpretation and thus tends to be subjective. This study's primary goal was to experiment on a tailored, uncomplicated workshop-based foresight process that relied on the insights of staff members in a contemporary, turbulent business environment.

The results' external validity was achieved through the detailed description of the experiment journey in the case company and by grounding this study on the previous research. Internal validity was attained with different types of triangulation [16]. First, data triangulation was applied by using various information sources in terms of people with different roles who participated in the workshops. Second, methodological triangulation combined two types of data collection methods, that is, workshops and meetings. Third, investigator triangulation was employed; several people from different backgrounds participated in the analysis, including the company professionals with varying areas of competence and the researchers outside the company. Fourth, theory triangulation involved diverse fields of research, comprising foresight, new service development, and innovation.

At the time of writing this paper, it is not yet known how the results of the foresight experiment will be used at Elisa Appelsiini; Hammoud et al. [1] and Mazurkiewicz et al. [6] make similar claims in their articles. Future research topics could include how the outputs of foresight activities would be utilized. The follow-up on the foresight results would mean long-term research and include some visibility on the decision making, strategy process, and even business impact. Additionally, it would be interesting to expand this research to a multiple-case study with this or slightly modified process and possibly use other data collection methods. A web-based interactive tool would be applicable if more people could attend. The transparency of the process could be enhanced as well if the intermediate results would be available to the staff and their comments would be solicited in the company's Intranet. The participant roles could also include representatives from customers, partners, competitors, and so on.

Acknowledgements. This research has been carried out under the Dimecc Need for Speed program and has been partially funded by Tekes (the Finnish Funding Agency for Technology and Innovation).

References

1. Hammoud, M.S., Nash, D.P.: What corporations do with foresight. Eur. J. Fut. Res. **2**(1), 1–20 (2014)
2. Vitalari, N., Saughnessy, H.: The Elastic Enterprise. The New Manifesto for Business Revolution. Telemachus Press (2012)
3. Moqaddamerad, S.: Corporate foresight: A contribution to innovation management, Turku 2014, Master thesis (2014)
4. Grant, R.M.: Strategic planning in a turbulent environment: evidence from the oil majors. Strat. Manag. J. **24**, 491–517 (2003)
5. Suomalainen, T., Kuusela, R., Tihinen, M.: Continuous planning: an important aspect of agile and lean development. Int. J. Agile Syst. Manag. **8**(2), 132–162 (2015)
6. Mazurkiewicz, A., Poteralska, B., Sacio-Szymańska A.: Implementation and evaluation of foresight results. In: The XXIV ISPIM Conference – Innovating in Global Markets: Challenges for Sustainable Growth, Helsinki, 16–19 June 2013
7. Rohrbeck, R.: Corporate Foresight Contributions to Management Science. Springer, Berlin (2011)
8. Popper, R.: How are foresight methods selected. Foresight **10**(6), 62–89 (2008)
9. Pina e Cuncha, M., Palma, P., Guimaraes da Costa, N.: Fear of foresight: Knowledge and ignorance in organizational foresight. Futures **38**, 942–955 (2006)
10. Horton, A.: Fore front: a simple guide to successful foresight. Foresight, J. Fut. Stud. Strat. Think. Policy **1**(1) (1999)
11. Voros, J.: A generic foresight process framework. Foresight **5**(3), 10–21 (2003)
12. Bishop, P., Hines, A., Collins, T.: The current state of scenario development: an overview of techniques. Foresight **9**(1), 5–25 (2007)
13. Keenan, M., Popper, R.: Combining foresight methods for impacts. In: NISTEP 3rd International Conference on Foresight, Tokyo (2007)

14. Teece, D.J.: Explicating dynamic capabilities: the nature and microfoundations of (sustainable) enterprise performance. Strat. Manag. J. **298**, 1319–1350 (2007)
15. Yin, R.K.: Case Study Research: Design and Methods. Applied Social Research Methods Series, 3rd edn., vol. 5. Sage Publications, Inc., Thousand Oaks (2003)
16. Järvinen, P.: On Research Methods. Opinpajan kirja, Tampere (2001)
17. Runeson, P., Höst, M.: Guidelines for conducting and reporting case study research in software engineering. Empirical Softw. Eng. **14**(2), 131–164 (2009)
18. Avison, D.E., Lau, F., Myers, M., Nielsen, P.A.: Action research. Commun. ACM **42**(1), 94–97 (1999)
19. Nardi, P.M.: Doing Survey Research, A Guide to Quantitative Methods. Pearson Education Inc., Boston (2003)
20. Osterwalder, A., Pigneur, Y., Bernarda, G., Smith, A.: Value proposition Design. Wiley. https://strategyzer.com/books/value-proposition-design
21. Stanford Research Institute. https://nielschrist.wordpress.com/2012/07/13/the-nabc-method-standford-research-institute-sri/
22. Voss, C., Tsikriktsis, N., Frohlich, M.: Case research in operations management. Int. J. Oper. Prod. Manag. **22**(2), 195–219 (2002)

DevOps Adoption Benefits and Challenges in Practice: A Case Study

Leah Riungu-Kalliosaari[1]([⊠]), Simo Mäkinen[1], Lucy Ellen Lwakatare[2],
Juha Tiihonen[1], and Tomi Männistö[1]

[1] Department of Computer Science, University of Helsinki,
Gustaf Hällströmin katu 2b, P.O. Box 68, 00014 Helsinki, Finland
`riungu@cs.helsinki.fi`
[2] Department of Information Processing Science,
University of Oulu, P.O. Box 3000, 90014 Oulu, Finland

Abstract. DevOps is an approach in which traditional software engineering roles are merged and communication is enhanced to improve the production release frequency and maintain software quality. There seem to be benefits in adopting DevOps but practical industry experiences have seldom been reported. We conducted a qualitative multiple-case study and interviewed the representatives of three software development organizations in Finland. The responses indicate that with DevOps, practitioners can increase the frequency of releases and improve test automation practices. DevOps was seen to encourage collaboration between departments which boosts communication and employee welfare. Continuous releases enable a more experimental approach and rapid feedback collection. The challenges include communication structures that hinder cross-department collaboration and having to address the cultural shift. Dissimilar development and production environments were mentioned as some of the technical barriers. DevOps might not also be suitable for all industries. Ambiguity in the definition of DevOps makes adoption difficult since organizations might not know which practices they should implement for DevOps.

1 Introduction

Software and product development in the modern era of interconnected, highly available systems requires close collaboration between members of the development team. Software distribution has changed and recurring software updates can happen to the point that software releases are served at the same time as when software is being used [12]. Because of the nature and frequency of the releases, possible issues in the production systems need to be monitored closely in order to provide optimum user experience [12]. Software organizations need to adapt their practices to various changes brought about by new concepts such as DevOps.

Our working definition of DevOps is: "a set of practices intended to reduce the time between committing a change to a system and the change being placed into

P. Abrahamsson et al. (Eds.): PROFES 2016, LNCS 10027, pp. 590–597, 2016.
DOI: 10.1007/978-3-319-49094-6_44

normal production, while ensuring high quality" [3]. The DevOps phenomenon has two core principles: (1) emphasis on collaboration between development and operations; (2) the use of agile principles and automation to configure and manage deployment environments [8]. DevOps extends collaboration between development and operations teams which eases the handling of changes in the production environment.

Industry reports on the DevOps practices have been rare in the past [9], although more studies have surfaced lately. What potential do practitioners see in DevOps, and what kind of challenges are there in adopting the DevOps? To answer these questions, we performed a multiple-case study of three software companies in Finland. We conducted semi-structured interviews with representatives from the companies and report the results of our analysis in this article.

The article is structured as follows. Section 2 describes previously reported DevOps experiences, benefits and challenges. Section 3 presents the applied research method. Section 4 focuses on the results whereas Sect. 5 discusses the results and considers the validity threats. Section 6 concludes the work.

2 Related Work

Several recent studies have recognized the importance of DevOps. Developer and operations teams can streamline development processes in order to fine-tune the performance of services and increase scalability with virtualization [6]. Monitoring the production systems at real-time enables developers to react whenever anomalies are detected [2,6,11]. On-demand infrastructures and timely feedback from monitoring support continuous software delivery and deployment. Release cycles can shorten to hours instead of weeks and months [11], which is seen as a definite advantage of DevOps [4,7]. Monolithic architectures restrict the release frequency [13] but microservice architectures help to break down components into smaller pieces suitable for frequent releases [2,13].

Combining the expertise and knowledge of software experts from different functions can be challenging. The lack of cooperation between developers and operations personnel results in uncoordinated activities [9,14]. This causes serious problems which include: (1) IT operations not being involved in the requirements specification, (2) poor communication and information flow, (3) unsatisfactory test environments, (4) lack of knowledge transfer, (5) immature systems, and (6) operational routines not being established prior to deployment [9].

Poor communication between the development and operations functions produces undesirable results. Non-functional requirements e.g. performance or availability might be overlooked as the responsibility of running the product is shifted to the operations team, letting developers off the hook [14]. Without proper access to production systems and error logs, developers become frustrated [13,14]. Such challenges are only exacerbated if the development teams are distributed [13].

Table 1. Characteristics of the organizations involved in the case study

Org.	Domain	Personnel	Unit size	Interviewee position
A	Software development and big data analytics	90	20	Senior Consultant 1 & 2
B	Digital service development	100	20	Senior Developer
C	Software development and research	>900	10	Lead Architect for Cloud

3   Research Method

We employed an explorative, qualitative research approach in our case study. We wanted to find out how the industry sees DevOps along with its advantages and limitations. Our research questions are:

- RQ1: How do industry practitioners perceive the benefits of DevOps practices in their organization?
- RQ2: How do industry practitioners perceive the adoption challenges related to DevOps?

We targeted software development organizations with sufficient DevOps experience. Three Finnish development organizations were selected for the study. Two of them were participants in a joint industry-academia program called Need for Speed [1]. The sampling for the study can be considered as convenience sampling. Table 1 introduces the organizations.

Organization A is a consultancy company with a specific DevOps unit. Its customers' operations environments ranged from private servers and clouds to the application of public cloud services. In Organization B, developers work as consultants in customer projects, bringing their expertise as required. Organization C is an international organization with a technological expertise services unit dedicated to cloud platform services. It sees DevOps as feasible for areas with direct control of the operations environment.

Semi-structured interviews were the data collection method. The themes related to views on the DevOps phenomenon, along with its advantages and limitations. Two interviews were conducted on-site and one remotely. The interviews lasted from one to two hours. The interviews were recorded and transcribed.

Thematic analysis and synthesis [5] was used to support data analysis. The method can be used to find patterns in the data by assigning codes to segments of text, translating the codes into higher-order themes and finally creating a model of the themes [5]. The interview transcripts were coded and a set of themes created as a result which allowed to construct a model of the benefits and challenges of DevOps.

4 Results

After analyzing the interview transcripts, we identified several themes. The higher-level themes considered were the benefits and challenges of adopting DevOps. Figure 1 illustrates the thematic map and the themes covered in this section.

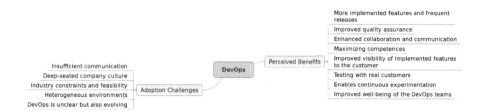

Fig. 1. Thematic map for the perceived benefits and adoption challenges of DevOps

4.1 Perceived Benefits of DevOps

The respondents thought that DevOps practices lead to a number of benefits. Broadly speaking, DevOps was seen to positively affect the pace at which software products could be delivered and the quality of products for instance by intensifying feedback cycles. The internal mechanics of engineering products in the organization including aspects such as communication were perceived to be affected, too.

As a definite advantage, the respondents highlighted *more implemented features and frequent releases.* Powered by automated build, testing and deployment processes, one of the main advantages of DevOps is that organizations are able to channel more features into the production and delivery pipelines as noted by an interviewed Lead Architect. Automation also reduces the effort required for setting up releases, making it possible for organizations to churn out the releases as frequently as required.

"There are multiple factors, relating to this but yes, definitely one of the key drivers of DevOps is actually that you can get more commits of code into each day basically." (Lead Architect, Org C).

Subsequently, higher levels of automation were found to drive *improved quality assurance.* The automated DevOps production pipeline helps to ensure that every change is verified before it is pushed forward for delivery. Because every change in the code is checked at every stage of the development, and errors are discovered and resolved on the fly, the end products have fewer bugs and the software can be readily released.

One of the major impacts of DevOps is that it forces the development and operations teams to interact with each other more than before, which was seen to lead to *enhanced collaboration and communication.* The walls between the traditional development versus operations silos are slowly broken down, and as a result encouraging a unified way of working. Increased collaboration accelerates the exchange of knowledge and experiences between the teams. Multi-functional teams with a variety of capabilities that boost productivity result in *maximizing competences* since a broader set of the skills is utilized.

The respondents felt that when applying DevOps practices, the possibility to release frequently has implications to the whole development process. Shorter development cycles were seen as beneficial for the customers who can enjoy newly developed features faster than before. Smaller releases made more often promote *improved visibility of implemented features to the customer*. In addition, due to frequent releases, the development and operations teams are able to receive early feedback from the end users and able to do *testing with real customers*, which helps in improving the end products.

Working with real customers, companies are better equipped with knowledge on customer preferences and are ultimately able to tailor their products to meet the market demands. According to the perceptions of the interviewees, DevOps can help companies to test different ideas quickly and make decisions accordingly. The constant testing of hypotheses in order to determine the value gains for both the customer and the organization is referred to as continuous experimentation [10]. An efficient DevOps process supports and *enables continuous experimentation* which requires well set up experimental infrastructure and environments.

DevOps can impact occupational welfare, too. A senior developer noted that frequent releases help to reduce the stress levels because the anxiety related to handling huge releases is minimized. So, DevOps processes not only bring benefits to the organization, but they also improve the way of working, hence positively contributing to the *improved well-being of the DevOps teams*.

4.2   DevOps Adoption Challenges

Due to many factors, DevOps might not always be successful. The respondents raised challenges related to communication patterns, organization cultures which are not malleable, different constraints stemming from the domain and environments, and the obscurity of the meaning of DevOps.

A key impediment for successfully adopting DevOps is *insufficient communication*. For instance, it was mentioned that operations teams do not always monitor or pass all the performance and other metrics that can be of use to developers, which can cause problems. In sub-optimal cases, operations engineers and developers care about different, and possibly conflicting, metrics: operations personnel worry about the uptime of servers whereas developers are concerned with the release frequency. It was noted that communication between the two groups may also be lacking if it occurs only through electronic systems, causing delays in reaction times to issues. In person communication is hard to replace with electronic tools.

DevOps adoption also highlights cultural matters. Profound changes to the cultural mindset are required and the *deep-seated company culture* can be a challenge. As mentioned in the interviews, roles merge, responsibilities shift, and people have to rethink their established roles. Developers have to take on tasks they are not used to and might have reservations on accepting new responsibilities for the operations environment like being on call for system failures. At the same time, operations people may be wary of the developers taking over their turf or overly taxed with handling more frequent releases. Changing people's behavior can be difficult, especially if they have had long careers. Smaller organizations might be in a better position to change their practices, though. As mentioned by one of the interviewees, people need to be receptive towards changing the company culture to fit the DevOps ideal since it is hard to push such initiatives through if, for instance, the management is not supportive. A Lead Architect stated the importance of culture and hardships in DevOps adoption.

"I think that's a big cultural shift that we are also seeing, difficult to address and what is probably the biggest blocker in moving ahead with this, bigger than the actual technical competences or processes. For me, I see it as two traditional roles that suddenly need to merge and we just need to find ways to, work towards one common goal." (Lead Architect, Org C).

DevOps practices might not be suitable in all circumstances. Access to production systems can be legally or contractually restricted so the *industry constraints and feasibility* in different domains need to be considered when applying DevOps. In specific cases, the environments such as databases used in production systems can be complex enough to make replicating the environments for verification and testing difficult as mentioned by a respondent. As a consequence, automated testing becomes less trustworthy meaning that *heterogeneous environments* provide a challenge for successful DevOps adoption.

While there is agreement about certain characteristics of DevOps, its true essence is still somewhat vague. Since there is not a standard set of fixed practices related to DevOps, practitioners find it hard to say what practices they should take into use for DevOps. It was seen that the meaning of DevOps has shifted in the previous years and new tools for DevOps keep coming up so one of the challenges is that *DevOps is unclear but also evolving*.

5   Discussion

The interviewees saw that adopting DevOps had some benefits. They saw DevOps as a means to increase the implemented features and generate more releases. The idea of rapid delivery aligns with the DevOps notion of reducing the time it takes for a software release to reach the production environment [3]. DevOps encourages automation, which was seen to help in improving the quality of releases.

DevOps helped to bridge the communication gap between developers and operations engineers. This fosters collaboration towards improving the development process and end product. Furthermore, the existing different skills can be readily utilized hence increasing the team's reactivity to problems.

The respondents thought that DevOps practices support real-time monitoring which helps to foster fast feedback loops and an experimental culture that engages more interaction with the end users. Real-time monitoring has also been previously highlighted by developers as a factor which helps to create fault-aware systems [2,6] and DevOps has been seen to encourage experimental culture [11].

Shortcomings in communication and the prevailing company culture were some of the challenges that we identified. The lack of knowledge and information sharing can result in obscuring vital facts. Guidelines suggesting how to share information can help but changing the culture of a company can be a challenge. The cultural aspects are significant, as has been previously stated [7,13]. The size of the company or having company-wide support for the change might matter. Smaller companies are in a better position to react faster to changes.

Constraints in the environment can prove challenging, too. Working habits emphasizing e.g. security can prevent some companies from using DevOps practices. Technical environments that are difficult to replicate add up to the challenges. Both challenges in the environment have been highlighted earlier [13].

As DevOps evolves, its definition, practices and tools are expected to change – a challenge that is expected to remain in the long run. As organizations continue to adjust to changes, Bass et al. [3] advise that DevOps should not be tied to any specific must-have tools or communication practices, but it should be aligned to the higher-level goals an organization wishes to achieve.

As an exploratory case study, there are no strong claims for causality and threats to internal validity are not central. The interviewees' responses are their own opinions on DevOps. Hence, the reported benefits and challenges are not universal. External validity could be threatened by the selection of the cases as two of the companies were consultancies. Consultants may see the situation differently because they can draw experiences from multiple clients. Still, considering external validity, it is possible that a company adopting DevOps might observe similar benefits and challenges as presented in the study.

The most notable threats to validity are related to construct validity and the operationalization of the concept of DevOps. Lacking a clear definition, respondents might have understood DevOps differently. Factors contributing to the benefits and challenges could have been left out if a respondent had a narrow understanding of DevOps which could affect the interpretation of its implications.

6   Conclusions

The study indicates some benefits and challenges involved in adopting DevOps. The benefits include more frequent releases, improved test automation, better communication and enhanced occupational welfare. DevOps can also support an experimentation culture in software development.

The factors inhibiting DevOps adoption were along human aspects e.g. lack of communication and resistance to change; and technical aspects e.g. the complexity of development and production environments. Suitability of DevOps might be questioned for certain domains and industry sectors, at least for now. The fuzzy definition of DevOps also prevents companies from having clear targets.

It would be interesting to learn about further implications of DevOps. Frequent releases are an advantage, but what are the effects of short release cycles and other DevOps practices? How does DevOps affect the end users, or is it just an internal matter for the development organizations? Understanding the effects in a larger scale could help in assessing the real value of DevOps.

Acknowledgments. This article was supported by TEKES as part of the N4S Program of DIMECC (Digital, Internet, Materials & Engineering Co-Creation).

References

1. Digile N4S (2016). http://www.n4s.fi/en. Accessed Sep 2016
2. Balalaie, A., Heydarnoori, A., Jamshidi, P.: Microservices architecture enables DevOps: migration to a cloud-native architecture. IEEE Softw. **33**(3), 42–52 (2016)
3. Bass, L., Weber, I., Zhu, L.: DevOps: A Software Architect's Perspective. Addison-Wesley, Boston (2015)
4. Callanan, M., Spillane, A.: DevOps: making it easy to do the right thing. IEEE Softw. **33**(3), 53–59 (2016)
5. Cruzes, D., Dyba, T.: Recommended steps for thematic synthesis in software engineering. In: International Symposium on Empirical Software Engineering and Measurement (ESEM), pp. 275–284, September 2011
6. Cukier, D.: DevOps patterns to scale web applications using cloud services. In: Proceedings of the 2013 Companion Publication for Conference on Systems, Programming, & Applications: Software for Humanity, pp. 143–152, SPLASH 2013. ACM, New York (2013)
7. Ebert, C., Gallardo, G., Hernantes, J., Serrano, N.: Devops. IEEE Softw. **33**(3), 94–100 (2016)
8. Humble, J., Farley, D.: Continuous Delivery: Reliable Software Releases Through Build, Test, and Deployment Automation. Addison-Wesley Professional, Boston (2010)
9. Iden, J., Tessem, B., Päivärinta, T.: Problems in the interplay of development and IT operations in system development projects: a Delphi study of Norwegian IT experts. Inf. Softw. Technol. **53**(4), 394–406 (2011)
10. Lindgren, E., Münch, J.: Software development as an experiment system: a qualitative survey on the state of the practice. In: Lassenius, C., Dingsøyr, T., Paasivaara, M. (eds.) XP 2015. LNBIP, vol. 212, pp. 117–128. Springer, Heidelberg (2015). doi:10.1007/978-3-319-18612-2_10
11. Neely, S., Stolt, S.: Continuous delivery? Easy! just change everything (well, maybe it is not that easy). In: Proceedings of the 2013 Agile Conference, pp. 121–128, AGILE 2013. IEEE Computer Society, Washington, DC (2013)
12. Roche, J.: Adopting DevOps practices in quality assurance. Commun. ACM **56**(11), 38–43 (2013)
13. Smeds, J., Nybom, K., Porres, I.: DevOps: a definition and perceived adoption impediments. In: Lassenius, C., Dingsøyr, T., Paasivaara, M. (eds.) XP 2015. LNBIP, vol. 212, pp. 166–177. Springer, Heidelberg (2015). doi:10.1007/978-3-319-18612-2_14
14. Tessem, B., Iden, J.: Cooperation between developers and operations in software engineering projects. In: Proceedings of the 2008 International Workshop on Cooperative and Human Aspects of Software Engineering, pp. 105–108, CHASE 2008, NY, USA. ACM, New York (2008)

Towards Continuous Customer Satisfaction and Experience Management: A Measurement Framework Design Case in Wireless B2B Industry

Petri Kettunen[1]([⊠]), Mikko Ämmälä[2], Tanja Sauvola[3],
Susanna Teppola[4], Jari Partanen[2], and Simo Rontti[5]

[1] Department of Computer Science, University of Helsinki, Helsinki, Finland
petri.kettunen@cs.helsinki.fi
[2] Bittium Wireless Ltd., Oulu, Finland
{mikko.ammala,jari.partanen}@bittium.com
[3] Department of Information Processing Science,
University of Oulu, Oulu, Finland
tanja.sauvola@oulu.fi
[4] VTT Ltd., Oulu, Finland
susanna.teppola@vtt.fi
[5] Faculty of Art and Design, University of Lapland, Rovaniemi, Finland
simo.rontti@ulapland.fi

Abstract. Customer satisfaction (CS) is continuously important in modern industrial business environments. However, it is inherently affective even in B2B contexts and thus not directly controllable. Satisfaction impacting customer experiences (CX), respectively, can be managed by the supplier company. The company should first define its strategic CX vision, and then set the value-based CX goals accordingly. The goals have to be made transparent to the entire organization for producing the experiences with their current status and projected progress. A transparent measurement system is thus needed. In this research work, we have investigated how satisfying experiences (chiefly UX) can transparently be gauged in a B2B case company. Following our prior research approach, instead of attempting to cover all possible experience touchpoints in customer-supplier relationships, we focus on the main experience factors of the case company. A real-time predictive CS/CX measurement framework design is proposed. A use case is illustrated for initial evaluation.

Keywords: Customer experience · B2B · Key performance indicator · Transparency · Service design · User experience

1 Introduction

Customer experience (CX) is expected to become an increasingly important competitive advantage. In the digital economy business-to-business (B2B) companies must also take that more consciously into account to succeed, following the B2C trends. By emphasizing the customer perspective, leading industrial B2B companies are

© Springer International Publishing AG 2016
P. Abrahamsson et al. (Eds.): PROFES 2016, LNCS 10027, pp. 598–608, 2016.
DOI: 10.1007/978-3-319-49094-6_45

endorsing superior user experience (UX) and CX as their differentiating competitive strategies.

In this paper we aim to develop towards such ideals in one particular case company context. Bittium, www.bittium.com (later referred to as "the company") offers innovative products and solutions based on own platforms for defense, public safety and other authorities markets, IoT markets (Internet of Things), as well as for industrial use. For the wireless communication markets and companies who need wireless connectivity to their products, the company offers R&D services based on latest wireless technologies and applications. The company also offers high-security solutions for mobile devices.

The strategic targets and challenges of the company are as follows: to achieve constant transparency to the performed work as close to real-time as possible with collaborative feedback system from the product development results, customer satisfaction, and developers to cover the whole value chain towards analytics supported customer experience in B2B context. Therefore, dashboards representing the work and its value are created. Customer involvement (understanding) and service design are key means.

The contribution of this paper is in showing how B2B customer experience can be systematized and, consequently, strategically managed throughout the organizational levels and lifecycle processes to continuously satisfy the customers. We design a proposal for a CS/CX measurement framework to realize it in practice, as demonstrated in the company case. The CX workflow gets transparency of the R&D and the KPI targets.

2   Background and Related Works

2.1   Customer Satisfaction and Experience in B2B

The key distinction of B2B contexts compared with business-to-consumer (B2C) is that the clients are other companies and organizations with formal acquisition processes run by professional buyers. Thus, in this paper, customers refer to users and acquirers of the products, including the delivery project and service-related operations stakeholders.

Customer experience stems from the perceptions of all the cognitive and emotional touchpoint encounters. Following their subjective experience judgements, the customers are satisfied in various degrees. This may then affect their future behaviors.

While traditional CS measurements (surveys, in particular) have been used for years, more prompt and forward-looking measures are just emerging. Currently, there are some published CX measurement models and frameworks (e.g., the Forrester's CX Index), but in B2B, only few exist and none are standardized. In B2B, the customer-supplier dependencies are more complex, requiring more comprehensive measures [1]. Measuring the customer value delivery and realization is still not often practiced [2, 3].

In general, it is not possible for industrial companies to control all the factors affecting their customer experiences. However, each company can make strategic choices of the particular experiences they want to deliver to their customers. They can select the experience components to focus on accordingly [3, 4]. There are various CX improvement models proposed, but no generally agreed, validated standard references exist (not even *de facto*). Some publicly available are the CXMM and Naïve to Natural.

2.2   Transparency of Customer Experience and Satisfaction

As mentioned, CX has a direct link to the customer behavior towards company's products and services, and therefore it requires careful planning and management throughout the organizational levels and lifecycle processes of the product/service. However, comprehensive and continuous CX management requires that the company has transparency built in their engineering processes, touchpoints, and customer interaction so that the realisation of positive CX can continuously be followed and planned as a whole.

In this research, we link transparency to the management of CX throughout the product lifecycle, from the design to the build and delivery, and related information system support. In recent research, transparency is connected to Lean thinking, continuous deployment and process visibility [5, 6]. However, it is still unclear how increased data and process transparency contributes to process performance, and under what circumstances transparency is needed and brings performance effects or business value [6].

In the research of customer satisfaction in information systems development, process transparency has also been identified as important [7]. Often, customer satisfaction information is not widely shared across the organization with all the employees, affecting the customer experiences. In B2B contexts, formalities and even restrictions may limit.

2.3   Continuous Customer Experience Development with Service Design

The sources and drivers of B2B customer satisfaction become more diverse. Service design (SD) is a methodological approach that can be used for customer involvement during the development process [8]. It is a holistic, multidisciplinary field that helps improve customer satisfaction by improving existing products and services, as well as making them more useful and desirable for customers with UX centric practices. Service design has already taken place in the B2C context, but it is also recognized as a useful approach in the B2B context, as well as in the internal development of processes.

SD serves as a platform and facilitator for cross-functional user-driven identification of product opportunities and features as well as enabling early concretization of ideas and their effect to the holistic customer experience. The consequent UX goals can be defined and managed systematically [9]. The translation of the findings into measurable CX/UX key performance indicators (KPI) is the critical phase in order to truly enable real-time, data-driven, and transparent management of user experience throughout the subsequent development, manufacturing, delivery, and service processes.

2.4 Customer Involvement and Feedback

Customer involvement in the development process and the understanding of customers' needs and behaviors are essential when building successful products and services. There are various methods and tools to involve customers. For instance, agile methods focus on improving customer satisfaction through collaboration and active participation of relevant stakeholders [8]. Ideally, the customer and the supplier treat themselves as partners with mutually beneficial commits to value creation. Customer involvement provides an opportunity to enhance the product's technical performance, as well as overall user experience, based on a better understanding of customers' needs, resulting in a better alignment of R&D resources. Also, throughout different touchpoints, there are opportunities to collect customer feedback. For example, continuous deployment and rapid feature validation cycles with customers are seen compelling for learning to improve R&D efficiency and customer satisfaction after deployment [8, 10].

3 Framework Design

This work is a continuation of our previous research with the case company. Initially, we investigated certain elements of the company R&D process and identified a set of strategies to improve the customer satisfaction (e.g., keeping customer promises) [11, 12]. In principle, real-world management research can be either description-driven (explanatory) or prescription-driven (design sciences). Our previous work with the case company has primarily followed the former thread, but in this paper, we advance with the latter, solution-focused approach. We propose the measurement framework as a design artefact and evaluate the innovation.

Based on the case company needs and challenges in particular (Sect. 1), and grounding on the extant literature in general (Sect. 2), the purpose of this research work is to design a solution for the following questions:

1. What valuable customer experiences does the company want to bring and focus on?
2. How to achieve and sustain them?
3. What measurements indicate and predict them?

To begin with, Fig. 1 depicts a conceptual model for the CS/CX measurement framework design. The reasoning is that the customers will be satisfied when they experience (CX) to get value from the supplied products (UX) and services considering the benefits and costs. The aim for the supplier firm is to provide that optimally. Ideally, all benefit from mutual value creations – leading to manageable and economically optimal CX. We thus propose four goal areas (exemplified in Sect. 4) to be attained (CS/CX vision):

   I. Excellent product solution (design; portfolio)
  II. High-quality implementation, manufacturing (capability, technology)
 III. Reliable transactions, customer care (includes validation of the products/ services)
 IV. Successful customer relationship (satisfaction, feedback; business/partner cases)

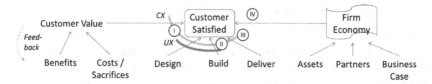

Fig. 1. Conceptual model of CS/CX management: goal spheres and contributing factors

Figure 2 visualizes our design solution model for the CS/CX measurement framework to manage the above. There are four measurement sections corresponding the goal areas I–IV. For each section, there are the following components to device: KPI displays (actuals and predicted), Information sources (feedbacks and feedforwards). The left-hand side of each grid displays the current state of the CX goals based on their associated measurement data (real-time) sources. The right-hand sides in turn reflect their future predictions based on the selected indicator signals. Effectively, the upper-half of each grid addresses research questions 1 and 2, and the lower-half – question 3, respectively.

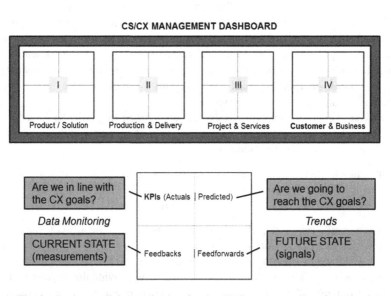

Fig. 2. Design model visualization for the CS/CX measurement framework

The added value of our framework is in combining the high-level CX goal areas and gauging them with both monitoring and predictive measures. Existing methods (like GQM⁺Strategies) can then be used to define them for each section [12].

4   Realization

This section shows how the CS/CX measurement framework design presented in Sect. 3 can be utilized in practice in the case company introduced in Sect. 1. The company has systematically managed its business-level and project-level satisfaction feedback since 2003. Most techniques used were based on collecting customer feedback and satisfaction data through familiar means such as surveys. Also, log files, bug reports, change requests, and feature assessment were used to guide product management decisions. At the time of this investigation the company development focus is to improve company enterprise data management[1] for product portfolio, transparency, traceability, and foresight purposes. Updated company portfolio and service offerings also have brought improvements to the company's UX and product feedback processes.

Table 1 exhibits how all the four sections (I–IV) of the measurement frame (see Fig. 2) can be instantiated with the actual company data sources and reports (displays). With this, the following company-specific CX goals and factors can be gauged end-to-end:

- Product/Solution: UX design use cases linked to product requirements; Proven UX factors applied into product features and usage
- Production & Delivery: Support for test case management to ensure early use case feedback both internally and externally
- Projects & Services: To react faster, adapt and improve – to be able to cope with the customer's requirements, technology, competences and way-of-working.
- Customer & Business: To create better knowledge and understanding of the customer in order to improve the services provided. With the help of creating better CX, customers will be more happy and loyal, and the customer relationship will be better.

An actual business case (confidential) can be characterized as following mapping of the total CX into the four main components of the measurement framework (Fig. 2):

– *Develop customized* (III) *mobile devices and solutions* (I) *for special authority* (IV) *use based on the company's special device platform* (II) *having enhanced security.*

For each component area, the company shall then define specific CX goals to be followed. The following is an excerpt of the consequent goal definition and flowdown:

- CX VISION: Pleasant user experience
  - CX GOALS:
    - o The end-user can use the device efficiently
      - UX GOALS:
        - o UX Design for Rugged keyboard
          - "Seamless navigation via rugged keypad"
          - ...
        - o ...
    - o ...

---

[1] Company's Product Master Data program.

Table 1. Framework realization

	ACTUALS	Feedback Sources	PREDICTORS	Feedforward Sources
I: Product / Solution	Customer Care Portal (product statistics); UX monitoring (evaluation of user stories); Prototype test statistics	Customer Care Portal (product feedback); Verification of user stories; Prototype tests (real-life)	Feature Assessment with Value Tool [13]; Lead user experience (trials); Product performance metrics translated from specific UX requirements	Technology and business evaluations; Usability expert evaluation data; Prototype trials (with SD); Product Master Data applications
II: Production & Delivery	Reports of *Product delivery related enquiries*; Product/delivery realization data monitoring	*Product Delivery related Enquiries* to product orderer, on deliveries; Delivery co-planning; Enterprise Data applications[1] (shared solution data)	Solution data management and Product content updates; Product release and trend management; Enterprise Data modeling and visualization	Company development environment for Continuous Integration/Deployment (SW & HW); Product Master Data and Enterprise Data applications[1]
III: Project & Services	Customer Feedback Summary – Trends (reports of *Project or Service related CS Enquiries*)	*Project or Service related CS Enquiries* to project management and teams / service orderer, during finalization (long cases multiple)	*Impact Mapping Grid* [12]	Project progress trends, estimates; Process audits; Employee feelings surveys
IV: Customer & Business	Reports of *Customer Satisfaction Surveys*	*Customer Satisfaction Surveys* to business / account management, annually or by plan	Customer Care Portal (statistics)	Customer Care Portal (customer feedback)

With the four sections (I–IV) of the CS/CX measurement framework, the particular goal above can transparently be monitored and steered accordingly throughout the entire product value chain and lifecycle as follows (c.f., Table 1):

   I. "Seamless navigation" designed and incorporated into the product requirements
   II. Software and hardware implementation fulfilling the requirements, production-to-design, related user documentation
   III. Customer perceptions: The quality of deliverables is/was good.
      Firm factors: The processes of the projects are/were well defined and tailored to fit the case, and followed (UX plan). Design tools and networks are/were utilized effectively. Verification and validation of deliverables is/was functional (UX tests).
   IV. Customer feedback concerning the navigation and the keyboard

5 Discussion

Our research and development work can be judged both in general and locally in the case company context with informed arguments. There are theoretical and practical implications leading to future research avenues, as well as suggestions for the company.

5.1 Evaluation

Our proposition is generic in that it only suggests the four main component areas, but it does not prescribe the specific goal-setting to be instantiated by the particular B2B company. This configuration work alone is expected to be beneficial for the company, since it forces to make strategic choices (question 1 in Sect. 3) and touchpoint analysis.

The proposed four component sections build transparency to the customer experience information over the organizational levels (Sect. 2.2) supporting the common awareness of the customer experience targets and their realisation during lifecycle processes. However, we acknowledge that such sectors as marketing and sales (brand experience) exist. Naturally, in different companies for instance the different types of products may lead to different weightings of the sections. Moreover, with B2B customers there are typically different persons (including primary/secondary/indirect users) involved at different stages (pre/post-delivery, use) of the customer journey (stakeholder analysis). The ISO/IEC 25010 standard advocates promoting such different stakeholder perspectives and types of users (quality in use).

At the time of this writing, the case exhibited in Sect. 4 is under development, so we do not have enough feedback from practitioners to conclusively assess, how beneficial our CS/CX measurement framework proposal could be to use. However, the proof-of-concept configuration described in Table 1 reflects its application potential *ex ante*.

Comparing, there is some conceptual research published although more in the B2C contexts. Choi, et al. investigated consumer service experiential components (including price) [4]. In B2B, for example one of the seminal works by Eggert and Ulaga tests the impact of customer perceived value on customer satisfaction [14]. Basten and Pankratz distinguish between the overall customer satisfaction of the organization and the end-user perceptions of the product performance [7]. Payne et al. advocate designing the different customer encounters considering the forms and apt metrics [3]. Our framework promotes that line of thinking, focusing on the usage and service touch-points. Value-in-use is the key component in the research model of Lemke et al [1]. Understanding the deep customer needs, co-creating the solution, and monitoring the actual value realization are principal satisfier factors. This mirrors the four sections of I, II–III, and IV of our CS/CX measurement framework, respectively (c.f., Fig. 1). In contrast to the conceptual research, the main contribution of our approach is operational.

A general limitation of this investigation is that it is based on a single company case. Consequently, the suggestions and findings cannot be generalized to the entire B2B industry: rather they are meant to provide insight into similar companies.

5.2   Implications

The prime lesson of our research work is in discerning how industrial B2B customer experience can systematically be framed and managed in practice. The conceptual model (Fig. 1) is for the design reasoning, not theory development and testing.

As customer experience is a summary of various organizational levels of customer interaction (Sect. 2.4) during the product/service lifecycle (Sect. 2.2), the case company main focus has been on enhancing the content and the accessibility of information through the information systems, which would support the efficient management and even prediction of customer experience by utilizing data sources that were accurate, timely, and relevant. A key target is to systematize product data and the aftersales operations. Our CS/CX measurement framework is aimed at facilitating that line of development – leaning on the assumption that the higher the process transparency, the more accurate the solution realization foresight.

In general, we can delineate the following customer experience management strategies with our CS/CX measurement framework: Design for Customer (IV in Fig. 1), Design with Customer (I, II), Design by Customer (III). In B2B, a R&D project can be considered a service to be codesigned and gauged (Sect. 2.3). Several counterparts from both the supplier's and the client's side can be asked considering each four section of our CS/CX framework: what knowledge, technology (assets), and resources they bring – and why (motivation). That is, in addition to the customer's view, we may also continuously appreciate the supplier's view, including the firm's economy (see Fig. 1). These can also be supported by SD. In the case company, the project level can be seen as the continuation of introducing design thinking. The first step has been paying attention to usability of software user interfaces and individual devices. On the next level the design focus expands to more holistic UX including fluent end-user work processes.

The basic premise of our research (Fig. 1) is that positive customer experiences improve customer satisfaction, which in turn, positively influences the business relationship outcomes (e.g., loyalty). However, such causal linkages are complex to validate. Nevertheless, each company should be able to discern the cost/benefit ratio of their different CX components. Customer value(-in-use) is the key concept [1].

While firm economy and business performance are out of the scope of our research work, we suggest that the company considers the potential negative impacts of poor customer experiences in the four sections of our CS/CX measurement framework both from the customer's and the firm's points of views. By systematically measuring the distinct touchpoints, the company is able to improve the performance impacts.

5.3   Future Work

We plan to strengthen the company case. More feedback from practitioners of applying our framework would be appreciated to judge its value and to discover most suitable internal and external (customer) data collection points as the sources of the measurements. Like exhibited in Sect. 4, we can record successful configuration templates (Table 1) for the known customers. In all, the predictive power of different indicators (the right-hand sides of the grids in Fig. 2) could be validated in the company's context. New internal information sources could be employee insights (of product realization) and employee satisfaction. Finally, we intend to follow the recent research stream of co-creating customer value [1–3]. This spans our entire CS/CX measurement framework space, but in our case company, the product value is the current focus area [13].

6   Conclusion

This paper suggests continuous customer experience management for modern B2B companies. While CX measurement cannot be fully standardized, with individual B2B customers it is possible for the company to control their selected touchpoints by their contributing factors and the associated experience components to gauge for customer satisfaction. By systematically measuring them, the company is armed to improve the performance with impact-oriented customer experience management. In this paper, we have designed a CS/CX measurement framework proposal to facilitate those aims as demonstrated in our target company case.

Acknowledgements. This work was supported by TEKES as part of the Need 4 Speed Program of DIMECC (Finnish Strategic Centre for Digital, Internet, Materials & Engineering Co-Creation).

References

1. Lemke, F., Clark, M., Wilson, H.: Customer experience quality: An exploration in business and consumer contexts using repertory grid technique. J. Acad. Mark. Sci. **39**(6), 846–869 (2010)

2. Keränen, J.: Customer Value Assessment In Business Markets. Doctoral Dissertation, Lappeenranta Univ. of Tech, Acta Universitatis Lappeenrantaensis 579 (2014)
3. Payne, A.F., Storbacka, K., Frow, P.: Managing the co-creation of value. J. Acad. Mark. Sci. **36**, 83–96 (2008)
4. Choi, E.K., Wilson, A., Fowler, D.: Exploring customer experiental components and the conceptual framework of customer experience, customer satisfaction, and actual behavior. J. Foodservice Bus. Res. **16**, 347–358 (2013)
5. Rodriquez, P., et al.: Continuous deployment of software intensive products and services: a systematic mapping study. J. Syst. Softw. (in press, 2016)
6. Berner, M., Augustine, J., Maedche, A.: The impact of process visibility on process performance. Bus. Inf. Syst. Eng. **58**(1), 31–42 (2016)
7. Basten, D., Pankratz, O.: Customer satisfaction in IS projects: assessing the role of process and product performance. Commun. AIS **34**, 430–447 (2015)
8. Yaman, S.G., Sauvola, T., Riungu-Kalliosaari, L., Hokkanen, L., Kuvaja, P., Oivo, M., Männistö, T.: Customer involvement in continuous deployment: a systematic literature review. In: Daneva, M., Pastor, O. (eds.) REFSQ 2016. LNCS, vol. 9619, pp. 249–265. Springer, Heidelberg (2016). doi:10.1007/978-3-319-30282-9_18
9. Kaasinen, E., et al.: Defining user experience goals to guide the design of industrial systems. Behav. Inf. Technol. **34**(10), 976–991 (2015)
10. Sauvola, T., Lwakatare, L.E., Karvonen, T., Kuvaja, P., Holmström Olsson, H., Bosch, J., Oivo, M.: Towards customer-centric software development: a multiple-case study. In: 41st Euromicro Conference on Software Engineering and Advanced Applications (SEAA), pp. 9–17. IEEE (2015)
11. Münch, J., Fagerholm, F., Kettunen, P., Pagels, M., Partanen, J.: Experiences and insights from applying gqm+strategies in a systems product development organisation. In: Demirors, O., Turetken, O. (eds.) 39th Euromicro Conference on Software Engineering and Advanced Applications (SEAA), pp. 70–77. IEEE (2013)
12. Kettunen, P., Ämmälä, M., Partanen, J.: Towards predictable B2B customer satisfaction and experience management with continuous improvement assets and rich feedback. In: Lassenius, C., Dingsøyr, T., Paasivaara, M. (eds.) XP 2015. LNBIP, vol. 212, pp. 205–211. Springer, Heidelberg (2015). doi:10.1007/978-3-319-18612-2_18
13. Mendes, E., Turhan, B., Rodriguez, P., Freitas, V.: Estimating the value of decisions relating to managing and developing software-intensive products and projects. In: 11th International Conference on Predictive Models and Data Analytics in Software Engineering (PROMISE). ACM (2015)
14. Eggert, A., Ulaga, W.: Customer perceived value: a substitute for satisfaction in business markets? J. Bus. Ind. Market. **17**(2/3), 107–118 (2002)

Emerging Research Topics

Gamification of Software Testing - An MLR

Mika V. Mäntylä[1]([⊠]) and Kari Smolander[2]

[1] University of Oulu, Oulu, Finland
mika.mantyla@oulu.fi
[2] Aalto University, Espoo, Finland
kari.smolander@aalto.fi

Abstract. This paper presents an initial multi-vocal literature review that extracts ideas for gamification of software testing. We surveyed the type of testing, system under test, role of individuals, gamification elements, challenges and drawbacks, support constructs and tools, and empirical evidence from academic sources and grey literature. Ideas were given to both automated unit-testing, and end-user related testing done by exploratory testers and beta testers. The most frequent gamification elements were points (13 sources), awards (4), stories (4), badges (3), rankings (3), levels (3) and time-pressure (3).

Keywords: Gamification · Testing · Multi-vocal literature · Grey literature

1 Introduction

Gamification is the utilization of game elements outside the context of computer games. Its purpose is to increase the engagement, motivation and performance of the participants [1]. We study gamification of software testing as software testing costs are high (35 % of the IT costs [2]), testing is often an undervalued job, and testing produces lots of information in the form of numbers. The numbers can be turned to points that are a fundamental gamification element. The high cost, low appreciation, and the apparent gamifiability of testing make it an excellent target for gamification.

Our research method was a multi-vocal literature review (MLR). MLRs aim at studying all types of writings on a particular topic [3]. Thus, in comparison to traditional systematic literature review they also include grey literature such as web-pages, blog posts and discussion forum content. They are suitable for topics where academic literature is lacking due to the recent emergence of the topic or for some other reason.

When searching the literature, we performed two main steps. First, we used a recent SLR of gamification in Software Engineering [1] as a starting point for forward and backward snowballing academic literature. We studied the SLR and all primary studies it was refereeing and found three papers that were related to software testing, verification and validation. Forward snowballing additionally revealed two additional studies. Second, we used Google Search Engine to search for relevant grey literature. Our search string was "gamification software testing". We utilized the page-rank algorithm. During the process, the quality of the grey literature quickly deteriorated as we progressed further. Our final included grey literature source was 34th hit provided by Google.

© Springer International Publishing AG 2016
P. Abrahamsson et al. (Eds.): PROFES 2016, LNCS 10027, pp. 611–614, 2016.
DOI: 10.1007/978-3-319-49094-6_46

Overall, our goal was not to cover all possible corners but to find a reasonable amount of sources (n = 20) to enable the collection of potential ideas and requirements for a full design science project, where a software testing gamification environment is built. Our resulting spreadsheet is online [4] and sources are referred with "S" and a number of the reference, e.g. S1 refers to the first source.

2 Results

2.1 Types of Testing, Systems Under Test (SUT) and Roles of Individuals

First, we wanted to understand what types of testing gamification has been proposed for gamification. Unit testing was the most popular option mentioned in six sources (see our online spreadsheet for details). In particular, Test-driven development, a specialized way of unit testing was mentioned in three out of the six papers that mentioned unit-testing. Six sources did not mention the type of testing or talked about testing in general with no particular focus area. Two sources mentioned beta-testing as the type of testing suitable for gamification. Two mentions were also given to exploratory testing. To summarize, gamification was mostly suggested to the very opposite ends of testing. Unit-testing is technical and typical performed by developers who also develop the software. On the other hand, beta-testing and exploratory testing is often done from end-users' perspective to find out problems particularly related to the user or the customer or the domain rules were the software is used.

Second, SUT can influence whether the gamification of software testing is desirable. However, the majority of our sources (13) did not specify the system under test in detail or claimed that is applicable to all systems types. The only type of system receiving more than one mention were Games with two sources. Other systems mentioned once were: Data-center software, Inter-active system with complex workflows, Enterprise Systems, Java, and an artificial element with linked list for education purposes. Overall, it appears that any type of SUT would be suitable for gamification.

Third, as past work suggests that testing is also performed by many roles (testers, developers, customers, product managers and help-desk personnel) [5, 6], we investigated the roles who participate in the gamified testing. Nine sources mentioned developers. Software testers were another notable group mentioned in eight sources. Other roles received considerably less mentions: students were mentioned three times, beta-testers and managers were mentioned in two sources and one source mentioned customer support, designers, and crowdsourced workers. Additionally, one source was ambiguous with respect to roles.

Although the literature of gamification recognizes that multiple roles can participate in gamified software testing efforts, still majority of our source focus on the two obvious groups developers and testers.

2.2 Gamification Elements

We classified the type of gamification elements [1, 7] of our sources. Gamification elements refer to constructs that try to transform work, i.e. software testing in our case, to a game. Transforming work that is supposedly boring and tedious to a game that supposedly is fun and engaging is the key motivator of gamification.

As in prior work [1] points were the most frequently mentioned gamification element with 13 sources. Points are a basic element in gamification that can be turned to other elements such as awards (4 sources), badges (3), and rankings (3). Empirical evidence of the effect of the gamification elements was limited in our sources, but for example S20 mentioned that a leaderboard (a public ranking based on points) was the most effective gamification element.

Other game elements were also frequently present. Stories or quests were mentioned in four sources. For example, S5 states that *"Testers will be impersonating different characters from a detective in industrial London...."* Time-pressure was an element mentioned in three sources. Time-pressure can increase efficiency and make games more engaging. Levels, mentioned in three sources, enable iterative progress and adjust the difficulty of the game so that a suitable challenge is always present, e.g. to complete level 1 one must have one unit-test for all classes, for level 2 one must have unit-tests for all methods and so on. Tips, mentioned in one source, can be also be used to make the games engaging and reduce deadlocks.

For an organization, games may require task distribution mechanics (mentioned in two sources). Rules, mentioned in two sources, are also important as otherwise someone can start getting points with inappropriate ways, e.g. to write meaningless code to increase unit-test coverage.

2.3   Empirical Evidence, Support Constructs, and Challenges

Only three sources provided properly reported empirical results. S12 presents two industrial case studies with impressive numbers that support the adoption of gamification. The first increased the defect fixing speed while the other focused on using static analysis results to motivate developers to create higher code quality. S13 presents a student experiment in unit-testing showing that the treatment group (gamified) found significantly more defects and had higher requirements coverage than the control group. Finally, S20 performed an industrial case study and found that their system was successful in motivating developers to write more and higher quality unit tests.

Twelve sources presented support constructs to gamification. S3 tells how their tool for gamification of testing failed and how it could be improved. S4 provides a storytelling scaffolding with roles and principles that help with gamification of testing. S7 connects gamification idea to the testers' career path. S15 provides a rule system. Actual tools were provided as JIRA add-ons (S8), Eclipse plugins (S10, S11, S13), web-based learning environments (S18), and as GUnit tool (S20).

From our sources, we found three challenges in the gamification of software testing that we consider notable. First, S6 highlighted that people have different ways to achieve the same goal. If one then starts to measure things like the quality of defect reports in the defect tracking system, then other qualities like excellent face-to-face communication that can be used as a substitute for the poor quality of written reports would be ignored. Thus, the game would reward only a selected subset of the bug reporting process, i.e. the one that is visible in the defect tracker. This ignores many relevant parts of the process as pointed out in the literature [8]. Second, even counting bugs will introduce challenges, for example counting and awarding based on the bug count could lead to a situation where five spelling mistakes in the application would result in five bug reports (S1). Such issues need to be dealt with some types of rules and game referees that decide what is right. Third, S2 pointed out a need for balance to give individuals enough freedom so that the game stays engaging and allows creativity to blossom, while still maintaining control and coordination.

3   Conclusions

We make four findings in this paper. First, gamification proposals were given to both ends of testing – automated unit-testing that is technical, and end-user related testing, i.e. beta-testing and exploratory testing. Second, the multitude of different roles and crowdsourcing in testing were recognized. Third, numerous gamification elements were present. Points were the most popular while stories appeared as something that could be used to increase the engagement in ways that are not possible for numeric point based approaches. Fourth, problems of gamification were discussed, e.g. the gamified approach might not allow employees to work in a way that is the most natural for each individual, thus, resulting in unfairness and lower productivity.

References

1. Pedreira, O., García, F., Brisaboa, N., Piattini, M.: Gamification in software engineering – a systematic mapping. Inf. Softw. Technol. **57**, 157–168 (2015)
2. Buenen, M., Walgude, A.: World Quality Report 2015–2016. Capgemini, Sogeti und HP (2015)
3. Garousi, V., Felderer, M., Mäntylä, M.V.: The need for multivocal literature reviews in software engineering: complementing systematic literature reviews with grey literature, p. 26. ACM (2016)
4. Mäntylä, M.V., Smolander, K.: Spreadsheet of sources: Gamification of Software Testing - an MLR [Internet]. Figshare. doi:10.6084/m9.figshare.3756600
5. Mäntylä, M.V., Itkonen, J., Iivonen, J.: Who tested my software? Testing as an organizationally cross-cutting activity. Softw. Qual. J. **20**, 145–172 (2012)
6. Prechelt, L., Schmeisky, H., Zieris, F.: Quality experience: a grounded theory of successful agile projects without dedicated testers, pp. 1017–1027. ACM (2016)
7. Hamari, J., Koivisto, J., Sarsa, H.: Does gamification work? – A literature review of empirical studies on gamification, pp. 3025–3034. IEEE (2014)
8. Aranda, J., Venolia, G.: The secret life of bugs: going past the errors and omissions in software repositories, pp. 298–308. IEEE Computer Society (2009)

Internationally Distributed Software Development: On the Impact of Distance Based on a Case Study

Harri Sten[✉], Hannu Jaakkola, and Kari Systä

Department of Pervasive Computing, Tampere University of Technology, Tampere, Finland
{harri.sten,hannu.jaakkola,kari.systa}@tut.fi

Abstract. Distribution of software development is increasingly global and crosses the geographical and cultural borders. As software development is creative teamwork, the distribution is not about mechanical division of work. The poster presents on on-going study on internationally distributed software development. Based on a literature and experiences from a case company, investigates the motivations, models of distribution and the most problematic areas.

Keywords: Distributed development · Software development · Management

1 Introduction

Software development is often an international activity. Distributed software development is in many ways different from the situation where developers work in a co-located fashion. While all the disadvantages associated with international distribution cannot be eliminated in full, their effects can be reduced. Therefore, finding a balance between the various benefits, disadvantages, and successes is the most important aspect for a successful international and distributed software development project. Carmel and Tjia [1] describe the problems in terms of five centrifugal forces, each of which alienate project staff from each other and make the work more difficult. These forces are culture, communication, coordination, control, and cohesion.

In this paper, these five centrifugal forces are used as a framework for analyzing distributed software development. In particular, we focus on the attributes of distance in distributed software development. This research analyzes the effects of these two dimensions, centrifugal forces and distance attributes by using a concrete case company that develops a product family in the globally distributed environment.

2 Research Methods and Data Collection

We address the aspects of distribution of software development in the light of earlier studies in the form of the literature review [2], and reflect the findings to a case company using an ethnographic study approach [3].

The ethnographic study is based on the main author' long (12 years) career in the case company. In addition, retrospectives have been important for development and

© Springer International Publishing AG 2016
P. Abrahamsson et al. (Eds.): PROFES 2016, LNCS 10027, pp. 615–620, 2016.
DOI: 10.1007/978-3-319-49094-6_47

improvement of the process. These retrospectives been conducted both in project and team level. As a genuine insider, the main author has collected data and analyzed the changes and documented conclusions in the internal wiki pages of the organizations.

3   Background

3.1   Attributes of Distance

The distance between developers has many attributes. One categorization of those attributes includes *geographical, temporal, socio-cultural and organizational distance* [4, 5]. When considering *geographical distance,* the physical distance does not explain all the impact to the software development. Effort, time, and cost of travelling are more relevant than simple physical distance [4, 6]. *Temporal distance* means that the developers work on different time zones and therefore have only few or no common working hours. Similarly, to geographical distance it hinders real-time communication [4], but also opens new possibilities like "follow-the-sun" [7] development.

Socio-cultural distance refers to a person's ability to understand and adapt to another person's values and normative practices. Factors of socio-cultural distance include e.g. national culture, language, politics, organization and employee motivation [4, 6]. One attribute of distance is *organizational.* The software development can be distributed to different parts of the company or even outsourced to another company. The organizational aspect can both decrease and increase the distance. Company culture can help organizational distribution to overcome socio-cultural differences [4].

3.2   Centrifugal Forces of Distributed Model

The literature mentions few reference models for distributed software development. Carmel [8] sees globalization of software development as a set of centrifugal forces that propels things outwards from the center as it disperses developers to the far corners of the world. Each of these five forces alienates project staff from each other and makes the work more difficult. Those forces are now introduced one by one.

Culture. Cultural effects are most visible in long and multi-national projects. Cultural diversity can have several dimensions like corporate, project, or national. Even small cultural mistakes may lead to culture clashes, mistrust and later to conflicts. Organizational culture has an impact to development environment, however the regional culture has still a much greater impact than organizational culture [9].

Communication. Communication requires special attention in distributed software development, because there is less or no informal communication.

Coordination. Software development is a set of complex tasks with complex interdependencies. Well thought division of labor is important in the distributed software project. Software project and /or the product must be sufficiently modular so that it can be divided into separate and independent work packages for each site to help the coordination of software development [4, 10, 11]. Also working time arrangements should be coordinated so that common working time between sites can be arranged to guarantee simultaneous work.

Control. Control ensures that the work is consistent with the objectives and selected standards and practices. Control is best achieved when the project managers can be and work among his subordinates (i.e. management by walking). That cannot be implemented in distributed software development project. To improve control in distributed software project must be prepared both financially and in terms of time for frequent travelling as often as possible to all sites [1, 12].

Cohesion. If a software development team has good cohesion, members can rely on each other, like each other and to help one another. All the members of the project team should trust each other, so that efficient co-operation is at all possible.

4   A Validating Case Study

Description of the organization. The case company had a really distributed organization with sites in Asia, North America and Europe. Headquarter and executive management was in Finland. Distribution to Asia and subcontracting were used to enable the growth but also due to cost pressures. Site in North America was established and acquisition in a Southern European country was implemented to access necessary technological know-how. Fast increase of distribution inevitably causes a lot of difficulties. Most of the problems during the development were consequences of geographical and temporal distances. Physical distance increased traveling related costs and temporal distance led to difficulties in communication (coordination and control).

Culture. The development work in the case company was distributed to three continents and seven countries. Cultural diversity required the management to familiarize and understand the cultures of the different countries. The main part of the software was developed in Finland, India and the USA. In the Lewis' LMR model [13], all these countries are on different edges of the triangle. Cooperation between these offices appeared very difficult. A strong corporate culture helped to decrease some implications in the area of culture, but in the subcontracting model it does not help.

Communication. The case company faced a lot of communication challenges. Long temporal and geographical distances lead to asynchronous communications. The main communication tool was e-mail. Synchronous communication was accompanied mainly with regular telephone and videoconferencing, but lack of mutual face-to-face meetings prevented successful of the communication.

Coordination. Coordination of work required special attention from the management. Product architecture was created to support distribution of tasks to different sites and subcontractor. As competencies and practices were very different at sites work slit was not ideal. The one positive consequences opportunity to use "follow-the-sun" while establishing their continuous integration and testing so that China tested every day what other sites had accomplished.

Control. Strong company and project culture helped organization to establish operational control of projects. But still some problems occurred during project related to oral reporting in the meetings. Culture differences made interpretation of daily oral reporting very hard as delivered quite often through some filtering. Also daily reporting had delays based on temporal differences.

Cohesion. Negative side effects of cultural differences, communication problems were lack of trust on each other's knowledge and competences. Lack of confidence and trust was already seen at early stages of development project. Organization started to establish kick-off meetings at the beginning of each project to create confidence on competencies and creating trust between sites and people.

5   Results and Analysis

Different organizational and project structures cause combinations of attributes of distance with many implications, both positive and negative. With good processes and development methods the organizations can decrease the negative impacts and at the same time to help managing the problematic areas of distributed development.

Table 1 shows how different distance attributes affect distributed work through the centrifugal forces. The table is based on earlier studies and their key findings e.g. [14–17], hypothesis of a main author and the case study (ethnographic study) presented in Sect. 3. Strength of these impacts has been estimated with four values (low/medium/high/very high). In very high level impact success of development work require serious actions to eliminate problems. Low level impact is not a serious threat needs to be taken into account. The most problematic areas are indicated with grey background in Table 1.

Table 1. Strength of impacts in the distribution

Centrifugal forces in areas of distribution	Culture	Communication	Coordination	Control	Cohesion
Geographical	High	High	Very High	Very High	Very High
Temporal	Low	Very High	Very High	Very High	Very High
Socio-cultural	Very High	High	Medium	Medium	High
Organizational	Very High	High	High	High	High

Low/Medium/High/Very High = Level of impact
Grey areas = Most problematic areas

The *geographical distance* has always impacts due to wasted time and costs of travel. The biggest impact is on coordination, control and cohesion. Controlling of the work and people from a long physical distance is hard to implement and oral two-way communication is often replaced with written reporting. It is not easy to use the management-by-walking method or true co-operation across distributed sites. Cohesion over long geographical distance is very difficult to establish and needs extra effort from the management.

The high *temporal distance* has a major impact to key areas of software development project. The case and earlier studies have shown that temporal distance leads to delayed and asynchronous communication, and lack of informal communication [1]. In addition to weak collaboration and trust all this makes implementation management mechanisms difficult [18]. On the other hand, the case has been shown that "follow-the-sun" development can take an advantage of temporal distance.

Different *socio-cultural distances* have a major impact on the working culture of the project. This effect can be reduced by introducing a strong company or project culture. Communication is difficult when people do not have common language or their cultural behavior is significantly different. It is hard to build trust and co-operation between people who have different backgrounds and believes. Our case showed that without prior collaboration or knowing and understanding competencies and ways of working in different cultures, developers cannot work together successfully during the project. Cultural problems are most harmful in outsourcing because no shared company culture to compensate resulting problems is present [1].

Organizational distance impacts all centrifugal forces, but mostly cultural. That can be seen clearly in the case of outsourcing where company cultures differ. When the company needs to distribute teams to different cultures, the management mechanisms, communication channels, practices and tools need to be upgraded and take into account national and company culture differences. [1]

To summarize, Table 1 shows how different attributes of distance and centrifugal forces impact the success of distributed work and it seems that common impact is even stronger in the presence of multiple attributes of distance.

6   Conclusions

Distributed software development is a daily routine in software industry. In this research we analyzed four selected attributes [4] of distance in internationally distributed software development and how those attributes influence the affects the centrifugal forces. In addition to geographical distribution, distributed development covers other factors, such as temporal and socio-cultural distribution, out of which the temporal distance has been shown to be the most problematic attribute of distance.

Acknowledgments. The research has been supported by Tekes-funded Digile project Need for Speed.[1]

---

[1] http://www.n4s.fi/en/.

References

1. Carmel, E., Tjia, P.: Offshoring Information Technology: Sourcing and Outsourcing to a Global Workforce. Cambridge University Press, Cambridge (2005)
2. Kitchenham, B.: Procedures for Performing Systematic Reviews. Keele University Technical report. Keele, Staffs, UK, Software Engineering Group, Department of Computer Science, Keele University. TR/SE 0401 (2004)
3. Randall, D., Harper, R., Rouncefield, M.: Fieldwork for Design: Theory and Practice. Springer, Heidelberg (2007)
4. Ågerfalk, P.J., Fitzgerald, B., Holmström, H., Lings, B., Lundell, B., Conchuir, E.O.: A framework for considering opportunities and threats in distributed software development. In: Proceedings of the International Workshop on Distributed Software, Austrian Computer Society (2005)
5. Gumm, D.C.: Dimensions of distribution in software development projects: a taxonomy. IEEE Softw. Spec. Issue Glob. Softw. Dev. 23, 45 (2006)
6. Holmström, H.Ó., Conchúir, E., Ågerfalk, P.J., Fitzgerald, B.: Global software development challenges: a case study on temporal, geographical and socio-cultural distance. In: International Conference on Global Software Engineering (ICGSE2006), Costão do Santinho, Florianópolis, Brazil, 16–19 October 2006
7. Carmel, E., Espinosa, J.A., Dubinsky, Y.: "Follow the Sun" Workflow in Global Software Development. J. Manag. Inf. Syst. 27(1), 17–38 (2010)
8. Carmel, E.: Global Software Teams: Collaborating Across Borders and Time Zones. Prentice Hall PTR, Upper Saddle River (1999)
9. Auch, F., Smyth, H.: The culture heterogeny of project firms and project teams. Int. J. Manag. 3(3), 443–461 (2010)
10. Lings, B., Lundell, B., Ågerfalk, PJ., Fitzgerald, B.: A reference model for successful distributed development of software systems. In: Proceedings of the 2nd International Conference on Global Software Engineering (ICGSE 2007), Munich, Germany, 27–30 August 2007
11. Ågerfalk, P.J., Fitzgerald, B., Olsson, H.H., Ó Conchúir, E.: Benefits of global software development: the known and unknown. In: Wang, Q., Pfahl, D., Raffo, D.M. (eds.) ICSP 2008. LNCS, vol. 5007, pp. 1–9. Springer, Heidelberg (2008). doi:10.1007/978-3-540-79588-9_1
12. Ramasubbu, N., Krishnan, M.S., Kampalli, P.: Leveraging global resources: a process maturity framework for managing distributed development. IEEE Softw. 22(3), 80–86 (2005)
13. Lewis, R.: When Cultures Collide. Leading Across Cultures, 3rd edn. Nicholas Brealey International, Boston (2006)
14. Noll, J., Beecham, S., Richardson, I.: Global software development and collaboration: barriers and solutions. ACM Inroads 1(3), 66–78 (2010)
15. da Silva, F.Q.B, et al.: Challenges and solutions in distributed software development project management: a systematic literature review. In: 2010 5th IEEE International Conference on Global Software Engineering (ICGSE), IEEE (2010)
16. Jiménez, M., Piattini, M., Vizcaíno, A.: Challenges and improvements in distributed software development: a systematic review. Adv. Softw. Eng. 2009, 3 (2009)
17. Šmite, D., et al.: Empirical evidence in global software engineering: a systematic review. Empirical Softw. Eng. 15(1), 91–118 (2010)
18. Fox, S.: Information and communication design for multi-disciplinary multi-national projects. Int. J. Managing Proj. Bus. 2(4), 536–560 (2009)

Using Scrum to Develop a Formal Model – An Experience Report

Marta Olszewska[✉], Sergey Ostroumov, and Marina Waldén

Faculty of Natural Sciences and Engineering, Åbo Akademi University, Turku, Finland
{marta.plaska,sergey.ostroumov,marina.walden}@abo.fi

Abstract. The benefits of merging agile and formal methodologies have been discussed on the conceptual level for several years now, also in our previous work. This paper presents a hands-on investigation on the synergy of the Event-B formal method within the Scrum development process. A case study of the landing gear critical system is used to investigate the feasibility of such a merge. We provide the quantitative and qualitative analysis of the case study by measuring developer's effort, size and complexity of the created model, as well as observing the development process. Our results show that the merge increases quality, in terms of sustaining the creation of correct and reliable systems (Event-B) and at the same time smoothens the modelling process, enhances comprehension of the system domain and requirements (Scrum).

Keywords: Scrum · Event-B · Agile development process · Formal methods

1 Background

Agile methods, dated back to Agile Manifesto [1], are known for enabling rapid, flexible and evolutionary development with a strong emphasis on its social aspect (team work and communication) [2]. They all have provided practices and values, which can be tailored with respect to the context of their application. Due to the flexibility and certain degree of freedom when using such methods, they are not considered as a first choice for supporting the development of critical systems. However, the quality and correctness of critical systems [3, 4] have been assured with formal methods for over 40 years now. The mixture of these methods would create a development setting, which can ensure high quality of the system being created in a process that supports iterativeness and response to change. This combination would benefit from providing transparency in the project by increasing the interaction between team members and improving comprehension of the requirements of the system to be developed.

In our previous work, we investigated several agile methods with respect to their feasibility in the development of critical systems [5]. We explored the values, principles and practices of agile development methods and placed them in the context of formal,

---

This work was carried out within the project ADVICeS (https://research.it.abo.fi/ADVICeS/), funded by the Academy of Finland, grant No. 266373.

P. Abrahamsson et al. (Eds.): PROFES 2016, LNCS 10027, pp. 621–626, 2016.
DOI: 10.1007/978-3-319-49094-6_48

refinement-based developments. We provided a mapping between the characteristics of these two, which established FormAgi – a high-level framework consisting of (i) guidelines on what concerns should be tackled before committing to a certain agile method and (ii) pointers in which aspects an agile method can be a facilitator in the formal development.

We chose to use Event-B [6, 7] as a formal method and modelling language and to apply it within the Scrum [8] agile process. We find Event-B particularly useful, as it supports the iterative creation of systems in a correct-by-construction manner. We are able to model software, hardware, as well as environment [9]. Scrum matches well Event-B and its idea of stepwise development of a system, since it is time-framed, iterative and incremental. Although Event-B is not considered as a lightweight approach, in this work we apply it in a rapid manner by conducting the development in small refinement steps [6], and by decomposing the models [10], as well as by using component-based visual development [11]. The goal is to achieve a development of a high quality and correct system in an adaptive, flexible, continuous and timely way.

In this work, we validate our claims we made in the previous conceptual study [5, 12]: (i) a refinement step (formal modelling) and a development iteration (agile process) are not exactly corresponding, (ii) in order to fit the iterations, the requirements may need to be decomposed, (iii) Scrum smoothens the development by facilitating communication and improving understandability in the project, as well as providing control over development (supports progress and steady pace). We perform a hands-on investigation on the Event-B development in a Scrum setting by using a case study (Landing Gear System – later referred to as LGS) from the industry from the aerospace domain. The LGS case study is well described in [13] and modelled using various formalisms. In our work we concentrate on the Scrum development process and how it can facilitate the Event-B formal modelling.

2   Event-B Within Scrum

Event-B provides rigour to the specification and design phases of the development process of critical systems. It enables us to gradually introduce more details and functionality to the constructed system via refinement steps. The formal development starts by modelling a set of requirements as an abstract specification which is then refined in a number of steps. The consistency between the refinement levels is verified by mathematical proofs. An Event-B specification uses a pseudo-programming notation (Abstract Machine Notation) and consists of a dynamic and a static part, which are linked to each other. Event-B is supported by the Eclipse-based, open source tool called *Rodin* [14] that is a "rich client platform" extendable with plug-ins.

We benefit from the way software systems are developed with Event-B. The gradual introduction of properties to the system enabled by refinement allows us to comply with the iterative, incremental and time-framed nature of agile development. Moreover, we can handle complexity issues more efficiently by decomposing the problems to simpler and smaller ones. The quality aspect of development is assured by the correct-by-construction approach and strengthening the work on requirements (elicitation). Finally, modelling and proving properties of the system contributes to building a well-defined system and diminishing the risk of unnecessary re-work due to misunderstanding or not sufficiently described requirements.

Formal development (herein modelling activity) differs from traditional development not only in the rigour of the development, but also in how the progress of the development can be seen and measured. For instance, the progress of the development is determined by the artefacts being created during the development (like requirements, specifications, models on specific abstraction levels or implementation of a feature), as opposed to recognising executable code as the main measure of progress.

A set of requirements to be developed, acting as product backlog, is called the *item pool*. It contains high- and low-level requirements, safety cases, environmental and context descriptions. A subset of the item pool comprising of requirements chosen for the current sprint is a *backlog*. The requirements are only prioritised within the sprints. The reasoning is twofold: (i) we do not want to rush decisions which would lead to a complex and hard to prove model and (ii) the work on the requirements and their structuring with respect to the modelling strategy will pay off later, when the model needs to be extended. Therefore, a sprint includes modelling of the requirements, as well as developing and proving a model. Finally, model animation and simulation, validation mechanisms supported by Rodin, can also be a part of the sprint.

Finally, although not present in the original Scrum, a tool-supported and proactive feedback system is included in the sprints via the *Monitoring and Metrics mechanisms* (M&M). It is to raise understanding on the current status of the iteration, facilitate the process improvement and provide control and evidence on the development, by measuring the number of proof obligations and the time that is used for modelling, as well as the size and complexity of the model.

3   Formally Modelling Landing Gear System in Scrum

We demonstrate the proposed synergy using the Landing Gear System case study LGS [13]. We focus on the process of formally building the model and how it can be smoothened by utilising Scrum. Further details of the LGS case study and the context of our investigation are given in [15]. The construction details of the formal model, its componentization and patterns are described in detail in [11].

The LGS system consists of a digital controller and a few actuators. The function of the system is to operate the landing gears and associated doors. Depending on the reactions from the pilot, the digital controller manipulates the mechanical part. The mechanical part, in its turn, consists of front, left and right landing sets. Each set includes a door, a landing gear and hydraulic cylinders that are attached to and move the corresponding doors and gears. In addition, the system has an analogical switch to prevent an abnormal behaviour of the digital part.

We performed our hands-on investigation in academic setting that involved three persons with the following expertise: formal methods, formal modelling of systems, quality assurance and quality measurements. The roles, to some extent shared, were as follows: (i) product owner: role shared by the modeller, due to the familiarity with the requirements in [13], and the senior expert; (ii) scrum master: quality assurance expert and agile expert; (iii) team: role shared by all three members. The participants were selected based on their familiarity with formal methods, as our goal was to make the work environment close to the one of the engineers from safety-critical domains.

Due to other work-related commitments of the team members, we set up a two-week restriction time for the development, divided into two sprints, each one week long (long sprint), where every work-day was treated as a short sprint. We held an introductory planning meeting, "sprint 0", to familiarise the non-agile members with the concepts of Scrum, as well as to ensure that the goals and vocabulary of the case study were clear for all of the team members.

The item pool and backlog were managed in an Excel form, which was constructed as a simplified tracking system. The safety, functional, equipment and other requirements of the case study [13] were added to the item pool/backlog in "sprint 0". The team planned the modelling by first prioritising the features listed in the item pool (assigning priorities 0-3) and then scheduling them for certain iterations (1st or 2nd). However, more requirements were added to the item pool/backlog by the team and product owner/ stakeholder later on, since some additional properties were revealed during the development. A requirement was assigned status *Done* when it was both modelled and proven. Only then the model could be submitted to the SVN-repository. Note that this study was not the sole activity of the development team during the workdays, so one cannot relate the collected data to the complete workday.

4   Analysis and Observations

The quantitative data we report on were collected and computed automatically and are describing: the development process (including meetings), the modeller's effort, the number of automatic and interactive proof obligations, and finally the size and complexity of the model (the dynamic and static parts). We also gathered some qualitative data about the development process and its suitability for the Event-B development based on the statements of the modeller.

In the *quantitative study*, we were particularly interested in the effort required for modelling and proving such system and how it reflects in perspective of Scrum. Some preparatory activities were needed at the beginning of the development (sprint "0"). Since the choice of modelling strategy and the sequence of modelling artefacts and properties has an impact on how easy it will be to prove the model, there is an overhead that should be taken into account when the system is being studied and the modelling is planned. Therefore, investing some time at the beginning of the sprints is beneficial in the long run and does not contradict the idea of an agile development process. On the contrary, any progress, also involving eliciting and reworking the requirements, conforms to the agile philosophy by supporting value creation (and indirectly eliminating waste by constructing the system in such a way that it does not need to be remodelled). In order for some requirements to obtain the status "Done" the developer needed to spend more than one day of work per requirement; whereas several other requirements could be completely modelled and proven within one day.

Whenever analysing a formal development, it is particularly interesting to investigate the *proof statistics*, which may shed some light on the development complexity or required effort. Proof statistics for our model consist of data representing the interactive, automatic and total number of Proof Obligations (POs) in each refinement step. Amongst the 504 proof obligations, only 13 required interactive proving. This was due to the redundancy of components and the well-definedness condition.

The *size and complexity of the model*, as well as the *difficulty* and *effort* of its creation, were calculated according to the set of metrics we established for Event-B [16] for each model submitted to the repository (*Done* status) for all refinement steps. The final model consists of ten refinement steps, each having a dynamic and static part. We observed that the dynamic part of the model had a steady pace of development (no sudden peaks in measures), which denotes that the requirements were well decomposed into features and that they were modelled in an iterative way following the refinement process. Thus, the development was well reflecting the agile principles. Moreover, the difficulty measures were not changing throughout the modelling, which signifies that the strategy for the development was well chosen. The static part of the model was considerably growing with respect to size, complexity and effort measures whenever a component was introduced, which was expected.

Additionally, we explored the *effort distribution* over the refinement steps based on the model metrics. When compared to the effort reported by the developer, the effort based on model metrics takes into consideration not only modelling and proving activities, but also the effort necessary to comprehend the model. It shows gradual growth concerning the development progress. Finally, the size and complexity of the complete model, as well as the effort computed from the model correlated.

Our *qualitative analysis* is based on the observations noted in our development diary during the sprints and a post-mortem interview with the developer. We observed that a refinement step does not correspond to an iteration, regardless of the definition of iteration (otherwise the length of the iteration would have to be fluctuating). When a refinement step takes longer than one iteration, i.e., it involves a problem that is too intricate, the problem needs to be decomposed into several smaller ones; otherwise; there may be several refinement steps in a single iteration. Since the "Done" status might not necessarily be obtained at the end of the working day, submissions to the subversion control system may not occur on a daily basis. Finally, the sequential nature of refinement does not fully conform to rapid and iterative development suggested by agile methodologies (a new feature request may require re-engineering the model). However, we noticed that Scrum is particularly helpful when it comes to monitoring and managing the development with respect to the planned modelling, due to requirements prioritisation and continuous control of progress (backlog). Communication and transparency of the development (a weak point in formal methods application) is facilitated, which is attributable to the set of meetings proposed by Scrum.

The quantitative and qualitative data confirmed that the synergy of Event-B and Scrum is beneficial for safety-critical developments, since the well-defined development methods are complemented with efficient and flexible development process. We are aware that our work is limited to two Scrum iterations, performed in a controlled, academic environment by one team and thus the development may seem of a small-scale. However, not only the case study was provided by industry and represented real life requirements from the aerospace domain, but also the team was of experience similar to the one of the engineers working in industry.

Due to the nature of our study, we cannot generalise our findings, nor validate them statistically. There are many variables that can impact the investigation, e.g., experience of the developer with a formal method or the tool that supports it; familiarity with agile processes; domain knowledge of the problem to be modelled. However, we believe that our results can be transferable to other formalisms and agile methods, as we show: (i) what kind of issues need more attention when choosing Event-B as a modelling language in an agile setting and (ii) what kind of fine-tuning of an agile process is needed to benefit the most from the agile and formal combination.

References

1. Manifesto for Agile Software Development. http://agilemanifesto.org/. Accessed 11–13 Feb 2001
2. Agile Alliance: What is Agile? In: Agile Alliance. https://www.agilealliance.org/agile101/what-is-agile/
3. Butler, R.: What is formal methods? In: NASA LaRC Formal Methods Program (2001)
4. Holloway, M.: Why engineers should consider formal methods. In: AIAA/IEEE16th Digital Avionics Systems Conference (1997)
5. Olszewska, M., Waldén, M.: FormAgi – A Concept for More Flexible Formal Developments. TUCS TR, Åbo Akademi University, Turku (2014)
6. Abrial, J.-R.: Modeling in Event-B: System and Software Engineering. Cambridge University Press, New York (2010)
7. Abrial, J.-R.: Extending B without changing it (for developing distributed systems). In: Proceedings of 1st Conference on the B Method, Nantes (1996)
8. Schwaber, K., Sutherland, J.: Scrum. The Official Guide (2010). http://www.Scrum.org
9. Event-B: Home of Event-B and the Rodin Platform (2008). http://www.event-b.org/index.html
10. Abrial, J.-R.: Event Model Decomposition. http://wiki.event-b.org/images/Event_Model_Decomposition-1.3.pdf
11. Ostroumov, S., Waldén, M.: Facilitating Formal Event-B Development by Visual Component-based Design. TUCS Technical report 1148, Turku Centre for Computer Science, Turku (2015)
12. Olszewska, M., Waldén, M.: DevOps meets formal modelling in high-criticality complex systems. In: 1st International Workshop on Quality-Aware DevOps (QUDOS 2015), Collocated with 10th Joint Meeting of the ESEC and ACM SIFSOFT FSE (2015)
13. Boniol, F., Wiels, V., Ait Ameur, Y., Schewe, K.-D. (eds.): ABZ The Landing Gear Case Study. CCIS, vol. 433. Springer, Heidelberg (2014). doi:10.1007/978-3-319-07512-9
14. Rodin Platform (2006). http://www.event-b.org/platform.html
15. Olszewska, M., Ostroumov, S., Waldén, M.: Synergising Event-B and Scrum - Experimentation on a Formal Development in an Agile Setting. TR 1152, TUCS, Turku (2016)
16. Olszewska (Pląska), M., Sere, K.: Specification Metrics for Event-B Developments. In: 13th International Conference on Quality Engineering in Software Technology (CONQUEST 2010), Dresden (2010)

Towards Better Selection Between Moving Windows and Growing Portfolio

Sousuke Amasaki[1]([⊠]) and Chris Lokan[2]

[1] Department of Systems Engineering, Okayama Prefectural University, Soja, Japan
amasaki@cse.oka-pu.ac.jp
[2] School of Engineering and Information Technology,
UNSW Canberra, Campbell, Australia
c.lokan@adfa.edu.au

Abstract. BACKGROUND: Several studies in software effort estimation have shown that it can be effective to use a window of recent projects, rather than the growing portfolio of all past projects, as training data. Practitioners need a method for choosing between those approaches when estimating effort for a target project. OBJECTIVE: This study examined the usefulness of the fitted values for choosing between moving windows and the growing portfolio. METHOD: An empirical experiment was conducted with a single-company ISBSG dataset. RESULTS: The fitted values could be useful for the selection on average. CONCLUSIONS: This positive result contributes to understanding when windows may be appropriate.

1 Introduction

Accurate effort estimation is essential to software project success. Intuitively, it may make sense to discount older projects as training data, as they may be less representative of an organization's current practices.

Recent studies [1,2] have shown that selecting only newer projects, using a moving window, could improve estimation accuracy. Several factors affect the usefulness of moving windows. As moving windows do not work for every situation, practitioners need a method to decide when they may be appropriate.

This paper investigates a method which gives a hint for selecting between moving windows and the growing portfolio.

2 Fitted Values Based Selection

Figure 1 depicts how a dataset is used as a growing portfolio, with moving windows, and with the selection method we examine here. The horizontal line represents a timeline of project data collection in an organization. The circle represents a target project to be estimated. The growing portfolio approach uses all project data collected in the past. The moving windows approach uses recent projects segmented by a window of size w.

© Springer International Publishing AG 2016
P. Abrahamsson et al. (Eds.): PROFES 2016, LNCS 10027, pp. 627–630, 2016.
DOI: 10.1007/978-3-319-49094-6_49

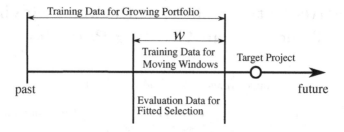

Fig. 1. The use of data with the growing portfolio, moving windows, and the selection method

The use of moving windows assumes that recent project data represents an organization's current situation better than older project data, and can thus train a good effort estimation model for a target project. It is also reasonable to suppose that an effort estimation model would fit more recent training data better than older training data, if it better reflects the current situation of the organization. In other words, the hypothesis is that if a model can learn characteristics of recent projects, it can fit them, and a new project, well.

Therefore, the fitted values of recent projects can give a hint for choosing between the growing portfolio and moving windows.

This study examined a simple method based on that idea:

Step 0: Make two training datasets; one holds all past project data, and the other holds a part of past project data segmented by a window of size w such that it only holds recent projects.

Step 1: Train two models: one uses all past project data, and the other uses the window of recent data.

Step 2: Evaluate the fitting performance (accuracy) of both models, for the projects in the window (shown as "Evaluation Data for Fitted Selection" in Fig. 1).

Step 3: Select the model that best fits the projects in the window.

At Step 2, the model based on the growing portfolio is evaluated on part of its training data, while the moving window is evaluated with all of its training data, as shown in Fig. 1. Note that we did not use any unseen or future projects: accuracy is based on fitted values for past projects, thus we call this *fitting performance*. Note also that we did not use a validation dataset in addition to a training dataset. This is because separating a validation dataset from recent projects may degrade the representativeness of the training dataset. Furthermore, this treatment would introduce the complication of determining the size of the validation dataset in addition to the size of the moving window.

We adopted mean absolute error ("MAE") for evaluating estimation accuracy. MAE is widely used in evaluation of effort estimation models.

3   Experiment

We conducted an experiment for examining the effect of using the fitted values based method. The experiment used the single-company ISBSG dataset of 228 projects investigated in past studies [1,2].

We used linear regression for building effort estimation models. The linear regression model used a log-transformation for effort and size, to improve the normality of residuals. Feature selection was also adopted for performance improvement.

The experiment evaluated the effects of using the selection method along with a timeline of projects' history. The sizes of moving windows were varied, as in past studies, because it significantly affected the accuracy. This study considered windows of 20 to 120 projects, as in [2].

For each window of size w, the experiment was performed as follows:

1. Sort all projects by starting date.
2. For a given window size w, find the earliest project p_0 for which at least $w + 1$ projects were completed prior to the start of p_0 (projects from p_0 onwards are the ones whose training set could be affected by using a window, so they form the set of evaluation projects for this window size).
3. For every project p_i in chronological sequence, starting from p_0, form estimates using the growing and windowing approaches. For the growing approach, the training set is all projects that finished before p_i started. For moving windows, the training set is the w most recent projects that finished before p_i started. If multiple projects finished at the same date, projects that started more recently are prioritized.
4. Evaluate estimation accuracy with MAE.

To test for statistically significant differences between accuracy measures, we use the two-sided Wilcoxon signed-rank test (`wilcoxsign_test` function of the `coin` package for R) and set the statistical significance level at $\alpha = 0.05$. We also controlled the false discovery rate (FDR) of multiple testing [3] with the "qvalue" function of the `qvalue` package in R. FDR is a ratio of the number of falsely rejected null hypotheses to the number of rejected null hypotheses.

4   Preliminary Result

As a preliminary experiment, we compared the fitted values based method and the growing portfolio. Figure 2 shows the difference in mean absolute error against window sizes. The x-axis is the size of the window, and the y-axis is the subtraction of the accuracy measure value with the growing approach from that with the fitted selection at the given x-value. The fitted selection is advantageous where the line is below 0. Circle points mean a statistically significant difference, with the fitted selection being better than the growing approach. At these points, the corresponding q-value is below 0.05 (this means that the number of falsely rejected hypotheses was at most 5 % of rejected hypotheses.)

Figure 2 shows that the proposed method can improve estimation accuracy, and improvements are significant with larger windows.

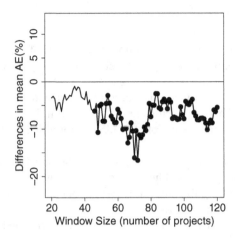

Fig. 2. The difference of accuracy between growing portfolio and fitted-selection

5   Conclusion and Future Directions

This paper investigated a method which gives a hint for choosing between moving windows and the growing portfolio, using data from one organization in the ISBSG dataset. We have shown that it has a statistically significant effect, compared to always using the growing portfolio. This result supported using fitted values in making the decision.

Examining the method with duration-based moving windows, enhancing the selection method in the effectiveness, and generalizing the results under other situations are future directions for this research.

Acknowledgment. This work was partially supported by JSPS KAKENHI Grant #15K15975.

References

1. Amasaki, S., Lokan, C.: On the effectiveness of weighted moving windows: experiment on linear regression based software effort estimation. J. Softw. Evol. Process **27**(7), 488–507 (2015)
2. Lokan, C., Mendes, E.: Investigating the use of duration-based moving windows to improve software effort prediction: a replicated study. Inf. Softw. Technol. **56**(9), 1063–1075 (2014)
3. Storey, J.D.: A direct approach to false discovery rates. J. R. Stat. Soc. Ser. B (Stat. Methodol.) **64**(3), 479–498 (2002)

Assessing the Behavior of Software Analysis Tools

Lerina Aversano, Carmine Grasso, Pasquale Grasso,
and Maria Tortorella[✉]

Departement of Engineering, University of Sannio, Via Traiano,
82100 Benevento, Italy
{aversano,carminegrasso,pasgrasso,
tortorella}@unisannio.it

Abstract. Quality models and metrics permit an objective evaluation of the quality level of a software product. Moreover, the adoption of software analysis tools that facilitate the measurement of software metrics can ease the evaluation tasks. However, the available tools do not interpret and measure metrics in the same manner. This paper proposes a preliminary investigation on the behavior of existing software metric tools and shows that the evaluation of the metrics of a software system by using different analysis tools provides different values. This aspect could impact on the overall software quality evaluation.

1 Introduction

A software project is an important investment for an organization. The commitment of financial resources and the expected time to get the final result is only justified by the necessity of addressing a need. On the other side, the software quality is "how well" the problem has been solved. Therefore, develop and/or select software products of an good quality represents a relevant activity. For knowing the quality level of a software system, it is important to adopt a quality model and metrics permitting an objective evaluation of the quality of a software product, and the availability of software analysis tools facilitating the measurement of software metrics can ease the evaluation tasks. Many software analysis tools measuring metrics exists. They have different characteristics concerning the programming language they analyse and measurement they perform, then the evaluator can have difficulties in identifying the software analysis tool that better addresses his needs.

This paper aims at investigating if the software analysis tools achieve similar results when they are used for assessing a software system, so as to be able to indifferently choose a tool instead of another. In particular the paper analyses a set of software analysis tools and verifies if they consider the same set of metrics and the way they are assessed. Therefore, the chosen tools are used for measuring a set of selected metrics on a software systems, and the obtained results are compared.

Next section describes the experimental setup of the study and lists the chosen software analysis tools and the selected metrics. Results of the evaluation is presented in the subsequent section, and final considerations are given in the last section.

© Springer International Publishing AG 2016
P. Abrahamsson et al. (Eds.): PROFES 2016, LNCS 10027, pp. 631–635, 2016.
DOI: 10.1007/978-3-319-49094-6_50

2　Experimental Setup

This section presents the planning of the presented analysis.

The first performed step regards the **Scope definition**. As already stated, the goal is to analyze and compare a set of software analysis tools evaluating software quality metrics with the aim of verifying if they consider the same metrics and interpret and evaluate them in the same manner.

The following step is **Selection of the evaluation tools**. The goal is to select the software tools to be analyzed and compared. They were chosen among the most used open source systems used for measuring software metrics. Such a kind of tools was considered for economical reasons. The tools were also chosen on the basis of the programming language they could evaluate, as the measurements obtained by the different tools had to be comparable. The Java programming language was chosen.

A free search in the SourceForge.net site brought to the identification of forty software analysis tools. The preliminary analysesd characteristics regarded: name, manufacture, link to the home page, license type, availability, supported programming languages, supported operating system/environment and evaluated metrics. This information permitted to considered the following nine software analysis tools:

Eclipse Metrics Plug-in 1.3.6. A metrics calculation and dependency analyzer Eclipse plugin.
CCCC. A command-line tool generating reports on various metrics.
Understand. A reverse engineering, code anylizer and metrics tool for different programming languages. It evaluates a set of standard metrics and visualizes them in different ways.
JArchitect. A static analysis tool for Java code evaluating different code metrics.
Stann4j. An Eclipse plug-in that allows for analysis of the dependencies between classes and packages, and provides code metrics.
CodePro Analytix. An Eclipse plug-in, freely offered by Google, regarding software quality improvement and reduction of development costs and schedules. It also supports code analysis, test cases, dependency analysis and metric measurement.
LocMetrics. A freeware simple tool, measuring the size of a software program by counting the number of lines in the source code
SourceMonitor. A tool for code exploration, including the measurement of a set of metrics related to the identification of module complexity.
CodeAnalyzer. A Java application for C, C++, Java, Assembly, Html. It calculates metrics across multiple source trees as one project.

Some of the tools above use a graphical interface, such as, JArchiect, Undertand, LocMetrics, CodeAnalyzer, and SourceMonitor; others are Eclipse plug-in, such as Metrics, Stan4j, CodePro Analytix, while CCCC software is a command line analysis tool.

Then, the **Metrics selection** task followed. It required the analysis of standards and evaluation models for open-source software systems to identify features, sub-features and metrics to be automatically evaluated by using the considered software analysis tools [4]. The considered metrics can be classified as it follows:

- Dimensional Metrics, used to evaluate the software quality analyzing the software system dimensions. Examples of this kind of metrics are: LOC (Lines of Code), TLOC (Total Lines of Code), NOP (Number of Packages), NOM (Number Of Methods), MLOC (Medium LOC per method), NOA (Number Of Attributes), etc.
- Object Oriented Metrics, such as the object oriented metrics proposed by Chindamber and Kermerer in 1991 [1], CK Metrics. Some example are: WMC (Weighted Methods for Class), CBO (Coupling between Objects), RFC (Response For Class), LCOM (Lack of Cohesion of Methods), DIT (Depth of Inheritance Tree), NOC (Number of Children) [2].
- Complexity Metrics, for assessing the complexity of the software, such as CC (McCabe's Cyclomatic Complexity) [1, 3].

Other important metrics are: AC (Afferent Coupling), EC (Efferent Coupling), I (Instability), A (number of abstract classes respect to the one of the concrete classes), D (distance from the ideal quality). Table 1 lists on the first column the metrics divided of the basis of the classification above, and on the first line the considered software analysis tools. The list is not complete, as the included metrics are those ones evaluated by at least three analysis tools. A number in a table cell indicates that the tool on the column evaluated the metric on the row.

Table 1 shows that the software analysis tools do not evaluate all the metrics. Three tools (Metrics, Jarchitect and CodePro) measure the large part of the metrics; while LOCMetrics, SourceMonitor and CodeAnalyzer consider only the dimensional metrics, and only six tools on nine consider the CK metrics. Definitively, none of the considered tools can be used to perform a complete evaluation of a software system quality, and it can be necessary to integrate them in a common evaluation strategy.

After defining what and how to make the analysis, task **Selection of the software systems to be evaluated** aimed at choosing the software systems to be analyzed. An open source software system was considered, as many metrics to be evaluated consider the source code. A software system named SimpleWeb was chosen. Then, the **Metric evaluation** task was performed for calculating the chosen metrics by using the considered software analysis tools. Finally, a **Results analysis** was executed for comparing the values of the metrics obtained by using the different software analysis tools, with the aim of verifying to which extent the evaluation tools interpret the metrics in a similar manner, by applying the same rules.

3 Evaluation

This section reports the analysis of the metric values evaluated by considering the chosen software analysis tools. Table 1 reports the values obtained by evaluating *SimMetrics*. Most of the values are given as mean, while few metrics have an integer value, such as: Class and Interface, SourceFile, LOC, TLOC, CommentWord and Blank Line. Table 1 indicates that in some cases the metrics have different values. This happen, for example, for the metric LCOM, that ranges from a minimum value of 0.28 to a maximum value of 46 measured with *JArchitect*. Similarly, the metric DIT passes from a value of 2.48 obtained with *CodePro* to a value equal to 1.17 measured with *CCCC*. Moreover, other metrics have mean values quite different between them.

Table 1. Metric values obtained for simmetrics

Software Analysis Tool/Metric	Metrics	Stan4j	LOC Metric	Source Monitor	JArchitect	CodePro	CCCC	UnderStand	Code Analyzer
AC	6.79				0	0			
EC	3.89				7.04	47			
D	0.38	0.42			0.14	0.19			
I	0.51				1	1			
A	0.11				0.19	19.10			
Object-Oriented metrics									
CBO		1.15			3.19		5.72	2.75	
DIT	1,71	1.71	1.47		1.49	2.48	1.17	1.68	
LCOM	0.28	5.49			0.28			46.46	
NOC	0.61	0.53			0.55	0.74	1.19	0.61	
WMC	10.39	9.26					5.12		
Dimensional metrics									
TLOC			7326	7280		7280		7279	7280
LOC	2238	2467	2238	1683	1191	2238	2283	2237	2238
NOM	6.05	6.79		5.85	6.72	5.23	5.12	6.39	
MLOC	4.66			3.63	4.49	5.92			
NOA	1.24	2.15			2.14	1.08			
NOP	9	9			9	9			
CWords			4351		2679	755	4389	4357	4358
Blank Lines			737					722	722
% Lines with Comments				60.30	69.22	33.70		1.95	
Source File			47	47	47			47	47
Class and Interface	47	47		47	47	47	58	47	
Complexity metrics									
CC	1.63	1.36			1.86	1.55	2.83	1.53	
NBD	1.22			1.85		0.91			

It is not possible to provide a more detailed description of the evaluation of some metrics, such as, CBO, DIT, LCOM, NOC, WMC, AC, EC, NOA, DC, MLOC, NBD, D, NOM, I, as their assessment depends on the specific definition adopted by the different tools. For example, this occurs for the differences detected in Class and Interface metric that with *CCCC* obtains a value of 58 differently from all the other tools, which provide 47 as a value.

A manual inspection of the source code allowed to deduce that *CCCC* tool, for the evaluation of Class and Interface metric, considers classes and interfaces but even the packages. Moreover, unlike the other tools, only tool *Metrics* returns a separate value for the number of classes and the one of interfaces.

In the case of metric TLOC, not all tools consider all the lines from the first to the last bracket. In particular *Understand* does not consider the first white line, while *LocMetrics* considers all the lines including those after the last curly bracket, so it provides a highest value. With regard to the LOC metric it ranges from a minimum value of tool *JArchitect* with 1191 lines of code to a maximum value of tool *Stan4j* with 2467 lines of code. This occur because *JArchitect* considers a method as a single statement, while *Stan4j* considers also the white lines of the methods as statement. Finally the *CCCC* tool considers a statement written on multiple successive lines as more lines of code. Performing a manual inspection of the source code it emerged that the actual number of lines of code value is 2238. as evaluated by tools *Metrics*, *Loc Metrics*, *CodePro*, *Analytix* and *CodeAnalyzer*. Regarding the Comment words metric, It can be observed that it ranges from a minimum value of 755 lines obtained by *CodePro* to a maximum value of 4389 obtained by *Understand*. This is due to the fact that some software counts as comments the lines included from the start to the end delimiters of the comments (/* - */).

4   Conclusions

Nowadays. software engineering managers always more often needs to deal with quantitative data regarding the quality of a software system. Indeed a number of metrics are generally adopted and measured during maintenance and evolution processes to predict effort for maintenance activities and/or identify parts of a system needing attention. Numerous software metrics tools have been implemented for evaluating the software metrics, however their use in practice requires their validation for understanding if they are really useful for achieving the evaluation goal. With this in mind, this paper investigates if different software analysis tools perform the same kind of assessment on a software system, and verifies if they consider the same set of metrics and interpret them in the same way. The performed analysis indicates that at least for the investigated software analysis tools differences exist. Actually, the evaluation of certain metrics with some tools delivered similar results, and they were not assessed as intended with other tools. This is because each metric is interpreted differently by each tool and then is differently calculated. Therefore, when a tool is chosen for performing a quality measurement, it is necessary to consider that this choice can be also misleading during the evaluation task.

Future work will consider more case studies and additional tools and metrics. Indeed, a larger base of software systems should be measured to increase the practical relevance of our results.

References

1. Chidamber, S.R., Kemerer, C.F.: A metrics suite for object-oriented design. IEEE Trans. Softw. Eng. **20**(6), 476–493 (1994)
2. Henderson-Sellers, B.: Object-Oriented Metrics: Measures of Complexity. Prentice-Hall Inc., Upper Saddle River (1996)
3. Li, W., Henry, S.: Maintenance metrics for the object oriented paradigm. In: IEEE Proceedings of the 1st International Software Metrics Symposium, pp. 52–60, May 1993
4. Lincke, R.: Validation of a Standard - and Metric-Based Software Quality Model – Creating the Prerequisites for Experimentation. Licentiate thesis, MSI, V äxj ö, University, Sweden, April 2007

Driving Academic Spin-off by Software Development Process: A Case Study in Federal Institute of Rio Grande do Norte - Brazil

Claudia M.F.A. Ribeiro[✉], Fellipe A. Aleixo, and Marília A. Freire

Federal Institute of Rio Grande do Norte – IFRN, Natal, RN, Brazil
{claudia.ribeiro,fellipe.aleixo,marilia.freire}@ifrn.edu.br

Abstract. This paper presents, as a case study, the experience of Federal Institute of Rio Grande do Norte (IFRN) in using software process, as a means to create institutional ambience for technological innovation and new start-ups formation. As a professional qualification institution, IFRN has succeeded during its century-old existence in providing good job opportunities for its students. However, the same educational model has proved not to be as adequate to give the students the same opportunity to run their own businesses. Having this in mind, significant institutional arrangements and curriculum innovations were made, mainly related to software development disciplines, in order to support the gradual transition of academic requirements (e.g. knowledge acquisition and best practices) into business and more market-oriented ones. This paper reports this trajectory, the main lessons learned, and the new challenges ahead.

Keywords: Software development process · Start-up · Academic spin-off

1 Introduction

Professional education aims at providing proper conditions for job activities. In this context, excellence of professional qualification is a key instrument to guarantee the best job opportunities. This is particularly true for technological areas, such as software development, where the pace of advances in technology dictates adjustments on curriculum.

Entrepreneurship also poses some challenges for curriculum planning, designing and implementation. Cutting-edge technologies and classes are not the single requirement. It must be complemented with real-world problems discussions, activities beyond the classroom, and other business-related subjects to give students the proper conditions to embark on a career in private equity.

Regarding these two educational aspects, Federal Institute of Rio Grande do Norte (IFRN) has played an important role in professional context, mainly for Brazilian Northeast region, where it is located. Over the last century, IFRN has changed to match the necessities of Brazilian economy and marketplace. This document covers part of this experience presenting curriculum and institutional adjustments made, to support

© Springer International Publishing AG 2016
P. Abrahamsson et al. (Eds.): PROFES 2016, LNCS 10027, pp. 636–639, 2016.
DOI: 10.1007/978-3-319-49094-6_51

students formation program. More specifically, we investigated these two following research questions:

RQ1. How can software process chain drive the maturity of software projects?
RQ2. Can the adoption of a software process in undergraduate curriculum influence the derivation of academic spin-off?

The answer for these two questions represents qualitative indicators that show how adjusted the curriculum is to the new professional demands. To support students during the many activities of software development, it was initially adopted RUP as the software development process. Despite the clear benefits of the process adoption and RUP itself, it became clear that to accomplish the curriculum demands, both academic and business requirements, it is critical to adapt the software process. In this paper, we share the lessons learned during a decade when such an adaptation process occurred.

This paper is organized as follows. Section 2 deals with academic spin-off models. Section 3 is dedicated to design and procedures of the case study. Results, conclusions and future work are subject of Sect. 4.

2   Academic Spin-off

Academic institutions all over the world have been the place where knowledge is created, acquired, transferred, combined, and converted into different types of knowledge (Gamble and Blackwell 2001; Waugaman 2014). As such capabilities have increasingly become critical for companies, mostly those concerned about innovative products and services, it is reasonable to think of academic environment as the natural crib for nurturing new businesses. This kind of institution is commonly named academic spin-offs (Corbett et al. 2014).

Academic spin-off model is not a novelty in many countries (Wright 2007), however, it is a quite new movement in Brazilian institutions. To support a proper environment for business inspiration, an academic spin-off has to make institutional arrangements, in order to give students a variety of extra-classes activities to complement entrepreneurship skills. Some of these arrangements include incubators, technology transfer officer, and the establishment of effective relations with external agents. In fact, closing the gap between academy and society is critical to provide a clear sense of real demands, and inspire new and successful business solutions.

IFRN has made significant efforts in this direction. However, as many institutions worldwide, culture is still one of the biggest challenges to overcome (Waugaman 2014). As stated in (Rasmussen and Borch 2010) "While leadership is about making things happen; organizational culture is the juice that makes people want to make things happen". It is worth noting that in the context of this case study, cultural aspect exceeds academic limits, as only recently (in 2016), discussions about intellectual property licensing, originated from research projects, gained legal support in Brazil. After that, researcher's productivity at universities and institutes, traditionally measured by the number of published paper, was revised to embrace also entrepreneurial activities, as well.

3   Case Study Design and Procedures

In this case study, the collected data refer to an interval of 10 years, from 2006 to 2016, of TADS (Technology of Software Analysis and Development) course. TADS is a three-year undergraduate course, which offers modules that embrace the main subjects related to software development. A key component of TADS curriculum is a Software Development Project (PDS). The main goal of PDS is to allow the students the opportunity to practice the theory covered in the formal disciplines. PDS was conceived as a bridge that intends to gap the distance between academic and marketplace requirements. The teams involve five or six members, who play different roles according to a proposed software process.

During this decade of TADS history, many adjustments on the software process were made, in order to maximize the quality level of resultant software products. So that, it is fair to say TADS history can be explained through software process evolution, which ended up to originate a family of (academic agile) processes. This process family was formally defined at 2014 and is composed by three processes: (i) PAWEB (Web Application Development); (ii) PAAD (Distributed Application Development); and (iii) PAAC (Enterprise Application Development).

To understand a case study that involves subjective aspects, such as here described, it is critical to understand the context that surrounds and involves the participants. IFRN has many institutional instruments to support innovation and start-up formation, such an officer dedicated to technology transfer (NIT), a technological incubator (ITNC), and a mentoring program. These organizational units have developed many activities to install a culture of innovation at IFRN. While the exercise of assessment is not a trivial task, revisiting the seven principles used by successful academic spin-off (Corbett et al. 2014) it is an interesting way to investigate how IFRN is going on implanting innovation-friendly environment. During the past decade, discussions about innovation and how to create academic spin-off to stimulate new business occurred, involving typical entities in the triple helix model (Etzkowitz 2008).

In a very broad sense, this case study aims to investigate the effectiveness of IFRN as an academic spin-off agent. To tackle this problem, it is necessary to deal with both objective and subjective issues. For the assessment of objective attributes of projects, all of software artefacts, such as code and documents, are saved in a repository under Redmine system. Additionally, the supervisors' notes cover subjective aspects on the projects. Finally, information about program mentoring and incubator processes are also recorded and evaluated, as an innovation.

This case study embraces a qualitative approach to organizing its data into three criteria. These criteria have been identified from the researchers' experience in conducting supervision of software development projects. They were defined as follows: (1) Project's success per cycle; (2) Project evolution through out cycles; and (3) Student's innovation engagement. The results of this case study are subject of next section, along with the main findings that came out from this analysis.

4   Results, Conclusions and Future Work

The case study presented described a decade of experience of Federal Institute of Rio Grande do Norte (IFRN) in using software process, as a means to guide students towards individual qualification and entrepreneurial initiatives. The main findings achieved pointed out towards the two research questions, as follows.

RQ1. How can software process chain drive the maturity of software projects?
Answer: In academic institutions, a software process chain can promote higher levels of maturity of software projects, by introducing gradually and consistently a minimum set of fundamental requirements, artefacts, roles, and activities, specially defined to observe the same level of intellectual students maturity.

RQ2. Can the adoption of a software process in undergraduate curriculum influence the derivation of academic spin-off?
Answer: For the sake of our experience described in this case study; the answer depends on the observance of rigorous application of software process. This is due the level of confidence acquired by students, not only about their own skills, but also on the potential market opportunities for the resultant product. While the former matches individual educational purposes, the latter also depends on how the innovation culture is disseminated in the institution.

More information about the results can be found at (Ribeiro 2016). As future work, we intend to make continuous analysis to improve our processes, and also plan to investigate automatic software metrics to attest the increment of quality on software artefacts. At the institutional level, we intend to make effort to implement the seven principles that guide innovative academic institutions (Waugaman 2014).

References

Corbett, A.C., Siegel, D.S., Katz, J.A.: Academic Entrepreneurship: Creating An Entrepreneurial Ecosystem. Emerald Group Publishing, Bingley (2014)

Etzkowitz, H.: The Triple Helix: University-Industry-Government Innovation in Action. Routledge, London (2008)

Gamble, P.R., Blackwell, J.: Knowledge Management: A State of the Art Guide. Kogan Page Publishers, London (2001)

Rasmussen, E., Borch, O.J.: University capabilities in facilitating entrepreneurship: a longitudinal study of spin-off ventures at mid-range universities. Res. Policy **39**(5), 602–612 (2010)

Ribeiro, C.M., Aleixo, F.A., Freire, M.A.: Academic Spin-off (2016). Accessed August 2016 from Software Development Research Group/CNAT/IFRN. http://nudes.ifrn.edu.br/index.php/projetos/academic-spin-off/

Waugaman, P.G.: Innovation U 2.0 reinventing university roles in a knowledge economy. J. Res. Admin. **45**(1), 125 (2014)

Wright, M.: Academic Entrepreneurship in Europe. Edward Elgar Publishing, Cheltenham (2007)

Future of Computing

The CRUSOE Framework: A Holistic Approach to Analysing Prerequisites for Continuous Software Engineering

Teemu Karvonen[1]([✉]), Tanja Suomalainen[2], Marko Juntunen[3],
Tanja Sauvola[1], Pasi Kuvaja[1], and Markku Oivo[1]

[1] Information Technology and Electrical Engineering,
University of Oulu, Oulu, Finland
{teemu.3.karvonen,tanja.sauvola,pasi.kuvaja,
markku.oivo}@oulu.fi
[2] VTT Technical Research Centre of Finland Ltd, Espoo, Finland
tanja.suomalainen@vtt.fi
[3] Oulu Business School, University of Oulu, Oulu, Finland
marko.juntunen@oulu.fi

Abstract. Continuous software engineering (CSE) is used for customer experiments and repetitive integrated processes within and between business planning and software development. First, this paper defines a new framework, called CRUSOE, for analysing CSE prerequisites. The framework allows for a more precise analysis of the interrelations and estimation of the changes that are prerequisites for moving from traditional product development to CSE. CRUSOE addresses prerequisites associated with and interdependencies among (1) the strategy, (2) architecture and (3) organisation. Second, this paper describes a case study conducted as part of a smartphone platform project to investigate the CSE prerequisites for product-focused software development. The results are synthesised together with recent related studies using the CRUSOE framework. The findings confirm challenges in moving towards CSE in embedded system development. Moreover, context-specific prerequisites should be considered, while it is still unclear as to how CSE can be systematically applied to the non-website development context.

Keywords: Continuous software engineering · Strategy · Architecture · Organising · BizDev · Software ecosystem

1 Introduction

Embedded and product-intensive software development project teams are becoming increasingly interested in applying practices and tools for continuous software engineering (CSE) [1]; e.g., the Lean Startup method [2], DevOps [3], continuous delivery (CD) [4] and continuous experimentation [5]. Although many of these practices are widely acknowledged in the field of website development [6, 7], there are only a few frameworks that describe how CSE can be applied in product-focused embedded system development (e.g. smartphones, cars etc.). Moreover, there is still very little

© Springer International Publishing AG 2016
P. Abrahamsson et al. (Eds.): PROFES 2016, LNCS 10027, pp. 643–661, 2016.
DOI: 10.1007/978-3-319-49094-6_52

empirical evidence of the actual usage of these practices in this context. The existing studies have mostly indicated severe challenges in adopting these practices in business-to-business (B2B) and embedded system development [8–11] contexts. In addition, CD and continuous experimentation still seem to mostly be used for small-scale website development projects [6, 8, 12]. Fagerholm et al. [5] have recently investigated continuous experimentation in university software laboratory projects with two case companies and have introduced a model for explaining how the continuous experimentation can be organised. However, more empirical studies are needed to increase our understanding of how these practices could be implemented in different software development contexts. Consequently, in this paper, our goal is to clarify the key prerequisites for applying CSE in product-focused software development.

The sustainable success of a company can be linked to its capabilities in terms of bringing new innovations to market. In today's competitive and turbulent business environment, time to market has also become very important. Consequently, business stakeholders have identified rapid fielding and continuous experimentation as important elements of their long-term strategies. Development stakeholders are tasked with finding a balance between development speed and stability, as the development process speed can often be temporarily increased by collecting *technical debt* (e.g., skipping some steps in the process), followed by a slowdown in development due to having to pay off the debt later. Consequently, companies need practices for maintaining a consistently high velocity. Bellomo et al.'s [13] suggests that companies must develop *combined practices* such as "release planning with architecture considerations" and a "prototype/demo with [a] quality attribute focus" to balance process speed and stability. Efficient integrative activities between software development and other functions (e.g., business and operations) are needed in all stages of the product lifecycle.

Fitzgerald and Stol [3] have emphasised continuous integration (CI) between software development and its operational deployment (i.e., DevOps) as well as continuously assessing and improving the link between the business strategy and software development (i.e., BizDev). However, they do not explicitly define how such a business strategy should be carried out or how it is enacted in a continuous manner. In this paper, we want to clarify strategy planning activities and their interrelationship with CSE. The focus of our study is on investigating CSE prerequisites in product-focused (e.g., embedded systems) software development projects. Our research contributions are as follows. First, we review the literature on CSE, strategy planning and models for analysing holistic aspects of software-intensive product development. Second, we construct and specify the CRUSOE framework (Continuous inteRdependencies in prodUct-focused SOftware Engineering) for analysing CSE in software-intensive projects. Third, we conduct a case study from a smartphone product platform project to validate the framework. The research question for the case study is: *What are the prerequisites for using the CSE approach in software-intensive product development?* Finally, we synthesise the case-study findings with recent related studies by applying the CRUSOE framework.

2 Background

2.1 Holistic Models for Analysing the Development of Software-Intensive Products

Various aspects of business and software ecosystems have been identified as important research topics in the context of CSE [1, 3]. In addition, as explicitly stated by Fitzgerald and Stol [3], continuity is required in all stages of the product lifecycle. Subsequently, they stress that it is necessary to constantly evaluate and improve software development interfaces with adjacent business-oriented activities. Previous CSE studies [3, 14] have suggested that delays in product development are often caused by a lack of holistic thinking and/or models for analysing software product development in a holistic manner. For example, inefficiencies and delays related to "handoffs" [15], as addressed by lean thinking, have been identified as a typical form of waste in software development, and thus the planning and engineering aspects of software product development should not be decoupled in separate silos for efficiency reasons. Still, information gaps and waste in between the business planning and development cycle could become evident when organisations are pushed towards faster (e.g., daily) or continuous software release cycles.

There are only a few documented approaches for analysing software product development in a holistic manner. As stated by Bosch et al. [17], few, if any, models exist that can analyse both the internal and ecosystem dimensions of research and development (R&D). The Business, Architecture, Process and Organisation (BAPO) [16] model (the left-hand side of Fig. 1) has been used for evaluating software product families and for analysing four main concerns addressed in product development: (1) how to make a profit from products, (2) the technical means to build the software, (3) responsibilities and relationships within software development and (4) the mapping of roles and responsibilities to organisational structures. As an update and extension to the BAPO model, the Ecosystem, Strategy, Architecture and Organizing (ESAO) [17] model (the right-hand side of Fig. 1) addresses both the *internal* and *ecosystem* dimensions for analysing company *strategy*, *architecture* and *organising*. Recently, both the BAPO and ESAO model dimensions have been applied to describe the *evolutionary steps* in the transition from traditional development towards an innovation experiment system (IES) [18]. Figure 1 illustrates the key dimensions of the BAPO and ESAO models. Later in this paper, we elaborate on the dimensions of the ESAO model as we construct the CRUSOE framework to analyse the CSE prerequisites. The CRUSOE framework illustrates possible interrelationships among ESAO dimensions that we consider to be important for CSE. These interrelationships (links) have also been previously addressed by the BizDev and DevOps concepts [3].

2.2 CSE in a Nutshell

When we use the term "CSE", we are referring to an emerging software development paradigm recently characterised by Bosch [14] (e.g., *Stairway to Heaven*, IES, and continuous deployment) and Fitzgerald et al. [3] (e.g., *Continuous**). IES is

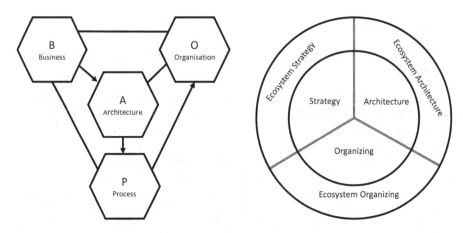

Fig. 1. The BAPO [16] and ESAO [17] models.

characterised by three coexisting aspects [19]: (1) "continuously evolving the software by frequently deploying new versions", (2) "customers and customer usage data play [ing] a central role throughout the development process", and (3) "development ... focus [ing] on innovation and testing as many ideas as possible with customers". To be able to frequently deploy new versions, it is necessary to be capable of CD, which, as defined by Humble and Farley [4], is an array of software development, CI and continuous deployment patterns for enabling fast, reliable and automated deployments to produc-tion. Consequently, the CSE paradigm can be associated with the Lean Startup method [2] (i.e., rapid validated learning) and enterprise agility [20] *sensing* (i.e., the capability of continuously determining what is the most valuable feature for the customer) and *response* (i.e., the capability of continuously deploying new versions to production). Underlying agile principles emphasise collaborative work methods between business people and developers: "Business people and developers must work together daily throughout the project" [21]. Interdependencies between the business and development aspects are often addressed via the need for establishing frictionless information flow and decision making in product development [3, 15] (e.g., fast information flow, transparency and continuous planning practices). Continuous information flow and smaller batch sizes allow for better synchronisation of business planning with iterative release planning methods and tools [22] (e.g., iterative feature prioritisation and road mapping) and for breaking down requirements into small chunks that can be imple-mented, tested and deployed in approximately 1- to 2-week sprints, as emphasised in Scrum methodology [23]. Finally, shorter iterations allow for faster customer feedback cycles, thereby reducing the risk of developing the wrong product. In website devel-opment, continuous automated deployment can even enable rapid controlled experi-ments [7] (e.g., A/B tests) with end users.

2.3 Business Management Views on Strategy and Strategic Planning

When juxtaposing the ideology of CSE practices [1, 3] with the traditional, *rationalistic* view of strategy and organisations [24], they appear ill-matched. Whereas CSE stresses the importance of real-time actions and continuous change, the rationalistic view of the strategy process [24] focuses on the creation of a structured future plan that is temporally and practically separated from its implementation [26, 27]. This separation thus relies on the assumption of a comparatively static and predictable business environment that allows the rational managers [26] to first create a plan based on systematic scanning and positioning [25] and then implement it while having sufficient control over the consequences of their actions [27]. The usefulness of such theories for practice has been questioned, as they do not sufficiently reflect today's volatile organisational reality [28, 29]. Therefore, there is a need for creating an understanding of strategy-making that better addresses the turbulent organisational reality.

Strategic planning is all about answering the questions of *where you are, where you want to be* and *how you get there*, as well as defining *how these aspects are connected* [30]. The strategy process varies across companies, but at the company level, it should be a continuous and issue-driven process [31]. In addition, the ways in which the strategy can be implemented fall into specific routines and work patterns that vary from firm to firm and between different types of firms [32]. Similarly, Brömmelstroet [33] defines how strategic planning phases can vary widely in terms of how they are organised (i.e., bottom up or top down), but all strategic planning processes can be seen as multilevel company processes in which planning actors work together towards a shared outcome. Even though the value of formal strategic planning has been strongly questioned [34], it is still an activity that is widely carried out in companies [35]. Formal strategy has power in affecting organisational actions and practices, as it defines roughly what is done and what is not done [36]. Eisenhardt and Brown [37] state that strategy should be seen as temporary, complicated and unpredictable and that strategy-making is a continuous process that is more oriented towards real-time operations than long-term stable goals [37].

From the software development perspective, and especially from the agile and lean software organisational perspective, Mavengere [38] clarifies that supply chain participants should have their own strategic plans which should be related to the whole supply chain's plan, but he does not go into detail about how these plans are created (i.e., the planning process in detail). On the other hand, Koenigsaecker [39] presents a lean strategic organisational process in which strategic planning is typically done once per year and is a learning experience in and of itself. In addition, monthly strategy deployment meetings are held to review progress and create opportunities for sharing lessons learned. The monthly strategy deployment reviews also help get the enterprise thinking about how to make the work process fundamentally better every month.

According to [40], among software development companies, the time frame for long-term strategic planning is commonly 3 years plus the current year. One of the case companies in this study used continuous strategic planning in which strategic plans were reviewed quarterly and monthly. The two other case companies reviewed and updated their strategic plans annually. Their strategic planning practices were closer to traditional project-based strategies than to continuous strategy practices – because the planning was performed annually, management approved plans which were then implemented for the rest of the year. Continuous strategy is extremely vital in a business environment that is constantly changing [41]. Suomalainen et al. [41] clarify that even though a strategy exists all the time, it should be iteratively and continuously updated based on market and customer demands. For example, past financial crises have forced companies to realise that continuous planning is required throughout their organisations; not only at the software development level, but also at the strategic, business and financial levels.

3   The CRUSOE Framework

In this section, we introduce a new framework called CRUSOE that we later use to analyse the CSE prerequisites.

Figure 2 provides a simplified illustration of the CRUSOE framework, which utilises the dimensions of the ESAO model [17]: (1) Strategy: ecosystem strategy (ES) and company internal strategy (CIS); (2) Architecture: ecosystem architecture (EA) and company internal architecture (CIA); and (3) Organising: ecosystem organising (EO) and company internal organising (CIO). The CRUSOE framework is an enhancement of the ESAO model that, according to the principles of CSE [1, 3], highlights the interdependencies between the three dimensions. These interdependencies are illustrated in Fig. 2, in which Areas 4, 5, 6 and 7 overlap with two adjacent dimensions. These areas illustrate interdependencies (e.g., integrative activities and combined practices) between dimensions. Area 7 illustrates the most overarching, holistic practices for company governance. Consequently, Areas 4, 5 and 6 illustrate more explicit integrative activities between dimensions, such as the BizDev concept addressed by Fitzgerald et al. [3]. We argue that the BizDev activities are associated with Areas 4, 5 and 7. According to Linden et al. [16], due to the interrelationships among the dimensions, any change in one dimension may have consequences in another dimension. These interrelationships have also been illustrated in the BAPO model with arrows and lines (Fig. 1). In the rationalistic view of the strategy process, and as stated by Bosch et al. [17], strategy should "idealistically" drive architecture and architecture should drive organising. However, in practice, "one has to allow for bi-directional dependencies" [17]. Moreover, the strategy must conform to *empiricism* and business realities; e.g., seemingly irrational customer behaviour and the existing constraints and capabilities of information technology (IT) and R&D. To summarise the notions referred to earlier about the need for a flexible and dynamic strategy process, we argue that the strategy process should not be seen as the process governing "only business" or "all company processes", but rather as a process that can, and should, be continuously influenced by other company processes. Subsequently, there are also bi-directional interactions and dependencies illustrated as overlapping areas between each dimension and highlighted with numbers 4 to 7 in Fig. 2. Although the CRUSOE framework is used herein to analyse the CSE prerequisites, we anticipate that the framework could also be used for analysing other kinds of software-intensive product development processes.

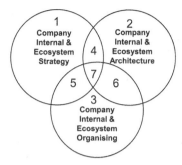

Fig. 2. Simplified illustration of the CRUSOE framework.

In Table 1, we further elaborate on the key aspects of each area of the CRUSOE framework. Areas 1 to 3 are adopted from the ESAO model definitions. Our contribution to this area of study relates to the questions associated with establishing integrative practices among the various ESAO dimensions (Areas 4–7). These questions highlight relations between the ESAO dimensions and choices that the company has available to it. For example, there could be a vast number of choices for how to build a software-intensive product. However, only a few of the choices perhaps allow for the proper means with which to generate revenue in the future (e.g. providing a proper platform for a service business based on continuous deployment). Meanwhile, different ecosystems could provide different technical and procedural capabilities for CSE. In this paper, the purpose of the framework is to aid in analysing CSE in software-intensive product development.

4   Case-Study Design

To investigate CSE in a real software development context and to validate the CRU-SOE framework, we applied the case-study method [42]. Our goal in conducting interviews was to gather data for a comprehensive understanding of the project's goal and of development and deployment practices. In addition, we asked about information flow and interactions among company stakeholders, customers and suppliers. In eight semi-structured face-to-face interviews, we asked participants to describe company strategy planning practices and product development processes. We also explicitly asked interviewees to identify the benefits and barriers associated with using the CSE approach to product development.

The unit of analysis in our case study was the project; i.e., developing a smartphone platform. Due to confidentiality reasons, we cannot provide a very detailed description of the features of the product. The platform included both software and hardware components. Consequently, this project is large, employing over 100 people directly inside the case company and also several partners involved in hardware and software development. We interviewed company personnel who were directly involved in the product development or company-level strategy planning. We also collected data from the organisation's public webpages for a better understanding of the project's purpose,

Table 1. CRUSOE framework areas explained.

CRUSOE framework Areas 1–7	Analysis scope: company internal (I)	Analysis scope: ecosystem (E)
1* - Strategy	What are the options for how the company generates revenue now and in the future? [17]	What are the options that the company has available in its current role in the ecosystem? [17]
2* - Architecture	What are the options for technology choices, technical means and technical structures to build software-intensive products? [17]	What are the options for how to design interfaces between the company's internal architecture and related ecosystem partners, such as suppliers providing solutions and firms that build software on top of a product or platform? [17]
3* - Organising	What are the options for ways of organising work, ways of working, roles, responsibilities, processes and tools within software development? [17]	What are the options for how a company works with customers, suppliers, and ecosystem partners in terms of processes, tools used, ways of working and ways of organising the collaboration? [17]
4 - Strategy & Architecture interdependencies	What are the options to connect the internal strategy and architecture? E.g. what are the practices for continuously validating technology choices, technical means and technical structures that generate revenue now and in the future?	What are the options to connect the ecosystem strategy and architecture? E.g. what are the practices for continuously comparing different ecosystems' technical capabilities and interfaces that generate revenue now and in the future?
5 - Strategy & Organising interdependencies	What are the options to connect the internal strategy and organising? E.g. practices for continuously adopting efficient ways of organising work, ways of working, roles, responsibilities, processes and tools.	What are the options to connect the ecosystem strategy and ecosystem organising? E.g. practices for continuously validating investments in ecosystem processes, tools, ways of working and ways of organising the collaboration in the ecosystem.
6 - Architecture & Organising interdependencies	What are the options to connect the architecture and organising? E.g. practices for continuously refactoring technical structures that provide efficient organising ways of working, roles,	What are the options to connect the ecosystem architecture and organising? E.g. practices for providing appropriate technical structures for continuous deployments and collaboration

(*continued*)

Table 1. (*continued*)

CRUSOE framework Areas 1–7	Analysis scope: company internal (I)	Analysis scope: ecosystem (E)
	responsibilities, processes and tools.	with customers and ecosystem partners.
7 - Strategy & Architecture & Organising interdependencies	What are the overarching company governance options for connecting the company strategy with technical architectures and with ways of organising? E.g. practices for enabling a company culture of continuous improvement, experimentation and innovation.	What are the overarching company governance options for connecting the company strategy with ecosystem interfaces and ways of collaborating with customers and ecosystem partners? E.g. practices for enabling a culture of continuous improvement, experimentation and innovation with customers and ecosystem partners.

*Areas 1 to 3 are the same as in the ESAO model [17].

company vision and strategic significance at the organisational level. We used convenience sampling for selecting interviewees and projects (i.e., those involving the company that we could easily access). In addition, related workshop materials such as video clips, photos and field notes were collected and stored to support the analysis. All of the data was collected in 1- to 1.5-hour semi-structured interviews with eight company employees. The interviewed employees' job titles and responsibilities are summarised in Table 2. All interviews were recorded for later transcription and a

Table 2. Interviewees' job titles and responsibilities.

Job title	Job responsibilities	Interview duration
Senior product manager	Responsible for delivering product programs to customers	117 min
Software platform product owner	Platform software component–related supervising	103 min
Quality manager	Product quality management including conformance to product safety standards and environmental regulations	105 min
Senior specialist	Design and implementation of continuous deployment processes and tools	104 min
President of the business segment	Chief Executive Officer for the business segment	67 min
Business developer	Product business development	78 min
Scrum master	Responsible for coordinating software development team work	86 min
Product manager	Responsible for coordination of the product program	92 min

qualitative data analysis was conducted using the NVivo tool [43]. The analysis was performed by considering the CRUSOE framework dimensions and the questions presented in Table 1.

5 Findings

In this section, we analyse the prerequisites for applying CSE through case-study data and by applying the CRUSOE framework areas introduced in Sect. 3.

5.1 ESAO Overview: Strategy (1), Architecture (2) and Organising (3)

The case company offers a wide range of products, platforms and R&D services that typically involve radio technologies and wireless data transfer. Consequently, the company is involved in multiple ecosystems. The company is also an active contributor to several open source software projects. Recently, the company has expanded its product portfolio towards Internet of Things (IoT) solutions and data analytics services. Its main customers are from the B2B domain, including both private- and public-sector organisations. Hence, when analysing the strategy and connected software development practices, it is necessary to explicitly specify which product category and customer segment is under analysis. The company has an established position in manufacturing systems for public safety and the military. However, more recently, the company has adopted a strategy for developing product platforms that allow tailored products to be created that could be sold to consumer markets (B2C). The smartphone platform project that we analysed in this case study is an example of this type of product.

We consider this company to be a very interesting research context for CSE because the company has many products in their portfolio and there are many different kinds of customers involved. This clearly addresses the challenges in defining product- and company-level processes.

In this way, the company has systematically developed capabilities to adapt to different customer contexts and software ecosystems and also to rotate employees among projects to develop the employees' skills and technical knowledge. Consequently, the interviewees often referred to other projects that they were aware of or had worked on previously. The interviewees emphasised that although there was a company-wide defined product development process that was, in principle, guiding all company projects, individual projects often improvised; i.e., very different methods were used or they worked in collaboration with specific customers and other ecosystem partners. Hence, when asked about the benefits of and barriers to using the CSE approach in product development, the interviewees considered opportunities for using the CSE approach as highly context-sensitive. Different products and customer segments were considered as having very different CSE prerequisites. These customer segments could be characterised by two extremes: "conservative public-sector customers" and "fast-moving private-sector customers". Different product segments could be characterised by "large and complex multivendor legacy systems" and "compact consumer products".

5.2   CRUSOE Area 4: Connecting Strategy and Architecture for CSE

This section analyses the options for connecting the internal and ecosystem strategy with the architecture for CSE; i.e., interfaces and technical structures to create revenue. The Android operating system (OS) [44] was selected as the software baseline for the smartphone project. When considering the various smartphone OS ecosystems, the Android OS currently has by far the largest market share, dominating markets with over 80 % of the total market share [45]. Hence, the selected platform also allowed for opportunities to generate future revenue as additional product applications could be continuously provided via the Google Play store (http://play.google.com/store/apps).

The project budget and product strategy management-level planning occurred in monthly cycles. The development teams organised their work into 2-week sprints that also guided and synchronised several planning-related activities such as the planning associated with validating technical interfaces, features and release-content prioritisation. The project actively used a CI system, thus new versions of the product could be produced several times a day. These new software versions were mainly used for internal testing purposes. Nevertheless, the project was considered capable of continuously delivering new versions to demonstrate the latest interfaces and product features for customers and ecosystem partners. We consider that interdependency with business planning (i.e., *continuous synchronisation of development sprints with continuous strategic planning and budgeting cycles*) was clearly a key prerequisite for using the CSE approach because it allowed for continuous feedback cycles and transparency in terms of how the project was progressing.

5.3   CRUSOE Area 5: Connecting Strategy and Organising for CSE

This section analyses the options for connecting the company's internal and ecosystem strategy with internal and ecosystem organising for CSE. The interviewees emphasised how the transition towards CSE was a strategic decision that governed practices relating to how products were designed and how the company was organised. Moreover, adopting CSE was considered as a competitive advantage in that it provides better transparency, efficiency and flexibility when working with different customer projects.

When considering the smartphone project-level CSE strategy, we could see that the CSE approach was mainly limited to software development practices such as CI and test automation. The interviewees also pointed out that while the company was a small player in the Android OS ecosystem, it had to adjust its internal plans according to supplier schedules and technology roadmaps. Meanwhile, larger smartphone vendors had more power to affect their supplier's plans. Consequently, the interviewees considered *supply chain support* as a key CSE prerequisite and also as a key hindrance to not being able to fully implement the CSE approach (e.g., CD in the project).

To summarise our findings regarding strategic dimension interdependencies with organising, we consider that currently, the company's internal strategy is to adopt a CSE capability. This is also the main driver for using CSE in the company projects. The company had already made significant investments in terms of promoting CI and CD solutions (e.g., automation) for use in software-intensive product projects.

As concrete evidence of the strategic decision, the company had established a *team of experts to implement the technical CI and CD framework (toolbox)* so that it could be adopted in all company projects. This expert team was also in charge of *coaching projects on how to adopt CI development practice*. We consider this activity as a key interdependency between the strategy and organising aspects that was clearly contributing to the company's transition towards CSE.

When considering other aspects of the ecosystem, some of the existing customers showed very little interest in using the CSE approach in product development projects. So far, only a few private-sector B2B customers had insisted on using the CSE approach in the development of consumer products. One interviewee pointed out that some customers have very little knowledge of and experience in agile product development methods. Meanwhile, public-sector customers in particular often have established and formal staged processes for acquiring software-intensive products; e.g., communication equipment for the military and for public safety must go through rigorous testing and certification processes before it can be put into actual use. Consequently, an *educated and motivated customer* was considered as an important CSE prerequisite.

5.4   CRUSOE Area 6: Connecting Architecture and Organising for CSE

This section analyses the options for connecting the company's internal and ecosystem architecture with organising for CSE. The interviewees considered the selected Android OS platform architecture (e.g., the hardware and software technology platforms and associated tools) to provide an adequate technical capability in terms of delivering software to end users rapidly and *over-the-air* (OTA) [46]. We consider this as a key prerequisite associated with the interdependency between the organising and architecture dimensions.

Several interviewees emphasised how the technical capability of providing updates continuously must be aligned with *quality assurance practices and cycles for testing*. The interviewees stated that the prerequisite of frequently delivering new updates to the end user would have to precede the rigorous internal testing period. One interviewee stated that some bugs can be identified only after using the product for a long period of time, which could be a challenge for CD. System updates that require rebooting or interrupting end-user product usage were also considered problematic since they could easily annoy end users. Moreover, updates in business and critical safety systems cannot interrupt or compromise the availability of the service. Consequently, it is a prerequisite to *minimise breaks in service availability and deliver updates so that the end user is not interrupted*.

We consider the interviewees' previous experiences in using rapid prototyping and demoing to be somewhat controversial. Although rapid prototyping was acknowledged as very important and good practice for identifying key functionalities and requirements for the product in the early phases of development, there were also drawbacks such as undisciplined processes for bug fixes and feature prioritisation. Two interviewees identified the problem known as the HiPPO; i.e., the "Highest Paid Person's Opinion" [7]. One interviewee emphasised how the processes for building prototypes and actual products were very different. Although prototypes can often be used for demonstrating new functionalities, they do not typically meet the proper internal quality criteria that are required for real products. Consequently, some managers are often too optimistic about how much work is still to be done in order to finalise the product. Therefore, the company needs to develop balanced processes that integrate speed and stability in order to build actual products in an experimental manner. An important CSE prerequisite is thus that the company *increases its understanding of the experimentation process* and that it *reviews current best practices, milestones and checklists for product development*. Methods for *managing technical debt* are particularly important prerequisites for CSE.

5.5   CRUSOE Area 7: Overarching Governance for CSE

Finally, this section analyses the options for overarching company governance for CSE. As stated earlier, we considered that the company management had clearly made a strategic decision to promote the CSE approach in all of its company projects. Two interviewees stated that any investment promoting CSE was an important "investment for the future". The interviewees considered it important to establish and improve systems for company-wide information transparency and for the real-time availability of customer feedback and product quality metrics. We consider the *company's senior management's commitment* to promoting the capability of using the CSE approach in product development as a key CSE prerequisite. We can identify several activities that indicate the company management's commitment to investing in CSE, such as an investment in people, tools and processes for enabling the rapid deployment of CI in all company projects; increasing test automation coverage; developing methods for end-user data collection (product platform instrumentation for data collection); systematising customer feedback collection (e.g., customer surveys); and developing tools and processes for analysing user data and sharing information internally in the company via IT systems. The company also arranged regular sessions for employees to promote *internal experience sharing and bottom-up strategic planning*.

5.6   Findings' Summary

In summary, we identified the following key CSE prerequisites in a smartphone platform project: *(1) customer education and motivation, (2) software ecosystem support, (3) supply chain stakeholder support, (4) leadership commitment, (5) process rigor for experimentation, (6) quality assurance process cycle duration, (7) technical debt management, (8) OTA updates with minimised breaks in service availability, and (9) internal experience sharing and bottom-up strategic planning*. The CRUSOE framework has significantly helped us to systematically categorise and more clearly articulate the prerequisites for using CSE in the case-study (smartphone platform) project. Based on our case-study findings, applying CSE to product-oriented development can involve a complex organisational change within and between software development and business activities. Whereas the adoption of technical infrastructure and development practices is an important starting point for CSE, one should also consider the company's culture, leadership and key stakeholder relations.

6   Discussion

This section continues our interpretation of the case-study results and synthesis of the prerequisites for CSE in software-intensive projects together with recent related empirical studies on the research topic. In Table 3, we list the main findings from the studies.

6.1   Synthesising the Prerequisites for CSE

As identified in previous studies referred to in Table 3, the challenges associated with CSE are often multidimensional. Incorporating pilot or lead customers in the development process and business-model change is clearly a commonly identified prerequisite for CSE that involves both the company's internal and ecosystem processes. In addition, the supply chain (e.g., the component and technology platform suppliers) must be incorporated in the development cycle to be able to continuously integrate all of the product components and test the product.

As stated by Facebook's release engineering manager, "Mobile deployments are more challenging than Web deployments because we don't own the ecosystem, so we can't do all the things that we would normally do" [12]. A company's role in the ecosystem can significantly affect how feasible it is to use the CSE approach. Earlier case studies have identified ecosystem-related challenges in CD, such as dependencies on the hardware platform component supply process and interrelated customer processes, such as periodic tendering, periodic budgeting, product piloting and acceptance

Table 3. Recent empirical studies on obstacles and challenges for CSE.

Leppänen et al. [8] Obstacles for CD: "resistance to change", "customer preferences", "domain constraints", "developer trust and confidence", "legacy code considerations", "[test automation] duration, size and structure", "different development and production environments", "manual and non-functional testing".
Lindgren et al. [9] Domain-independent challenges associated with continuous experimentation: "organizational culture", "availability and sharing of data", "data analysis", "identifying metrics", "release cycle speed", "defining product roadmap", "time [resources]", funding [resources], "technical obstacles".
Rissanen et al. [10] B2B specific challenges of CD: "technical challenges", "customer challenges", "procedural challenges".
Olsson et al. [47] Challenges identified in the adoption of CD: "diverse adoption of agile practices among teams", "complexity of team resource allocation", "dependence on resources outside of the team", "difficulties in analyzing and maintaining automated tests", "difficulty in removing or reducing old tests", "difficulties in establishing efficient rollback mechanisms", "no effective mechanism for analysis of customer data", "lack of understanding about feature use", "no pro-active use of customer data".

testing practices. These ecosystem-related constraints could require overarching changes in a company's business model, architecture and organising.

As identified in previous case studies, the product architecture must provide capabilities for adequate componentisation for partial and staged release, including roll-back mechanisms. Additionally, internal and ecosystem stakeholder needs must be addressed in the architecture; e.g., enabling CI and partial deliveries of products without updating the whole product. Technical capabilities for CD and continuous testing in production-like (staging) test environments are prerequisites for pushing reliable, bug-free releases into the customer's production environment. While deployment to the production environment can technically be similar to deployment to the staging environment, it involves risks directed towards the customer's business. Consequently, deployment to production must ensure the rapid identification of any abnormalities in the system and, if needed, an immediate roll-back to the previous functional configuration.

The experimentation of new functionalities on Facebook is conducted via "canarying" [12]; i.e., collecting user data from alpha and beta test groups before engaging in mass deployments, where changes are pushed out to all production systems (servers). As identified by Rahman et al. [6], CD is used almost solely for deploying websites. Hence, we consider that Internet- and cloud-based virtualisation technologies provide the best technical capabilities for CSE. Cloud-based services are nowadays often integrated with embedded systems and consumer products (e.g., sports-tracking and health-monitoring applications). Consequently, this trend may also enable the increasing use of the CSE approach in the future.

As identified in previous studies, it is a prerequisite that a project must have the capability for continuous integration and testing of the whole product. The existing system for CI can often be incrementally upgraded for automated delivery; i.e., a continuous release process also involving the release of the decision-making (e.g., acceptance) process for customer deliveries. As the release cycle may shorten quite dramatically, it is paramount that the user experience (UX) and system design functions are integrated into the development team to enable the efficient planning of features.

From a release planning point of view, in traditional software projects, the customer's role is to be involved in the planning and freezing of requirements at the start-up stages of the project. Consequently, the customer accepts project delivery based on customer validation at the end of the project. From the development process point of view, a customer's role and responsibilities could change radically when moving from periodic traditional methods towards CSE. Although a product owner can represent the customer, the actual customer must also take a more active stakeholder role throughout the project because deliveries can be experimental (tentative and prone to change) and they can occur more frequently. Subsequently, the delta between deliveries to be accepted by the customer is smaller. CD, however, depending on the industry domain, may radically impact how value is delivered to users.

Moving away from periodic delivery (large releases) often leads to inevitable business-model transformation. CD involves customer use and purchase processes. Internal business planning, requirement prioritisation and release delivery processes are also involved. However, organisational capabilities for CD must be considered. As stated by Facebook's release engineering manager, "CD works for small teams, within

20 to 30 changes per day". Hence, more complex systems and large projects (i.e., with more than 100 developers) working in a common code base may have to settle for a lower continuous deployment frequency.

6.2 Study Limitations, Future Studies and Threats to Research Validity

The main limitation in our study relates to the constructed CRUSOE framework because it has only been validated through one case study. More empirical studies are needed to validate the framework's true utility. Moreover, as our goal was to understand the holistic prerequisites for CSE, we acknowledge that is it also beneficial to investigate explicit CSE practices and also dependencies within individual dimensions. Consequently, for future studies, it might be useful to either scope the research topic and/or apply the framework in a different software project context. Applying the CRUSOE framework in a different context would also provide information on how to improve the framework.

The main threats to validity and the limitations in case studies are typically addressed by the data-collection methods, data interpretation, reliability and generalisability of the results. Due to the nature of the case-study method, the results are not generalisable to the whole industry. To mitigate the risks associated with construct validity (e.g., misunderstandings and misinterpretations between the interviewer and interviewees), we started each interview with a 5- to 10-min introduction on the research topic and key concepts of CSE (e.g., CD and continuous experimentation). The semi-structured interview method allowed us to ask clarifying questions throughout the interview. We also arranged for an interactive feedback session with the case company representatives to share interview summaries and to get feedback on our analysis; i.e., how we (the researchers) interpreted the interviewees' answers. The company stakeholders confirmed that our findings were correct.

7 Conclusion

In this paper, we have applied the case-study method to a smartphone platform project to investigate the prerequisites for CSE. First, we specified the CRUSOE framework in terms of it allowing for a holistic, systematic and structured investigation of the prerequisites for CSE. We consider that the CRUSOE framework enabled us to more precisely articulate and analyse the prerequisites for CSE. The framework can further aid in developing estimations regarding the changes that are needed when moving from traditional product development to CSE. Finally, the case-study findings were synthesised alongside related recent studies. The results indicate that using the CSE approach in product-focused software development could involve several areas within and between the strategy, architecture and organising dimensions. Moreover, novel integrative activities are needed for eliminating disconnects and for balancing speed and stability (e.g., feature-driven development and managing cumulating technical debt). Although these are initial ideas on how to organise continuous experimentation in software development, rigorous processes are needed between the customer and the supplier. Our case study indicated that opportunities for using the CSE approach in product development are often context-sensitive (e.g., customer and product dependent). Moreover, customer motivation and ecosystem support for CSE are important. Although the CSE approach is mostly used for website development, more systematic use of CSE could enhance the competitiveness of product-oriented companies. However, more prescriptive models and best practices are clearly needed to describe how CSE should be implemented in product-oriented software development.

Acknowledgments. This work was supported by TEKES as part of the Need for Speed Project (http://www.n4s.fi/) of DIMECC (Digital, Internet, Materials & Engineering Co-Creation).

References

1. Bosch, J.: Continuous Software Engineering: An Introduction. In: Bosch, J. (ed.) Continuous Software Engineering, pp. 3–13. Springer, Switzerland (2014)
2. Ries, E.: The Lean Startup: How Today's Entrepreneurs Use Continuous Innovation to Create Radically Successful Businesses (2011)
3. Fitzgerald, B., Stol, K.J.: Continuous software engineering: a roadmap and agenda. J. Syst. Softw. (2015). doi:10.1016/j.jss.2015.06.063
4. Humble, J., Farley, D.: Continuous Delivery: Reliable Software Releases through Build, Test, and Deployment Automation (2010)
5. Fagerholm, F., Guinea, A.S., Mäenpää, H., Münch, J.: The RIGHT model for continuous experimentation. J. Syst. Softw. (2016). doi:10.1016/j.jss.2016.03.034
6. Rahman, A.A.U., Helms, E., Williams, L., Parnin, C.: Synthesizing continuous deployment practices used in software development. In: 2015 Agile Conference, pp. 1–10. IEEE (2015)
7. Kohavi, R., Henne, R.M., Sommerfield, D.: Practical guide to controlled experiments on the web. In: Proceedings of the 13th ACM SIGKDD International Conference on Knowledge Discovery and Data Mining - KDD 2007, p. 959. ACM Press, New York (2007)
8. Leppänen, M., Mäkinen, S., Pagels, M., Eloranta, V.-P., Itkonen, J., Mäntylä, M.V., Männistö, T.: The highways and country roads to continuous deployment. IEEE Softw. **32**, 64–72 (2015)
9. Lindgren, E., Münch, J.: Software development as an experiment system: a qualitative survey on the state of the practice. In: Lassenius, C., Dingsøyr, T., Paasivaara, M. (eds.) XP 2015. LNBIP, vol. 212, pp. 117–128. Springer, Heidelberg (2015). doi:10.1007/978-3-319-18612-2_10
10. Rissanen, O., Münch, J.: Transitioning towards continuous delivery in the B2B domain: a case study. In: Lassenius, C., Dingsøyr, T., Paasivaara, M. (eds.) XP 2015. LNBIP, vol. 212, pp. 154–165. Springer, Heidelberg (2015). doi:10.1007/978-3-319-18612-2_13
11. Lwakatare, L.E., Karvonen, T., Sauvola, T., Kuvaja, P., Olsson, H.H., Bosch, J., Oivo, M.: Towards DevOps in the embedded systems domain: why is it so hard? In: 2016 49th Hawaii International Conference on System Sciences (HICSS), pp. 5437–5446. IEEE (2016)
12. Adams, B., Bellomo, S., Bird, C., Marshall-Keim, T., Khomh, F., Moir, K.: The practice and future of release engineering: a roundtable with three release engineers. IEEE Softw. **32**, 42–49 (2015)
13. Bellomo, S., Nord, R.L., Ozkaya, I.: A study of enabling factors for rapid fielding combined practices to balance speed and stability. In: Proceedings of the International Conference on Software Engineering, pp. 982–991 (2013)

14. Bosch, J. (ed.): Continuous Software Engineering. Springer, Switzerland (2014)
15. Poppendieck, M., Poppendieck, T.: Implementing Lean Software Development: From Concept to Cash (2006)
16. Van Der Linden, F., Bosch, J., Kamsties, E., Känsälä, K., Obbink, H.: Software product family evaluation. In: Nord, R.L. (ed.) SPLC 2004. LNCS, vol. 3154, pp. 110–129. Springer, Heidelberg (2004). doi:10.1007/978-3-540-28630-1_7
17. Bosch, J., Bosch-Sijtsema, P.: ESAO: a holistic ecosystem-driven analysis model. In: Lassenius, C., Smolander, K. (eds.) ICSOB 2014. LNBIP, vol. 182, pp. 179–193. Springer, Heidelberg (2014). doi:10.1007/978-3-319-08738-2_13
18. Olsson, H.H., Bosch, J.: Climbing the stairway to heaven: evolving from agile development to continuous deployment of software. In: Bosch, J. (ed.) Continuous Software Engineering, pp. 15–27. Springer, Switzerland (2014)
19. Bosch, J.: Building products as innovation experiment systems. In: Cusumano, M.A., Iyer, B., Venkatraman, N. (eds.) ICSOB 2012. LNBIP, vol. 114, pp. 27–39. Springer, Heidelberg (2012). doi:10.1007/978-3-642-30746-1_3
20. Overby, E., Bharadwaj, A., Sambamurthy, V.: Enterprise agility and the enabling role of information technology. Eur. J. Inf. Syst. 15, 120–131 (2006)
21. Beck, K., Beedle, M., Van Bennekum, A., Cockburn, A., Cunningham, W., Fowler, M., Grenning, J., Highsmith, J., Hunt, A., Jeffries, R., Kern, J., Marick, B., Martin, R.C., Mellor, S., Schwaber, K., Sutherland, J., Thomas, D.: Agile Manifesto. http://agilemanifesto.org/
22. Ruhe, G.: Product Release Planning Methods, Tools and Applications. Auerback Publications, Taylor and Francis Group, LLC (2010)
23. Schwaber, K., Beedle, M.: Agile Software Development with Scrum (2001)
24. Hutzschenreuter, T.: Strategy-process research: what have we learned and what is still to be explored. J. Manage. 32, 673–720 (2006)
25. Tsoukas, H., Chia, R.: Philosophy and Organization Theory. Emerald Group Publishing Limited (2011)
26. Vaara, E., Kleymann, B., Seristo, H.: Strategies as discursive constructions: the case of airline alliances. J. Manag. Stud. 41, 1–35 (2004)
27. MacKay, R.B., Chia, R.: Choice, chance, and unintended consequences in strategic change: a process understanding of the rise and fall of NorthCo Automotive. Acad. Manag. J. 56, 208–230 (2012)
28. Sandberg, J., Tsoukas, H.: Grasping the logic of practice: theorizing through practical rationality. Acad. Manag. Rev. 36, 338–360 (2011)
29. Chia, R.: A "Rhizomic" model of organizational change and transformation: perspective from a metaphysics of change. Br. J. Manag. 10, 209–227 (1999)
30. Bryson, J.M.: Strategic Planning for Public and Nonprofit Organizations: A Guide to Strengthening and Sustaining Organizational Achievement (2011)
31. Bogsnes, B.: Implementing Beyond Budgeting: Unlocking the Performance Potential (2008)
32. Nordqvist, M., Melin, L.: The promise of the strategy as practice perspective for family business strategy research. J. Fam. Bus. Strateg. 1, 15–25 (2010)
33. te Brömmelstroet, M.: Performance of planning support systems. Comput. Environ. Urban Syst. 41, 299–308 (2013)
34. Mintzberg, H.: The Rise and Fall of Strategic Planning (2000)
35. Whittington, R., Cailluet, L.: The crafts of strategy. Long Range Plann. 41, 241–247 (2008)
36. Balogun, J., Huff, A.S., Johnson, P.: Three responses to the methodological challenges of studying strategizing. J. Manag. Stud. 40, 197–224 (2003)
37. Eisenhardt, K.M., Brown, S.L.: Competing on the edge: strategy as structured chaos. Long Range Plann. 31, 786–789 (1998)

38. Mavengere, N.B.: Information technology role in supply chain's strategic agility. Int. J. Agil. Syst. Manag. **6**, 7–24 (2013)
39. Koenigsaecker, G.: Leading the Lean Enterprise Transformation (2009)
40. Suomalainen, T.: Defining continuous planning through a multiple-case study. In: Abrahamsson, P., Corral, L., Oivo, M., Russo, B.⬤(eds.) PROFES 2015. LNCS, vol. 9459, pp. 288–294. Springer, Heidelberg (2015). doi:10.1007/978-3-319-26844-6_21
41. Suomalainen, T., Kuusela, R., Tihinen, M.: Continuous planning: an important aspect of agile and lean development. Int. J. Agil. Syst. Manag. **8**, 132 (2015)
42. Runeson, P., Höst, M.: Guidelines for conducting and reporting case study research in software engineering. Empir. Softw. Eng. **14**, 131–164 (2008)
43. QRS International: NVivo (2016). http://www.qsrinternational.com/
44. Google: Android. https://www.android.com/
45. Gartner: Gartner Says Worldwide Smartphone Sales Grew 9.7 Percent in Fourth Quarter of 2015. http://www.gartner.com/newsroom/id/3215217
46. Hoffman, T.L.: Over-the-air programming of wireless terminal features (2003). https://www.google.com/patents/US6622017
47. Olsson, H.H., Bosch, J.: Towards agile and beyond: an empirical account on the challenges involved when advancing software development practices. In: Cantone, G., Marchesi, M. (eds.) XP 2014. LNBIP, vol. 179, pp. 327–335. Springer, Heidelberg (2014). doi:10.1007/978-3-319-06862-6_27

Software Development in the Post-PC Era: Towards Software Development as a Service

Sami Alajrami[1(✉)], Alexander Romanovsky[1], and Barbara Gallina[2]

[1] Newcastle University, Newcastle upon Tyne, UK
{s.h.alajrami,alexendar.romanovsky}@newcastle.ac.uk
[2] Mälardalen University, Västerås, Sweden
barbara.gallina@mdh.se

Abstract. Over the years, software development has evolved to meet the needs of new types of applications and to embrace new technological disruptions. Today, we witness the rise of mobility where the role of the conventional high-end PC is declining. Some refer to this era as the Post-PC era. This technological shift, powered by a key enabling technology, cloud computing, has opened new opportunities for human advancement. Consequently, the evolving landscape of software systems drives the need for new methods for conceiving them. Such methods need to: (a) address the challenges and requirements of this era and (b) embrace the benefits of new technological breakthroughs. In this paper, we list the characteristics of the Post-PC era from the software development perspective and describe two motivating trends of software development processes. Then, we derive a list of requirements for the future software development from the characteristics of the Post-PC era and from the motivating trends. Finally, we propose a reference architecture for cloud-based software process enactment as an enabler for Software Development as a Service. The architecture is the first step addressing the needs that we have identified.

Keywords: Software Development · Post-PC Era · Process Enactment · Clouds

1 Introduction

Software systems are playing a critical role in modern society. Many aspects of our lives (e.g. transport and health care) are dependent on software. In a way, software is *smartifying* our lives through the smart X trend (phones, watches, glasses, cars, grids and cities). The list goes on leading to a *smart society* where every aspect of the society is connected to, influenced by, and dependent on software. Although, this helps addressing several societal challenges, it comes with the cost of increased software complexity. This complexity is then reflected on the way software is conceived where the expectations of quality, reliability, security, safety and fast delivery are higher than ever.

© Springer International Publishing AG 2016
P. Abrahamsson et al. (Eds.): PROFES 2016, LNCS 10027, pp. 662–671, 2016.
DOI: 10.1007/978-3-319-49094-6_53

Driven by challenges and opportunities, software development will continue to evolve to address the *smart society* needs and beyond. For example, the Internet has made Global Software Engineering (GSE) possible while economical factors and market needs have motivated the rise of new development paradigms.

As Maximilien and Campos point out [10], we are entering the *Post-PC* era. This era is characterized by the increasing mobility and connectivity of people and devices, and the use of the Internet as a computing delivery medium. The role of the traditional personal computers (high-specification desktops) is gradually declining. Personal computers are becoming mobile and low-specification devices. Users can use any Internet-connected low-specification device to perform their tasks on powerful computing resources delivered over the Internet (using tools which are delivered as services). With this mobility, the relevance of OSs/platforms becomes less [7] as many software applications are offered in an OS/platform neutral fashion (e.g. services or HTML5). Cloud computing provides the enabling computing infrastructure on demand for such applications.

Accordingly, the way software is conceived needs to adapt to the rising *Post-PC* era. Software development is a complex socio-technical process which involves multiple stakeholders. Development teams use a wide range of tools/platforms for development, testing, deployment and operation of software. Some of these tools are already offered through the Internet (e.g. Eclipse Orion[1]). This paradigm is often referred to as Tools as a Service (TaaS). TaaS, however, overlooks the organizational aspects of the process. Therefore, there is a need for *Software Development as a Service (SDaaS)* which uses the cloud to support modelling, managing and enacting software processes in a model-driven fashion. SDaaS can utilize cloud as an execution and distribution medium where tools are offered as services and orchestrated in workflows. Development environments will be created on the fly and scaled as needed. Engineers will be able to do their work on-the-go from anywhere. Furthermore, modelling and monitoring the process itself will integrate the organizational and management aspects into the development environment.

In this paper, we propose a reference architecture for cloud-based software process enactment as an enabler for Software Development as a Service (SDaaS). This architecture brings the benefits of clouds and modelling to support development processes. We describe two industry-inspired development trends from the two themes: Continuous Delivery and Global Software Engineering. We highlight the impact of the *Post-PC* era on software development and identify the requirements of software development in that era. Based on these requirements, we design the proposed SDaaS architecture.

2 Motivating Trends

In this section, we list and discuss two industry-inspired motivating trends which describe different development/business needs a modern software vendor is facing. For each trend, we discuss its impact on software development.

---

[1] https://orionhub.org/.

2.1   Continuous Delivery

Continuous Delivery [9] has become a trendy software development paradigm along with DevOps. Together, they aim at bridging the gaps between development and operations teams and automate the build-test-deploy-release cycle. The motivation is to achieve frequent releases, reduce conflicts and therefore, reduce cost. To achieve such automation, teams should follow certain practices and use supporting tools/platforms. Humble and Farley [9] set the principles and technical practices for successful implementation of Continuous Delivery. We use Facebook's deployment pipeline [6] as an example of a Continuous Delivery process for large projects. Facebook is an example of a complex software that requires rapid innovation and release of new features. As shown in Fig. 1, the release cycle for each new feature starts by engineers coding a new feature or a bug fix. The code is then reviewed by a different engineer using the *Phabricator* code review tool. Tools such as distributed source control and automated testing packages are used. The code is released on stages: first it is released to internal employees to test it and is also tested for performance issues using *Preflab*. Then (after fixing any discovered issues), it is released to a small portion of users using the *Gatekeeper* tool. Only after these stages have passed successfully, the new feature would be released to all users.

Discussion. Facebook is delivered through the Internet and changes and new features are continuously pushed to users transparently. This means that developers will be committing and integrating code very often (sometimes on daily basis). The benefits of such frequency includes maintaining a bug-free code base and easier bug fixing (since searching for bugs is limited to last pushed code). Automation and repeatability of the software build-test-deployment-release are a key enabling factor to Continuous Delivery. To pick up the fruits of Continuous Delivery, the social/organizational aspect must be considered. For example, if developers do not commit their code regularly, the Continuous Delivery chain is broken. Therefore, there is a need for convergence and monitoring support to ensure certain processes and practices are followed.

2.2   Software Outsourcing

The *Post-PC* era is also a globalized era. Software development outsourcing was driven by business and economic factors (e.g. exploiting low-cost developers

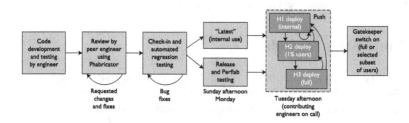

Fig. 1. Facebook's deployment pipeline [6].

and reducing the time-to-market). In addition, companies tend to outsource the tasks that they lack the skills or expertise to perform. Outsourcing can take place either within the same organization (intra-organization) or across organizations (inter-organization).

This example is inspired by the railway system development. In this scenario, there are two companies cooperating on system development. Company A is a contractor that runs large industrial projects for designing/redesigning railway networks. Among various tools the company uses a number of simulation tools to visualise and analyse the systems it is building, to debug them, to check their characteristics (such as throughput, energy consumption, performance and capacity). During such projects company A develops a wide range of models, diagrams, documents and blueprints that will be used for building the network. As part of this work, company A needs to develop a safe signalling software to operate the network by following a stringent software process. To ensure the system safety, company A would like to use industry-strength formal technologies. Company A does not have expertise in conducting large-scale formal verification of complex systems so it decides to outsource this work to small independent company B that has the right skill set. Conducting this type of verification is the main business of company B. The artefacts to be used by company B include layouts, infrastructure data, service patterns, timetables and control tables. Due to the confidential nature of these artefacts, company B signs a non disclosure agreement and a Service Level Agreement (SLA) with company A and as a precaution, it undertakes all its processes on a private infrastructure. Both companies (A and B) only exchange relevant artefacts and do not know each other's internal processes.

Discussion. In reality, large scale projects may include intra and inter-organization outsourcing with other teams/partners. Management of such projects can be tedious and consumes enormous resources (time and effort) to monitor and synchronize the different outsourced sub-projects. Several issues may arise. Small issues such as using different tool versions by different teams may easily go unnoticed till a late stage of the project at which it will become very costly to fix. Other concerns include how to ensure the quality of the outsourced tasks and how to monitor that they have been performed according to SLAs. Process-state-awareness and communication is vital for the success of such distributed development projects [7]. Therefore, there is a need for efficient management and monitoring of such projects.

3   Characteristics of the *Post-PC* Era

The term *Post-PC* era was used to describe the fall of PC sales due to the rise of mobile devices. When David Clark used the term for the first time in a talk called "The *Post-PC* Internet" in 1999, he predicted that the future will be "inevitably heterogeneous" and "a network full of services"[2]. Today, we can see this prophecy taking place in the form of heterogeneous mobile devices and services while PCs are becoming more portable and low-specification. The technology shift in this era is enabled by cloud computing technology and the Internet. This shift has changed the way users access and interact with technology. We categorize the characteristics of the *Post-PC* era into two categories: (a) technical and (b) organizational.

3.1   Technical Characteristics

The Rise of Mobility. Over the past few years, mobile devices have been shaking the dominance of PCs. Users use mobile devices for many daily activities. This has enabled new business models and new software distribution platforms (e.g. app stores) [7]. Consequently, users have become more mobile and have adopted new interaction patterns for interacting with technology (e.g. touch and voice). This increasing mobility impacts software development in two ways: one impacts the produced mobile software (e.g. to have less power consumption) and the other impacts the development process itself. The new interaction paradigms that came with mobile devices have driven new works on unconventional development methods. Microsoft *TouchDevelop* [4] platform enables programming on the go using only mobile phone touch screens. Another trend is using voice recognition to input code[3]. **The Cloud as the Development and Operation Platform.** Mobile devices have limited computing power. To overcome this challenge, mobile applications delegate the processing and storage to cloud platforms over the Internet. Cloud computing allows acquiring computing resources on the fly and on a pay-as-you-go pricing model. This paradigm has enabled Software, Platform (hardware, OS, etc.) and Infrastructure to be offered as services over the Internet. Consequently, software development is increasingly relying on Internet services which enable collaboration and integration between development teams (e.g. Github[4]). Open source software and crowdsourcing are examples of how the Internet (powered by the cloud) enables collaborative development. In addition, many software systems are now built by aggregating other services from the Internet. Cloud is becoming the development and the operation environment for software. This trend raises the need for alternative methods and technologies to conceive, design, implement, test, deploy and evolve software [7].

3.2   Organizational (Business) Characteristics

On Demand Infrastructure and Tools Acquisition. With cloud and services, traditional software distribution models have changed. Desktop clients are being changed to cloud-based tools and mobile applications.

---

[2] http://www.nytimes.com/1999/04/18/business/economic-view-is-mr-gates-pouring-fuel-on-his-rivals-fire.html.
[3] https://www.youtube.com/watch?v=8SkdfdXWYaI.
[4] https://github.com/.

Computing infrastructure is now only acquired and scaled up/down as needed. Along with this shift, pricing models have also changed from the desktop client licence model to in-app purchases and pay-as-you-go models. **Globalized Development.** As mentioned earlier, the *Post-PC* era is driving the development and operation to take place in the cloud. This has facilitated undertaking global software development projects. Software development outsourcing helps reducing costs and development time, but also introduces management challenges to overcome spatial, cultural and geographical distances in order to ensure the quality of the product and effective communication between development teams. **Dissolving Boundaries.** The Internet has made geographical boundaries within or between companies disappear. In addition, team boundaries are also fading [7]. Design, development, testing and operations are no longer isolated tasks. Trendy development paradigms such as DevOps calls for tight collaboration and integration across these tasks.

4 Software Development in the *Post-PC* Era

The characteristics listed in the previous section affect how software development is going to be conducted in the near future and raises the need for new methods and tools for software development. Here, we list a non-exhaustive list of requirements (derived from Sects. 2 and 3) for the next software development environments: **Process Monitoring & Management.** Regardless of which process model you use, the need for process visualization, monitoring the process status and detecting/predicting problems and deviations becomes vital. Considering the outsourcing scenario in Sect. 2, visual models of the process would ease communication and understanding between distributed teams. Process monitoring and status checking would help project managers to identify bottlenecks in the process; **Tools as a Service.** The process models contain the tools needed to support the process. To achieve executability of models, the required tools should be available as a service over the Internet. While some tools can be automated, others can be interactive. Interactive tools should provide interaction patterns over the Internet. Consistency of tool versions used by distributed teams for development and production is vital. As Humble and Farley [9] demonstrate (using their experience from real-world projects), using different versions of the same package by collaborating teams could create very costly problems; **Provenance, Governance & SLA monitoring.** Software development is a human-centric process and when the involved humans are distributed within the same or across different companies, effective management becomes essential. As mentioned earlier, process monitoring and consistency checks are important, but they are not enough. Data about the process, its enactment environment, the tools used, the stakeholders involved and the artefacts produced/consumed should be logged. Such data can be useful for process improvement and accountability. Moreover, when multiple companies are involved in a project, the processes followed by both parties should comply with the agreed SLA. Therefore, there is a need for SLA monitoring to assist the management of such collaborative projects and ensure all parties are compliant; **Artefacts Management.** Artefacts are tightly related to the previous needs and process models are artefacts themselves. Therefore, artefacts should be managed and stored effectively. They should be accessible from anywhere and available at any time. Changes made to them should be tracked and different versions of an evolving artefact should be kept; **Automation.** The question about how much automation one can have in a software process is important. The answer is indeed, a limited portion. However, automation when possible is beneficial. Repetitive tasks such as the build-test-deploy-release cycle are error-prone and their automation can prevent errors and save time. Non-interactive tasks (e.g. testing or model checking) can be automated. Furthermore, automated background service can be run to check consistency and compliance and monitor SLAs.

5   Reference Architecture for Enabling SDaaS

Aggregating the previous needs leads to Software Development as a Service (SDaaS). SDaaS provides tools for modelling, enacting and managing software processes. It enables orchestrating tools on the fly as services and manage and store artefacts in the cloud. In addition, it enables utilizing the scalable cloud resources to run automated processes and meet the needs of computing-intensive tasks (e.g. code analysis and testing). In this section, we propose a reference architecture for SDaaS. The architecture is model-driven where processes are modelled and enacted as workflows.

The architecture complies with the Workflow Management Coalition (WfMC) reference model [8] and is designed as a service. It consists of three main components: (a) **The modelling and management** interface is offered as Software as a Service (SaaS) and allows distributed teams to access, model, enact and manage processes. (b) **The enactment service** is offered as a Platform as a Service (PaaS) and handles the instantiation, enactment and monitoring of process models. And (c) **Workflow Engines** are deployed in a set of hybrid clouds and enact the individual workflow tasks/activities.

5.1   Process Modelling (Build Time)

Software processes consist of a set of different types of (e.g. interactive or automated) activities, which are to be enacted by different stakeholders with different enactment requirements (e.g. privacy, computing power). These process details need to be captured. Software & Systems Process Engineering Meta-model (SPEM2.0) [11] is the Object Management Group (OMG) standard for modelling software processes. SPEM2.0 lacks explicit support for expressing cloud-based process enactment and control flow semantics. Consequently, we proposed EXE-SPEM [2] which is an extension of SPEM2.0 for cloud-based enactment. Software process models modelled in EXE-SPEM can be mapped to an executable XML notation.

Figure 2 shows the software process build time components which are packed as a SaaS solution. The **Model Authoring** module allows constructing process models using EXE-SPEM constructs. The **Access & Sync. Service** applies access management policies and ensures the consistency of models that are being authored by distributed teams simultaneously. This module also notifies collaborators when a model is changed/updated. Once the model is authored, the **Model Storage Service** allows saving/retrieving the model into the cloud-based repository through the enactment service API. Finally, models can be transformed into the executable XML notation from EXE-SPEM using the **Model Transformations** module.

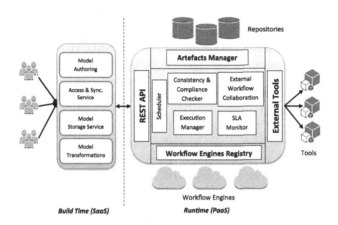

Fig. 2. Detailed architecture for the Software Development as a Service (SDaaS) platform.

5.2   The Enactment Service (Runtime)

The enactment service has an API to interact with the process modelling service. This way, modelling can be done from SaaS or a plug-in for a legacy desktop client. Behind the API, the service is responsible for the runtime instantiation and execution of process models. To do this, the service consists of several modules as illustrated in Fig. 2. These modules are: **The REST API** provides endpoints for process enactment and monitoring and artefacts storage and retrieval; **The Artefacts Manager** stores the artefacts and meta-data about them into the artefacts repository. Software processes involve producing large number of artefacts such as: code, models and documentation. These artefacts capture invaluable information about both the software process and product evolution. The artefact meta-data includes: actors involved, version, tools used and the date and time the artefact was created/modified; **The External Tools** are service blocks performing the process activities. These blocks are either: interactive, control points (providing control flow during the process execution) or automated fire-and-forget activities. This module provides the necessary information on these activities when needed for process execution; **The Execution**

Manager orchestrates the enactment of process models. First, an instance of the model is created and the ready-to-execute activities are passed to the scheduler. The scheduled activities are then executed on workflow engines. During the execution of the process, the execution manager tracks of the status of the process instance being executed. This module also logs all the provenance data about each process instance execution; **The Workflow Engines Registry** is responsible for starting, stopping and monitoring workflow engines based on the activities scheduling policies used by the scheduler. Workflow engines are independent applications running on different cloud providers. Activities get executed in a workflow engine that is deployed on a public or private cloud. The workflow engine has to meet the execution requirements expressed in the process model. The execution of activities is a black-box execution which means that the workflow engine would not know any information about the process being executed. This reduces the risks of privacy and confidentiality breaches. In order to decouple the enactment service from the workflow engines, asynchronous communication between them is achieved through message oriented middleware; **The Scheduler** handles the planning of process execution. This involves checking the needed resources (from the process model). The scheduler should operate using a policy to meet the enactment requirements (e.g. enacting an activity on a private cloud) while minimizing the cost. Several cloud-based workflow scheduling algorithms exist and can be used (e.g. [1]). The schedules generated by the scheduler determine the expected load of execution and is used by the workflow engines registry to dynamically scale the number of workflow engines; **The Consistency Checker** automatically checks the process consistency during its execution which can alleviate problems early and save time and cost (as explained in Sect. 4). Discussion of consistency checking techniques is beyond the scope of this paper; **The SLA monitor** transparently ensures that all parties collaborating on a project are not breaching the agreed SLA (as explained in the software outsourcing scenario in Sect. 2). While each organization can have its own SDaaS environment, these environments can exchange data about the process state and execution using the External Workflow Collaboration module; Finally, **The External Workflow Collaboration** allows process execution to incorporate invoking processes managed by another workflow system (e.g. from a different company).

6   Conclusion

The *Post-PC* era is here and software is embedded in almost every aspect of our daily life. Software systems have evolved but the way they are conceived still needs to be rethought to adapt to the new era's challenges and to embrace its technological breakthroughs.

In this paper, we have described the characteristics of the new era and its impact on software development. We also proposed the SDaaS reference architecture for supporting software processes enactment. To become a reality, this proposal requires tools to be offered as services. We have developed a prototype of the proposed architecture consisting of an enactment engine that executes software processes, a number of off-the-shelf tools deployed as services in our tool repository and an artefact store. The prototype was used to enact a safety-related process [3] and a number of verification/modelling processes. Our ongoing work focuses on implementing larger and more complex processes and evaluating the architecture proposed. In a longer run we aim at creating a community of developers extending the architecture and applying it for the development of complex software systems.

Additionally, Empirical studies are needed to study the effects of this proposal on the organizational, technical and economical aspects of software development processes. Furthermore, the effect on different development process models (e.g. Agile) also needs to be analysed and benchmarked. Usability studies can determine the effects this approach may have on individual developers, managers and other stakeholders. Indeed, as Fred Brooks put it, *"There is no silver bullet"* and we can only eliminate accidental difficulties in software development. Inherent difficulties will continue to exist as software and its development evolve [5].

References

1. Abramson, D., Lees, M., Krzhizhanovskaya, V., Dongarra, J., Sloot, P.M., Wang, J., Korambath, P., Altintas, I., Davis, J., Crawl, D.: Workflow as a service in the cloud: architecture and scheduling algorithms. Procedia Comput. Sci. **29**, 546–556 (2014)
2. Alajrami, S., Gallina, B., Romanovsky, A.: EXE-SPEM: towards cloud-based executable software process models. In: Proceedings of the 4th International Conference on Model-Driven Engineering and Software Development, MODELWARD 2016, pp. 517–526 (2016)
3. Alajrami, S., Gallina, B., Sljivo, I., Romanovsky, A., Isberg, P.: Towards cloud-based enactment of safety-related processes. In: Skavhaug, A., Guiochet, J., Bitsch, F. (eds.) SAFECOMP 2016. LNCS, vol. 9922, pp. 309–321. Springer, Heidelberg (2016). doi:10.1007/978-3-319-45477-1_24
4. Ball, T., Burckhardt, S., de Halleux, J., Moskal, M., Tillmann, N.: Beyond open source: the TouchDevelop cloud-based integrated development environment. Technical report MSR-TR-2014-127, Microsoft Research, September 2014
5. Brooks, F.P.: No silver bullet: essence and accidents of software engineering. IEEE Comput. **20**, 10–19 (1987)
6. Feitelson, D., Frachtenberg, E., Beck, K.: Development and deployment at facebook. IEEE Internet Comput. **17**(4), 8–17 (2013)
7. Fuggetta, A., Di Nitto, E.: Software process. In: Proceedings of the on Future of Software Engineering, pp. 1–12. FOSE, ACM (2014)
8. Hollingsworth, D.: Workflow Reference Model. No. TC00-1003, Workflow Management Coalition (WfMC), January 1995
9. Humble, J., Farley, D.: Continuous Delivery: Reliable Software Releases Through Build, Test, and Deployment Automation, 1st edn. Addison-Wesley Professional, Boston (2010)
10. Maximilien, E.M., Campos, P.: Facts, trends and challenges in modern software development. Int. J. Agil. Extrem. Softw. Dev. **1**(1), 1–5 (2012)
11. OMG: Software and Systems Process Engineering Meta-Model Specification, V2.0, April 2008

Invited Papers

The Origins of Design Thinking and the Relevance in Software Innovations

Matilde Bisballe Jensen$^{(\boxtimes)}$, Federico Lozano, and Martin Steinert

Department of Engineering Design and Materials, NTNU, Richard Birkelandsvei 2B,
7491 Trondheim, Norway
{matilde.jensen,federico.lozano,martin.steinert}@ntnu.no

Abstract. This paper argues that the methods used in the trending buzzword Design Thinking have deeper roots and bigger application potential, beyond product development IDEO and the Stanford University d.school style. The conscious combination of these Design Thinking methods and rapid iteration sessions is also of value when deploying it to software development. It is a powerful approach for requirement discovery and hence becomes relevant when developing novel solutions. This argument is supported by the case of SAP AppHaus and their experience on implementing the Design Thinking process for HANA related software development. Here Design Thinking forces to holistically explore a solution space with the customer, but also to bring different internal disciplines together early. Hence anybody who is interested in software innovations might want to consider the core ideas behind Design Thinking.

Keywords: Design thinking · Software development · SAP case study · Product discovery

1 Introduction

This paper provides an introduction and justification of the activities behind Design Thinking. Although the "buzzword-factor" of Design Thinking has increased in recent decades[1] the methods applied origins from older academic research fields such as the design research group of Stanford University, Social Science, and Mechanical Engineering. Hence it is more than a brief management trend praising post-its, pipe cleaners and play dough, but in combination a powerful method for developing radical innovations. First we present the origins of the most domesticated Design Thinking Rules: Empathize; Define; Ideate; Prototype and Test. Moreover, we provide the reader with insights from Silicon Valley based SAP AppHaus and argue why any Software Innovation could benefit from the Design Thinking process.

---

[1] According Google Trends the number of google searches on *Design Thinking* is 10 times higher today than 10 years ago.

© Springer International Publishing AG 2016
P. Abrahamsson et al. (Eds.): PROFES 2016, LNCS 10027, pp. 675–678, 2016.
DOI: 10.1007/978-3-319-49094-6_54

2 The Research Domains Behind Design Thinking

The d.school Bootcamp Bootleg describes 5 essential activities covering the process of Design Thinking; Empathize, Define, Ideate, Prototype, Test. Below we briefly describe the origins of these activities.

Empathize and Define. In Design Thinking you are to empathize with not only the end-user, but also any stakeholder of you product. You are looking for relevant pain points to address in your solution. One should be able to put him/her-self in the place of a stakeholder and understand their motivations and frustrations. This demand for under-standing and empathy are traditional skills required in the field of anthropology and sociology. Actor Network Theory was introduced in the early 80's and argues the value of seeing problems in the context of actor-networks and identifying the misalignments in this network (Callon 1984, 1986; Latour 1996). This is the basic idea behind need finding and the holistic approaches taught in Design Thinking.

Ideate. Ideation originates from the field of creativity research and the ability to consciously focus on either divergent or convergent processes (Runco and Okuda 1988). Ideation covers developing several solutions to an initial challenge. It is not enough to stop at the first idea at hand, but instead one have to explore the solution space. Onarheim and Biskjaer (2015) describe ideation as much more than just a eureka moment. They argue that one of the most important skills when ideating are to be aware of your creativity constraints that are surrounding the context and might you constrain you.

Prototype and Test. Prototypes make ideas tangible. This changes the design dialogue from abstract to concrete. Bringing in a physical object to talk about is the principle of *boundary objects* introduced by sociologist Star and Griesemer (1989). They argue the value of bringing stakeholders together around a boundary object opening up for view-points across disciplines and interests.

Moreover in Design Thinking prototyping are a strategy to learn. In this way it relates to active learning or action research, where you built representations or small experi-ments to challenge and test context hypotheses (Berg 2004; Bonwell and Eison 1991; Cameron 2009). Hence you get feedback on your ideas very early on in the project. The process of testing specific ideas as hypotheses origins from the scientific method it self with Karl Popper as the main spokes person (Popper 1959).

3 The Case of SAP AppHaus

Agreeably Agile Development and the Design Thinking process are similar. Both favor user involvement, rapid prototyping and testing. Yet Design Thinking is for discovery hence requirement defining. Agile development methods take a starting point in coding for semi-well-defined requirements. Hence the two methods compliment each other - Design Thinking fitting the early stage of product discovery followed by Agile processes when the right "it" has been defined. To illustrate this claim, the case of AppHaus Silicon

Valley is being presented. The insights were kindly provided through a semi-structured interview with Design & Innovation Executive Philipp Skogstad from SAP AppHaus.

Design Thinking for Product Discovery, Early Co-Collaboration and Business Strategy Considerations

At SAP Design Thinking is a core nominator for the early stage product development. The core values of implementing design thinking have been to allow rapid iterative development involving the three-dimensional product core; customer, technology and business. This allows much faster to reframe the actual problem of the customer. SAP's benefit of Design Thinking is to gain the holistic overview of a problem. Hence a project always starts with a discovery phase conducting research on customers, end-user as well as current technological solutions. In order not to start coding immediately several future interactions are physically prototyped through role-plays and paper wireframes. SAP even developed the tool *Scenes* that allow a tangible dialogue among customers, developers and designers. Through story-boards and scenes the dialogue reflect future scenarios rather than detailed specifications[2].

> *"One of the core values when implementing Design Thinking in our development process was actually not only to bring in external stakeholders early on in the process, but actually to get programmers and UI designers to meet earlier as well. This improves the understanding of specific design choices and to what degree certain solutions are flexible. This saves us a lot of time."* Philipp Skogstad SAP

Involving customers early on in the development influenced the communication topics as well. Helping the customers seeing the bigger context of their products transformed the dialogue from being product to strategy or underlying problem focused.

> *"First you might see yourself having a meeting with the people from product development. Next time you find your self being brought to business strategy meetings."* Philipp Skogstad, SAP

This indicates that Design Thinking is more than a process to develop innovative products, but a mindset that allow you to explore and foresee uncertainties as well. This is supported by recent scholars arguing that design thinking covers a much broader field than solely product development (Cooper et al. 2009).

Implementing Design Thinking

SAP made strategic efforts to implement the exploring and testing mindset of Design Thinking. Their core initiative covers the so-called three P's: *People*, *Process* and *Place*. *People* means making sure you are working in an interdisciplinary environment. *Process* means having a conscious knowledge on which methods to use when and being able to switch between methods taken from Design Thinking as well as Agile Development processes. In SAP Design Thinking is hence not something to stand alone, but it complemented supported by process such as Agile Development. *Place* covers having a physical workspace that creates and atmosphere of openness to idea sharing, experimenting and prototyping. At SAP they aimed at creating an art studio rather than a gallery.

---

[2] https://experience.sap.com/designservices/scenes.

"Many companies fail at creating such a space and end up with fancy chairs etc. like an art gallery. We seek to create the feeling of an art studio where you are allowed to test, experiment and get things dirty," Philipp Skogstad, SAP

4 Conclusion

In this paper we describe the original research fields behind the methods applied in the Design Thinking Process in order to remove the term from a brief buzzword to a credible innovation method. We argue that though these methods are not new, the favor of rapid iteration and stakeholder involvement supports the exploratory mindset any innovator needs in the early stages of product development. They are powerful in defining the product requirement that in term form the foundation for applying agile development methods. This description is supported by the case of Silicon Valley based AppHous that in their daily work successfully apply Design Thinking methods for product discovery and agile method for test and implementation.

References

Berg, B.: Qualitative Research Methods for the Social Sciences, 4th edn. (2004)

Bonwell, C.C., Eison, J.A.: Active Learning: Creating Excitement in the Classroom. School of Education and Human Development, Washington, DC (1991)

Callon, M.: Some elements of a sociology of translation: domestication of the scallops and the fishermen of St Brieuc Bay. Sociol. Rev. **32**(S1), 196–233 (1984)

Callon, M.: The Sociology of an actor-network: the case of the electric vehicle. In: Callon, M., Law, J., Rip, A. (eds.) Mapping the Dynamics of Science and Technology: Sociology of Science in the Real World, pp. 19–34 (1986)

Cameron, M.: Review Essays: Donald A. Schon, The Reflective Practitioner: How Professionals Think in Action. Basic Books, New York (1983, 2009)

Cooper, R., Junginger, S., Lockwood, T.: Design thinking and design management: a research and practice perspective. Des. Manage. Rev. **20**(2), 46–55 (2009)

Latour, B.: On actor-network theory: a few clarifications. Soziale Welt **47**, 369–381 (1996)

Onarheim, B., & Biskjaer, M.: Balancing Constraints and the Sweet Spot as Coming Topics for Creativity Research. Creativity in Design: Understanding, Capturing, Supporting **1**, 1–18 (2015)

Popper, K.: The Logic of Scientific Discovery (1959)

Runco, M.A., Okuda, S.M.: Problem discovery, divergent thinking, and the creative process. J. Youth Adolesc. **17**(3), 211–220 (1988)

Star, S.L., Griesemer, J.R.: Institutional ecology, 'translations' and boundary objects: amateurs and professionals in Berkeley's museum of vertebrate zoology, 1907–1939. Soc. Study Sci. **19**, 387–420 (1989)

Playing Protection Poker for Practical Software Security

Martin Gilje Jaatun$^{(\boxtimes)}$ and Inger Anne Tøndel

Department of Software Engineering, Safety and Security,
SINTEF ICT, 7465 Trondheim, Norway
martin.g.jaatun@sintef.no
http://www.sintef.no/sos-agile

Abstract. Software security is about creating software that keeps performing as intended even when exposed to an active attacker. Secure software engineering is thus relevant for all software, not only security software. We describe Protection Poker, a tool for risk estimation to be used as part of the iteration planning meeting, and discuss some preliminary experiences.

1 Introduction

Protection Poker is a security risk assessment technique for agile development teams proposed by professor Laurie Williams and colleagues at NCSU [1]. The idea is to play Protection Poker as part of every iteration[1] planning meeting, in order to rank the security risk of each feature to be implemented in that iteration, and possibly identify additional security mechanisms that have to be implemented to maintain an acceptable risk level.

1.1 Risk in Protection Poker

Protection Poker uses a slight variation of the traditional computation of risk:

$$risk = \left(\sum \text{value of assets that could be exploited}\right) \times (\text{the exposure}) \quad (1)$$

Risk is always related to the requirements that are to be implemented in the next iteration, often this will be some new, enhanced or corrected functionality. Exposure relates to how hard or easy this change in functionality makes it to attack the system, and in the evaluation of exposure, one should consider the possible ways in which attackers can attack the system (attack surface), what type of breaches they can perform (confidentiality, integrity, availability) and the skill level required. For asset value, the value of the asset for various groups should be considered: the value of the asset for an attacker is important for attacker motivation, whereas the value of the asset for customers, users, the business, etc. highly determines the consequences that a successful attack may

---

[1] e.g., a "sprint" in Scrum.

© Springer International Publishing AG 2016
P. Abrahamsson et al. (Eds.): PROFES 2016, LNCS 10027, pp. 679–682, 2016.
DOI: 10.1007/978-3-319-49094-6_55

have. Assets are typically considered to be database tables or system processes that the new functionality controls.

Our dialect of Protection Poker[2] uses the following numbers to determine asset value or system exposure: <10, 20, 30, 40, 50, 60, 70, 80, 90, 100. In calculations, "<10" is counted as 10. To be able to prioritize between different requirements, it is important to be able to get a spread in the numbers assigned. This is to avoid that, e.g., high risk projects rate every requirement with a high number. That would make it very hard to prioritize within the project.

1.2 Calibration

With Protection Poker, the security risk of a requirement is compared to other requirements of the same system. The goal is not to establish a "perfect" and "universal" risk value, but to rate the security risk of the requirements in order to be able to better prioritize security effort. Before starting to play Protection Poker for a system, it is thus recommended to perform calibration in order to arrive at a common understanding of the end-points of the scale, i.e., what does a <10 or a 100 mean for this product? This is done the following way:

Asset value: The team asks itself: what assets are most important in this system, and what assets are of little value. The asset they can think of as most important is given a '100' and the asset they can think of with little value is given a '<10'.
Exposure: The team asks itself: what types of functional requirements can open up most for attacks, and which functional requirements can limit exposure, and assign a '100' and a '<10' accordingly.

In the evaluation of asset value and exposure, numbers should be assigned relative to these endpoints, as well as the values assigned for previously assessed requirements.

2 Playing the Game

Protection Poker is played during an iteration planning meeting, and it is recommended that the full development team participates. One person should have the role as moderator, and this person will be responsible for leading the team through the game, and point the discussions in a good direction. Ideally, a separate person should be tasked with recording important security solutions and ideas that emerge during play. Focus is on the specific requirements the team will likely implement during the next iteration.

Step 1 – Common understanding of the requirements: The requirements to be implemented in the iteration are explained to the team (e.g., by the product manager or business owner) and the team members discuss or ask questions to clarify the requirements.

---

[2] http://www.sintef.no/protection-poker.

Step 2 – Initial discussion of security implications: The team performs a first discussion of the security implications of the requirements. The moderator can ask leading questions, e.g., "Who would want to attack this system?"; "What would an attacker do if he got access to this data?"; or "What damage could an insider do with this functionality?"

Step 3 – Identify assets: Everybody together identify which assets are created or touched upon by the requirement under consideration. Some of these may have already been assigned a value, and then this value can be reused.

Step 4 – Assign value to assets: For identified assets that have not previously been assigned a value, each participant picks the Protection Poker card (individually and without telling anybody about which card has been picked) that best describes their understanding of the asset's value. All participants show their selected card to the whole team, and the team discusses the rationale for selecting the cards; the team members with the highest and lowest cards explain them to the group, followed by an open discussion until the team is ready to revote (if there is disagreement). When the team has reached a consensus on the asset value (or when there is no use in discussing any further – in these cases the moderator is responsible for making a suggestion for what value to assign to the asset), the moderator notes the asset value. The team now moves on to the next asset (if there are more left to assess) or to the exposure evaluation.

Step 5 – Evaluate exposure: As for asset value, the team bids to evaluate to which extent the requirement increases the exposure of the system and assets to attack.

Step 6 – Calculate risk: The numbers assigned for asset values and exposure are used to calculate a risk value as given in Eq. 1.

Step 7 – Compare risk related to other requirements: The risk value for the requirement can be compared to the risk value of other requirements to see for which requirements security should be given specific priority.

Step 8 – Prioritize security activities: Based on the risk value and the discussion decision should be made on how to address security for this requirement. The decision should be documented. If there is a need for specific security activities or functionalities, these should be documented together with other requirements (e.g. in the backlog).

3 Experiences and Challenges

We made some small adjustments to the Protection Poker cards and terminology. Whereas the original Protection Poker uses the term "ease of exploitation", we found that this concept was distracting or not properly understood by some pilot players, e.g., leading them to focus too much on threats such as "shoulder surfing". In order to focus more on how a feature increases the attack surface of an application, we decided to change it to "exposure".

The original Protection Poker[3] uses the same cards as Planning Poker [2,3] (also known as Scrum Poker), used for effort estimation in agile teams. Planning

---

[3] http://collaboration.csc.ncsu.edu/laurie/Security/ProtectionPoker/.

Poker cards follow a Fibonacci-like sequence, after the rationale that it is easier to have an opinion on whether a task takes 1 or 2 days than whether it takes 40 or 41 days. We argue, however that the same is not true when it comes to relative value of assets or degree of exposure, and since we are less concerned about small risks and more interested in the bigger risks, we opted for an even scale instead. This enables us to differentiate between big risks, not just the small ones.

We have tried out Protection Poker with representatives from various Norwegian organizations and in general it has been well received. However, some have indicated that they feel it takes too long to play the game, especially when considering that planning meetings already are perceived as being too full. Laurie Williams [1] found that the time required for playing dropped significantly after the team gained familiarity with the technique, but we need more experience with our partner companies to determine whether that will also be the case here. We remain open to the possibility of changing how and when Protection Poker is played in order to maximise the benefit.

For some development groups, we have observed that asset identification can be difficult, and particularly the *granularity* of assets can be challenging. It is important that at least within a development team, the assets have a consistent granularity, as this otherwise might skew the risk calculations.

Acknowledgment. This work was supported by the SoS-Agile: Science of Security in Agile Software Development project, funded by the Research Council of Norway, grant number 247678.

References

1. Williams, L., Meneely, A., Shipley, G.: Protection poker: the new software security game. IEEE Secur. Priv. **8**(3), 14–20 (2010)
2. Grenning, J.: Planning poker or how to avoid analysis paralysis while release planning. Hawthorn Woods: Renaissance Softw. Consult. **3**, 1–3 (2002)
3. Moløkken-Østvold, K., Haugen, N.C., Benestad, H.C.: Using planning poker for combining expert estimates in software projects. J. Syst. Softw. **81**(12), 2106–2117 (2008). Best papers from the 2007 Australian Software Engineering Conference (ASWEC 2007), Melbourne, Australia, 10–13 April 2007

Exploring Expectations About Risk-Based Testing: Towards Increasing Effectiveness and Efficiency

Michael Felderer[1](✉) and Rudolf Ramler[2]

[1] Institute of Computer Science, University of Innsbruck, Technikerstrasse 21a,
6020 Innsbruck, Austria
michael.felderer@uibk.ac.at

[2] Software Competence Center Hagenberg GmbH, Softwarepark 21, 4232 Hagenberg, Austria
rudolf.ramler@scch.at

Abstract. Risk-based testing is sometimes reduced to an approach that focuses on cutting costs and time in testing. While the high effort involved in testing makes efficiency an important issue, for many companies the main concern is still to find the critical defects in their software products. Such defects can cause costly remedial upgrades and fixes, and they threaten the company's long-term business success. In this paper we explore how the two goals "effectiveness" and "efficiency" motivate a risk-based testing approach in different organizations. Furthermore, we identify a third goal, summarized as "management support". In a survey conducted as part of a tutorial on risk-based testing we investigated common expectations and potential benefits associated with these three goals. The results indicate that the main motivation for a risk-based approach is making testing more efficient. Nevertheless, efficiency and effectiveness are not conflicting goals and the main challenge is therefore finding strategies that increase the overall benefit of including risk information in testing.

Keywords: Test management · Software risk management · Software testing · Risk-based testing · Test process improvement · Effectiveness · Efficiency

1 Introduction

Software testing is an essential and widely practiced measure for assuring software quality. By accounting for up to 50 % of the overall project effort, testing is also a highly costly and time-intensive activity in software development. Hence, an adequate test strategy plays a key role in balancing product quality with cost and time-to-market. Ideally this balance is achieved by taking the risks into account, which are associated with the consequences of poor quality caused by software defects. A systematic consideration of the involved risks is suggested by risk-based testing [1].

However, risk-based testing is sometimes (mis-)understood as an approach that focuses primarily on minimizing costs and time – according to the pun "cut testing and take the risk". The high effort involved in software testing makes efficiency an important management goal. Although important, for many companies the main concern is still to miss critical bugs. Critical bugs can significantly delay time-to-market, result in costly

© Springer International Publishing AG 2016
P. Abrahamsson et al. (Eds.): PROFES 2016, LNCS 10027, pp. 683–688, 2016.
DOI: 10.1007/978-3-319-49094-6_56

hotfixes, and threaten the acceptance of software products and services by customers on the long run. In such a case, effectiveness is often the primary goal in software testing. It has to be balanced with short-term economic constraints such as limited time and or resources available for software testing.

The need to balance effectiveness and efficiency requires adequate management support. Providing management supports is therefore a further, commonly observed goal of risk-based testing. It is also found in contexts where testing is determined by the need to fulfill industry standards and organizational regulations.

In this paper we explore these main goals associated with risk-based software testing. Section 2 provides an overview of the relevant concepts and links them to findings from related work. Section 3 shows the results from a survey conducted as part of a previous tutorial held at the Software Quality Days 2016[1]. The paper is concluded by a summary and discussion in Sect. 4.

2   Background

Risk-based testing is a testing approach which considers risks of the software product as the guiding factor to support decisions in all phases of the test process [2]. In previous studies we investigated the potential of risk-based testing in large enterprises [3] as well as in small and medium enterprises [4]. We also studied the introduction of risk-based testing in an organization [5], where an essential first step is to establish a risk-based test strategy with clear goals and expectation for all testing activities. Among other research questions we explored "What is the benefit and improvement potential that defect prediction can provide for software testing?" in these different contexts. Our findings can be summarized as follows.

The general motivation is that information about fault-prone modules, i.e., those that have a high risk of causing critical failures, allows focusing the testing effort on selected parts of the software system instead of testing the entire system with the same rigor (Fig. 1). The associated improvement potential is based on the observation that the majority of the faults (usually approximated as "80 % of the defects") comes from a relatively small amount of the code (usually approximated as "20 % of the modules") and that "about half the modules are defect free" [6, 7].

2.1   Effectiveness

One of the resulting benefits of risk-based testing is its ability to *increase the effectiveness of testing*, which can be defined as the degree to which testing is able to detect all defects in the system under test (e.g., defects actually detected per total defects). Testing is an investment in the quality of a software product [8, 9]. Even though resources are limited in general, it is important to achieve quality requirements such as functional correctness, reliability, performance etc.

---

[1] https://2016.software-quality-days.com/en/.

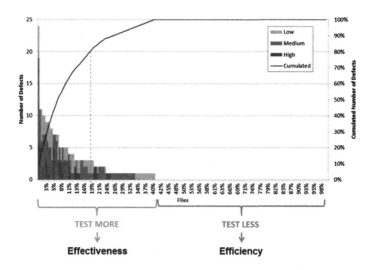

Fig. 1. Increasing effectiveness and efficiency with risk-based software testing.

A risk-based approach can help to make testing more effective by including information about high-risk components in test planning from the very beginning. Directing the main testing effort to high-risk components to pursue a thorough, systematic testing approach (1) *increases the likelihood that the existing defects are detected.* Besides an improvement of the product's quality, (2) setting priorities based on risk considerations fosters the *detection of critical defects* first. Risk-based prioritization also ensures that (3) defects are found *in the early iterations of testing.*

In our study on risk-based testing in industry [3] we found that the investigated companies use risk information to further increase the range of testing with additional risk-based test cases. These test cases are added to the existing set of tests that were systematically derived from the requirements in order to boost the chance of detecting additional defects. It is expected that fewer defects will slip through to the field.

2.2 Efficiency

Another potential benefit of risk-based testing is its ability to *increase the efficiency of testing*, which can be defined as ratio between output and input (e.g., detected defects per time spent). Time and manpower are constrained resources in the development of software systems. This also affects the resource allocation in software testing, which has to cope with the fundamental challenge that exhaustive testing of a software system is not possible in a realistic timeframe [10]. Therefore, it is sensible to allocate (prioritize) the available resources in a way so that most output can be generated.

Most organizations use testing as a means to reduce the risk of delivering software with critical bugs. However, a harsh competitive environment can imply severe time and resource constraints that outweigh quality risks. In the struggle to meet strict release deadlines or to maintain short-term business opportunities, companies may be forced to (1) *reduce testing time* and (2) *cutback resources* allocated for testing. In this context, the understanding of risks is typically used to make testing more efficient, i.e., to adjust the amount of testing to optimally use the available time and resources for covering at least the most critical parts.

Small and medium enterprises (SME) seem to be most affected by time and resource constraints. In our study on risk orientation in software testing processes of SME [4] we observed cases where risk information has been used to increase test efficiency, i.e., to adjust the amount of testing to reduce cost and time. Larger organizations seem to tackle time and resource constraints by using risk information to increases the chance of finding critical defects in the early iterations of testing and, in consequence, to reduce the overall costs and time required for stabilization [3].

2.3 Management Support

Finally, we also found that companies benefit from the risk information used in risk-based testing for supporting management in decision making and in pursuing process improvement initiatives. A risk-based approach helps to make the balance between cost and quality transparent and easier to communicate. These benefits were observable in small, agile organizations [4] as well as in large enterprises [3] that have to cope with the fulfillment of industry standards and organizational regulations.

One example is the use of risk-burndown carts [5]. Traceability between the executed test cases, the test results and the risk items enables reliable release quality statements as well as the estimation of residual risks. In risk-based evaluation and reporting, risk burn-down charts, which illustrate the development of risk exposure for a system or specific artifacts over time, are a suitable measure for release quality and residual risk estimation. The risk that is estimated in the beginning is reduced with every test cycle until a risk level is reached where it is acceptable to release the software application. This method based on risk burn-down charts proposed in the studied project has been found intuitively accessible and suitable for supporting release decisions by project management.

3 Preliminary Survey Results

A list of commonly observed expectations and potential benefits that motivate the adoption of a risk-based testing approach has been collected from previous projects (e.g. [5]) as well as related literature (e.g., [11, 12]). In a survey conducted as part of a tutorial held at the Software Quality Days 2016, one of the biggest industry-academia conventions on software quality in Europe, we asked the participants about their motivation for risk-based testing in their projects or products.

The survey showed 20 different motivations for risk-based testing. Each participant was asked to select all motivations considered relevant in context of his or her work. The participants' main roles were software tester, test manager, project manager, quality manager, team lead or head of QA, software architect and developer with practical experience in software testing ranging from 1 to more than 10 years; majority in the range of 3 to 5 years. We received answers from 23 participants ($N = 23$).

Figure 2 shows the results sorted by the number of times a motivation has been selected by a survey participant. Motivations related to *effectiveness* are shown in blue, motivations related to *efficiency* are shown in orange, and motivations related to organizational and *management support* are shown in green color.

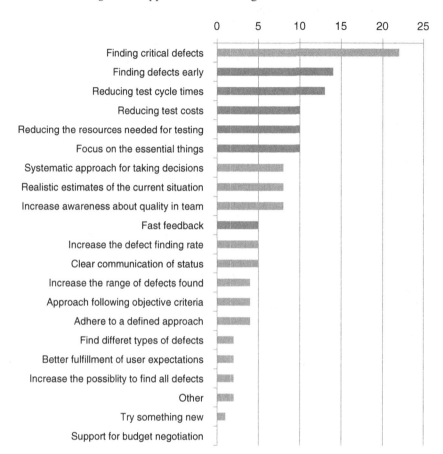

Fig. 2. Number of times a motivation has been selected by a survey participants ($N = 23$). Motivations are related to effectiveness (blue), efficiency (orange) or management support (green). (Color figure online)

4   Conclusions and Future Work

Despite its preliminary character, the survey indicates that the main motivation for introducing or conducting risk-based testing is making testing more efficient. Weighted over all possible motivations selected by the participants, 48 % can be related to *efficiency* aspects, 29 % to *effectivity*, and 23 % to *management support*. The emphasis on efficiency is also visible from the ranking of the motivating factors. It is, however, worth noting that the top most motivation selected by 22 out of 23 participants is "finding critical defects", which is remarkable since we consider this motivation to be associated more with effectiveness than with efficiency.

Efficiency and effectiveness are not conflicting objectives in risk-based testing. From a research perspective, thus, the main question for future work is to explore which strategies that maximize the overall benefit of testing with risk information.

Acknowledgements. This work has been supported by the COMET Competence Center program of the Austrian Research Promotion Agency (FFG), and the project QE LaB – Living Models for Open Systems funded by the Austrian Federal Ministry of Science, Research and Economy.

References

1. Ramler, R., Felderer, M.: A process for risk-based test strategy development and its industrial evaluation. In: Abrahamsson, P., Corral, L., Oivo, M., Russo, B. (eds.) PROFES 2015. LNCS, vol. 9459, pp. 355–371. Springer, Heidelberg (2015). doi:10.1007/978-3-319-26844-6_26
2. Felderer, M., Schieferdecker, I.: A taxonomy of risk-based testing. Int. J. Softw. Tools Technol. Transf. **16**(5), 559–568 (2014). Springer
3. Felderer, M., Ramler, R.: A multiple case study on risk-based testing in industry. Int. J. Softw. Tools Technol. Transf. **16**(5), 609–625 (2014). Springer
4. Felderer, M., Ramler, R.: Risk orientation in software testing processes of small and medium enterprises: an exploratory and comparative study. Softw. Q. J. **24**(3), 519–548 (2016). Springer
5. Felderer, M., Ramler, R.: Integrating risk-based testing in industrial test processes. Softw. Q. J. **22**(3), 543–575 (2014). Springer
6. Boehm, B., Basili, V.R.: Software defect reduction top 10 list. IEEE Comput. **34**(1), 135–137 (2001). IEEE
7. Shull, F., Basili, V.R., Boehm, B., Brown, A.W., Costa, P., Lindvall, M., Port, D., Rus, I., Tesoriero, R., Zelkowitz, M.: What we have learned about fighting defects. In: 8th Symposium on Software Metrics, METRICS 2002, p. 249. IEEE (2002)
8. Huang, L.G., Boehm, B.: How much software quality investment is enough: a value-based approach. IEEE Softw. **23**(5), 88–95 (2006)
9. Ramler, R., Biffl, S., Grünbacher, P.: Value-based management of software testing. In: Value-Based Software Engineering, pp. 225–244. Springer, Heidelberg (2006)
10. Ramler, R., Wolfmaier, K.: Economic perspectives in test automation: balancing automated and manual testing with opportunity cost. In: International Workshop on Automation of Software Test, AST 2006, pp. 85–91. ACM (2006)
11. Amland, S.: Risk-based testing: risk analysis fundamentals and metrics for software testing including a financial application case study. J. Syst. Softw. **53**(3), 287–295 (2000)
12. Redmill, F.: Theory and practice of risk-based testing. Softw. Test. Verification Reliab. **15**(1), 3–20 (2005). Wiley

2nd International Workshop on Human Factors in Software Development Processes

Human Factors in Software Development Processes: Measuring System Quality

Silvia Abrahao[1], Maria Teresa Baldassarre[2], Danilo Caivano[2], Yvonne Dittrich[3],
Rosa Lanzilotti[2], and Antonio Piccinno[2(✉)]

[1] Universidad Politecnica de Valencia (UPV), Valencia, Spain
sabrahao@dsic.upv.es
[2] Università degli Studi di Bari Aldo Moro, Bari, Italy
{mariateresa.baldassarre,danilo.caivano,rosa.lanzilotti,
antonio.piccinno}@uniba.it
[3] IT University of Copenhagen, Copenhagen, Denmark
ydi@itu.dk

Abstract. Software Engineering and Human-Computer Interaction look at the development process from different perspectives. They apparently use very different approaches, are inspired by different principles and address different needs. But, they definitively have the same goal: develop high quality software in the most effective way. The second edition of the workshop puts particular attention on efforts of the two communities in enhancing system quality. The research question discussed is: who, what, where, when, why, and how should we evaluate?

Keywords: Human Computer Interaction · Software Engineering · Human factors · Development process

1 Introduction and Motivation

Software Engineering (SE) and Human-Computer Interaction (HCI) look at development processes of interactive software systems from different perspectives. Efforts to reduce the gap between the two communities for what concerns the introduction of human factors in software development processes have started to be discussed in the first edition of the workshop, held in Bolzano in 2015 [1]. One aspect that emerged from the discussion pointed out concerns on how system quality should be measured, in order to satisfy both communities. Indeed, the software product industry emphasizes how important it is to involve users and customers to evaluate quality in terms of functionality and usability of software products [2].

Although researchers and practitioners from the two communities share the same goal of developing high quality systems, the methodologies, methods and metrics they use to evaluate such quality are very different due to their background and expertise.

The second edition of the workshop on Human Factors in Software Development Processes aims at providing a forum for discussing measuring system quality from both perspectives. In particular, the following research issues are addressed:

© Springer International Publishing AG 2016
P. Abrahamsson et al. (Eds.): PROFES 2016, LNCS 10027, pp. 691–696, 2016.
DOI: 10.1007/978-3-319-49094-6_57

- key methods that allow to integrate human factors in the evaluation of the software quality;
- methodologies and techniques currently used in software development teams to engage users in the evaluation process;
- how the level of human factor involvement can be objectively verified during and after software development;
- how Software Engineering and HCI researchers and practitioners can overcome the communication gap when evaluating system quality.

Researchers and practitioners who face the problem of integrating human factors in software quality evaluation should have a place to discuss their experiences, lessons learned and future intentions to reach a common understanding on evaluation topics.

2   Filling the GAP Between SE and HCI

SE and HCI apparently use very different approaches, are inspired by different principles and address different needs. Ultimately though they have the same goal: developing high quality software in the most effective way.

Based on the discussions of the previous edition and of the contributions received, the authors of this paper have classified some gaps between the two communities that can be seen as two sides of the same medal. In the following, we illustrate and discuss: (i) the main differences between SE and HCI approaches adopted, (ii) categorize the common wisdoms and (iii) explore possible ways to reduce the gap and converge.

2.1   The Differences

2.1.1   User vs. Market Oriented Systems

One of the most popular claims in the two communities is that they address different types of software products.

The HCI products are User Oriented Systems where typically there is some type of "users" (user, lead user, customer and so on) to refer to during the development. Here the source of requirements (functional and non functional) is primarily the "user" himself who is actively involved in the design, review and validation, i.e. ingrained in the entire development process right up until delivery. The systems are very focused on specific domains, they offer the functions that are specialized on users' needs.

The SE products are Market Oriented Systems that address a wide range of needs and are used by tons of users that differ for functions used, language, culture, ability, competences and skills. Here the source of requirements are the laws, domain and business rules, books, the already existing legacy systems, competitors and, in general, the so called stakeholders. The "users" are rarely involved and typically a "customer" doesn't exit because the developed product is addressed to an entire market segment with hopefully hundreds of customers. The systems are so big that there isn't a single "user" that knows all the requirements to develop and thus the "users" are simply not essential.

2.1.2 Vertical vs. Layered or Horizontal Architecture

An assertion emerged in the previous workshop is that the differences between User and Market Oriented product imply the use of different software architectures. The HCI architectures were perceived as "vertical" in that they address specific needs of specific users from specific domains. Due to these characteristics the system development starts from interface until database without particular attention to maintainability and reuse. The resulting systems are generally characterized by a high coupling between data functions and interfaces and a possible low internal cohesion.

The SE architectures are usually layered architectures inspired by principles such as modularization, separation of interest, information hiding, reuse etc. and the resulting systems are assumed to be maintainable and robust. The interface is only one of the system layers and it is often considered less important than others such as the data layer or business layer. Here the belief is that the obtained systems are so maintainable that their interfaces can be adjusted or completely changed in a short time and fashionable way without particular problems. Common architecture styles are Software Product Lines, Enterprise Architectures, Service Oriented Architectures etc. A software system is naturally perceived along the horizontal dimension because it covers a wide range of domains, from business to technical. A typical example is an Enterprise Resource Planning.

2.1.3 User Time - Ex Ante vs. Ex Post

A crucial point in the SE-HCI debate is the decision on when the users should be involved. The HCI philosophy is "as soon as possible" while the SE face states that the "users are rarely involved". This is the result of a numbers of convictions; for HCI: the interface and usability are crucial for system success and the nature and type of interface strongly influences the architecture style; The interface cannot be simply pushed into a system right after being developed; The source of requirements is also the "user" and thus drives system development from the start (User Driven Development) [7].

SE: in this community a Process/Product Driven Development is adopted. The source of requirements "can also" be the user but he/she is generally not considered particularly important, rather time consuming and misleading. If the system is developed according to the SE processes and principles the user interface can be easily pushed into the system at the end of development when the critical and most important layers are completed. The final users can be involved before software delivery to carry out pilot studies aimed at validating user satisfaction and product correctness. All the suggestions coming from users are then quickly and effectively incorporated.

2.2 Common Wisdom

Following to discussions of the previous edition we have outlined some "common wisdom" points spread within the communities, just to mention a few:

- HCI systems are more usable than SE ones;
- HCI systems are less maintainable than SE ones
- HCI systems are less performing than SE ones

Obviously these are anecdotal assertions and with lack of any evidence with the only intent of soliciting and marking the differences and distance between the two communities.

2.3 Bridging the Gap

How do we reduce the gap? What approaches, techniques or processes should we use? Discussion and information collected among participants of both communities were trivial in some cases and original in others. They have been summarized in the following list:

- make use of short iterations, meetings and focus groups between "stakeholders" during system development in order to reduce the risks of omitted requirements and deliver unusable systems. Stakeholders obviously include among others, users, lead users and customers as well as developers and experts. To this end during the discussion of this point was clear that there is a misleading use of terms in the two communities and that most likely terms like user, lead user or customer as intended by HCI are included and considered by SE as stakeholders;
- use of lightweight processes, especially those ones proposed in HCI community that starting from the well known agile processes, such as SCRUM or XP, extend them by actively involving the "user" or "customer";
- concepts such as experimentation and empirical evaluation can represent a common means for both communities. Action research, ethnographic studies, Cooperative Method Development, formal experiments, case studies [6], surveys, qualitative and quantitative evaluations etc. could become a shared platform of methods for a joint evaluation of what is done in the two communities;
- use of interdisciplinary teams that include both HCI and SE experts;
- definition and use of shared quality models able to objectively evaluate the quality of the system developed.

In the end we can observe that in the recent years the two communities are progressively converging towards a set of common practices, process and empirical techniques. The considerations above and the outcomes of the discussions enhanced during the first edition of the workshop suggest to refer to empirical approaches [5] and evaluation of software quality [3, 4] as a way for enhancing the convergence between communities and improves software quality overcoming skepticism and common wisdoms.

Despite the discussion, the research problem still remains: who, what, where, when, why, and how should we evaluate quality?

Nowadays software quality approaches are also converging towards product evaluation from different point of views: internal, external quality, quality in use. For example, if we refer to ISO/IEC 25000 we can observe that it standardizes the processes and models for product evaluation and provides useful guidelines for addressing system quality in a more objective way. This has been one of starting points for triggering further discussion in the current edition.

3   Audience and Expected Outcomes

The overall goal of this interdisciplinary workshop has been to raise the level of engagement and discussion about human factors in software quality measurements. A further goal of the workshop has been to identify opportunities to improve the synergy of the two communities on the scientific discourse and progress on human aspects of software evaluation, as well as to better identify opportunities able to educate practitioners and researchers about how to conduct sound human-centered evaluations in the context of software engineering. Indeed, the organizers of the workshop are a synergic composition of active researchers belonging to both communities. The expected outcome is a descriptive framework that helps to organize the current best practices and a set of recommendations for formalizing and verifying software system quality.

The workshop has received a positive response from both HCI and SE communities with several interesting and valuable contributions. The submissions were peer-reviewed by international committee members for their quality, topic relevance, innovation, and potentials to foster discussion. Finally, five papers were accepted.

In the first paper, "Gamification and Functional prototyping to Support Motivation towards Software Process Improvement" authors discuss commitment in software process improvement initiatives in the context of people-driven processes to help ensure software quality. Gamification and functional prototyping are used as a means to boost motivation and commitment.

The second paper "Exploring Mobile User Experience through Code Quality Metrics" presents a set of features for evaluating the code quality of Android applications. The discussion points out how user experience varies in mobile ecosystems and who developers should focus on software quality to assure usable applications from a user perspective.

In the third paper "Early-Usability in Model-Driven Game Development", authors propose a model that can be used to evaluate the usability of video games in early stages of development. Moreover, the method relies on a model that decomposes usability into measurable attributes and metrics specific to the video game domain, bridging de facto a gap between SE and HCI.

In the fourth paper "What aspects of context should be described in case studies about software teams? Preliminary results from a mapping study", authors illustrate the results of a mapping study aiming at addressing human-based factors that influence the selection and composition of software engineering teams and how these can influence and impact final quality.

Finally, in the fifth contribution "Miscommunication in Software Projects: Early recognition through tendency forecasts", authors address issues of team communication and how miscommunication can lead to delay of software releases and especially hamper customer satisfaction. Aspects related to team composition and their interaction with users is also addressed.

Acknowledgment. We would like to thank the organizers of PROFES 2016 for giving us the opportunity to organize this workshop. We are also grateful to our international program committee of experts in the field for their reviews and collaboration.

References

1. Abrahao, S., Baldassarre, M.T., Caivano, D., Dittrich, Y., Lanzilotti, R., Piccinno, A.: Human factors in software development processes. In: Abrahamsson, P., Corral, L., Oivo, M., Russo, B. (eds.) Proceedings of the Product-Focused Software Process Improvement: 16th International Conference, PROFES 2015, Bolzano, Italy, 2–4 December 2015, pp. XIV–XVI. Springer, Switzerland (2015)
2. Costabile, M.F., Fogli, D., Lanzilotti, R., Mussio, P., Piccinno, A.: Supporting work practice through end-user development environments. J. Organ. End User Comput. **18**(4), 43–65 (2006)
3. Pardo, C., Pino, F.J., García, F., Piattini, M., Baldassarre, M.T.: A process for driving the harmonization of models. In: ACM International Conference Proceeding Series, pp. 51–54 (2010). doi:10.1145/1961258.1961271
4. Pardo, C., Pino, F.J., García, F., Piattini Velthius, M., Baldassarre, M.T.: Trends in harmonization of multiple reference models. In: Maciaszek, L.A., Loucopoulos, P. (eds.) ENASE 2010. CCIS, vol. 230, pp. 61–73. Springer, Heidelberg (2011). doi: 10.1007/978-3-642-23391-3_5
5. Ardimento, P., Caivano, D., Cimitile, M., Visaggio, G.: Empirical investigation of the efficacy and efficiency of tools for transferring software engineering knowledge. J. Inf. Knowl. Manag. **7**(3), 197–207 (2008). doi:10.1142/S0219649208002081
6. Baldassarre, M.T., Bianchi, A., Caivano, D., Visaggio, G.: An industrial case study on reuse oriented development. In: IEEE International Conference on Software Maintenance, ICSM 2005, Art. No. 1510124, pp. 283–294 (2005). doi:10.1109/ICSM.2005.20
7. Ardito, C., Buono, P., Caivano, D., Costabile, M.F., Lanzilotti, R., Bruun, A., Stage, J.: Usability evaluation: a survey of software development organizations. In: International Conference on Software Engineering and Knowledge Engineering (SEKE 2011), Miami, Florida, USA, pp. 282–287, 7–9 July 2011

Gamification and Functional Prototyping to Support Motivation Towards Software Process Improvement

Mercedes Ruiz[✉], Manuel Trinidad, and Alejandro Calderón

Department of Computer Science and Engineering, University of Cádiz, Cádiz, Spain
{mercedes.ruiz,manuel.trinidad,alejandro.calderon}@uca.es

Abstract. The topic of commitment in software process improvement (SPI) has been a recurrent topic of research that has not received enough attention in the recent years. In many situations, the lack of commitment in SPI initiatives is appointed as the major cause leading to failure. In this paper, we propose the use of simulation-based process functional prototyping as a tool to design and test SPI initiatives in a risk-free environment together with gamification, as a means to boost motivation and commitment. The paper shows the conceptualization of the proposal and the design of the gamification strategy, describes the tools built at the technical implementation of the strategy and summarizes the main results of a pilot study conducted to initially evaluate the proposal.

Keywords: Gamification · Process prototyping · Simulation · Software process improvement · Motivation · Commitment

1 Introduction

This work is part of a research endeavor aimed at exploring the application of simulation techniques and gamification in the context of people-driven processes to help ensure software quality. In this paper, we explore the aspects related to commitment in software process improvement initiatives and how simulation techniques, as a means of functional process prototyping, and gamification can be used to help improve attitude and commitment.

The topic of commitment in software process improvement (SPI) has been a recurrent topic of research that has not received enough attention in the recent years. Abrahamssom and Iivani [2] conclude that even with investments of billions of dollars in SPI, the results show that two thirds of the efforts fail in reaching the objectives. In many situations, the lack of commitment in SPI initiatives is appointed as the major cause leading to this failure. This sounds at least paradoxical since it is undoubted that SPI has to be present whenever an organization attempts to improve its efficiency and results.

In this paper, we propose the use of process functional prototyping as a tool to design and test SPI initiatives in a risk-free environment together with gamification, as a means to boost motivation and commitment. This paper is structured as follows: Sect. 2 provides the background for this study and describes similar works to ours highlighting the differences between other initiatives and our proposal. Sections 3 and 4 describe our

© Springer International Publishing AG 2016
P. Abrahamsson et al. (Eds.): PROFES 2016, LNCS 10027, pp. 697–704, 2016.
DOI: 10.1007/978-3-319-49094-6_58

proposal and the tools that have been already developed to technically support this approach, respectively. Section 5 describes the pilot study conducted to initially assess the proposal and the main results. Finally, Sect. 6 summarizes the paper, draws our conclusions and describes our future work.

2 Background

2.1 Software Process Prototyping

In the context of this work, we define a functional prototype as a fully functional model used to test an idea or process in order to learn from its use and provide the specifications to implement this idea or process in the real world. As an element of functional prototyping, the use of simulation models has been an active research topic over the past two decades. Simulation applied to software development projects was introduced in the field of software engineering in the pioneering work of Abdel-Hamid and Madnick [1]. Zhang and his colleagues conclude in their review of the literature that it is an effective tool for the assessment and management of changes made in the projects and software organizations [23]. Similarly, Raffo and Wakeland [16] define the process simulation software as 'possibly the most useful tool to improve the maturity and capability of processes, allowing increasing the level of maturity in CMMi'. In addition, another important advantage of using this type of functional prototyping is its integration with other techniques that promote analysis and knowledge extraction from its results.

2.2 Gamification

It was not until 2011 when gamification was defined in a way that is formally accepted. Deterding and his colleagues [7] defined gamification as the application of the design elements of games in different environments, such as websites, education or social networks.

In the field of software engineering, some applications of gamification have already been published. For example, Singer and Schneider [19] proposed a gamified experience to enhance the practice of software engineering and control versions or Dubois [9] suggested the use of self-organizing models for the gamification of context-sensitive applications. In [14], a case study that shows a real application of game mechanics in software engineering processes is collected. In the context of software testing, some applications of gamification have been also published. For example, Jonathan Khol [12] indicates that gamification helps testing activities to be more interesting, creative, productive and fun, leading to more effective results.

Some companies in the sector are already beginning to apply gamification in its working methods. A comprehensive systematic mapping of the field of gamification in software engineering is shown in [15].

Gamification and SPI. In this section, we focus on the works about the use of gamification in the specific scope of SPI. Dorling and McCaffery [8] propose using gamification in the context of SPICE. In this work, gamification is presented as a solution 'for better user engagement, faster feedback of achievement and more visible progress indicators of process improvement'. Herranz and his colleagues [10, 11] define a methodological gamification framework to guide organizations to apply gamification in the scope of organizational change management of SPI.

To the best of our knowledge, these are the only works reported in the literature that are specifically focused on the application of gamification in the scope of SPI. Our proposal is also placed in the scope of promoting the application of gamification in SPI. However, our contribution takes a further step by conceptually and formally designing a gamification strategy that, based on the use of process functional prototyping, is intended to boost motivation and commitment towards SPI. The technical platform to support the implementation of the strategy is also described.

3   Gamification Framework for SPI

This section describes the process we have followed to design a gamification strategy. The strategy's aim is to gamify the use of process functional prototyping in order to bring together the best of both worlds into the area of SPI initiatives design and test.

First, before starting any process leading to the implementation of a gamification strategy, it must be clear that the benefits intended to be obtained meet your needs. Even though this may sound obvious, a poorly designed gamification strategy leads most probably to failure in meeting your business objectives [5]. In their book, Werbach and Hunter [21] go deeper into this problem and state that gamification is not a solution to every business problem. Hence, the very first stage in the design of a gamification effort is to value if it will help to meet your objectives.

In order to perform the initial evaluation of our approach, we followed Werbach and Hunter's proposal [21] consisting on providing an answer to the following questions:

Q1: Motivation: Where would you derive value from encouraging behavior?

Some studies have highlighted the importance of motivation in the software engineering practice. Beechama et al. [4] performed a systematic literature review to find, among other things, what motivates software developers to be more productive. Furthermore, when analyzing the specific field of SPI, there is a common agreement in the published literature about the importance of commitment and motivation in the success of any SPI initiative [2, 13, 20].

Therefore, the works reported support the thesis that the improvement of motivation is among the most crucial issues in SPI and, consequently, gamification is a suitable tool to be used in this area.

Q2: Meaningful Choices: Are your target activities sufficiently interesting?

When designing a gamification strategy one should concern about the participant's autonomy. For this reason, and based on the fact that change and challenge drive software engineers motivation, we decided to design an environment where the participant could design and explore the result of as many different SPIs initiatives as they could imagine.

Q3: Structure: Can the desired behaviors be modeled through a set of algorithms?
Every gamification strategy needs to be measurable. In our proposal, we track and record measures regarding the complexity of the SPI initiative designed by the participant and the level of success of that initiative. Later, the structure of feedback information and rewards received by the participant are based on these measures.

Q4: Potential Conflicts: Can the game avoid conflicts with existing motivational structures?
Practice shows that some game mechanics intertwined with other organization rewards, such as salary, lead to demotivation [21]. For this reason, we decided that our reward system should be built on the basis of promoting self-improvement, team-improvement and, therefore, organizational improvement.

Once we can provide a positive answer to each of the previous questions, we can conclude that gamification can help solve our problem of improving motivation and commitment towards SPI initiatives.

3.1   Designing the Gamification Strategy

In order to design our gamification strategy, we followed the process described by Werbach and Hunter [21]. The process and the results of each step are described below:

Step 1. Define your business objectives.   In our case, we pursue the following objectives: (a) improve the attitude of participants towards SPI initiatives, (b) increase their motivation towards the design and implementation of SPI, and (c) improve the quality of SPI initiatives.

Step 2. Delineate your target behaviors.   We pretend the participants to use the technique of process functional prototyping to design and evaluate different SPIs initiatives.

Step 3. Describe your players.   We include in our strategy intrinsic motivators aimed at: (a) rewarding individuals for the knowledge and mastery shown when designing process prototypes, (b) promoting effective communication, by rewarding the quality of the solutions proposed, and (c) encouraging competition among teams of participants, to enhance team building.

Step 4. Devise your activities cycles.   Actions such as using the technique, creating prototypes, adding components and complexity to their prototypes, etc. are examples of actions placed in this low-level cycle that are monitored, recorded and awarded. As the data associated to these actions become available, the actions placed at the high-level cycle can be performed. These actions are mostly to challenge the participant with a SPI problem of a higher complexity.

Step 5. Don't forget the fun!   Our current and next software engineers belong to the so-called Generation Y (also known as Millennials). According to their features described in [18], we decided to provide a technological environment that meets their expectations, mostly flexibility provided by a mobile application, instant feedback and collaborative culture.

Step 6. Deploy the appropriate tools. Since our strategy is not based on the interaction of the user with a web-like platform, we decided to develop a particular technical implementation to support the strategy, as described below.

4   Technical Implementation

The technical implementation consists of three tools: *SysDyn*, *OpenBadgesUCA* and *GamAnalyze* that work collaboratively.

The main features of each tool are the following:

1. *SysDyn*. Its main function is to allow the user to create functional simulation-based process prototypes on touch devices such as tablets. It is a mobile application for Android implemented as a hybrid system, i.e., combining native code Android (Java), with HTML5, CSS3 and JavaScript.
2. *OpenBadgesUCA*. *OpenBadgesUCA* aims to effectively send the user's badges awarded by *SysDyn* to their account in Mozilla OpenBadges platform [3]. It is implemented as a web app with a PHP script that receives encrypted data sent by *SysDyn* and decrypts them to allow the user upload their awards to their account in Mozilla OpenBadges. *OpenBadgesUCA* uses HTML5, JavaScript, CSS3 and PHP.
3. *GamAnalyze*. *GamAnalyze* aims to help analyze the data collected by mostly *OpenBadgesUCA* to provide information about the results of the gamification strategy. *GamAnalyze* is a web 2.0 application built using Yii Framework [22].

5   Evaluation of the Proposal

In this section, we present the preliminary results based on a pilot study carried out with a small number of users. For this study, we designed a pilot evaluation based on [17], in which the participants used the framework to solve a given SPI problem and provided their feedback using a post-experience questionnaire.

In order to measure the motivation, we selected the following seven core indicators, partially based on Chou's proposal [6]: (a) Accomplishment, (b) Empowerment, (c) Ownership, (d) Curiosity, (e) Control, (f) Creativity and (g) Social influence. The questionnaire is answered individually. The information is collected by asking the participant to rate, in a Likert-like scale ranged from 1 (lowest value) to 5 (highest value), their agreement with a total of 20 statements.

Five professors of software engineering related subjects and five students attending a course in software processes at the University of Cádiz in Spain took part in the study. They were selected by invitation and participated voluntarily in the pilot study. All of them completed the post-experience questionnaire.

Figure 1 shows the results obtained in this pilot study regarding the motivation indicators. The indicators related to Accomplishment and Empowerment were the best rated. The use of *SysDyn* helped participants make progress and motivated them to overcome the challenges, since the feedback to the SPI initiatives they were designed was immediate thanks to the in-built simulator in *SysDyn*. This automate feedback assisted them in the adjustment of their solutions, helping them feel more creative and engaged in the process.

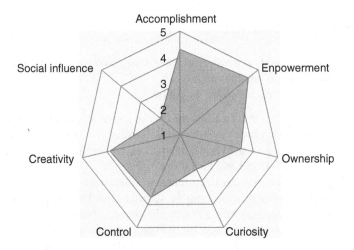

Fig. 1. Radial diagram of the motivation indicators

The indicators of Ownership and Control were also positively rated, since the sense of creating your own solution, by increasing and improving it was present in the experience.

The social influence and the curiosity were the indicators that received the lowest rate. The factor of curiosity is highly influenced by the sense of the unknown, i.e. not knowing what is going to happen after you have made a decision. We consider that this result may be due to the fact that in this stage, our tools did not implement any kind of uncertain or random event that may happen during the simulation of a SPI initiative, making them more unpredictable and fostering the curiosity of the participants. As for the social influence, our tools help the user to share their achievements via Twitter. This is a good option for participants who are motivated by trying to achieve what others have. However, not all our participants seem to have that competitor profile.

6   Conclusions

This paper presents a novel approach towards the improvement of commitment and motivation in SPI initiatives. The main contributions of this work are the following:

1. The application of the technique of simulation-based functional process prototyping to provide a risk-free environment where software engineers can design, test, and evaluate the effect of the SPIs initiatives.
2. The integration of the mentioned technique with gamification as a means of boosting motivation and commitment in SPI.

3. A gamification strategy that supports this integration and that has been conceptually created and designed following the process suggested by Werbach and Hunter [21].
4. A suite of tools that implement and support the technical implementation of the strategy.
5. A pilot study conducted to initially assess the validity of the proposal.

Our future work is mostly focused on the enrichment and improvement of the strategy and the tools developed based on the results of the pilot study. Next, we are planning to develop more experiments to help us validate our proposal.

Acknowledgements. This work has been partially supported by the Spanish Ministry of Science and Technology (grant TIN 2013-46928-C3R) with ERDF funds and the Andalusian Plan for Research, Development and Innovation (grant TIC-195).

References

1. Abdel-Hamid, T., Madnick, S.: Software Project Dynamics: An Integrated Approach, 1st edn. Prentice-Hall, Upper Saddle River (1991)
2. Abrahamssom, P., Iivari, N.: Commitment in software process improvement - in search of the process. In: Proceedings of the 35th Annual Hawaii International Conference on System Sciences (HICSS-35 2002), vol. 8. IEEE Computer Society, Washington (2002)
3. Atkins, T.: It's Raid Night! Gamification for Software Test Teams? http://think testing.files.wordpress.com/2012/05/pqa-gamificationtesting-v120426.pdf. Accessed 9 March 2016
4. Beechama, S., Baddooa, N., Halla, T., Robinsonb, H., Sharpb, H.: Motivation in software engineering: a systematic literature review. Inf. Softw. Technol. **50**(9–10), 860–878 (2008)
5. Burke, B.: Gamification 2020: What Is the Future of Gamification? http://www.grow thengineering.co.uk/what-is-the-future-gamification/. Accessed 9 March 2016
6. Chou, Y.K.: Octalysis – complete Gamification framework. http://yukaichou.com/gamifi cation-examples/octalysis-complete-gamification-framework/. Accessed 9 March 2016
7. Deterding, S., Dixon, D., Khaled, R., Nacke, L.: From game design elements to gamefulness: defining "Gamification". In: MindTrek 2011, 28–30 September, Tampere, Finland (2011)
8. Dorling, A., McCaffery, F.: The gamification of SPICE. In: Mas, A., Mesquida, A., Rout, T., O'Connor, R.V., Dorling, A. (eds.) SPICE 2012. CCIS, vol. 290, pp. 295–301. Springer, Heidelberg (2012). doi:10.1007/978-3-642-30439-2_35
9. Dubois, D.J.: Toward adopting self-organizing models for the gamification of context-aware user applications. In: 2012 2nd International Workshop on Games and Software Engineering (GAS), vol. 9(15), p. 9 (2012)
10. Herranz, E., Colomo-Palacios, R., Amescua-Seco, A.: Towards a new approach to supporting top managers in SPI organizational change management. Procedia Technol. **9**, 129–138 (2013)
11. Herranz, E., Colomo-Palacios, R., de Amescua Seco, A., Yilmaz, M.: Gamification as a disruptive factor in software process improvement initiatives. J. Univ. Comput. Sci. **20**(6), 885–906 (2014)
12. Khol, J.: Software Testing Is a Game. Better Software, pp. 7–8, January/February 2013
13. Niazi, M.: Software process improvement implementation: avoiding critical barriers, CROSSTALK. J. Defense Softw. Eng. **22**(1), 24–27 (2009)

14. Passos, E.B., Medeiros, D.B., Neto, P.A.S., Clua, E.W.G.: Turning real-world software development into a game. In: 2011 Brazilian Symposium on Games and Digital Entertainment (SBGAMES), vol. 260(269), 7–9 November 2011
15. Pedreira, O., García, F., Brisaboa, N., Piattini, M.: Gamification in software engineering – a systematic mapping. Inf. Softw. Technol. **57**, 157–168 (2015)
16. Raffo, D.M., Wakeland, W.: Moving up the CMMI capability and maturity levels using simulation. Technical report CMU/SEI-2008-TR-002 ESC-TR-2008-002, January 2008
17. Runeson, P., Host, M., Rainer, A., Regnell, B.: Case Study Research in Software Engineering: Guidelines and Examples. John Wiley & Sons, Hoboken (2012)
18. Saxena, P., Jain, R.: Managing career aspirations of generation Y at work place. Int. J. Adv. Res. Comput. Sci. Softw. Eng. **2**(7), 114–118 (2012)
19. Singer, L., Schneider, K.: It was a bit of a race: gamification of version control. In: 2012 2nd International Workshop on Games and Software Engineering (GAS), vol. 5(8), p. 9, June 2012
20. Stelzer, D., Mellis, W.: Success factors of organizational change in software process improvement. Softw. Process. Improv. Pract. **4**(4), 227–250 (1998)
21. Werbach, K., Hunter, D.: For the Win. How Game Thinking can Revolutionize your Business. Wharton Digital Press, Philadelphia (2012)
22. Yii framework. The Fast, Secure and Professional PHP Framework. http://www.yii framework.com/. Accessed 9 March 2016
23. Zhang, H., Kitchenham, B., Pfahl, D.: Software process simulation modeling: facts, trends and directions. In: Proceedings of the 15th Asia-Pacific Software Engineering Conference, pp. 59–66. IEEE Computer Society (2008)

Exploring Mobile User Experience Through Code Quality Metrics

Gerardo Canfora[2], Andrea Di Sorbo[2], Francesco Mercaldo[1(✉)],
and Corrado Aaron Visaggio[2]

[1] Institute for Informatics and Telematics,
National Research Council of Italy (CNR), Pisa, Italy
francesco.mercaldo@iit.cnr.it
[2] Department of Engineering, University of Sannio, Benevento, Italy
{canfora,disorbo,visaggio}@unisannio.it

Abstract. Smartphones have been absorbed into everyday life at an astounding rate, and continue to become more and more widely used. Much of the success of the mobile paradigm can be attributed to the discover of a huge market. Users may pick from a large collection of software, in domains ranging from games to productivity. Each platform makes the task of installing and removing apps very simple, further inciting users to try new software. Smartphone users may download applications from the official Google Play market, but those applications do not pass any review process, and can be downloaded very shortly after submission. Google Play does not offer any mechanism to ensure the user about the quality of the installed app, and this is particularly true for user experience: the user simply downloads and runs the application. In this paper we propose a features set to evaluate the code quality of Android applications to understand how user experience varies in mobile ecosystem. Our findings show that developers need to focus on software quality in order to make their applications usable from the user point of view.

Keywords: Software quality · Mobile applications · User experience

1 Introduction and Background

Since its inception, the smartphone has quickly become one of the most ubiquitous technological artifacts in today's society.

Global sales of smartphones to end users totaled 349 million units in the first quarter of 2016, a 3.9 percent increase over the same period in 2015, according to Gartner: smartphone sales represented the 78 percent of total mobile phone sales in the first quarter of 2016[1]. Sales continue to increase year after year, as the smartphones become even more accessible and intertwined in day-to-day life. Such phones have achieved success due in part to easily available applications (apps), typically provided by official market.

---

[1] http://www.gartner.com/newsroom/id/3323017.

© Springer International Publishing AG 2016
P. Abrahamsson et al. (Eds.): PROFES 2016, LNCS 10027, pp. 705–712, 2016.
DOI: 10.1007/978-3-319-49094-6_59

Apps have major implications for both end users and software developers, especially in terms of software quality and user experience.

Indeed, mobile device users may download applications from the official Google Play store (formerly the Android Market). Apps on the Play Store are not reviewed in any way, and can be downloaded very shortly after submission. This unrestricted model is often called the "wild west" [1]. In this paradigm, more responsibility is placed on the user to screen an app and determine whether it is safe and whether it meets his needs. This can be problematic as the app may be new, and the user likely has little insight into how the app works.

No criteria is given as to how these apps should be scored, so the decision is left completely to the user. Users may also leave comments regarding the app. Many of these indicate the user's feelings toward the quality of the app, often advising others on whether the app is worth downloading.

With such a large presence of apps and markets, and their ever-increasing popularity, the question of how to determine the quality of an app and its marketplace is one that warrants consideration.

In this paper we evaluate mobile applications extracting a set of code quality features in order to investigate the user experience evolution in Android environment.

Different authors propose metrics for evaluating the user experience on mobile devices. Authors in [2] apply a set of features with the aim at understanding whether there are differences in terms of usability between trusted and malware mobile samples. Researchers in [3] developed a platform named ATE for supporting design of UX tests. User perception is obtained by measuring the smartphone's resources (i.e. time, memory occupation). The main difference with these works is that both of the papers do not address the problem of UX evaluation through code quality metrics.

The paper poses the following research question:

- RQ: is there a difference in user experience among mobile applications developed in different years?

The paper is organized as follows: the next section describes the methodology, the third section discusses the results and, finally, conclusion and future works are given in the last section.

2   The Methodology

In this section we explain the rationale behind the features set we extracted and the approach we used to extract them.

We defined a set of features for evaluating the quality of Android mobile applications from users' side, i.e. user experience (UX) related.

We consider following categories with their respective features:

- *Separation of View and Controller*: we compute these features in order to assess the conformance of each app to the model-view-controller (MVC) architectural pattern. In this pattern, commonly used for user-interface software, there are three components. The model contains the data for the application. A view presents something to the user, generally based on the model, and allows interaction. Finally, the controller implements the program logic, mediating the interaction between the view and the model. Android development is based around this pattern. Activities are the controllers, plain old Java objects (POJO) comprise the model, and the previously discussed mechanisms (XML or Java) comprise the view. A fundamental tenet of the pattern is that views should not be defined in controllers. We compiled a list of view objects from the Android.widget package[2], and used it to determine where view objects were defined.

In this category fall following metrics:

- $SVC1$: this feature represents the number of views in controllers;
- $SVC2$: this feature represents the number of views not in controllers;
- $SVC3$: this feature represents the percentage of views defined outside of controllers.

While the previous features are related to software quality, the following categories directly influence the user's experience. We detail each of these features.

- *Unchecked Bundles.* On any given day, one in five Android users will experience a crash, and up to half will uninstall the offending app[3]. Research has shown that the most common reason for app crashes is the occurrence of a NullPointerException [4]. Many of these are left uncaught and thus cause crashes. The NullPointerException is often manifested in the implementation of the application lifecycle. In order to pass data among views, the developer can use a custom object, the Intent, to wrap data. The developer must call the putExtras() method of the Intent class, which creates a Bundle, another custom object, to wrap the data. From the receiving end, there is a class-level Intent. A Bundle can accessed from the Intent using the getExtras() method. In some cases this method might return null[4], meaning that if left unchecked it may lead to a crash. Thus, the developer should handle the possibility of the exception being thrown when using Bundles from Intents to prevent the app from crashing. This can be accomplished using a try-catch block or an if statement. We counted the number of Bundles in each application.

In this category the following features fall:

- UB1: this feature counts the number of Bundles in each application;
- UB2: this feature counts the number of Checked Bundles in each application;
- UB3: this feature counts the number of Unchecked Bundles in each application.
- *Token Exceptions.* In Android development, the Context object is used to store information regarding, as expected, the current context of the application[5].

---

[2] https://developer.android.com/reference/android/widget/package-summary.html.
[3] http://visual.ly/android-errors-real-time?utm_source=visually_embed.
[4] https://developer.android.com/reference/android/content/Intent.html.
[5] https://developer.android.com/reference/android/content/Context.html.

This is necessary to perform certain actions, such as showing a notification. In order to show a dialog, the context of an Activity must be used. Using any other context, such as that of a service, will throw a Window-Manager.BadTokenException[6]. We counted the number of dialogs shown from classes other than activities, which might lead to crashes.

This category includes the following metric:

- **TE:** this feature represents the number of potential bad token exception.
- *Number of Fragments.* The Fragment was added to the Android SDK level 11. It represents a behavior or a portion of user-interface in an Activity. This can be combined to create a fragmented interface[7]. Since these are new to the platform, we determined that they might be useful in determining quality, as developers may have trouble adjusting to new techniques.

In this category falls following metric:

- **NF:** this feature counts the number of fragments in each application.

In order to study the evolution of UX, relying on the assumption for which apps presenting a previous packaging date have been developed earlier than apps presenting a subsequent packaging date, (i) we grouped together apps presenting same packaging year, and (ii) for each resulting group we computed the correspondent set of descriptive statistic indicators for all the features we computed, in order to describe the evolution trends of each feature belonging to the dataset. Specifically, we computed for each feature: (i) Minimum, (ii) 1st Quartile, (iii) Median, (iv) 3rd Quartile, (v) Maximum, and (vi) Mean.

3   Evaluation

We designed an experiment [5,6] in order to evaluate the effectiveness of the proposed feature set, expressed through the research question RQ stated in the introduction. More specifically, the evaluation is aimed at verifying whether the eight features are able to highlight differences from the UX point of view in Android mobile applications developed in different years.

We conducted measurements on a dataset containing 15,426 Android trusted apps downloaded from the Google's official app store[8]. We identified Google Play as a target for our study for several reasons. This is by far the largest and most used source for Android applications, with over a million apps in July 2013 and was most recently placed at 2 million apps in February 2016[9]. The majority of devices sold are compatible and come with the market preinstalled, making it the most accessible. In fact, using other markets requires the explicit permission of the user. In order to download applications we crawled the Google Play market using an open-source crawler[10]. The obtained dataset includes samples belonging

---

[6] https://possiblemobile.com/2013/06/context/.

[7] https://developer.android.com/guide/components/fragments.html.

[8] https://play.google.com/store.

[9] http://www.statista.com/statistics/266210/.

[10] https://github.com/liato/android-market-api-py.

to all different categories available on the market. The crawler is configured to equally download applications from the different categories of apps.

The .apk file of an Android application is basically a zip archive containing all the resources an application needs to run, such as the application binary code and images. Using this package format all the files that makes an application go from the computer of the developer to end user devices without any modification. In particular, all metadata of the files contained in the .apk package, for instance the last modification date, are preserved. All bytecode, representing the application binary code, is assembled into a classes.dex file that is produced at packaging-time. Thus the last modification date of this file represents the packaging time.

We retrieve the date of the compilation at which the Dalvik bytecode was produced in order to infer the historical distribution of the samples in our dataset. Specifically, we retrieve application packaging in: 2008 (178 samples), 2009 (143 samples), 2010 (167 samples), 2011 (629 samples), 2012 (1548 samples), 2013 (3640 samples), 2014 (2448 samples), 2015 (6423 samples), 2016 (250 samples).

We provide a comparison of descriptive statistics of the populations of applications.

Figure 1 shows the boxplots related to the features $SCV1$, $SCV2$, $SCV3$, $UB1$, $UB2$, $UB3$, TE and NF (from left to right).

The boxplots related to $SCV1$ feature show that the value of the views in controller is very similar between apps developed in different years. The implementation of a view in a controller is considered a bad programming practice, the boxplot suggests that this practice is quite diffused in Android programming indifferently from the packaging year. The boxplots related to the $SVC2$ feature, i.e. the number of views that are not in the controller, is symptomatic of the fact that Android programmers employ frameworks for developing applications, especially in the more recent year (i.e., 2016): this is reflecting the increasing trend in the $SCV2$ feature. The trend is also considerable in 2009 but, as explained by previous boxplots, developers anyway make use of view embedded into controllers. The boxplots related to the $SVC3$ feature, i.e. the percentage of views defined outside of the controllers, confirm the trend we highlighted in discussing $SVC2$: Android developers take into account the best practices of software engineering when they design the application, as matter of fact newer and older mobile applications present the 100 % of percentage of view correctly defined outside of controllers.

Bundles are generally used for passing data between various Android activities, this is the reason why a not handled bundle may cause NullPointerException whether expected data are not returned. Boxplots show that when the packaging year is increasing, the number of bundled employ by the application is increasing: this may happen because mobile applications are quickly increasing in complexity and functionality to offer to end users. Applications developed in 2010, 2015 and 2016 exhibit an overusing of bundles if compared with previous packaging years, as demonstrated by boxplots related to the $UB1$ feature, i.e. the number of Bundles in each application.

Boxplots related to the $UB2$ feature, i.e. the number of Checked Bundles in each application show that developer do not take into account that the

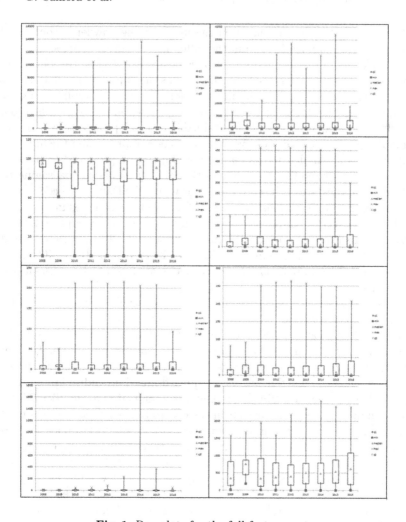

Fig. 1. Box plots for the full features set.

application can cause a NullPointException due for a Bundle, i.e. the usage of check related to Bundle is very limited and it is almost similar between different packaging years. The boxplots related to the $UB3$ feature, i.e. the number of Unchecked Bundles in each application, reflect the results of the $UB2$ feature: we denote an increment of Unchecked Bundles in newer Android applications. With the increase of functionality and the usage of web-services required by new applications developers have to employ more and more Bundles in order to exchange data between activities: when developers do not handle bundle exception, they make their applications sensitive to unpredictable crashes due to NullPointerException. This result has a dramatic impact on UX, because the application may crash at any time unnoticed by the user.

To show a dialog, the context of an Activity must be invoked. Using any other context, such as that of a service, will throw a WindowManager.BadTokenException. The boxplots boxplots related to the TE feature, i.e. the number of potential token exception in each application, do not exhibit an increment between different packaging years: this happens because developer do not increasing employ dialogs shown from classes other than activities, that may cause unexpected crashes.

Fragments represent a behavior or a portion of user-interface in an Activity. This can be combined to create a fragmented interface. Basically a fragment is a modular section of an activity, which has its own lifecycle, receives its own input events: it is a sort of "sub activity" that it is possible to reuse in different activities. The boxplots related to the NF feature, i.e. the number of fragments in each application, show that the trend increases when the packaging year increases. This happens for a two-fold motivation: the first one is that developers learn quickly how to use enhancements provided by new SDK version, but on the other side they don't care of software quality. As matter of fact, Fragments were created to embed small user-interface portion in an Activity but they do not exceed with using them. Indeed, an extensive use of Fragments is not in line with the Separation of View and Controller.

Table 1 shows the results obtained for each median indicator we considered in the study.

Table 1. Median indicator for each feature we computed for the packaging year.

Feature	2008	2009	2010	2011	2012	2013	2014	2015	2016
$SCV1$	49	137	73	82	81	86	73	81	90
$SCV2$	711	1327	810	755,5	924	1010	1099	1178	1487
$SCV3$	95,51	91,87	87,08	90,56	88,79	89,95	91,82	91,56	91,14
$UB1$	0	22	10	10	10	13	11	15	10
$UB2$	0	8	1	4	4	6	5	6	6
$UB3$	0	11	4	5	4	6	5	9	4
TE	0	1	2	2	1	2	2	1	0
NF	345	764	348	378,5	404	512	490	548	628

From results we denote that $SVC2$ median feature exhibits greater values if compared with the $SVC1$ median i.e., the number of views not in controllers exceed the number of views in controllers. From the software engineering side this is a result representative that developer take into account MCV pattern when they developer mobile applications, and from the UX ones, being the view not coupled from business logic, the application will be easily adaptable by the developer to run on a plethora of devices with different screen size with the same UX level from the user point of view. The $SVC3$ feature median, i.e. the percentage of views defined outside of controllers, confirms this software quality positive trend.

The $UB1$, $UB2$ and $UB3$ features median exhibits that recent mobile application make less use of Bundles if compared with previous developed ones. Considering that a non handled bundle can cause a NullPointerException and the consequently crash of the application with the correspondent lose of data, we conclude from this analysis that developer take into account to caught exceptions from Bundle, in order to guarantee an high UX to the users.

Relatively to TE feature median, the table shows that the number of potential to token exceptions in each application is almost the same between different Android application. Developers are aware that this may cause unexpected crashes and they avoid to use them, for the benefit of either software quality and UX. The NF feature median increments occur in recent packaging years. The excessive usage of Fragment is a bad programming practice, because it pushes to include small portions of graphics interface into business logic classes. As matter of fact, an extensive use of Fragments, merging view and controllers, is resulting in a consequently poor software quality and UX.

4   Conclusions and Future Works

In this paper, we extract from 15,426 applications a set of features in order to evaluate the quality of user experience in the software for mobile devices.

Results obtained show that Android mobile applications present several indicators that make us think that the developers do not care about the quality of user experience in a systematic way. Future works concern the evaluation of the review mechanism on Google Play to verify whether the user reviews are coherent with the software quality and user experience.

References

1. Higa, D.: Walled gardens versus the wild west. Computer **41**(10), 102–105 (2008)
2. Mercaldo, F., Visaggio, C.A.: Evaluating mobile malware by extracting user experience-based features. In: Abrahamsson, P., Corral, L., Oivo, M., Russo, B. (eds.) PROFES 2015. LNCS, vol. 9459, pp. 497–512. Springer, Heidelberg (2015). doi:10.1007/978-3-319-26844-6_37
3. Canfora, G., Mercaldo, F., Visaggio, C.A., DAngelo, M., Furno, A., Manganelli, C.: A case study of automating user experience-oriented performance testing on smartphones. In: 2013 IEEE Sixth International Conference on Software Testing, Verification and Validation, pp. 66–69. IEEE (2013)
4. Kechagia, M., Spinellis, D.: Undocumented and unchecked: exceptions that spell trouble. In: Proceedings of the 11th Working Conference on Mining Software Repositories, pp. 312–315. ACM (2014)
5. Carver, J.C., Juristo Juzgado, N., Baldassarre, M.T., Vegas Hernández, S.: Replications of software engineering experiments. Empirical Softw. Eng. **19**(2), 267–276 (2014)
6. Ardimento, P., Caivano, D., Cimitile, M., Visaggio, G.: Empirical investigation of the efficacy and efficiency of tools for transferring software engineering knowledge. J. Inf. Knowl. Manage. **7**(03), 197–207 (2008)

Early Usability in Model-Driven Game Development

Silvia Abrahão$^{(\boxtimes)}$, Emilio Insfran, José Ángel Carsí,
and Adrián Fernandez

DSIC – Universitat Politècnica de València, Camino de Vera s/n,
46022 Valencia, Spain
{sabrahao,einsfran,jcarsi,afernandez}@dsic.upv.es

Abstract. Video games are one of the most influential types of software today. However, they are becoming more and more complex to design and evaluate. In this context, Model-Driven Development approaches seem to be very promising since a video game can be obtained by transforming platform-independent models into platform-specific models that can be in turn transformed into code. In previous work, we defined a usability evaluation method specifically tailored to this type of development process. This paper shows how this method can be used to evaluate the usability of video games in early stages of a model-driven development process. The method relies on a model that decomposes usability into measurable attributes and metrics specific for the video game domain. To show the feasibility of the method, we performed an early usability evaluation of a video game for the XBOX360 platform.

Keywords: Video game · Usability inspection · Model-Driven Development

1 Introduction

Video games are one of the most influential types of software today. Games are being used for far more than entertainment, with applications including social marketing, education, and specialist training. The video game development industry is a strong economic sector that deals with the development of highly interactive software, i.e., video games, for a wide variety of technology platforms.

The interaction between the game and the players is a critical factor in the success of a video game. Usability and playability are considered to be the most important quality factors of video games [10]. *Usability* is defined as the degree to which the video game can be understood, learned, used and is attractive to the user, when used under specified conditions [6]. *Playability* is defined as a collection of criteria with which to evaluate a product's gameplay or interaction [7]. Playability is often evaluated by using early prototypes and iterative cycles of playtesting during the entire video game development cycle. However, the evaluation of usability in current video game

This research work is funded by the Value@Cloud project (MINECO TIN2013-46300-R).

© Springer International Publishing AG 2016
P. Abrahamsson et al. (Eds.): PROFES 2016, LNCS 10027, pp. 713–722, 2016.
DOI: 10.1007/978-3-319-49094-6_60

development practices is often deferred to late stages in the game development cycle, thus signifying that usability problems from early stages may be propagated to late stages of the development, and consequently making their detection and correction a very expensive task. The state of the art for game development in software engineering has been summarized in a systematic literature review [1]. The results of this review show a significant lack of studies in the key dimensions of video game quality: playability and usability.

Today there is no common agreement what kind of usability evaluation methods can and should be used to enhance the design of games [3]. Traditional video game development approaches do not take full advantage of a usability evaluation of the game design artifacts that are produced during the early stages of the development. These intermediate artifacts (e.g., screen mock-ups or screen flow diagrams) are used to guide game developers but not to perform usability evaluations.

This problem may be alleviated by using a Model-Driven Development (MDD) approach due to its intrinsic traceability mechanisms that are established by the transformation processes. Platform-independent models (PIM) or platform-specific models (PSM) can be evaluated during the early stages of video game development to identify and correct some of the usability problems prior to the generation of the source code of the final video game application. We are aware that not all the usability problems can be detected based on the evaluation of models since they are limited by their own expressiveness and, most important, they may not predict the user behavior and preferences. However, the use of inspection methods for detecting usability problems can be complemented with other evaluations performed with end-users. In previous work, we defined a usability evaluation method specifically tailored to model-driven video game development. In this paper, we show how this method can be used to evaluate the usability of a video game for the XBOX360 platform.

This paper is organized as follows. Section 2 discusses our usability inspection method. Section 3 describes a strategy to apply this method for performing early usability evaluations in model-driven video game development. Section 4 presents the evaluation of a specific game to illustrate the inspection method. Finally, Sect. 5 presents our conclusions and further work.

2   Usability Inspection Method

Our usability inspection method relies on a Video Game Usability Model [5] which contains a set of usability attributes and measures that can be applied by the designer in the following phases of a MDD development process: (i) in the PIM, to assess different models that specify the video game application independently of platform details (e.g., screen flow diagrams, screen mock-ups, screen navigation diagrams); (ii) in the PSM, to assess the concrete design models related to a specific platform (if they exist); and (iii) in the code model, to assess the generated video game.

The goal of this usability model is to extend the Software Quality Model proposed in the ISO/IEC 25010 (SQuaRE), specifically the usability characteristic, for specifying, measuring, and evaluating the usability of video games that are produced throughout a model-driven development process from the end-users perspective.

The SQuaRE states that the usability of a software product can be decomposed into the following sub-characteristics: *Appropriateness Recognisability*, which refers to how the software product enables users to recognize whether the software is appropriate for their needs; *Learnability*, which refers to how the software product enables users to learn its application; *Ease of Use*, which refers to how the software product makes it easy for users to operate and control it; *Helpfulness*, which refers to how the software product provides help when users need assistance; *Technical Accessibility*, which refers to how the software product provides help when users need assistance; and *Attractiveness*, which refers to how appealing the software product is to the user.

Since these sub-characteristics are too abstract we decompose them into usability attributes and measures as showed in the second and third column of Table 1. The attributes have been defined by considering and adapting ergonomic criteria for user interfaces [2] as well as knowledge from other domains such as Web development [4], and the underlying usability principles from game development [8]. The measures are generic to ensure that they could be operationalized in different software artifacts from any model-driven video game development method.

It is worth to mention that we cannot guarantee that our usability model covers all the possible usability attributes for the video game domain. Our model is an attempt to operationalize subjective heuristics, usability guidelines and recommendations into usability attributes that can be quantified by means of measures.

3 Evaluation Process

In order to apply the Video Game Usability Model to a specific model-driven video game development, we follow a usability evaluation process. A typical video game development process consists in the following activities: requirements specification, game design, implementation, and playtesting, along with the usability evaluation. The usability evaluation is conducted by applying the following steps:

1. The establishment of evaluation requirements. *Evaluation profiles* are chosen to specify which model-driven game development method is employed, which type of video game is developed, what the target technological platform is, and at which target players the game is aimed. Given a specific model-driven game development method, *software artifacts (models)* and *usability attributes* from the Video Game Usability Model are selected to perform early usability evaluations. The measures associated with the selected attributes are instantiated for a specific software artifact of the game development method, and the thresholds for the measures are established.

2. Early usability evaluation. Each selected game software artifact is evaluated with a set of measures. Each measure returns a numeric value within a specific threshold that indicates whether there is a usability problem in the video game. A usability report is generated with the usability problem details and suggestions to solve them.

3. Usability evaluation in-use. Even when early usability evaluation is performed on models, the game should also be further evaluated with end-users in specific

Table 1. Decomposition of the SQuaRE into measurable attributes and generic measures

Sub-characteristics	Attributes	Measures
Appropriateness Recognisability	Visibility	Percentage of screen usage
	Interface Simplicity	Total number of GUI elements
	Control Simplicity	Total number of control mappings
	Consistency	Ratio of similitude between screens
Learnability	Feedback	Total number of GUI elements displaying state changes
		Ratio of GUI elements highlighting state changes
		Ratio of meaningful messages
	Tutorial Support	Tutorial interactivity
		Tutorial coverage
Ease of Use	Control Consistency	Ratio of similitude between colliding game actions
	Internal Navigational Simplicity	Internal menu navigation depth
		Internal menu navigation breadth
	External Navigational Simplicity	Shortest Path To Gameplay
		Shortest Path To Exit
		Shortest Return Path To Gameplay
Helpfulness	Hint Support	Availability of hints
		Hint understandability
	Goal Support	Goal visibility
		Goal understandability
Technical Accessibility	Subtitle Support	Availability of subtitles
		Subtitle support for hearing impaired players
		Subtitle style differentiation
	Magnifier Support	Subtitle resize support
Attractiveness	Customization	Control remapping
		Interface customization
	Wait Reduction	Inactive wait
		Skip capability of non-interactive content

contexts of use. Since this paper focuses on early usability evaluation in model-driven development, usability evaluation in-use is not within the scope of this work.

After usability evaluations, game designers should perform changes to the models in order to solve the usability problems. Early usability problems detected in the game design can be corrected in each model of the corresponding development stage (e.g., PIM, PSM) prior to the code generation.

4   Applying the Usability Inspection Method

The usability model was applied to a 2D fighting game for the XBOX 360, which is similar to the commercial Capcom's Street Fighter V™ for the same platform.

4.1   Model-Driven Video Game Development

Model-driven video game development [9] is a game development methodology that focuses on defining platform-independent models which provide a precise high-level specification of the gameplay, control, and graphical user interface of the video game under development. We focus only on the following platform-independent models that offer the most suitable modeling primitives for usability evaluation:

Screen Navigation Diagram. Video games display visual information on different game screens through which players can navigate. Figure 1 shows the screen navigation metamodel. A screen navigation diagram can be specified by using *screen nodes* and *screen transitions*.

A game screen represents a game state in the screen navigation. Two special screen nodes denote the *initial* and *final* states that define the screens on which a video game starts and ends. Screen transitions represent a change of state in the screen navigation, i.e., moving from one screen to another. Screen transitions are triggered by *screen events* such as control interactions, time, or rule executions.

Screen Layout Diagram. When the flow of screens is clearly defined in a navigation diagram, each game screen GUI should be further specified by using a screen layout diagram. Figure 2 shows the screen layout metamodel. A screen layout diagram can be specified by different GUI *display primitives* that can be positioned and sized on the screen. These primitives provide a visual representation of a game attribute which is previously defined in the gameplay perspective. There are four types of GUI display primitives: *numeric containers* and *textual containers* which represent information as plain numbers or text, *image containers* which represent information using 2D images

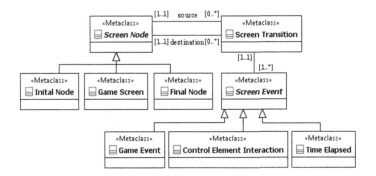

Fig. 1. Excerpt of the Screen Navigation metamodel

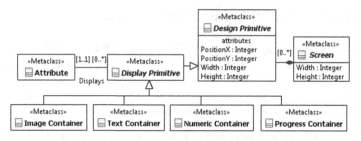

Fig. 2. Excerpt of the Screen Layout metamodel

or animations, and *progress containers* which represent the progress of information as a relative percentage of a colored bar or a succession of small icons.

Control Mapping Diagram. A game control mapping defines how players interact with controller devices to communicate with the game. Figure 3 shows the control mapping metamodel. A *controller* is a device that players use to communicate with the game. Controllers are made up of smaller *control elements* such as keys, buttons, joysticks and triggers that players use to communicate atomic game interactions. *Control element interactions* such as pressing or releasing a button, moving a joystick, or pulling a trigger, activate the specific action rules of a player's character. A control mapping diagram specifies which *control elements* and *interactions* are associated with gameplay *actions*.

4.2 Establishment of the Usability Evaluation Requirements

The evaluation profile of the 2D fighting game example used is as follows:

- Game development method: the game is designed by using a model-driven development method. The software artifacts involved in the usability evaluation are the screen navigation, the screen layout and the control mapping diagrams.
- Type of video game: the game belongs to the 2D fighting genre.

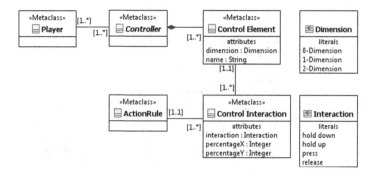

Fig. 3. Excerpt of the Control Mapping metamodel

- Target technological platform: the game is developed for the XBOX 360.
- Target audience: the game, like most 2D fighting games, is targeted at a hardcore audience of players who have a great deal of previous experience in games of the same genre, and who thus know and expect certain common genre conventions.

Table 2. Operationalized measures for the case study

Measure	Percentage of Screen Usage (PSU)
Attribute	Appropriateness Recognisability/Visibility
Artifact	Screen Layout Diagram (PIM)
Operationalization	Each display primitive of the Screen Layout Diagram has attributes for its width and height. The screen meta-class also has attributes for its width and height. Both the primitive display size and the screen size can be defined as the product of their width and height
Formula	PSU = (Sum of all display primitives width x height) / (screen width x height)
Thresholds	The XBOX 360 is typically played on a high-resolution TV, which benefits visibility. Hardcore players are also well trained in the specific genre conventions of 2D fighting games, thus minimizing the space needed to convey the game's visual information. **Critical** Usability Problem: [PSU > 0.5] **Low** Usability Problem: [0.1 < PSU ≤ 0.2] **Medium** Usability Problem: [0.2 < PSU ≤ 0.5] **No** Usability Problem: [PSU ≤ 0.1]
Measure	Total Number of GUI Elements (TNGUIE)
Attribute	Appropriateness Recognisability/Interface Simplicity
Artifact	Screen Layout Diagram (PIM)
Operationalization	Each display primitive of the Screen Layout Diagram is a GUI of the screen
Formula	TNGUIE = Sum of all display primitives of the Screen Layout Diagram
Thresholds	Hardcore players are experienced in the genre conventions of 2D fighting games and they expect their typical interface layout, with a number of GUI elements between 3 and 10. **Critical** Usability Problem: [TNGUIE > 10] **Low** Usability Problem: [3 < TNGUIE ≤ 5] **Medium** Usability Problem: [5 < TNGUIE ≤ 10] **No** Usability Problem: [0 ≤ TNGUIE ≤ 3]
Measure	Shortest Return Path To Gameplay (SRPTG)
Attribute	Ease of Use/External Navigational Simplicity
Artifact	Screen Navigation Diagram (PIM)
Operationalization	Each screen primitive of the Screen Navigation Diagram can be associated with a game screen.
Formula	SRPTG = minimum number of transitions between the game over screen node and the gameplay screen node.
Thresholds	Hardcore players value immediateness of menu interfaces. **Medium** Usability Problem: [SRPTG > 2] **No** Usability Problem: [0 ≤ SRPTG ≤ 2]

For the sake of simplicity, only two usability sub-characteristics were evaluated: *Appropriateness Recognisability* and Ease *of Use*. The selected attributes were *Visibility*, *Interface Simplicity*, and *External Navigation Simplicity*, whose associated measures are shown in Sect. 2. The operationalization of the aforementioned measures are presented below in Table 2. Note that the measure thresholds are defined in accordance with specific information from the evaluation profile for the video game evaluated in this case study. We gather this information from game developers but we are aware that these values need to be empirically validated to determine which thresholds are more appropriate for pre-defined evaluation profiles.

4.3   Early Usability Evaluation of Software Artifacts

Figure 4 shows the main GUI elements of the game rendered in a Screen Layout Diagram. Figure 5 shows the game screens and transitions in a Screen Flow Diagram. The Control Mapping Diagram is not rendered as a figure for the sake of simplicity: the game uses a 2-dimensional control element (the left thumbstick associated with character movement), and six 1-dimensional control elements (the buttons associated with light/medium/strong punches and kicks).

With regard to the Screen Layout Diagram (see Fig. 4), we apply the two specific measures shown for this artifact in Sect. 4.2 in order to evaluate the *Visibility* and *Interface Simplicity* of the video game. By applying the **Percentage of Screen Usage** formula we obtain PSU = 0.09 (by dividing the sum of the size of all the display primitives by the screen size). This indicates that there is no usability problem related to the *Visibility* attribute since PSU is in the threshold [PSU ≤ 0.1]. By applying the **Total Number of GUI Elements** formula we obtain TNGUIE = 13 (by counting all the display primitives in the diagram), which leads to a critical usability problem related to the *Interface Simplicity* attribute since the value obtained is [TNGUIE > 10]. Table 3 shows the usability report associated to this usability problem (UP001).

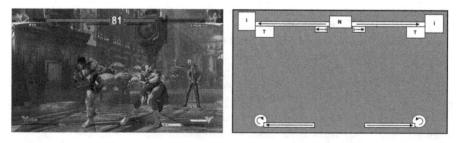

Fig. 4. *Street Fighter V* screenshot and the corresponding Screen Layout Diagram

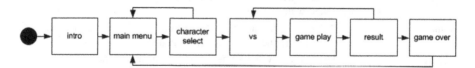

Fig. 5. *Street Fighter V* Screen Flow Diagram

Table 3. Usability report for usability problem UP001

ID	UP001
Description	There are too many GUI Elements on the same game screen.
Affected attribute	Appropriateness Recognisability/Interface Simplicity
Severity level	Critical [TNGUIE = 13 > 10]
Artifact evaluated	Screen Layout Diagram
Problem source	Screen Layout Diagram
Recommendations	Collapse GUI elements that render the same information, such as the image and the text container that portray the fighter portrait and name

Table 4. Usability report for usability problem UP002

ID	UP002
Description	Players need to navigate through several screens to restart the game
Affected attribute	Ease of Use/External Navigational Simplicity
Severity level	Medium [SRPTG = 4 > 2]
Artifact evaluated	Screen Flow Diagram
Problem source	Screen Flow Diagram
Recommendations	Add a shortcut (e.g., retry) from the game-over screen to the gameplay screen

With regard to the Screen Flow Diagram (see Fig. 5), we can use up to three specific measures in order to evaluate the *External Navigation Simplicity* attribute belonging to the video game's *Ease of Use* sub-characteristic. In this example, we use the **Shortest Return Path To Gameplay** formula obtaining a SRPTG = 4 (by counting the screen transitions from *gameplay*, *result*, and *vs* screens), which leads to a medium usability problem related to the *External Navigation Simplicity*, since the value obtained is in the threshold [SRPTG > 2]. Table 4 presents this usability problem (UP002).

After applying the measures, we can conclude with regard to the *Appropriateness Recognisability* sub-characteristic that the video game has poor *Interface Simplicity* but very good *Visibility*, i.e., the game has a complex interface but effectively manages to keep gameplay visible. With regard to the *Ease of Use* sub-characteristic, we realize that the video game has poor *External Navigational Simplicity*, i.e., the game has a complex flow of screens which makes it difficult to restart the game.

5   Conclusions

We presented a usability inspection method that can be used in early stages of model-driven video game development. The method relies on a usability model that has been developed specifically for the video game domain. This model is aligned with the SQuaRE standard and allows the evaluation of the usability of video games developed according to a model-driven development process. Usability is considered throughout the entire game development, thus enabling a more usable video game to be developed and thereby reducing effort during the maintenance stage.

The inherent features of model-driven development provide a suitable context in which to perform usability evaluations since usability problems that may appear in the final application can be detected and corrected at the model level. Although the proposed usability inspection method has been operationalized to a specific model-driven development process that has been used to develop a video game for the XBOX360 platform, it can also be integrated into other model-driven video game development processes by establishing the relationships between the generic measures from the usability model and the modeling primitives of the different software artifacts of the selected development process.

Nevertheless, we are aware that a further comparison with the users' perception on the usability of a video game obtained by applying a model-driven development process is needed. For this reason, we are currently performing an empirical study to compare the predicted usability of two video games measured using a set of metrics from the Usability Model with the perceived usability of these video games.

Future work includes the application of the method to industrial case studies, the definition of aggregation mechanisms for combining the values obtained from individual measures into usability indicators. We also plan to empirically validate the effectiveness of the proposed usability inspection method by means of controlled experiments in which the results of the evaluations obtained at the model level will be compared to the ones obtained when players interact with the generated video game.

References

1. Ampatzoglou, A., Stamelos, I.: Software engineering research for computer games: a systematic review. Inf. Softw. Technol. **52**(9), 888–901 (2010). doi:10.1016/j.infsof.2010. 05.004. ISSN:0950-5849
2. Bastien, J.M., Scapin, D.L.: Ergonomic Criteria for the Evaluation of Human-Computer Interfaces, version 2.1 (1993)
3. Bernhaupt, R., Eckschlager, M., Tscheligi, M.: Methods for evaluating games: how to measure usability and user experience in games? In: Proceedings of the International Conference on Advances in Computer Entertainment Technology, pp. 309–310. ACM Press, Salzburg (2007)
4. Calero, C., Ruiz, J., Piattini, M.: Classifying web metrics using the web quality model. Emerald Group Publishing Limited **29**(3), 227–248 (2005)
5. Fernandez, A., Insfran, E., Abrahão S., Carsí J.A., Montero, E.: Integrating usability evaluation into model-driven video game development. In: 4th International Conference on Human-Centered Software Engineering (HCSE), Toulouse, France (2012)
6. ISO/IEC 25010: Systems and software engineering, Systems and software Quality Requirements and Evaluation (SQuaRE), System and software quality models (2011)
7. Järvinen, A., Heliö, S., Mäyrä, F.: Communication and Community in Digital Entertainment Services. Prestudy Research Report, Hypermedia Laboratory, University of Tampere, Tampere (2002). http://tampub.uta.fi/tup/951-44-5432-4.pdf
8. Microsoft: Best Practices for Indie Games 3.1. http://create.msdn.com/en-US/education/catalog/article/bestpractices_31
9. Montero, E., Carsí, J.A.: A platform-independent model for videogame gameplay specification. In: Digital Games Research Association Conference (DiGRA 2009), London, UK (2009). http://www.digra.org/dl/db/09287.28003.pdf
10. Nacke, L.: From playability to a hierarchical game usability model. In: FuturePlay at Game Developers Conference Canada, Vancouver, Canada (2009)

What Aspects of Context Should Be Described in Case Studies About Software Teams? Preliminary Results from a Mapping Study

Maria Teresa Baldassarre[1]([✉]), César França[2], and Fabio Q.B. da Silva[3]

[1] Department of Informatics, University of Bari, Bari, Italy
mariateresa.baldassarre@uniba.it
[2] Department of Statistics and Informatics, Federal Rural University of Pernambuco, Recife, PE, Brazil
cesar@franssa.com
[3] Center of Informatics, Federal University of Pernambuco, Recife, PE, Brazil
fabio@cin.ufpe.br

Abstract. In this article, we report the findings of a systematic literature mapping study aimed at identifying contextual factors that should be described in case studies about teams in software engineering. As a result, we identified 26 factors, which we organized in five dimensions: characteristics of individuals, groups, team processes, projects and organizations. These dimensions and factors can guide future reports to present better descriptions of the context in which their software teams are studied.

1 Introduction

Understanding how software teams work, and how best to design them is an issue of high relevance for industry in general [1]. However, given the specificities of the software development activity, several theories from organizational behavior do not apply directly in this field [2], which has recently attracted attention and effort from software engineering researchers. However, given the large variety of soft factors and uncontrollable variables involved in studies with human subjects, it has been challenging to software engineering researchers to elaborate reliable and general theories or predictive models on software development teamwork [3]. Recent secondary studies [3–5] point out that the main weakness of those studies is that they still miss potentially relevant contextual information. Enriching research reports with more contextual information could bring many benefits, such as increasing the strength of the presented evidences; enhancing their transferability; and enabling future work to synthesize knowledge following more systematic procedures, such as meta-ethnographies [6] and others [7].

In this research, we are interested in documenting the concrete characteristics of the context that should be described in teamwork case study reports, to support the improvement of this type of research. The currently available qualitative research guidelines [8–11] are not very specific about that basically because they are designed

© Springer International Publishing AG 2016
P. Abrahamsson et al. (Eds.): PROFES 2016, LNCS 10027, pp. 723–730, 2016.
DOI: 10.1007/978-3-319-49094-6_61

to be independent of the research subject. To this end, we designed a systematic literature mapping study with a twofold complementary approach: first, we review papers that contain methodological recommendations on what the characteristics of teams should be included in rich descriptions of contexts in studies involving software engineering teams; second, we look at papers that conducted case studies with software teams to map what characteristics they actually have reported.

This is yet an in progress research. In this short article we present the results of the first part of the study, which is a thematic synthesis made in the six papers, manually selected out from the 4,915 reviewed titles published between 2008 and 2014 in relevant journals and conferences. Our results uncovered 26 different contextual factors that should be described in studies on software teams. These factors are organized in five dimensions: characteristics of individuals, of groups, of team processes, of projects and of organization. Although these factors are of high relevance to this type of research, several of them, particularly those related to individuals and groups, were only briefly mentioned in the previously existing checklists. This paper is organized as follow: in Sect. 2, we briefly detail the referential work that motivated our research; in Sect. 3 we describe our mapping study protocol and its threats to validity; in Sect. 4 we present preliminary results of this study, which a discussed in more details in Sect. 5, where we also conclude and posit our future steps.

2 Background

According to Yin [12], a case study is defined as "an empirical inquiry that investigates a contemporary phenomenon in depth and within its real life context, especially when the boundaries between the phenomenon and context are not clearly evident". Dybå et al. [11] define context as "the circumstances, conditions, situations, or environments that are external to a specific phenomenon and that enable or constrain it". However, sometimes, the context interfere in, or interacts with, the phenomenon of interest. Thus, case studies reports must provide in-depth description of the natural settings, offering rich, qualitative data, to enable researchers to draw appropriate interpretations of the data. A rich description of the context also help case studies to improve their transferability, making easier to readers or user to decide whether the findings are likely be applied to other situations or not [13]. Dybå et al. [11] also distinguishes two types of context: the discrete context refers to specific contextual variables, such as organization size, or product complexity; and the omnibus context refers to a broad perspective, drawing attention to who, what, when, where, and why involved in the activities under observation. In order to make the context description in case studies reports more straightforward, Petersen and Wohlin [10] proposed a checklist of 21 discrete characteristics of context, organized in six different context facets: product, processes, practices and techniques, people, organization, and market. They suggest, however, that this checklist should be extended, and adapted according to the object of study and to the consensus of the specific community. In this article, we are specifically interested in the characteristics of the discrete context of case studies that address teamwork related phenomena. According to Marks et al. [14] there are at least three approaches to characterize a team: describing the characteristics of the team members; describing the properties of the team that vary as a function of team context, and the environment in which the team is acting; and describing the processes through which the team works. Those approaches are only partially covered in Petersen and Wohlin's [10] checklist.

3 Review Protocol

We have taken a different approach from Petersen and Wohlin [10]. While they have proposed a checklist from scratch, we decided to carry out a systematic literature mapping study on scientific papers addressing teamwork in software engineering published in highly qualified venues, looking for methodological recommendations on what the characteristics of context should be described in future reports. A mapping study is defined as a type of systematic literature review whose the aim is "to identify all research related to a specific topic" either to answer broad research questions or to picture trends in a given area [16, 19]. In this paper, we aim to answer the following research question:

RQ1. What characteristics of the context should be described in case studies about teams in software engineering?

To this end, we designed a mapping study protocol based on Kitchenham and Charters' [17] guidelines. The thematic synthesis followed the recommendations of Cruzes and Dybå [18]. Overall, our study was conducted in three main steps. *First*, we carried out a manual search in the proceedings of the last seven years (2008–2014) of four conferences (ICSE, ESEM, EASE, CHASE) and four journals (EMSE, IST, JSS, TSE). We chose this time period because the main known guidelines for qualitative research in software engineering data from 2008 [15]. This initial selection was based on reading titles and abstracts, resulted in the list of 71 potentially relevant studies. That activity was done independently by two researchers. *Second*, we read full texts, and applied inclusion and exclusion criteria. We included both theoretical articles addressing case studies or other qualitative approaches in software engineering research; and secondary research reviewing case studies or other qualitative methods, presenting a detailed discussion on how primary research software engineering teams or teamwork in software projects reports should improve. We excluded papers not written in English or not available on the web as well as invited papers, keynotes, workshop reports, books, theses and dissertations. We also excluded papers of computer science domain but clearly out of the software engineering scope or papers that did not target software engineers, software engineering teams, or that did not relate to teamwork or software teams. Each paper was judged by two researchers, independently, and conflicting opinions were individually discussed and resolved. In the end, six papers were selected to analysis and synthesis. In the *third* step, we extracted relevant segments of the papers, labeled them with representative codes. Two researchers read and analyzed all the six papers independently. Then, these two researchers, together, grouped the labels in higher order categories, following an iterative and incremental process. The research team was composed of four researchers. The data management was conducted using Google Forms and worksheet files in Microsoft Excel ™. A quality assessment was not carried out because we assumed the papers to have high quality given the sources where they were published.

4   Results

In this section we present the results of the thematic synthesis conducted in the six selected papers. The references are listed at the appendix in the end of this article. The results are organized according to Marks et al. [14] dimensions in the subsections below, and summarized in Table 1.

Table 1. Contextual factors

A. Individual	<ul><li>Perception of the organization</li><li>Level of expertise</li><li>Demographics</li><li>Personality traits</li><li>Individual interests</li><li>Interpersonal / Technical skills</li></ul>	
B. Group	<ul><li>Group Composition (expertise/competence)</li><li>Management Style</li><li>Team Climate (Commitment/Motivation/Identification)</li><li>Group structure / organization</li><li>Geographical dispersion</li></ul>	
C. Team Processes	<ul><li>Customer relationship</li><li>Communication Dynamics</li><li>Management and coordination activities (project, requirements, configuration, change, etc.)</li><li>Software development process</li><li>Researcher involvement</li><li>Working schedule</li></ul>	
D. Environment	D1. Project	<ul><li>Stakeholders / Sponsors</li><li>Project importance / criticality</li><li>Project complexity / variability</li><li>Project Duration / Size</li></ul>
	D2. Organization	<ul><li>Working facilities / office outline</li><li>Organizational Culture</li><li>Business model</li><li>Human resources-related policies</li><li>Organization Size / Structure</li></ul>

4.1   Characteristics of the Individuals

This dimension groups individual characteristics of the team members, which characterize the people in the team individually, and are independent of others. These characteristics are relevant, because as pointed out in P4:

"The success of a software development project depends on people and human resource factors (…) Not only the experience and competency of the team members is important, but also their personal characteristics such as honestly, collaborative attitude, sense of responsibility, readiness to learn, and work with others are considered equally important, if not more" (P4, p. 1872, Sect. 3.2).

Thus, in addition to the basic demographics (age, education, gender, function, etc.) it seems to be relevant to characterize the individuals in the teams in terms of their technical and interpersonal skills [P1, P3, P4, P5]; perceptions that they hold about the organization [P1, P2, P3, P5]; level of career experience and expertise [P1, P4, P5]; personality traits and behavioral patterns [P2, P4]; and individual interests [P5].

4.2 Characteristics of the Group

When the individuals are put together to work as a team, there are characteristics that pertain to the collectivity. In this dimension, we sought to cluster these properties of the group that only make sense when the team is formed. In this dimension, we identified five categories: Group composition refers to how the group is balanced in terms of combined individual characteristics (knowledge, expertise, personality, etc.) [P1, P2, P3, P4, P6]; Group structure regards the size, functions, and power allocated to the team members [P1, P3, P4]; Geographical dispersion describes the physical configuration of the participants [P3, P4, P6]; Management style describes formal and informal relationships established between the group and its leader [P2, P3]; and finally Team climate describes the relationship between the individuals and the group, such as commitment with others, collective identity or team spirit, motivation to work, cohesion, trust, etc. [P1, P2, P3, P6].

4.3 Characteristics of the Team Processes

The dimension of Team Processes is intended as the way of doing things on behalf of teams, or how teams work and operate, and what they do. According to P6: "Besides, to understand the level of coordination practices, communication process and technology should be described as well. While availability of collaboration technology and its adoption level could be a mediate factor of team dispersion on perform" (P6, p. 136, Sect. 5.1).

This dimension includes six characteristics: Customer relationship clarifies the type of relationship that the team has with its customers as well as the role that a customer play in the team [P1, P3, P4, P5]; communication dynamics relates to how team members communicate among each other [P2, P3, P4, P5, P6] includes communication processes, interactions of the various participants, members interaction and how they share work and so on; management and coordination activities [P3, P5, P6] describes the types of activities and procedures that management puts in practice during a project involving software development teams such as devolution of project responsibility to project business owners, measure team performance to assure team is working on schedule and within budget, adopt standard procedures, software development process [P1, P2, P3, P4, P5, P6] details the characteristics of the processes teams adopt, some examples are: amount of documentation, code ownership, development practice, coding standards, planning game activity; researcher involvement [P1, P2, P3, P4, P5, P6] discusses how an external researcher should coordinate in a development team, and working schedule [P5] articulates the mechanisms that should characterize team members' schedule such as dynamic schedule, no overtime, 40-h working weeks.

4.4 Characteristics of the Environment

The Environment dimension was intended as inclusive of all those factors that characterize the context in which a project is carried out and where a team operates. As we defined the categories and coded the papers in our synthesis analysis we agreed on the fact that this dimension actually was more appropriate to be divided into two dimensions: Project and Organization as the categories coded fit better. So, as it can be seen in Table 1, Environment category has been divided into Project and Organization.

The first comprises features that a project should have, just to give an example: "Initial characterization of a software development project can play an important role in shaping participant's attitudes and actions in the development process." (P5, p. 11, Sect. 5.2.1). It includes categories such as: stakeholders [P3, P5, P6]; project importance and criticality [P3, P5]; project complexity and variability [P3, P5]; project duration and size [P5].

The Organization dimension relates to the characteristics that the organization should have with respect to software development teams [P2]. "Thus changing the culture of an organization is not a trivial task, since it requires changes on members' ways of thinking, communicating, relating to each other, as well as consolidated habits and working manners." (P2, p. 1956, Sect. 3.)

This dimension includes categories such as: working facilities and office outline [P1, P3, P5, P6] that define in some way how the office should be organized like logistical arrangements, physical and temporal settings, spaces distribution and so on The organizational culture category includes details relating to aspects such as ways of thinking, historical organizational practices, corporate culture [P1, P2, P3, P4, P5]; Business model category includes information of the models adopted such as organization type, setting of the industry or of the study carried out [P1, P5]; Human-resources related policies includes aspects about rewarding system adopted for staff and company policies related to the employees' motivation [P2, P3]. Finally, organizational size and structure provides insight on the dimensions of the company with codes on multiple independent teams, organization structure and size, as well as having projects with small teams [P1, P3].

5 Discussion and Conclusion

This research was motivated by the fact that research reports and studies of software development teams ignore potentially relevant information of the particular context in which they are conducted, which may directly compromise the transferability of this type of research [20]. Less obviously, it also impacts the ability of the whole field to accumulate knowledge, learning from comparative synthesis of different studies [19].

Dybå et al. [11] warns that what counts as context depends on the substantive problem under scrutiny, so it is not possible to draw checklists that are general enough. Our checklist is looking specifically to the study of software development teams, but even so the relevance of the elements in the list may vary. It is indeed a long list of contextual factors. Petersen and Wohlin [10] suggest that the importance of the discrete checklist is to help the researchers to make informed decisions about what to describe in their reports.

Compared to previous work carried out by other authors [10, 14] we have particularly focused on the characteristics that address teamwork related phenomena. To this end, our categories related to organization, processes and project are common to the ones in Petersen and Wohlins' checklist [10] labeled as organization, processes/practices and market; while other Petersen and Wohlin categories such as product have not been considered in our dimensions as they may be not central to teamwork features. Our categories are more oriented to human aspects, rather than the general context. This motivates the identification of both individual and group categories in the sense that they focus on team member characteristics as single elements and as components of a group immersed in an environment where the team acts and works through specific processes.

The contextual factors listed in Table 1 are also of some importance to the software engineering practice, because they reveal a variety of aspects that software engineers must deal with, and that managers should care about, because they can somehow impact the effectiveness of the team [20]. It was not our objective to map how different properties affect the effectiveness of the team, but that information can be found in the six papers that we analyzed (Appendix A). Dutra et al. recently presented a synthesis of these factors [4].

Finally, this study is part of a larger effort to document characteristics of the context that should be described in teamwork studies. This work was limited to identify other authors' suggestions, but it is not yet an exhaustive list. In the next step, we will look at what factors have actually been reported in these types of studies, and why. We hope that, by enriching their context descriptions, in the future we will be able to address more sophisticated questions such as what software engineering approaches work best for a given type of team, or how a team should be assembled and organized, given a set of characteristics of the environment.

A Appendix: List of Selected Papers

[P1] T. Dybå and T. Dingsøyr. "Empirical studies of agile software development: A systematic review". IST, 50 (9–10), pp. 833–859 2008.

[P2] C. Tolfo and R. Wazlawick. "The influence of organizational culture on the adoption of extreme programming". JSS, 81 (11), pp. 1955–1967 2008.

[P3] T. Chow and D. Cao. "A survey study of critical success factors in agile software projects". JSS, 81 (6), pp. 961–971 2008.

[P4] S. Misra, V. Kumar and U. Kumar. "Identifying some important success factors in adopting agile software development practices". JSS, 82 (11), pp. 1869–1890 2009.

[P5] L. Mcleod, S. Macdonell and B. Doolin. "Qualitative research on software development: a longitudinal case study methodology". EMSE, 16 (4), pp. 430–459 2011.

[P6] N. Anh, D. Cruzes and R. Conradi. "Dispersion, coordination and performance in global software teams: a systematic review". ESEM, pp. 129–138 2012.

References

1. Sawyer, S.: Software development teams. Commun. ACM **47**(12), 95–99 (2004)
2. Sharp, H., Badoo, N., Beecham, S., Hall, T., Robinson, H.: Models of motivation in software engineering. IST **51**, 219–233 (2009)
3. Moe, N., Dingsøyr, T., Dybå, T.: A teamwork model for understanding an agile team: a case study of a Scrum project. IST **52**(5), 480–491 (2010)
4. Dutra, A., Prikladnicki, R., França, C.: What do we know about high performance teams in software engineering? Results from a systematic literature review. In: SEAA 2015
5. Ribeiro, D., Cardoso, M., da Silva, F., França, C.: Using qualitative meta summary to synthesize empirical findings in literature reviews. In: ESEM 2014
6. da Silva, F., Cruz, S., Gouveia, T., Capretz, L.:. Using meta-ethnography to synthesize research: a worked example of the relations between personality on software team processes. In: ESEM 2013
7. Cruzes, D., Dybå, T.: Research synthesis in software engineering: a tertiary study. IST **53**(5), 440–455 (2011)
8. Seaman, C.: Qualitative methods in empirical studies of software engineering. IEEE TSE **25**(4), 557–572 (1999)
9. Runeson, P., Höst, M.: Guidelines for conducting and reporting case study research in software engineering. EMSE **14**, 131–164 (2009)
10. Petersen, K., Wohlin, C.: Context in industrial software engineering research. In: ESEM 2009
11. Dybå, T., Sjøberg, D., Cruzes, D.: What works for whom, where, when, and why? On the role of context in empirical software engineering. In: ESEM 2012
12. Yin, R.: Case Study Research: Design and Methods: Applied Social Research Methods Series, vol. 5, 4th edn. SAGE Publications, Thousand Oaks (2009)
13. Merriam, S.: Qualitative Research: A Guide to Design and Implementation, 2nd edn. Jossey-Bass, [S.l.] (2009)
14. Marks, M., Mathieu, J., Zaccaro, S.: A temporally based framework and taxonomy of team processes. Acad. Manage. Rev. **26**(3), 356–376 (2001)
15. Dittrich, Y., John, M., Singer, J., Tessem, B.: Editorial for the special issue on qualitative software engineering research. IST **49**, 531–539 (2007)
16. da Silva, F., Santos, A., Soares, S., França, C., Monteiro, C., Maciel, F.: Six years of systematic literature reviews in software engineering: an updated tertiary study. IST **53**, 899–913 (2011)
17. Kitchenham, B., Charters, S.: Guidelines for performing systematic literature reviews in software engineering. EBSE Technical Report (2007)
18. Cruzes, D., Dybå, T.: Recommended steps for thematic synthesis in software engineering. In: ESEM (2011)
19. Carver, J.C., Juristo, N., Baldassarre, M.T., Vegas, S.: Replications of software engineering experiments. Empir. Softw. Eng. J. **19**(2), 267–276 (2014). doi:10.1007/s10664-013-9290-8
20. Ardimento, P., Caivano, D., Cimitile, M., Visaggio, G.: Empirical investigation of the efficacy and efficiency of tools for transferring software engineering knowledge. J. Inf. Knowl. Manage. **7**(3), 197–207 (2008)

Miscommunication in Software Projects: Early Recognition Through Tendency Forecasts

Fabian Kortum[✉], Jil Klünder, and Kurt Schneider

Software Engineering Group, Leibniz Universität Hannover,
Welfengarten 1, 30167 Hannover, Germany
{fabian.kortum,jil.kluender,kurt.schneider}@inf.uni-hannover.de

Abstract. Efficient team communication is essential for software project success. Misunderstood or underestimated demands on customer requirements and insufficient information sharing within a team can rapidly cause the delay of software releases, hamper customer satisfaction or even endanger the project succeed. The challenges remain to quantify the right amount of communication according to durations, necessary effort, and the ambitions to avoid firefighting situations. Especially newly build or less experienced teams often struggle with their information flow. To improve team communication performances for these teams, we build an experience based classifier model that interpolates tendency forecasts with five approved team communication metrics from related work. The model matches archival project communications with present team conditions and computes tendency forecasts for the ongoing project. These future trends can indicate critical communication conditions right from early phases. Hence, they can reduce risks of miscommunication during a project.

Keywords: Machine learning · Team communication · Experience-base

1 Introduction

Successful software projects and today's development processes are primarily grounded on efficient team communication. Communication within software developing teams consists of several psychological facets, practical use of technologies and organizational expertise [5, 12]. Tightened project costs and reduced resources require further improvements to stay internationally competitive. Software projects with zero margins for errors, misunderstandings or functionality issues lead to higher pressuring rates of developer conditions [11]. Risks of later improvements or potential delay of releases can cause a radical loss of customer satisfaction and probably the cancellation or failure of a project. Therefore, team communication and the flow of information seem to be a prerequisite for project

---

This work was funded by the German Research Foundation (DFG) under grant number *263807701* (Project TeamFLOW, 2015–2017).

© Springer International Publishing AG 2016
P. Abrahamsson et al. (Eds.): PROFES 2016, LNCS 10027, pp. 731–738, 2016.
DOI: 10.1007/978-3-319-49094-6_62

success [5]. The challenges remain in scheduling the right amount of communication according to durations, necessary effort and the ambitions of a team to avoid firefighting situations. Especially new build or less experienced teams often struggle with their communication management. Tuckman [15] revealed that teams typically change and expose their social behavior over time, settled by the experiences made during each phase by the team members. Furthermore, most project teams suffer stressful or troubling situations differently due to individual team characters and communication styles [11,12].

In this approach, we introduce a technique that enables future tendencies of team communication behavior for ongoing software projects, resulted from present team communication characteristics and experience-based support from archival projects. We build a machine learning classifier that operates on relevant data records and interpolates a multi-week communication tendency with five significant metrics describing a team's simplified communication behavior. The applied archival data and communication metrics used within this approach refer to a field study from previous investigations with retrospectives on team communication in student software projects [12]. A machine learning classifier which is developed in Java is realized through a k-nearest neighbor (kNN) model with predictive characteristics to involve training and testing data. This kNN model accesses archival project information from the training set and matches them with present team communication conditions. After all, it interpolates communication trends based on best matches with closely related conditions. The resulting future trends can indicate critical communication behavior right after early project phases and enable early adjustments. Due to dynamic changes of a team's communication behavior over time, the kNN model considers the entire course of team communication since the project start. We validated our model through leave-one-out-cross-validations (LOOCV), also encountered its overall accuracy on team communication tendencies, measured as the aggregated error rates between the model's forecasts and real testing data references of archival project records.

The model currently interpolates tendency forecasts with future perspectives up to 14 weeks and operates with high accuracies during several project phases. We present validating results and insights gained from applying both psychological and software engineering perspectives, additionally to their respective interpretations. It would be highly desirable to obtain improved team communication for project success based on experience-based tendency assistances with archival records and ongoing team communication conditions. In our vision, this terminology can be especially helpful for newly formed teams and allow a better understanding in scheduling and planning meeting quantities during different phases of project.

2 Related Work

This approach is grounded on several previous publishing from psychological perspectives on socio-interactive team communications and predictive analytics.

Kauffeld et al. [5] investigated that the interaction and meeting intensities of software developing teams shows strong affects to the project's overall success.

Klünder et al. [6,7] and Schneider et al. [12] monitored and explored socio-interactive communication behaviors of students in software projects. The authors applied a multi-week field study with real software projects and environmental framework to elicit project information with unsynthesized origin. In cooperation with psychological experts, the authors derived and manifested five relevant communication metrics which have a direct impact on team communication behavior.

Kumar et al. [10] describe the importance of training and guidance of communication ways for software engineering students. The authors use comparison methods on two student software projects to determine their communication style. The authors also explored pitfalls and indicate the communication difficulties for newly formed teams. This was out motivation to apply an assistance approach combining both experience-based guidance and predictive analytics on communication behavior.

Jørgensen et al. [4] elaborated the significance of forecasts for effort-scaling in software projects. They established a sequential approach with distinctions of measurable project outcomes under lessons learned circumstances. The author's goals were to validate whether experience-based information from a previous project will affect the following project based on the additional available source of experienced data.

Sharma et al. [13] approached the accuracy of priority handler for occurring bugs by using machine learning methodologies and cross-validations with an experience base of earlier prioritized bugs. They analyzed and validated the accuracy of 76 sample studies using support vector machines.

We use the author's conceptual theory on experience-based approaches supported by machine learning to forecast team communication tendencies that consider a team's ongoing communication condition. In a previous approach, we applied psychological perspectives and analytical methods to explore the feasibility of a first simplified forecasting tool that can compute tendencies on team communication intensities in support of a machine learning classifier [6,9].

3 Methodology

3.1 Study Design

We accessed 34 student software projects from a previous field study [12] that provides a series of small, yet complete software projects including team communications in a variety of psychological and software project metrics. All software projects were comparable in their framework conditions, complexity, and duration. Most importantly, they did not consist of synthetic made or biases and intended for real use in their respective context by the customer.

We use five manifested metrics [7,12] to describe team communication behavior through relevant expressions and attributes from the field study records.

These metrics are compounds of communication attributes with matter for teams like mutual network structures, communication paths, proportions of communication media channels and their intensity of use, as well as meeting distances, team moods, and spirits. We extracted a synergistic conjunction with these five metrics as predictable subjects involving FLOW distance [7], FLOW centralization [7], and team spirits [14]. We also consider the positive and negative moods which have been previously proven to be relevant factors for team communication [12].

An application realized in this approach uses the kNN algorithm. Furthermore, it supports the integration of entire collections with communication metrics for training the model and compute communication tendencies. An internal diagnose functionality resolves the model's predictions accuracy automatically due to actually loaded training data, its quality and significance of the raw information. The latter, it can help teams to validate whether their training data is qualified as experience data for tendency forecasts or not.

3.2 Team Communication Metrics

FLOW distance is a metric considering different kind of communication channels like e-mail, meetings and phone calls and the perceived communication intensity [7]. We applied it as central metric for communication behavior [6] since it indicates potential problems in the communication way of a team [12].

FLOW centralization combines the quantitative distribution of all communication ways between team members and resolves the dominance positioning of the single members. It indicates the degree to which communication is focused on a subset of an entire team [7].

During a software project, *team moods* yield impressive information with significant reflection during releases, quality gates, issues and similar [11]. In this approach, each team member's mood is covered by positive and negative affects describing the feelings during a week [12]. A team's emotional expression reflects a direct condition about the project's status and thus provides important information with impact to project success [3]. The positive and negative attributed mood were aggregated into two central metrics [2].

In analogy to the team's mood, *team spirit* represents a further emotional reflection about the status of socio-interacting conditions. The metric used in this approach is aggregated from each team's responded atmosphere and subset to inner team's mutual trusts, creativity with innovative thinking, satisfaction on team results, time availability, and schedulability, as well as inner performances and productivity [12,14]. The aggregated team spirit metric presents a subjective opinion indicating the balance of a team's overall atmosphere and satisfaction. Therefore, it can be expressed as the mean value for each teams rating.

Figure 1 presents a plot of the differences in 34 student software projects and the weekly provided metrics. The figure shows normalized ranges from 0.0 to 1.0 of the selected metrics. Verifying the ranges and variances of data is a first necessary demand before building and training classifier models.

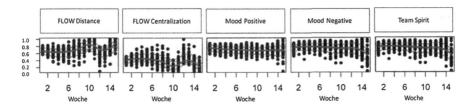

Fig. 1. Distribution of communication metrics from field study reports

3.3 Machine Learning Classifier

Predictive analytics and its machine learning subset provide powerful algorithms with different characteristics on experience based forecasts. The kNN algorithm is one of these representatives with outstanding qualities in information matching [1]. In a previous approach [9], we introduced the feasibility of a simplified prediction model that considers team communication intensities. According to the goals of this approach, we wanted to improve the model's level of maturity and realize a Java application with a higher accuracy under consideration of five selectable metrics.

The developed application consists of several auto features, e.g. data normalizing for k-nearest training and testing data as well as an upload function for a training set. We integrated an accuracy validation function that enables teams to forecast different tendencies under limitation to selected metrics. This functional feature is associated with an inner process detecting the best fitting k-value to achieve most accurate forecasts. The algorithm measures the vector distance between communication metrics from the experience base and the new inputs from ongoing communication conditions during a project [6,9]. Both information are proceeded by matching a k-number of archival projects from the training data that fulfill the closest team communication similarities with the real communication in the past weeks. These best matches are used to interpolate tendencies.

With respect to changing communication styles, this model considers the matching with other communication metrics on a multi-span of time. The accuracy of weekly communication forecasts is limited to the model's training data and matching comparability. The k-value of matching algorithm manages a number of required matches with the reference inputs that are necessary to interpolate a new tendency. Different k-values can have more or less good predictions. We included a diagnostic support for the training data to extract a best operational k-value due to the quality and significance of the training data. This ensures the highest precision outcome due to the measured significance of the experience data.

4 Validation and Forecast Results

The accuracy of forecasts remains to the quality and significance by the applied training data and the selected k-value. We applied the leave-one-out-cross-validation (LOOCV) to our forecasting application and approved its overall accuracy [8] on team communication tendencies. The training data of our kNN model consists of 34 student software projects; each providing 15 weeks of weekly submitted team communication information. LOOCV folds a single team project from the training set and inserts its communication information iteratively as weekly inputs to the model. This resolves tendency forecasts for different weekly progressing stages during the lifespan of a project. The error between the fold records and the forecast delivers a measurable prediction deviance. The average deviance of the application through all weekly forecasts is defined as the forecast's overall error rate. This rate represents so far only the overall errors for a single fold project. Afterward, LOOCV iterates and folds again for every further team project from the entire training data.

In fact, this procedure results from 34 single overall error rates which reveal an average total error rate of the current forecasting model of 11.5 %. The mean precision of our model operates with 88.5 % on a maximum forecast horizon of up to 14 weeks. Compared with the results from the previous approach [9], we increased the models precision by 5.5 % while operating with five communication metrics. The applied best k of 6 is auto-detected from the highest forecast's overall precision due to the training data. The integrated auto k-finder updates its k-value with every change of training data to ensure the highest accurate forecast. Figure 2 shows the distribution of all measured error rates according to the progressed weeks during the project and decrease of the forecast horizon. The decrease is linked to the reduce of left weeks until the projects ending.

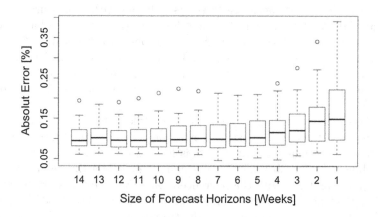

Fig. 2. Overall error rates

The forecast's accuracy has an almost constant error rate of 9 % exception for the last two weeks. The data quality of team records and submission decreases towards project's end, which has a direct affect to training data.

The wide spread of communication styles with weak correlation dependencies to the previous weeks costs a total loss of 3 % from the model's overall precision.

Nevertheless, the application still computes remarkable forecasts over multiple weeks with high accuracy and a final overall precision of 88.5 %. The data quality issues at the end seem hereby marginal. The almost constant level of error rates during changing forecast horizons is an indicator for well-performing tendency forecasts with the chosen team communication metrics.

5   Conclusion

5.1   Discussion

Meanwhile our approach leads to good results, the results cannot be over-generalized.

A generalized support for any type of software project with team communication forecast cannot be granted. Although, this approach on student software projects and its applied communication metrics presents parallels with software projects in industrial environments. However, the team's communication behavior and tendency errors strongly depend on the applied training data and should be so far only used with student software project approaches. A practical validation has not been established yet. We plan to extend our model with data taken from industrial projects. At this moment, our tool only works great for projects with a duration of 15 weeks.

5.2   Conclusion

In this approach, we presented the feasibility of team communication forecasts with the FLOW distance, FLOW centralization, team spirit, positive and negative moods as significant team communication metrics. We developed a Java application that enables the integration of various data collections and normalizes its data content to perform predictive operations. The core is based on a kNN model that computes the correlation between a team's present communication course and finding for k-nearest communications condition within the models training data. The k-best matches become interpolated as future communication tendencies during a project.

The precision of current tendency forecasts is validated through LOOCV and resulted in mean precisions of 88.5 %. The application is designed to consider future types of numeric metrics with dependencies to team communication in software projects. This approach is an encouraging step to support new software developing teams in finding their optimal communication structures. Experience based tendency forecasts in combination with continuous team communication can help hereby to reduce risks of miscommunication and promote for better software quality due to less pressuring phases.

References

1. Beyer, K., Goldstein, J., Ramakrishnan, R., Shaft, U.: When is "Nearest Neighbor" meaningful? In: Beeri, C., Buneman, P. (eds.) ICDT 1999. LNCS, vol. 1540, pp. 217–235. Springer, Heidelberg (1999). doi:10.1007/3-540-49257-7_15

2. Flory, J.D., Manuck, S.B., Matthews, K.A., Muldoon, M.F.: Serotonergic function in the central nervous system is associated with daily ratings of positive mood. Psychiatry Res. **129**(1), 11–19 (2004)
3. Graziotin, D., Wang, X., Abrahamsson, P.: Happy software developers solve problems better: psychological measurements in empirical software engineering. CoRR abs/1505.00922 (2015)
4. Jørgensen, M., Gruschke, T.M.: The impact of lessons-learned sessions on effort estimation and uncertainty assessments. IEEE Trans. Softw. Eng. **35**(3), 368–383 (2009)
5. Kauffeld, S., Lehmann-Willenbrock, N.: Meetings matter effects of team meetings on team and organizational success. Small Group Res. **43**(2), 130–158 (2012)
6. Klünder, J., Karras, O., Kortum, F., Schneider, K.: Forecasting communication behavior in student software projects. In: Proceedings of the The 12th International Conference on Predictive Models and Data Analytics in Software Engineering, PROMISE 2016, pp. 1–8. ACM, New York (2016)
7. Klünder, J., Schneider, K., Kortum, F., Straube, J., Handke, L., Kauffeld, S.: Communication in teams - an expression of social conflicts. In: Bogdan, C., Gulliksen, J., Sauer, S., Forbrig, P., Winckler, M., Johnson, C., Palanque, P., Bernhaupt, R., Kis, F. (eds.) HCSE/HESSD -2016. LNCS, vol. 9856, pp. 111–129. Springer, Heidelberg (2016). doi:10.1007/978-3-319-44902-9_8
8. Kohavi, R., et al.: A study of cross-validation and bootstrap for accuracy estimation and model selection. In: IJCAI, vol. 14, pp. 1137–1145 (1995)
9. Kortum, F., Klünder, J.: Early diagnostics on team communication - experience-based forecasts on student software projects. In: 10th International Conference on the Quality of Information and Communications Technology (Quatic). IEEE (2016)
10. Kumar, S., Wallace, C.: A tale of two projects: a pattern based comparison of communication strategies in student software development. In: 2013 IEEE Frontiers in Education Conference (FIE), pp. 1844–1850. IEEE (2013)
11. Liskin, O., Schneider, K., Kiesling, S., Kauffeld, S.: Meeting intensity as an indicator for project pressure: exploring meeting profiles. In: 2013 6th International Workshop on Cooperative and Human Aspects of Software Engineering (CHASE), pp. 153–156. IEEE (2013)
12. Schneider, K., Liskin, O., Paulsen, H., Kauffeld, S.: Media, mood, and meetings: related to project success? ACM Trans. Comput. Educ. (TOCE) **15**(4), 21 (2015)
13. Sharma, M., Bedi, P., Chaturvedi, K., Singh, V.: Predicting the priority of a reported bug using machine learning techniques and cross project validation. In: 2012 12th International Conference on Intelligent Systems Design and Applications (ISDA), pp. 539–545. IEEE (2012)
14. Sudhakar, G.P.: Software Development Teams: Performance, Productivity and Innovation. Prentice-Hall India, Delhi (2016)
15. Tuckman, B.W., Jensen, M.A.C.: Stages of small-group development revisited. Group & Organization Management **2**(4), 419–427 (1977)

Doctoral Symposium

A Research Proposal: Tracking Open Source Software Evolution for the Characterization of Its Evolutionary Behavior

Munish Saini[✉] and Kuljit Kaur Chahal

Department of Computer Science, Guru Nanak Dev University, Amritsar, Punjab, India
munish_1_saini@yahoo.co.in, kuljitchahal@yahoo.com

Abstract. Open Source Software (OSS) has attracted a lot of attention in the last decade. Due to the rising dominance of OSS in the software industry; not only practitioners, but researchers as well as academicians are also keen to understand the OSS development and evolution process. Several studies have been conducted in the past in this regard. Most of the existing work relates to growth analysis of OSS projects using source code level metrics. Lately, metrics related to change activity have also been included to understand OSS evolution. Change activity as recorded in Source Code Management (SCM) systems is used in a few cases. Most of the work deals with finding change size, and change effort distributions. A few studies do change profile analysis as OSS systems evolve. But that is restricted to a few of the change categories, e.g., adaptive v/s non-adaptive changes, corrective v/s non-corrective changes. This research study explores change profiles of 106 OSS systems by extracting change type information from their SCM repositories and then categorizing these changes automatically into five different categories - corrective, adaptive, perfective, preventive, and enhancement related. The idea is to understand the way OSS projects undergo change through long periods of time. The results indicate that change behavior of the OSS projects is different for different types of changes.

Keywords: Open Source Software (OSS) · Software evolution · Change classification · Cluster analysis · Commit quality

1 Introduction

Software evolution refers to the phenomenon of continuous software change and growth after its initial development. Understanding software evolution in general and OSS projects evolution in particular has been of wide interest in the recent past. A wide range of research studies has analyzed the OSS evolution from different points of views such as growth [1] quality [2], and group dynamics [3]. Several research studies, in the past have studied the historical records of changes of OSS projects and found them useful for understanding the software evolution. In this study, we explore the change evolution of OSS projects focusing on their different types, e.g. corrective, adaptive, perfective, preventive, and enhancement.

© Springer International Publishing AG 2016
P. Abrahamsson et al. (Eds.): PROFES 2016, LNCS 10027, pp. 741–745, 2016.
DOI: 10.1007/978-3-319-49094-6_63

2   Problem Definition

Kemerer and Slaughter [4] explore the evolution of commercial systems on the basis of detailed change events. The study shows that systems pass through several evolutionary phases. However, all the systems do not follow the same evolutionary paths. There are few studies that explore the change evolution in OSS projects from this point of view. Meqdadi et al. [5] study trends only in the adaptive changes in 3 OSS projects. As per their analysis, adaptive changes decrease over the period of time. Most of the change analysis studies in OSS projects investigate only the distributions of changes types, change size, and change frequency. In this study, a large set of OSS projects are analyzed to explore trends in their evolution corresponding to different types of changes over a period of time. The trend analysis indicates patterns in which different change types evolve. We have traced the evolution behavior of OSS projects at two distinct levels of detail: fine grained and coarse grained. In the fine-grained analysis, OSS projects and their repositories are explored in depth to analyze the repository level metrics; whereas for coarse-grained analysis only project level metrics are explored for evaluation.

Following are the main objectives of this study:

A. Fine-grained analysis

- Analyzing the change profiles of OSS projects using their change logs.
- Change profiling of OSS projects to explore the evolutionary patterns with respect to the types of changes performed over a period of time.
- Prediction of commits with respect to previous commits.
- Examining the change activity in OSS projects from three points of view: change purpose (type), change size, and change effort.
- Analyzing commit quality of OSS projects.

B. Coarse-grained analysis

- Understanding the programming language profile of an OSS project.
- Analyze the existence of similar (or dissimilar) pattern in single and multiple contributor projects in terms of: (a) main programming languages, (b) licensing, (c) number of different languages used, (d) identifying the relationship (between the number of user, contributors, total commit, and LOC).

3   Significance of the Work

Commits, and other related data in the SCM of OSS projects can be analyzed to see the development activity, technical effervescence and popularity of the projects [6]. All stakeholders, including project managers, developers, and end users can use commit evolution trends to understand the post implementation activities of a project (such as enhancements of the old features of the project, the addition of new features, or improvements in its performance). When an end user selects an OSS project for use, he should be able to see the history of change of the software project. How are changes handled in the past? The kind of changes a software system encounters can indicate the health of the software project (though it is not in the scope of this paper, but we believe that our work creates a base for further discussion in this direction). This information is also of interest to researchers and academicians as the OSS development paradigm offers them an opportunity to understand the software evolution process with the help of the large data sets available in the public domain. What change patterns does an OSS system follow? Can these change patterns be generalized across the problem domains or the development paradigms? These are still open questions.

4 Results so Far

4.1 Fine-Grained Analysis of the OSS Projects

Analyzing the Change profiles of Software Systems using their Change Logs [8]
The change distribution and change pattern analysis of commit logs of six OSS projects have shown that the corrective changes are most often performed in the OSS projects, whereas the preventive changes have the minimum share in all the change logs except for Twitter MySQL and Apache Tomcat as the code restructuring has been taken up in these projects. In all the OSS projects, the enhancement activity is second among the change activity performed. It is observed that change activity in all the projects follows the up and down trend. It does not remain constant in any of the OSS projects.

Change Profile Analysis using Cluster Analysis to identify the Evolution trends (the paper under review)
Cluster analysis of all the change type of 106 OSS projects gives broadly three categories of change activity: high activity, moderate activity, and low activity. In high activity clusters, pressure to add more features dominates at the beginning followed by corrective actions. Corrective changes stabilize before all other change types. Adaptive and perfective changes catch slowly. It may be that developer teams focus on (problem-specific) features of projects first, and the adaptive and perfective changes are implemented later to gain a competitive edge. In projects with moderate activity for different change types, enhancement changes are again dominating in the beginning and stabilize later. Corrective changes increase at a moderate rate and surpass the enhancement changes towards the end of the observation period. Interestingly, adaptive and perfective changes, both, start at the same level.

Fuzzy Analysis and Prediction of OSS Projects Commit Activity [9, 10]
The computational method [7] of forecasting based on fuzzy time series is used to predict the commit activity in OSS projects. The results have shown that the computational method performs better than the best fitted ARIMA model for the commit data set of seven OSS projects. The error values in the case of the computational method remain close to the zero, whereas they fluctuate a lot in the case of the ARIMA.

Analyzing Change Profile of OSS Projects using Burst Detection (the paper under review)
The empirical investigation using the burst detection technique, in the change activity and other change related attributes such as change effort, and change size reveals

that they follow almost same patterns of occurrence. The high or moderate activity projects have significant peak correlation for the change attributes. But it is not so in projects with low levels of activity.

4.2 Coarse Grained Analysis

Understanding Language Profile of OSS Projects using Association Rule Mining [11]

The process of mining the most frequent associated group of languages from the data set is performed by exploring the KDD approach and using Apriori association rule mining algorithm. It provides combinations of the programming languages which are often used together in a project. The generated rules indicate that the languages like C, C++, C#, Java, PHP, Perl, Java Script, Python, Tcl, and Assembly are widely used in the development of the OSS projects.

Empirically Investigating Evolution Trends of Single and Multiple Contributor OSS Projects [12]

Popular languages (like Java, C, C++, PHP, Python, C# Perl, JavaScript, and Ruby) and licenses (like GPL, GPL3 MIT, LGPL, BSD3-Clause, and GPL3-late) have shown high usage trends in both types of projects. The average number of languages used in single and multiple contributor projects is 4.60 and 8.51 respectively. The relationship analysis between the attributes (user, LOC, commits, contributors) of single and multiple projects indicates that multiple contributor projects have strong relationship between contributors and commits; whereas contributor-LOC, user-commit, commit-LOC have shown a moderate relation and user-LOC, user-contributor has shown a weak relation. In single contributor projects, there is no strong relationship between different sets of attributes.

4.3 Work to Be Done

The commit messages of seven OSS projects (two large projects, three medium projects, and two small projects) are to be analyzed by focusing on the syntactical wellness and effectiveness of commit messages. A new approach is proposed to calculate the commit quality of a commit message by using 11 syntactical metrics of a commit message. The commit quality of software projects helps developers and project analysts to better understand the way OSS projects evolve. We will explore if there is any relation between software evolution and the commit quality of OSS projects. We plan to correlate the commit quality with number of contributors, and number of commits for large, medium and small OSS projects.

References

1. Godfrey, M., Tu, Q.: Evolution in open source software: a case study. In: Proceeding of the IEEE International Conference on Software Maintenance (ICSM), pp. 131–142 (2000)
2. Zhang, H., Kim, S.: Monitoring software quality evolution for defects. IEEE Softw. **4**, 58–64 (2010)
3. Fang, Y., Neufied, D.: Understanding sustained participation in open source software projects. J. Manag. Inf. Syst. **25**(4), 9–50 (2009)
4. Kemerer, C.F., Slaughter, S.A.: An empirical approach to studying software evolution. IEEE Trans. Softw. Eng. **25**(4), 493–509 (1999)
5. Meqdadi, O., Alhindawi, N., Collard, M., Maletic, J.: Towards understanding large-scale adaptive changes from version histories. In: IEEE International Conference on Software Maintenance, pp. 416–419 (2013)
6. Gonzalez-Barahona, J., Robles, G., Herriaz, I., Ortega, F.: Studying the laws of software evolution in a long-lived FLOSS project. J. Softw. Evol. Process. **26**(7), 589–612 (2014)
7. Singh, S.R.: A computational method of forecasting based on fuzzy time series. Math. Comput. Simul. **79**(3), 539–554 (2008)
8. Saini, M., Kaur, K.: Analyzing the change profiles of software systems using their change logs. Int. J. Softw. Eng. (IJSE-Egypt) **7**(2), 39–66 (2014)
9. Saini, M., Kaur, K.: Fuzzy analysis and prediction of commit activity in open source software projects. IET Softw. J. **10**(5), 136–146 (2016). doi:10.1049/iet-sen.2015.0087
10. Saini, M., Kaur, K.: Software Evolution Prediction using Fuzzy Analysis. EAIT. 349-354. Indian statistical institute Kolkata, India (2014). doi:10.1109/EAIT.2014.66
11. Saini, M., Kaur, K.: Understanding languages profile of open source software using association rule mining. In: IEEE International Conference on Future Technologies Conference, Fisherman's Wharf San Francisco, United States (2016)
12. Saini, M., Kaur, K.: A study to find significant evolution trends in OSS projects with single or multiple contributors. In: SCESM 2016, Heirank Business School, Noida, India (2016)

Transition from Plan-Driven to Agile:
An Action Research

Mohammad Abdur Razzak[(✉)]

Lero–the Irish Software Research Centre, University of Limerick, Limerick, Ireland
abdur.razzak@lero.ie

Abstract. Nowadays, many individuals and teams involved on projects are already using agile development techniques as part of their daily work. However, we have much less experience in how to scale and manage agile practices in distributed software development. At this level, there is an increasing need to standardize best practices to avoid reinvention and miscommunication across artifacts and processes. So, the emerging growth of frameworks i.e.; Scaled Agile Framework (SAFe[®]) in industry requires an academic attention because SAFe[®] does not cover all aspects of agility required in a distributed environment context. Early adopter of SAFe[®] also reported that, geographically distributed teams experience lower productivity due to lack of alignment and solid program execution. On the other hand, Global Teaming Model (GTM) places particular emphasis on the organization and management of globally distributed development teams, it does not specify *how* to develop software using Agile and Lean principles. Furthermore, the GTM recommended practices are normative, and do not prescribe how to implement the practice. Thus, we hypothesize that combining SAFe[®] practices, together with GTM recommendations will provide practitioners with a framework of implementable practices.

Keywords: Global software development · Agile · Scaled agile framework · Global Teaming Model

1 Background

1.1 Global Software Development

Improved communication technologies, access to global talent, cheaper labour, proximity to new markets and legal requirements have all contributed to the growth in Global Software Development (GSD) [24]. GSD is software work undertaken in different geographical locations, across national boundaries in a coordinated fashion through synchronous and asynchronous interaction [12]. As a result, a growing number of software companies started to implement GSD to reduce

Supervisor: Dr. John Noll, Research Fellow, Lero–the Irish Software Research Centre, University of Limerick, Limerick, Ireland; john.noll@lero.ie

P. Abrahamsson et al. (Eds.): PROFES 2016, LNCS 10027, pp. 746–750, 2016.
DOI: 10.1007/978-3-319-49094-6_64

time-to-market, increase operational efficiency, improve quality, and many more. Over the years several recommendations have been published in support of this complex development paradigm [6]. But, industrial experience shows that, GSD is reputed to suffer from communication breakdowns, low morale and delays due to teams being geographically, culturally and temporally separated [4,5,16].

1.2 Agile Methods

Traditionally Global Software Development has followed a plan driven, structured, waterfall approach, where tasks are allocated according to where they appear in the software lifecycle [8]. It was considered that agile methods envisaged for *small projects* and *co-located teams* [1] would be a poor fit for Global Software Development because both Agile and distributed development approaches differ significantly [18]. Agile methods tend to rely on informal processes to facilitate coordination whereas distributed software development relies on formal mechanisms. There is a growing trend for companies to adopt agile methods as reported in a tertiary study of Global Software Development [11]. However, setting up an Agile team is usually motivated by benefits such as increased productivity, innovation, and employee satisfaction [21] but introducing an Agile method can change the culture (command and control model) in a company; so to implement the Agile practices in global software environment developers need to have more autonomy as well as decision-making power [9].

1.3 Agile Framework

The choice of scaling agile framework adopted or how the framework is tailored will depend on the organization's size or on "what works" based on their own business goals, operative model, and needs. The Agile Scaling Knowledgebase (ASK) (http://www.agilescaling.org/home.html) developed a matrix of different Agile frameworks namely *Scrum-of-Scrum (SoS)*, *Large Scale Scrum (LeSS)*, *Scaled Agile Framework (SAFe®)*, *Disciplined Agile Delivery (DAD)*, *Spotify Model*, and *Scrum at Scale*. This matrix shows that SAFe®, launched in 2012 by Dean Leffingwell [13], focuses on large enterprises and takes a scaled approach to Agile adoption.

The SAFe® framework includes [13,14]: a process model that covers the highest and the lowest level in the enterprise; Associated Agile values and practices, including Scrum [20], eXtreme Programming [3], Kanban and Lean Software Development [17], and the Agile Manifesto [10]; four core values: code quality, alignment, program execution and transparency.

1.4 Global Teaming Model

The Global Teaming Model (GTM) is a model for global software engineering, with a particular emphasis on organization, governance and management of globally distributed development teams [19]. The Global Teaming Model follows the hierarchical structure and nomenclature of the CMMI [22]. At the highest level there are two broad goals, "Define Global Project Management" and "Define Management Between Locations". These goals are decomposed into Specific Practices that define broad categories of practice that lead to the parent goals. Specific Practices are further elaborated into Sub-practices. Finally, Sub-practices have one or more recommendations that specify detailed actions to be taken. In total, the GTM has five Specific Practices, twenty Sub-practices, and 64 recommendations, that have been validated against a real industrial case [4, 7].

2   Research Problem

Software development is still driven by *Infinite Diversity in Infinite Combinations*– as a consequence of that, practitioners do not ask themselves *why to adopt* these practices instead they ask *how to scale* these practices. So, there are two visible challenges–first one is, *Scaling Practices* and second one is, *Combining multiple development methodologies*. Scaling Agile continues to be a challenge in software development because when more teams works together then its required strong coordination among teams as well as on the project [1, 15, 23]. Scott W. Ambler [2] pointed out several factors, that needs to taken into consideration when scaling Agile such as team size, geographical distribution, entrenched culture, system complexity, legacy systems, regulatory compliance, organizational distribution, governance and enterprise focus.

To resolve the stated issues, a number of frameworks have been proposed to provide guidance for scaling agile across the enterprise and SAFe® is one of the commonly known models. SAFe® has gained a rapid attention and an important choice for organization that are in need of approaches for scaling agile development. However, SAFe® focuses merely on describing the best practices, roles and artifacts of agile and lean principles but no attempt has been made to describe implementation strategy. SAFe® also does not cover all aspects of agility required in a distributed environment context. Early adopter of SAFe® also reported that, geographically distributed teams experience lower productivity due to lack of alignment and solid program execution. On the other hand, while the GTM places particular emphasis on the organization and management of globally distributed development teams, it does not specify *how* to develop software using Agile and Lean principles. Furthermore, the GTM recommended practices are normative, and do not prescribe how to implement the practice. So, we hypothesize that combining SAFe® practices, together with GTM recommendations will provide practitioners with a framework of implementable practices. Thus, our research going forward is driven by following hypothesis:

> *Scaled Agile Framework can provide concrete implementations of GTM recommendations for Agile development*

3   Methods

This research will undertake a cycle of action research. The action research process can be defined as a number of learning cycles consisting of predefined stages. Within the action research a number of sub-methods will be use, namely interviews and workshops for data collection, and grounded theory as well as statistical analysis. Alongside, we will also gather data through participant observations, informal meetings, informal communications (e-mails) and documents from the organization and specific projects. This research will comprise multiple iterations over in three stages namely–*Identify, Develop, and Implement & Measure*:

- **Stage 1–*Identify***
  - Identify the current "As-is" process in the industrial settings. (Via interviews, observation, Global Teaming survey, documentation inspection)
  - Extract SAFe® practices at 4 levels (Team, Program, Value Stream, Portfolio), and stakeholder roles and responsibilities
  - Identify SAFe® practices that implement GTM Recommendations
  - Identify GTM Recommendation that is not implemented

- **Stage 2–*Develop***
  - Create "To-be" process model incorporating SAFe® practices that implement unimplemented GTM recommendations
  - Develop a process "Roadmap", that shows how to transition from the current "As-is" process, to the desired "To-be" process

- **Stage 3–*Implement and Measure***
  - Implement "To-be" process within the industrial settings and collect the KPI's
  - Evaluate the implementation and revise Roadmap and "To-be" models accordingly.

Acknowledgement. I would like to thanks Dr. Sarah Beecham, Senior Research Fellow, Lero. This work was supported, in part, by Science Foundation Ireland grants 10/CE/I1855 and 13/RC/2094 to Lero - the Irish Software Research Centre (www.lero.ie).

References

1. Abrahamsson, P., Conboy, K., Wang, X.: Lots done, more to do: the current state of agile systems development research. Eur. J. Inf. Syst. **18**, 281–284 (2009)
2. Ambler, S.W.: Agile software development at scale. In: Meyer, B., Nawrocki, J.R., Walter, B. (eds.) CEE-SET 2007. LNCS, vol. 5082, pp. 1–12. Springer, Heidelberg (2008). doi:10.1007/978-3-540-85279-7_1
3. Beck, K.: Extreme Programming Explained: Embrace Change. Addison-wesley professional, Boston (2000)
4. Beecham, S.: Motivating software engineers working in virtual teams across the globe. In: Ruhe, G., Wohlin, C. (eds.) Software Project Management in a Changing World, pp. 247–273. Springer, Heidelberg (2014)
5. Beecham, S., Noll, J.: What motivates software engineers working in global software development? In: Abrahamsson, P., Corral, L., Oivo, M., Russo, B. (eds.) PROFES 2015. LNCS, vol. 9459, pp. 193–209. Springer, Heidelberg (2015). doi:10.1007/978-3-319-26844-6_14

6. Beecham, S., O'Leary, P., Richardson, I., Baker, S., Noll, J.: Who are we ng global software engineering research for? In: IEEE 8th International Conference on Global Software Engineering (ICGSE), pp. 41–50. IEEE (2013)
7. Beecham, S., Richardson, I., Noll, J.: Assessing the strength of global teaming practices: apilot study. In: 2015 IEEE 10th International Conference on Global Software Engineering (ICGSE), pp. 110–114. IEEE (2015)
8. Estler, H.C., Nordio, M., Furia, C.A., Meyer, B., Schneider, J.: Agile vs. structured distributed software development: a case study. Empirical Softw. Eng. 19(5), 1197–1224 (2014)
9. Fowler, M.: Using an agile software process with offshore development. Capturado em (2006). http://martinfowler.com/articles/agileOffshore.html
10. Fowler, M., Highsmith, J.: The agile manifesto. Softw. Dev. 9(8), 28–35 (2001)
11. Hanssen, G.K., Šmite, D., Moe, N.B.: Signs of agile trends in global software engineering research: a tertiary study. In: Sixth IEEE International Conference on Global Software Engineering Workshop (ICGSEW), pp. 17–23. IEEE (2011)
12. Herbsleb, J.D., Moitra, D.: Global software development. Software 18(2), 16–20 (2001). IEEE
13. Leffingwell, D.: Scaled Agile Framework® 3.0 (2015). http://v3.scaledagileframework.com/. Accessed 15 Mar 2016
14. Levy, R., Short, M., Measey, P.: Agile foundations: principles, practices and frameworks. In: BCS (2015)
15. Maples, C.: Enterprise agile transformation: the two-year wall. In: Agile Conference, AGILE 2009, pp. 90–95. IEEE (2009)
16. Noll, J., Beecham, S., Richardson, I.: Global software development and collaboration: barriers and solutions. ACM Inroads 1(3), 66–78 (2010)
17. Poppendieck, M., Poppendieck, T.: Lean Software Development: An Agile Toolkit. Addison-Wesley, Boston (2003)
18. Ramesh, B., Cao, L., Mohan, K., Xu, P.: Can distributed software development be agile? Commun. ACM 49(10), 41–46 (2006)
19. Richardson, I., Casey, V., McCaffery, F., Burton, J., Beecham, S.: A process framework for global software engineering teams. Inf. Softw. Technol. 54(11), 1175–1191 (2012)
20. Schwaber, K., Beedle, M.: Agile Software Development with Scrum. Prentice Hall, Upper Saddle River (2002)
21. Šmite, D., Moe, N.B., Ågerfalk, P.J.: Fundamentals of agile distributed software development. In: Šmite, D., Moe, N.B., Ågerfalk, P.J. (eds.) Agility Across Time and Space. Springer, Heidelberg (2010)
22. Team, C.P.: Capability maturity model integration for development. Software Engineering Institute Technical report CMU/SEI-2006-TR-008 (2006)
23. Turk, D., France, R., Rumpe, B.: Limitations of agile software processes. In: Third International Conference on Extreme Programming and Flexible (2014)
24. Vizcaíno, A., García, F., Piattini, M., Beecham, S.: A validated ontology for global software development. Comput. Stand. Interf. 46, 66–78 (2016)

Software Product Innovation Through Startup Experimentation in Large Companies

Henry Edison$^{(\boxtimes)}$

Free University of Bozen-Bolzano, Bolzano, Italy
henry.edison@inf.unibz.it

Abstract. Startups are king of innovation. Their innovative products not only have changed our lives today but also put long-established players under pressure. Corporate management is now looking for ways to innovate like startup. Along with it, awareness and use of the Lean startup method has grown rapidly amongst the software startup community and large companies in recent years. However, how large companies could benefit from this method is still not fully understood. To shed a light on this issue, we conducted a multiple case study with 5 internal startups from different large companies.

Keywords: Innovation · Software product innovation · Internal startup · Lean startup · Method in action

1 Introduction

The world has changed. With their innovative products, startups are disrupting traditional markets and replacing long-established players. Uber, Spotify, AirBnB, to name a few, are examples of startup that have changed the way we do business today. Today, Alibaba, a Chinese online retailer has become the largest retail business in the world, which has greater revenues than Wal-Mart. Startups offer new product, business model and customer value at high speed and with cutting edge technology. To identify an opportunity, startups continuously communicate with their potential users, iterate and experiment to find a repeatable and scalable business. When the opportunity seems not going anywhere, startups are willing to pivot immediately, by redirecting and reshaping the product and the market. To compete in this age of disruption, companies cannot rely on efficiency on both cost and time-to-market and quality improvement anymore [1]. Corporate management is now looking for ways to innovate like startup. With a greater resource in-house, they hope that they are able to bring innovative product to market with the speed and new technology as startups do.

Along with it, awareness and use of the Lean startup method has grown rapidly amongst the software startup community in recent years. Like most previous methods, the development and promotion of these methods have been almost entirely driven by practitioners and consultants, with little participation

P. Abrahamsson et al. (Eds.): PROFES 2016, LNCS 10027, pp. 751–756, 2016.
DOI: 10.1007/978-3-319-49094-6_65

from the research community during the early stages of evolution. These methods are now the focus of more and more research efforts.

Even though Lean startup method is originated in software startup, it has also gained interest from large companies i.e. General Electric, 3M, Intuit, etc. Recent survey on 170 corporate executives reveals that 82 % of them are using some elements of Lean startup in their context [2]. Marijarvi et al. [3] report on Finnish large companies' experience in developing new software through internal startups. Ries [4] claims that Lean startup bears potential to improve the innovativeness of large companies. However, scientific and empirical studies regarding the implementation of Lean start-up in large software organisations are rare [5]. Based on this observation, the research questions investigated in this study are:

- RQ1: How Lean startup approach is applied to internal startup?
- RQ2: What are the challenges that Lean startup based internal startup faced by?
- RQ3: What are the key factors affecting Lean startup based internal startup?
- RQ4: How does Lean startup approach applied by internal startup support software product innovation?

2 Related Work

Software product innovation (SPI) refers to the introduction of new software product to an existing or new market [6]. Due to its nature, SPI is different with product innovation in general. Software is intangible and time is the main resource consumed to write, compile and test the code [7]. As in other industry, SPI is triggered by technology or market opportunity [8]. Technology is used to improve the current or offer new functionality. Market opportunity is arisen out of the unmet customer needs from the current offer or to address the newly revealed customer needs. SPI differs from software process innovation, which refers to the implementation of new process (i.e. OO development, CASE tools, open source, etc.) [9]. Software process innovation does not lead to SPI.

Our previous work reveals that the current research streams on SPI focus on five different areas: grassroot innovation, early user integration, agile-based innovation, startup experimentation and open innovation [9]. The first two areas are looking at how to capture new ideas from outside companies i.e. users, customers, competitors, etc., and turn them into product in-house. Agile-based innovation seeks a way to generate innovation using agile practise. Rather than developing new product internally, research on open innovation suggests to collaborate with external entity i.e. through living lab.

Startup experimentation approach is one of emergent themes in SPI which is inspired by Lean startup method [10,11]. In this approach, software is developed and validated in a continuous experiments with all stakeholders. Bosch [12] introduces an innovation experimentation system to minimise Research and Development (R&D) investment and increase customer satisfaction. In this system, R&D is responsible to develop the product iteratively (2–4 weeks) based on customer feedback. However, the method is limited to SaaS and embedded system. Based on Bosch's study, Fagerholm et al. [10] and Lindgren and Münch [11] propose a continuous experimentation system, which continuously testing the value of the product to users. These studies emphasise more on product development itself and how to capture the product's value. In this study, we do not only look at product development but also business development.

Current research on Lean startup method is centred on applying its method in software startup context to develop new product i.e. [13–15]. Very few peer-reviewed studies investigate how Lean startup method support SPI in large companies. Our study is one of the first effort to establish the empirical and scientific evidence of Lean startup method to support SPI in large companies.

3   Research Approach

Due to the uniqueness and complex nature of the phenomenon and the intention to achieve an in-depth understanding of it, a multiple case study is considered a suitable research approach. The case companies is selected based on the following criteria: (1) the company develops software in-house, (2) a dedicated team is responsible from ideation to commercialisation of a new software, and (3) the software falls out of the current main product line. The unit of analysis in this study is a development team or internal startup.

There are five cases involved in this study. Two of them are in the same company. Some of the case companies will remain anonymous at the request of the companies. The profile of five internal startups are shown in Table 1.

Table 1. The profile of the five cases

	Lokki	Team A	Team B	Team C	Team D
Company	F-Secure	XCo	YCo	ZCo	ZCo
Business domain	Cyber security and privacy	Print directory publisher	Telecommunication	Classified advertisement	
Member	6–7	7–10	5–18	5–6	3–5
Product	Location sharing	Prepayment platform	Audio & video conversation	e-Commerce platform (general)	e-Commerce platform (used cars)
Customer	Family	Merchant's owners	Segmented users	Segmented users	Segmented users
Current status	Terminated	Scaling	Scaling	Development	Terminated
Timeframe	2012–2014	2014-now	2013-now	2016-now	2014–2016
#interviews	8	2	3	2	1

Semi-structured interviews were used as the primary data collection method. To better understand the phenomenon, several members were interviewed (see Table 1). The interviewees were selected based on their involvement in the development and their availability in the interview process. In the case of Team A, the team lead did not recommend us to talk to other current members. She argued that they recently joined the team.

Most of the interviews were done in their office, but some of them were done through Skype due to geographically constraint. Each interview lasted between one and two hour, and was recorded. All interviews were transcribed verbatim. Notes were taken during the interviews. Other supporting materials, such as presentation, white papers, etc. were also collected to triangulate the interview data.

To guide the study process, we employ method in action framework [16] as the conceptual framework. The framework recognises the complex nature of software development and each component affects the overall system. However, the framework does not prescribe detailed and specific action to use. It allows us to reflect on the software development as rich and complex phenomenon influenced by the components and interactions [17].

4 Initial Results

Except Team B and Team C, the startup experimentation was initiated by corporate management as part of strategy exercise to look for growth through product innovation. In these cases, management was responsible to mobilise the resources needed by the team. In the cases of Team B and Team C, the initiative came from the employees who found a gap in the current market and technology. As consequences, they had to find a way to convince the management and get all the resources needed. Hence, an internal startup was established to develop and bring the new product to market. Based on Lokki case, the detail process on how Lean startup method is applied to internal startup has been published in [18]. The framework used in this study is used to analyse the remaining cases.

Using method in action framework, our initial results identify the challenges faced by internal startups. The initial key challenges are presented in Table 2.

In all cases, the core team members were recruited internally and assigned dedicatedly to that team. In the case of Team B, the team found difficulties to recruit new members externally because YCo is not known as software developing company. Moreover, YCo was struggling with attracting new talent to join the company. In the case of Lokki, it was not clear to the employees what it means by working in internal startup. Moreover, not everybody has entrepreneurial mindset.

During the development process, all teams had to report the progress to corporate management periodically. The role of founder is found in Team B and Team C case. A founder is the one who has a vision about the new product. In the other cases, there was no founder role inside the team. Hence they had to figure it out what product should be developed. In Team A case, the internal startup employed Design Thinking approach to seek for new idea. In both Lokki case and Team D, no specific method was employed. The team members were brainstorming to collect and decide ideas to be implemented. No metrics were collected during that period until they had approval from management to start the development.

Table 2. The key challenges of Lean based internal startups

	Key challenges
Organisational context	Overhead communications
	Potential internal conflict of interest
Company strategy	Strategy change
	Organisational championship
	Aligning between new product and company strategy
Human resources	Entrepreneurial mindset
	No "real" founder, no vision
	Recruiting new talent
Development/Business context	Fear of cannibalisation
	Autonomy in decision making process
	Balancing the needs of all stakeholders

Our initial results show that only Team A had freedom in both product and business development, whereas in the other cases, the team only had freedom in product development. When it comes to defining business model, the team needed approval from management. In the case of Team A, the team was supported by the CEO. When new management came in, the CEO protected the initiative. They were allowed to continue the project even though at that time, the product did not bring any revenue. In the case of Team D, they did not get approval for validating new business model, thus the initiative was closed. In the case of Lokki, due to the strategy change, the new product had fell beyond the core business. Moreover, no organisational championship that were able to protect them led to the termination of that initiative.

5   Conclusion and Future Work

With the conceptual framework presented herein, we are able to understand better how Lean startup method is used in large companies. This study proposes several specific contributions. Firstly, the framework should facilitate companies to better use Lean startup method suited to their needs. Secondly, based on the identified key challenges companies can prepare and undertake any preemptive actions to overcome or minimise these challenges. Third, using the common key factors, companies can maximise its potential to support product innovation through internal startup.

The next step of this study is to continue in-depth data analysis to all cases using the same protocol to answer all research questions. Based on the analysis, the framework will be refined and extended. A cross-case comparison will be performed to identify the common pattern among the cases.

References

1. Rejeb, H.B., Morel-Guimaraes, L., Boly, V., Assiélou, N.G.: Measuring innovation best practices: improvement of an innovation index integrating threshold and synergy effects. Technovation **28**, 838–854 (2008)
2. Kirsner, S.: The barriers big companies face when they try to act like lean startups (2016). https://hbr.org/2016/08/the-barriers-big-companies-face-when-they-try-to-act-like-lean-startups
3. Marijarvi, J., Hokkanen, L., Komssi, M., Kiljander, H., Xu, Y., Raatikainen, M., Seppanen, P., Heininen, J., Koivulahti-Ojala, M., Helenius, M., Jarvinen, J.: The cookbook for successful internal startups. In: DIGILE and N4S (2016)
4. Ries, E.: The Lean Startup: How Today's Entrepreneurs Use Continuous Innovation to Create Radically Successful Businesse. Crown Business, New York (2011)
5. Edison, H., Wang, X., Abrahamsson, P.: Lean startup: why large software companies should care. In: XP 2015 Scientific Workshop Proceedings, pp. 2:1–2:7 (2015)
6. Lippoldt, D., Stryszowski, P.: Innovation in the Software Sector. OECD, Paris (2009)
7. Moe, N.B., Barney, S., Aurum, A., Khurum, M., Wohlin, C., Barney, H.T., Gorschek, T., Winata, M.: Fostering and sustaining innovation in a fast growing agile company. In: Dieste, O., Jedlitschka, A., Juristo, N. (eds.) PROFES 2012. LNCS, vol. 7343, pp. 160–174. Springer, Heidelberg (2012). doi:10.1007/978-3-642-31063-8_13
8. Desouza, K.C., Awazu, Y., Kim, J.: Managing radical software engineering: leverage order and chaos. IJTPM **8**(1), 22–40 (2008)
9. Edison, H., Duc, A.N., Jabangwe, R., Wang, X., Abrahamsson, P.: An investigation into software product innovation: a systematic literature review. In: ICE/IEEE International Technology Management 2016 Proceedings (2016)
10. Fagerholm, F., Guinea, A.S., Mäenpää, H., Münch, J.: Building blocks for continuous experimentation. In: RCoSE 2014 Proceedings, pp. 26–35 (2014)
11. Lindgren, E., Münch, J.: Software development as an experiment system: a qualitative survey on the state of the practice. In: Lassenius, C., Dingsøyr, T., Paasivaara, M. (eds.) XP 2015. LNBIP, vol. 212, pp. 117–128. Springer, Heidelberg (2015). doi:10.1007/978-3-319-18612-2_10
12. Bosch, J.: Building products as innovation experiment systems. In: Cusumano, M.A., Iyer, B., Venkatraman, N. (eds.) ICSOB 2012. LNBIP, vol. 114, pp. 27–39. Springer, Heidelberg (2012). doi:10.1007/978-3-642-30746-1_3
13. Efeoglu, A., Moller, C., Sérié, M.: Solution prototyping with design thinking - social media for sap store: a case study. Commun. Comput. Inf. Sci. **447**, 99–110 (2014)
14. Haniotis, J.: Innovation jams: lessons in agile product development - an experience report. In: Agile Conference 2011 Proceedings, pp. 223–229 (2011)
15. May, B.: Applying lean startup: an experience report - lean & lean ux by a ux veteran: lessons learned in creating & launching a complex consumer app. In: Agile Conference 2012 Proceedings, pp. 141–147 (2012)
16. Fitzgerald, B., Russo, N.L., Stolterman, E.: Information Systems Development: Methods in Action. McGraw-Hill Education, Boston (2002)
17. O'Neill, S., Morgan, L., Conboy, K.: A framework for investigating open innovation processes in ISD. In: ICIS 2011 Proceedings (2011)
18. Edison, H., Wang, X., Abrahamsson, P.: Product innovation through internal startup in large software companies: a case study. In: Euromicro SEAA 2016 Proceedings (2016)

Erratum to: Supporting Management of Hybrid OSS Communities - A Stakeholder Analysis Approach

Hanna Mäenpää[1]([✉]), Tero Kojo[2], Myriam Munezero[1],
Fabian Fagerholm[1], Terhi Kilamo[3], Mikko Nurminen[3],
and Tomi Männistö[1]

[1] University of Helsinki, Helsinki, Finland
{hanna.maenpaa,myriam.munezero,fabian.fagerholm,
tomi.mannisto}@cs.helsinki.fi
[2] The Qt Company, Espoo, Finland
tero.kojo@qt.io
[3] Tampere Technical University, Tampere, Finland
{terhi.kilamo,mikko.nurminen}@tut.fi

Erratum to:
Chapter 7 in: P. Abrahamsson et al. (Eds.)
Product-Focused Software Process Improvement
DOI: 10.1007/978-3-319-49094-6_7

In the paper starting on page 102 of this volume, the word "communities" was spelled incorrectly in the main title. It has to read "Communities" instead of "Communnities".

The updated original online version for this chapter can be found at
DOI: 10.1007/978-3-319-49094-6_7

Tutorials

Tutorials at PROFES 2016

Daniela S. Cruzes[1]([⊠]) and Sabrina Markzac[2]

[1] SINTEF-ICT, Trondheim, Norway
danielac@sintef.no
[2] Computer Science School – PUCRS, Porto Alegre, RS, Brazil
sabrina.marczak@pucrs.br

Abstract. PROFES 2016 hosts nine exciting tutorials that will complement and enhance the main conference program, offering a wider knowledge perspective around the conference topics. The tutorials provide insights into special topics of current and ongoing relevance to the conference focus areas. We have divided the program in five special tracks: innovation and speed, software security, software quality, regulated software, DevOps and Lean Startups. Our goal is to have practitioners from different companies participating on this day.

1 Introduction to the Tutorials

PROFES 2016 hosts nine exciting tutorials that will complement and enhance the main conference program, offering a wider knowledge perspective around the conference topics. We have divided the program in five special tracks: Innovation and Speed, Software Security, Software Quality, Regulated Software, DevOps and Lean Startups (See Table 1).

On Track 1, Innovation and Speed are the focus. On the Design Thinking tutorial, the presenters will give a hands-on introduction into Design Thinking and rough physical prototyping in the early stages of any kind of product development – physical as well as digital. On the Continuous experimentation tutorial, insights on how to use continuous experimentation to steer development towards rapid value creation and to avoid unnecessary development efforts will be the focus.

On Track 2, Software Security will be addressed on a full day tutorial, which will provide a brief introduction to the core principles of software security, threat modeling using data flow diagrams, attack trees and misuse cases. On the second part of the tutorial, the participants will have a hands-on on Protection Poker, a tool for risk estimation to be used as part of the sprint planning meeting.

On Track 3, Software Quality will be addressed on the perspective of Risk-Based Testing and Architecture Evaluation. In the Risk-based Software Testing, the presenters introduce the concept of risk in software testing as well as a practical approach for developing a risk-based test strategy. The tutorial is based on results from previous research and studies investigating the introduction of risk-based testing in large organizations as well as small and medium enterprises. On the Architecture Evaluation tutorial, there will be a presentation of a method for architecture evaluation, with a walk-through in an example of a previously performed evaluation.

P. Abrahamsson et al. (Eds.): PROFES 2016, LNCS 10027, pp. 759–760, 2016.
DOI: 10.1007/978-3-319-49094-6

Table 1. Tutorials at PROFES 2016

	Morning	Afternoon
Track 1: Innovation and Speed	Design Thinking for Software Innovations – a crash course in rough physical prototyping (*Martin Steinert, Federico Lozano & Matilde Bisballe*)	Continuous Experimentation: Accelerating Innovation through Highly Effective Experiments (*Jürgen Münch*)
Track 2: Software Security	Practical Software Security in a Continuously Deploying World (*Martin Gilje Jaatun & Inger Anne Tøndel*)	
Track 3: Software Quality	Risk-Based Software Testing: Increasing Effectiveness and Efficiency in Testing (*Michael Felderer & Rudolf Ramler*)	Architecture Evaluation – Threat or opportunity? (*Even-Andre Karlsson*)
Track 4: Regulated Software	Experience from integrating Agile Development with process standards like ASPICE and ISO 26262 (*Even-Andre Karlsson*)	Safe Scrum (*Geir K. Hanssen, Thor Myklebust, Tor Stålhane & Børge Haugset*)
Track 5: DevOps and Lean Startups	Creating Champions and battling Dragons – How to create a DevOps culture? (*Pål Thomassen & Ingrid Sorgendal*)	Lean startups in established companies: How to make it really happen and how to avoid common pitfalls? (*Nils Moe & Tone Merethe Aasen*)

On Track 4, the tutorials focus on Regulated Software; Safety-critical software is becoming an increasingly larger part of safety systems, such as fire-detection, dynamic positioning, and autonomous driving. In the morning, the presenters will introduce the basic principles of process standards like ASPICE and ISO 26262, and also practical experience how to incorporate them in an agile environment, how to incorporate safety activities into sprints, handling of traceability in an agile environment, handling of reviews, change management, etc. These standards have not been adapted to agile development, and many of the underlying assumptions are based on a waterfall model and many organizations have problems joining these two words. In the afternoon, the tutorial will explain the specific challenges related to development of safety-critical systems and explain how Scrum may be adapted to create a flexible and efficient process for both development and certification, based on the SafeScrum process framework.

On Track 5, the two tutorials will focus on two very actual topics in software companies, DevOps and Lean Startups. The term DevOps is still often misunderstood, and is typically associated with many types of automation tools. However, while a key strategy in many well performing teams, automation is a consequence of DevOps workflows – not the main point. In this tutorial the presenters will demystify the term and give some insights on how to change an organization towards DevOps culture. In the afternoon, the tutorial will describe the idea and motivation behind Lean Startup, why many agile companies are implementing this approach today, and how they do it. Further, the tutorial will highlight challenges companies face when adopting the Lean Startup approach, and explain why the Lean Startup team needs a high degree of autonomy, and how to enable such autonomy.

Continuous Experimentation: Accelerating Innovation Through Highly Effective Experiments

Jürgen Münch[1,2(✉)]

[1] Herman Hollerith Center, Reutlingen University,
Danziger Straße 6, 71034 Böblingen, Germany
Juergen.Muench@Reutlingen-University.de,
Juergen.Muench@cs.helsinki.fi
[2] Department of Computer Science, University of Helsinki,
P.O. Box 68, 00014 Helsinki, FI, Finland

Abstract. Finding the right scope for product development in order to build innovative products that customers want is crucial for success. Continuous experimentation is an important means to steer development towards rapid value creation and to avoid unnecessary development efforts. Insights from such experiments can directly influence frequent iterative deliveries. Continuous experimentation helps companies to gain competitive advantage by reducing uncertainties and rapidly finding product roadmaps that work. However, defining a product strategy in a testable way and running the right experiments in an effective way is hard. Setting up experiments wrong can lead to false results and wrong business decisions.

1 What You Will Learn

In this hands-on tutorial you will learn the tactics and habits for highly effective experiments and how to introduce them into your company. Join this tutorial to learn how to get out the most out of continuous experimentation.

- How to identify the relevant questions we need to answer for making good product decisions.
- How to find and formulate the right hypotheses to test.
- What are the components of a good hypothesis?
- How to define metrics that inform product decisions.
- How to select the right experiments.
- How to justify the efforts for experimentation.
- How to align experiments with your product decisions and product strategy.
- How to transition your organization towards continuous experimentation.

© Springer International Publishing AG 2016
P. Abrahamsson et al. (Eds.): PROFES 2016, LNCS 10027, pp. 761–762, 2016.
DOI: 10.1007/978-3-319-49094-6

2 Who Should Attend

This presentation is aimed at

- product managers,
- innovation managers,
- startup founders,
- business people,
- software developers,
- consultants,
- coaches, and
- anyone who is interested in making an impact with their products through experimentation.

3 Who is Teaching This Tutorial

Jürgen Münch is a Professor of Software Engineering at Reutlingen University, Germany, and a Research Director in the Department of Computer Science at the University of Helsinki, Finland. He regularly teaches product management courses and helps companies to develop innovation capabilities and new digitally-enabled products and services. He specializes in software engineering, in particular data- and value-driven software development, product management, agile engineering, and startups. Results are documented in five books and more than 150 refereed publications.

4 Outline

1. Why Experiments?
2. Setting up Highly Effective Experiments
3. Achieving Breakthrough

5 What Former Attendees Said

- One of the most enriching courses.
- Jürgen has a very profound practical and theoretical knowledge.
- Definitely recommendable.

Integrating Agile Development with Process Standards Like ASPICE and ISO 26262

Even-André Karlsson[(⊠)]

Addalot Consulting AB, Gråbrödersgatan 8, 211 21 Malmö, Sweden
even-andre.karlsson@addalot.se

Abstract. In many industries there is dual pressure on both being more agile and adaptive to changing requirements at the same time as being compliant with process standards like ASPICE and ISO 26262. These standards have not been adapted to agile development, and many of the underlying assumptions are based on a waterfall model. Many organizations have problems joining these two words. In this tutorial we will look at the basic principles in these some standards, and also practical experience how to incorporate them in an agile environment. Examples that we will show are e.g. how to incorporate safety activities into sprints, handling of traceability in an agile environment, handling of reviews, change management, etc.

1 Biography and Contact Information of Tutorial Presenters

Even-André Karlsson has over 20 years' experience as a consultant for larger software companies. One of his areas of expertise is evaluating, documenting and development of processes for software architecture. Even's experience includes modelling Ericsson GPRS and BTS systems. He served as adjunct professor at the Lund Technical University for three years teaching an industrial course in Software Architecture.

2 Description, to be Used for Evaluation, Including Aims and/or Learning Objectives

Learning objectives

- Understand how to be compliant with process standards in an agile process.
- Understand the major obstacles, and possible ways to handle them
- Get some practical experience from real world organizations that have addressed these issues.

3 Target Audience and Desired Number of Participants (Minimum and Maximum)

This presentation is interesting for developers and managers that have to tackle this challenge. A basic understanding of agile development and process standards is useful. No restriction on number of participants.

© Springer International Publishing AG 2016
P. Abrahamsson et al. (Eds.): PROFES 2016, LNCS 10027, pp. 763–764, 2016.
DOI: 10.1007/978-3-319-49094-6

4 Tentative Agenda

Introduction (50 min)

- Who am I? Who are you?
- Agile development
- Process standards, e.g. ISO 26262, ASPICE

Areas of concern with examples (2 × 50 min)

- Documentation
- Traceability
- Up front analysis and design
- Planning and support processes
- Safety activities

Architecture Evaluation - Threat or Opportunity?

Even-André Karlsson[(✉)]

Addalot Consulting AB, Gråbrödersgatan 8, 211 21 Malmö, Sweden
even-andre.karlsson@addalot.se

Abstract. Addalot has in many contexts been commissioned to evaluate the architecture of a product. There may be situations where you want to buy a company, taking over a product, or that you have purchased a product, but are not satisfied and want to gain a deeper understanding of the evidence and weaknesses. The purpose of the architecture evaluation is to obtain an objective analysis for future product decisions. We usually say that an architecture evaluation of a system is that an inspection of a car or a transfer inspection of a house - something that should be mandatory. In this tutorial we want to go through the method we use to do this, what areas we analyze, and common weaknesses and risks that we often encounter. We conclude by walking through an example of an evaluation as we recently did for Swedish Radio.

1 Biography and Contact Information of Tutorial Presenters

Even-André Karlsson has over 20 years' experience as a consultant for larger software companies. One of his areas of expertise is evaluating, documenting and development of processes for software architecture. Even's experience includes modelling Ericsson GPRS and BTS systems. He served as adjunct professor at the Lund Technical University for three years teaching an industrial course in Software Architecture.

2 Description, to be Used for Evaluation, Including Aims and/or Learning Objectives

Areas that we evaluate are:

- Functionality
- Logical structure, interface, dynamic architecture, documentation and traceability
- Flexibility, comprehensibility and maintainability
- Scalability, performance, redundancy, security and safety (if relevant)
- Code structure and quality
- Testability, test strategy, automation and coverage
- Future plans

© Springer International Publishing AG 2016
P. Abrahamsson et al. (Eds.): PROFES 2016, LNCS 10027, pp. 765–766, 2016.
DOI: 10.1007/978-3-319-49094-6

Learning objectives

- Understand how an architecture evaluation is done
- Understand when it can be useful to perform one
- Practical experience from evaluations that can help in your own work as architect, both on current and future systems

3 Target Audience and Desired Number of Participants (Minimum and Maximum)

This presentation is interesting for both architects who want to evaluate products and architects who want to prepare themselves and their system of evaluation.

It is also useful for managers and decision makers that needs to understand what an architecture evaluation is and when it can be useful to do.

4 Tentative Agenda

- Introduction (50 min)
  - Who am I? Who are you?
  - Why do we do architecture evaluations?
  - How do we do it?
- SR example (30 min)
- Areas and examples (50 min)
  - Functionality
  - Architecture and documentation
  - Non functional aspects
  - Code, testing and environment
  - Management of architecture
- Examples of conclusion (20 min)

SafeScrum Tutorial

Geir Kjetil Hanssen[1(✉)], Thor Myklebust[1], Tor Stålhane[2],
and Børge Haugset[1]

[1] SINTEF, Department of Software Engineering, Safety and Security,
Postboks 4760 Sluppen, 7465 Trondheim, Norway
{ghanssen,Thor.Myklebust,Borge.Haugset}@sintef.no
[2] Informatics Department, Norwegian University of Science and Technology,
Sem Sælandsvei 9, 7491 Trondheim, Norway
tor.stalhane@idi.ntnu.no

Abstract. Safety-critical software is becoming an increasingly larger part of safety systems, such as fire-detection, dynamic positioning, and autonomous driving. Such systems normally needs to be certified according to international safety standards, such as IEC 61508 which provides details on *how* the system and the software is to be built in order to be considered safe. In order to achieve a certificate by in independent assessor, the system provider needs to provide comprehensive documentation to demonstrate proof of conformance to the standard. This makes the development process complex and documentation costs very high. Traditionally this has been managed by the use of plan-based approaches, typically variants of the V-model. This has been a viable approach for decades as safety systems have largely been hardware based. The ongoing software growth however calls for a new take on the development process and the industry has picked up an interest in agile development methodologies to address a growing need for flexibility in development. As an answer to this we have proposed the SafeScrum process framework in order to meet new challenges in development and certification of safety critical software. The tutorial will explain the specific challenges related to development of such systems and explain how Scrum may be adapted to create a flexible and efficient process for both development and certification.

The software tends to be very complex which also affects the development process.

1   Biography and Contact Information of Tutorial Presenters

Geir Kjetil Hanssen is a senior research scientist at SINTEF ICT, Norway. He has a PhD in software engineering from the Norwegian University of Science and Technology (NTNU). His main areas of interest are software engineering methodologies – in particular agile methods, software process improvement, and safety critical systems. He is currently involved in industry-oriented research projects addressing the implementation and effect of agile methods for developing systems that will undergo certification according to the IEC61508 and DO178C standards. Founder of SafeScrum. Contact information: ghanssen@sintef.no, +47 92492454.

© Springer International Publishing AG 2016
P. Abrahamsson et al. (Eds.): PROFES 2016, LNCS 10027, pp. 767–769, 2016.
DOI: 10.1007/978-3-319-49094-6

Thor Myklebust works as research and certification manager at SINTEF ICT. He is a Cand. Scient. in physics with an additional two years at university level on Psychology and Statistics. He has experience in certification of products and systems since 1987 and has been a member of several international committees since 1988.

- Safety (NEK/IEC 65),
- IEC 61508 committee,
- Railway (NEK/CENELEC/TC 9) and
- NB-rail (notified bodies) since 2007.

He was vice-chairman and chairman of NB-rail in the period October 2013 – October 2015. Founder of SafeScrum. Contact information: thor.myklebust@sintef.no, +4795779869.

Tor Stålhane holds a master degree in physical electronics and a PhD in statistics. He worked as a developer at SINTEF from 1969 to 1988 and as a safety analyst of software intensive systems from 1988 to 2000. He then moved to NTNU where he was a professor in software engineering, teaching software engineering, process improvement and safety analysis of software-intensive systems up to 2014. He is now professor emeritus at NTNU. Founder of SafeScrum. Contact information: stalhane@idi.ntnu.no, +47 97595326.

Børge Haugset is a research scientist at SINTEF ICT, Norway. He has a Master in software engineering from the University of Oslo (UiO). His main areas of interest is agile software development and where safety meets security – in particular the complex problems that modern safety-critical software systems face when introduced to open networks and the Internet of Things. Contact information: borge.haugset@sintef.no, +47 93420190.

2   Description, to Be Used for Evaluation, Including Aims and/or Learning Objectives

The tutorial will describe the SafeScrum process and then go through the important steps in agile development of safety critical systems according to SafeScrum and IEC 61508 – safety analysis, the application of the agile practices and examples of applied tool chains. The tutorial will end with a presentation of how we can adapt the agile process to other relevant standards. After having attended the tutorial, the participants should be able to:

- Basic understanding of safety-critical software and the IEC 61508 standard
- Understand and apply the basic ideas of agile development of safety-critical systems
- Create a SafeScrum process that is compliant to other relevant safety standards

3 Target Audience and Desired Number of Participants (Minimum and Maximum)

Target audience is developers and project managers who (1) are, or will be involved in the development of safety-critical systems and (2) will introduce agile development methods into the process. The tutorial will focus on Scrum and development according to IEC 61508 but can be adapted to most safety-critical standards and agile methods.

- Minimum number of participants: 5
- Maximum number of participants: 50

4 Special Requirements, Such as Facilities, Equipment, and Materials, if Applicable

Necessary equipment is:

- Video equipment and screen
- Whiteboard and pens

5 Tentative Agenda

Time	Topic	Responsible
13:00	Scrum and agile software development Introduction to safety-critical systems	GH
13:30	The SafeScrum process	GH
13:50	Safety analysis, hazard logs and SafeScrum	TS
14:20	Coffee break	
14:35	Use of Agile Practices when developing Safety-Critical Software	TM
15:05	The SafeScrum tool chain and tool classification	BH
15:30	Adapting SafeScrum to other standards than IEC 61508	TS
16:00	End of tutorial	GH

6 Acknowledgments

This work was partially funded by the Norwegian research council under grant #228431 (the SUSS project). Research has been done in collaboration with Autronica Fire & Security AS and Kongsberg Maritime AS. We are grateful for valuable input from TÜV Nord and TÜV Rheinland.

Creating Champions and Battling Dragons – How to Create a DevOps Culture

Pål Thomassen$^{(\boxtimes)}$ and Ingrid Sorgendal

Bekk Consulting AS, Ferjemannsveien 10, 7042 Trondheim, Norway
pal.thomassen@bekk.no, ingrid.sorgendal@bekk.no
http://www.bekk.no

Abstract. The term DevOps is a vague and often misunderstood term. It is typically associated with many types of automation tools. However, while a key strategy in many well performing teams, automation is a consequence of DevOps workflows – not the main point. In this tutorial we will demystify the term and give some insights on how to change an organization towards DevOps culture.

1 Introduction

Are you curious about what DevOps is, and how its practices can benefit your organization – or are you ready to implement a DevOps workflow, but struggling to break up an unyielding silo mindset?

The DevOps movement is rapidly spreading throughout the software community. A group of concepts, inspired and catalyzed by Agile and Lean approaches, there are many misconceptions of what DevOps is, and how it can be implemented to benefit the development and operation of software. Oftentimes, a shift to a DevOps oriented workflow requires organizational culture changes that can be difficult or even painful to undertake.

Join us for this tutorial, where we will demystify the term (and dispel some myths), and give you the tools to identify how you can change your organization into a smooth, well tuned DevOps machine.

2 Biography of Presenters

Pål Thomassen is Practice Lead for DevOps at BEKK Trondheim, and board member for the Trondheim DevOps meetup. Pål draws from his experience as a developer in projects for small and large Norwegian businesses, both in private and public sectors. Pål is dedicated to improving the workflows and efficiency of development teams, all the while spreading his enthusiasm and love for the software community.

Ingrid Sorgendal is Practice Lead for User Experiences at BEKK Trondheim, and board member for the Trondheim IxDA meetup. As a User Experience Designer, Ingrid is a seasoned facilitator with experience from a broad array

© Springer International Publishing AG 2016
P. Abrahamsson et al. (Eds.): PROFES 2016, LNCS 10027, pp. 770–771, 2016.
DOI: 10.1007/978-3-319-49094-6

of projects and customers. She oftentimes finds herself working with improving organizational cultures – enabling her customers to meet user needs, in addition to creating better working conditions for the developers.

In this tutorial, Ingrid and Pål team up to share their experiences with DevOps and organizational change.

3   Learning Objectives

- To give partipants an introduction to what DevOps is (and isn't)
- To make participants confident with improving the culture of their own organizations
- To challenge participants on how to implement and streamline a DevOps workflow

4   Target Audience and Prerequirements

The tutorial targets practitioners interested in shifting to a DevOps workflow; especially those struggling with change resistant cultures and/or silo cultures. However, interested researchers will also benefit from presentations as well as activities. The tutorial will be hands on with specific techniques aimed at preparing tutorial participants on working with the cultures of their own organizations, in order to implement the DevOps Concept into their software development and operations.

There are no requirements, though participants should in advance decide on a business or organization (your own workplace, customer, institute; as long as you know it well) that can be use for the individual tutorial activities.

5   Tentative Agenda

- Introduction: DevOps
- Introduction: Actor mapping
- Activity: Map your organization
- Introduction: Creating champions and battling dragons
- Activity: Identify champions and dragons
- Activity: Create your battle strategy
- Wrap up: DevOps in your day-to-day workflow

Lean Startups in Established Companies: How to Make it Really Happen and How to Avoid Common Pitfalls

Nils Brede Moe[(✉)] and Tone Merethe Aasen

SINTEF, 7465 Trondheim, Norway
nils.b.moe@sintef.no

Abstract. Sustaining innovation in a company delivering services based on software is difficult. One common challenge is developing new products and services when well-defined requirements are lacking due to a high level of uncertainty of what the customer really wants. This tutorial presents one approaches to handling this uncertainty by relying on continuous experimentation and validated learning. The method "Lean Startup" is about cross-functional teams given the authority to set directions for the new product, and continuously testing out the assumptions and ideas on real customers. However, the Lean Startup team is seldom able to solve all tasks by themselves. While doing continuous experimentation, the team must align many decisions regarding with the rest of the company, which usually slows them down. Further, the team's autonomy is reduced due to multiple dependencies, which in turn reduces the innovation potential of the team. The question is how do we have Lean Startup teams which overcome these difficulties and reap the benefits using the method. Also: Who should be part of the cross-functional Lean Startup team? Should the team be isolated? What are the consequences if the team operating independently form the rest of the organization?

1 Biography and Contact Information of Tutorial Presenters

Nils Brede Moe works with software process improvement, agile software development, Lean-startup and global software development at SINTEF. His research interests are related to organizational, socio-technical, and global/distributed aspects. His main publications include studies on self-management, decision-making, innovation and teamwork. He wrote his thesis on "From Improving Processes to Improving Practice — Software Process Improvement in Transition from Plan-driven to Change-driven Development". He is also holding position at Blekinge Institute of Technology.

Tone Merethe Aasen works with innovation management, and knowledge processes and strategies at SINTEF. Her research interests are related to innovation as participative processes, including new models and practices for collaborative innovation work. Her main publications include books and papers on innovation as collective processes in and between organizations, and on employee-driven-innovation. She wrote her thesis on "Innovation as social processes A participative study of the Statoil R & D program Subsea Increased Oil Recovery (SIOR)".

© Springer International Publishing AG 2016
P. Abrahamsson et al. (Eds.): PROFES 2016, LNCS 10027, pp. 772–773, 2016.
DOI: 10.1007/978-3-319-49094-6

2 Description, to Be Used for Evaluation, Including Aims and/or Learning Objectives

The tutorial will describe the idea and motivation behind Lean Startup, why many agile companies are implementing this approach today, and how they do it. Further, the tutorial will highlight challenges companies face when adopting the Lean Startup approach, and explain why the Lean Startup team needs a high degree of autonomy, and how to enable such autonomy. After having attended the tutorial, the participants should be able to:

- Have basic understanding of Lean Startup and how to apply it.
- Understand the challenges of such approaches in established companies related to the product owner, management, and other departments.
- Understand the need for and how to empower the Lean Startup team.

3 Target Audience and Desired Number of Participants (Minimum and Maximum)

Target audiences are team members, team leads, project and department managers, business analysts, and HR. The tutorial will focus on Lean Startup, agile software development, and empowered cross-functional teams. Minimum number of participants: 5, Maximum number of participants: 40.

4 Special Requirements, Such as Facilities, Equipment, and Materials, if Applicable

Necessary equipment: Video equipment and screen, whiteboard, markers and pens.

5 Tentative Agenda

13:00   Introduction to the workshop and Lean Startup
13:50   The challenges of Lean Startup in an established company – a story
               from an Norwegian bank
14:40   The self-managing cross functional Lean Startup team
15:00   Strategies for implementing Lean Startup
15:45 – 16.00 Summing up and closing the tutorial

Acknowledgments. This work was supported by the Smiglo project, partly funded by the Research Council of Norway under grant 235359/O30, and by the Agile 2.0 project which is supported by the Research council of Norway through grant 236759/O30.

Author Index